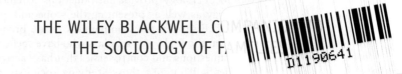

THE WILEY BLACKWELL CO
THE SOCIOLOGY OF F

D1190641

WILEY BLACKWELL COMPANIONS TO SOCIOLOGY

The *Wiley Blackwell Companions to Sociology* provide introductions to emerging topics and theoretical orientations in sociology as well as presenting the scope and quality of the discipline as it is currently configured. Essays in the Companions tackle broad themes or central puzzles within the field and are authored by key scholars who have spent considerable time in research and reflection on the questions and controversies that have activated interest in their area. This authoritative series will interest those studying sociology at advanced undergraduate or graduate level as well as scholars in the social sciences and informed readers in applied disciplines.

The Blackwell Companion to Major Classical Social Theorists
Edited by George Ritzer

The Blackwell Companion to Major Contemporary Social Theorists
Edited by George Ritzer

The Blackwell Companion to Criminology
Edited by Colin Sumner

The Blackwell Companion to Social Movements
Edited by David A. Snow, Sarah A. Soule, and Hanspeter Kriesi

The Blackwell Companion to Law and Society
Edited by Austin Sarat

The Blackwell Companion to the Sociology of Culture
Edited by Mark Jacobs and Nancy Hanrahan

The Blackwell Companion to Social Inequalities
Edited by Mary Romero and Eric Margolis

The New Blackwell Companion to Social Theory
Edited by Bryan S. Turner

The New Blackwell Companion to Medical Sociology
Edited by William C. Cockerham

The New Blackwell Companion to the Sociology of Religion
Edited by Bryan S. Turner

The Wiley Blackwell Companion to Major Social Theorists
Edited by George Ritzer and Jeffrey Stepnisky

The Wiley Blackwell Companion to Sociology
Edited by George Ritzer

The Wiley Blackwell Companion to Political Sociology
Edited by Edwin Amenta, Kate Nash, and Alan Scott

The Wiley Blackwell Companion to the Sociology of Families
Edited by Judith Treas, Jacqueline Scott, and Martin Richards

Also available:

The Blackwell Companion to Globalization
Edited by George Ritzer

The New Blackwell Companion to the City
Edited by Gary Bridge and Sophie Watson

THE WILEY BLACKWELL COMPANION TO

The Sociology of Families

EDITED BY
**JUDITH TREAS, JACQUELINE SCOTT,
AND MARTIN RICHARDS**

WILEY Blackwell

This edition first published 2017
© 2014 John Wiley & Sons Ltd

Edition History: Judith Treas, Jacqueline Scott, and Martin Richards. (Hardback: 9780470673539 – 2014)

Registered Office(s)
John Wiley & Sons, Inc., 111 River Street, Hoboken, NJ 07030, USA
John Wiley & Sons Ltd, The Atrium, Southern Gate, Chichester, West Sussex, PO19 8SQ, UK

Editorial Office
9600 Garsington Road, Oxford, OX4 2DQ, UK

For details of our global editorial offices, customer services, and more information about Wiley products visit us at www.wiley.com.

Wiley also publishes its books in a variety of electronic formats and by print-on-demand. Some content that appears in standard print versions of this book may not be available in other formats.

Library of Congress Cataloging-in-Publication Data

The Wiley Blackwell companion to the sociology of families / edited by Judith Treas, Jacqueline Scott, and Martin Richards.
     pages   cm
  Includes index.
  ISBN 978-0-470-67353-9 (cloth) | ISBN 978-1-119-40603-7 (paper)
1. Families.   2. Families–Research.   I. Treas, Judith.   II. Scott, Jacqueline L.
III. Richards, Martin, 1940 January 26–
  HQ519.W547 2014
  306.85–dc23
                                                                              2013049095

Cover Image: Laura James, *Family Portrait*, 1998, acrylic on canvas. Private Collection / The Bridgeman Art Library
Cover Design: Wiley

Set in 10/12.5pt Sabon by SPi Publisher Services, Pondicherry, India

Printed in Singapore by C.O.S. Printers Pte Ltd

10 9 8 7 6 5 4 3 2 1

Contents

CONTENTS

Contributors

Irma Arriagada is a Chilean Sociologist. She graduated from the University of Concepción and pursued her studies at the London School of Economics and I.D.E.A., University of Santiago, Chile. She worked at ECLAC-United Nations from 1974 to 2008, is an international consultant for the UN, and a researcher at the CEM-Chile (Women's Studies Center) on gender and family topics. She has published more than 70 papers and edited 5 books. She coauthored *Cadenas globales de cuidados: el papel de las migrantes peruanas en la provisión de cuidados en Chile*, 2012, UN-Women (*Global Care Chains: The Role of Peruvian Migrants in the Provision of Care in Chile*).

Loretta Baldassar is Professor in the Department of Anthropology and Sociology at the University of Western Australia and Adjunct Principal Research Fellow, School of Political and Social Inquiry, Monash University. Loretta has published extensively on transnational families, including *Families Caring Across Borders* (with Baldock & Wilding, Palgrave 2007), *Intimacy and Italian Migration* (edited with Gabaccia, Fordham Uni Press 2011), and many journal articles. Her most recent book is *Transnational Families, Migration and the Circulation of Care* (edited with Merla, Routledge, 2013).

Ulrich Beck is Professor of Sociology at Ludwig Maximilian University of Munich, and since 2013, the Principal Investigator of the ERC project: "Methodological Cosmopolitanism—In the Laboratory of Climate Change." Since 1997, he is *British Journal of Sociology* Visiting Centennial Professor at the London School of Economics and since 2011 has served as a Professor at the Fondation Maison des Sciences de l'Homme, Paris. Her publications include *Risk Society* (Sage, 1992), *Individualization* (with Elisabeth Beck-Gernsheim; Sage, 2002), *The Cosmopolitan Vision* (Polity, 2006), and *A God of One's Own* (Polity, 2010).

Elisabeth Beck-Gernsheim is Professor of Sociology at the Norwegian University of Science and Technology/University Trondheim. Her research focuses on migration and ethnicity, medicine and health, and the sociology of love and family. Her publications include *The Social Implications of Bioengineering* (Humanities Press, 1995), *The Normal Chaos of Love* (with Ulrich Beck; Polity, 1995), *Reinventing the Family: In Search of New Lifestyles* (Polity, 2002), *Wir und die Anderen* (Suhrkamp, 2007), and *Distant Love* (with Ulrich Beck; Polity, 2013).

Timothy J. Biblarz is Associate Professor of Sociology at the University of Southern California. His research investigates the roots and consequences of social inequalities in the United States over time, with an emphasis on social mobility and family and intergenerational issues.

Susan L. Brown is Professor of Sociology and Codirector of the National Center for Family and Marriage Research at Bowling Green State University. A family demographer, her research interests focus on how family structure is tied to individual well-being. In particular, she examines how new family forms, including cohabitation, are related to the health and well-being of children and adults. Much of her recent work addresses intimate partnership transitions in later life.

Nathaniel Burke is a PhD student in Sociology at the University of Southern California. A New Directions in Feminist Research Fellow, he studies gender, masculinity, sexuality, labor, and inequality. His research investigates the division of childcare in families headed by gay fathers and the labor experiences of gay male sex workers.

Deborah Carr is Professor of Sociology at Rutgers University and the Institute for Health, Health Care Policy and Aging Research. She studies families in later life, with an emphasis on the psychological consequences of widowhood and divorce. Her recent work includes an NIA-funded project exploring the ways that family relationships affect older adults' preparations for end-of-life medical care and decision-making.

Megan Carroll is a PhD Candidate in the Department of Sociology at the University of Southern California. She is interested in gender, sexuality, and the politics of family change. Her dissertation explores the triumphs and challenges of gay fathers' collective identity formation, drawing from ethnographic research of gay parenting groups.

Yen-Chun Cheryl Chen is a PhD student in the Department of Sociology, University of Cambridge. She is a Cambridge Gates Scholar, entering in 2010. She has been trained within political science, social work, and sociology. She had applied social identity theory to look at ethnic relations in the Russian Federation and has always been inspired by interdisciplinary work related to family lives, especially women's life course development. Her current research focuses on familial ideology, intergenerational relationships, and the trend of marriage postponement in Taiwan.

Emily M. Douglas, PhD, is an Associate Professor of Social Work at Bridgewater State University. Her areas of expertise include male victims of partner violence, fatal child maltreatment, corporal punishment, and divorced families. She has authored more than 30 articles and 3 books on social policies for divorced families, family policy, and corporal punishment. She is the founder and director of the National Research Conference on Child and Family Programs and Policy.

Thomas Alan Elliott is a PhD candidate in Sociology at the University of California, Irvine. His research interests include sexuality, culture, and social movements. He is currently working on his dissertation about national newspaper coverage of homosexuality since 1950 and the role the LGBT movement has played in changing that coverage.

Christopher G. Ellison is Professor of Sociology and Dean's Distinguished Professor of Social Science at the University of Texas at San Antonio. He has published widely on religious variations in family life, with particular attention to child-rearing attitudes and practices and marital and relationship functioning. His other major areas of interest include the implications of religiousness and spirituality for mental and physical health and mortality risk, as well as the role of religion within racial/ethnic minority populations in the United States.

Rys Farthing is currently a DPhil Candidate in the Department of Social Policy and Intervention at the University of Oxford. Her research focuses on child poverty and explores the impacts of growing up in low-income families from young people's perspectives.

Juho Härkönen is University Lecturer of sociology at Stockholm University and Visiting Professor of sociology at the University of Turku. His research interests cover the life course, family sociology and demography, and social stratification. His recent works have been published in *Demography*, *European Journal of Population*, *European Societies*, *European Sociological Review*, *Social Forces*, *Social Politics, and Social Science and Medicine*.

Joshua A. Hendrix is a doctoral student in Sociology at North Carolina State University. His research interests concern the ways that parental work schedules and household characteristics influence individual, family, and child outcomes, with special emphases on child psychological well-being and delinquency. A forthcoming publication examines how the timing of parental work schedules influences adolescent delinquent behaviors and will appear in the *Journal of Family Issues*.

Denise A. Hines, PhD, is an Associate Research Professor in the Department of Psychology department at Clark University, where she is also director of the Massachusetts Family Impact Seminars and the Clark Anti-Violence Education Program. She has authored over 30 articles and 2 books on family violence. She has been the principal investigator on five federal grants, focusing on the etiology of partner violence, prevention of interpersonal violence, and the health of male partner violence victims.

Melanie N.G. Jackson is a doctoral student in the Department of Family Social Science at the University of Minnesota, specializing in Couple and Family Therapy. Melanie's research interest is in family gerontology. She is working on projects focusing on issues in families and aging, including dementia caregiving, family inheritance decisions, and health decision-making among older rural women.

Matthijs Kalmijn is Professor of Sociology at the University of Amsterdam and member of the Netherlands Royal Academy of Sciences. He is known for his work on marriage, divorce, and intergenerational relationships and involved in the development of several large-scale survey projects such as the Netherlands Kinship Panel Study (NKPS). He recently published on intergenerational support in the *Journals of Gerontology* (2013) and on marriage in *Demography* (2013). More information is available on www.matthijskalmijn.nl.

Majella Kilkey is Reader in Social Policy at the University of Sheffield, UK. Her research interrogates family policies and practices through the lens of migration. Recent publications include *Gender, Migration and Domestic Work* (with Perrons, Plomien, Hondagneu-Sotelo, and Ramirez, Palgrave, 2013) and articles in *Global Networks* and *International Migration*. With Lutz and Palenga-Möllenbeck she edited the 2010 special issue "Domestic and care work at the intersection of welfare, gender and migration regimes: European experiences" (*Social Policy and Society*, 9 (3)).

Rhiannon A. Kroeger is a postdoctoral fellow at the Population Research Center at the University of Texas at Austin. Her research focuses on the ways in which socio-economic stratification fundamentally shapes the influences of other institutions, such as the family, on health. Her current research examines how socioeconomic stratification shapes the structure and quality of intimate unions, and whether any socioeconomic differences in intimate union experiences contribute to socioeconomic health disparities throughout the life course.

Jack Lam is a PhD candidate in the Department of Sociology at the University of Minnesota-Twin Cities. He conducts research at the intersection of work and organizations, the life course, and health and well-being. He has recently published in *Work and Occupations* and *Journal of Occupational Health Psychology*. His dissertation research is a longitudinal study focusing on antecedents, patterns, and the health consequences of job insecurity for a cohort of individuals in their early adulthood.

Trude Lappegård is a senior researcher in the Research Department of Statistics Norway. Her research focuses on gender issues, family policy, and fertility behavior. Her current projects investigate the relationship between new family dynamics, gender equality, and fertility choices in Western societies and demographic consequences of the Nordic family policy.

Sean R. Lauer is an Associate Professor of Sociology at the University of British Columbia. In his research, he applies institutional approaches from sociology to the study of families and communities. His current research on communities examines community-based organizations. His research on family has focused on the institution of marriage, including money management.

Jui-Chung Allen Li holds a joint appointment in the Institute of European and American Studies and the Institute of Sociology, Academia Sinica, and is an Associate Professor of Social Research and Public Policy, New York University Abu Dhabi. His primary research interests include marriage formation and disruption, the causes and conse-quences of population aging (and related policy responses), and justice and inequality.

Hadas Mandel is a Senior Lecturer in the Department of Sociology and Anthropology at Tel Aviv University. Her research focuses on cross-country variations in gender inequality and their relationship to class inequality and the role of the welfare state. Selected publications on this topic appeared in the *American Journal of Sociology*, *American Sociological Review*, *Social Forces*, and *The British Journal of Sociology*. Her current research project deals with the role of gender in the determination of wage inequality between occupations.

Wendy D. Manning is a Distinguished Research Professor in the Department of Sociology at Bowling Green State University. She is the Codirector of the National Center for Family and Marriage Research and Director of the Center for Family Demographic Research. She is a family demographer with a research emphasis on family structure, union formation and stability, and relationships among adolescents as well as adults.

Laura Merla is Deputy Director of the Interdisciplinary Research Centre on Families and Sexualities (CIRFASE) at the Catholic University of Louvain, Belgium. Her pub-lications include a special issue of *Recherches sociologiques et anthropologiques*, 41 (1) (coedited with Baldassar); papers in *Autrepart*, 57–58 and *International Migration* (published online); and *Transnational Families, Migration and the Circulation of Care* (edited with Baldassar, Routledge, 2013). Her forthcoming publications include the book *Transnational Family Solidarity in Local Contexts* (Routledge, Transnationalism Series).

Phyllis Moen holds a McKnight Presidential Endowed Chair and is Professor of Sociology at the University of Minnesota, arriving there in 2003 after 25 years as a professor at Cornell University where she held the Ferris Family Chair in Life Course Studies. Dr. Moen investigates the relationship between institutions, health, and the gendered life course. Her most recent book (2005) was *The Career Mystique: Cracks in the American Dream*. She is part of the Work, Family and Health Network and is currently writing a book on the experiences of Boomers.

Toby L. Parcel is Professor of Sociology at North Carolina State University. She is recognized for her research on parental working conditions' effects on child out-comes and for her studies of family and school effects on academic achievement and social adjustment. Recent publications on these topics have appeared in the *Journal of Health and Social Behavior*, *Journal of Marriage and Family*, and *Research in Social Stratification and Mobility*.

Karen D. Pyke, PhD, an associate professor of Sociology at the University of California, Riverside, studies second-generation Asian Americans and internalized oppression. She has recently published on gender inequity among faculty, power dynamics in age-different marriages (with Michele Adams), and the taboo on the study of internalized racism. Her research appears in *Gender & Society*, *Journal of Marriage and Family*, *Journal of Family Issues*, *Sociological Perspectives*, etc.

Martin Richards is Emeritus Professor of Family Research, Centre for Family Research, University of Cambridge. His recent books include *Reproductive Donation: Practice, Policy and Bioethics* (edited with Guido Pennings and John B. Appleby, 2012), and *We Are Family? Relatedness in Assisted Reproduction: Families, Origins and Identities* (edited with Tabitha Freeman, Fatemeh Ebtehaj, and Susanna Graham, 2014).

Kevin M. Roy, PhD, is Associate Professor of Family Science at the University of Maryland College Park School of Public Health. His research focuses on the life course of men on the margins of families and work. Through participant observation and life history interviews, he explores the intersection of policy systems with caregiving and with providing roles in kin networks. He received a PhD in Human Development and Social Policy at Northwestern University in 1999.

Jacqueline Scott is Professor of Empirical Sociology in the Faculty of Human, Social and Political Sciences, University of Cambridge and a Fellow of Queens' College. Her recent edited books include *Gendered Lives: Gender Inequalities in Production and Reproduction* (with Shirley Dex and Anke Plagnol, 2012); *Gender Inequalities in the 21st Century: New Barriers and Continuing Constraints* (with Rosemary Crompton and Clare Lyonette, 2010); and *Women and Employment: Changing Lives and New Challenges* (with Shirley Dex and Heather Joshi, 2009).

Alison Shaw is a Senior Research Fellow in Social Anthropology at the University of Oxford, UK. She is recognized for research with Pakistani families in the United Kingdom. Her research interests include ethnicity and health; social aspects of genetics; as well as kinship, gender, and transnational marriages. Her most recent book is *Negotiating Risk: British Pakistani Experiences of Genetics* (2009).

Wendy Sigle-Rushton is a Reader in Gender and Family Studies and an Associate at the Centre for Analysis of Social Exclusion (CASE) at the London School of Economics where she convenes an MSc program in Gender, Policy, and Inequalities. She has published extensively on the relationship between family structure and the well-being of children and adults. Ongoing work considers the interaction of family structure, ethnicity, and nativity in the production of child health outcomes in the United States and the United Kingdom.

Pamela J. Smock is Professor of Sociology at the University of Michigan-Ann Arbor and Research Professor at the Population Studies Center of the Institute for Social Research. Her research focuses on changing family patterns in the United States and the implications of social class and gender inequality for families. She has published on an array of topics including cohabitation, the economic consequences of divorce and marriage, nonresident fatherhood, and the motherhood wage penalty.

Kristen W. Springer is Associate Professor of Sociology at Rutgers University and the Institute for Health, Health Care Policy and Aging Research. She studies gender, families, and health with an emphasis on gendered dynamics in families and men's health. Her recent research includes an NIA-funded project examining the relationship between health outcomes and income dynamics across 30 years of marriage. She is also using experimental methods to explore how masculinity threats affect men's health.

Murray A. Straus, PhD, is Professor Emeritus of Sociology and founder and Codirector of the Family Research Laboratory at the University of New Hampshire. He has been President of the National Council on Family Relations, the Society for the Study of Social Problems, and the Eastern Sociological Society. He is the author or coauthor of over 200 articles on the family and research methods, as well as 17 books on partner violence, family violence, and corporal punishment.

Göran Therborn is Professor Emeritus of Sociology at Cambridge University, to which he is still partly attached, and Affiliated Professor at Linnaeus University, Sweden. He has published extensively on regionally and globally comparative issues, including, in recent years, *Between Sex and Power: Family in the World, 1900–2000* (2004), *Inequalities of the World* (2006), *Les sociétés d'Europe du XX au XXIe siècle* (2009), *The World: A Beginner's Guide* (2011), and *The Killing Fields of Inequality* (2013). He is currently working on a global study of Cities of Power.

Judith Treas is Chancellor's Professor of Sociology and Director of the Center for Demographic and Social Analysis at the University of California, Irvine. Her previous book, edited with Sonja Drobnič, is *Dividing the Domestic: Men, Women and Household Work in Cross-National Perspective* (2010).

Pernilla Tunberger is a PhD student in the Department of Government, University of Uppsala, Sweden. She has an MSc in Gender and Social Policy from London School of Economics and has previously published (with Wendy Sigle-Rushton) "Continuity and Change in Swedish Family Policy Reforms," *Journal of European Social Policy*, 21 (3) (2011). Her current research investigates how labor market flexibilization in different European welfare states affects the conditions for individuals' combination of earning and caring.

Eric D. Widmer is Professor of Sociology at the University of Geneva. His long-term interests include family and other interpersonal relations, life course research, and social networks. Along with others, he has been developing for two decades research on families in a configurational perspective. His most recent book is *Family Configurations: A Structural Approach to Family Diversity* (2010). Information on his work and publications are available at www.edwidmer.org.

Raelene Wilding is a Senior Lecturer in Sociology at La Trobe University, Melbourne, Australia. Her research uses a range of qualitative methods to focus on the intersections of mobilities, relationships, and communication technologies. Her publications include *Families Caring Across Borders* (with Baldassar and Baldock, Palgrave, 2007) and *Race and Ethnic Relations* (with Fozdar and Hawkins, OUP, 2009), as well as numerous articles in journals, including in *Global Networks* and the *Journal of Refugee Studies*.

Kristi Williams is Associate Professor of Sociology at The Ohio State University and Research Associate at the Institute for Population Research. She studies the influence of family and other social relationships on health and well-being. Her recent work includes an NICHD-funded project examining the consequences of nonmarital and early fertility for the health of women and their offspring and identifying the role that subsequent marriage plays in shaping these outcomes.

Xiaohe Xu is Professor of Sociology at the University of Texas at San Antonio. He has published extensively on comparative family and family studies. His recent publications examine the multifaceted linkages between religion and dating, marriage timing, and child development.

Carrie Yodanis is an Associate Professor of Sociology at the University of British Columbia. In her research she examines gender and inequality from a cross-national perspective, including such topics as the division of housework, management of money in marriage, violence against women, and occupational and class segregation. Her current research examines the change and lack of change in the institution of marriage.

Preface

We live in extraordinary times. Even the youngest readers of the *New Wiley Blackwell Companion to the Sociology of Families* can mine their personal experiences for numerous examples of revolutionary change. Those among us who are a little older can recall when telephones were always tethered to a wall and long-distance calls were too expensive for the casual catch-ups with kin that we now take for granted. Certainly, in the decade since the publication of the first *Companion to the Sociology of Families*, the world has moved on with blinding speed.

Beginning in 2008, a global economic crisis shook the security of households. It derailed the retirement hopes of older family members. It upended young adults' plans to strike out on their own, marry, and start families. It frustrated family men, who struggled not only to meet traditional expectations to provide for their families, but also to live up to new ideals as hands-on, involved fathers and gender egalitarian mates. The scope of the crisis reflected global economic integration. Globalization was already being played out in high levels of international migration, creating transnational families no longer calling a single country home.

Although the great recession left few families unscathed, it drew attention to persistent and growing inequalities between families. From the United States in the developed North to Latin American countries in the developing South, the lifestyles and life chances of family members were increasingly defined by their educations, incomes, and occupations. Where marriage is valued, it was becoming more and more the province of the rich. In some places, marriage had lost its cachet. Cohabitation was filling the void as a pragmatic partnering arrangement for younger and older couples alike.

Even if progress toward gender equality sometimes slowed, there was no sign that the gender revolution would be rolled back. Male privilege was challenged even in such patriarchal societies as East Asia. Despite enduring differences in the gendered life course, men's and women's responsibilities in the workplace and the home converged. Employment and motherhood seldom mesh seamlessly, however. Advanced welfare states embraced work–family reconciliation policies that might encourage childbearing and help them out of an unsustainable sinkhole of subreplacement fertility and negative population growth.

Demographic and family change was often read in terms of its implications for the care and support of the youngest and oldest family members. One hallmark of the last decade has been a continuing movement toward greater diversity in family forms. Cohabitation, divorce, nonmarital childbearing, and child-free unions made talk of *the family* seem a quaint anachronism. The question is not so much whether innovations in family life offers personal fulfillment for adults, but rather whether new family forms meet the needs of children. The continuing growth of female-headed families with limited means underscores the depth of this problem. With welfare state retrenchment, there are similar concerns that loneliness and insecurity await unmarried and childless older adults in coming decades.

Prompted by economic, political, cultural, legal, and technological developments, transformations in families have played out on a global stage. On the one hand, globalization means the diffusion of family innovations. For instance, revisionist Western ideas about gender intrude on East Asian societies. On the other hand, a worldwide perspective shows the region-by-region, country-by-country differences in key features of family life. Cultures retain defining aspects of their family systems. Countries do not necessarily trend together in the same direction. Even in the West, divorce started to rise in some places, just as it seemed to be topping out among countries that were early adopters.

Against the tumult of the last decade, there is a clear imperative to reassess what we know about families. Fortunately, research on families has thrived during this period. According to a recent online title search on *family* and *families* in the *Sociological Abstracts* data base, 10,184 articles were published in scholarly journals just since the first *Companion to Sociology of Families* debuted in 2004. This figure does not do justice to books or to the many important works published in other disciplines or in languages besides English. The challenge of this volume, then, is to synthesize a wealth of new findings in order to understand changing families in the context of a longer historical tradition of research and theory.

The new *Companion* is fortunate to have a distinguished team of family specialists as contributors. Drawn from five continents, there are old hands and fresh voices, all committed to making sense of family change around the world. Each chapter is new or significantly revamped. Each addresses a central issue or domain, describing the state of the field and emerging concerns. A comparison with the earlier *Companion* underscores transformations in families and in family scholarship.

The earlier volume emphasized Europe and North America. Markedly more global in outlook, this *Companion* leads off with an introduction to the distinctive family systems of world regions and cultures. To Europe and the United States, this new book adds dedicated chapters on families in East Asia and Latin America. While it is fair to say that European and American families are the subject of the most research and, hence, receive the most attention, the contributions in the new *Companion* are concertedly comparative. Some chapters are genuinely cross-national in scope. Others have a narrower scope but take care to point out enlightening contrasts. Where the emphasis is on a particular country, the country case is carefully chosen. For instance, in an engaging chapter on religion, the US experience stands as an intriguing exception to secular trends elsewhere in the developed world.

The previous collection anticipated the rising interest in globalization with chapters on immigrant families in the United States and the United Kingdom. This edition returns to these subjects, but it now also provides an overarching review of the much broader concept of transnational families. Importantly, immigrant families have ceased to be a side bar in family studies. Rather than merely an auxiliary topic with its own review, the families of immigrants are incorporated into essays across this book. We learn, for example, about the increase in foreign brides in East Asian countries, the intergenerational conflicts between immigrant parents and their native-born children, and the growing use of DNA testing to prove family relationships for purposes of immigration.

In the 2004 *Companion*, a thoughtful essay on lesbians and gays analyzed how a marginalized community nonetheless overcame the lack of institutional models and support to craft their own distinctive family lives. Picking up the theme here, a new chapter describes the much more welcoming environment for today's same-sex couples. This chapter builds on the growth in scholarship, a development leading toward a positive consensus on once disputed questions such as gay and lesbian parenting. A new review turns to new topics, namely, the family lives of GLBT youths and grandparents. As in the case of immigrant families, same-sex couples have been mainstreamed in the sociology of families and take their place in chapters ranging from assisted reproduction technologies to partner violence to the health of children and adults.

The important connection of feminism and family demanded a chapter in 2004, but gender permeates every new chapter in this volume. Although women are at the center of virtually every family policy debate, research now recognizes men as integral to families, too. Today, fathers are the subject of their own chapter. In other chapters, the interest in men extends to protective marital health effects, the importance of male earnings for the transition to marriage, and changing attitudes toward male infertility. A similar case can be made for the successful colonization of family studies by the life course perspective. In the *New Wiley Blackwell Companion to the Sociology of Families*, there are chapters on age groups and intergenerational relations, and the life course appears as an important organizing theme for understanding everything from poverty to sexual behavior.

Overview and Organization

Although North American and European scholarship receives the most attention in this *Companion*, the book takes a broad and global view of family life, particularly with respect to the developed world. This perspective is seen, on the one hand, in a set of chapters that explores points of difference and convergence between regions of the globe. On the other hand, it is evident in chapters that investigate the family implications of globalization, such as international migration, which gives rise to transnational families spanning national borders and to immigrant families adapting to new circumstances even as they change the host society.

Göran Therborn (Chapter 1) sets the stage with a sweeping historical examination of families across time and space. He argues for taking a long view of family change, one that recognizes the persistence of unique features of family systems in different parts of the globe. The chapter maps family systems that reflect the continuing influence of distinctive beliefs and practices, whether Christian-European,

Islamic West Asian/North African, Confucian East Asian, Sub-Saharan African, South Asian, Southeast Asian, or Creole. Shaped by economic transformations, political change, and cultural exchange, family systems are characterized by internal power dynamics in gender relations, generational bonds, and the regulation of sexuality, marriage, and fertility. A lively cross-national account of patriarchy, marriage, and fertility reminds us that the more things change, the more they stay the same.

Trude Lappegård (Chapter 2) turns the spotlight on Europe with family changes understood through a prism of the life course. Marriage and childbearing are postponed, their sequence altered, and their connection weakened. With some country-to-country variation in the level and pace of change, new family behavior is evident in the increase in cohabitation and decline in fertility. Important questions remain. As cohabitation becomes so widely practiced, why do couples still marry, and does it matter whether Europe's children are born within or outside marriage? *Wendy D. Manning* and *Susan L. Brown* (Chapter 3) focus on families in the United States, where official definitions miss the mark by failing to capture the diversity in contemporary family life. There have been increases in age at marriage, cohabitation, same-sex couples, and nonmarital births. Divorce remains high. Many children do not live with two married, biological parent. Given income inequality and a weak public safety net, these trends – already closely tied to social class – drive a wedge between well-off Americans and disadvantaged segments of the population. *Yen-Chun Cheryl Chen* and *Jui-Chung Allen Li* (Chapter 4) consider Japan, South Korea, Taiwan, and mainland China, where a Confucian heritage met modernization and rapid economic development in the twentieth century. East Asian societies defy scholarly predictions by maintaining values of Confucian familism. A system of mutual dependence survives, favoring males over females, the older generation over the younger one, and family members over unrelated individuals. Weaving a compelling story of assaults on male privilege, changing marriage practices, and a growing concern for family support of the aged, Chen and Li foresee the resilience of the East Asian family, even as it becomes increasingly egalitarian. *Irma Arriagada* (Chapter 5) analyzes Latin America, a case less well known than other regions. Her theoretical framework stresses the global forces of modernization that affect Latin American living standards, but also the processes of modernity that influence how individuals see themselves and their families. Living arrangements have become more diverse, dual-earner couples have increased, and female-headship has risen. Gender – together with ethnicity and social class – are key given the colonial legacy of Creole societies and the inequality and social exclusion in Latin America today.

A second set of chapters engages diversity, inequality, and immigration in the lives of families.

Timothy J. Biblarz, Megan Carroll, and *Nathaniel Burke* (Chapter 6) step up to remind us that same-sex families resemble other families in many ways. Their approach considers the distinctive features of same-sex families that may persist even when sexual pluralism is achieved. Most scholarship focuses on gays as partners and parents, but the authors highlight less studied groups, notably queer youth and gay elders. Moving beyond the narrow and misleading *difference is deficit* framework, they emphasize positive outcomes and relationship models that may prove instructive for heterosexual families. *Rys Farthing* (Chapter 7) provides a primer on family poverty for family sociologists. She approaches concepts of poverty not as a technical issue of methodology but as a deeper moral exercise to understand what poverty really means. Putting poverty in global context reveals unimaginable absolutes of *extreme poverty* alongside the relative deprivation underpinning social exclusion in the developed world. Life cycle stage, gender, and disability raise the odds of deprivation, but poor families show remarkable resiliency. Their fascinating and resourceful strategies include *getting by* with little, *getting out* of poverty, *getting back* at systems stacked against them, and, less often, *getting organized* to address their problems collectively.

Three chapters analyze diversity from the perspective of immigration. *Loretta Baldassar, Majella Kilkey, Laura Merla*, and *Raelene Wilding* (Chapter 8) consider transnational families. Tools developed to study families bound to one community are inadequate to understand families whose member do not even live in the same country. Focusing on family caregiving, they emphasize not only conceptual and methodological approaches but also the practical strategies for *doing family* from afar. New communication technologies, global care chains of immigrant caregivers, cultural differences in what make a good parent, and state impediments to transnational caregiving come in for thought-provoking analysis. *Alison Shaw*'s (Chapter 9) questions how well modern individualism – the reigning cultural explanation for the retreat from marriage in British society – explains the behavior of South Indians, Afro-Caribbeans, and Pakistani Muslims. Their family practices are neither as stable nor as uniform as popularly believed – nor is there as much convergence with British norms as expected. South Indians in cramped terrace houses still create joint families housing by moving kin next door. Pakistanis still marry a cousin from abroad but traditional values of family stability now call for accepting divorce when a marriage fails. *Karen D. Pyke* (Chapter 10) frames her essay on immigrant families in the United States around race. Racial inequality shapes the experience of immigrants, but immigrant families color conceptions of race. Against the historical black–white divide, she emphasizes the rapidly growing Asian and Hispanic populations, which, she argues, are moving closer toward symbolic and material whiteness. Pyke examines the rise in multiracial families formed by racial intermarriage, biracial children, and transnational adoptees. Particularly within Hispanic families, immigration law creates mixed status families in which unauthorized immigrant kin suffer persistent disadvantage and pose insecurity even for family members who are citizens.

Family forms and family influences define four chapters. *Rhiannon A. Kroeger* and *Pamela J. Smock* (Chapter 11) report on cohabitation, now a normative part of the life course in many countries. In the United States, older adults live together without marrying, babies are born to cohabiting parents, and nearly half of children are apt to be raised in a cohabiting union at some point. Questions remain: What is the best way to measure cohabitation? How are children affected? How does cohabitation compare to marriage? Does cohabiting before marriage raise the odds of divorce?

As *Eric D. Widmer* (Chapter 12) points out, who does and does not belong to the family is an open question, especially given divorce and remarriage. Approaching families as configurations, Widmer shows parent–child and husband–wife dyads embedded in interdependencies of social networks. With no less than nine family types (e.g., friends-as-family type, in-law oriented constellation, nuclear family of parents and children), configurations are the stuff that social capital is made of, predicting conflict and ambivalence in relationships. *Deborah Carr, Kristen W. Springer*, and *Kristi Williams* (Chapter 13) frame disparities in psychological and physical health as a legacy of family life. One concern is the impact on children's health of family structure, family transitions, and intrafamily processes, such as parenting style or marital conflict. Another is the influence on adults' health of marriage, widowhood, and parenthood. Although causal relations are often in doubt, research debunks popular beliefs, including notions that children bring happiness or that the risk of widowhood lies in death from a broken heart. *Christopher G. Ellison* and *Xiaohe Xu* (Chapter 14) emphasize the continuing influence of religion. Starting with a short overview of the United States, they compare the churched and unchurched, as well as members of different denominations. Religious beliefs and practices are linked to partnering – from dating and premarital sex to marriage and cohabitation to marital quality and divorce. As for parenting, religion colors whether people have children, how they go about raising them, and even how children ultimately turn out.

Four chapters emphasize processes within families, including divorce, violence, money management, and parental investments in children. *Juho Härkönen* (Chapter 15) examines divorce and its contradictions. The rise in women's employment seems a plausible explanation for divorce, but the evidence is less compelling. Some research detects negative effects of divorce on children, but many are modest and short-term. Under some conditions, divorce turns out to be a positive, not negative, influence on well-being. Better understood as a process than an event, the implications of the divorce decree are hard to distinguish from the consequences of a troubled marriage. *Emily M. Douglas, Denise A. Hines*, and *Murray A. Straus* (Chapter 16) place partner violence into global perspective with recent results from large cross-national studies. Theoretical approaches ranging from patriarchy to personality dysfunction come in for critical evaluation. Acknowledging the gains from 40 years of research, the authors argue against the dominant frame of violence as something men do to women. Researchers, they emphasize, need to consider men and women as perpetrators and victims. Programs must address same-sex, female-to-male, and reciprocal violence more effectively. *Sean R. Lauer* and *Carrie Yodanis* (Chapter 17) tackle money management as a window into bigger issues of couple solidarity and gender equality. The choice of the common pot or separate purses to organize finances speaks not only to a couples' relationship but also to dominant cultural conceptions of marriage as an institution where individual interests are subordinated or given free reign. Money management presents a grand paradox. Equal access to monies signals a gender egalitarian approach, but women's control over budgets can impose burdensome responsibility. *Toby L. Parcel* and *Joshua A. Hendrix* (Chapter 18) analyze the family's role in the transmission of social and cultural capital. Parents actively seek to give their children the cultural tools and social connections that prepare them for their future lives. Their efforts are linked to academic achievements as well as social adjustment, including the avoidance of delinquent behavior. Because parenting behaviors and the opportunities families depend on social class, schools and communities must do more to bolster parents' efforts.

Life course perspectives, which run through this *Companion*, receive special attention from one set of contributors. *Matthijs Kalmijn* (Chapter 19) considers the relations between adult children and their parents. Intergenerational solidarity, tempered by conflict and ambivalence, is the organizing theme. On intergenerational exchange, Kalmijn weighs the evidence for competing theories – self-interested exchange and altruism. Consistent with altruism, is it better to give than to receive, or does personal well-being result from being on the receiving end of exchanges, as a cost–benefit exchange paradigm suggests? Or, is a balance of giving and getting what really matters? *Jacqueline Scott* (Chapter 20) takes the youngest family members as her subject. She challenges family sociologists to study children as children, not just as the appendages of families to which they belong. Family circumstances, while not determinative, are certainly consequential for children's outcomes. Scott, however, argues for studying how children view their circumstances and how they act to influence the course of their own lives. This perspective demands we rethink the benefits and downsides of child labor and *home alone* self-care. *Kevin M. Roy* (Chapter 21) examines the changing roles of fathers in the family. The masculine provider role is still important, but it has become harder for some fathers to support their families. Furthermore, men today confront growing expectations that childcare and emotional involvement, not just providing economically, be part of their parenting portfolio. Although research on the importance of fathers for child outcomes, men are up against challenges, whether living apart from children or coping with incarceration, immigration, or depression. *Phyllis Moen, Jack Lam,* and *Melanie N.G. Jackson* (Chapter 22) turn to families of later life. Historical context, transitions and trajectories, linked lives, and adaptive strategies motivate their review. Against an historical backdrop of financial stress, the transition to retirement has become uncertain, demanding older workers adapt to careers cut short or unavoidably extended. With demographic changes altering the landscape of support, family members must pursue different strategies to cope with changes in the health and dependency of older relations – from quitting paid work to furnish care to finding a group residence for an infirm parent or spouse.

Families exist in broader contexts as the final section emphasizes with chapters on policy, science, and social change. *Pernilla Tunberger* and *Wendy Sigle-Rushton* (Chapter 23) consider family policies. Labor market conditions and family structures are needed to sustain any allocation of work and care to men and women. Each approach has its own logic, but as conditions change, each comes under pressure to change. Depending on employed wives and informal childcare is not sustainable when grandmothers, too, forsake homemaking for paid jobs. Below-replacement fertility, shrinking labor forces, and aging populations demand measures to raise fertility and women's employment rates. EU countries have converged on work–family reconciliation policies. Getting men to do more caring and helping women earn enough to support families remain elusive goals. As *Hadas Mandel* (Chapter 24) argues, women's earnings contribute to the household well-being and promote gender equality. Her cross-national analysis, however, challenges generalizations about the impact of family-friendly initiatives such as public childcare and parental leave. Work–family reconciliation programs benefit low-educated women by keeping them in the labor force and, thus, increasing their skills, experience, and earnings. Well-educated women with the greatest incentives to continuous employment are little affected by state efforts. *Martin Richards* (Chapter 25) places the family in the context of scientific developments, namely, genetic and assisted reproductive technologies. Richards' fascinating account covers the history of these scientific developments, the changing public response, and the implications for definitions of kinship. As genetic testing intrudes on mate selection, as parents craft a reassuring narrative for their nonbiological child, and as prenatal screening imposes painful choices, the implications for families increase. *Judith Treas* and *Thomas Alan Elliott* (Chapter 26) consider sexual behavior in a cross-national analysis of changes in the family institution and the broader society. The greater autonomy of adolescents and young adults is evident in their more active sex lives, but the risks associated with early sexual experience still elicit family concern. Compared to earlier generations, adults bring greater sexual experience to marriage. They no longer expect that sex lives will end with advancing age. Perhaps the most dramatic change is the increased acceptance of sex between two men or two women. As same-sex couples achieve marriage equality, it remains to be seen whether they will adopt the practices of the heterosexual institution (e.g., putting more stock in sexual exclusivity) or whether same-sex partners will pose marital models for others to follow.

Ulrich Beck and Elisabeth Beck-Gernsheim (Chapter 27) draw the volume to a close by returning to the overarching themes of global families and change. Although the questions of family sociology (What is a couple?) may be timeless, the answers are less obvious today. Globalization means that love is now cosmopolitan. It transcends a particular place and culture and is enmeshed with political and economic geo-conflicts of our times. For instance, a stalled gender revolution has left women in developed countries to rely on Third World immigrants to care for their homes and children, even as the household workers must leave loved ones in a distant homeland. Jettisoning methodological nationalism characterizing family scholarship, Beck and Beck-Gernsheim chart a course for far-ranging analyses of the *global chaos of love*.

Part I

Global Perspectives on Families

1

Family Systems of the World: Are They Converging?

Göran Therborn

Times of Change and Family Patterns

Two things, only, are certain about the future of the family. First, the family pattern will look different in different parts of the world, and the future will offer a world stage of varying family plays. Second, the future will not be like the past. The second point has an important corollary, which needs to be underlined. Times of change are seldom aware of their own proper significance. Interpreters of the present have a strong tendency either to underestimate (even to deny) what is going on or to exaggerate it (as a new era), caught up as they are in conflicting whirls of social processes and in a competitive race for attention. In the case of the family, exaggeration is the name of the game in public debate. The "End of the Family" contest is mainly between the positivists, hailing a triumph of "individualization" and the advent of "pure relationships," and the negativists, lamenting the dissolution of society, population decline, and the coming of an old-age ice age. To understand your own time of change, you need a strong dose of historical knowledge and a self-critical distance of reflectiveness.

On the basis of my research, then, I would like to present here two conclusions.

First, there are different family systems in the world today, and they are, on the whole, not converging and in some respects rather diverging; they will also characterize the world in the foreseeable future. Second, the recent changes in the Western European or American family must be comprehended with a longer time perspective than that of the standardized industrial family between the Depressions of the 1930s and the 1970s. The great world religions and the cultural history of civilizations provide us with a world map of major family systems, internally subdivisible and still very diverse but nevertheless discernible patterns of a manageable number.

Families in the global world, what do they look like in this new awareness of the intensive interconnectedness of the planet indicated by the word "global"? What meaningful world patterns are there, making sense of the infinite individual

The Wiley Blackwell Companion to the Sociology of Families, First Edition.
Edited by Judith Treas, Jacqueline Scott, and Martin Richards.
© 2014 John Wiley & Sons Ltd. Published 2017 by John Wiley & Sons Ltd.

variations? Are family patterns and behavior becoming more similar across the globe? How do families connect in today's world? Are families losing or gaining social importance in the early twenty-first century?

Family typologies have been developed mainly by anthropologists and historical demographers with a focus on premodern, preindustrial societies and their rules of descent and inheritance, of prohibited and preferred partners of marriage, and of inter-generational rules of residence (cf. the recent magisterial overview by Todd, 2011, chapter 1). For purposes of modern and contemporary understanding, another approach may be more practical. With a searchlight on power relations, between generations and between spouses, and regulations and practices of sexuality, marital and nonmarital, we may try to discern a few large geocultural family areas of the world. Then, we can find at least seven such family systems, most of them with ancient roots, albeit historically changing in their processes of evolving reproduction. Each of them contains not only a myriad of individual variants but also distinguishable subsystems.

The World's Seven Major Family Systems and Their Twentieth-Century Mutations

For brevity's sake, I shall talk about "family systems," but what I have in mind might be more adequately rendered as family–sex–gender–generation systems. A family is a product of sexuality, and one of its modes of functioning is regulating who may or may not have sex with whom. Historically, if not by necessity or future, the family is at the very center of male–female social gendering, of husband and wife, mother and father, daughter and son, and sister and brother. Thirdly, the family sets the stage of intergenerational relations, of actual fertility, and of rights and obligations of social-ization, support, and inheritance. The brief overview in this chapter derives from a book-length and fully referenced study (Therborn, 2004).

1. The *Christian–European* family, exported also to European settlements overseas and therefore also known as the "Western" family, was historically distinctive, because of its monogamy norm and of its insistence, by the Catholic Church above all, on the right to free choice of marital partner while also legitimizing nonmarriage. In Western Europe, one of the distinguishing features, transported overseas, was the norm of neolocality, transported over-seas, with new couples forming their own households. Also, descent and inheritance were bilateral, with the female lineage as important as the male, with some notable exceptions, like the British aristocracy.

Social gendering was basically asymmetrical, patriarchal, and masculinist, like in most parts of the world, but its patriarchal gendering was uniquely fragile, among all major family systems. Freedom to marry, or not, monogamy, neolocality, and bilateral descent and inheritance (even if unequal), each and all gave Western European women a much stronger hand than their sisters elsewhere.

Among internal European variations, the most noteworthy historical one, very much in evidence at the beginning of the past century, was an East–West divide running from Trieste to Saint Petersburg (Hajnal, 1953) and traceable back to the frontiers of

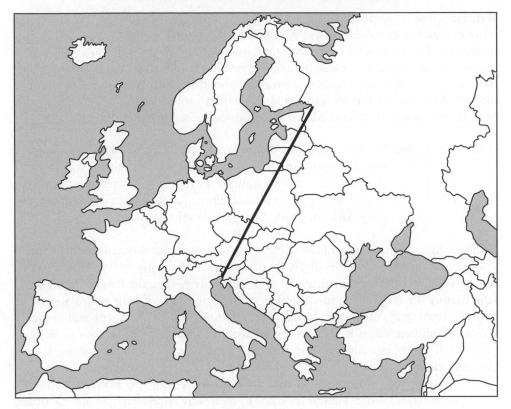

Figure 1.1   The Hajnal line.

early medieval Germanic settlements (Kaser, 2000, see Figure 1.1). With nonnegligible simplification – overriding significant exceptions in Latin Europe – the line divided a Western variant of a norm of neolocality or household headship change upon marriage, late marriages, and a sizeable proportion, >10%, of women never marrying, from an Eastern one of frequent patrilineal descent (in Russia and the Balkans), patrilocality, a female mean age at first marriage 4–7 years lower, and almost universal marriage.

From the world hegemony of North Atlantic powers since the eighteenth century, we should expect this family system to be a global pacesetter of change, and so, it has turned out. Large-scale birth control first emerged in the aftermath of the great North Atlantic revolutions, the American and the French, spreading to the rest of Europe in the late nineteenth century and reaching the rest of the world only after World War II (WWII), into sub-Saharan Africa only in the 1990s. Western European and North American women's rights began to expand in the nineteenth century, again before anywhere else, and from a basis of historically circumscribed patriarchy. But even the theoretical principle of male–female family equality took a long time to conquer all of Western Europe, West Germany only in 1976 – when privileged paternal authority was abolished – and all aspects of French family law only by 1985, after a basic breakthrough in 1970, when "parental authority" replaced "paternal power" (Therborn, 2004, pp. 98, 100).

In the course of the twentieth century, other aspects of the European family developed in an inverted V trajectory. The marriage rate rose dramatically, peaking after WWII, in most countries of Western Europe in 1965–1973, in the United States in the early 1960s.

Birthrates rose correspondingly, reaching a top in the United States in 1957, when a woman could be expected to have 3.8 children (US Bureau of the Census, 2012), and in Western Europe around 1965. After that, marriage and births went downhill, with a massive rise of nonmarried cohabitation, pioneered in Scandinavia, and birthrates plummeting to far below reproduction, above all in Southern Europe. Under Communism after WWII, Eastern Europe pioneered egalitarian family legislation, together with Scandinavia, and pushed female labor force participation. Birthrates decreased.

2. The *Islamic West Asian/North African* family. Islam, more than Christianity, is, of course, a world religion, spread across continents. But outside its historical homelands, the Islamic family institution has been importantly affected by other cultures, and subjected to other regional processes of twentieth-century change, including African, South Asian, and Southeast Asian.

While Islamic marriage is a contract, and not a sacrament, it, as well as family, gender, and generation relations generally, is extensively regulated by holy law. This law does not only express a general principle of male superiority – like the Pauline tradition of Christianity – but specify it in a number of concrete rules, of male guardianship, of delimited polygyny, of divorce by male repudiation, and of the patrilineal appurtenance of children. But it is also concerned with the protection of women as individuals, of daughters' inheritance rights – although half of sons' – and recognizing female property rights, including property rights and legal capacity of married women.

Sexuality as such is not seen as morally destructive, but it is taken as a serious threat to the social order. Therefore, it has to be strictly regulated by a marital order. Forced marriages are forbidden, but the bride's assent may, according to Islamic law, be legitimately implied from her silence, and her marriage contract is signed by her guardian. Families are tightly knit because of close endogamy. By the end of the twentieth century, between a fifth (Egypt) and a third (Arabian Peninsula) of all marriages were between first cousins (Todd, 2011, 506ff).

Endogamy started to decline in the last decades of the past century, but the major change of the Islamic West Asian/North African family, also recent, has been the rise of the female marriage age – up to 26–29 in the Maghreb and to 22 in Egypt and Iran by the turn of the century – and the spread of birth control, beginning in Tunisia and Egypt in the 1960s. The region has been subjected to global antipatriarchal influence, in the wake of the UN 1979 Convention of the Elimination of All Forms of Discrimination Against Women, ratified by most countries, save Iran and Saudi Arabia, but around 2000, only Tunisia and Turkey had done away with explicit legal norms of male family superiority.

3. The *South Asian* family pattern covers major subdivisions, geographical – first of all, North versus South – and religious, mainly if not exclusively Hindu and Muslim. Pakistan, northern India, and Bangladesh are more patriarchal, across religious religions, than the (Indian) South. Hindu marriage is a sacrament and as such in principle indissoluble, whereas marriage to Muslims is a this-worldly contract. Pakistan tops the world league of cousin marriages, whereas the northern Hindi belt of India is governed by kin as well as village exogamy. On the other hand, cousin marriages are twice as frequent, around fourth of all, in Hindu southern India as in Muslim Bangladesh (Todd, 2011,

pp. 507, 244). Caste is a Hindu phenomenon, and Hindu marriages are caste endogamous, but caste has also penetrated South Asian Muslims, and caste considerations can be fit into the equality of status norms of Islamic family law.

However, the region of Bangladesh, India, Nepal, and Pakistan also has a distinctive family commonality. It is the world center of misogyny; in the 1970s, it was the only one in the world in which female life expectancy was lower than male (World Bank, 1995). In the first half of the twentieth century, the subcontinent also stood out for its low female age of marriage, most girls marrying before the age of 15. Arranged marriages constitute the prevailing mode of Muslim as well as of Hindu and Sikh marriages. Patrilineal and patrilocal families are predominant all over the region.

In the last third of the twentieth century, the female marriage age moved upward, most strongly in Pakistan, least in Bangladesh. In the 1990s, female life expectancy overtook the male, but the natural female advantage is still unnaturally small. Postindependence antidiscriminatory family legislation was without much practical effect.

4. The *Confucian East Asian* family comprises the vast area historically shaped or heavily influenced by Sinic civilization, Japan, Korea, and northern Vietnam, as well as China. Classical Confucian patriarchy had been modified in Japan, softened in Vietnam, and was by 1900 most orthodoxly endorsed in Korea. In world history, it was the summit of normative patriarchy. The relation between father and son is the primary of the "Five Relationships" in human life, and filial piety the cardinal virtue, to which all other family and social norms are subordinate. Ancestor worship was the focus of ritual devotion.

Marriage was a contract between families, dissoluble by mutual agreement or by the husband. Bigamy was illegal, but "concubines" had a formal family status as second-rank wives, and their children were legitimate. The patrilineal joint family was the Chinese ideal, the patrilineal stem family – with married sons expected to branch off – the main Japanese one.

In the twentieth century, the Confucian East Asian family model experienced two major political shocks. One was the US occupation of Japan, and the other was the Communist revolution in China, with autonomous extensions to South Korea, Taiwan, and North Vietnam, respectively. Converging on individual autonomy and gender equality, American occupying Liberalism and Chinese Communism attacked paternal power and male dominance head on, introducing and endeavoring to implement norms of choice and equality. Neither was fully successful, but after a generation, marital choice had become prevalent, and women's rights had been clearly enhanced, if not on par in practice with male rights.

5. The *sub-Saharan African* family pattern was to the structural anthropologists of premodern families a mosaic of fundamentally different systems, of descent, marriage rules, and conceptions of kinship. From a vantage point of contemporary comparison, rather some striking similarities stand out. Most conspicuously, by the late twentieth century, Africa south of the Sahara was the only region of the world with mass polygyny. By the end of the past century, it was also outstanding by its birthrate, much higher than the rest of the world. In contrast to the South Asian predominant dowry of marital alliance exchange, African marriages

have historically required payment and/or services rendered to the family of the future bride. Fertility is a high positive value, and there is, in most countries, no control system of premarital female sexuality comparable to the Asian patriarchies or to that of historical Southern Europe. Nevertheless, in spite of an economic autonomy within marriage wider than that of many Euro-American women, sub-Saharan families are widely subject to strong and harsh male power.

Within contemporary sub-Saharan Africa, mass polygyny is primarily, if not only, a West African practice. Stern marital regulations of sexuality are kept above all in the Sahel-savannah belt across the continent south of the desert, from Muslim Mauretania and Northern Nigeria to Christian Ethiopia. Female economic autonomy has grown along the West Coast, above all. Long-time premarital sex, with the longest periods between sexual debuts and marriage, is a southern practice, of South Africa and its surroundings (cf. Bongaarts, 2007).

Polygyny began to decline, substantially, with the female birth cohorts of the 1950s (Fenske (2011, appendix B). Birth control reached parts of the continent in the 1990s. For the rest, the main twentieth-century impact was probably that of the postindependence crises of the last third of the century; of economic disasters, wars, and social disruption with ensuing rapid nondevelopmental urbanization; and of the hecatomb of HIV–AIDS, particularly in the southern part. Taken together, these calamities meant an enormous family disruption, of orphanage, sexual violence, and breaks of marital exchanges and alliances.

6. The *Southeast Asian* type of family, like the African, draws on several formative cultural sources, religiously on Buddhism, Islam, and Christianity (Philippines mainly) and ethnoculturally on Malay customs. The less strict, though not egalitarian, norms of the latter and Buddhism's unique lack of interest in the family and in sex–gender relations have in interaction and overlapping shaped a cultural area outside of the three strongly patriarchal and patrilineal Asian regions, East, West, and South. Descent is usually bilateral. A freedom of marital choice evolved in the course of the twentieth century, without social upheavals or political drama. The virtual universality of marriage in the rest of Asia was here qualified by a minority abstention from marriage, rising sharply with female education (Therborn, 2006).

By current Euro-American standards, Southeast Asia is still a male-dominated sexist society. Egalitarian UN influence has been modest. More important have been the Vietnam War inclusion of the Philippines and Thailand into the US sex economy and the establishment of Filipinas as major producers in the global care chain (Hochschild, 2000).

7. The *Creole family* is a product of a violent encounter, of subjugated, enslaved, or enserfed African and American Indian populations with European conquerors and masters. Out of it came historically, on one side, a particularly rigid and elaborate European patriarchy and, on the other, a system of white male sexual predation and of informal, little regulated intraracial African–American and Indo-American sexuality, mimicking the ruling predators, with informal, matrifocal families. Most of the special white patriarchy, with its

male display and female seclusion, once prevailing at the top of the US ante-bellum South, of the colonial Caribbean and Ibero-America, and imperial Brazil, is now gone. Residues of it are discernible, though, in the lingering Latin American bans of abortion and (lately somewhat loosened) divorce.

The popular side of the dual Creole system, on the other hand, has continued to reproduce itself, among US blacks and among Latin American and Caribbean "people of color." It is manifested in much lower rates of marriage, much higher rates of informal cohabitation and extramarital births, more union instability, and more mother-centered families and kin than among white compatriots and comparable overwhelmingly white societies.

Over the past century, there was a tendency toward more marriage among the Creole populace, culminating sometime in midcentury or around 1960 and reversed into more informalization (Castro Martin, 2002; Tolnay, 2004). The precarity of living in the American ghettos and the Latin American slums has reproduced family–sex–gender practices of the old plantations and landed estates.

The dynamics of family change

Family systems do not have an intrinsic dynamics of their own, but are subjected to pressures for change from their changing environments. Economic changes have been important: structural transformations, such as deagrarianization, proletarianization – undermining traditional rural patriarchies – industrialization, and deindustrialization and economic conjunctures, closing or opening opportunities and options – like the European Depression of the 1870s, that of the 1930s, the African crisis of the 1970s–1980s, the post-WWII Euro-American boom, the East Asian growth "miracles" from Japan to China, and the oil-rent windfall in West Asia/North Africa. Cultural developments, such as schooling and secularization, have had strong impacts. Old and new forms of rural and urban living mean major family effects from urbanization. Political changes have also played important roles, from the indirect birth control effects of the French and American Revolutions to the often much lagged effects of deliberate normative interventions, from early twentieth-century Scandinavian reformism and the Russian Revolution, the US occupation of Japan, and the Chinese Revolution to the late twentieth-century egalitarian efforts of the United Nations.

All the world's family patterns have changed in modern times. But distinctive traditional practices and relations have been reproduced most successfully in the most rural regions of the world, South Asia and sub-Saharan Africa, and in the least secularized, that is, the same areas plus secluded parts of West Asia, like the Arab Peninsula or Iran, although even there patriarchy is being undermined by a large expansion of female higher education.

Current Tendencies: Are the Family Systems Converging?

Whether recent changes are making family patterns more similar around the world is a question still unsettled by scholarship (cf. Ruggles, 2007, 436f). In my view, diversity still predominates.

Patriarchy/masculinism

Patriarchy and masculinism were major losers of the twentieth century, in particular of its second half. Egalitarian advances were considerable in Europe, the Americas, and East Asia, while changes were minor or marginal only in South Asia, West Asia, and Africa, north as well as south of the Sahara (Therborn, 2004, chapters 2 and 3).

Since the UN Conference on Women in Beijing in 1995, there has been no significant international effort at promoting more egalitarian family and gender patterns. But the increasing concern of the OECD with work–family relations, in particular with facilitating the combination of two-worker families and having children, bears upon intrafamily divisions of labor (OECD, 2008).

Politically, the big question of recent change pertains to the effects of post-Communism, of the implosion (Eastern Europe), abandonment (China and Vietnam), and military defeat (Afghanistan) of Communism. The Communists were in principle antipatriarchal and spent much effort on widely unpopular measures of family reform, from the Russian Bolsheviks in 1918 to the Chinese Communists some 30 years later to the Afghan Communists a good 60 years later (Therborn, 2004, p. 74, 83ff, 93ff). How far their achievements went, in the face of often ferocious resistance and gradually in the swamp of their own complacent authoritarianism, still has to be unraveled. But it was clearly enough to lead into a post-Communist backlash; post-Communist Europe has a clearly more maternalist and home-centered view of women than Western Europe (Haavio-Mannila and Rotkirch, 2010, 487ff). Post-Communist China has also taken steps back to its pre-Communist family past, of arranged marriages, ancestor worship, and misogynist discourse (Davis and Harrell, 1993; Xu et al., 2007; Cook and Dong, 2011). Again, however, comprehensive studies of how far this backlash has gone are still in the waiting. And there are movements of feminist resistance, even in current Afghanistan.

One area where resurgent patriarchy and masculinism can be measured is in the sexual ratio of births, of surviving children, and of male–female life expectancy. Low fertility, an enforced public policy in China and a chosen option in other parts of the world, patriarchal/masculinist son preference, and prenatal scanning technology have recently skewed sex ratios of births in a distinctive set of countries. They have been spotted in South Asia; South Korea; China; Vietnam; the Caucasian republics of Armenia, Azerbaijan, and Georgia; and the western Balkans of Albania and Montenegro (UNFPA, 2011a). As the two first-mentioned countries indicate, the phenomenon is not just post-Communism, but it provides some hard evidence of the effect of the latter.

In India, the sex ratio of 0–6-year-olds has increased from a normal distribution of 104–106 boys per 100 girls in 1981 and 1991 to 109 in 2011 (UNFPA, 2011a, 15ff). The masculinist push has been strongest in post-Communist China, soaring to a sex ratio at birth of 120 in 2005, and so far stabilizing there, up from 107 in 1982 (UNFPA, 2011a, p.13).

Marriages arranged by fathers and/or mothers remain important in the twenty-first century, although their exact prevalence is unknown. Such marriages are still predominant in South Asia, that is, in India, Pakistan, Nepal, and Bangladesh (Moody, 2008; WLUML, 2006, chapter 3; Jones, 2010; Bhandari forthcoming), a practice carried into the current diaspora (Charsley and Shaw, 2006; Penn, 2011).

It is widespread in rural Central Asia; in West Asia, including rural Turkey; in North Africa; and in sub-Saharan Africa. It is occurring in substantial parts of Southeast Asia, such as Malaysia and Indonesia, backed up by permissive national or provincial law (WLUML, 2006, chapter 3). Islamic law forbids forced marriages, but no active consent is required of the bride. Parental marriage arrangements remain important in China, particularly in the rural west (Xu *et al.*, 2007; Judd, 2010).

However, it is important to underline the contemporary inadequacy of the binary conception of arranged and choice marriages. Classical arranged marriages without the future spouses – or at least not the bride – being consulted have largely disappeared in East Asia (Jones, 2010; Tsutsui, 2010; Zang, 2008) and is eroding in the other parts as well (WLUML, 2006; Bhandari forthcoming). In Arab countries such as Egypt and Morocco, there is overwhelming support for the idea that women should have a right to choose their spouse and also an overwhelming perception that this is currently the case (UNDP, 2005, pp. 263–264).

What is prevailing in most of Asia and Africa is the conception of *marriage as a family business*, not just a decision of two individuals. Within this familistic conception and practice of marriage, there is a whole range of intergenerational power constellations and of considerations of status, income, and opportunities. (For two illuminating illustrations from two different cultures and from opposite social poles, see the Indian bestseller novel by Chetan Bhagat (2009) and the novelesque China reportage by Leslie T. Chang (2009).)

The world's two major redoubts of male family power are sub-Saharan Africa and South Asia, in both cases particularly their northern parts. According to survey data reported by UNICEF (2007, pp. 19–20) in countries like Nigeria and Mali, about two-thirds of wives say husbands alone make decisions on daily household expenditure and alone decide if the wife can visit a friend or a relative. In Uganda and Tanzania, this is reported by just under half of all wives, in Kenya and Ghana by about a third of all married women, and down to a fifth in Zimbabwe. (South Africa was not part of the survey.) In Bangladesh, corresponding conditions are experienced by a third of women and in Morocco and Egypt by a good fourth. (The Indian survey worded its questions somewhat differently, but only a third of married Indian women said they could go alone to the market, to a heath facility, and outside the community.) A good half of Indian women age 15–49 agreed, in 2005–2006, that there was at least one specific reason for which a husband was right in beating his wife (Ministry of Health and Family Welfare, 2012, pp. 68, 81).

Under UN auspices and domestic feminist pressures, patriarchal power laws were scrapped in Western Europe and the Americas in the last third of the twentieth century (Therborn, 2004, 100ff). While not without influence on official norms, this global process had a much more limited impact on Africa and Asia. Arab countries and many African countries, for example, Congo-Kinshasa, have laws of wifely obedience and requirements of husband/father/male relative consent, for a passport, for example (Banda, 2008, 83ff). A Mali government bill repealing the obedience clause was withdrawn in 2009 after conservative male opposition, although it had been passed by the parliament (WLUML, 2012).

Like political power, patriarchy has also a soft dimension, not only commanding obedience but also enlisting respect, veneration, love, sacrifice, and support. Ancestor worship was a widespread practice outside the messianic world religions, from

China to sub-Saharan Africa and to Indo-America. As a social norm, this patriarchy of respect was most articulate in East Asia, in the supreme Confucian norm of "filial piety." What has happened to it and its more diffuse equivalents elsewhere?

In the succeeding text, we shall take notice of one important breach of it, the refusal of a substantial minority of Hong Kong, Taiwanese, and Japanese women and couples to maintain the ancestral bloodline. Nevertheless, residential patterns and value polls show that filial piety, even if weakened, remains an internationally distinctive feature of the East Asian family.

According to the 2006 East Asian Social Survey, about half of adult household heads in Mainland China and in Taiwan were coresiding with a parent, in Japan about 40%, and in South Korea a third. Intergenerational money transfers show a net gain for elderly parents, except in Japan, with its older prosperity (Yang n.d., figure 2). Other studies tell of strong support among youth and adults for supporting parents (Deutsch, 2006). In Vietnam at the end of the past century, three-fourths of retired men (60+) and women (55+) lived with one of their children (Cobb-Clark, 2009, p. 95). Around 2000, about a fifth of Indian households had more than one married couple, with an additional portion of extended families (Palriwala and Neetha, 2011, p. 1068). In Latin America, as well as in Africa, extended families remain important. In Mexico, they make a fourth of all households, pretty constantly since the 1970s, and 13% of households have more than three generations (Montes de Oca Zavala, 2009, p. 108) In 2009, 16 million Brazilians, 8.5% of all, were living in a household of more than six members (CEPAL, 2012, table 1.1.21).

However, family values and resources may fail to keep up the enormous economic change in recent times. Among all the countries of the Luxembourg Income Study, South Korea has by far the highest amount of relative income poverty among the elderly; 42% of them are below half the median income, which may be compared to 28% in Taiwan, 27 in Mexico, 20 in the United States, and 9% in Germany (www.lis.org/key-figures). Coresidence of elderly with children is rare in Western Europe, 5–8% in France and Germany, but more frequent in Eastern Europe, 20% in Russia and around 25% in Bulgaria (de Jong Giervold, 2009, figure 1).

Marriage

In Europe, the 1000-year-old divide between areas east and west of the Trieste to Saint Petersburg line has by and large survived also the implosion of Communism and the restoration of capitalism, as comes out of Table 1.1. The divide was never perfectly clear-cut, and a couple of recent developments do provide a few new exceptions, but the pattern is still there, younger and more marriages in the east than in the west.

The east–west marriage divide of Europe, first pointed out by John Hajnal (1953), is still there. Hungary has caught up with neighboring Austria on the other side of the Hajnal line, and Bulgarian marriages have plummeted below Western rates, at least in large part due to massive outmigration. (Slovenia, on the other hand, actually straddles the line and seems to have been west of it at least by the mid-nineteenth century (Svab, Rener, and Kuhar, 2012).) Between France and Germany, on one hand, and Russia and the Ukraine, on the other, the age difference is actually larger now than a century ago, in the mid-2000s 8 years and around 1900 5–6 years (Therborn, 2004, table 4.1).

Table 1.1   Marriage age and marriage rates in Eastern and Western Europe, in circa 2005–2007

Female marriage age[a]		Marriage rates, per thousand population	
East ≤25	West ≥30	West ≤5	East ≥7
Albania	Denmark	Austria	Belarus
Belarus	Finland	Bulgaria	FYR Macedonia
Bulgaria	France	France	Romania
Estonia	Germany	Germany	Russia
Moldova	Ireland	Hungary	Ukraine
Russia	Italy	Italy	
Ukraine	the Netherlands	the Netherlands	
	Norway	Norway	
	Slovenia	Portugal	
	Sweden	Slovenia	
		Spain	
		Sweden	
		the United Kingdom	

[a]Singulate mean age at marriage (SMAM).
Source: Data from UNFPA, World Marriage Data, available online from www. UN.org/esa/population/publications/WMD2008.

Marriage in the United States was, in terms of age and frequency, historically more similar to Eastern than to Western Europe and has remained so, with a crude marriage rate in 2006 of 7.2 and a mean marriage age of never-married women at 26 years. The age of marriage continues to differ in the world. About half of African and South Asian girls born around 1980 were married by the age of 18 (UNICEF, 2006, p. 46). There is no catching up at the poles. In Mali, the marriage age remained unchanged between 1976 and 2006; in Bangladesh and India it rose by 2 years from the mid-1970s to the mid-2000s. For about the same period, the rise in France and Sweden was 8–9 years (UNFPA, 2008).

New marital tendencies have appeared in East Asia, though mainly outside Mainland China. The norm of universal marriage has been abandoned in metropolitan East Asia, above all by highly educated women. Whatever nonmarital sex is going on, it is very discrete. Single mothers are few; informal cohabitation is largely hidden from view (Jones, 2007, 2010).

The marital regulation of sexuality and of reproduction has changed considerably. In several European countries, from Bulgaria to France, more than half of all babies are born outside wedlock. In Southern and Central Europe, it remains a clear minority phenomenon, though, and in South Korea and Japan, it is almost nonexistent (OECD, 2011). The latter is a common Asian and North African pattern, shared by China, Indonesia, India, and Egypt. Sub-Saharan Africa differs widely in this respect, between strongly predominant marital births in Nigeria, Ethiopia, the Sahel region, and Southern Africa with long periods of premarital sex and a current predominance of extramarital births (Bongaarts, 2006, table 2; Mensch, Grant, and Blanc, 2006, table 1; The Sustainable Democratic Dividend, 2012). The current fissiparous family behavior in postapartheid South Africa (Budlender and Lund, 2011) resembles the American Afro-Creole pattern.

In the Americas, the Creole pattern of informal unions and extramarital births has staged an uneven comeback. In the United States in 2007, 71% of births to Afro-American women were extramarital, as compared to 27% to white women. Taking cohabitation into account, in the early 2000s, about half of all births to black US women occurred outside both cohabitation and marriage but only one-tenth of white births (Manlove *et al.*, 2010, pp. 622, 628). Mexico is now near the very top in the OECD, having more than half of its babies born outside marriage (OECD, 2011). And the historical hemispheric cards are being reshuffled, with Jamaica experiencing a marriage boom and Chile, once a very conservative buttoned-up country, letting its marriage rate (3.3 in 2005) fall to less than half the Jamaican. Chile is here accompanied by Bolivia, Paraguay, and Peru, of the old Indo-Creole region. Since the early 2000s, the large majority of Chilean births take place outside marriage (Larrañaga, 2006, p. 139).

Fertility and the future of populations

Recently, birthrates have fallen strongly in most of Asia, in Eastern Europe, and in Latin America. In sub-Saharan Africa as a whole, fertility has also fallen recently, to 4.5, but not in all countries. For the whole world, women are now expected to bear 2.5 children in their lifetime. The rapid Arab adoption of birth control is worth noticing, with the Total Fertility Rate (TFR) falling from 6.7 in 1970–1975 (UNDP, 2005, p. 290) to 3.2 in 2010 (UNFPA, 2010, p. 105).

Is the world converging on a low fertility rate? Probably, but we are not quite there yet, and a new divide is emerging. Around 1900, the fertility differential between the United States and sub-Saharan Africa was something like 2.2 to 2.7 children. In 2010–2015, it was 2.7. In 2010–2015, the differential between India and Germany was 1.0; in 1896–1900, it was 0.8. On the other hand, the United States and Western Europe are now much closer to China, to Russia, and to Latin America than 100 years ago (historical data from Therborn, 2004, table 8.7, current ones from UNFPA, 2011b, pp. 116–121).

Currently, the birthrates of the world are hung up between one pole, not or only very marginally affected by birth control, and another of historically unprecedented low rates. Basically unaffected by birth control (TFR at 6 and higher) by 2010 were nine African countries plus Afghanistan and Timor Leste (UNFPA, 2010, 100ff). At the other end are populations far below natural reproduction. Following the lead of the Australian demographer Peter McDonald (2009), we may focus on countries with a fertility rate at or below 1.5. The extremely low-fertility countries are made up of two or three distinctive groups, situated in very different cultural and economic contexts.

One is European, which may be divided into two subsets. There is a Western, central and southern, cluster, comprising of Austria (1.4), Germany (1.3), Greece (1.4), Italy (1.4), Malta (1.3), Portugal (1.4), Spain (1.5), and Switzerland (1.5) and an Eastern, post-Communist cluster: Belarus (1.3), Bosnia and Hercegovina (1.2), Bulgaria (1.5), Croatia (1.5), Czech Republic (1.5), Hungary (1.4), Latvia (1.5), Lithuania (1.4), Moldova (1.5), Poland (1.3), Romania (1.3), Russia (1.4), Slovakia (1.3), Slovenia (1.4), FYR Macedonia (1.4), and Ukraine (1.4). All post-Communist Europe has fallen below the reproduction rate, and above the 1.5 cutoff are only Estonia (1.7) and Montenegro and Serbia (both at 1.6). The other group is East

Asian and includes Hong Kong (1.0), Japan (1.3), Singapore (1.3), South Korea (1.2), and Taiwan (1.0) (McDonald, 2009; UNFPA, 2010, 100ff).

Scholarship has not yet fully caught up with this new global phenomenon, which at first appears rather puzzling. It involves two and half historical family systems but so far no other. It spans, on the one hand, the European post-Communist area of mass impoverishment and insecurity, combined with soaring inequality, and the East Asian zone of spectacular economic development, with some post-1990 qualification for Japan. In family terms, the most radical change has happened in East Asia, partly breaking the ancient intergenerational line. For completed fertility cohorts, a third of women in Hong Kong and Japan and a fifth of women in Singapore and Taiwan have had no child at all (McDonald, 2009).

Economic adversity tends to affect birthrates, wherever they can be controlled. This is most likely a major reason for the plummeting birthrate of post-Communist Europe, a fall down to a TFR of 0.8 for 1993 and 1994 in the former GDR (Therborn, 2004, p. 258). But the bulk of explanation of very low fertility derives most likely from recent gender imbalances. The low-fertility areas are all strongly patriarchal, in relation to their region, with few facilities for accommodating dual-career couples and children, and in East Asia, male conceptions of marriage have not kept up with female successes in education and business. The result is a modern *Lysistrate* rebellion of career women, abstaining from marriage and children (cf. Jones, 2010; McDonald, 2009). Whether all these very low fertility rates are reversible is anybody's guess, but if they are not, the world is likely to divide between reproducing and shrinking populations.

Transnational familism

After globalization, transnationalism has become a buzzword of our times (Portes, 2001; Vertovec, 2009). In contrast to the economic and mass culture macroperspective of the former, the latter focuses on the microsocial dynamics of human actors crossing and straddling economic and cultural regions as well as state boundaries. The size and the novelty of transnationalism had better not be exaggerated by romantic fascination. Worldwide transnational migration today is about the same size as it was a good century ago – when the Americas got its mass population and when crowds of Chinese and Indians fanned out overseas – now and then about 3% of the world population living outside their country of birth (UNFPA, 2011b, p. 66). Largely new are the global care chains – of mothers from poorer countries migrating for caring work in richer ones while somebody else is caring for her children at home (Hochschild, 2000; Yeates, 2012) – and the East Asian transborder marriage mass markets. For 2005–2009, more than 10% of South Korean marriages were with foreign spouses. Between a fourth and a third of Taiwanese men's marriages were with wives from abroad (Choe, 2011).

This is not the place to enter into the now extensive literature on transnational families and the complex and varied effects on family process it has found (see, e.g., Beck-Gernsheim, 2007; Chamberlain and Leydesforff, 2004 Charsley and Shaw, 2006; Huang, Yeoh and Lam, 2008;Levitt and Jaworsky, 2007; Mazzucato and Schans, 2011; Yeoh, Huang, and Lam, 2005;Yeates, 2012). But migration as a transnational family raises two questions of a more general character which we shall touch upon. First, how far does family transnational migration affect the geocultural pattern of world family systems? Second, what does it tell us about the current importance of family in the context of alleged individualization?

What comes out of the literature earlier is that the transcontinental migration has not given rise to a new family species. On the contrary, in spite of new pressures and through various ways of accommodation – facilitated by new cheap and fast communication – so far, the main effect has been an extended reproduction of existing family patterns by spatial displacement. The territorial impact has been largest in Western Europe, where the long outmigration stream has been reversed. Within Europe, the Western European family pattern is now coexisting with arranged marriages and extended family households. In Europe as well as in North America, higher immigrant fertility rates are helping the reproduction of the resident population. While second-generation immigrant fertility rates and other practices tend to move closer to those of the surrounding population, the existing literature has not found any significant rapprochement between the families of sending and receiving territories produced by migration.

Highlighted by the literature, on the other hand, is the importance of family in the migratory process. Very often, migration is part of a family strategy for a better life, whether by migrant remittances, by international hypergamy, or by staged family outmigration. The latter is facilitated by family reunification permits in many receiving countries.

Conclusion: Persistent Diversity, Persistent Importance

Families continue to differ around the world, in size, in composition, in sexual regulation and marriage, in patriarchy or male sex–gender–generation power, in their stability, in their care for the elderly, and in their fertility and patterns of reproduction. Persistent global diversity should also be considered in relation to the ongoing processes of divergence by class in postindustrial societies. Successful industrialization once meant a stabilization and standardization of the Euro-American family (Therborn, 2004, 163ff). Currently, a new postindustrial sociocultural dynamic is driving family patterns apart between classes, through mounting educational and income homogamy and bifurcated paths of prosperity and insecurity. It has received most attention and is perhaps most pronounced in the United States (Murray, 2012; Brooks, 2012, reporting research by Robert Putnam).

From the persistent global diversity of systems of family–sex–gender relations, from transnational migratory familism, and from the growing divergence of family patterns in the postindustrial center of the world, we may also conclude a persistent, and in comparison with a generation ago probably increasing, importance of the family.

References

Banda, F. (2008) *Project on a Mechanism to Address Laws that Discriminate Against Women.* Geneva: Office of the High Commissioner for Human Rights, www.ohchr/documents/ publications (accessed July 20, 2012).

Beck-Gernsheim, E. (2007) Transnational lives, transnational marriages: a review of the evidence from migrant communities in Europe. *Global Networks*, 7 (3), 271–88.

Bhagat, C. (2009) *2 States: The Story of My Marriage*. Rupa, Delhi.

Bhandari, P. (Forthcoming) *Spouse Selection in New Delhi*. Department of Sociology, Cambridge University, PhD Thesis.

Bongaarts, J. (2007) Late marriage and the HIV epidemic in sub-Saharan Africa. *Population Studies*, 61 (1), 73–83.

Budlender, D. and Lund, F. (2011) South Africa: a legacy of family disruption. *Development and Change*, 42 (4), 925–946.

Brooks, D. (2012) The opportunity gap. *International Herald Tribune*, July 11, p. 9.

Castro Martin, T. (2002) Consensual Unions in Latin America: Persistence of a Dual Nuptiality System. *Journal of Comparative Family Studies*, 35 (1), 35–55.

CEPAL (2012) *Anuario Estadístico de América Latina y del Caribe*.CEPAL, Santiago de Chile.

Chamberlain, M. and Leydesdorff, S. (2004) Transnational families: memories and narratives. *Global Networks*, 4 (3), 227–241.

Chang, L.T. (2009) *Factory Girls: Voices from the Heart of Modern China*. Picador, New York.

Charsley, K. and Shaw, A. (2006) South Asian transnational marriages in comparative perspective. *Global Networks*, 6 (4), 331–344.

Choe, M.K. (2011) Family formation patterns among young people: general trends and emerging issues in East and Southeast Asia. www.un.org/esu/population/meetings/egm-adolescents (accessed July 29, 2012).

Cobb-Clark, D. (2009) *The Role of Support from Children and Own Labour Supply in Supporting the Elderly in Indonesia And Vietnam: A Comparison of Two Studies*. Doha International Institute for Family Studies and Development, Family Support Networks and Population Ageing, pp. 94–97, www.fsd.org.qu/app/media/224 (accessed October 30, 2013).

Cook, S. and Dong, X-y. (2011) Harsh choices: Chinese women's paid work and unpaid care responsibilities under economic reform. *Development and Change*, 42 (4), 947–965.

Davis, D. and Harrell, S. (eds.) (1993) *Chinese Families in the Post-Mao Era*. University of California Press, Berkeley.

Deutsch, F.M. (2006) Filial piety, patrilineality, and China's one-child policy, *Journal of Family Issues*, 27 (1), 366–389.

Fenske, J. (2011) African polygamy: past and present. LSE Research Online, http://eprints.lse.ac.uk/39246/ (accessed October 30, 2013).

Giervold, J. de Jong (2009) *Living Arrangements and Differences in Family Support: A Comparative Perspective*. Doha International Institute for Family Studies and Development, Family Support Networks and Population Ageing, pp. 72–76, www.fsd.org.qu/app/media/224 (accessed October 30, 2013).

Haavio-Mannila, E. and Rotkirch, A. (2010) Sexuality and family formation in *Handbook of European Societies: Social Transformations in the 21st Century* (eds S. Immerfall and G. Therborn), Springer, New York, pp. 465–497.

Hajnal, J. (1953) Age at marriage and proportions marrying. *Population Studies*, 7, 2, 111–136.

Hochschild, A.R. (2000) Global care chains and emotional surplus value, in *On the Edge: Living with Global Capitalism* (eds W. Hutton and A. Giddens),Jonathan Cape, London, pp. 130–146.

Huang, S., Yeoh, B.S.A. and Lam, T. (2008) Asian transnational families in transition: the liminality of simultaneity. *International Migration*, 46 (4), 3–13.

Jones, G.W. (2007) Delayed marriage and very low fertility in Pacific Asia. *Population and Development Review*, 33 (3), 453–478.

Jones, G.W. (2010) Changing marriage patterns in Asia, Singapore: Asia Research Institute Working Paper No. 131, arigwj@nus.edu.sg (accessed October 30, 2013).

Judd, E.R. (2010) Family strategies: fluidities of gender, community and mobility in rural West China. *China Quarterly*, 204, 927–938.

Kaser, K. (2000) *Macht und Erbe*. Böhlau, Vienna.

Larrañaga, O. (2006) Comportamientos reproductivos y fertilidad, 1960–2003, in *El Eslabón Perdido: Familia, modernización y bienestar en Chile* (eds J. Samuel Valenzuela, E. Tironi and T.R. Scully), Aguilar, Santiago de Chile, pp. 137–176.

Levitt, P. and Jaworsky, B.N. (2007) Transnational migration studies: past development and future trends. *Annual Review of Sociology*, 33, 129–156.

Luxemburg Income Study (2012) Key Figures, www.lisproject.org/key-figures (accessed July 26, 2012).

McDonald, P. (2009) Explanations of low fertility in East Asia: a comparative perspective, in *Ultra-Low Fertility in Pacific Asia: Trends, Causes and Policy Issues* (eds G. Jones, P.T. Straughan and A. Chan), Routledge, London, pp. 23–39.

Manlove, J., Ryan, S., Wildsmith, E. and Franzetta, K. (2010) The relationship context of nonmarital childbearing in the U.S. *Demographic Research*, 23/22, 615–654.

Mazzucato, V. and Schans, D. (2011) Transnational families and the well-being of children: conceptual and methodological challenges. *Journal of Marriage and the Family*, 73 (4), 704–712.

Mensch, B.S., Grant, M.J. and Blanc, A.K. (2006) The changing context of sexual initiation in sub-Saharan Africa. *Population and Development Review*, 32 (4) 699–727.

Ministry of Health and Family Welfare, Government of India (2012) *Gender Equality and Women's Empowerment in India*. Mumbai: International Institute for Populations Sciences. www.measurehs.com/pubs/pdf/0057 (accessed July 24, 2012).

Moody, P. (2008) *The Intimate State: Love Marriage and the Law in Delhi*. Routledge, New Delhi.

Montes de Oca Zavala, V. (2009) *Families and Interpersonal Solidarity in Mexico: Challenges and Opportunities*. Family Support Networks and Population Ageing UNFPA, pp. 107–111.

Murray, C. (2012) *Coming Apart: The State of White America, 1960–2010*. Crown Forum, New York.

OECD (2008) Policy Brief. Babies and Bosses: Balancing Work and Family Life, www.oecd.org/employment/34566853.pdf (accessed August 5, 2012).

OECD (2011) OECD Family Database, www.oecd.org/elssocial/family/database (accessed July 20, 2012).

Palriwala, R. and Neetha, N. (2011) Stratified familialism: the care regime in India through the lens of childcare. *Development and Change*, 42 (4), 1049–1078.

Penn, R. (2011) Arranged marriages in Western Europe: media representation and social reality. *Journal of Comparative Family Studies*, 42(5), 637–650.

Portes, A. (2001) Introduction: the debates and significance of immigrants transnationalism. *Global Networks*, 1 (3), 181–193.

Ruggles, S. (2007) The future of family demography. *Annual Review of Sociology*, 18, 423–441.

Svab, A., Rener, T. and Kuhar, M. (2012) Behind and beyond hajnal's line: families and family life in Slovenia. *Journal of Comparative Family Studies*, 43 (3), 419–437.

The Sustainable Demographic Dividend (2012) Global Children's Trend, http://sustaindemographicdividend.org/articles/international-family-indicators (accessed July 26, 2012).

Therborn, G. (2004) *Between Sex and Power: Family in the World, 1900–2000*. London: Routledge.

Therborn, G. (2006) Family's in today's world- and tomorrow's, international. *Journal of Health Services*, 36 (3), 593–603.

Todd, E. (2011) *L'origine des systèmes familiaux: I. L'Eurasie*. Gallimard, Paris.

Tolnay, S.E. (2004) The living arrangements of African American and immigrant children, 1880–2000. *Journal of Family History*, 29 (4), 421–437.

Tsutsui, J. (2010) *The Transitional Phase of Mate Selection in East Asian Countries*. Presentation at the ISA World Congress in 2010, obtained from the author: junya_tsts@nifty.com (accessed October 30, 2013).

UNDP (2005) *Arab Development Report 2005*. UNDP, Geneva.

UNFPA (2008) *World Marriage Data 2008*, www.un.org/esa/population/publications/WMD2008 (accessed October 30, 2013).

UNFPA (2010) *State of World Population 2011*. UNFPA, New York.

UNFPA (2011a) *State of World Population 2011*. New York: UNFPA.

UNFPA (2011b) *Report of the Global Meeting on Skewed Sex Ratios at Birth*, www.unfpa.org/home/publications/pubs/data (accessed on July 19, 2012).

UNICEF (2006) *The State of the World's Children 2006*. UNICEF, New York. www.unicef.org/sowc06 (accessed October 30, 2013).

UNICEF (2007) *The State of the World's Children 2006*. UNICEF, New York. www.unicef.org/sowc07 (accessed October 30, 2013).

US Bureau of the Census (2012) Statistical Abstract of the United States: 2012, www.census.gov/compendia/statab/cats/birthsdata (accessed October 30, 2013).

Vertovec, S. (2009) *Transnationalism*. Routledge, London.

Women Living Under Muslim Law (WLUML) (2006) *Knowing Our Rights: Women, Family Laws and Customs in the Muslim World*, 3rd edn. www.wluml.org/node/588 (accessed July 20, 2012).

WLUML (2012) Mali: "Women's rights in Mali set back 50 years" by new "Family Code" law, www.wluml.org/news/mali-womens-rights-mali-se-back (accessed July 25, 2012).

World Bank (1995) *Social Indicators of Development*. World Bank Books, Washington, D.C.

Xu, A., Xie, X., Liu, W. *et al.* (2007) Chinese family strengths and resiliency. *Marriage and Family Review*, 41 (1–2), 143–164.

Yang, J. (n.d.) Parent–child dynamics and family solidarity: a comparative study of East Asian societies. Renmin Univerisy, Beijing. Juhua_Yang@yahoo.com (accessed July 20, 2012).

Yeates, N. (2012) Global care chains: a state-of-the-art review and future directions in care transnationalization research. *Global Networks*, 12 (2), 135–154.

Yeoh, B.S.A., Huang, S. and Lam, T. (2005) Transnationalizing the "Asian"family: imaginaries, intimacies and strategic intents. *Global Networks*, 5 (4), 307–315.

Zang, X. (2008) Gender and ethnic variation in arranged marriages in a Chinese city. *Journal of Family Issues*, 29 (5), 615–638.

2

Changing European Families

TRUDE LAPPEGÅRD

Introduction

The most dramatic change in families is the disconnection between marriage and childbearing. Family formation has traditionally been related to a certain sequence of events including marriage as the main context for childbearing, while now, more children are born within cohabitation. Over the last four decades, men and women have delayed becoming parents and are having fewer children. The transformation of the family also includes new family arrangements such as cohabiting unions, same-sex marriages, single-parent families, and living alone. This chapter will examine the main features of these changes across Europe and discuss differences and similarities across nations in light of gender equality and developments in public policy.

Becoming a Family

Nowadays, most young people start their first union in cohabitation, but there are great variations across Europe. In just a few decades, cohabitation has gone from being a marginal phenomenon to a more accepted way of coresiding. In the recent past, childbearing has been closely linked to marriage, and the increase in childbearing in cohabitation is one of the most remarkable demographic changes to have occurred in Europe. The meanings of family and marriage have changed over time, and even though marriage rates are decreasing, most couples seem to end up married, especially when they become parents.

The Wiley Blackwell Companion to the Sociology of Families, First Edition.
Edited by Judith Treas, Jacqueline Scott, and Martin Richards.
© 2014 John Wiley & Sons Ltd. Published 2017 by John Wiley & Sons Ltd.

Cohabitation

Cohabitation has become a generally accepted living arrangement across Europe (Liefbroer and Fokkema, 2008). In most countries, very few young couples move directly into marriage, and in many countries, the majority of first unions are now within cohabitation (Sobotka and Toulemon, 2008; Billari and Liefbroer, 2010). However, the degree of cohabitation and the degree of acceptance of couples living together without planning to marry differ between countries. There are also differences in the length of time couples cohabit, if they have marriage plans and if children are born within cohabitation. Consequently, the character and meaning of cohabitation vary between individuals, countries, and over time.

The increase in cohabitation is identified as perhaps the most important of the new family behaviors described in the second demographic transition (Lesthaeghe, 1995). Ideational change and shifts toward individualism and secularism (Bumpass, 1990; Lesthaeghe, 1995; Surkyn and Lesthaeghe, 2004) are often used to explain changing lifestyle choices. It can also be attributed to factors such as increasing female economic empowerment and the contraceptive revolution (Kiernan, 2004). In addition, cohabitation may symbolize "the avoidance of the notion of dependency that is typically implicit in the marriage contract" (Kiernan, 2004, p. 52). This might be more so for women than for men. Finally, young people's expectations toward partnerships and marriage are changing, and it is claimed that relationships have moved away from the realm of normative control and institutional regulation giving rise to the new idea of reflexive "pure relationships" based on love and mutual attraction (Giddens, 1992).

Cohabitation as we observe nowadays is new, but unmarried coresiding partnerships are not a new phenomenon. Historical sources suggest that couples across Europe cohabited for various reasons, for example, cohabitation after a marriage breakdown and in between marriages (Kiernan, 2004). For instance, in Sweden, Trost (1978) identified two types of cohabitation from the eighteenth century. One practiced by a group of intellectuals opposed to church marriage was known as a "marriage of conscience." The other practiced among poor people who could not afford to marry was known as a "Stockholm marriage." While the first group was a highly marginal phenomenon, the "Stockholm marriage" was the most common group of cohabitation reported from several countries (Noack, 2010).

Various classifications have been developed over the years to understand the meaning of cohabitation. The aim has been to improve knowledge about its development over time, across nations, and between individuals. One basic and often identified distinction is made between cohabitation as a stage in the marriage process and cohabitation as an alternative to marriage. First, cohabitation as a stage in the marriage process means that sharing a household is viewed as a preface to moving into a seriously committed relationship. In this way, unmarried cohabitation becomes an experiment in committing to a long-term relationship (Seltzer, 2000). One advantage of sharing a household for young couples is that they can pool resources and benefit from the economies and convenience of sharing a household (Seltzer, 2000; Smock, 2000; Perelli-Harris *et al.*, 2010). Second, cohabitation as an alternative to marriage means that cohabitation lasts longer and has become a socially accepted way of living, both as a living arrangement for young people and also as a family form in which to have and raise children (Smock, 2000). Countries are developing along different trajectories. There is great variation in the prevalence of cohabitation, and cohabiting couples express different perceptions of the prospects for their cohabitation, that is, there is great variation in the proportion of cohabitating unions that do or do not have plans for marriage. To describe trends over time, Sobotka and Toulemon (2008) suggest three main stages that are widely shared across countries. In the first stage, which is described as *diffusion*, an increasing proportion of young adults enter a consensual union at the beginning of a partnership, and this eventually becomes a majority practice. In the second stage, described as *permanency*, cohabitation lasts longer and is less frequently converted into marriage. In the last stage, *cohabitation as a family arrangement*, pregnancy gradually ceases to be a strong "determinant" of marriage among cohabiting couples, and as a result, childbearing among cohabiting couples becomes common.

Using data from the 2008 European Social Survey, Noack, Berhardt, and Wiik (2013) distinguish between three cohabitation patterns. One cluster of countries (Greece, Romania, Croatia, Slovenia, Bulgaria, and Poland) represents a "traditional" pattern of living arrangements in which cohabitation is relatively rare, that is, 5% or less of the total population cohabit and 11% of those unmarried are cohabiting. At the other end of the scale, the Nordic countries, primarily Norway and Sweden, and France are clustered into "high-prevalence countries" where 20% or more of the total population are cohabiting and 34% or more of those unmarried live in cohabitation. The countries that represent a "middle group" of level of cohabitation include the Netherlands, Belgium, Luxembourg, the United Kingdom, Ireland, Germany, Switzerland, Hungary, Portugal, Spain, the Czech Republic, and Slovakia. In these countries, between 6% and 14% of the total population cohabit, and between 13 and 22 of those unmarried are cohabiting (Noack, Berhardt, and Wiik, 2013).

Despite these variations across countries, there is generally a relatively high acceptance of cohabitation across Europe. According to Noack, Berhardt, and Wiik (2013), in most countries, more than half of the population in the age range 15–55 does not disapprove of couples living together without being married. The highest acceptance was found in the Nordic countries and particularly Denmark where as many as 96% of the population agreed that cohabitation is completely acceptable.

Although unmarried cohabitation reaches a stage at which it becomes an alternative to marriage, substantial differences between the two partnership arrangements remain. First and foremost, men and women report a different quality of relationship in cohabitation and marriage. That is, comparative studies of European countries suggest that cohabitants have a lower level of general life satisfaction and happiness compared with married couples (Soons and Kalmijn, 2009), and cohabitants live in relationships of less commitment (more breakup plans) and less partnership satisfaction than married couples (Wiik, Keizer, and Lappegård, 2012). Importantly, in both studies, the "cohabitation gap" was narrower in countries where cohabitation is most widespread and institutionalized than in countries where cohabitation was a marginal phenomenon. This suggests that cohabitation has become "marriage-like" in relationship quality in countries where cohabitation is considered more as an alternative to marriage.

Evidence of lower relationship quality in unmarried cohabitation (Soons and Kalmijn, 2009; Wiik, Keizer, and Lappegård, 2012) including in countries where cohabitation is more widespread, and the high likelihood of cohabiting relationships dissolving (Liefbroer and Dourleijn, 2006), including those in which children are born (Andersson, 2002, 2003), can be related to cohabitation and marriage being qualitatively different unions. That is, there may be more selection into marriage because cohabiting couples who are more satisfied with their relationship are more likely to marry and those less satisfied more likely to remain cohabiting or break up.

Regulations and rights around cohabitation differ significantly. In many countries, cohabiting couples cannot access many of the normative and legal benefits that married individuals enjoy. The registration of fathers is not compulsory in some countries, and unmarried couples must negotiate bureaucratic obstacles to gain joint custody (Perelli-Harris and Sánchez Gassen, 2012). In some countries, for example, Germany, the tax code favors married couples, while in countries where cohabitants and married couples have the same rights and obligations in relation to social security, pensions, and taxations, for example, Norway, there are still differences in private law (Noack, 2010).

The transition to marriage

Marriage has undergone a remarkable transformation in its character and meaning (Sobotka and Toulemon, 2008). Even though there is an almost universal ongoing decline in marriage rates across Europe, marriage still seems to be a desirable living arrangement. However, the reasons for marriage may have changed, and the transition into marriage occurs at different stages in people's lives than it has in the past. Available Eurostat statistics show that the mean age at first marriage in the middle of the 1970s was 22–24 years. At that time, Sweden was the forerunner, where postponement had already started and had reached a mean age of 25. By the new millennium, the mean age at women's first marriage had increased rapidly and was found mostly in the later twenties. Setting age 30 as a threshold, only Sweden had reached this level by 2000, while 10 years later in 2010, the mean age for first-time brides was 30 years or older in the Nordic countries, France, Germany, Ireland, Luxemburg, the United Kingdom, Spain, and Italy. In Sweden, it has now reached age 33. Even though marriage ages across Europe have increased, the mean age at first marriage remains widely differentiated, especially along the "East–West divide" with lower mean ages in Eastern European countries (Sobotka and Toulemon, 2008).

The marriage decline has been one of the main markers of the second demographic transition, which is seen as being driven by changes in values (Surkyn and Lesthaeghe, 2004). The decline in marriage rates or the number of marriages per 1000 population can be seen in Table 2.1. In 1970, the marriage rates were between 7.0 and 9.0 across most of Europe. Twenty years later in 1990, marriage rates for most countries had decreased to between 5.0 and 6.0. The general trend into the new century has been a continuing decrease in marriage rates to between 3.0 and 4.0. However, there have been a few exceptions where the marriage rate has increased over the last 10 years in Sweden, Finland, and Greece. There is a clear connection between the decline

Table 2.1   Total period marriage rates 1970–2010 for selected European countries

Country	1970	1980	1990	2000	2010
Ireland	7.0	6.4	5.1	5.0	4.6
France	7.8	6.2	5.1	5.0	3.8
Sweden	5.4	4.5	4.7	4.5	5.3
Norway	7.6	5.4	5.2	5.0	4.8
United Kingdom	8.5	7.4	6.6	5.2	4.3
Denmark	7.4	5.2	6.1	7.2	5.6
Finland	8.8	6.2	5.0	5.1	5.6
Belgium	7.6	6.7	6.5	4.4	3.9
Netherlands	9.5	6.4	6.5	5.5	4.5
Luxemburg	6.4	5.9	6.1	4.9	3.5
Switzerland	7.6	5.6	6.9	5.5	5.5
Greece	7.7	6.5	5.8	4.5	5.0
Bulgaria	8.6	7.8	6.8	4.3	3.2
Czech Republic	9.2	7.6	8.8	5.4	4.4
Austria	7.1	6.2	5.9	4.9	4.5
Italy	7.4	5.7	5.6	5.0	3.6
Germany	7.9	6.3	6.5	5.1	4.7
Spain	7.3	5.9	5.7	5.4	3.6
Portugal	9.4	7.4	7.2	6.2	3.8
Hungary	9.4	7.5	6.4	4.7	3.6

Source: Data from Eurostat.

in marriage rates and postponement of marriage. This means that some of the declines in marriage rates are due to people postponing marriage, so a reversal may have a "catching-up" effect. A recent study of the reverse marriage trend in Sweden suggests that the popularity of marriage in Sweden is increasing (Ohlsson-Wijk, 2011). As a forerunner of new family behavior and the first country in which young people started to postpone marriage, Sweden makes an interesting case study. When marriage is no longer the conventional form of union formation based on social norms and values, people are marrying for other reasons, and marriage can be seen as a manifestation of individual values and preferences (Sobotka and Toulemon, 2008). An interesting question is whether other countries will also experience a similar marriage turnaround in the future. It has been argued that the symbolic value of marriage may still be high even though its practical importance has decreased (Cherlin, 2004). Thus, marriage may mark a new stage in couple's relationships and may symbolize its distinction from cohabitation (Noack, Berhardt, and Wiik, 2013).

Same-sex marriage

Same-sex marriage is the newest type of family formation. It did not exist before the twenty-first century, but has emerged in several countries over the last decade. Legalizing same-sex marriage has been more controversial in some countries than others. Before same-sex marriages were legalized, the Nordic countries and the Netherlands introduced the so-called registered partnership where same-sex couples were given more or less the same legal rights and duties as heterosexual marriages (Noack, Berhardt, and Wiik, 2013). Since 2000, same-sex marriages have been legalized in seven European countries: the Netherlands (2001), Belgium (2003), Spain (2005), Norway and Sweden (2009), and Iceland and Portugal (2010) (Chamie and Mirkin, 2011). Same-sex marriages have also been legalized in Canada and some states in the United States.

In European countries, same-sex marriages constitute a very small proportion of all marriages. The proportion was somewhat larger in the first year following its legislation but is now in the range of 1.8% (Spain) and 3.2% (Sweden) (Chamie and Mirkin, 2011). Some analyses have shown that same-sex marriages in Scandinavia are somewhat different to heterosexual marriage in that couples are older when they marry and female couples have a higher divorce risk than male couples (Andersson *et al.*, 2006; Andersson and Noack, 2010).

The increase in childbearing in cohabitation

Following the increase in unmarried cohabitation among young people, there has been a dramatic rise in childbearing in cohabitation. With a few exceptions, official statistics in most countries have not picked up on these trends and are still publishing only the proportion of births outside marriage. The vast majority of the increases in births have been in cohabiting couples, rather than to single mothers (Perelli-Harris *et al.*, 2010). Childbearing outside any union constitutes 5% of births observed in Italy, Spain, and Switzerland; about 10% in Norway, West Germany, and the United Kingdom; and about 20% in the United States and Austria (Kennedy and Bumpass, 2008; Sobotka and Toulemon, 2008).

Figure 2.1 shows the proportions of births outside marriage in 1970, 1985, 2000, and 2010 for European countries. There has been a clear increase in nonmarital childbearing in all nations, but there are extensive variations across nations in the level of nonmarital childbearing and in the time period during which the changes occurred. Before 2000, there was a clear North–South divide. The highest proportions of births outside marriage were found in the Nordic countries where 50% of all births were nonmarital, while the lowest proportions were found in Southern European countries, for example, Greece, where still less than 10% of children were born outside marriage. After 2000, only small changes appeared in the Nordic countries, with Iceland and Sweden experiencing small decreases, whereas more countries had reached 50%. For instance, France increased from 43% in 2000 to 54% in 2010. During the last 40 years, countries have followed different trajectories in the increase of nonmarital childbearing. Among the Nordic countries, Iceland and Sweden had reached a level of almost 20% or higher already in 1970, while Norway had a lower level from the outset and increased at a slower pace until 2000. Another group is France, the United Kingdom, and Bulgaria, which have almost reached the same level as the Nordic countries. These countries had their most rapid increase in the period 1985 to 2000, where the level continued to increase after 2000. The next group is the Netherlands, the Czech Republic, and Austria, which have now reached a level of 40% or more; the Netherlands and the Czech Republic have increased rather rapidly over the last 10 years. Austria is somewhat different in already having a relatively high

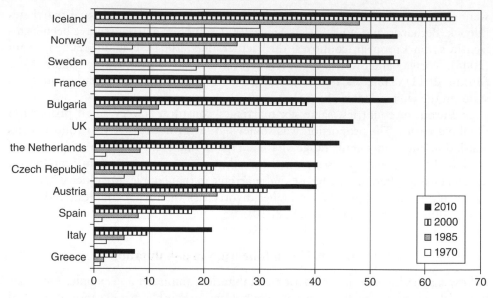

Figure 2.1 Percentage of births outside marriage 1970–2010 for selected European countries. *Source*: Data from Eurostat.

proportion (13%) in 1970 and increasing more gradually. Southern European countries have witnessed more variation in the last decade. While Greece has experienced only small changes, there have been rather rapid increases in both Italy and Spain, with Spain having already started to increase in the period 1985–2000.

New research has shown that childbearing in cohabitation across Europe is associated with a negative educational gradient, that is, cohabiting women with low levels of education (less than completed basic secondary school) have a significantly greater risk of first births than women with medium levels of education (completed secondary school and any school beyond secondary school but less than completed college), while cohabiting women with high levels of education (bachelor's or university degree or higher) have a significantly lower risk (Perelli-Harris et al., 2010). These authors interpret this as a "pattern of disadvantage." Across Europe, life has become more uncertain in the labor and housing markets. Young people have responded to these conditions by postponing family-related events including leaving the parental home, marrying, and childbearing (Kohler, Billari, and Ortega, 2002; Sobotka and Toulemon, 2008). Perelli-Harris et al. (2010) argue that if cohabitation can be linked to this uncertainty, "marriage signifies stability, and the least educated have been the most severely affected by economic uncertainty and globalization, then it seems to follow that the least educated would be more likely to cohabit, while the most highly educated would be more likely to marry. This association should become even more pronounced at the birth of a couple's first child, when the stability of marriage and the commitment of two parents may be perceived as especially crucial for childrearing" (2010, p. 796).

Childbearing and marriage

The increase in childbearing in cohabitation raises the question of the role of marriage in the childbearing process. When cohabitation functions as a stable relationship for raising children, marriage may become more irrelevant (Heuveline and Timberlake, 2004; Kiernan, 2004). The fact that most children born into cohabitation will experience the marriage of their parents (Heuveline and Timberlake, 2004) indicates that marriage and childbearing continue to be inter-related, although in a manner different to previously. When the normative pressure to follow the standard sequencing of marriage followed by childbearing becomes weaker, it might lead to a greater variety in sequences of events (Billari and Liefbroer, 2010). The perception of what constitutes a family has also changed. Kiernan's (2004) analysis of 1998 Eurobarometer data shows that children, rather than partnership status, appear to be more salient in defining families.

To understand the meaning of marriage vis-à-vis childbearing, four categories of marriage have been proposed by Holland (2013). In the first category, the standard sequence of marriage and then children, defined as the *family-forming marriage*, follows normative thinking that childbearing should take place in marriage. Marriage that occurs in tandem with or shortly after the beginning of childbearing is defined as a *legitimizing marriage*. The so-called "shotgun" marriage or bridal pregnancy has become less common, but marriages occurring shortly after the birth of a child can be placed into this category. In the next category, marriage is not seen as necessary for childbearing, and the transition to parenthood is viewed as a stronger relationship commitment than marriage. However, marriage may be seen as indicating *reinforcement* of the marriage contract as a formalization of the commitment and adds an additional layer of security to the union. Finally, marriage is seen as the *capstone* of the family-building process and occurs when the couple has achieved a desired family size.

In new analysis, Perelli-Harris *et al*. (2012) show how childbearing is interrelated with marriage and cohabitation. As presented in Table 2.2, they followed a subsample of women who had their first birth within a union. Their results show the percentage of women who were cohabiting with the father of their first child, the percentage of these women who were cohabiting at conception and birth, and the proportion of women who were cohabiting 1 and 3 years after birth. For the last two columns in Table 2.2, both marriage and dissolution were possible alternatives. First, the results confirm that across Europe cohabitation has become the most common way of starting a union that produces children, with a few exceptions. Second, in most countries, most cohabitation that involves childbearing couples still moves into marriage before the birth of the first child. This is the period of the most changes. Third, couples who are cohabiting at the first birth make fewer changes later and are more likely to continue cohabiting as they did before the birth. For all the countries included in this study, cohabitation may still be regarded as a temporary state, at least when childbearing is involved (Perelli-Harris *et al*., 2012). Following the categories proposed by Holland (2013), it is clear that family-forming marriage and legitimizing marriages are most present across Europe. This pattern is less evident in Norway, which together with the other

Table 2.2 Among women who gave birth within a cohabiting or marital union, the percentage remaining within cohabitation at different stages in the life course in 11 European countries, 1995 to the early 2000s

	Start of union	Conception	First birth	One year after birth	Three years after birth	
	Percent of women who began their unions with cohabitation	Percent still cohabiting at conception	Percent still cohabiting at birth	Percent of women in cohabitation 1 year after birth, based cumulative incidence curves	Percent of women in cohabitation 3 years after birth, based cumulative incidence curves	Percent who started union with cohabitation and stayed in cohabitation up to 3 years after birth
Norway	90	61	56	49	35	39
France	90	51	47	41	33	37
Austria	88	55	38	30	23	27
Netherlands	78	33	26	25	22	28
United Kingdom	75	34	26	22	15	20
Bulgaria	77	45	24	21	20	26
Russia	57	40	18	13	8	14
Hungary	46	28	18	17	15	33
Romania	29	18	12	9	7	24
Italy	18	10	8	7	4	22

Source: Data from Perelli-Harris *et al.* (2012).

Nordic countries is often described as the forerunner in family change. Using another approach, similar distributions are found for Sweden, another forerunner in new family behavior (Holland, 2013).

Transition to Parenthood

Becoming parents is one of the most important decisions couples make and has become an important way of expressing partnership commitment. Better access and improved contraception have made couples and especially women more able to choose when and how many children they want. Young people wait longer until they become parents and have fewer children than in the past. To better understand changing fertility trends across Europe, three main features are explored: the diversity of family behavior, gender equality, and family policy.

Fewer and later childbirths

Throughout Europe, there is great concern for present fertility levels and trends. Since the 1960s, birth rates across Europe have dropped dramatically, and fertility below replacement levels has captured the attention of researchers, policy makers, and society at large. Low fertility puts more pressure on the welfare state by increasing the age-dependency ratio, thus also creating a larger burden for future generations. Total Fertility Rate (TFR) is the main indicator of fertility. TFR is the mean number of children born alive to a woman during her life course under the provision that the childbearing pattern in the period applies to the woman's entire reproductive period. A TFR of around 2.1 children per woman is considered to be the replacement level, that is, the average number of children per woman required to keep the population size constant in the absence of migration.

Table 2.3 shows the TFR across Europe for the period 1970–2010. Currently, the highest rates are in Ireland, France, the United Kingdom, and the Nordic countries, and the lowest rates are to be seen in Central and Southern European countries. In the trend of decreased fertility across Europe, many countries have experienced fertility rates at "very low" (below 1.5) or "lowest low" (below 1.3) levels (Frejka and Sobotka, 2008). Since 2000, fertility levels seem to be increasing in almost all countries, albeit slightly. This may be partly due to a catching-up process, following postponement of having children. Since the beginning of the 1970s, women across Europe, especially in Western Europe, have been postponing motherhood. In the early 1970s, the average age at first birth for most Western European women was 23–24 years, while in 2000, it was 27–28 years (Council of Europe, 2005). Since 2000, women have still been postponing childbirth, but there are some signs of stabilization with a lessening pace of postponement. For instance, during the 1990s, the mean age at first birth increased by 1.8 years among Norwegian women, while it only increased by 0.8 years during the 2000s. Numbers for men are rare, but in general, they are following the same movement at slightly higher ages. There is little evidence that delayed entry into parenthood plays a significant role in the shifts toward low and very low fertility levels in many parts of Europe (Frejka and Sobotka, 2008).

Table 2.3   Total period fertility rates 1970–2010 for selected European countries

Country	1970	1980	1990	2000	2010
Ireland	3.85	3.21	2.11	1.89	2.07
France	2.47	1.95	1.78	1.89	2.03
Sweden	1.92	1.68	2.13	1.54	1.98
Norway	2.50	1.72	1.93	1.85	1.95
United Kingdom	2.45	1.90	1.83	1.64	1.94
Denmark	1.95	1.55	1.67	1.77	1.87
Finland	1.83	1.63	1.78	1.73	1.87
Belgium	2.25	1.68	1.62	1.67	1.84
Netherlands	2.57	1.60	1.62	1.72	1.79
Luxemburg	1.97	1.50	1.60	1.76	1.63
Switzerland	2.10	1.55	1.58	1.50	1.50
Greece	2.40	2.23	1.40	1.26	1.51
Bulgaria	2.17	2.05	1.82	1.26	1.49
Czech Republic	1.92	2.08	1.90	1.14	1.49
Austria	2.29	1.65	1.46	1.36	1.44
Italy	2.38	1.64	1.33	1.26	1.41
Germany	2.03	1.56	1.45	1.36	1.39
Spain	2.88	2.20	1.36	1.23	1.38
Portugal	3.01	2.25	1.56	1.55	1.36
Hungary	1.98	1.91	1.87	1.32	1.25

Source: Data from Eurostat.

Childlessness

Parallel to the trend in young people of postponing parenthood is a trend of increased childlessness. As illustrated in Figure 2.2, 10–20% of women born in 1950–1965 will never have children. The highest numbers are found in Austria, Finland, the Netherlands, Sweden, Switzerland, and the United Kingdom, where about one in five women born in either 1960 or 1965 is childless. Data for men are relatively rare; however, in Norway and Sweden where such data are available, higher proportions of men relative to women in the same cohorts are childless. More than one in five men born in 1960 had not fathered a child. These numbers are based on reliable register data and not a result of poor quality or missing data on men's fertility histories. Childlessness is a concern not only because of its implications for maintaining stable populations but also because it has consequences for individuals, including access to support in old age (Dykstra and Hagestad, 2007; Rowland, 2007).

Delaying parenthood has been seen as a strategy, especially among women, to pursue goals such as higher education, become established in the labor market, and accumulate material resources (Sobotka, 2005). Using period and cohort fertility data for 17 European countries and the United States, Sobotka (2005) analyzed and projected trends in final childlessness among women born between 1940 and 1975. Although final childlessness will gradually increase across all European countries, there will be national variations in the magnitude of these changes. The Nordic countries and France have relatively low childlessness compared with other European countries. Sobotka argues that the generous family policies typical in these countries may have an enabling

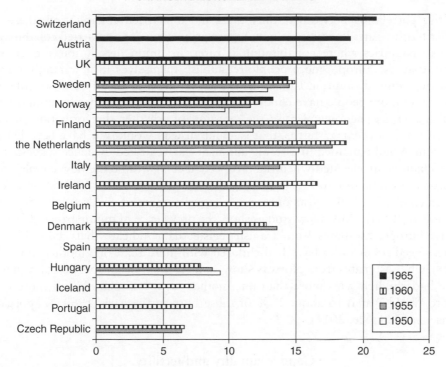

Figure 2.2 The proportion of childless women at age 40, women born 1950–1965, selected European countries.
Source: Data from OECD; Statistics Sweden; Statistics Norway.

effect as "by reducing some constraints child rearing imposes upon people's lives, they enable more couples to decide to become parents" (Sobotka, 2005, p. 28).

The social acceptance of childlessness has increased over time. Using data from the 2006 European Social Survey, Merz and Liefbroer (2012) show that approval of voluntary childlessness was highest in Northern, followed by Southern Europe and lowest in former communist Eastern European countries. They also find that approval of childlessness is related to advancement in the second demographic transition. According to this theory, increased emphasis on autonomy and self-realization lead to greater acceptance of new demographic behavior that deviates from traditional family norms (Lesthaeghe, 2010). There is an important gender dimension in attitudes toward childlessness where Merz and Liefbroer (2012) also find that women are more approving of voluntary childlessness than men and the educational gradient in approval of childlessness is steeper for women.

The diversity of family behavior and fertility

An appropriate line of inquiry is to examine linkages between changing fertility trends and the diversity of family behavior across Europe. It is argued that one of the central parts of the second demographic transition, the decline in marriage rates, cannot be considered an important cause of the current low fertility levels in many European countries (Sobotka and Toulemon, 2008). Nowadays, we observe a positive correlation between fertility rates and unmarried cohabitation; there are higher fertility rates in countries with higher proportions of unmarried cohabitation than in countries where cohabitation is rarer. As union dissolution and divorce increase across Europe, more people reestablish themselves in new family unions following family dissolution. Consequently, more children are born within a stepfamily union, and more people have children with more than one partner (multipartnered fertility). These phenomena raise the question of whether the formation of new unions produces "extra" births, that is, children who would not have been born if the woman had remained in a stable union. So far, scattered evidence suggests that birth chances are elevated when the prospective child will be the new couple's first or second common offspring, indicating that the unique value of a first or second shared child exceeds the costs of rearing a larger number of children in stepfamilies (Thomson, 2004). Only a few studies show the prevalence of multipartnered fertility across Europe. Estimates from Danish register data indicate that about 10% of fathers aged 38 or older have had children with more than one mother (Sobotka, 2008), while estimates from Norway show an increase in the proportion of men who have had children with more than one mother, from less than 4% of those born before World War II to about 11% of those born in the early 1960s (Lappegård, Rønsen, and Skrede, 2011).

Gender equality and fertility

Gender practices in paid and unpaid work have changed over the past decades. In most Western countries, there has been a move away from the traditional male bread-winner model toward various degrees of dual-earner models in which both men and women participate in the labor market. An essential question is whether gender equality matters for fertility. Low fertility is often seen as the result of gender inequality in areas of life that have been recognized as essential for childbearing in modern societies, namely, employment, economic resources, and household and care work. The European Commission recognizes that the future of the welfare states depends on women's willingness to insure a reproduction function and proposes a wide range of policies to improve the possibilities for women and men to found a family, including financial support and work arrangements (European Commission, 2007).

In previous decades, low fertility in industrialized countries has been linked to increasing female labor force participation (Becker, 1981). More recently, the relationship seems to have reversed, and there is a positive macrolevel correlation between female work in the labor market and fertility. To illustrate this, Figure 2.3 shows the correlation between the percentage of women aged 25–54 who are found in the labor force and the TFR. There is a clear South–North division, where the Nordic countries have both high fertility levels and high proportions of women in the labor force, while in Southern European countries, there is both low fertility and low female labor force participation. Eastern European countries also have low fertility but have a longer history of female employment. In the countries where we can see a positive fertility reversal, gender equality is also very high. In some countries, the gender egalitarian model has become the norm, that is, the political goal of gender equality is implemented through welfare state interventions in family arrangements. Fertility in these countries is also high.

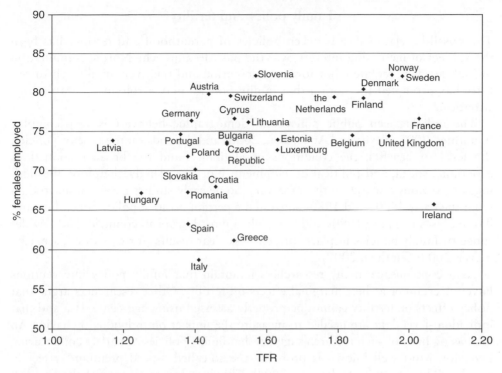

Figure 2.3 The correlation between the percentage of females in the work force (aged 25–54) and total fertility rate 2010 for selected European countries.
Source: Data from Eurostat.

The Nordic countries are suitable examples since they generally score high on gender equality indexes such as the UN gender empowerment measurement and have relatively high fertility compared with other industrialized countries. These phenomena might be explained by the Beckerian model where improved female empowerment predicts fertility decline (Becker, 1981), but as we move toward the egalitarian model where the dual-earner couple is the norm, gender equality might generate higher fertility.

Most modern societies are moving toward higher gender equality, a process often referred to as the "gender revolution." Many describe this as a two-step process, with the first step being developing gender equality in education and employment and better integration of women in the political process. This is followed by higher gender equality in the private sphere of the family (Goldscheider, Oláh, and Puur, 2010), implying that men take a more active role in the family, that is, participation in housework and childcare. Where the process of gender equality within the family sphere is not occurring at the same pace as gender equality at the societal level, families are put under pressure, thereby limiting fertility (Goldscheider, Oláh, and Puur, 2010). A similar argument is made by McDonald (2000); low fertility in developed countries is the result of a high level of gender equality in individual-oriented social institutions, for example, the educational system and the labor market, and a low level or at best a moderate level of gender equality in family-oriented institutions, especially in the family.

Family policy and fertility

The possible relationship between policies of parenthood and fertility has been the subject of increasing interest over the past decades. The Nordic combination of high levels of female labor force participation and relatively high levels of fertility has prompted the notion that family policies play a role in generating this situation.

The link between public policy and demographic behavior is very complex (Gauthier, 2007; Neyer and Andersson, 2008) and depends on the type of policies, the level of benefits, the conditions of eligibility, and the broader context of economic, social, and political development. Not surprisingly, therefore, the findings of previous research in this area vary. Some early studies based on macrodata from the early 1970s and 1980s suggested a certain positive policy effect, but similar analyses from the 1990s and later, when most European countries had a wider range of family policies in place, present less clear results (for overviews, see, e.g., Neyer, 2003; Gauthier, 2007).

As a consequence, many researchers maintain that family policy interventions have uncertain or at best marginal effects on fertility. Other researchers argue that policy effects on fertility cannot be properly assessed using aggregate data and that individual-level data are needed to measure the impact on individual behavior. An increasing body of such research suggests that family policies can affect childbearing behavior. Most well known is probably the so-called "speed premium" effect in Sweden (Hoem, 1990; Andersson, 2004). This is a unique feature of the Swedish parental leave system that has encouraged mothers to space their childbirths more closely together. Evidence from Norway indicates that there may be a slight positive effect on fertility of increasing day-care supply (Rindfuss *et al.*, 2007). Studies from other parts of Europe also suggest that family policies play a role in fertility decisions. For Italy, Del Boca (2002) finds that the availability of childcare and part-time work increases both the probability of working and having a child; estimates for France suggest that fertility is quite sensitive to financial incentives in the French family benefit package (Laroque and Salanié, 2008).

Family Dissolution

While staying together until separated by death is the norm, marriages are increasingly dissolving, resulting in more diverse living arrangements and family forms including more people living alone for longer periods, more parents living as single parents, and more people repartnering. This may have consequences not only for the parents (mostly the fathers) who are not living full time with their children but also for children's welfare.

Increasing and decreasing divorce rates

Nowadays, all European countries experience higher divorce rates than they did just a few decades ago. During this period, there have been considerable changes in divorce policy and divorce laws. Throughout Europe, there are large differences

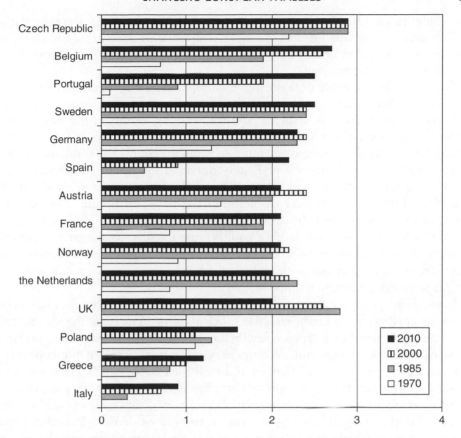

Figure 2.4 Crude divorce rates per 1000 population 1970–2010 for selected European countries. *Source*: Data from Eurostat.

in the tempo of the increase and the level of divorce rates, and some countries have even experienced a reversal trend over the last 10 years. This is illustrated in Figure 2.4, which shows the number of divorces per 1000 population for several European countries for the period 1975–2010. Many countries experienced a major increase in the divorce rates in the 1970s (e.g., the United Kingdom, the Netherlands, Norway, Germany, Belgium, and France) and reached a level of 2.0 or above in 1985. Sweden, Austria, and the Czech Republic already had higher levels in 1970 but were found to have higher levels in 1985. In 1985, the highest levels were found in the United Kingdom and the Czech Republic with 2.8 and 2.9, respectively. The Czech Republic continued this high level in 2000 and 2010, while the United Kingdom together with several other countries has experienced a decrease in the divorce rates, especially since 2000. Divorce rates started to increase somewhat later in both Spain and Portugal, but they have now reached divorce rates at the higher end of the scale. Poland, Italy, and Greece also experienced an increase in divorce rates, but not to the same level as other European countries. These trends show that there is no consistent East–West differentiation in divorce rates as there were in other indicators of family behavior (Sobotka and Toulemon, 2008). Consequently, as cohabitation is increasingly gaining ground across Europe, it becomes more difficult to interpret divorce rates, especially the decrease that we can observe in parts of Europe. As more couples start unmarried cohabitation, there is more selection into marriage as many of the less committed couples break up before they enter marriage.

There are few available data on trends in separation among unmarried cohabitants, mainly because it is an informal behavior; only a few countries have the option to register cohabitation as a living arrangement, for example, the Netherlands. Generally, cohabiting unions have a higher breakup risk than marriage, especially when there are no children involved but also when the couple has common children. Using data from the Fertility and Family Survey 1989–1997, Andersson (2002, 2003) compared disruption risks depending on the family status at childbirth. He finds that children born within cohabitation have higher disruption risks than children born in marriage, but the differences between cohabitation and marriage are smaller in Sweden where the level of childbearing in cohabitating couples was the greatest. This indicates that when childbearing in cohabitation becomes more common, cohabiting unions with children become a less selective group and more similar to married couples in union stability.

Interestingly, people's acceptance of divorce does not follow divorce rates as one may expect (Rijken and Liefbroer, 2012). The authors argue that "the idea that the more one is exposed to a type of new behavior, the more tolerant one's attitudes towards this type of behavior become, may not be applicable if the behavior is evaluated as largely negative" (Rijken and Liefbroer, 2012, p. 43). There are, however, two characteristics of a country that they find correlate with acceptance of divorce involving young children. First, the poverty rate among single-parent households is negatively associated with acceptance of divorce involving young children. Second, higher enrolment in childcare is positively associated with acceptance of divorce involving young children. This means that the financial consequences for the single parent, mostly the mother, are a factor people take into account when forming attitudes toward divorce. In addition, childcare protects children's upbringing and provides mothers with opportunities for paid work (Rijken and Liefbroer, 2012).

Single-parent families

A consequence of higher divorce rates is more children not living with both parents. As illustrated in Table 2.4, there is great variation across Europe. Data from the Health Behavior in School-Aged Children Survey 2005/2006 report on children aged 11, 13, and 15 combined show that, among the countries included here, Italy has the highest proportion of children living with both parents (87%) and Denmark the lowest (66%). The majority of children not living with their parents are living with one parent, most likely their mother. There is considerable diversity in the distribution of children living in single-parent families compared with stepfamilies. In Italy, the proportion of single parents is 67% and in Denmark 37%, with the rest living in stepfamilies. The higher prevalence of stepfamilies compared with single-parent families is more pronounced in countries where the proportion not living with both parents is greater. This indicates that repartnering or remarrying is more common in countries where family dissolution is more common.

Table 2.4 Family structure for children aged 11, 13, and 15 combined, 2005/2006, for selected European countries

Country	Both parents	Single parent	Stepfamily	Other
Italy	87	9	3	1
Greece	86	11	2	1
Spain	84	11	4	1
Poland	83	12	3	1
Portugal	82	10	6	2
Ireland	81	13	5	2
Netherlands	80	12	7	1
Switzerland	79	12	8	1
Austria	76	14	8	1
Luxemburg	76	14	8	2
Belgium (Flemish)	74	14	10	1
Germany	74	15	9	1
Hungary	74	16	9	2
France	73	14	11	1
Norway	73	16	10	2
Sweden	73	14	12	1
Finland	71	16	13	1
Czech Republic	70	16	12	2
United Kingdom (England)	70	16	12	1
Denmark	66	19	13	3

Source: Data from Health Behaviour in School-aged Children Survey 2005/2006 in Chapple 2009.

One of the consequences of family dissolution and divorce is that one of the parents is not living, at least not full time, with their children. This is often the father as mothers are more likely to have their children living with them on a daily basis after separation or divorce. On the other hand, more repartnering means that more adults – also more so among men – are living in families with children who are not their biological children. Family dissolution may have a direct consequence for the welfare of children. Single-parent families are less likely to have as much income as families of both parents. Separation often means the direct loss of a family earner but may also increase the difficulty and cost for the custodial parent in supplying labor and generating income.

Discussion

Family behavior across Europe is changing. Most countries are following the same trends, but there is extensive variation in level and tempo of change. Decreasing marriage rates and fertility rates, increasing divorce rates, and more children born within cohabitation indicate that "new" family behavior is becoming more popular across Europe. There is also a general postponement of family events, that is, increasing ages of transition to marriage and parenthood, but also more variation, indicating a diverging pattern of timing and sequencing of events (Billari and Liefbroer, 2010). In this chapter, we have seen how these changes vary over time and across nations. In this discussion, I will raise two issues from this review, namely, the relationship between marriage and childbearing and the situation with low fertility across Europe.

The most profound changes are the disconnection of marriage and childbearing and family events not following a traditional sequence. This raises two main questions concerning the role that marriage will have in the future and whether there are different consequences for children born within or outside marriage. The main role of marriage as an institution has been the ritual of forming a new couple (Heuveline and Timberlake, 2004) and as a way to sanction the link between parents and their children (Sobotka and Toulemon, 2008). As most young couples nowadays start living together outside marriage and more children are born within cohabitation, the meaning of marriage has changed. Marriage is perceived as a private matter, and couples are entering marriage at different stages in the family formation process. Even though cohabitation is practiced as an alternative to marriage in some groups, most couples eventually marry. As we have seen in this chapter, marriage remains the main context for raising children, and most children will experience their parents being married. For some, marriage remains the main arena for childbearing, and for others, marriage is a capstone to the family formation process (Holland, 2013). When cohabitation becomes completely accepted and there are no legal differences in marriage and cohabitation, an appropriate question is: why do couples still choose to marry? The fact that Sweden, one of the forerunners in new family behavior, is witnessing a reverse marriage trend makes this question even more relevant. In the future, there is a need for more research and new theories about the changing meaning of marriage and the role of cohabitation in the family formation process.

Does it matter whether children are born within or outside marriage? The main distinction is whether a child is born to a single mother, not whether he/she is born to cohabiting or married parents. There is evidence that cohabiting unions are more fragile than marriage, also when children are involved. However, the differences are smaller in countries where cohabitation is more common. The prevalence of cohabitation and childbearing in cohabitation is generally associated with changing values and norms that are more accepting of new family behavior (Lesthaeghe, 2010). However, as we have seen in this chapter, childbearing in cohabitation is associated with a negative educational gradient also in countries where cohabitation is more common, suggesting also a pattern of disadvantage (Perelli-Harris et al., 2010). In the future, there is a need for more research on how different social groups are adapting new family behaviors and the meanings given to cohabitation and marriage by different groups.

Lower fertility has been part of the shift in family behavior, but some countries have lower fertility levels than others and there are real concerns for the imbalance in the age structure and the consequences of low fertility. Young people still have a strong desire to have children, and having children together seems to be a more important expression of relationship commitment for couples than marriage. The decision about having children is embedded in economic, structural, and normative conditions. It is not difficult to imagine that it would be easier to bring a child into the world when certain aspects are in order, such as having a decent place to live and having a stable and economically secure job. For many women, the prospect of being able to remain in the labor market after childbirth may also be of importance. In some countries, the state has become a central actor in the sense that they provide families with economic compensation for the cost of having children and offer child-care to parents. The debate continues over whether the state should spend money on children and to what extent they should make arrangements for families that reconcile family and work life. At an aggregate level, there is a positive correlation between the use of family policies and fertility rates in Europe. There is still a need for more research on how these mechanisms are working and whether arrangements that are working in some societies can be transferred to others.

To conclude, European families are changing in terms of more diverse ordering of life events and continued postponement of events. Despite some variations, countries appear to be following similar trajectories in how partnership and parenthood are organized.

Acknowledgment

This work was supported by the Research Council of Norway and constitutes a part of the research project "Family dynamics, fertility choices, and family policy" (202442/S20). We would like to thank Jennifer Holland, Netherlands Interdisciplinary Demographic Institute (NIDI); Gerda Neyer, Stockholm University; Turid Noack, Statistics Norway; and Tomáš Sobotka, Vienna Institute of Demography for valuable insights.

References

Andersson, G. (2002) Children's experience of family disruption and family formation: evidence from 16 FFS countries. *Demographic Research*, 7, 343–364.

Andersson, G. (2003) Dissolution of unions in Europe: a comparative overview. *MPIDR working paper WP2003–004*, Max Planck Institute for Demographic Research, Rostock.

Andersson, G. (2004) Childbearing developments in Denmark, Norway and Sweden from 1970s to the 1990s: a comparison. *Demographic Research*, 3, 155–176.

Andersson, G. and Noack, T. (2010) Legal advances and demographic developments of same-sex unions in Scandinavia. *Zeitschrift für Familienforschung (Journal of Family Research)*, 22 Sonderheft, 87–101.

Andersson, G., Noack, T., Seierstad, A. and Weedon-Fekjær, H. (2006) The demographics of same-sex marriages in Norway and Sweden. *Demography*, 43, 79–98.

Becker, G. (1981) *A Treatise on the Family*, Harvard University Press, Cambridge.

Billari, F.C. and Liefbroer, A.C. (2010) Towards a new pattern of transition to adulthood. *Advances in Life Course Research*, 15, 59–75.

Bumpass, L.L. (1990) What's happening to the family? Interactions between demographic and institutional changes. *Demography*, 27, 483–498.

Chamie, J. and Mirkin, B. (2011) Same-sex marriage: a new social phenomenon. *Population and Development Review*, 37, 529–551.

Chapple, S. (2009) Child Well-Being and Sole-Parent Family Structure in the OECD: an Analysis. *OECD social, employment and migration working paper, no. 82*, OECD, Paris.

Cherlin, A.J. (2004) The deinstitutionalization of American marriage. *The Journal of Marriage and Family*, 66, 848–861.

Council of Europe (2005) *Recent Demographic Developments in Europe*, Council of Europe, Strasbourg.

Del Boca, D. (2002) The effect of child care and part time opportunities on participation and fertility decisions in Italy. *Journal of Population Economics*, 15, 549–573.

Dykstra, P.A. and Hagestad, G.O. (2007) Roads less taken: developing a nuanced view of older adults without children. *Journal of Family Issues*, 28, 1275–1310.

European Commission (2007) *Europe's Demographic Future: Facts and Figures on Challenges and Opportunities*, Office of Official Publications of the European Communities, Luxembourg.

Frejka, T. and Sobotka, T. (2008) Overview chapter 1: fertility in Europe: diverse, delayed and below replacement. *Demographic Research*, 19, 15–46.

Gauthier, A.H. (2007) The impact of family policies on fertility in industrialized countries: a review of the literature. *Population Research and Policy Review*, 26, 323–346.

Giddens, A. (1992) *The Transformation of Intimacy. Sexuality, Love & Eroticism in Modern Societies*, Polity Press, Cambridge.

Goldscheider, F., Oláh, L.S. and Puur, A. (2010) Reconciling studies of men's gender attitudes and fertility: response to Westoff and Higgins. *Demographic Research*, 22, 189–198.

Heuveline, P. and Timberlake, J.M. (2004) The role of cohabitation in family formation: the United States in comparative perspective. *Journal of Marriage and Family*, 66, 1214–1230.

Hoem, J.M. (1990) Social policy and recent fertility change in Sweden. *Population and Development Review*, 16, 735–748.

Holland, J.A. (2013) Love, marriage, then the baby carriage? Marriage timing and child-bearing in Sweden. *Demographic Research*, 20 (11), 275–306.

Kennedy, S. and Bumpass, L. (2008) Cohabitation and children's living arrangements: new estimates from the United States. *Demographic Research*, 19, 1663–1692.

Kiernan, K. (2004) Unmarried cohabitation and parenthood in Britain and Europe. *Law & Policy*, 26, 33–55.

Kohler, H-P., Billari, F.C. and Ortega, J.A. (2002) The emergence of lowest-low fertility in Europe during the 1990s. *Population and Development Review*, 28, 641–680.

Lappegård, T., Rønsen, M. and Skrede, K. (2011) Fatherhood and fertility. *Fathering: A Journal of Theory, Research, and Practice about Men as Fathers*, 9, 103–120.

Laroque, G. and Salanié, B. (2008) *Does Fertility Respond to Financial Incentives?* Discussion paper no. 5007, Centre for Economic Policy Research, London.

Lesthaeghe, R. (1995) The second demographic transition in western countries: an interpretation, in *Gender and Family Change in Industrialized Countries*, (ed. K.O. Mason and A.-M. Jensen), Clarendon Press, Oxford, pp. 17–62.

Lesthaeghe, R. (2010) The unfolding story of the second demographic transition. *Population and Development Review*, 36, 211–251.

Liefbroer, A.C. and Dourleijn, E. (2006) Unmarried cohabitation and union stability: testing the role of diffusion using data from 16 European countries. *Demography*, 43, 203–221.

Liefbroer, A.C. and Fokkema, T. (2008) Recent trends in demographic attitudes and behaviour: is the second demographic transition moving to southern and eastern Europe? in *Demographic Challenges for the 21st Century: A State of Art in Demography* (ed. J. Surkyn, P. Deboosere and J. Van Bavel), VubPress, Brussels, pp. 115–141.

McDonald, P. (2000) Gender equity in theories of fertility transition. *Population and Development Review*, 26, 427–439.

Merz, E.-M. and Liefbroer, A.C. (2012) The attitude toward voluntary childlessness in Europe: cultural and institutional explanations. *Journal of Marriage and Family*, 74, 587–600.

Neyer, G. (2003) Family policies and low fertility in Western Europe. *Working paper, 2003–021*, Max Planck Institute for Demographic Research, Rostock.

Neyer, G. and Andersson, G. (2008) Consequences of family policies on childbearing behaviour: effects or artefacts? *Population and Development Review*, 34, 699–724.

Noack, T. (2010) *En stille revolusjon: det moderne samboerskapet i Norge* [A Quiet Revolution: The Modern Form of Cohabitation in Norway], University of Oslo, Oslo.

Noack, T., Berhardt, E. and Wiik, K.A. (2013) Cohabitation or marriage? Contemporary living arrangements in the West, in *Contemporary Issues in Family Studies: Global Perspectives on Partnerships, Parenting, and Support in a Changing World* (ed. A. Abela and J. Walker), Wiley Blackwell, Oxford, pp.16–30.

Ohlsson-Wijk, S. (2011) Sweden's marriage revival: an analysis of the new-millennium switch from long-term decline to increasing popularity. *Population Studies: A Journal of Demography*, 65, 183–200.

Perelli-Harris, B. and Sánchez Gassen, N. (2012) How similar are cohabitation and marriage? The spectrum of legal approaches to cohabitation across Western Europe. *Population and Development Review*, 38 (3), 435–467.

Perelli-Harris, B., Sigle-Rushton, W., Kreyenfeld, M. *et al.* (2010) The educational gradient of childbearing within cohabitation in Europe. *Population and Development Review*, 36, 775–801.

Perelli-Harris, B., Kreyenfeld, M., Sigle-Rushton, W. *et al.* (2012) Changes in union status during the transition to parenthood in eleven European countries, 1970s to early 2000s. *Population Studies: A Journal of Demography*, 66, 167–182.

Rijken, A.J. and Liefbroer, A.C. (2012) European views of divorce among parents of young children: understanding cross-national variation. *Demographic Research*, 27, 25–52.

Rindfuss, R.R., Guilkey, D., Morgan, S.P. *et al.* (2007) Child care availability and first-birth timing in Norway. *Demography*, 44, 345–372.

Rowland, D.T. (2007) Historical trends in childlessness. *Journal of Family Issues*, 28, 1311–1337.

Seltzer, J.A. (2000) Families formed outside of marriage. *Journal of Marriage and the Family*, 62, 1247–1268.

Smock, P.J. (2000) Cohabitation in the United States: an appraisal of research themes, findings, and implications. *Annual Review of Sociology*, 26, 1–20.

Sobotka, T. (2005) Childless societies? Trends and projections of childlessness in Europe and the United States. Paper presented at Population Association American Annual Meeting in Philadelphia,April,2005,http://paa2005.princeton.edu/download.aspx?submissionId=50352 (accessed October 31, 2013).

Sobotka, T. (2008) Does persistent low fertility threaten the future of European populations? in *Demographic Challenges for the 21st Century: A State of Art in Demography* (eds. J. Surkyn, P. Deboosere and J. Van Bavel), VubPress, Brussels, pp. 22–89.

Sobotka, T. and Toulemon, L. (2008) Overview chapter 4: changing family and partnership behaviour: common trends and persistent diversity across Europe. *Demographic Research*, 19, 85–138.

Soons, J.P.M. and Kalmijn, M. (2009) Is marriage more than cohabitation? Well-being differences in 30 European countries. *Journal of Marriage and Family*, 71, 1141–1157.

Surkyn, J. and Lesthaeghe, R. (2004) Value orientations and the second demographic transition (SDT) in Northern, Western and Southern Europe: an update. *Demographic Research*, 3, 45–86.

Thomson, E. (2004) Step-families and childbearing desires in Europe. *Demographic Research*, 3, 115–134.

Trost, J. (1978) Attitudes toward and occurrence of cohabitation without marriage. *Journal of Marriage and Family*, 40, 393–400.

Wiik, K.A., Keizer, R. and Lappegård, T. (2012) Relationship quality in marital and cohabiting unions across Europe. *Journal of Marriage and Family*, 74, 389–398.

3

American Families: Demographic Trends and Social Class

Wendy D. Manning and Susan L. Brown

American Families: Demographic Trends and Social Class

American families have undergone a radical transformation even in the last decade. A critical factor that may have influenced some of the recent change in families is the economic recession. In the wake of the recession, the middle class has become smaller, and it has become harder to maintain their standard of living (Pew Research Center, 2012a). All education groups have experienced the loss in income; however, those with only a high school degree have experienced the greatest loss (Pew Research Center, 2012a). This chapter examines recent demographic trends and specifically focuses on changes in the family according to socioeconomic status. We begin with a discussion of what constitutes a family and then provide a description of change in the timing and composition of families. Finally, we consider how those trends have differed according to social class and reflect on what this might mean for future generations.

Defining American families

A wide variety of families exist in the United States; there is certainly no singular American family. Families have been in flux, and our definitions of families have had to keep pace with increasingly common and emerging family forms. As demographers, we often rely on the US Census Bureau data and their definitions of a family. The following is used to define families in a Census Brief titled, "Households and Families: 2010" (Lofquist et al., 2012).

> A family consists of a householder and one or more other people living in the same household who are related to the householder by birth, marriage, or adoption. Biological, adopted, and stepchildren of the householder who are under 18 are the

The Wiley Blackwell Companion to the Sociology of Families, First Edition.
Edited by Judith Treas, Jacqueline Scott, and Martin Richards.
© 2014 John Wiley & Sons Ltd. Published 2017 by John Wiley & Sons Ltd.

"own children" of the householder. Own children do not include other children present in the household, regardless of the presence or absence of the other children's parents.

A family household may also contain people not related to the householder. A family in which the householder and his or her spouse of the opposite sex are enumerated as members of the same household is a husband-wife household. In this report, husband-wife households only refer to opposite-sex spouses and do not include households that were originally reported as same-sex spouse households. Same-sex spousal households are included in the category, "same-sex unmarried partner households" but may be either a family or nonfamily household depending on the presence of another person who is related to the householder. The remaining types of family households not maintained by a husband-wife couple are designated by the sex of the householder.

A nonfamily household consists of a householder living alone or with nonrelatives only, for example, with roommates or an unmarried partner.

This definition does not count same-sex cohabiting couples without children or different-sex couples without children as a family. Further, cohabiting couples (same sex or different sex) that have a child in the household who is not related to the head of household (basically a stepchild to the head) are not counted as families. Most Americans have a somewhat more expansive definition of families (Powell *et al.*, 2010). Even more recent data collected by Powell, Steelman, and Pizmony-Levy (2012) find that the presence of children continues to dramatically increase the likelihood that heterosexual cohabiting and same-sex living arrangements are counted as "family." In addition, increasing numbers of children have more than one home, which is the result, in part, of shifts in policies determining physical custody arrangements (Kelly, 2007; National Center for Family & Marriage Research, 2012). Some states even have adopted presumption of joint custody in divorce cases. Depending on relationships, family members may "claim" children and adults who only spend part of the year living with them. Further, members of families do not always agree on who is in their family as families are perceived and constructed differently by each person (White, 1998). Specifically, research on stepfamilies indicates that there often is not consensus on who is in and out of the family (Furstenberg, 1987; Pasley, 1987; White, 1998). Along a similar vein, we find variation in mother–child dyad reports of cohabitation with at least a third of dyads not sharing the same view of their family structure (Brown and Manning, 2009). Standardization in the measurement of household relationships and families is desirable but remains challenging as families are socially constructed entities and continually shifting (Brown and Manning, 2009; National Center for Family & Marriage Research, 2012). One of the best ways to reference the contemporary family climate may be "Sustained Diversity" (Gerson, 2000).

Family change

The age at first marriage is at a historic highpoint and approaching levels observed in Europe (Elliot *et al.*, 2012). In 2011, the median age at first marriage is 27 for women and 28.7 for men (U.S. Bureau of the Census, 2012). Just in the last decade, the age at first marriage has increased by almost 2 years for both men and women. In contrast, many European countries have median ages of marriage in their 30s. The proportion of the population who has never married has also slightly increased in the last decade rising among men ages 40 to 44 from 15.7% in 2000 to 20.4% in 2010 (author's calculations http://www.census.gov/hhes/families/data/cps2010.html Table A1 and http://www.census.gov/hhes/families/data/cps2000.html Table A1). The levels of never marrying among middle-aged Americans (45 and older) are approaching the historic highpoints observed in 1940 (Elliott *et al.*, 2012). Currently, over one-quarter (28%) of Americans have never been married, which represents a peak over the last half a century; in 1960, 15% of Americans had never been married (Pew Research Center, 2011). The shifts in marriage are due to both delays in marriage and a modest increase in the proportion of the population who never marries. As described later, these delays in marriage provide greater opportunities for cohabiting relationships in young adulthood.

At the same time, marriage is declining among the US population; the last decade has witnessed dramatic struggles over the legalization of marriage for same-sex couples. Public opinion has shifted with nearly half of Americans as well as President Obama reporting support for same-sex marriage (Pew Research Center, 2012b). This has not been supported at the federal level but has been legally endorsed (as of March 2013) in nine states (Connecticut, Iowa, Maine, Maryland, Massachusetts, New Hampshire, New York, Vermont, and Washington) and Washington, D.C. A number of states permit civil unions and domestic partnerships, which provide many of the same protections as legal marriage; about half of same-sex couples have a legally recognized partnership option (Pizer and Kuehl, 2012). Recent estimates based on Census 2010 data indicate there are nearly 650,000 same-sex-couple households (Gates, 2012). The number of same-sex-couple households has increased by 80% over the last decade in contrast to a 40% increase in different-sex unmarried couples and 4% rise in different-sex married couples (Gates, 2012). There is little work relying on nationally representative data on the stability of these couples. About one in six (16%) same-sex-couple households includes biological, step, or adopted children, and about half of same-sex parents have only one child (Burgoyne, 2012). Same-sex couples are less likely to have children and tend to have fewer children than opposite-sex couples. Federal data collections have incorporated new ways of measuring same-sex marriage and unions in the United States (National Center for Family & Marriage Research, 2012). Yet these indicators focus on resident children in same-sex parent couple households, so single lesbian and gay parents are excluded as well as nonresident gay and lesbian mothers and fathers.

The number of different-sex cohabiting couple households has been on a steady rise with 7.5 million couples in 2010 (Kreider, 2010). The increase in age at first marriage has left more early adult years free for cohabitation, and cohabitation levels are also high following a divorce. Between 2006 and 2010, two-thirds of women ages 30–34 had ever cohabited in contrast to only 40% 25 years earlier (Manning, 2010). Increasingly, cohabitation is the first union formed by Americans rather than marriage; three-quarters (73%) of women who formed a union since

2000 cohabited rather than married first (Kennedy and Bumpass, 2011). Even though cohabiting unions are experienced by a large proportion of the population, on average, the unions do not last long. Just about half (45%) of women remained cohabiting with their first partner after 2 years (Kennedy and Bumpass, 2011). From a child's perspective, nearly half have experienced their parents' cohabitation, but these families are much more short-lived than marriages (Manning, Smock, and Majumdar, 2004; Kennedy and Bumpass, 2011). Cohabitation is not just a form of family life experienced by the young. An age group that has witnessed an increase in cohabitation is older Americans with a doubling between 2000 and 2010 in cohabitation among adults over the age of 50 (Brown, Bulanda, and Lee, 2012). Roughly 8% of older unmarried adults are cohabiting. The meanings and implications of cohabitation are likely different for younger and older cohabiting men and women (King and Scott, 2005; Brown, Lee, and Bulanda, 2006). While cohabitation has been integrated into much family research, there is variation in the experiences of cohabitation.

Marriage without prior cohabitation (direct marriage) is an increasingly rare event as the modal pathway into marriage is through cohabitation. Two-thirds of women who recently married had lived together prior to marriage (Manning, 2010). This represents a departure from the levels observed 25 years ago when only half of women had lived together prior to marriage (Bumpass and Sweet, 1989). Yet cohabitation is not always a promise of marriage. Fewer cohabiting unions are resulting in marriage (Kennedy and Bumpass, 2011). About one-quarter of recent cohabitations resulted in marriage within 2 years of beginning of living together in contrast to 40% a decade earlier (Kennedy and Bumpass, 2008; Kennedy and Bumpass, 2011). Further, young men and women are experiencing more cohabiting partnerships (serial cohabitation) (Lichter, Turner, and Sassler, 2010). One-quarter of a recent birth cohort of women who had cohabitation experience lived with more than one partner (Cohen and Manning, 2010). This means that young adults are spending more time not in any one cohabiting relationship but in a greater number of cohabiting relationships (Cohen and Manning, 2010). The United States appears to be moving toward patterns in Europe in terms of increases in cohabitation and declines in direct marriages. Taken together, these trends in cohabitation suggest that research needs to move away from anchoring analysis of family change around only marriage.

These changes in marriage and cohabitation patterns have not led to substantial changes in divorce. The US divorce rate is among the highest in the world, but it has plateaued (Raley and Bumpass, 2003; Kreider and Ellis, 2011). Between two-fifths and half of first marriages are expected to end in separation or divorce (Stevenson and Wolfers, 2007). In 2010, about one in seven or 14% of Americans were divorced or separated in contrast to only 5% 50 years ago (Pew Research Center, 2011). In 2009, about one-quarter (22.4%) of women were ever divorced, and the median age at first divorce was 30 (Kreider and Ellis, 2011). About one-quarter (24%) of children born to married parents are expected to experience the dissolution of their parents' marriage by age 12 (Kennedy and Bumpass, 2011). The divorce rate among the Baby Boom generation (ages 50–64) has spiked. Today, one-quarter of those who divorce are over age 50, while 20 years ago, only 10% of those getting divorced were over age 50 (Brown and Lin, 2012). High divorce rates remain an experience unique to the United States, but increases are occurring in many countries, such as Japan and the Netherlands.

Once Americans divorce, they typically do not stay single (Sweeney, 2010). Schoen and Standish (2001) reported that 69% of women and 78% of men remarry after divorce. In 2009, the time to remarriage from divorce was about 4 years for women and men (Kreider and Ellis, 2011). In 2010, nearly one in three (30%) of marriages were remarriages (Cruz, 2012). The trend from the 1940–1944 and 1960–1964 birth cohorts suggests that similar proportions of men and women have been married at least twice (Kreider and Ellis, 2011). These remarriages are more fragile than first marriages and are more likely to end in dissolution (Teachman, 2008). The decline in remarriage after divorce has been offset by increases in post-marital cohabitation (McNamee and Raley, 2011). Thus, repartnering is an important part of the relationship landscape but has received relatively little research attention.

The proportion of Americans who are widowed has declined from 9% in 1960 to 6% in 2010 (Pew Research Center, 2011). In 2009, most spouses who experienced widowhood were over age 65 (70% among men and 66% among women). Over 70% experienced the death of their first spouse (i.e., were in a first marriage). Roughly 80% of recent widow(er)s are white and over half have no more than a high school diploma. Fewer than 7% are residing with their own minor children (Elliott and Simmons, 2011). Union formation following widowhood is more common among men than women and more likely to be marriage than cohabitation (Brown, Bulanda, and Lee, 2012).

Living Apart Together (LAT) describes long-term committed couple relationships that do not involve coresidence. Some couples are not able to live together because of geographical separation for work or school. Others prefer to maintain some autonomy and independence by living separately. It is difficult to obtain good estimates of the prevalence of LAT relationships in the United States since nearly all social surveys restrict their focus to household members. Nonetheless, a study using the General Social Survey suggests that roughly 7% of adults were involved in LAT relationships in the late 1990s, and more recent estimates from the state of California indicate about 12% of adults are in LAT relationships (Strohm et al., 2009). LATs are comparable to cohabitors in terms of average age (and younger than marrieds) but tend to be more highly educated than cohabitors. They are less likely than cohabitors to report plans to marry their current partner (Strohm et al., 2009). While LATs have received greater attention in the European context, there is increasing recognition that these relationships need to be integrated into our understanding of health and well-being of American adults.

Most adult Americans do not report a preference for sharing their home with their parents or adult children, even if there is an economic need (Seltzer, Bianchi, and Lau, 2012). Yet about 16.5% of households in 2000 and 17.7% in 2010 consisted of at least two generations of adults sharing a residence (Payne, 2012). There has been attention to the young adults who return home (boomerang children) (Newman, 2012). About half of young adults (18–24) lived with their parents in 2010 (53%) and in 2000 (52%) (US Census Bureau, 2012). A modest increase occurred among 25–34-year-olds from about 10% in 2000 to 14% in 2011 (Furstenberg,

2011; Jacobsen and Mather, 2011; Qian, 2012). The delay in marriage has provided more opportunities for returning home because unmarried young adults live with their parents more often than married young adults (Qian, 2012). The change in multigenerational living has not shifted much among older Americans in the last decade with nearly one-fifth living in multigeneration households. There may be growing parallels between American and European young adults who experience delays in independent living.

A group of Americans that has not received much attention is those who live alone. In 2000, 13% of adults lived alone, and today, about 14.3% live alone, which represents a historic high point since 1950 (Pew Research Center, 2010b). In terms of households, the levels have remained quite stagnant with about 25.8% of households in 2000 and 27.4% in 2010 composed of singles living alone (Lofquist *et al.*, 2012). Klinenberg (2012) reports that Americans prefer to live alone but still value their social relationships and are not socially isolated. Among older Americans, there is remarkable stability in the proportion who live alone: 28.1% lived alone in 2000 and 27.4% did so in 2008 (Pew Research Center, 2010a). Further, much higher proportions of older women live alone (34%) than men (18%). As solo living increases, it may be more important to consider relationships that exist across household boundaries. For instance, the growing popularity of LAT relationships corresponds with the worldwide increase in solo living. At the same time, it is important to uncover the extent to which those living alone have access to social support, particularly with the aging of the population (Lin and Brown, 2012).

Our assessments of family change are often centered on the living arrangements of children because the family is the primary socializing unit and source of economic and emotional support for children. The initial living arrangements are measured at birth. In the last decade, the proportion of children born to unmarried mothers has increased from 33.2% in 2000 to 40.8% in 2010 (Martin *et al.*, 2011). The current levels are at a historic peak. The share of births that are nonmarital doubled from 1980 when less than one-fifth (18.4%) of children were born to unmarried mothers (Martin *et al.*, 2011). Driving this increase in nonmarital childbearing has been childbearing to cohabiting mothers. There has been a shift in the occurrence of non-marital births to cohabiting women; in the late 1990s, about 40% compared with 58% in the early 2000s (Martinez, Daniels, and Chandra, 2012). Basically, there have been small declines in births to single mothers and married mothers with increases in children born to cohabiting mothers (Kennedy and Bumpass, 2011). This trend of most nonmarital births occurring to cohabiting mothers is similar to patterns in Europe.

Children's family living arrangements at birth provide only a snapshot of their family experiences with many going on to experience parental (re)marriages, separations and divorce, and cohabitation. Estimates indicate that 24% of children experience the breakup of their parent's marriage and two-thirds experience their cohabiting parent's separation (Kennedy and Bumpass, 2011). About 50% of children born to unmarried mothers experience their mother's marriage and nearly half (46%) their mother's cohabitation (at birth or later) (Kennedy and Bumpass, 2011). As a result of all these family changes, the trends indicate a continual decline in children living in two biological married parent families. In 2001, 69.1% of children were living in two married biological parent families, while in 2010, 65.7% did so (US Bureau of the Census, 2011). The increasing complexity of family life from children's perspectives requires assessments that account for this growing array of experiences, which have enduring consequences for child well-being (Brown, 2010).

Social class and family change

As socioeconomic inequality has risen in the United States, the divergence in family patterns has grown. A unique feature of American society is the vast divide in social class with a weak safety net for the disadvantaged. Several researchers have commented on how this growing income inequality has led to a divergence in American family patterns according to social class (Ellwood and Jencks, 2004; McLanahan and Percheski, 2008; Smock and Greenland, 2010; Cherlin, 2011). We draw on recent literature and reports on demographic trends along with our own analysis of Census and ACS data to track shifts in family patterns according to education level. For the purposes of this chapter, we consider educational attainment as a proxy for social class. We understand the concept of social class is complex and that a more nuanced portrait would include indicators of occupation, income, wealth, investments, and power. In the United States today, 15% of adults over age 25 have not graduated from high school, 29% only have a high school degree, 28% have some vocational education or some college, and 29% have a college degree or more (Julian and Kominski, 2011; Ryan and Siebens, 2012). Figure 3.1 shows the distribution of households with children

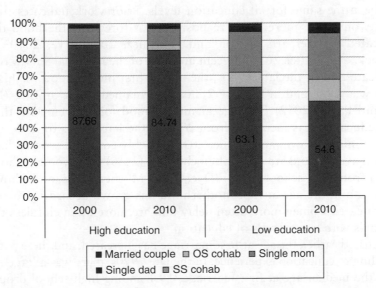

Figure 3.1 Family households with children: family structure and education of parents.
Source: Decennial Census (2000) and American Community Survey (2010): IPUMS.

according to family type for the most educated and least educated Americans. In 2000, we draw on Census data and in 2010 data from the American Community Survey. Among highly educated family households (the head and/or spouse/partner has a college degree) with children, the shift in family composition has been quite small with the vast majority (85%) of highly educated family households consisting of married couples. In contrast, there has been a decline among Americans with the lowest levels of education (the head and/or spouse/partner does not have a high school degree) in the proportion of family households with children that include married couples, from 63% in 2000 to 55% in 2010. Figure 3.1 shows that the education divide is apparent in 2000 and is becoming larger.

Another lens on this question has been illustrated from the perspective of children. Elwood and Jencks (2004) discuss the education divide in family patterns and, in an analysis of Current Population Survey data, present the percentage of children living in single-mother homes over time and according to maternal educational attainment. An increase in children's experience at time of interview in single-mother families occurred for children who have mothers with low levels of education, from about 30% in 1980 to 46% in 2010 (Elwood and Jencks, 2004; Author's calculations CPS 2010). Children with mothers who were high school graduates or had some college education witnessed even sharper increases in single-motherhood experience. For example, 15% of children who have a mother with a high school degree lived in a single-mother home in 1980, and 40% did so in 2010. In contrast, about one-tenth of children who have mothers with college degrees have lived with a single mother, and this has remained stable over the last 30 years (Ellwood and Jencks, 2004; author's calculations http://www.census.gov/hhes/families/data/cps2010.html Table C3).

The median age at entry into motherhood has increased; however, the increase has not been the same for all education levels. Prior work indicates that highly educated women are more likely to postpone or forego motherhood than their less educated counterparts (Abma and Martinez, 2006; Dye, 2010; England, McClintock, and Shafter, 2011). Recent analyses of the National Survey of Growth data indicate that in the late 1970s, the age at first motherhood for high school dropouts was 19.0, and in the late 2000s, it remained stable at 19.2 (Manning, Brown, and Payne, 2012). The age at motherhood for women with the highest levels of education has increased from 27.7 in the late 1970s to 29.9 in the late 2000s (Manning, Brown, and Payne, 2012). Highly educated women have fewer children on average and are more often childless (22%) than women who have not graduated from high school (15%) (Dye, 2010; Mosher, Jones, and Abma, 2012). Thus, the gap in the age at first motherhood has grown according to education. Highly educated women more often delay and are more often childless than their counterparts with lower levels of education.

As discussed earlier, the age at first marriage has increased, and these patterns differ according to education experience. In the late 1970s, there was a large education divide in the median age at first marriage, 19.1 among high school dropouts and 24.7 among college graduates (Manning, Brown, and Payne, 2012). The education gap in the median age at first marriage during the late 2000s is comparatively small, ranging from 24.3 among women without high school degrees to 26.8 among college graduates (Manning, Brown, and Payne, 2012). The proportion of 30–44-year-old women who ever married declined from 82% in 1970 to 69% in 2007 among college graduates, while during the same time frame, the proportion who ever married among those without a college degree declined from 83% to 56% (Fry and Cohn, 2010). In 2010, the marriage rate was over twice as high among college graduates as women with less than a high school degree (Payne and Gibbs, 2011). Thus, just as Goldstein and Kenney (2001) argued over 10 years ago, the marriage decline has occurred for all women, but it has been greater among those who have lower levels of education.

The divorce rate has remained relatively stable; however, there have been striking education differentials in divorce. The most educated appear to have experienced small gains in the stability of marriages (Martin, 2006; Amato, 2010; Copen *et al.*, 2012). The education gap observed in the late 1980s has increased slightly today with a greater decline in divorce among college educated women than women without a high school degree (Raley and Bumpass, 2003; Martin, 2006; Isen and Stevenson, 2010; Copen *et al.*, 2012). Drawing on 2006–2010 data, the probability a first marriage will disrupt by the tenth anniversary is lowest for college graduates (0.15) and graduate degrees (0.18), while the probability of disruption among women with only a high school degree or without a high school degree is 0.40 and with some college education is 0.37 (Copen *et al.*, 2012). In contrast in the late 1980s, the probability of disruption within the first decade of marriage was 0.20 among college graduates and 0.39 among women without a high school degree (Raley and Bumpass, 2003). Based on 2010 data, the rate of divorce is lowest among college graduates and highest among women with some college education (Gibbs and Payne, 2011). The education gradient in divorce is not linear; women without a high school degree have divorce rates that fall between those with college degrees and those who have some post-high school educational attainment.

To understand the education gradient among women who have low levels of education requires acknowledging that foreign-born Latinas have the lowest educational attainment and relatively low dissolution rates. Assessments that exclude foreign-born Latinas indicate women without a high school degree have a much higher rate of dissolution than college graduates (Martin, 2006); however, inclusion of the foreign-born lowers the dissolution rates among women without a high school degree (Gibbs and Payne, 2011). Overall, the marriages of highly educated women are becoming more stable, while women who are less educated are experiencing rising disruption rates (Martin, 2006).

The result of the delays in marriage and almost no change in the age at parenthood has been growth in nonmarital childbearing. The education divide in premarital fertility has grown among more recent birth cohorts (England, Shafer, and Wu, 2012). Analyses of the National Survey of Family Growth indicate that in the late 2000s (2005–2010), 65% of all births to women with less than a high school degree were to unmarried women, and only 8% of births to college graduates were to unmarried women (Payne, Manning, and Brown, 2012). Most children born to college graduates accrue the benefits of parental marriage, while only one-third of children born to the least educated do so. Kennedy and Bumpass (2008) report that in the early 1990s, about half (52%) of births to

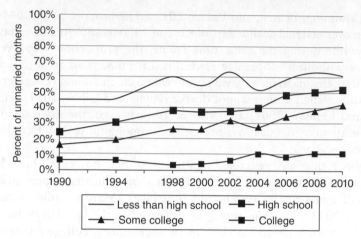

Figure 3.2   Percent of unmarried mothers.
Source: Data from Current Population Survey, June Fertility Supplements.

women with less than a high school degree were to unmarried women, and only 5% of births to college graduates were to unmarried women. As Kennedy and Bumpass (2011) argue, most of the growth in unmarried motherhood is due to births to cohabiting women. The education gap in births to single mothers has remained constant, but the education gap in births to cohabiting mothers has grown. In the early 1990s, one-quarter (25%) of women with less than a high school degree had a birth while cohabiting, whereas in the late 2000s, 36% did so (Kennedy and Bumpass, 2008; Payne, Manning, and Brown, 2012). The shift in childbearing during cohabitation over the same time period among college graduates increased from 1% to 5%. The implications for child well-being are important to consider as children may benefit from the additional income and greater caretaking involvement that a second adult, cohabiting partner may provide.

Another illustration of trends in nonmarital fertility according to educational attainment is based on our use of the Fertility Supplement of the Current Population Survey data. These data do not precisely measure the union status at time of birth but indicate whether a birth occurred in the last year and the union status at the time of interview. Figure 3.2 shows that the trend has been sustained high levels of unmarried motherhood among the least educated and sustained low levels among the most educated. High school graduates and women with some college have experienced sharp increases in unmarried motherhood. Taken together, these studies confirm that there has been a long-standing educational divide and the greatest growth in nonmarital fertility may be among the working class.

Cohabitation has increased more rapidly among those with lower levels of education. Twenty-five years ago, the education gap in cohabitation experience was relatively small (43% among those with less than 12 years of education versus 31% among college graduates) (Bumpass and Sweet, 1989). More recently, three-quarters of women with less than a high school degree had ever cohabited in contrast to half (47%) of college graduates (Manning, 2010). Cohabitation has increased for all women; however, it has become the overwhelming majority experience among the least educated and experienced by about half of college graduates today. In terms of trends in the type of first coresidential union formed, women who were working class (highest education was high school graduate or some college) experienced the greatest increase in cohabitation. In the mid-1980s, about half (56%) of high school graduates who formed a union first cohabited, while in the late 1990s, the vast majority (89%) did so (Manning, Brown, and Payne, 2012). Further, children's experience in cohabiting-parent families has also increased such that in the late 2000s, about 70% of children with a mother with a high school degree or less lived in a cohabiting-parent family and only 10% of the children of college graduates did so (Kennedy and Bumpass, 2011). These findings illustrate that cohabitation has a different role in family formation according to social class. Cohabitation most often serves as a setting for childbearing and rearing among the less educated.

Although many young adults cohabit, others reside with their parents. Young adults are increasingly living with their parents across education groups with the greatest increase among 20–24-year-olds (Qian, 2012). Qian (2012) reports that over one-third of young adults in their early twenties with a high school degree (38%) or some college (37%) lived with their parents in 2000, and this increased to nearly half (45% and 46%, respectively) in 2007–2009. In 2000, 29% of college graduates lived with their parents, and in 2007–2009, 37% did so. The most disadvantaged young adults without a high school degree experienced only a modest change in parental coresidence, from 32% in 2000 to 35% in 2007–2009 (Qian, 2012). The working class appears to have experienced the greatest increase in parental coresidence. These findings suggest that parental coresidence is the result of economic need rather than personal preference. As young adults continue to suffer the aftereffects of the recent Great Recession, we can expect to see a rise in coresidence with parents as an economic survival strategy.

Conclusion

This chapter reviews the recent trends in family change in the United States and documents the dramatic shifts that have occurred in the last decade. A critical event shaping families over the last decade is the Great Recession that began at the end of 2007 and has played a large role in the shrinking of the middle class. For the first time in history, the middle class lost ground in recent years, leaving them with fewer resources to help weather further financial crises. The precarious status of the middle class may exacerbate the social class divide in family patterns in the near future. In fact, the recession may have added fuel to family trends that were already underway. The slow economic recovery means the lingering effects of the economic crisis persist today, affecting how Americans form and sustain families and contributing to even more pronounced diverging destinies for parents and their children (McLanahan, 2004). The hollowing out of the middle class will arguably contribute to the rise of fragile families, who are economically unstable, often unmarried families. At the other end of the spectrum, marriage may be more elusive for a growing share of Americans, reinforcing the notion that marriage is a luxury good or capstone event that is attainable only among the elite (Cherlin, 2004). This chapter has focused on how social class, operationalized by education, structures family life. We acknowledge that other indicators of social inequality such as race/ethnicity and nativity status as well as gender are also integral to family behaviors and experiences but maintain that education is a key marker of social status and is especially germane to understanding recent patterns and trends in US families.

The decline of marriage and rise of cohabitation are two of the most dramatic family changes in the last decade. Given economic stability is typically a prerequisite for marriage, it is not surprising that the age at marriage continues its steady ascent. The most educated have the oldest median age at first marriage; however, the education divide has narrowed with high school graduates often waiting as long as college graduates to get married, perhaps reflecting the growing propensity for disadvantaged young adults to substitute cohabitation for marriage. Delays in marriage may eventually lead to foregone marriage, especially for those who are disadvantaged economically.

At the same time, cohabitation is still on the rise, perhaps because it provides a way to form a joint household without the economic qualifications necessary for marriage. Most marriages are preceded by cohabitation, but this is much more common among women with only a high school degree (82%) than women with a college degree (59%). In other words, direct marriages (without cohabitation) occur primarily among the most educated. Further, serial cohabitation is increasing and is more common among those without college degrees. Thus, women who have lower levels of education have more complex relationship biographies than women who are more advantaged. In general, it seems cohabitation is less tied to marriage than it was a few decades ago as fewer cohabiting unions eventuate in marriage. We anticipate this trend will continue as cohabitation's status as a family form becomes increasingly recognized and more widely shared (and marriage becomes out of reach for a growing share of Americans).

We highlight the growing diversity of family experiences. The legal recognition of same-sex marriage is spreading. At the same time, the legal and social recognition of other forms of relationships, for example, civil unions and domestic partnerships, is widespread and has implications for both same- and different-sex couples and parents. New relationship types have emerged, such as LAT, and may become entrenched as another form of intimate partnership. Intimate partnerships increasingly span household boundaries. New relationships may also extend across generations. Partly in response to the economic crisis, young adults who return to (or have never left) their parental home may need to forge new types of relationships with their parents. Additionally, older adults are likely to face challenges and opportunities as they draw on their more complex families for support in old age. One-third of Baby Boomers are unmarried and thus on the cusp of old age without a spouse available to provide care and support (Lin and Brown, 2012).

Children are now exposed to a wider array of family experiences that may include cohabiting and married stepparents, half-siblings, stepsiblings, and other relationships that we are less well able to label and identify. They also experience less stability in their families' lives; family living arrangement transitions are increasingly common, even among young children. Living with two stable biological married parents remains on the horizon for the children of college graduates but has become a more elusive goal that is difficult for those with low education to attain.

One implication of these changes in the family landscape is a continued shift in expectations and attitudes toward varying family living circumstances. As children increasingly live in a wider range of families, their own family behaviors may be more diverse. Family change may operate as a feedback loop that generates further family change in the next generation.

A second implication of these trends concerns the health and well-being of children, adults, and families. The well-known advantages of married-couple families are not available to as many adults and children in 2010 as 2000. This is not to say that cohabiting, single-parent, and other types of families do not offer healthy home environments; rather, the legal and social protections that marriage affords children and parents are not an option for the majority. Many countries do not observe sharp differentials in the well-being of children according to family type because their children are buffered against disadvantage by universal and generous health and welfare benefits to all children. In the United States, it is possible that comparisons across family types may become less relevant as they are increasingly experienced by large and varied groups of children.

The landscape of US families continues to shift, and this transformation has been exacerbated by the recent economic crisis. Marriage is now just one of an array of options; families are increasingly formed outside the boundaries of marriage and often span across households. The declining centrality of marriage in the United States is fundamentally reshaping the family experiences of children and adults whose family life courses are increasingly variable and complex. Family change is especially pronounced among the most disadvantaged groups in the United States, and these patterns are likely to intensify as the sluggish economy continues to whittle away at the middle class. Our task as researchers is to document the trends and patterns characterizing US family life and link them to population health and well-being.

References

Abma, J.C. and Martinez, G.M. (2006) Childlessness among older women the United States: trends and profiles. *Journal of Marriage and Family*, 68, 1045–1056.

Amato, P.R. (2010) Research on divorce: continuing trends and new developments. *Journal of Marriage and Family*, 72, 650–666.

Brown, S.L. (2010) Marriage and child well-being: research and policy perspectives. *Journal of Marriage and Family*, 72, 1059–1077.

Brown, S.L. and Manning, W.D. (2009) Family boundary ambiguity and the measurement of family structure: the significance of cohabitation. *Demography*, 46 (1), 85–101.

Brown, S.L. and Lin, I.-F. (2012) The gray divorce revolution: rising divorce among middle-aged and older adults, 1990–2010. *Journals of Gerontology, Series B: Psychological Sciences and Social Sciences*, 67, 731–741.

Brown, S.L., Lee, G.R. and Bulanda, J.R. (2006) Cohabitation among older adults: a national portrait. *Journal of Gerontology: Social Sciences*, 61, S71–S79.

Brown, S.L., Bulanda, J.R. and Lee, G.R. (2012) Transitions into and out of cohabitation in later life. *Journal of Marriage and Family*, 74, 774–793.

Bumpass, L.L. and Sweet, JA. (1989) National estimates of cohabitation: cohort levels and union stability. *Demography*, 26, 615–625.

Burgoyne, S. (2012) Demographic profile of same-sex parents. FP-12-15. National Center for Family & Marriage Research, http://ncfmr.bgsu.edu/pdf/family_profiles/file115683.pdf (accessed September 25, 2012).

Cherlin, A.J. (2004) The deinstitutionalization of American marriage. *Journal of Marriage and Family*, 66, 848–861.

Cherlin, A.J. (2011) Between poor and prosperous: do the family patterns of moderately-educated Americans deserve a closer look? in *Social Class and Changing Families in an Unequal America* (eds. M.J. Carlson and P. England), Stanford University Press, Stanford, pp. 68–84.

Cohen, J. and Manning, W.D. (2010) The relationship context of premarital serial cohabitation. *Social Science Research*, 39, 766–776.

Copen, C.E., Daniels, K., Vespa, J. and Mosher, W.D. (2012) First marriages in the United States: data from the 2006–2010 national survey of family growth (number 40). *Division of Vital Statistics*, www.cdc.gov/nchs/data/nhsr/nhsr049.pdf (accessed September 25, 2012).

Cruz, J. (2012) Remarriage rate in the U.S., 2010. FP-12-14. National Center for Family & Marriage Research, http://ncfmr.bgsu.edu/pdf/family_profiles/file114853.pdf (accessed September 25, 2012).

Dye, J.L. (2010) Fertility of American women: 2008. *Current population reports* (20–536), www.census.gov/prod/2010pubs/p20-563.pdf (accessed September 25, 2012).

Elliott, D.B. and Simmons, T. (2011) Marital events of Americans: 2009. *American Community Survey*, http://www.census.gov/prod/2011pubs/acs-13.pdf (accessed September 25, 2012).

Elliott, D.B., Krivickas, K., Brault, M.W. and Kreider, R.M. (2012) Historical marriage trends from 1890–2010: a focus on race differences. Presented at the Annual Meetings of the Population Association of America, San Francisco.

Ellwood, D.T. and Jencks, C. (2004) The uneven spread of single-parent families: what do we know? in *Social Inequality* (ed. K.M. Neckerman), Russell Sage Foundation, New York, pp. 3–78.

England, P., McClintock, E.A. and Shafer, E.F. (2011) Birth control use and early, unintended births: evidence for a class gradient, in *Social Class and Changing Families in an Unequal America* (eds. M.J. Carlson and P. England), Stanford University Press, Stanford.

England, P., Shafer, E.F. and Wu, L.L. (2012) Premarital conceptions, postconception ("shotgun") marriages, and premarital first births: education gradients in U.S. cohorts of white and black women born 1925–1959. *Demographic Research*, 27 (6), 153–166.

Fry, R. and Cohn, D. (2010) Women, men and the new economics of marriage. *Pew Research Center Social and Demographic Trends*, http://www.pewsocialtrends.org/files/2010/10/new-economics-of-marriage.pdf (accessed September 25, 2012).

Furstenberg, F.F., Jr. (1987) The new extended family: the experience of parents and children after remarriage, in *Remarriage and Step-Parenting: Current Research and Theory* (eds. K. Pasley and M. Ihinger-Tallman), Guilford, New York.

Furstenberg, F.F., Jr. (2011) The recent transformation of the American family: witnessing and exploring social change, in *Social Class and Changing Families in an Unequal America* (eds. M.J. Carlson and P. England), Stanford University Press, Stanford, pp. 192–220.

Gates, G.J. (2012) Same-sex couples in census 2010: race and ethnicity. *The Williams Institute*, http://williamsinstitute.law.ucla.edu/wp-content/uploads/Gates-CouplesRaceEthnicity-April-2012.pdf (accessed September 25, 2012).

Gerson, K. (2000) Resolving family dilemmas and conflicts: beyond utopia. *Contemporary Sociology*, 29 (1), 180–188.

Gibbs, L. and Payne, K.K. (2011) First divorce rate, 2010. FP-11-09. National Center for Family & Marriage Research, http://ncfmr.bgsu.edu/pdf/family_profiles/file101821.pdf (accessed September 25, 2012).

Goldstein, J.R. and Kenney, C.T. (2001) Marriage delayed or marriage forgone? New cohort forecasts of first marriage for U.S. women. *American Sociological Review*, 66 (4), 506–519.

Isen, A. and Stevenson, B. (2010) Women's education and family behavior: trends in marriage, divorce and fertility. Cambridge, MA. *NBER working paper no. 15725*.

Jacobsen, L.A. and Mather, M. (2011) Population bulletin update: a post-recession update on U.S. social and economic trends, www.prb.org/pdf11/us-economic-social-trends-update-2011.pdf (accessed September 25, 2012).

Julian, T. and Kominski, R. (2011) Education and synthetic work-life earnings estimates. *American Community Survey Reports*, www.census.gov/prod/2011pubs/acs-14.pdf (accessed September 25, 2012).

Kelly, J.B. (2007) Children's living arrangements following separation and divorce: insights from empirical and clinical research. *Family Process*, 46, 35–52.

Kennedy, S. and Bumpass, L.L. (2008) Cohabitation and children's living arrangements: new estimates from the United States. *Demographic Research*, 19, 1663–1692.

Kennedy, S. and Bumpass, L.L. (2011) Cohabitation and trends in the structure and stability of children's family lives. Paper presented at the Annual Meeting of the Population Association of America, New Orleans, April 1, 2011.

King, V. and Scott, M.E. (2005) A comparison of cohabiting relationships among older and younger adults. *Journal of Marriage and Family*, 67, 271–285.

Klinenberg, E. (2012) *Going Solo: The Extraordinary Rise and Surprising Appeal of Living Alone*, Penguin Books, New York.

Kreider, R.M. and Ellis, R. (2011) Number, Timing, and Duration of Marriages and Divorces: 2009. *Current population reports*, pp. 70–125, www.census.gov/prod/2011pubs/p70-125.pdf (accessed September 25, 2012).

Lichter, D.T., Turner, R.N. and Sassler, S. (2010) National estimates of the rise in serial cohabitation. *Social Science Research*, 39, 754–765.

Lin, I.-F. and Brown, S.L. (2012) Unmarried boomers confront old age: a national portrait. *The Gerontologist*, 52, 153–165.

Lofquist, D., Lugaila, T., O'Connell, M. and Feliz, S. (2012) Households and Families 2010. U.S. Census Bureau, http://www.census.gov/prod/cen2010/briefs/c2010br-14.pdf (accessed September 25, 2012).

Manning, W.D. (2010) Trends in cohabitation: twenty years of change, 1987–2008. FP-10-07. National Center for Family & Marriage Research, http://ncfmr.bgsu.edu/pdf/family_profiles/file87411.pdf (accessed September 25, 2012).

Manning, W.D., Smock, P.J. and Majumdar, D. (2004) The relative stability of marital and cohabiting unions for children. *Population Research and Policy Review*, 23, 135–159.

Manning, W.D., Brown, S.L. and Payne, K.K. (2012) Stability and change in age at first union formation over the last two decades: a research note. *Working paper*. National Center for Family & Marriage Research Bowling Green State University, Bowling Green, Ohio.

Martin, M.A. (2006) Family structure and income inequality in families with children: 1976 to 2000. *Demography*, 43, 421–445.

Martin, J.A., Hamilton, B.E., Ventura, S.J. *et al.* (2011) Births: final data for 2010. *National Vital Statistics Reports*, 61, 1, www.cdc.gov/nchs/data/nvsr/nvsr61/nvsr61_01.pdf (accessed September 25, 2012).

Martinez Gladys, D., Daniels, K. and Chandra, A. (2012) Fertility of men and women aged 15–44 years in the United States: national survey of family growth, 2006–2010. *National Health Statistics Reports*, 51, www.cdc.gov/nchs/data/nhsr/nhsr051.pdf (accessed September 25, 2012).

McLanahan, S.S. (2004) Diverging destinies: how children are faring under the second demographic transition. *Demography*, 41, 607–627.

McLanahan, S.S. and Percheski, C. (2008) Family structure and the reproduction of inequalities. *Annual Review of Sociology*, 34, 257–276.

McNamee, C.B. and Raley, R.K. (2011) A note on race, ethnicity and nativity differentials in remarriage in the United States. *Demographic Research*, 24 (13), 293–312.

Mosher, W.D., Jones, J. and Abma, J.C. (2012) Intended and unintended births in the United States: 1982–2010. *National Health Statistics Report*, 55, 1–28.

National Center for Family & Marriage Research (2012) Counting Couples, Counting Families: Full Report, Bowling Green State University, Bowling Green, http://ncfmr.bgsu.edu/pdf/Counting%20Couples/file115721.pdf (accessed September 25, 2012).

Newman, K.S. (2012) *The Accordion Family: Boomerang Kids, Anxious Parents, and the Private Toll of Global Competition*, Beacon Press, Boston.

Pasley, K. (1987) Family boundary ambiguity: perceptions of adult stepfamily members, in *Remarriage and Stepparenting: Current Research and Theory* (eds. K. Pasley and M. Ihinger-Tallman), Guilford, New York, pp. 206–224.

Payne, K.K. (2012a) Median age at first marriage, 2010. FP-12-07. National Center for Family & Marriage Research, http://ncfmr.bgsu.edu/pdf/family_profiles/file109824.pdf (accessed September 25, 2012).

Payne, K.K. (2012b) Young adults in the parental home, 1940–2010. FP-12-22. National Center for Family & Marriage Research, http://ncfmr.bgsu.edu/pdf/family_profiles/file122548.pdf (accessed September 25, 2012).

Payne, K.K. and Gibbs, L. (2011) First marriage rate in the U.S., 2010. FP-11-12. National Center for Family & Marriage Research, http://ncfmr.bgsu.edu/pdf/family_profiles/file104173.pdf (accessed September 25, 2012).

Payne, K.K., Manning, W.D. and Brown, S.L. (2012) Unmarried births to cohabiting and single mothers, 2005–2010. FP-12-06. National Center for Family & Marriage Research, http://ncfmr.bgsu.edu/pdf/family_profiles/file109171.pdf (accessed September 25, 2012).

Pew Research Center (2010a) Pew research center tabulations of the decennial U.S. census data, 1950–2000, and current population survey, annual social and economic supplement, 2001–2009, http://pewsocialtrends.org/files/2010/10/752-multi-generational-families.pdf (accessed September 25, 2012).

Pew Research Center (2010b) The Return of the Multi-Generational Family Household. http://pewsocialtrends.org/files/2010/10/752-multi-generational-families.pdf (accessed September 25, 2012).

Pew Research Center (2011) New Marriages Down 5% from 2009 to 2010: Barely Half of U.S. Adults Are Married – A Record Low, http://www.pewsocialtrends.org/2011/12/14/barely-half-of-u-s-adults-are-married-a-record-low/?src=prc-headline (accessed September 25, 2012).

Pew Research Center (2012a) Fewer, Poorer, Gloomier: The Lost Decade of the Middle Class, http://www.pewsocialtrends.org/2012/08/22/the-lost-decade-of-the-middle-class/ (accessed September 25, 2012).

Pew Research Center (2012b) Two-Thirds of Democrats Now Support Gay Marriage. http://www.pewforum.org/Politics-and-Elections/2012-opinions-on-for-gay-marriage-unchanged-after-obamas-announcement.aspx (accessed September 25, 2012).

Pizer, J.C. and Kuehl, S.J. (2012). Same-Sex Couples and Marriage: Model Legislation for Allowing Same-Sex Couples to Marry or All Couples to Form a Civil Union. The Williams Institute, http://williamsinstitute.law.ucla.edu/wp-content/uploads/Pizer-Kuehl-Model-Marriage-Report.pdf (accessed September 25, 2012).

Powell, B., Steelman, L.C. and Pizmony-Levy, O. (2012) Transformation or continuity in Americans' definition of family: a research note. *Bowling Green State University NCFMR working-paper 12–12*. http://ncfmr.bgsu.edu/pdf/Brian%20Powell%202012/file119560.pdf (accessed October 31, 2013).

Powell, B., Bolzendahl, C., Geist, C. and Carr Steelman, L. (2010) *Counted Out: Same Sex Relations and Americans' Definition of Family*. Russell Sage Foundation, New York.

Qian, Z. (2012) During the great recession, more young adults lived with parents. Census brief prepared for project US 2010, http://www.s4.brown.edu/us2010/Data/Report/report08012012.pdf (September 25, 2012).

Raley, R.K. and Bumpass, L.L. (2003) The topography of the divorce plateau: levels and trends in union stability in the United States after 1980. *Demographic Research*, 8, 245–259.

Ryan, C.L. and Siebens, J. (2012) Educational Attainment in the United States: 2009, Population Characteristics, www.census.gov/prod/2012pubs/p20–566.pdf (accessed September 25, 2012).

Schoen, R. and Standish, N. (2001) The retrenchment of marriage: results from marital life tables for the united states, 1995. *Population and Development Review*, 27, 553–563.

Seltzer, J.A., Lau, C.Q. and Bianchi, S.M. (2012) Doubling up when times are tough: a study of obligations to share a home in response to economic hardship. *Social Science Research*, 41 (5), 1307–1319.

Smock, P.J. and Greenland, F.R. (2010) Diversity in pathways to parenthood in the U.S.: patterns, implications, and emerging research directions. *Journal of Marriage and Family*, 72 (3), 576–593.

Stevenson, B. and Wolfers, J. (2007) Marriage and divorce: changes and their driving forces. *Journal of Economic Perspectives*, 21 (2), 27–52.

Strohm, C.Q., Seltzer, J.A., Cochran, S.D. and Mays, V.M. (2009) Living apart together relationships in the United States. *Demographic Research*, 21, 177–214.

Sweeney, M.M. (2010) Remarriage and stepfamilies: strategic sites for family scholarship in the 21st century. *Journal of Marriage and Family*, 72, 667–684.

Teachman, J. (2008) Complex life course patterns and the risk of divorce in second marriages. *Journal of Marriage and Family*, 70, 294–305.

U.S. Census Bureau (2011) U.S. Census Bureau CPS, Families and Living Arrangements: 2010, http://www.census.gov/hhes/families/data/cps2010.html (accessed September 25, 2012).

U.S. Census Bureau (2012) U.S. Census Bureau CPS, Families and Living Arrangements: 2011, http://www.census.gov/hhes/families/data/adults.html (accessed September 25, 2012).

White, L.K. (1998) Who's counting? Quasi-facts and stepfamilies in reports of number of siblings. *Journal of Marriage and the Family*, 60, 725–733.

4

Family Change in East Asia

Yen-Chun Cheryl Chen and Jui-Chung Allen Li

Modernization and Mystiques about East Asian Families

In this chapter, we examine family change in Japan, South Korea, Taiwan, and China. These four countries have shared similar cultural heritages, all being heavily influenced by the Confucian teachings, and have been through rapid industrial and economic developments in the twentieth century. In many respects, these societies are modernized, but families in these countries have all preserved certain cultural traditions that seem resistant to influences of external social and economic forces. Undoubtedly, the family confers a unique significance for people in East Asian societies. The family not only occupies a symbolic center place in their cultural systems but also affects their behaviors. The proliferation of a family's lineage is also highly valued. Familism – individuals must yield their respective interests to the prosperity of their family as rooted in the Confucian teachings – still dominates in East Asia.

East Asian familism has four major emphases: (i) the father–son axis of the extended family, (ii) the hierarchical power structure of offspring's submission to parental authority, (iii) the intergenerational mutual dependence, and (iv) the dominance of social interactions and favor exchanges with family members over unrelated individuals (Yang, 1988, p. 98). The hierarchical family relationship in the name of filial piety has been a crucial aspect in organizing people's lives and in coordinating production in the agrarian past in East Asian societies. The value of patriarchal filial piety gives the power to the husbands over wives, to parents over their children, and even to the sons over their widowed mothers and their sisters. The ethos of familism demands the younger generation be obedient to the elder

Authors are listed in alphabetic order to indicate equal contributions. An earlier version was presented at the 2012 meeting of the National Council on Family Relations, Phoenix, AZ.

The Wiley Blackwell Companion to the Sociology of Families, First Edition.
Edited by Judith Treas, Jacqueline Scott, and Martin Richards.
© 2014 John Wiley & Sons Ltd. Published 2017 by John Wiley & Sons Ltd.

generation. It assigns the responsibility of caring for the older generation to the younger generation and often prevents East Asian governments from welfare state legislation as such policies are considered to undermine functions traditionally served by the family. The primogeniture convention favors firstborn sons in inheritance and makes a son preferable to a daughter, thus further reinforcing the patriarchal hierarchy in the East Asian family system.

The father–son axis is fundamental to the family relations in East Asian societies. In these societies, the sons are the heirs who will carry the family name down the generations and therefore have the ultimate right of inheritance, whereas the daughters will eventually become members of other families after marriage and carry the family names of their husbands. Traditionally, when the family resources are limited, the family will invest a disproportionate amount of resources in their sons rather than daughters, because only their sons' social status and upward mobility will benefit the family (Parish and Willis, 1993). The family is also a religious group in terms of rituals worshiping the ancestors that remain common practice in these societies. The family lineage plays a crucial role in connecting the family members together, transcending time and space (Eastman, 1988; Thornton and Lin, 1994; Sugimoto, 2010).

The traditional family-based ideology was especially welcomed by the rulers/emperors because it provided a narrative framework to maintain a top-down social order. For example, historians argued that the *Ie* system – which has often been referred to as *the* "traditional" Japanese family – is indeed a recent invention established only during the Edo and Meji era (from the sixteenth to the nineteenth century) (Hashimoto and Traphagan, 2008).

Mystiques about East Asian families

Western scholars have long been interested in exploring and understanding family development in East Asia. Goode (1963) expected that both China and Japan would see increases in divorce and remarriage among the widowed, the nuclearization of the family, and the loosening ties between the generations, though at different speeds owing to contextual differences. These predictions were based on the functionalist idea that the nuclear family fits better in an industrialized society and gender egalitarianism would eventually follow as women and men gradually fulfilled the same set of functions through paid work in industrial societies. Thornton, Binstock, and Ghimire (2008) proposed that as the countries across the world become industrialized, they will gradually embrace "modern" ideologies, commonly defined as those originated from Western Europe and Northern America. The second demographic transition perspective suggests that an attitudinal shift from emphasizing the family and parenthood toward individualism will follow social and economic developments, which will in turn lead to the emergence, or even prevalence, of more diverse family forms such as cohabitation and nonmarital childbearing (Lesthaeghe and van de Kaa, 1986).

Although industrial and economic developments in East Asian countries have led scholars to speculate that they will eventually move their emphasis from familism to individualism, such speculations based on a unidirectional linear development cannot fully explain what we have observed in these societies. To examine the validity of modernization theory in a non-Western context, Whyte, Hermalin, and Ofstedal (2003) compared several family-related issues between Taiwan and China. Although Taiwan would be considered as more advanced in socioeconomic development than China, Taiwan seems to preserve more traditional behaviors toward filial duty than their Chinese counterpart, in terms of intergenerational support. Moreover, in spite of their divergent views on such topics as marriage formation or division of household tasks, older and younger generations in Taiwan express a strong support for filial obligations. Whyte therefore argued that we should take into account the role of the state in understanding family change, apart from economic development and cultural diffusion. In addition, he also suggested that filial piety seems to be a rigid value passed down from generation to generation.

Similarly, in South Korea, Confucianism remains an important guidance in people's daily lives. Norms of seniority determine how two people interact with each other. The emphasis of Confucianism on education has resulted in a nearly universal aspiration for higher education among individuals and behind government's expansion of its tertiary education system (Park, 2013). Nevertheless, due to its patriarchal tradition, education may be beneficial for women in their spousal search but may matter little in their career advancement (Chang, 2010). The "Chaebol" conglomerates, the main business enterprise entities in South Korea, fully represent the patriarchal system in the economy and largely restrict women's upward mobility in the career ladder. Chang (2010) used the term "compressed modernity" to describe the struggles between the preservation of Confucian teachings and the modernization faced by the South Koreans.

Among the four East Asian societies covered in this chapter, Japan was the first to experience modernization and industrialization and has become the most economically prosperous. Nevertheless, the transition from the dominance of the extended family system to the nuclear family has not totally changed people's imagination of what a family should look like. In her ethnographic work, White (2002) illustrated how Japanese people negotiate between the "harmonious and beautiful family" in ideal and the "sometimes broken and not-so-perfect family" in reality. Because the concept of *Ie* has not only been used as a framework for the family system but also for organizing the order of the society and for defining one's cultural identity, its influences can hardly be removed simply by changes in the social and economic conditions (Kuwayama, 2001). The Japanese government has recognized the need to adjust the family law to accommodate family lives in the modern days, by stressing individual choices on family formation and by abolishing the traditional ideology on gendered division of labor in a report that forecasts the outlook of Japanese family in 2030.[1] Nevertheless, the nuclear family and the *Ie* system remain the cornerstone in this report (Hiroko, 2011, p. 54).

In the process of modernization, familism has often been criticized as outdated and conservative. In the four countries discussed in this chapter, legal changes that permit both men and women to inherit and to divorce with equal power have taken place only in the past 50 years (Hyunah, 2003; Chen and Yi, 2005; Atoh, 2008; Evans, 2008). These changes in the legal settings do not exert their effects immediately, but have gradually become ingrained in people's ideology and have been present in the differences between older and younger generations in their views toward family lives. Despite their similarities to family change in the West for a long time, family change in East Asia may result from totally different mechanisms. These societies have gone even further in fertility declines, but people remain disapproving of cohabitation and nonmarital childbearing. These phenomena may have to be understood via an acknowledgment or even appreciation of the family ideology deeply rooted in their cultures. In the next sections, we review recent studies about family change in different domains in East Asia, first focusing on women's status and gender equality, as we believe it is the key to understand how culture plays a role. We also discuss marriage formation and dissolution, migrant families, fertility decline, living arrangements, and population aging. We conclude by discussing the challenges faced by East Asians and the opportunities they may take in response to the challenges.

Women's Status and Gender Equality in East Asia

Women's status has always been inferior due to the tradition of filial piety rooted in East Asian cultures (Chang, 2010). Women were expected to confine themselves to their household and be submissive to their fathers, husbands, and sons. Until recent decades, they had no right of inheritance and were required to carry the family name of their husbands. An important mission of women is to give birth to children, especially sons, in order to continue the family lineage of their husbands. A large family was considered a blessing that would bring good fortune.

Modernization and women's status in East Asia

Inglehart and Norris (2003) proposed that modernization and economic development will eventually bring gender equality to all societies. The demographic transition theory (see, e.g., Kirk, 1996) posits that the decreasing fertility and mortality rates emancipate women from their family roles and free their time to participate in the labor market. The second demographic transition theory (Lesthaeghe and van de Kaa, 1986) predicted further changes in social norms, moving toward a more individualized society. In East Asia, we observe some of these phenomena happening, but the explanations may be different from the dominant theories.

Women's participation in the labor force has contributed to the industrialization and economic development in Japan, South Korea, and Taiwan. In the 1950s (in Japan) and 1960s (in Taiwan and Korea), women's labor force had filled the labor demands in export-driven industry (Brinton, 2001). In China, the Communist Party encouraged women's labor force participation during the Cultural Revolution and the Great Leap Forward Movement as a means to accelerate economic development and to achieve gender equality by eliminating all kinds of gender differences (Johnson, 1983). Nevertheless, women's labor force participation has always been regarded as supplementary. Their employment is often treated as flexible and disposable, and thus, fringe benefits and long-term commitment are considered optional. During economic downturns, women workers absorb the crisis by being the first to be laid off. When work and family collide, women are expected to take the family as their priority. Brinton (2001) documented an M-shaped age pattern of women's labor force participation in Japan and South Korea. The first hump of the M-shape indicates that women tend to leave the labor market upon marriage and childbearing. Although the M-shape was less clear for women's labor force participation in Taiwan due to differences in labor market structures and different degrees of emphasis on motherhood among the countries (Brinton, 2001), the rate still decreased gradually after marriage. Recently, the M-shaped patterns in women's labor force participation have remained clear, though weaker, and the bottom of the M-shape has shifted toward 30 to 34 years of age, consistent with later ages of marriage and child-bearing. Recent rapid fertility declines do not reduce much of the childbearing burden on East Asian women. Instead, parents invest even more time and money in educating their "future hopes" (Fong, 2004), emphasizing the quality of their offspring. At the same time, increasing longevity means that more elderly people will be in need of care for a longer period of time, and this care is usually provided by female family members. Many women nowadays still disproportionately take on "the second shift" (Hochschild, 1989), and this may contribute to postponed or even foregone marriages and childbearing in East Asia.

Legal settings and changes in gender role ideology

Equal employment legislation has been passed in Japan (in 1985), South Korea (in 1989), and Taiwan (in 2002). It was not until the late 1990s, however, that the legal authorities in Japan started to prohibit companies from discriminating against women in recruitment and promotion. China, unfortunately, has not passed any similar legislation at the national level so far. Parental leave and child-care policies were introduced only recently in these societies, as part of the governmental strategies to promote childbearing to combat rapid population aging (Rebick and Takenaka, 2006; Lee, 2009; Chin et al., 2012). Even though more women nowadays will return to or stay continuously in the labor force after childbearing, they are more likely to be in part-time jobs, which provide them with the flexibility to combine domestic and paid work (Holloway, 2010). Women are also more likely to be concentrated in clerical jobs and the service sector; they are less likely to be in managerial positions; they earn lower salaries than men even in the same position and have worse career prospects (Yoo, 2003; MIC, 2011). While women's participation in the labor force may have changed the dynamics and the share of household tasks between spouses in the Western societies (Cunningham, 2007), the same seems not to be true in East Asia (Frejka, Jones, and Sardon, 2010).

The differences among the sameness

Although families in East Asia commonly share the influences of patriarchal ideology and filial piety rooted in Confucianism, the outlook for women's status in these societies is quite different due to the differences in each country's historical context. Women's movements in these societies have also taken on different agendas – deriving from Western feminism while accommodating to local issues. In Japan, the postwar period was still characterized by the male breadwinner/ female-homemaker ideal, even though during wartime, many women had been drawn into the labor force. The women's movement started in the 1960s, focusing first on environmental and consumer issues; in the late 1970s and 1980s, it began to challenge women's domestic roles, promote equalities between males and females in the labor market and the implementation of family-friendly measures, and raise women's self-awareness (Buckley, 1994). In South Korea, the women's movement was initiated by the nationalist movement in the 1970s and 1980s, but the focus has gradually shifted toward the meaning of womanhood and sex-related issues in the 1990s (Hampson, 2000). In China, a women's movement was part of the broader government agenda. As early as in the 1950s, the marriage law entitled women to marriage by personal will and to the right of divorce (Croll, 1981), even though it took longer for the society to adjust its attitude toward the conjugal relationship after the legislation (Yan, 2003). In Taiwan, the women's movement has been growing since the lifting of the martial law in the late 1980s. Prosperity goes hand in hand with democratization in Taiwan, and the feminists have pressed for gender equality and helped raise women's self-awareness in all aspects (Chang, 2009).

The Gender Gap Report 2011 (Hausmann, Tyson, and Zahidi, 2011) shows that in general women's status in East Asian countries has remained stable since 2006 and more efforts are needed for improvement. In terms of health and educational level, Japan, South Korea, and Taiwan have all reached the standard comparable to other developed countries. Even though son preference remains crucial in determining the sex ratio at birth or the distribution of family resources, its importance seems to have decreased in recent years (Chu and Yu, 2010). Nevertheless, Japan and South Korea, despite their stunning economic performance, are both ranked near the bottom among developed countries on the overall gender gap index. Among these four countries, South Korea has the lowest female-to-male ratio on wages and tertiary educational enrollment; Japanese women have the least say in the public sphere; China's sex ratio at birth remains the most imbalanced in the world; and Taiwan is the last to establish the legal infrastructure that supports gender equality among the three countries (OECD, 2012). While the gender gaps in different domains in East Asian societies remain relatively wide in comparison with their Western counterparts, these societies have taken a long road to complete these achievements. We will discuss how change in women's status in these societies is related to family change in East Asia in the following sections.

Marriage Formation and Dissolution

Who marries whom

In the past, marriages were arranged by parents in Taiwan and China. Women and men nowadays, like those in the modern Western countries, also embrace the ideal of romantic love and are free to choose their spouses (Coontz, 2005). Unlike the widespread traditional wisdom that valued the match on family background, independence in spousal choice based on love has led to a higher level of marital satisfaction than in arranged marriages (Xu and Whyte, 1990). Despite the trend toward diminishing influence of the parents, this does not, however, mean that the normative constraints ubiquitous in the past no longer exist in modern Chinese societies. The norms used to be for women to marry a man with higher status. The norms have over time weakened in Taiwan – with increasingly fewer marriages in which the husband had either the same or a higher educational attainment than the wife – but they have remained largely unchanged in China (Chu and Yu, 2010, chapter 5). We speculate that the constraints imposed by the persistent norms of females-marrying-up (hypergamy) and males-marrying-down may have also led to the decline in marriage rates in East Asia because women's higher educational attainments make it harder for them to marry up.

Focusing specifically on spousal choice in terms of educational attainment, Smits, Ultee, and Lammers (1998) found that educational homogamy is associated with religious and cultural factors characterizing each society. While the stereotype suggests that educational homogamy in East Asia may be much higher than in the Western countries, it is indeed similar to that in Catholic societies but stronger than that in Western countries of Protestant heritage. Among the four countries discussed in this chapter, South Korea has the highest level of educational homogamy (Smits and Park, 2009).

Educational homogamy in East Asia has declined over time (Satoshi, 2005). Rather than looking at the strength of the overall associations between wife's and husband's educational attainments, Smits and Park (2009) delineated a much more nuanced story about trends in educational homogamy in East Asian societies and note that different processes occur in different segments of the society. They found that those with the highest level of education tend to invoke a social closure to protect their status by marrying only spouses with the same level of educational attainment. People in the lowest education category are marginalized from the mainstream society and have relatively little chance of marrying up. Across time, educational homogamy has continuously decreased, except for the two extremes of education level, indicating the increasing importance of romantic love over social status in most people's spousal choices.[2] The argument of the increasing salience of romantic love is further supported by the fact that higher female employment is associated with a lower level of educational homogamy. Employment empowers women so that they can marry someone outside their education category. Smits and Park concluded that, along with modernization, individuals in East Asian societies nowadays enjoy a higher level of personal freedom and they exercise this freedom by choosing a spouse on the basis of romantic love that may occur beyond educational boundaries.

One limitation of the literature is that few studies have examined the gender asymmetry in educational homogamy. For example, the Confucianism hypothesis in Smits and Park (2009) stipulates only that Confucianism emphasizes the values of education and family, and they predicted that educational homogamy will therefore be stronger in societies under the greater influence of Confucianism. They did not, however, discuss the patriarchal character of Confucian culture in which gender equality is not expected and so maintaining the patriarchal order by marrying a

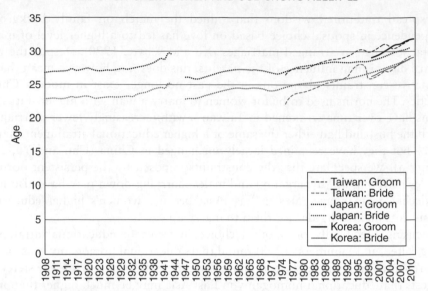

Figure 4.1   Age at first marriage: Japan, Taiwan and Korea, 1908–2010.
Note: The figure represents data from countries that reported mean age.
Source: For Japan, Statistics and Information Department, Ministry of Health, Labour and Welfare, *Handbook of Health and Welfare Statistics 2012*; for Korea, Statistic Korea, *Marriage and Divorce Statistics in 2009 and 2011*; for Taiwan, Department of Household Registration, Ministry of Interior, *Household Statistics 2012*.

spouse with some particular level of educational attainment may not be as desirable. Another limitation of the literature about who marries whom is that it rarely takes into account nonmarriage. All of the previous studies we are aware of exclude respondents who were never married and only describe the patterns of homogamy for those who had ever been married. This practice may not have been a problem when marriages were universal across all countries in all periods, but may no longer be appropriate when men and women increasingly retreat from marriage. We will now turn to this trend.

Trends toward later and fewer marriages

Extremely high percentages of people in East Asian countries intended to be married, ideally before age 30, but the percentages have been in decline. Despite nearly universal intention to marry before age 30 and strong preference for marriage over singlehood or cohabitation, an increasing number of East Asians have failed to achieve their marriage goal; some of them never marry. As Figure 4.1 shows, in Japan, Taiwan, and South Korea, the mean ages at first marriage for ever-married men and women have increased.[3] These statistics may be distorted by the rise of never-married men and women, and thus, we present the crude marriage rates for all four countries in Figure 4.2. Despite more noise in the trends, the crude marriage rates have clearly been in decline. These statistics are consistent with the speculation that not only have East Asian women increasingly

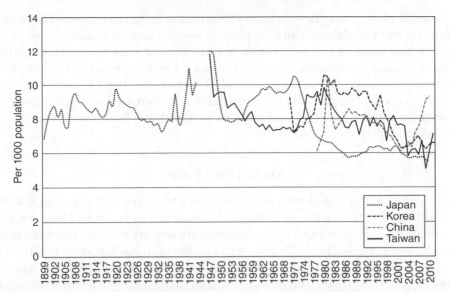

Figure 4.2 Crude marriage rate: Japan, Korea, China and Taiwan, 1899–2010.
Source: For Japan, Statistics and Information Department, Ministry of Health, Labour and Welfare, *Vital Statistics 2011*; for Korea, Korean Statistical Information Service (KOSIS), *Crude Marriage Rate, Vital Statistics, Population/Household*; for Taiwan, Department of Household Registration, Ministry of Interior, *Household Statistics 2012*; for China, China Statistical Yearbooks Database, *China Statistical Yearbook 2011*.

delayed their first marriages, but also an ever-growing proportion of them will likely remain single for the rest of their lives (Jones, 2007). Beyond speculations, two empirical studies on marriage formation in East Asia have documented that women in Japan (Raymo, 1998) and Taiwan (Chang and Li, 2011) have increasingly foregone marriage.

Trends toward later and fewer marriages are ubiquitous across all levels of educational attainment in Japan (Raymo, 2003), but the educational differentials have increased in Taiwan (Chang and Li, 2011). Raymo (2003) argued that enrollment in tertiary education was the main reason Japanese women delayed their marriage, although he also alluded to the possibility that such marriage delays may reflect the difficulty for women to balance work and family. As Raymo and Iwasawa (2008) further noted, while Japanese women are increasingly likely to be pregnant when they marry, lower-educated Japanese women have become more likely to enter a "shotgun" marriage than more educated women. Ethnographic evidence suggests that Japanese women express ambivalent feelings toward marriage. On the one hand, strong norms persist so that marriage is regarded as essential to the transition to adulthood and the fulfillment of filial obligations. On the other hand, women view marriage as being inherently sexist and inhibiting their autonomy – specifically restricting their career development and taking away control over their finances (Nemoto, 2008).

Scholars have speculated that the rise of individualism, which no longer treats women as purely family members, along with the erosion of parental influences on spousal choice, may help explain these trends in marriage formation in East Asian societies. Educated and employed women are not only economically independent but also able to live a decent life without men. In contrast, marriage brings a woman back to the constraints imposed by the patriarchal culture and a husband who may not treat her as equal. Reduced social and financial pressures to marry, coupled with changes in attitudes and increased divorce rates, make women reconsider the costs and benefits of marriage (Retherford, Ogawa, and Matsukura, 2004).

Marital dissolution

In the United States and elsewhere, divorce rates were low and rose almost mono-tonically until very recently. In contrast, divorce rates in Japan had been high and observed no apparent trend from the seventeenth century to the nineteenth century (Goode, 1993; Fuess, 2004). Divorce rates in Japan, indeed, had declined to very low levels during the first half of the twentieth century due to the implementation of the *Ie* system. Since the end of World War II, they bounced back to levels similar to those in the Western world (Kumagai, 2008) – with about one in three marriages being projected to end in divorce. Recent trends in divorce in Japan also show a divergence by education, with women of no more than a high school diploma far more likely to divorce than those of higher education (Raymo, Iwasawa, and Bumpass, 2005).

As Figure 4.3 shows, the crude divorce rates for the four countries are all on the rise in recent decades. Japan is a special case. We can trace data all the way back to 1899 when a new family registration law enacted in the prior year made the data more reliable; before the enactment, cohabiting unions were excluded from the official statistics. Historical trends in divorce rates in Japan are an anomaly in that they are not monotomic; they do not rise along with industrialization, urban-ization, and modernization. Divorce trends in Japan also confirm a finding that changes in divorce-related legislation or policies (e.g., the Meiji Restoration of 1868, the 1898 Civil Code) do not have any lasting impact on marital disruption, even though they might temporarily change the divorce rates immediately follow-ing the implementation of the particular law or policy (Fuess, 2004). Moreover, as noted by Kumagai (2008) in a number of other family domains, there is a tremen-dous amount of variation in divorce rates not only across historical periods but also across localities in Japan.

We know little about divorce in South Korea until recently. Lee (2006) found that college-educated women had a much lower divorce rate than those who had only attended elementary school. Using vital statistics data for all marriages and divorces registered between 1991 and 2006, Park, Raymo, and Creighton (2009) documented a much stronger negative educational gradient in divorce rates among Korean women, and the gradients have grown even wider across successive marriage cohorts.

Many studies on divorce in East Asia have been either motivated by or, in some sense, reactions to the hypothesis about social change and class differences in divorce prevalence proposed by Goode (1993). Goode argued that divorce in the early phase would be more prevalent among those with high socioeconomic status.

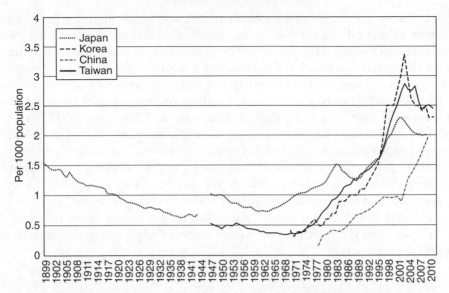

Figure 4.3 Crude divorce rate: Japan, Korea, China and Taiwan, 1989–2010.
Source: For Japan, Statistics and Information Department, Ministry of Health, Labour and Welfare, *Vital Statistics 2011*; for Korea, Korean Statistical Information Service (KOSIS), *Crude Divorce Rate, Vital Statistics, Population/Household*; for Taiwan, Department of Household Registration, Ministry of Interior, *Household Statistics 2012*; for China, China Statistical Yearbooks Database, *China Statistical Yearbook*.

Since divorce incurred high financial and social costs, this population was better able to secure sufficient resources to overcome legal and economic barriers to divorce. As the costs of divorce gradually declined, divorce would diffuse to individuals of lower social classes. Eventually, it is those at the lower end of the class echelon who would have higher divorce rates. Chen (2012) found support for Goode's hypothesis by observing the full historical development of an educational crossover in Taiwanese divorce trends from a positive gradient by education to a negative gradient. Other studies documenting recent trends in Japan and South Korea found a negative differential by education in divorce, consistent with the latter development hypothesized by Goode. These studies on marital disruption in East Asia also addressed issues commonly referred to as the second demographic transition (Lesthaeghe and van de Kaa, 1986) and, in particular, implications for social inequality (McLanahan, 2004). For example, a unique difference between Japan and the United States is in living arrangement following a marital disruption. In Japan, as many as one in four divorced Japanese women in their late 30s (and about 80% of divorced mothers having child custody) were living with their parents, whereas only 1 in 50 divorced American women were living with their parents (Raymo, Iwasawa, and Bumpass, 2005). This may lead us to expect greater emotional and socioeconomic support for divorced women and their children in Japan than in the United States.

More studies are needed for us to understand marital disruption in East Asia, but a major problem that has substantially limited the progress in this area is data quality. Surveys conducted in East Asian societies all suffer high degrees of under-reporting of marital disruptions, as compared with official vital statistics. While part of the discrepancy between survey estimates and official statistics may be due to marital separations that have not become a legally registered divorce, underre-porting remains large even in surveys that distinguish between a separation and a legal divorce. While some have turned directly to registration data to study marital disruptions in East Asia (e.g., Raymo, Iwasawa, and Bumpass, 2005; Park and Raymo, 2013) and others maintain an agnostic attitude toward data quality, improved survey methodology with better measures of marital disruption is essential for making real progress in this area of research. The same logic also applies to measuring cohabitation and other marital statuses. For example, research on remar-riages in East Asia is particularly thin, mostly due to data limitations. Social surveys often only ask about current marital status, but do not inquire about the order and marital history of the respondents, thereby substantially constraining quantitative analysis of remarriages.

Migrant Families

Regional migration has existed in East Asia for a long time. Yet, it was not until the 1970s that marriage migration caught scholarly attention (Kamiya and Lee, 2009). In Taiwan, Japan, and South Korea, the proportion of marriage between a local man and a foreign woman from a less developed country has been on the rise. In Taiwan, 13% of newly wedded couples are cross-national (NIA, 2012). A similar pattern can be found in South Korea, where 11% of the total marriages in 2010 are between a Korean and a foreigner (Statistic Korea, 2010). In Japan, around 3% of those who married in 2009 were composed of a Japanese groom and a foreign bride. Common to those marriages is that the brides are most likely from South and Southeast Asian countries, and these couples tend to be located in lower social strata.

Marriage migration in East Asia is a unique phenomenon that highlights the cultural importance of the proliferation and extension of lineages as well as the patriarchal culture. As "hypergamy" remains the ideal promulgated in marriage, the increase in women's educational levels and their potential economic independence via employment have gradually weakened the marriage market privilege of men, especially those with inferior social and economic status. Compared to women, men are less likely to forgo marriages because the pressures from cultural traditions for them to maintain their family lineage are especially strong (Constable, 2005).

The improvement in women's educational level and economic conditions means men from inferior socioeconomic status face difficulty sustaining the hypergamy marriage pattern. This results in an insufficient pool of potential partners for these men, and marrying a foreign bride provides a solution to this dilemma. The world system, which arranges countries in a hierarchy by their level of development, enables them to fulfill the hypergamy ideation (Constable, 2005). Moreover, the advertised and stereotyped docile and submissive images of these foreign women fulfill the traditional gender division of household labor (Kojima, 2001). As a foreigner in the first few years of their marriages, brides are forced to be subordinate to their husbands, since most countries require their husbands to be the guarantors of their wives during the process of natu-ralization. This legal requirement enforces an unequal relationship between the partners. Ng (2005) criticized marriage migration for reinforcing gender inequality in the patriarchal tradition. The stigma attached to these foreign brides, derived from negative images about their countries of origin and the women's perceived economic motivations to migrate, is ubiquitous in media reports and even in daily language. The stigma may have a strong impact not only on the married couples but on their families as well (Belanger, Lee, and Wang, 2010).

Nevertheless, recent studies on marriage migration have gradually shifted from the view of victimized women to one revealing the active agency that the female migrants play in the process of migration (Kim, 2010). By marrying someone from, and migrating to, an economically more developed country, migrant women also fulfill their dreams of pursuing modernity, romantic love, and upward mobility (Thai, 2008; Faier, 2009). Moreover, their upward economic mobility, resulting from the structural differences between origin and destination countries, has given them the ability to assist their families in their countries of origin (Jones and Shen, 2008).

Since East Asian countries are culturally and ethnically more similar in comparison with Western societies, marriage migrants have brought challenges to their destina-tion countries on how to integrate the diverse cultures. Language with subtle dis-criminatory connotations is substituted with neutral ones. Studies on parenthood and child development among migrant families have also moved from a pathological perspective to one emphasizing the strength of these families, which can be empow-ered by government and community supports (Kamiya and Lee, 2009). Although China has been the major sending country of foreign spouses, whether its own serious imbalance in sex ratio at birth will alter the pattern of population flow will be of interest to demographers (Jones and Shen, 2008). Overall, we see the adjust-ment in actions taken by governments toward accepting a culturally diversified family pattern as having helped change people's attitudes and ideations toward what a family should look like.

Fertility Decline

Closely related to marriages postponed and forgone is fertility decline. Women in East Asian countries have reduced their Total Fertility Rate (TFR) to very low levels of about 1.2. The TFR refers to the total number of children an average woman in the society is expected to have in her life if she survives throughout the end of her reproductive years and if she experiences the currently observed age-specific fertility rates. In developed countries where mortality rates are low, a TFR of 2.1 is considered "the replacement level" at which the size of each gen-eration will remain constant. Figure 4.4 shows that, unlike fertility trends in

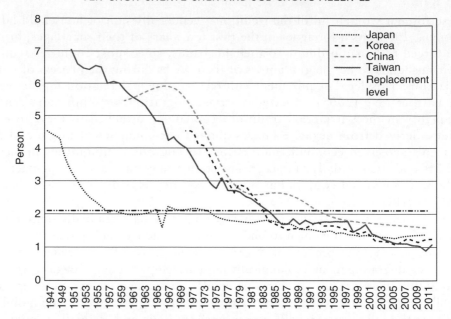

Figure 4.4   Total fertility rate: Japan, Korea, China and Taiwan, 1947–2011.
Source: For Japan, Statistics and Information Department, Ministry of Health, Labour and Welfare, *Vital Statistics 2011;* for Korea, Korean Statistical Information Service (KOSIS), *Total Fertility Rate, Vital Statistics, Population/Household;* for Taiwan, Department of Household Registration, Ministry of Interior, *Household Statistics 2012;* for China, The World Bank Total Fertility Rate, China.

European countries, the drop in fertility rates among East Asian societies seems to go deeper without showing any sign of recuperation.

Trends in fertility rates are very similar between Taiwan, South Korea, and China. The trend in fertility rates in Japan, however, shows some unique patterns. We can trace Japanese TFRs all the way back to 1947. According to Takahashi (2004), the "baby boom" years in Japan were restricted to a very short period of 1947–1949. The TFRs in Japan dropped quickly to around the replacement level in the late 1950s and remained there until the mid-1970s when another round of fertility declines started. The fertility decline in the early twentieth century implies the existence of family limitation practices, and similar family limitation practices occur fairly early in other East Asian societies, too. In addition, a unique phenomenon about East Asian trends in fertility is the sometimes cyclical period fluctuations, often reflecting zodiac astrology. For example, the TFRs tend to be higher in the year of the dragon, which is considered an auspicious symbol in the Chinese culture (e.g., Goodkind, 1991). Conversely, the TFR in Japan abruptly dipped to 1.58 in 1966 due to the year of Hinoe Uma (which means the "fire horse"). The Hinoe Uma occurs once every 60 years, and women born in that year are believed to possess a difficult personality and to bring misfortune to their husbands. Thus, many Japanese couples avoided childbearing in 1966. Similarly, Lee and Paik (2006) found that the male-to-female sex ratio at birth increased, whereas fertility decreased in the year of the horse in Korea since 1970.

Explanations of fertility decline

Although long-term TFRs for East Asian countries may seem to decline monotonically, we only understand the first part of the decline. The demographic transition theory suggests that as mortality rates fall and the number of surviving children in the family increases, a rational response is to practice family limitation. A somewhat unique feature of this explanation to be applied in East Asia must consider the patriarchal culture in which parents in the agrarian past had power over offspring, and this power weakened as education expanded and nonfarm employment became prevalent (Feeney, 1994). Moreover, we do not know how effective family planning programs are in altering childbearing intentions and behaviors of East Asian women (Pritchett, 1994), because fertility rates started to drop *before* the implementation of these programs. Unlike what is widely believed, governmental family planning programs in Japan, Taiwan, and Korea, and the "later, longer, fewer" policy in China (during the 1970s) may have played only a negligible role in instigating fertility declines. They have at best increased the speed of fertility decline in these countries (Pearce, 2011). The only exception is the one-child policy started in 1979 in China, which has effectively reduced the proportions of women having a second child (i.e., period parity progression ratios) in certain parts of the country (Feeney, 1994). Note, however, that Figure 4.4 also shows that TFRs started to fall in the late 1960s, and fertility decline slowed down in the 1980s and onward. A recent survey by Gu *et al.* (2007) highlights the substantial variation in family planning policies at the local level. Their study also confirms the tremendous convergence between what the state family planning policies intend to achieve and the actual fertility rates that occurred in China. In other words, the government plays a much greater role in influencing women's childbearing behaviors in China than in other places, despite the prominent role of socioeconomic determinants of fertility. China's one-child policy, along with changes in socioeconomic conditions, has led to its rapidly aging population, also found in other East Asian countries without such a state policy. Another serious consequence of this policy is an extraordinary imbalance in sex ratio at birth. Li, Yi, and Zhang (2011) estimate that the one-child policy results in seven extra boys per 100 girls for the 1991–2005 birth cohorts and accounts for more than half of the total increase in sex ratios. What we do not understand about fertility declines in East Asia is the continuing trend toward the lowest low fertility, which results in rapid population aging. This will pose real challenges to these societies because the family, rather than government welfare programs, has traditionally shouldered most, if not all, the responsibilities of caring for the elderly.

Living Arrangements and Aging Society

Comparative studies of the family have often made a dichotomy between extended and nuclear families as the typical family types in the East and in the West, respectively. However, such a dichotomy may be misleading, if not stereotypical. Based on historical data in China, for example, Martin (1990) argued that the multigenerational family has never been the most prevalent family structure due to high mortality rates limiting the availability of kin. Lower mortality rates nowadays make it more likely for multigenerational households to exist. It is important to separate "family in ideals" and "family in practice" in order to see the real changes in family structure in East Asia (Martin, 1990; Hashimoto and Traphagan, 2008).

Aging society and elderly care

Declining coresidence between adult children and their elderly parents has sent a cautious alarm to the governments on how to deal with the issue of elderly care in the future. It also provokes scholarly attention on whether people's responsibility toward family obligation has declined (Chueng and Kwan, 2009). Although filial piety is performed with different forms, most people still consider taking care of elderly parents to be an important family value (Ikels, 2004). At the same time, more and more parents of the younger generation say they do not want to rely on their adult children for care in the future.

How will this change in people's ideation about family ties influence long valued intergenerational relationships in East Asian societies? In fact, upward intergenerational resource transfers are no longer dominating the intergenerational relationship. In recent years, downward transfer is becoming more prominent. Since the governments in these countries continue to place a great amount of care work on families, dual-earner families rely heavily on the childcare provided by the elderly parents. The childcare provided by elderly parents supports women's labor force participation and helps them to balance work and family. Moreover, because "leaving the parental home" to assert one's independence is not common in East Asian societies, unmarried adult children are more likely to stay with their parents until they marry than in the West. Nowadays, it takes longer for the younger generation to become financially independent. Especially after experiencing a few economic crises, trends in youth unemployment and underemployment have all made obtaining lifelong stable employment and long-term economic security more difficult. This trend may contribute to the prolonged period in which the younger generation has to rely on parental support (Xenos et al., 2006).

Adaptation between ideation and reality

Practice in real life is the behavior people perform in reconciling their new situation with their ideational conventions (Tilly and Scott, 1978). Traditional stem families of a married son living with aging parents may be declining, but this does not immediately reflect the decline in people's regard for the family. What is more often seen is the change in people's definition of coresidence. The term "proximate residence" is used to depict the living arrangement whereby adult children live in the same neighborhood, instead of the same household, as their parents (Zimmer and Korinek, 2008). This living arrangement is a practical adjustment to the needs family members face over the life course (Chen, 2005) and to the housing constraints in big cities (Logan and Bian, 1999). It also reflects the change in people's concepts about privacy and helps avoid the potential conflicts between the mother and the daughter-in-law living under that same roof. In China, the implementation of the one-child policy has had a huge influence on the composition of the family. What was traditionally deemed atypical, such as coresidence with the wife's instead of the husband's parents, is now becoming more acceptable. The new living arrangements prompt people to redefine and modify the meaning of filial obligation and how this family value should be carried out.

Aging is an important challenge. According to the United Nations' projection, these East Asian societies rank at the top among all the aging societies due to the combination of low mortality rates and lowest low fertility rates. Given that the proportion of the elderly in the population is becoming larger, discussions about population aging have focused on the pension system or other alternative support systems. This issue is expected to be particularly severe in East Asian societies due to their strong emphases on families' caring roles.

Challenges and Opportunities

Families in East Asian countries have long been guided by the familism rooted in the Confucian teachings. Our review suggests that modernization does not necessarily predict changes in family lives in this region. Filial piety has remained essential but is gradually being compromised. Women's status has improved in some aspects, but there is still a long way to go in terms of providing full legal protections or changing people's gender role attitudes.

Will the family lose its importance in East Asia? Our review shows that marriage remains highly regarded but marriage based on romantic love has become dominant. Yet, there is a clear trend toward later and fewer marriages, as well as increasing acceptance of divorce. The below-replacement fertility rates have caught so much attention that nearly all the governments in this region have made boosting fertility a priority. Currently, families have continued to shoulder the main task of elderly care. At the same time, however, the older generation plays a key role in providing necessary resources to support the younger generation.

What will be the future of East Asian families? To reflect upon the debate regarding the deinstitutionalization of family (Amato, 2004; Beck and Beck-Gernsheim, 2007), we expect that the prominence of family will depend more on the emotional tie it provides and less on the structure of the family. With greater governmental support and attention paid to individual needs, as well as the gradual shift in people's ideas and expectations about what a family should look like and how it should function, the hierarchical and patriarchal tradition derived from filial piety will be challenged, but these challenges will hopefully create opportunities for a more equal society.

Acknowledgments

We thank the conference participants, Judith Treas and Jacqueline Scott for helpful comments and Sze-Chi Faye Huang for able research assistance. Partial research support from the National Science Council of Taiwan (NSC 101-2410-H-001-027) is gratefully acknowledged.

Notes

1 The report was made by The Future Life Discussion Council, Cabinet Office, and aimed to draw a picture of the everyday life of Japan in 2030. See Hiroko (2011) for a detailed description of this report.
2 Note, however, that this hypothesis seems to run contrary to Becker's (1991) claim that love is more likely to occur between individuals of similar levels of educational attainment (p. 327). Smits and Park (2009) believed, instead, that romantic love should be able to cross the educational boundaries.
3 Mean ages at first marriage are calculated for only those who have been married and thus are labeled as bride and groom. Data are not available for China.

References

Amato, P.R. (2004) Tension between institutional and individual views of marriage. *Journal of Marriage and Family*, 66, 959–965.

Atoh, M. (2008) The relevance of ideational changes to family transformation in postwar Japan, in *International Family Change: Ideational Perspectives* (eds. R. Jayakody, A. Thornton and W. Axinn), Lawrence Erlbaum Associates, New York/London, pp. 223–250.

Beck, U. and Beck-Gernsheim, E. (2007) Families in a runaway world, in *The Blackwell Companion to The Sociology of Families* (eds. J. Scott, J. Treas and M. Richards), Blackwell Publishing, Oxford, pp. 499–514.

Becker, G.S. (1991) *A Treatise on the Family*, Harvard University Press, Cambridge, MA.

Belanger, D., Lee, H.-K. and Wang, H.-Z. (2010) Ethnic diversity and statistics in East Asia: 'foreign brides' surveys in Taiwan and South Korea. *Ethnic and Racial Studies*, 33 (6), 1108–1130.

Brinton, M.C. (2001) *Women's Working Lives in East Asia*, Stanford University Press, Stanford.

Buckley, S. (1994) A short history of the feminist movement in Japan, in *Women of Japan and Korea: Continuity and Change* (eds. J. Gelb and M.L. Palley), Temple University Press, Philadelphia, pp. 150–186.

Chang, D.T. (2009) *Women's Movement in Twentieth-Century Taiwan*, University of Illinois Press, Chicago.

Chang, K.-S. (2010) *South Korea Under Compressed Modernity: Familial Political Economy in Transition*, Routledge, London/New York.

Chang, Y.-C. and Li, J.-C.A. (2011) Trends and educational differentials in marriage formation among Taiwanese women. RAND Labor and Population Working Paper #WR-891. RAND Corporation, Santa Monica.

Chen, F. (2005) Residential patterns of parents and their married children in contemporary China: a life course approach. *Population Research and Policy Review*, 24, 125–148.

Chen, W.-C. (2012) The changing pattern of educational differentials in divorce in the context of gender egalitarianization: the case of Taiwan. *Population Research and Policy Review*, 31, 831–853.

Chen, Y.-H. and Yi, C.-C. (2005) Taiwan's families, in *Handbook of World Families* (eds. B. Adams and J. Trost), Sage Publications, Thousand Oaks, pp. 177–189.

Chin, M., Lee, J., Lee, S. *et al.* (2012) Family policy in South Korea: development, current status, and challenges. *Journal of Child and Family Studies*, 21, 53–64.

Chu, C.Y.C. and Yu, R.-R. (2010) *Understanding Chinese Families: A Comparative Study of Taiwan and Southeast China*, Oxford University Press, Oxford.

Chueng, C.-K. and Kwan, A.Y.–H. (2009) The erosion of filial piety by modernisation in Chinese societies. *Ageing and Society*, 29, 179–198.

Constable, N. (2005) *Cross-Border Marriages: Gender and Mobility in Transnational Asia*, University of Pennsylvania Press, Philadelphia.

Coontz, S. (2005) *Marriage, a History: How Love Conquered Marriage*, Penguin, New York.

Croll, E.J. (1981) *The Politics of Marriage in Contemporary China*, Cambridge University Press, Cambridge.

Cunningham, M. (2007) Influences of women's employment on the gendered division of household labor over the life course. *Journal of Family Issues*, 28, 422–444.

Eastman, L.E. (1988) *Family, Fields and Ancestors: Constancy and Change in China's Social and Economic History*, 1550–1949, Oxford University Press, New York.

Evans, H. (2008) *The Subject of Gender: Daughters and Mothers in Urban China*, Rowman & Littlefield, Lanham.

Faier, L. (2009) *Intimate Encounter: Filipina Women and the Remaking of Rural Japan*, University of California Press, Berkeley and Los Angeles.

Feeney, G. (1994) Fertility decline in East Asia. *Science*, 266, 1518–1523.

Fong, V.L. (2004) *Only Hope: Coming of Age Under China's One-Child Policy*, Stanford University Press, Stanford.

Frejka, T., Jones, G.W. and Sardon, J.-P. (2010) East Asian childbearing patterns and policy developments. *Population and Development Review*, 36, 579–606.

Fuess, H. (2004) *Divorce in Japan: Family, Gender, and the State, 1600–2000*, Stanford University Press, Stanford.

Goode, W.J. (1963) *World Revolution and Family Patterns*, The Free Press of Glencoe, New York.

Goode, W.J. (1993) *World Change in Divorce Patterns*, Yale University Press, New Haven.

Goodkind, D.M. (1991) Creating new traditions in modern Chinese populations: aiming for birth in the year of the dragon. *Population and Development Review*, 17, 663–686.

Gu, B., Wang, F., Guo, Z. and Zhang, E. (2007) China's local and national fertility policies at the end of the twentieth century. *Population and Development Review*, 33, 129–147.

Hampson, S. (2000) Rhetoric or reality? Contesting definitions of women in Korea, in *Women in Asia: Tradition, Modernity, and Globalisation* (eds. L. Edwards and M. Roces), University of Michigan Press, Ann Arbor, pp. 170–186.

Hashimoto, A. and Traphagan, J.W. (2008) *Imagined Families, Lived Families: Culture and Kinship in Contemporary Japan*, SUNY Press, Albany.

Hausmann, R., Tyson, L.D. and Zahidi, S. (2011) The global gender gap report 2011, World Economic Forum, Geneva.

Hiroko, T. (2011) Chapter 3. Reforming families in Japan: family policy in the era of structural reform, in *Home and Family in Japan: Continuity and Transformation* (eds. R. Ronald and A. Alexy), Routledge, London/New York.

Hochschild, A. (with A. Machung) (1989) *The Second Shift: Working Parents and the Revolution at Home*, Piatkus, London.

Holloway, S.D. (2010) *Women and Family in Contemporary Japan*, Cambridge University Press, Cambridge.

Hyunah, Y. (2003) Gender equality vs. 'tradition' in Korean family law: towards a postcolonial feminist jurisprudence. *The Review of Korean Studies*, 6, 85–118.

Ikels, C. (2004) *Filial Piety: Practice and Discourse in Contemporary East Asia*, Stanford University Press, Stanford.

Inglehart, R. and Norris, P. (2003) *Rising Tide: Gender Equality and Cultural Change around the World*, Cambridge University Press, Cambridge.

Johnson, K.A. (1983) *Women, the Family and Peasant Revolution in China*, University of Chicago Press, Chicago.

Jones, G. (2007) Delayed marriage and very low fertility in Pacific Asia. *Population and Development Review*, 33, 453–478.

Jones, G. and Shen, H.-H. (2008) International marriage in East and Southeast Asia: trends and research emphases. *Citizenship Studies*, 12, 9–25.

Kamiya, H. and Lee, C.W. (2009) International marriage migrants to rural areas in South Korea and Japan: a comparative analysis. *Geographical Review of Japan Series B*, 81, 60–67.

Kim, M. (2010) Gender and international marriage migration. *Sociology Compass*, 4, 718–731.

Kirk, D. (1996) Demographic transition theory. *Population Studies*, 50, 361–387.

Kojima, Y. (2001) In the business of cultural reproduction: theoretical implications of the mail-order bride phenomenon. *Women's Studies International Forum*, 24, 199–210.

Kumagai, F. (2008) *Families in Japan: Changes, Continuities, and Regional Variations*, University Press of America, Lanham.

Kuwayama, T. (2001) The discourse of *Ie* (family) in Japan's cultural identity and nationalism: a critique. *Japanese Review of Cultural Anthropology*, 2, 3–37.

Lee, Y.-J. (2006) Risk factors in the rapidly rising incidence of divorce in Korea. *Asian Population Studies*, 2, 113–131.

Lee, M. (2009) Transition to below replacement fertility and policy response in Taiwan. *Japanese Journal of Population*, 7, 71–86.

Lee, J. and Paik, M. (2006) Sex preferences and fertility in South Korea during the year of the horse. *Demography*, 43, 269–292.

Lesthaeghe, R. and van de Kaa, D. (1986) Twee demografische transities? [Two demographic transitions?], in *Bevolking: Groei en Krimp, Special Issue of Mens en Maatschappij* (eds. D. van de Kaa and R. Lesthaeghe), Van Loghum Slaterus, Deventer, pp. 9–24.

Li, H., Yi, J. and Zhang, J. (2011) Estimating the effect of the one-child policy on the sex ratio imbalance in China: identification based on the difference-in-differences. *Demography*, 48, 1535–1557.

Logan, J.R. and Bian, F. (1999) Family values and coresidence with married children in urban China. *Social Forces*, 77, 1253–1282.

Martin, L.G. (1990) Changing intergenerational family relations in East Asia. *Annals of the American Academy of Political and Social Science*, 510, 102–114.

McLanahan, S. (2004) Diverging destinies: how children are faring under the second demographic transition. *Demography*, 41, 607–627.

Ministry of Internal Affairs and Communications (MIC) (2011) Statistical Handbook of Japan, http://www.stat.go.jp/english/data/handbook/index.htm (accessed October 13, 2012).

National Immigration Agency, Republic of China (NIA) (2012) Statistics on Marriage Between Taiwanese Citizens and Foreigners, http://www.immigration.gov.tw/public/Attachment/212016212134.xls (accessed February 9, 2012).

Nemoto, K. (2008) Postponed marriage: exploring women's views of matrimony and work in Japan. *Gender and Society*, 22, 219–237.

Ng, T. (2005) Migrant women as wives and workers in Singapore, in *Asian Migrations: Sojourning, Displacement, Homecoming and Other Travels* (ed. B.P. Lorente), Asia Research Institute, National University of Singapore, Singapore, pp. 99–107.

OECD (2012) Social Institutions and Gender Index: Chinese Taipei, http://genderindex.org/country/chinese-taipei (accessed October 11, 2012).

Parish, W.L. and Willis, R.J. (1993) Daughters, education, and family budgets. *Journal of Human Resources*, 29, 863–898.

Park, H. (2013) The transition to adulthood among Korean youths: transition markers in productive and reproductive spheres. *The ANNALS of the American Academy of Political and Social Science*, 646, 129–148.

Park, H. and Raymo, J.M. (2013) Divorce in Korea: trends and educational differentials. *Journal of Marriage and Family*, 75, 110–126.

Park, H., Raymo, J. and Creighton, M. (2009) Educational differentials in the risk of divorce and their trends across marriage cohorts of Korean women. *Gender Studies and Policy Review*, 2, 6–17.

Pearce, F. (2011) *Peoplequake: Mass Migration, Ageing Nations, and the Coming Population Crash*, Eden Project, London.

Pritchett, L.H. (1994) Desired fertility and the impact of population policies. *Population and Development Review*, 20, 1–55.

Raymo, J.M. (1998) Later marriages or fewer? Changes in the marital behavior of Japanese women. *Journal of Marriage and the Family*, 60, 1023–1034.

Raymo, J.M. (2003) Educational attainment and the transition to first marriage among Japanese women. *Demography*, 40, 83–103.

Raymo, J.M. and Iwasawa, I. (2008) Bridal pregnancy and spouse pairing patterns in Japan. *Journal of Marriage and Family*, 70, 847–860.

Raymo, J.M., Iwasawa, M. and Bumpass, L. (2005) Marital dissolution in Japan: recent trends and patterns. *Demographic Research*, 11, 395–419.

Rebick, M. and Takenaka, A. (2006) Changing Japanese family, in *The Changing Japanese Family* (eds. M. Rebick and A. Takenaka), Routledge, London/New York, pp. 3–16.

Retherford, R.D., Ogawa, N. and Matsukura, R. (2004) Late marriage and less marriage in Japan. *Population and Development Review*, 27, 65–102.

Satoshi, M. (2005) Educational homogamy in contemporary Japan. *Social Science Japan*, 33, 9–11.

Smits, J. and Park, H. (2009) Five decades of educational assortative mating in 10 East Asian societies. *Social Forces*, 88, 227–255.

Smits, J., Ultee, W. and Lammers, J. (1998) Educational homogamy in 65 countries: an explanation of differences in openness using country-level explanatory variables. *American Sociological Review*, 63, 264–285.

Statistic Korea (2010) International Migration in 2010, http://kostat.go.kr/portal/english/news/1/1/9/index.board?bmode=download&bSeq=&aSeq=271369&ord=3 (accessed February 14, 2013).

Sugimoto, Y. (2010) *An Introduction to Japanese Society*, 3rd edn, Cambridge University Press, Cambridge.

Takahashi, S. (2004) Demographic investigation of the declining fertility process in Japan. *Japanese Journal of Population*, 2, 93–116.

Thai, H.C. (2008) *For Better or For Worse: Vietnamese International Marriages in the New Global Economy*, Rutgers University Press, New Brunswick.

Thornton, A. and Lin, H.-S. (1994) *Social Change and the Family in Taiwan*, The University of Chicago Press, Chicago/London.

Thornton, A., Binstock, G. and Ghimire, D. (2008) International dissemination of ideas about development and family change, in *International Family Change: Ideational Perspectives* (eds. R. Jayakody, A. Thornton and W. Axinn), Lawrence Erlbaum Associates, New York/London, pp. 19–44.

Tilly, L.A. and Scott, J.W. (1978) *Women, Work, and Family*, Holt, Rinehart and Winston, New York/London.

White, M.I. (2002) *Perfectly Japanese: Making Families in an Era of Upheaval*, University of California Press, Berkeley.

Whyte, M.K., Hermalin, A.I. and Ofstedal, M.B. (2003) Intergenerational relations in two Chinese societies, in *China's Revolutions and Intergenerational Relations* (ed. M.K. Whyte), University of Michigan Press, Ann Arbor, pp. 225–254.

Xenos, P., Achmad, S., Khe, N.D. *et al.* (2006) Delayed Asian transitions to adulthood: evidence from national surveys of youth. *Asian Population Studies*, 2, 145–189.

Xu, X. and Whyte, M.K. (1990) Love matches and arranged marriages: a Chinese replication. *Journal of Marriage and Family*, 52, 709–722.

Yan, Y. (2003) *Private Life Under Socialism: Love, Intimacy, and Family Change in a Chinese Village 1949–1999*, Stanford University Press, Stanford.

Yang, C.-F. (1988) Familism and development: an examination of the role of family in contemporary China, in *Social Values and Development: Asian Perspectives* (eds. D. Sinha and H.S.R. Kao), Sage Publications, New Delhi/Newbury Park/London, pp. 93–123.

Yoo, G. (2003) Quality of life across population groups: women in the workplace: gender and wage differentials. *Social Indicators Research*, 62–63, 367–385.

Zimmer, Z. and Korinek, K. (2008) Does family size predict whether an older adult lives with or proximate to an adult child in the Asia-Pacific region? *Asian Population Studies*, 4, 135–159.

5

Changes and Inequalities in Latin American Families

Irma Arriagada

Introduction

To understand the changes in families in Latin America, this chapter adopts a gender-based perspective: while the family is analyzed as a field for the exercise of personal rights, individual family members interact with unequal and asymmetric power within it. Gender processes in Latin America reflect both the legacy of the Creole family system (described by Therborn, Chapter 1) and the transformations brought about by economic modernization and by new ways of thinking and acting associated with modernity. Typical of Latin American societies is a high degree of exclusion and poverty, which results in basic inequality in living conditions and in exposure to the region's integration into the global economy and culture. As a result, new combinations of gender inequality, family life cycles, and income are emerging, together with the new paradoxes that families display in the context of modernity and modernization tempered by exclusion.

This analysis draws on earlier work (Arriagada, 1998, 2002, 2007, 2012), which is updated for this volume. Because Latin American family trends may be less familiar to readers of this Companion, this diagnosis draws on data sources from the 1990 and 2009 household surveys, which have been processed by the Economic Commission for Latin America and the Caribbean (ECLAC, http://www.eclac.org) to make them comparable to one another. They correspond to the Latin American urban population (80.9%) (ECLAC, 2011b). As these consider only two recent points in time, they cannot be used to analyze the long-term evolution of the Latin American family. Accordingly, this paper makes only a cautious analysis of aspects derived from the data used, supplementing conclusions with other sources including studies that illustrate aspects that have not been investigated in surveys of internal family organization, together with references of a more historical nature. For a recent review on Latin American families with a particular emphasis on policy, see García and de Oliveira (2011).

The Wiley Blackwell Companion to the Sociology of Families, First Edition.
Edited by Judith Treas, Jacqueline Scott, and Martin Richards.
© 2014 John Wiley & Sons Ltd. Published 2017 by John Wiley & Sons Ltd.

Family studies: Main paradigms

The classic paradigms of sociological studies have stressed the family's central role in the functioning of society – either invoking a structural-functionalist tradition that relates family matters to the stability of institutions and ultimately society itself or a Marxist perspective that perceives close links between changes in the family and developments in other social institutions such as private property, social class, industrial society, and the State. The link between family change and modernization processes was thus recognized early in sociological analysis, in terms of the development of the nuclear family and individual income. Nonetheless, the associated concept of the patriarchal family was not addressed in depth in the leading theories on the family in vogue at the time, especially those in the North American structural-functionalist tradition.

More recently, and from the very start of gender studies, a more critical view has been taken of the asymmetries that exist among family members in terms of power, resources, and negotiating capacity. In this respect, the greatest power is generally associated with whoever generates the family's monetary income, or the person that cultural norms expect to do so – usually the male head of household. Attention has also been drawn to the way the distribution of resources, power, and time affects women's differential participation in the labor market, politics, and public life generally. The inequality among family members with different degrees of power on account of their sex and age has also been highlighted, thereby demonstrating the persistence of gender asymmetries.

The twentieth-century patriarchal family makes a clear distinction between the public and private domains, with a sharp division of labor between men and women. The man is responsible for establishing a family, based on very clear structural relations of authority and affection toward his wife and children, which are legitimized in the outside world and enable him to provide for, protect, and guide his family. Women, on the other hand, are expected to complement and collaborate with the husband/father (Olavarría and Parrini, 2000). In most Latin American countries, the law reflects this traditional family model, which displays a strong resistance to change. Nonetheless, there have been a number of positive changes, such as the Responsible Parenthood Act recently passed in Costa Rica and legislation against domestic violence passed in most countries of the region.

In Latin America, family formations in the Creole society were profoundly marked by the patriarchal Spanish colonial legacy and by a population model of informal constitution of couples that implied extramarital births and a socially accepted practice of male sexual predation (Therborn, 2007). The gender system in urban *mestizo* societies attached great importance to the separation between the public and the domestic domains, control of female sexuality, the concept of family honor, recognition by other men, and fatherhood as a means of asserting one's masculinity. Historically, class and ethnic differences intensified control over women's sexuality, allowing men the possibility of having relationships with women from different social groups according to different rationales and moral codes. On the other hand, the fragile nature of public institutions in those societies led to the domestic/public contrast being perceived in territorial terms: in the home or on the street. While the home is an ordered space where kinship relations and personal networks unfold, the street is an ambiguous space where personal desires override the common interest (Fuller, 1997; Ariza and de Oliveira, 2004). This patriarchal model of the family is currently being questioned in both public and private, and there is a striking variety in people's representations, discourses, and practices.

Thus, modern family studies see the interaction among gender, social classes, and ethnic groups as central pillars of inequality that define very different conditions of life and structures of opportunities while looking closely at the interrelations among individual time frames, family cycles, and social processes.

Modernity and Modernization in Latin America

The changes that have occurred in the family in relation to the incorporation of Latin America to a global economy and to processes of modernization and modernity are relatively unknown. These transformations arise from sociodemographic transitions, the upheavals of economic crises and their social repercussions, as well as changes in the cultural ambit and in the representations and aspirations in relation to the family.

Modernization and modernity with exclusion

In Latin American countries and elsewhere, a widely debated and recurring theme in sociology concerns modernization and the social and economic processes that accompany it. The consideration of modernity, in contrast, mainly focuses on normative aspects, cultural dimensions, and acceptance of the diversity of identities in pluralistic societies. In general, these two processes have not evolved in the same direction. The relation between the processes of subjectivization (as a perception of this process by individuals, characteristic of modernity) and modernization has proven to be unpredictable, asynchronous, and at times contradictory (Wagner, 1994; UNDP, 1998).

The distinguishing aspects of modernity include the changes that have occurred within the family and the dimensions most closely related to social identity processes that tend to generate increasing autonomy – especially the changing social roles of women.

The distinction between the processes of modernization and modernity is analytical, for the two concepts are closely interrelated (Calderón, Hopenhayn, and Ottone, 1993). Some dimensions are shared – for example, the progressive secularization of collective action, which began with the separation of powers between the State and the Church, but later, in the case of the family, involved recognition of the right to divorce, which is no longer condemned by religious authorities but seen as a "reflexive" personal choice.

Modernization processes and their effects on families include the following:

- *Changes in production processes*: These include economic growth generated by industrialization, by the transition from rural to urban work, and, today, by the development of preeminently market-based global service economies.

- *Changes in demographic structure*: Rapid urbanization processes, longer life expectancy, lower birthrates, and shrinking family size, reflected in changes in the population-age pyramid and family structure.
- *New patterns of work and consumption*: Families have increasing access to goods and services, and there are changes in the forms of work – expansion of the industrial and service sectors, of paid female work, of informal-sector employment, and of job instability.
- *Massive but segmented access to social goods and services such as education, social security, and healthcare*: The coverage of the services is expanded, but there is also greater social fragmentation and inequality due to the different qualities of services supplied.

These changes in basic living conditions caused by the large-scale processes related to globalization and modernization – especially urbanization associated with industrialization, the growth of female employment, new consumption patterns, and new forms of labor market participation – have a key influence on the organization of families and the way they perceive themselves.

With regard to modernity, other aspects are taken into account, such as the following:

- *Promotion of social and individual freedom (individualization)*: This involves expansion of the rights of women and children; questioning of the patriarchal system within the family; profound changes in the areas of intimacy and sexuality; and a search for new identities (Giddens, 1992). The thesis of individualization for analyzing the family, however, has been questioned even in developed countries (Smart and Shipman, 2004).
- *Progress of the social dimension in the development of individual potential*: This development is to the detriment of the importance accorded to the family.
- *Progressive secularization of collective action*: As more and more people distance themselves from religion-based codes of behavior, individual ethics are gaining force, especially with regard to the exercise of reproductive rights and sexual morality.
- *Spread of a formal and instrumental logic*: The emphasis on reasoning that is rational and calculated in pursuit of goals.
- *Reflexivity*: This refers to the fact that most aspects of social activity are continuously being reassessed in the light of new information or knowledge (Giddens, 1990). The family is not exempt from this reflexive approach, which changes people's courses of action and is particularly striking in the case of women (specifically in the feminist movement), representing the point at which male domination breaks down (Bourdieu, 2001).
- *The spread of democratic attitudes*: Defense of diversity and increased tolerance; broadening of citizenship to include other social sectors such as ethnic groups, women, young people, and children.
- *Democratic representation in government*: Marked by the presence of different social attitudes and values.
- *Generation of increasingly multicultural societies*: Embracing diversity in lifestyles and family forms and structures.

In brief, modernity in the family is likely to be reflected in the exercise of democratic rights and autonomy among family members, together with a fairer distribution of labor (domestic and social), opportunities, and family decision making. This implies a new relationship based on asymmetries tempered by democratic principles (Salles and Tuirán, 1996).

Some elements of modernization processes in Latin America have not developed fully, resulting in small groups being included in social and material benefits while large population sectors are left out. Many of the changes associated with modernization have been carried out in a segmented way without being accompanied by the processes characteristic of modernity, especially as regards the cultural and identity dimensions of those changes.

Modernity is essentially a posttraditional order, characterized by increasing diversity of lifestyles and modes of living, with heterogeneous influences affecting habits, values, images, and modes of thought and entertainment. This is boosted by globalization processes that have affected the social links among groups and have had powerful effects on the more personal aspects of our experience, where the security that traditions and customs used to provide has not been replaced by the certainty of rational knowledge (Giddens, 1991). Accordingly, the changes in the family caused by the processes of modernization and modernity become a breaking point in the private–public dichotomy and give rise to emerging forms of family life that redefine the relationship between the family and society. In the case of Latin America, this is accompanied by a process of hybridization to the extent that very traditional and patriarchal forms of the family persist alongside of new styles of family life. These styles overlap strongly with ethnic–racial identity and social class, which define not only material conditions of life but also symbolic forms and very different family values.

The present Latin American context and its impact on families

Socioeconomic changes
From an economic, social, and cultural standpoint, there are a number of worrying aspects in the structural situation of Latin America. Though there have been economic growth and increasing job opportunities during the last years, there have also been persistent informal employment and regressive income distribution that affect families differentially. The continuing process of neoliberalism that includes privatization of education, health, and social security requires more economic resources from families to cover their needs.

Social security coverage, for example, continues to be low; only 43% of households have at least one member affiliated with a social insurance system and in only 32% of households is the head of the household or spouse affiliated. Gender and generational gaps are evident, given that the level of social security coverage is significantly higher among households with a male head (49.5%) than households with a female head (41.3%). Likewise, young people have lower levels of coverage than adults (ECLAC, 2011a).

Alongside these processes, the expansion of the working-age population has generated simultaneous trends toward precarious employment and unemployment in the region. Unemployment is higher among the poorer segments, those with less education, young people, and women. Another worrying aspect is the contradiction between the increase in structural unemployment[1] and economic growth, with all the damage that this causes to family security and stability.

Recent trends also reveal the deteriorating situation, impoverishment, and indebtedness of middle-income groups. More and more family members (especially women, young people, and children) are finding work in traditionally precarious and low-productivity sectors. The entry of women into low-paid jobs offers them limited chance of improving their employment prospects. While paid employment is a way of enhancing their living standards and gaining greater self-sufficiency, it has the disadvantage that it further increases the total workload borne by women. They have to divide their responsibilities between the family and their job while receiving little support from their partner or from social institutions. This is particularly true of poorer women. Mothers with higher incomes can hire domestic workers for their homes or private services to take care of their children.

In addition to these aspects, there has been a revolution in expectations, fueled by the mass media. This has increased the sense of frustration at the widening gap between the growing desire for consumption and the real possibility of obtaining desired goods. Inequality in the region is growing and income differences are widening, which severely hinders the possibilities of the social integration of marginalized families into society and further aggravates the sources of differences among them.

Demographic changes

Alongside with the modernization process, there is massive access to modern contraceptive methods – derived from the first demographic transition, which involved a reduction in mortality and fertility rates and an increase in life expectancy. This transition has had major effects on Latin American families. Longer life expectancy has lengthened the duration of life as a couple. In Mexico, it is estimated that husband/wife roles can span up to 40 years of people's lives (Ariza and de Oliveira, 2001). In countries such as Argentina, Uruguay, and Chile, the period could be even longer, barring separation or divorce. Also, there are increasing numbers of single-person households, families made up of older adults, and households with no children. At present, one in every four Latin American households contains at least one older adult (ECLAC, 2000a). This increase in the number of older persons means an increase in the caregiving work performed by women in their homes.

Average family size has shrunk because couples are having fewer children and births are being spaced more widely apart. The number of multigenerational families is falling, while single-person households are on the rise. Migration, which may occur for a variety of reasons (economic considerations, armed conflict, and domestic violence, among others), is another factor leading to smaller households.

Fertility rates had fallen in most Latin American countries. The average Latin American Total Fertility Rate (TFR) was 5.9 children per woman in the 1950s, declined to 2.3 by the 2005–2010 period when the rate for Europe was 1.4 and 2.0 for the United States (ECLAC, 2007). Today, the Latin American rates are below the world average of 2.5 children per woman and similar to levels observed in Europe 40 years ago. Some countries already have fertility rates below replacement level. Recently, however, they have stabilized, and in some cases (Argentina, Chile, Panama, and Uruguay), there has been an increase in adolescent fertility rates, which reflects the fact that different countries are at different stages in the demographic transition.

The highest adolescent fertility rates are in the poorest population groups, among teenagers with little schooling, in rural areas, and in areas with high concentrations of indigenous people (ECLAC, 2000b; Guzmán, Hakker, and Contreras, 2001; ECLAC, 2011a). The factors that have contributed the most to the drop in fertility are associated with exposure to sexual relations, such as not entering a union or doing so later in life, or separating from a partner either temporarily or permanently. These account for nearly 50% of the decline compared to natural fertility. The use of contraceptives accounts for more than 40% of the decline (ECLAC, 2011a).

In some of the region's socially more developed countries (such as Argentina, Chile, and Uruguay), the models of sexual, marital, and reproductive behavior that are widespread in developed countries are beginning to take root among higher-income and more educated social groups. These include later marriage and reproduction among young people with high levels of schooling. In Chile, for example, the male age at marriage rose from 26.6 to 29.4 years between 1980 and 1999; the female age rose from 23.8 to 26.7. There were higher rates of divorce and cohabitation among Latin America's middle-income groups. In Chile, the number of divorces in 2009 (50,269) was almost equal to the number of marriages (52,834). The number of marriages decreased, the number of annulments increased, birthrates diminished, and the number of children born outside marriage increased. In 1999, 47.7% of Chilean children were nonmarital births, whereas the 1990 figure had been only 34.3%. The consolidation of similar patterns in Europe led some to suggest that they represent a second demographic transition.

This second transition is associated with a profound change in values, closely related to Giddens's concept of late modernity (Giddens, 1990, 1992). Demographers studying this subject have preferred to associate it with "postmaterialist values" (Inglehart, cited by Van de Kaa, 2001) and, more recently, with postmodernization and postmodernity (Van de Kaa, 2001). Apart from fertility indices that are well below replacement levels, this second transition includes the following features: (i) an increase in celibacy and voluntarily childless couples; (ii) postponement of first union; (iii) later birth of the first child; (iv) consensual unions increasingly seen as an alternative to marriage; (v) an increase in the number of children born and raised out of wedlock; (vi) greater frequency of marital breakdown (divorce); and (vii) diversification of family structures.

Some of these features have a long history in Latin America, and their existence has less to do with modernity than with socioeconomic exclusion and poverty and even with traditionalism. This is true of both consensual unions and marital abandonment, historically documented in the concept of the *huacho*, which refers to the child without a present or known father and born out of wedlock (also denominated "illegitimate"). In short, certain sociodemographic phenomena affecting Latin American families conceal differentiated and specific determinants, directions, and consequences that depend on the socioeconomic group in which they occur. Cohabitation, which is emerging as a modern lifestyle among the middle class today, long existed as a traditional pattern among poor segments of the population.

It has been asserted that all three dimensions of the classic definition of the family – sexuality, procreation, and cohabitation – have changed profoundly and have begun to evolve in different directions, resulting in a growing multiplicity of family and cohabitation models (Jelin, 1998). It is generally agreed that most of the changes in family structure are gradual and are influenced by family location (urban vs. rural), social class, and the various experiences that Latin American societies have gone through (Salles and Tuirán, 1997). Other changes have been very dynamic, however, including the extremely rapid evolution of the social roles of women both within and outside the family, the increase in their labor market participation, and the growing number of households headed by women.

The Main Changes in Latin American Families

In recent decades, different processes have produced changes in the structure and behavior of families in Latin America. From the economic point of view, the incorporation of Latin America into the global economy has modified forms of work and employment, which in turn have affected the organization and distribution of rights and responsibilities within the family. The demographic changes related to reduced fertility, increased life expectancy, and migration are also affecting family size and structure. The entry of women into the labor market triggered a cultural and subjective transformation that has been termed the "quiet revolution" (Goldin, 2006; Esping-Andersen, 2009) because of its scope. All these transformations have been marked by major cultural changes about the value of the family, acceptance of new forms of family structure, and increasing possibilities of choice, especially for women. As Jelin (1998) indicated, transformations in family formation, dynamics, and structure express the diffusion and adoption of new values related to a process of autonomy and a demand for individual interests and rights, in particular in gender and intergenerational relationships, that is, values linked to modernity.

New family structures: Type and family cycle

Analyses based on ECLAC data from 1990 and 2009 show significant changes in Latin American families in recent decades. The main transformations in family structures are synthesized in the following based on information from household surveys in urban areas in 18 Latin American countries.

Diversification of family types: Families and households moved away from the dominant two-parent-with-children model between 1990 and 2009. A family and household typology for family and nonfamily household types was constructed to analyze this diversification and is presented in Box 5.1.

The most important model in urban Latin America is the nuclear family, that is, the two-parent family with children. It decreased from 46.3% in 1990 to 41.1% in 2005. In 2005, this nuclear family coexisted with the extended family, usually with three generations, which represented slightly more than a fifth of all Latin American families (21.7%).

Another tendency, the increase in families with a female head, has acquired visibility and been analyzed extensively in the Latin American region, especially in Central America (López and Salles, 2000; ECLAC, 2004). The percent of households headed by women increased in each of 17 Latin American countries between about

> **Box 5.1** Family and household types based
> on household surveys
>
> • Nuclear families (two partners and/or a parent–child unit only)
> • Extended families (one or both parents present, with or without children,
>   together with other relatives)
> • Compound families (one or both parents, with or without children, with or
>   without other relatives, together with nonrelatives)
> • Single-person households (household consisting of just one person)
> • Nonnuclear households (without a couple or parent–child nucleus, although
>   other kinship ties may exist)
>
> Families include single-parent (usually the mother) or two-parent families
> (both parents present) as well as partners without children.

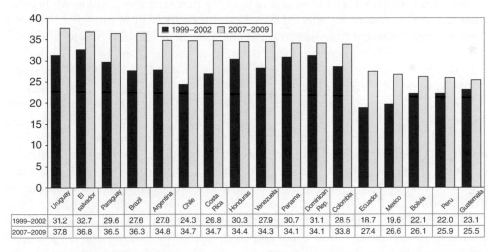

	Uruguay	El salvador	Paraguay	Brazil	Argentina	Chile	Costa Rica	Honduras	Venezuela	Panama	Dominican Rep.	Colombia	Ecuador	Mexico	Bolivia	Peru	Guatemala
1999–2002	31.2	32.7	29.6	27.8	27.8	24.3	26.8	30.3	27.9	30.7	31.1	28.5	18.7	19.6	22.1	22.0	23.1
2007–2009	37.8	36.8	36.5	36.3	34.8	34.7	34.7	34.4	34.3	34.1	34.1	33.8	27.4	26.6	26.1	25.9	25.5

Figure 5.1 Percentage of female headed households by country: 17 Latin American countries: 1999–2002 and 2007–2009.
Source: ECLAC (Economic Commission for Latin America and the Caribbean) (2010b) Social Panorama of Latin America 2010 (LC/G.2481-P), March 2011, Santiago, Chile. United Nations Publication, Sales No. E.11.II.G.6.

1999 and 2009 (Figure 5.1). From a demographic perspective, female headship is related to the increase in singleness, resulting from separations and divorces, from migration, and from extended widowhood, which reflects the increase in female life expectancy. From a socioeconomic and cultural perspective, this growth in female headship relates to women's increased levels of education and their growing economic participation, which allows them the economic independence and social autonomy to establish or continue households without partners. Women head almost a third of families in Latin America. In 2009, the lowest percentage was in Guatemala (25.5%), and the highest was in Uruguay (37.8%) (see Figure 5.1). The percentage of indigent households headed by women is higher than the average, reflecting the facts that such households tend to have more dependents, women's earnings in the labor market are lower, and obligations of childcare limit their possibilities in choosing employment.

Between 1990 and 2005, there has also been an increase in nonfamily households, among which one-person households have increased the most (6.7%–9.7%). The individualization that forms part of modernity is reflected in the increase in one-person households, that is, households of persons who opt not to live in a family. They are most commonly young people who postpone matrimony or cohabiting. Likewise, the aging of the Latin American population partly accounts for the increase in one-person households among elderly persons (especially widows due to their longer life expectancy) with sufficient resources to live apart from kin.

In effect, there are a wide variety of family arrangements today. Adults can opt to live alone, in a couple without children, in one-parent households, in consensual unions, in same-sex (gay or lesbian) unions, and so on. There are a growing number of blended families (couples who bring together their children by another partner from previous unions), as well as distant families as products of the migration of family members. However, the weight of many of these changes is unknown because their magnitude cannot be inferred based on information from household surveys. Case studies, however, show important changes in the perception of who are members of such families, greater individualization of the members of the family, and acceptance of distinct affective logics by members within the same family (Wainerman, 2005; Araujo and Martuccelli, 2012).

Decline in the male-provider family model: This male-provider model corresponds to the traditional concept of the nuclear family, in which both parents are present along with their children, the mother works as a housewife full time, and the father acts as the only breadwinner. Increased educational levels and the growing economic incorporation of women have led to a shift from the "male-provider" model to that of the "double-income family." The labor force participation rate of urban women in Latin America in 1990 was 42% and by 2010 increased to 52% (ECLAC, 2012). In effect, in the majority of Latin American families, women have ceased to be exclusively housewives and have entered the labor market, making an important new contribution to family income. This is reflected in the trend to a lower percentage of nuclear families in which there are children and the female spouse does *not* work (from 47.6% in 1990 to 30.2% in 2009); there is a higher percentage in which the female spouse does combine work and children (from 26.7% in 1990 to 33.5% in 2009). Figure 5.2 shows the situation in 2005. The most traditional model of the nuclear family, with two parents, children, and a female spouse who dedicates herself to domestic work (male-breadwinner model), represented one in five (20.9%) urban Latin American households.

This change means that a high proportion of Latin American family members seek to balance between work and family care responsibilities. Women are especially affected by this transition, given that the cultural expectation remains that mothers (whether real or potential, in effect, all women) continue to have the main responsibility for the care of the home and at the same time participate in the labor market. But while women's access to paid work has increased and consumes time to deal with family responsibilities, there has not been an equivalent change in the distribution of

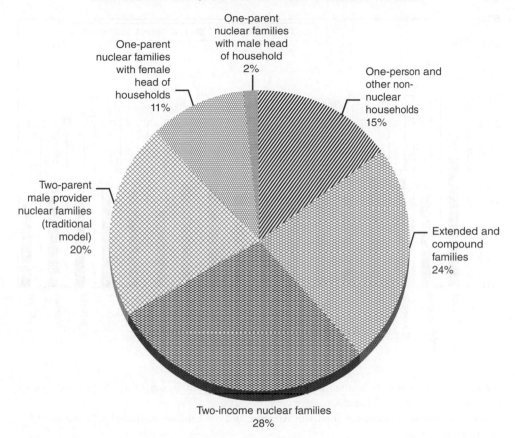

Figure 5.2   Percent distribution of urban families and households, by type and country: 18 Latin America countries, 2005.
Note: Includes Argentina, Bolivia, Brazil, Chile, Colombia, Costa Rica, Dominican Republic, Ecuador, El Salvador, Honduras, Guatemala, Mexico, Nicaragua, Panama, Paraguay, Peru, Uruguay and Venezuela.
Source: Irma Arriagada (coord.) (2007), "Familias y políticas públicas en América Latina. Una historia de desencuentros", Libros de la CEPAL, No. 96 (LC/G.2345-P), Santiago, Chile, Economic Commission for Latin America and the Caribbean (ECLAC), October. United Nations Publication, Sales No. S.07.II.G.97.

time that men dedicate to work and to the home. The work overload has fallen upon women, especially mothers with small children. This includes the segment of female-headed, one-parent families in Figure 5.2, which is much more numerous than their male-headed counterparts.

As already noted, the number of women living alone or as heads of households with dependents has been increasing in recent decades, so that the responsibility of women for their own survival and that of their family has also increased. Their children's fathers often do not support adolescent mothers, and older adults are not cared for by their male children, a tendency that increases the family caregiving load for women. Even when women live with a partner, men's incomes are often so inadequate that women and children must assume the double load of domestic work and work outside the home to round out the family budget. Even though Mexico has one

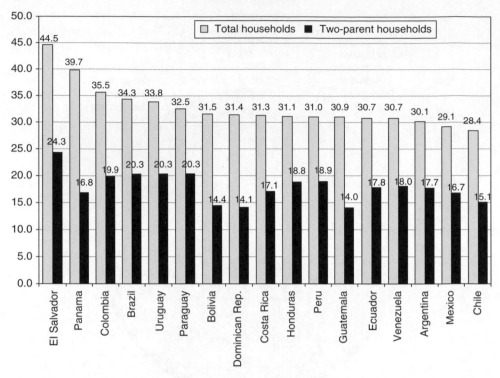

Figure 5.3 Women´s percentage contribution to household income for all and two-parent household by country: 17 Latin American countries, 2008.
Source: Economic Commission for Latin America and the Caribbean, special tabulations of the households surveys.

of the lowest percentages of households headed by women, a study found that the incomes of 17.1% of households, independent of the sex of head of the house, were earned exclusively or predominantly by women (Rubalcava, 1996). In 2008, the economic contribution of women in all households ranged between 44.5% of total household income in El Salvador and 28% in Chile (see Figure 5.3). Likewise, the economic contribution of women in two-parent households was lower but still significant for family budgets. In these households, women's contributions to total household income were 24.3% in El Salvador and 15.1% in Chile.

The economic contribution of the work by children, especially in indigent households, is also important for the survival of these households. Young people and children in the region work in variable percentages depending on the country and age group. The data underestimate the magnitude of child and youth participation in the labor market, given that legislation in the majority of countries prohibits employing persons under 18 years of age. Nevertheless, it is accepted that children under this age work for a few hours per day, provided they attend school and only perform light work. In the case of households where children work, the children contribute between 16% and 36% of household incomes (Arriagada, 1998).

Information about the labor force participation of women and youth reveals two tendencies: one virtuous and the other negative. The first refers to the fact that the participation of more adult members of the family, mainly women, allows the family to emerge from poverty. The labor participation of children under the age of 18 has negative long-run consequences, however, given that they drop out of the educational system. This results in social and economic limitations for them and their future families and thus reproduces the intergenerational cycle of poverty.

The changing composition of families: Latin American families have become smaller, and their distribution across family life cycle stages has also changed. The reduction in the size of families and households is noted in all Latin American countries, although with significant variations. In 2009, Uruguay has the lowest average household size (2.9 persons), while Peru and Ecuador has the highest (4.0). This is associated with the decrease in fertility, the improved general socioeconomic level allowing family members to live apart, and the increased labor participation rate of women. Other factors include couples marrying at an older age, delaying children, and increasing the space between births. Likewise, the increase in the number of consensual unions has been accompanied by shorter relationships, which suggests the importance of analyzing the characteristics of the affective bonds generated in relationships.

Couples' transitions over time have given rise to the concept of stages in the family life cycle, a heuristic idea based in procreation within stable unions. Despite the diversity in family structures and experience, the family life cycle remains a useful, if admittedly simplified, way of describing the different phases that couples' households can go through. Six stages, identified on the basis of the ages of the woman and the youngest child, provide insights into these developments. There is (i) *the young couple without children* (the woman younger than 40); (ii) then the *initial* stage of starting a family when the first children are born; (iii) the stage of family *expansion* when the number of children peaks; (iv) *consolidation*, when the couple is no longer having babies and the youngest children are adolescents; (v) the *departure stage* when children are grown and leave home to start their own households; and (vi) the *empty nest* when an older couple (the woman 40 years or older) no longer have children in the home (Arriagada, 2002).

Due to significant demographic changes, in particular declining birthrates and increased life expectancy, important changes have occurred in Latin America in the distribution of families over each stage in the family life cycle. Based on information from household surveys, the majority of Latin American families are in the stages of family expansion and consolidation, that is, in the stage when the family stops having more children. This is when family resources are under strong pressures given the size of the family and the economic dependence of children 6–18 years of age.

Comparing data from 1990 and 2009, it can be observed that there is an increase in the proportion of families in the stages when the children are over 18 and leaving home as well as when couples are older and have all left home. The increased number of families in the latter stages of the life cycle is explained by the fact that there are more countries in the advanced stage of demographic transition, with the consequent aging of the population. The highest proportions of such households in Latin America are found in Uruguay, Argentina, Chile, and Cuba (Figure 5.4).

Class and ethnic inequalities

The family has a long association with processes of social inequality. The reproduction of social inequalities originates in the family system and in the conditions of the class

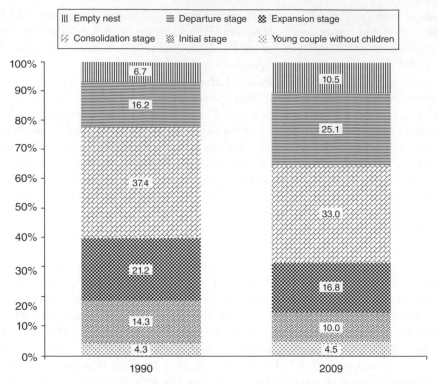

Figure 5.4   Percentage distribution of families according to the family life cycle: 18 Latin American countries, 1990–2009.

Note: Includes Argentina, Bolivia, Brazil, Chile, Colombia, Costa Rica, Dominican Republic, Ecuador, El Salvador, Honduras, Guatemala, Mexico, Nicaragua, Panama, Paraguay, Peru, Uruguay and Venezuela.

Source: Economic Commission for Latin America and the Caribbean, special tabulations of the households surveys.

origins of families which determine the future access of family members to social, economic, and symbolic assets.

Notably, in terms of income distribution as measured by the Gini coefficient, Latin America is one of the most unequal regions in the world. The type of family one belongs to conditions the possibility of well-being. In the distribution of household types according to income quintiles, given types of households tend to be concentrated among the poorest or the richest. In 2009, persons in the richest 20% were most in a position to constitute one-person households. Equally, nuclear households with a male head and without children were in the quintiles of families with more resources. In turn, one-parent nuclear families with women as household heads were concentrated in the lowest income quintile. The higher incidence of indigence and poverty among households with a female head is explained by the lower number of economic contributors to the family income and the generally lower incomes of working women.

Thus, the major tendencies observed among families occur with broad diversity among the social groups and classes. For example, the households of families that belong to the highest income quintile have two to three fewer members than families in the lowest quintile owing to the higher number of children among the poorest families. Likewise, extended households are concentrated among the poorest, while one-person households are concentrated among the richest. The levels of well-being are associated with the different stages of the family life cycle. The structures of household expenditures and consumption also vary according to the levels of family income.

Another major source of diversity and inequality is among families belonging to indigenous ethnic groups and Afrodescendents. It is estimated that there are around 670 indigenous groups in Latin America representing between 40 and 50 million persons, concentrated mainly in Mexico, Peru, Guatemala, Bolivia, and Ecuador. Information from some population censuses in or around 2010 indicate higher growth rates of the indigenous population than the nonindigenous, which is consistent with the higher number of children per family among indigenous people.

The information about indigenous people, although fragmented, consistently shows a higher incidence of poverty, lower incomes, lower levels of schooling, lower life expectancy, higher infant and maternal mortality, as well as less access to sewerage systems and potable water (Del Popolo and Oyarce, 2005). Similarly, their values and behaviors in relation to the family differ from those of nonindigenous peoples and also differ among distinct indigenous groups. For example, Aymaras and Quechuas in Bolivia tend to begin their reproductive cycle later than nonindigenous Bolivians and the Guarani in Paraguay. Likewise, the conception of the family and its ideal size varies with ethnic identity, as is shown in this testimony: *We have a distinct concept of the family. We can have 5, 6, or 7 children.... Children give the family its value. We appreciate large families. It is selfish to think of having only one child and to give that child everything...* (woman of the Ngöbe people). Consistent with this testimony, census data from six Latin American countries for the year 2000 show higher fertility rates among indigenous people than among nonindigenous peoples (Del Popolo and Oyarce, 2005).

It is estimated that 30% of the Latin American population is of Afrodescent, mainly located in Brazil (approximately 45% of the total population) and to a much lesser extent in Ecuador, Costa Rica, Guatemala, and Honduras. An estimated 75 million Afrodescendents live in these five countries. The socioeconomic situation of Afrodescendents varies according to the levels of inequality in the specific countries (Rangel, 2005). In addition to the demographic, social, and economic inequalities suffered by Afrodescendents and indigenous peoples, they face racism, xenophobia, and persistent discrimination by public institutions and the rest of the society.

Gender inequalities in allocation of time

One of the key concepts in the analysis of the interrelation between work and family is the sexual division of labor, which analytically links the two spheres and highlights the mechanisms of the work–family relationship in social reproduction. It refers to daily intergenerational and social care. Numerous studies have shown the unequal participation of men and women in both the labor market and domestic labor. To the extent that the increasing incursion of women into paid work has not been accompanied by an equivalent increase in the participation of men in domestic labor, the workload of women has risen (Ariza and de Oliveira, 2004).

The production of goods and services that takes place in the sphere of the family or through unpaid work does not have public visibility nor is it counted in labor records. Therefore, it has been considered as nonwork according to the usual definitions of work and paid employment. Likewise, the sexual division of labor as consolidated since industrialization associates (more in the collective imagination than in reality) men with economic activities and women with domestic and family activities (Carrasco, 2001). This rigid distribution of tasks hides the contribution of women's work to family and social well-being. The lack of monetary value attributed to unpaid domestic work impedes an assessment of the real economic contribution of women to the development of countries, to the reduction of poverty, and to the well-being of their families (ECLAC, 2004).

Surveys about time use are essential to understand changes and restructuring resulting from the participation of women in the labor market, because they provide essential quantitative information on the structure of domestic work as determined by the socioeconomic status of the family, its life cycle stage and the place of residence. There are significant differences between men and women in time use in general and particularly in relation to performing unpaid domestic tasks. The model upon which Latin American societies are structured relegates women to private space and the realization of reproductive labors. On the other hand, men are associated with the public space and productive functions. Another factor that influences the variations of the time assigned to reproductive work within the home is the life stage of various household members. The distribution of time dedicated to domestic work varies among women according to their age, marital status, and the number and age of children living in the home. The composition and functions of domestic work differ considerably if the woman is young, single, and with one child as opposed to married with more than two children and in charge of caring for older adults (Aguirre, 2009). Examining domestic work within the family requires incorporating as a central element the concept of the family life cycle, which enriches knowledge of domestic work and its functioning in diverse family structures.

In relation to paid work, women encounter more obstacles than men to entering the labor market and have higher rates of unemployment throughout their working lives. Women are subjected to the vertical and horizontal segmentation of occupations, that is, they work in a narrower range of occupations and are more concentrated than men in informal and low-productivity sectors such as domestic services: "feminized" occupations have consequently lower earnings. The income gap between men and women has been decreasing with time. While in the 1990s, women earned 69% of what men were earning, almost 20 years later in 2008, this gap had been reduced by 10 percentage points, that is, women made 79% of what men earn. Although the proportion of women without incomes of their own decreased by 11 percentage points between 1994 and 2008, over a third of women in urban areas and 44% in rural areas cannot sustain themselves economically. The majority cannot acquire their own monetary resources because of their domestic and caregiving activities at the home. In turn, the percentage of men without incomes has remained relatively stable at around 10%. This situation underlines the persistent vulnerability of women to poverty and inequality (ECLAC, 2010a).

Various time-use surveys that have registered the time dedicated to paid and unpaid activities have been conducted in 16 countries in the Latin American region.

Unfortunately, they do not lend themselves to cross-national comparisons owing to differences in recruitment, subject coverage, *in situ* data collection methods, study population (household, individual, minimum age of interviewees), reference period (day before, week), and, in particular, the activities making up household and caregiving work, and the reporting of simultaneous activities (Durán and Milosavljevic, 2012). Despite the methodological differences that impede comparability, there are a number of general tendencies in time use.

The total work time of women (paid and unpaid) is greater than the total work time of men. According to information from the ECLAC Gender Equality Observatory of Latin America and the Caribbean (www.cepal.org/oig), the average weekly paid and unpaid work time is seen for a number of countries. In Brazil in 2008, men worked 47h and women 57h. In Colombia in 2009, men worked 53h and women 64. In Ecuador in 2008, men worked 52h and women 66. In Mexico in 2009, men worked 64h and women 86. In Peru in 2010, men worked 62h and women 70. Finally, in Uruguay in 2007, men worked 56 and women 79.

Men, of course, are less likely to participate and they invest less time in domestic and caregiving activities than do women. For Mexico in 2010, 52% of men compared to 96% of women devoted at least some time to domestic tasks. The figures for the care of children, the sick, and disabled were 29% of men and 53% of women (INEGI, 2011). In 2002 in Mexico, where women contributed 85h to domestic work, men contributed only 15% of the total household labor. Women dedicated on average 14h a week exclusively to caregiving for children and other members of the household, while men contributed only 7.6h. The number of hours that women dedicate to work increases notably in the stages of the family life cycle associated with raising children, especially when the children are under 5 years of age. Despite the increase of work in the household with small children, the time men dedicate to household work remains constant over the different stages of the life cycle.

Women's paid workweek is shorter than that of men because women need to attend to domestic and family responsibilities. A survey in Chile in 2007 found that women accounted for 78.2% and men 22.8% of the total time dedicated to caregiving in the home, while women accounted for 66.4% of the time dedicated to household tasks, while men accounted for only 33.6%. On the other hand, the relation was the reverse for paid work: the rate of employment for men was 69% and the rate for women was only 38%.

Even when women have paid work, the distribution of domestic and caregiving work between women and men continues to be unequal. In Mexican families with both partners participating in the labor market, work time is divided in the following manner: on average, male partners work 52h weekly in their economic activity, and female partners work 37h. Male partners dedicate 4h weekly to cleaning house and female partners 15h; male partners 7h to cooking and female partners 15.5h; male partners 8h to childcare and female partners 12; and finally male partners dedicate 1.5h to cleaning and care of clothing and female partners 8h (INEGI, 2004).

Women who have children in one-parent households and who perform unpaid work are shown to work fewer unpaid work hours than women who live with a partner and children. Without a male breadwinner, more of their time is likely to go into paid employment. In 2007, single women with children in Uruguay dedicated

7 fewer hours weekly to unpaid work than women who live with a partner and children (Aguirre, 2009). In terms of increasing unpaid domestic and caregiving work, having a partner or being married is a bad option for women, and their unpaid workload increases in the case of women who belong to blended families.

Cultural changes

Cultural concepts and images regarding male power continue to prevail in the social domain, along with behavioral patterns based on those images. This helps to explain the inconsistencies that exist between the traditional discourse and new family practices. Nonetheless, certain dimensions of modernity have been emerging, such as redefined conjugal roles, in which the principle of equality is gradually gaining acceptance in keeping with the growing economic contribution to the household made by women and children. Changing parent–child relationships reflect a strengthening of the rights of the child and less emphasis on relations of hierarchy and submission. New individual choices (e.g., nonnuclear and single-person households) are emerging, made possible by individual access to economic resources. The institution of the nuclear family centered on paternal authority and supported by all social institutions is being called into question by a number of interrelated processes. These processes include changes in the organization of work in a global information economy; women's higher levels of education and labor market participation; increasing control over the frequency and spacing of pregnancies; circulation of people and ideas between different societies; and greater conscious awareness of their situation among women themselves (Guzmán, 2002).

Incipient processes of "individualization" are also emerging. Personal rights take precedence over family ones, and personal fulfillment overrides family interests. In these processes of cultural change, globalized images of different family types have fueled the move toward individual rights and autonomy. These go along with changes in models of sexuality and intimacy, especially among adolescents, and a greater emphasis on peer culture (in which young people identify first and foremost with other young people). A study in Chile claims that young people see family relations as problematic. They believe family conflict affects them negatively, and they blame parental attitudes for this. Authoritarianism, mistrust, and a lack of care and affection are children's most frequent complaints about their family environment (UNDP, 2002).

A number of changes in domestic relationships can also be identified. Compared to earlier studies, a case study conducted in Mexico City and Monterrey shows that women today have greater decision-making power over reproductive issues (use of contraceptives, attending clinics) than in other areas of family life (García and de Oliveira, 2001). The gender-based division of labor for domestic chores shows little change, however. Domestic violence persists in a variety of forms, together with a strong tendency for men to restrict women's freedom to carry on various types of activities. A large proportion of women still have to obtain permission to undertake paid work, join associations, or visit friends and family. There are still areas of exclusive male decision making, such as what major goods to purchase and where to live. Men and women have strikingly different perceptions of the various issues covered in the survey: in Mexico City, for example, the existence of domestic violence is perceived less clearly by men than by women – 16% compared to 33%, respectively (García and de Oliveira, 2001).

A study in Argentina that analyzed two generations of two-provider families concluded that "the division of labour has moved from the traditional model of segregated roles, to a transitional one...." The generational transition has not been uniform, as paternity gained many more supporters than domesticity. In other words, men increased their participation in childcare much more than in housekeeping chores, which remain largely a female preserve. Although women have not cut back on their participation in domestic and maternal chores, they have begun to encroach on traditionally male activities in the home (Wainerman, 2000, p. 149).

Rapid social, economic, and cultural changes have an impact on family relationships, attitudes, and social practices, given new opportunities (such as the greater autonomy, the possibility of choice with regard to childbearing, and the economic independence for women). These coexist, however, with traditional patterns of behavior, such as subjective feelings of dependency, teenage pregnancy, and gender-based division of domestic chores.

Latin American families have undergone major changes, but these have been more marked in some areas than in others. Patriarchal authority is being called into question, and very incipient democratic models of family reconstruction are emerging. This is increasingly necessary, because families provide psychological security and material well-being to their members in a world characterized by the individualization of work, the breakdown of civil society, and the loss of legitimacy of the State. Nonetheless, the transition to new family forms entails a fundamental redefinition of gender relations in all societies (Castells, 1998). Unlike developed countries, Latin America displays glaring inequalities between families at different economic levels. Public policy formulation therefore needs to consider the fact that the family structures of poorer households limit their chances of escaping poverty. For example, poor households tend to be at the expansion stages in the family life cycle, with fewer economic providers and a larger number of members to provide for. These socioeconomic differences are compounded by gender and ethnic inequalities. These are fundamental issues. When formulating policies and programs aimed at democratizing Latin American families, there is a need to alter the current balance of men's and women's rights and obligations in the family domain.

Conclusion

Within the framework of the *sui generis* modernization and modernity occurring in Latin America, this chapter has analyzed a number of cultural, socioeconomic, and demographic changes that families in the region have undergone. The changes occur against a general backdrop of gender, ethnic origin, and class inequality. Therefore, this paper has considered the historical evolution of family structures associated with modernization in terms of distinctive development paths in different social classes. It has considered the evolution of families over time as they pass through stages of the family life cycle, taking account of the fluidity of family structures and the changes taking place in them. Due to their systemic nature, gender inequities permeate the social fabric, such that overcoming them requires changes in other mechanisms that perpetuate social inequality, hence the analytical importance of an approach that focuses on the overlap between gender and other systems of inequality relating to class, ethnic origin, or life cycle (Salles and Tuirán, 1997; Ariza and de Oliveira, 2001).

There have also been changes in symbolic aspects, reflected in new types of families and family relationships. These occur in the context of societies undergoing continuous processes of change that question traditional family roles and raise new challenges and tensions for their members. In a context of modernization without modernity, family change does not follow a single line but unfolds along a variety of paths heading in different and sometimes opposite directions. The analytical frameworks used to study families reveal a number of limitations in approach and public policy design often because of the assumption that there is a single desirable family model.

In many discourses, the institution of the family is seen as the final bastion against the vicissitudes of modernity, overlooking the fact that the great demographic, social, and economic changes the family has undergone prevent it from adequately performing the changing functions demanded of it. This suggests the existence of unresolved traditional problems (such as domestic violence and rigid sexual division of roles), compounded by new challenges for families that require additional cognitive, material, and sociability resources to address (Güell, 1999). Modernity itself involves the possibility of accepting new forms of family structure and functioning that afford autonomy and reflexivity in decision making for all members. The fact that these processes of reflexivity and change, which often take place privately, are not being adequately reflected in public debate further widens the gap between people's representations, discourses, and practices.

Revealing the existence of a wide diversity of situations, findings relating to family structures and home life cast doubt on the dominant image of the traditional patriarchal family. At the same time, the separation of sexuality from reproduction, so that motherhood is now a matter of choice, has increased women's possibilities of gaining access to greater labor market opportunities (albeit often in precarious forms of employment) and taking part in social and political activities. With regard to family forms and functions in a Latin American setting of highly varied modernity, domestic gender inequalities are not only being challenged but also being rebuilt in the wake of the other changes taking place. These include a dual workload for women, the persistence of domestic violence, and more limited autonomy for women.

On the other hand, the stages of the demographic transition tend to overlap even within a given country, depending on whether one is considering sectors of high socioeconomic level or extreme poverty. The social, economic, and demographic changes taking place in Latin America display a number of basic pillars around which old forms of inequality are reproduced and new ones are created which require an integrated multidimensional approach to overcome.

Note

1   It refers to unemployment resulting from changes in the basic composition of the economy. These changes simultaneously open new positions for trained workers as, for example, in the case of introduction of new technologies.

References

Aguirre, R. (ed) (2009) *Las bases invisibles del bienestar social. El trabajo doméstico no remunerado en el Uruguay*, UNIFEM, Doble Clic editoras, Montevideo, Uruguay.

Araujo, K. and Martuccelli, D. (2012) *Desafíos Comunes. Retrato de la sociedad chilena y sus individuos, Tomo II, Trabajo, sociabilidades y familias*, LOM ediciones, Colección Ciencias Humanas, Santiago.

Ariza, M. and de Oliveira, O. (2001) Familias en transición y marcos conceptuales en redefinición. *Papeles de población*, 7 (28), 9–39, Mexico City, April–June.

Ariza, M. and de Oliveira, O. (2004) *Imágenes de la familia en el cambio de siglo. Universo familiar y procesos demográficos contemporáneos*, Instituto de Investigaciones Sociales, Universidad Nacional Autónoma de Mexico (UNAM), Mexico.

Arriagada, I. (1998) Latin American families: convergences and divergences in models and policies. *CEPAL Review*, 65, 85–102.

Arriagada, I. (2002) Changes and inequality in Latin American families. *CEPAL Review*, 77, 135–153.

Arriagada, I. (coord.) (2007) *Familias y Políticas públicas en América Latina: una historia de desencuentros*, ECLAC Book No. 96, UNFPA, Santiago.

Arriagada, I. (2012) *Diversidad y desigualdad de las familias latinoamericanas. Desafíos para las políticas públicas*, Editorial Académica Española, https://www.eae-publishing.com/catalog/details//store/es/book/978-3-8484-7737-1/diversidad-y-desigualdad-de-las-familias-latinoamericanas (accessed November 18, 2013).

Bourdieu, P. (2001) *Masculine Domination*, Polity Press, London.

Calderón, F., Hopenhayn, M. and Ottone, E. (1993) *Hacia una perspectiva crítica de la modernidad: las dimensiones culturales de la transformación productiva con equidad*, ECLAC Work Document No. 21, ECLAC, Santiago.

Carrasco, C. (2001) Hacia una nueva metodología para el estudio del trabajo: propuesta de una encuesta de empleo alternativa, in *Tiempos, trabajo y género*, (compiled by C. Carrasco), Barcelona Publicaciones Universitat, Barcelona.

Castells, M. (1998) *The Information Age: Economy, Society and Culture*, vols. II and III, Blackwell Publishers, Cambridge.

Del Popolo, F. and Oyarce, A. (2005) Población indígena de América Latina: perfil sociodemográfico en el marco de la CIPD y de las Metas del Milenio. Presented in the Seminario Internacional Pueblos indígenas y afrodescendientes de América Latina y el Caribe, ECLAC, Santiago, April 27–29, 2005.

Durán, A. and Milosavljevic,V. (2012) *Unpaid Work, Time Use Surveys, and Care Demand Forecasting in Latin America*, Fundación BBVA Work Document No. 7, Fundación BBVA, Madrid.

ECLAC (Economic Commission for Latin America and the Caribbean) (2000a) *Social Panorama of Latin America, 1999–2000*, ECLAC, Santiago.

ECLAC (2000b) *Juventud, población y desarrollo: problemas, oportunidades y desafíos*, ECLAC Book No. 59, ECLAC, Santiago.

ECLAC (2004) *Roads Towards Gender Equity in Latin America and the Caribbean*, ECLAC, Santiago.

ECLAC (2007) *Latin America and the Caribbean Demographic Observatory Fertility Year III*, No. 5, ECLAC, Santiago.

ECLAC (2010a) *What Kind of State? What Kind of Equality?* ECLAC, Santiago.

ECLAC (2010b) *Social Panorama of Latin America 2010 (LC/G.2481-P)*, March 2011, Santiago, Chile. United Nations Publication, Sales No. E.11.II.G.6.

ECLAC (2011a) *Social Panorama of Latin America, 2011*, ECLAC, Santiago.

ECLAC (2011b) *Statistical Yearbook of Latin America and the Caribbean*, ECLAC, Santiago.

ECLAC (2012) *El Estado frente a la autonomía de las mujeres*, Colección La hora de la Igualdad, Santiago.

ECLAC (2013) Gender Equality Observatory for Latin America and the Caribbean, http://www.cepal.org/oig/default.asp?idioma=IN (accessed June, 2012).

Esping-Andersen, G. (2009) *The Incomplete Revolution. Adapting to Women's New Roles*, Polity Press, Cambridge.

Fuller, N. (1997) *Identidades masculinas. Varones de clase media en el Perú*. Catholic University of Peru/Fondo Editorial, Lima.

García, B. and de Oliveira, O. (2001) Las relaciones intrafamiliares en la ciudad de México y Monterrey: visiones masculinas y femeninas. Paper presented at the Twenty-Third International Congress of LASA, Washington, DC, September 6–8, 2001.

García, B. and de Oliveira, O. (2011) Family changes and public policies in Latin America. *Annual Review of Sociology*, 37, 593–611.

Giddens, A. (1990) *The Consequences of Modernity*, Stanford University Press, Stanford.

Giddens, A. (1991) *Modernity and Self-Identity. Self and Society in the Late Modern Age*, Stanford University Press, Stanford.

Giddens, A. (1992) *The Transformation of Intimacy: Sexuality, Love and Eroticism in Modern Societies*, Polity Press, Cambridge.

Goldin, C. (2006) The quiet revolution that transformed women's employment, education, and family. NBER working paper no. 11953, American Economic Review, May 2, 2006, v 96, www.nber.org/papers/w11953 (accessed May 2, 2012).

Güell, P. (1999) Familia y modernización en Chile. Paper presented at the Comisión de Expertos en Temas de Familia, Servicio Nacional de la Mujer (SERNAM), Santiago, December.

Guzmán, V. (2002) *Las relaciones de género en un mundo global*. ECLAC Mujer y desarrollo series No. 38, ECLAC, Santiago.

Guzmán, J.M., Hakker, R., and Contreras J.M. (2001) *Diagnóstico sobre salud sexual y reproductiva de adolescentes en América Latina y el Caribe*, UNFPA, Mexico.

INEGI (2004) Encuesta Nacional sobre Uso de Tiempo 2002. Instituto Nacional de Estadística, Geografía e Informática, Aguascalientes: Press release, March 8, 2004.

INEGI (2011) Estadísticas de género Proyecto Interinstitucional. Presented at the XII Encuentro Internacional de Estadísticas de Género: empoderamiento, autonomía económica y políticas públicas, Aguas Calientes, octubre 2011.

Jelin, E. (1998) *Pan y afectos. La transformación de las familias*, Fondo de Cultura Económica, Argentina.

López, P. and Salles, V. (comps.) (2000) *Familia, género y pobreza*, Grupo Interdisciplinario sobre mujer trabajo y pobreza (GIMTRAP), México.

Olavarría, J. and Parrini, R. (eds) (2000) *Masculinidad/es: identidad, sexualidad y familia. Primer encuentro de estudios de masculinidad*, Latin American Faculty of Social Sciences (FLACSO)/University of the Academy of Christian Humanism, Santiago.

Rangel, M. (2005) La población afrodescendiente en América Latina y los Objetivos de Desarrollo del Milenio. Un examen exploratorio en países seleccionados utilizando información censal. Presented at the International Seminar on Pueblos indígenas y afrodescendientes de América Latina y el Caribe ECLAC, Santiago, April 27–29, 2005.

Rubalcava, R. (1996) *Hogares con primacía de ingreso femenino en Hogares, familias: desigualdad, conflicto, redes solidarias y parentales*, Sociedad Mexicana de Demografía (SOMEDE), México.

Salles, V. and Tuirán, R. (1996) Mitos y creencias sobre vida familiar, *Revista Mexicana de Sociología*, 59 (2), 117–144, Instituto de Investigaciones Sociales, National Autonomous University of Mexico, Mexico City, April–June.

Salles, V. and Tuirán, R. (1997) The family in Latin America: a gender approach. *Current Sociology*, 45 (1), 153–195, Sage Publications, London, January.

Servicio Nacional de la Mujer (SERNAM) (2001) *Mujeres chilenas. Estadísticas para un nuevo siglo*, Instituto Nacional de Estadísticas, Santiago.

Smart, C. and Shipman, B. (2004) Visions in monochrome: families, marriage and the individualization thesis, *The British Journal of Sociology*, 55 (4), England. http://eprints.whiterose.ac.uk/3764/2/Visions_in_Monochrome.pdf (accessed November 1, 2013).

Therborn, G. (2007) Familias en el mundo. Historia y futuro en el umbral del siglo XXI, in *Familias y Políticas públicas en América Latina: una historia de desencuentros* (coord. I. Arriagada), ECLAC Book No. 96, ECLAC, Santiago.

United Nations Development Programme (UNDP) (1998) *Desarrollo humano en Chile*. Las paradojas de la modernización, Santiago.

UNDP (2002) Human Development in Chile We, the Chileans: A Cultural Challenge. *Human development report Chile 2002*, Santiago.

Van de Kaa, D. (2001) Postmodern fertility preferences: from changing value orientation to new behaviour, in *Global Fertility Transition* (eds. R. Bulatao and J. Casterline), Population Council, New York.

Wagner, P. (1994) *A Sociology of Modernity: Liberty and Discipline*, Routledge, London.

Wainerman, C. (2000) División del trabajo en familias de dos proveedores. Relato desde ambos géneros y dos generaciones, *Estudios demográficos y urbanos*, 15 (1), 149–184, El Colegio de Mexico, Mexico City, January–April.

Wainerman, C. (2005) *La vida cotidiana en las nuevas familias ¿Una revolución estancada?* Ediciones Lumiere, Buenos Aires.

Part II
Diversity, Inequality, and Immigration

6

Same-Sex Families

TIMOTHY J. BIBLARZ, MEGAN CARROLL
AND NATHANIEL BURKE

At this writing, the majority of Americans support same-sex marriage (Powell *et al.*, 2010; King, 2012), and the US Supreme Court has just ruled that a federal law limiting marriage to that between a man and a woman is unconstitutional (*United States v. Windsor* 2013, No. 12–307; see also *Hollingsworth v. Perry* 2013, No. 12–144). President Obama's brief in the same case concluded that gay couples were demonstrably capable of rearing healthy children, and the Court found that denying marriage "humiliates tens of thousands of children now being raised by same-sex couples." The best point estimate is that currently 220,000 dependent children are being raised by same-sex couples (Gates, 2013a).

In its movement toward equalizing the distribution of marriage rights, the United States follows forerunner countries like the Netherlands, Spain, and six other European nations along with Argentina, Uruguay, South Africa, Canada, and, pending one final challenge, France. In these same countries and a few others, full joint adoption by same-sex couples is also legal, as it is in almost half of the US states.

Global trends are decidedly in the direction of incorporation. More than 25 of the 31 countries analyzed by Smith (2011) show greater proportions of national samples saying that same-sex sexual behavior is not wrong over the past 20 years. The observed age gap in attitudes has elders more disapproving than young people in every country; trends toward acceptance are expected to gain momentum with cohort replacement. In just the past 10 years, 17 US states, housing 38% of the population, have legalized same-sex marriage, some by popular vote. More states will surely follow as Williams Institute economists, for example, document the boost that marriage expansion brings to state economies (Kastanis, Badgett, and Herman, 2012; Kastanis and Badgett, 2013a, b). Indeed, signaling incorporation

The Wiley Blackwell Companion to the Sociology of Families, First Edition.
Edited by Judith Treas, Jacqueline Scott, and Martin Richards.
© 2014 John Wiley & Sons Ltd. Published 2017 by John Wiley & Sons Ltd.

are cover stories that are already moving past gay marriage and onto gay divorce (e.g., Green, 2013).

Three decades of steadily improving social science (mostly conducted in the United States) show fairly robustly that sexual orientation *per se* is not an important predictor of quality parenting, although research claiming to have found the damning evidence of putative ill effects of gay parenting continues to make its way into the public square (for a critique, see Perrin, Cohen, and Caren, 2013). Longitudinal research projects in the United Kingdom (e.g., MacCallum and Golombok, 2004), Belgium (e.g., Vanfraussen, Ponjaert-Kristoffersen, and Brewaeys, 2003), and the Netherlands (e.g., Bos, van Balen, and van den Boom, 2007) have reached similar conclusions on the benign outcomes of same-sex families. While from a very small sample of countries, the core findings have, with reasonable caution, been applied to different national circumstances. The general theories of parental genetic, behavioral, environmental, and attitudinal effects on child development offer no compelling reason to believe that parental sexual orientation *per se* bears an important influence on children's developmental health one way or another. In fact, becoming a parent after asserting a gay or lesbian identity often signals a heightened degree of child wantedness and child centeredness because of the great effort typically involved along less conventional paths to parenthood. Scholars have achieved a rare degree of consensus that unmarried lesbian parents are raising children who develop at least as well as their counterparts with married heterosexual parents (e.g., Stacey and Biblarz, 2001; American Academy of Pediatrics, 2002; Tasker, 2005). Others raise the question of whether they and gay fathers might even be doing a better job (Johnson and O'Connor, 2002; Goldberg, 2012; Pappas, 2012).

Even while marginalized from equitable legal protection, lesbian- and gay-male-headed families look like the mainstream in many ways; yet this chapter would tend toward dull if we wrote mostly about how same-sex families are like everybody else. At the risk of being accused of a bit of cherry picking, we focus on potentially interesting terrains of difference that may not be wholly owed to marginalization or as likely to soon disappear into the *historical dustbin* of a sexually pluralist society (Stacey and Biblarz, 2001). We try to accent scholarly gains made by research that is unbridled from the harm or *differences are deficits* framework. While (disproportionately white middle-class) working-age gay couples and parents, in relation to institutions like law and marriage, occupy the headlines, we give a bit more attention to other groups along the life course – for example, queer youth and gay elders – that are often overlooked. Finally, where possible, we consider the implications of findings emerging from Lesbian, Gay, Bisexual, and Transgender (LGBT) family studies for core questions in family sociology more generally.

Queer Youth

The gay male or lesbian parents in same-sex families began life as youth who experienced some degree of same-sex desire. For utility, we refer to these individuals as *queer youth* to indicate that they may engage in sex acts with persons of the same sex, experience same-sex attraction, or claim a nonheterosexual identity.

Research on queer youth often focuses on the most visible: those who self-identify as nonheterosexual. Respondents who meet this definition are usually older teens or adults reflecting on their adolescence. Those who experience same-sex desire or engage in same-sex sexual acts during adolescence but do not assert a nonheterosexual identity are underrepresented in research (Savin-Williams, 2001a), as are the voices of queer youth themselves (Mustanski, 2011). The youth in the study of Friedman *et al.* (2004) felt that sexual and romantic attraction were as salient a part of their sexual orientation as self-labeling and sexual behavior.

Most of the research on queer youth falls under one of two umbrellas – risk models and coming-out models. We discuss each in turn.

Risk models

Unfortunately, much of what we know is shaped by applied studies of pathologized, visible, victimized youth, and parents who seek support in understanding their child's sexual identity (Savin-Williams, 2001b). This literature explores average risks of suicide, sexually transmitted diseases, homelessness, and substance abuse (Rivers and D'Augelli, 2001; Russell, 2003, 2006; Marshal *et al.*, 2008) as concomitants of heterosexism and homophobia but less so their dispersion across class, race, gender, and place. Rasmussen *et al.* (2004) note how a partial narrative can become the entire view of a complex population.

The voices of queer youth and their strategies of resistance to victimization and abuse are limited in the literature. The minority of queer youth who attempt suicide, for example, could be served well by more scholarship on queer youth that are empowered, resilient, sexual, and exerting agency (Unks, 2003). Queer youth themselves may find the pathological narrative to be homophobic and not representative of the majority of their lives (Rofes, 2004). For example, Pachankis and Hatzenbuehler found that gay youth will frequently overachieve in domains like academics in an "adaptive shifting of domains in which one stakes his self-worth" (2013, 186). This may carry its own psychological costs but does not fit neatly into the conventional risk framework.

The problematic *heterosexual versus homosexual* framework (Savin-Williams, 2001a) which propels a great deal of the research on queer youth mutes within-group diversity and ignores the many places of overlap between queer youth and heterosexual youth. For these reasons, many scholars have begun building a new literature that explores resilience, incorporation, adaptation, and diversity among gay youth. Battle (2012), for example, deliberately moved away from risk-based models in designing the new *Social Justice Sexuality Survey* for LGBT people of color, which focuses in part on youth. Riggle *et al.* (2008, p. 210) also argue for more informed psychological approaches that can "help sexual minorities and their families envision and claim the positive aspects of their lives." Whether these efforts represent a lasting change in the frameworks applied to queer youth remains to be seen.

While the majority of literature on queer youth focuses on risk, fewer studies focus on risk reduction. Eisenberg and Resnick (2006), in a study of youth protective factors, indicate that reducing risk for queer youth lies in creating and strengthening resources that speak to family connectedness. They acknowledge that few studies have explored the significance of protective factors and how they can be strengthened for and by queer youth and their families. Girls may be better protected from suicide risk than boys as they generally identify their nonheterosexual identity later than boys, and gender nonconformance is typically more accepted by the families of girls than boys (van Wormer and McKinney, 2003). Future research must be carefully done to separate gender from sexuality and not assume that queer youth are gender nonconforming.

Coming-out models

The average age at which children experience sexual attraction, regardless of orientation, varies from study to study, though boys tend to experience first same-sex sexual attraction earlier than girls. Noteworthy is the tremendous variability in age (many youth do not begin disclosing to others until they are in their 20s and older) and in the meaning and experience of *coming out* itself. Like sexuality (gay/straight), coming out is often treated as a binary (concealment/disclosure) stand-in for something that is far more complex and diverse. Strong models or typologies of some of the general processes involved are Cass's (1979) *stages* (identity confusion, identity comparison, identity tolerance, identity acceptance, identity pride, identity synthesis) and D'Augelli's (1994) *identity processes* (exiting heterosexuality, developing a personal Lesbian, Gay, and Bisexual (LGB) identity, developing an LGB social identity, becoming an LGB offspring, developing an LGB intimacy status, entering an LGB community) (Bilodeau and Renn, 2005).

The age at which youth begin to disclose to others is on the decline, which may be a result of cohort changes and increased levels of social and familial acceptance (Floyd and Bakeman, 2006); cohorts born in the 1960s and 1970s disclosed at an average of 5 years later than contemporary cohorts (Kryzan, 2000). The young men and women in the study of D'Augelli (2002) experienced first awareness at an average age of 10 or 11 and first disclosures at around age 17. In contrast, the elders in the study of D'Augelli and Grossman (2001) remember first awareness occurring around age 14, on average, and first disclosures did not occur until they were close to 30 years old. Ironically, the trend toward early *coming out* is also leading to a decline in the number of LGBT parents, as many contemporary LGBT parents had children in heterosexual relationships at a young age, before asserting a nonheterosexual identity (Gates, 2011).

Queer youth's struggle for acceptance is apparent in literature which positions the heterosexual nuclear family as oppressive both before coming out and after as a result of rejection (Gorman-Murray, 2008). Families may respond negatively to a child's nonheterosexual identity, mistakenly assuming that the identity is diametrically opposed to marriage and children (Hammack, Thompson, and Pilecki, 2009). Withholding one's orientation can create feelings of distance with family members, and queer youth often disclose to parents out of desire for closeness with them. They often succeed, as families usually successfully move from conflict to acceptance. The length of time this takes and the actual processes involved are poorly understood. Tremble *et al.* (1989) indicate that families work to reinterpret their values in order to arrive at acceptance, while contemporary scholarship complicates this narrative. For example, many parents in the study of Fields (2001) did not so much accept their child's identity as they accepted their inability to change it, arriving at a place of tolerance.

An immediately positive parental response to a child's coming out is rare; the more frequent first response is that of loss (Fields, 2001). When a child comes out, many families go through a process of moving from loss to acceptance in rough parallel to grief models (Heatherington and Lavner, 2008). We still know little about what occurs within families after the initial response and how families adjust to the youth's identity over time.

Families with queer youth can tell us quite a bit about how families challenge stereotypes and navigate the coming-out process of their child. While queer youth typically disclose to their fathers after their mothers, Pilkington and D'Augelli (1995) found that mothers were more likely to respond with verbal abuse, though they are also more likely to be protective of their child. The gendered dynamics of these disclosures for both the parent and the child require further study. For example, following disclosure, fathers' reactions may be particularly important to the well-being of boys (LaSala, 2010).

Factors that predict parent's reactions include whether the child discloses or is discovered, the age of the child, the age of the parents, level of education, ethnicity, and religion. More recent data (Ryan *et al.*, 2010) indicate that youth's gender, sexual identity, or transgender identity does not influence family's acceptance as significantly as do the family's ethnicity, immigration and occupational status, and religious affiliation. Families whose parents had higher levels of occupational status, for example, were shown to be more accepting of their child's nonheterosexual identity. Family diversity, therefore, needs to be brought into the exploration of queer youth, pointing to the continued need for intersectional research rather than resting on the assumption that all families with queer youth operate and respond similarly.

Parents who accept their child's same-sex desires may ultimately join advocacy groups in order to create a more positive social climate for their child. This advocacy by the family is essential in communities that may have a lower degree of tolerance as a result of cultural or religious beliefs. Families can create a sense of local belonging and resist heterosexism by "threading the logic of the family through the few community-based organizational structures available" (Gray, 2009, p. 169). In all communities, families have been shown to be a tremendous buffer against the harmful effects of victimization that queer youth may face. Family acceptance predicts better self-esteem and guards against harm (Ryan, Russell, Huebner *et al.*, 2010).

All youth keep secrets. The secrets of sexual confusion and comparison are experienced to some degree by mostly all teenagers, but that of homoerotic desire is particularly weighty. This secret is often kept for years from self and for more years from others. The fear of the psychological violence that might accompany someone finding out, or telling someone, can be tremendous. Social reaction can range from kind to horrible; rarely is even the most accepting reaction ever completely free of homophobia because of the predominance of heterosexual institutions. In these contexts, many processes are not well understood. What strategies, for example, do queer youth utilize in order to navigate discussions of desire and attraction among their peers and their families? How do queer youth begin to explore their feelings of attraction and broach these topics with potential partners? How are the experiences and views of youth who experience both same-sex and different-sex attraction silenced or not by the heterosexual/homosexual binary?

Extended adolescence

In the transition to adulthood, gay youth face challenges not only in their local environments but in the considerable constraints imposed by the state regarding sexual orientation (e.g., constraints on marriage, adoption, and fertility services) and by the culture, around the meaning of adulthood and the markers that signal its full arrival. Focusing on what kind of an order queer people might belong to and following Foucault's suggestion that we contemplate why homosexuality is threatening as a lifestyle more than as a form of sexuality, Halberstam (2005) observed that queer lives often fall outside of the heteronormative time sequence of birth–marriage–reproduction–death. In a social structure where marriage and reproduction are the core markers of adulthood, queer temporality that falls outside of this sequence can be viewed as childish, self-centered, and immature or as a kind of extended adolescence. Queer culture is often represented by conventional institutions as a subculture, and subcultures are something one is eventually supposed to grow out of.

Similarly, Edelman's (2004) concept of *reproductive futurity* suggests that traditional Western politics are predicated on making the future a better place, and *the child* works as the symbolic image of that future. As queer people are symbolically separated from the act of reproduction, queerness "names the site of those not fighting for children" and is positioned as a "relentlessly narcissistic, antisocial, and future-negating drive" (2004, p. 3). Queers are positioned as a threat to the child and to the future the child belongs to. For queer youth, this can be experienced as a fatalistic message about their own futures.

Jones (2011) presents a more optimistic analysis of queer youth's actual futures, in which she argues that conventional life trajectories have simultaneously become more accessible to LGBT people and less compulsory overall. In her study of 33 bisexual young adults, many participants literally *drew* futures for themselves that were both positive and nonnormative. In Goltz's (2009) study, younger lesbian women were more likely to associate their own futures with positive meanings and images of family and children, compared to young gay men. A range of factors may influence these contradictions, such as the extreme variability in tolerance toward diverse sexualities over time and location, or the well-documented tendency for men to internalize homophobia at higher rates than women (Grossman, D'Augelli, and O'Connell, 2002; Fredricksen-Goldsen and Muraco, 2010). What applied scholars do tend to agree on is the importance of discussing positive aspects of gay and lesbian lives, compared to the negative life experiences that often dominate the literature (Riggle *et al.*, 2008).

Gay Parents

Millions of queer youth, while mostly barred from legal marriage, grow up and form families, have children, foster children, adopt children, coach children, teach children, care for their nieces and nephews, and otherwise undermine cultural assertions that being gay means being antichild. In the scholarship on how parental sexual orientation matters, the question has shifted from whether being raised by gay or lesbian parents is harmful to children (as against makes no difference at all) to less *report card* explorations of where parental sexual orientations and genders may and may not matter for parents' and children's lives and development along the life course. Unfortunately, in the current historical period, these questions cannot be fully answered by social science research because of arguably insurmountable selection problems, mostly rooted in the extrafamily environment.

Selection

Say, for example, that research detected higher levels of certain kinds of qualities in youth with gay parents than with straight parents. This might be due to the influence of some aspects of parents' sexualities and genders (disentangling those two itself is an intractable sort of overidentification problem), and home environments, but it could as well be due to parents' unequal access to the formidable public and material privileges of legal marriage, or children having to contend with vicarious social stigma at school, and so on. Researchers cannot *hold constant* (un)equal protection in law and the larger society. As same-sex marriage achieves full legal status nationally, or in states or provinces, our ability to discern whatever unique effects the sexual orientation and gender mix of parents have on family processes and child outcomes would, accordingly, be enhanced, because we could match samples on actual marriage and the opportunity to marry.

Social science finds consistently that children from groups that face prejudice and discrimination have tougher odds of scoring high on conventional *success* measures. In turn, the baseline expectation here would be that in a heterosexually privileged culture, children with straight parents would do better. This is partly why the many findings of equal (or better) outcomes of children with gay parents (e.g., Tasker, 2005) are noteworthy, an instance where nonfindings are unexpected findings.

This in turn points to another side of the stubborn selection issues that out gay parents in most of our samples to date are a relatively privileged group of whites who are comparatively educated, urban, and mature. Recent national evidence shows that gay couples are far more socioeconomically, racially, and spatially diverse than is often depicted. For example, 39% of adults in same-sex couples who have children under age 18 in the home are people of color (Gates, 2013b), and same-sex parenting couples have lower average incomes than comparable different-sex couples. At the same time, gay couples in the US population have regularly been found to be more educated than their heterosexual counterparts (Black *et al.*, 2000; Gates, 2013b).

The selection issues go well beyond sample bias. For example, the structure and form of different routes to parenthood require different amounts of resources and thus sort and select users almost by definition. Conceiving a child through heterosexual reproduction is the least expensive (and so least selective) route to parenthood. Other routes like donor insemination (sometimes *in vitro*), adoption, foster care, traditional surrogacy, gestational surrogacy, and elective coparenting take considerable time, work, money, reflection, intention, proaction, and want-edness. (In this book, see Chapter 25 on the development of assisted reproduction technologies.) The children produced by them are the result of especially high levels of parental investment (Bos, van Balen, and van den Boom, 2003). In a complex way, homophobia and marginalization come up against privilege and perseverance in many of these families.

Family life

What is it like raising kids outside of heterogender designs where, in accord with their different sexes, fathers and mothers tend toward different gender repertoires and domains of specialization? It appears that more egalitarian family lives unfold; research has repeatedly shown that lesbian parent couples, for example, have high levels of shared employment, decision making, parenting, parenting goals, and family work (see Biblarz and Savci, 2010; Biblarz and Stacey, 2010). This includes more parental partnering in time spent caring for children, talking with children, playing with children, disciplining children, helping with homework, and time spent in employment. One or another of these findings spans studies from four different western countries. Research coming out on gay fathers shows similar patterns (e.g., Goldberg, 2012).

Even so, unlike straight parents, gay parents have to be concerned with homophobia, and this in turn may inform decisions like choosing the child's pediatrician, parental involvement at school, opening up to the child's school teacher, and screening other persons in the child's life (Johnson and O'Connor, 2002). While personal choice and aptitudes tend to guide task sorting in *degendered parenting* arrangements (Silverstein, Auerbach, and Levant, 2002), some specialization or divi-sion of labor between partners still occurs of the sort typically characteristic of Western capitalist societies (e.g., differences between partners in relative time spent in public/employment and private/family arenas). That gender does not vary within lesbian coparents or between lesbian coparent families does not mean that these families are immune from other stubborn axes of inequality. One example is biological relatedness to the child: lesbian biological mothers often provide more of the primary childcare than comothers and may be afforded more recognition and legitimacy by others (e.g., Goldberg and Perry-Jenkins, 2007). Another is marital status: family fears, behaviors, contingencies, and interaction with institutions in the extrafamily environment may vary across married, domestic partner, civil union, or not recognized legal statuses (Rothblum, Balsam, and Solomon, 2008; Shapiro, Peterson, and Stewart, 2009). Another axis is route to parenthood. Within, for example, gay cofather families, some stratification of status and privilege may exist (from high to low) across gestational surrogacy, other kinds of surrogacy, adopting children, and families where children came out of former heterosexual relationships

(Carroll, 2012). Finally, race and class matter of course, as the very meaning of egalitarianism and sharing varies across LGBT families in different social locations (e.g., Moore, 2008, 2011).

Recent research examining the relationship between LGBT families carries important methodological and theoretical implications. For example, despite the expectation that LGBT people and their families would gravitate toward urban areas where they can more easily access LGBT-affirming resources, LGB families are geographically diverse and often reside in nonmetropolitan areas with varying levels of acceptance or support (Oswald and Lazarevic, 2011; Oswald and Holman, 2013a). In order to understand how space-specific social conditions can impact LGB families, Oswald *et al.* (2010) developed a methodology of *community climate* to measure the degree of support that LGBT people and families may receive in a particular location. Their scale was created using municipal-level data on the number of LGBT organizations and legal nondiscrimination ordinances, as well as county-level demographics that included the number of religious adherents and the number of same-sex partner households. Both were validated alongside the survey data of LGBT individuals' perceived community climate (see Oswald and Holman, 2013b), and the resulting scale is the first of its kind: a comprehensive tool to empirically assess the level of support for LGBT people and families within a particular zip code. Future studies conducted using this new data set may help researchers improve on minority stress models that link wellness outcomes to social support and other environmental circumstances as well as invite more visibility to geographically diverse (and intrinsically, racially, and economically diverse) LGBT individuals and families (Oswald *et al.*, 2010; Oswald and Holman, 2013a).

What aspects of family life might we expect will be conditioned by two parents of the same sex, and where would we expect patterns from the heterosexual family literature to obtain right across the gender mix of parents? We suspect that the gender mix of parents substantially moderates most dimensions of family process studied in mainstream family sociology, because gender matters that much. For example, the time bind and second shift (Hochschild and Machung, 1989, 1997) experienced by mothers in dual career couples are in some ways shaped by the fact that their partners are men; these kinds of work/family conflicts may take on different shapes when the partners are two mothers or two fathers (Burke, 2013). Domestic violence, intergenerational relations, kin keeping, class and families, race and families, the state and families, privatization of family life, religion and family life, courtship, etc., mostly everything we know about these and other textbook topics rests in one way or another on an assumption of heterosexuality. These topics need to be rethought and reexamined when parents are of the same gender. Accordingly, as heterosexual couples become less guided by gender, gay male and lesbian coparent families may be setting trends that family sociology can learn from more generally.

One particularly interesting aspect of this is that out gay parents generally have to go outside the family and bring a third party in to conceive children. Where legally permitted, some gay fathers hire surrogate *mothers* for pay, while others may have a friend who will surrogate. Still others may choose elective coparenting with a woman. Lesbian mothers may use an anonymous sperm bank donor, but they may also use a brother's or other man's donated sperm, making him a kind of potential biosocial father or uncle-like figure at the same time. Increasingly, adoptions are of the *open* or cooperative sort, where the birth mother and adopted family know who each other are and have the option of contact.

This raises the opportunity for more parents or parent-like people in the lives of children, and for the concomitant negotiations of new relationship boundaries and role definitions that gives rise to. That not all of the adults with an investment in the children live under the same roof makes same-sex families both part of and a bell-wether of the continuing separation of family and household (Cherlin, 2010). For some time now, out same-sex individuals have had to go outside of the household to achieve parenthood. Research might benefit by threading these experiences with those of the many other emergent families that move beyond traditional nuclear and especially beyond the purely private household – blended, step, multigenerational, elective, transnational, commuter, and so on.

Gay Elders

Though they are often left out of the academic conversation about same-sex families, gay and lesbian elders can also inform our broader understanding of families and sexuality. Attention toward gay and lesbian elders is becoming increasingly important as the boomer generation ages and large cohorts of gay and lesbian parents become grandparents (Whalen, Bigner, and Barber, 2000). The overall body of literature on gay and lesbian elders tells a story of diverse family structures and informal systems of social support (Fredriksen-Goldsen and Muraco, 2010). These dynamics emerge through a number of themes in the growing body of literature on LGB elders' families, each of which much be understood within the historical context of LGB elders' lives.

Historical contexts of LGB identities

Many elders came of age during a cultural shift in gay identity expression and meaning. Early homophile movements promoted an understanding of homosexuality as a private, intimate relation, but the gay liberation movement, most commonly associated with Stonewall, propelled gay identities into the realm of public and political action. Combined with other historical events that many gay elders witnessed, such as the AIDS crisis and the removal of homosexuality from the *DSM* (Diagnostic and Statistical Manual of Mental Disorders, published by the American Psychiatric Association), these competing discourses have shaped and divided elders' perspectives about the appropriate contexts for disclosing their sexual identities (Fox, 2007; Haber, 2009).

The current generation of gay and lesbian elders has lived through a historical period of intense homophobia, and research accordingly suggests that most gay and lesbian elders see *passing* as a practical resource for maintaining relationships with heterosexuals (Pollner and Rosenfeld, 2000; Heaphy, Yip, and Thompson, 2003; Almack, Seymour, and Bellamy, 2010). Many elders themselves have described the experience of being gay or lesbian as *not safe* or *dangerous* during the majority of their lifetime (e.g., Orel and Fruhauf, 2006). Other gay and lesbian elders, however, view passing as a betrayal of their authentic self. The proportions of each group seem to be changing as boomers continue to age and assert their identities (Grossman, D'Augelli, and O'Connell, 2002; Haber, 2009).

Many scholars have been careful to contextualize elders' experiences in reference to the historical period through which they have lived. Rosenfeld (1999, 2003) especially has documented the interplay between generational cohorts, identity expression, and social change. Studies that have reported the most positive outcomes of LGB elders have generally relied on participants who are involved in the broader gay and lesbian movement and therefore identify more strongly with the Stonewall era's philosophies of gay identity (e.g., Whitford, 1997; Orel, 2004; Henrickson and Neville, 2012). By contrast, elders who have not disclosed their sexual identities are generally characterized as having lower quality of life (Fredriksen-Goldsen and Muraco, 2010). To the extent that *internalized homophobia* can be measured, it has been correlated with worse mental health and increased suicidal ideation (D'Augelli *et al.*, 2001; Fredriksen-Goldsen and Muraco, 2010). These outcomes have been found to vary by gender, with men internalizing homophobia at higher rates than women and thus experiencing more severe outcomes with age (D'Augelli *et al.*, 2001). Research addressing racial diversity among LGB elders is extremely limited, but one study found that older black gay men perceived higher levels of racism than younger black gay men, as well as higher levels of ageism than older white gay men (David and Knight, 2008). Groups like Services and Advocacy for Gay Elders (SAGE) are working to combat these issues, though they are unlikely to be sought out by elders who do not affirm a positive gay identity (Friend, 1989; Haber, 2009).

Family dynamics are of course deeply intertwined with elders' decision to disclose their sexual identities. Many who chose not to disclose feared rejection from family members, in particular, whose reactions could be difficult to predict (Friend, 1989; Pollner and Rosenfeld, 2000). As the participants in Pollner and Rosenfeld's (2000) study pointed out, these anxieties contradict dominant discourses about the resiliency of family bonds, which were criticized by some elders as a strictly heterosexual privilege. Some elders also felt that disclosure was unnecessary because family members already *knew* but were equally invested in maintaining secrecy (Friend, 1989; Pollner and Rosenfeld, 2000). Again, this attitude is generally attributed to dominant, pre-Stonewall (a series of New York City riots often positioned as *the beginning* of the gay liberation movement) gay identity expression which viewed sexuality as a private aspect of the self (Rosenfeld, 2003).

Challenges of aging

LGB elders face the same bodily challenges of aging as their heterosexual counterparts and thus require similar aid from care providers. However, their distinct social needs present an added challenge during the aging process (Maylor *et al.*, 2007; Slevin, 2008). Whereas literature on families often focuses on the younger relatives of elders performing care work, LGBT elders are less likely to have children or grandchildren to care for them (Almack, Seymour, and Bellamy, 2010). Institutionalized homophobia and heterosexism in the healthcare system also constrain elders' ability to communicate with healthcare providers or receive quality care (Richard and

120

Brown, 2006; Blank *et al.*, 2009). Some LGB elders may even avoid professional care in anticipation of discrimination (Hash, 2006; Richard and Brown, 2006). For many, homophobia could exacerbate the rude or hostile treatment they could already expect from a healthcare system that has become *far too impersonal* (Hash, 2006, p. 132). Several studies have recommended separate retirement or care facilities for LGB elders as a solution to these challenges (Johnson *et al.*, 2005; Fredricksen-Goldsen and Muraco, 2010).

Many LGB elders rely on close friends and fictive kin, commonly referred to as *families of choice*, to meet their care needs (Grossman *et al.*, 2000; Blank *et al.*, 2009). *Families of choice* are often cited as an alternative to blood-related kinship available to LGBT individuals, though, as Heaphy (2009) notes, the *choices* involved in these relationships are often constrained by the availability of economic, social, and cultural resources. Furthermore, the formation of *families of choice* is highly dependent on one's level of *outness* and integration into a gay community, which is less common among elders. The dynamics between visibility, community ties, and aging can have far-reaching effects on LGB elders' access to care. For example, one study that recruited participants through community organizations and personal contacts found that a majority of gay men and lesbians over 65 perceived themselves to be healthy, happy, well adjusted, and ready to negotiate the challenges of aging (Orel, 2004). In another study that recruited elder LGB participants exclusively through churches, 51% had no support system and 70% feared that they lacked the financial means necessary to meet their needs through the aging process (McFarland and Sanders, 2003). Due to the challenges of recruiting participants who are not involved in institutionalized forms of LGBT support, it is difficult to more precisely measure the relationship between sexuality, aging, family, and care.

Despite such limitations, support systems based on choice have been found to offer similar rates of wellness to LGB elders, compared to heterosexual elders (Fredriksen-Goldsen and Muraco, 2011). LGB elders who rely on choice-based relationships for care have also reported better mental health and higher quality of life than those who relied on family members (Masini and Barrett, 2008). Despite these outcomes, *families of choice* are often cut off from the resources offered to families who are tied through blood or legally recognized marriages, such as insurance benefits, hospital visitations, decision-making rights, and the ability to use the Family and Medical Leave Act (Calhill and South, 2002; Blank *et al.*, 2009; Knauer, 2011).

End-of-life planning is especially challenging for LGB elders as a result of their legally unrecognized relationships. Not only are their preferred next of kin often excluded from end-of-life decisions, but an LGB person's will could even be contested on the basis that homosexuality itself is evidence of incompetence (Friend, 1989; Almack *et al.*, 2010). To prepare for these challenges, gay and lesbian elders often plan ahead for their futures by legally naming their *families of choice* as their next of kin, though there is no guarantee that their wishes will be upheld if challenged by a blood relative (Friend, 1989; Hash, 2006; Almack *et al.*, 2010). The grieving process is also exacerbated for elders' same-sex partners, whose loss may go unrecognized by those who were either not aware of the relationship or refused to acknowledge it (Hash, 2006; Almack *et al.*, 2010).

Marital status

Among those that suffer most from the challenges of aging are unmarried or widowed LGB elders, who are often isolated from any form of community. Research indicates that more LGB elders live alone than heterosexual elders, and those that do tend to experience more negative physical and mental outcomes (Heaphy, Yip, and Thompson, 2003; Blank *et al.*, 2009). However, Hostetler (2009) argues that maintaining a healthy single lifestyle may be difficult against strong normative expectations that privilege marriage and family. His study of 94 single gay men, ages 35–70, found that participants often justified their singlehood as a step along the way to establishing a family or as a result of unconscious choices they may have made. Very few participants reported that they actively intended to live a single lifestyle. While it is possible that a social desirability bias influenced interviewees to describe their singlehood in terms that conformed to strict societal expectations of marriage and family, Hostetler (2009) argues that these narrative strategies are indicative of a missing *single-by-choice* identity in society, which could be accompanied by more institutional forms of support. In other words, maintaining a healthy and happy single lifestyle is challenging within a society that views singlehood as an involuntary result of failed relationships.

The need for acceptance of a wide breadth of relational configurations is also reflected in interviews with partnered gay and lesbian elders. Elders who choose to *pass* and keep their sexual identities secret may have been more likely to marry heterosexually than younger generations, for whom marriage is seen as optional (Friend, 1989; Almack, Seymour, and Bellamy, 2010). Yet even older same-sex couples who have been together for 40 or more years have expressed diverse responses to the increased availability of legally recognized partnerships. For example, among the nine couples interviewed by Porche and Purvin (2008) about their attitudes toward marriage, the two couples who chose not to legally marry were the oldest. Both couples had formed their relationship before the Stonewall riots, and neither was involved in the gay or lesbian community. In explaining his reasons for not marrying, one participant expressed, "I'm old enough to know that civil rights – those laws don't change the way people act or think or anything, it's a much longer process" (Porche and Purvin, 2008, p. 155). He and his partner wore rings to symbolize their commitment but refused to define their marriage in terms of legal sanctions. The other participants who deliberately chose not to marry, a lesbian couple in their 60s, explained that they had already spent so much time and money arranging legal protections for themselves. They believed a marriage would only make those arrangements more complicated. This couple also did not feel that marriage was particularly important or necessary, and they expressed criticism toward the marriage movement.

In a study of 18 Canadian grandmothers, Patterson (2005) also uncovered a strong streak of ambivalence toward legal marriage via Bill C-38, which legalized same-sex marriage across Canada. Many couples appreciated the legislation as a sign of increased acceptance, but they were also concerned about the bill's potential to erase alternatives for gay and lesbian couples. As one couple reflected, "the loss about Bill C-38 is the loss of creativity; we are being fit into a box that we didn't create" (Patterson, 2005, p. 47). As Heaphy (2007) explains, the creative forms of kinship that permeate elders' lives are grounded in their resilience against hegemonic meanings of gender and sexuality. Even though gender inequalities can be found within these creative kinship patterns, they represent the diverse values and possibilities that can accompany social change (Patterson, 2005; Heaphy, 2007).

Same-sex grandparents

Researchers estimate that one to two million LGB Americans are either grandparents or soon to become grandparents (Orel and Fruhauf, 2006). Only recently, however, has scholarship begun to explore relationships between LGB grandparents and their grandchildren. These relationships are often mediated by LGB grandparents' adult children, whereas elders who are not accepted by their children may have less contact with their grandchildren or be less likely to disclose their sexual orientation (Orel and Fruhauf, 2006; Fruhauf, Orel, and Jenkins, 2009). For those that are involved in their grandchildren's lives, grandparents' sexual orientation influenced a range of dynamics in the relationship.

Six of the sixteen lesbian and bisexual grandmothers in Orel and Fruhauf's (2006) study had not disclosed their sexual orientation to their grandchildren out of worry that they would react negatively to their sexual orientation. These grandmothers characterized their relationship with their grandchildren as distant and dishonest, and they generally found it extremely stressful to maintain an illusion of heterosexuality. A study by Fruhauf *et al.* (2009) found similar dynamics among gay grandfathers, who had little to no contact with their grandchildren when their adult children did not approve of their sexuality.

Lesbian and bisexual grandmothers who had disclosed their sexual orientation to their grandchildren felt that honesty was essential in maintaining a warm and intimate relationship with their grandchildren (Orel and Fruhauf, 2006). Most of the grandfathers interviewed by Fruhauf *et al.* (2009) reported that coming out to their grandchildren was easier or *more natural* than coming out to other family members, including their own children. Adult children usually assisted in the grandfathers' coming-out process, and the process itself was often prompted by the grandchildren's questions. However, some grandfathers indicated that their grandchildren did not need to ask questions. As one participant said, his sexual orientation "became part of the fabric of life...as race, or hair color, or anything else" for his grandchildren (Fruhauf, Orel, and Jenkins, 2009, p. 110).

Orel and Fruhauf (2006) also found some inequalities between biological and nonbiological cograndmothers. Biological grandmothers were generally granted higher status and sometimes felt angry at their partners' lack of interest in the grandchildren. Other times, biological grandmothers were jealous that their partners were not obligated to assume as many responsibilities for the grandchildren. Biological grandmothers were also faced with the added challenge of maintaining a positive relationship and ongoing communication with their exhusbands, who had a strong influence over grandmothers' relationship to their adult children.

Participants in multiple studies did not feel that their sexuality significantly affected their role as grandparents (Whalen, Bigner, and Barber, 2000; Orel and Fruhauf, 2006). As Orel and Fruhauf (2006) explain, grandmothers' sexual orientation did not in itself have an impact on their relationship to their grandchildren, but their relationships were constrained by the heteronormative and homophobic context in which those relationships took place. Interestingly, grandmothers believed that cultural gender expectations, not sexual orientation, primarily influenced their role as grandmothers (Orel and Fruhauf, 2006). They were expected to take on a nurturing role with the grandchildren, in support of their adult children. Whalen *et al.* (2000) also emphasized the emotional support that grandmothers provided for their adult children and grandchildren. Fruhauf *et al.* (2009), by contrast, did not emphasize nurture in grandfather's roles, instead describing a diverse range of roles that included active grandparent, source of wisdom, father figure, and absent figure. A very small number of participants in each LGB grandparenting study referenced their attempt to challenge dominant notions of gender and sexuality through their role as grandparents, providing messages of gender role flexibility and tolerance. Many of the women in a Canadian study of 18 lesbian grandmothers were especially introspective regarding the alternatives to hegemonic meanings of gender and family that they had embraced in response to a homophobic society (Patterson, 2005). For these women, their role as grandmothers consistently included the presentation of diversity, self-acceptance, and successful nonconformity.

Elders' relations to youth and society

Aside from the body of research addressing LGBT grandparents, a few other scholars have begun to examine the relationship between LGBT elders and today's youth more broadly. This research raises critical questions concerning the impact of LGBT elders' invisibility on gay youth and identifies some of the communicative barriers across generations within the LGBT movement.

Ever since Berger (1982) referred to older gays and lesbians as *the unseen minority*, the invisibility of LGBT elders has been a very strong theme in the body of research addressing aging and sexual orientation. This invisibility has consequences within the families of LGBT elders, but it also has an impact on the families of others affiliated with the LGBT movement. In the absence of more positive images of LGBT elders, stereotypes of older gay men as lonely, self-loathing, and predatory have dominated relations between gay elders and gay youth. Fox (2007), for example, investigated the use of the term *troll* as a dehumanizing slang term referring to older gay men within the LGBT community. These stereotypes are widely available in the society, and they permeate beyond gay and lesbian individuals themselves. Many young gay and lesbian people, for example, have reportedly had family members discourage their sexuality by saying things like "imagine how lonely you will be when you are old" (Friend, 1989, p. 242).

In a society in which images of the future that are offered to young people are primarily tinted with heterosexual images of marriage and family, Goltz (2009, p. 562) asks of queer youth, "what does it mean to exist in a space outside of these blueprints and images, to be denied access to the dominant scripts?" Goltz thus argues that the negative stereotypes associated with gay elders, combined with the invisibility of LGBT elders' actual lived experiences, influence younger gay men's tendency to attach negative and gloomy meanings to their own futures. Goltz argues that the invisibility of LGBT elders is thus connected to some of the risk behaviors associated with queer youth (Goltz, 2009).

While many LGBT elders do struggle with loneliness (Grossman, D'Augelli, and Hershberger, 2002), a review of the last 25 years of LGBT aging literature found that the majority of published research described predominantly positive adjustment to the aging process among older gay men and lesbians (Fredrik-Goldsen and Muraco, 2010). Furthermore, research has found that there is not one normative life course for older gay men and lesbians, but rather a variety of life trajectories influenced by gender, cohort, marital status, coming out, and friendship networks (Herdt, Beeler, and Rawls, 1997). Using this information to dismantle stereotypes and offer greater visibility of LGBT elders could potentially improve young gay men's visions of the future, but improving relations between LGBT elders and the broader LGBT community also comes with its own challenges.

For many elders, even the term *queer* may have negative connotations strong enough to alienate them from the larger LGBT movement, which has reappropriated the term to describe a variety of ideologies and identities (Fox, 2007; Brown, 2009). Ageism is also a challenge within the gay and lesbian community, particularly for older gay men who face a well-documented emphasis on youth in gay subcultures (Heaphy, 2007; Goltz, 2009). Furthermore, as previously discussed, elders who have spent a lifetime learning to survive by hiding their sexuality may find it difficult to adjust to contemporary LGBT identity politics that stress outness and authenticity. This appears to be the case even when exposing their sexuality no longer threatens their survival (Fox, 2007). However, researchers predict that as LGBT boomers age, they will be more *out* than generations before them and more likely to assert their rights as LGBT Americans (Haber, 2009). In the meantime, more attention paid toward the diverse configurations of LGBT families at every life stage can not only inform our sociological understanding of families more broadly, but as Goltz (2009) argues, it may help set a standard for young people of a brighter future.

Discussion

A number of themes unfold from this chapter. First, the report card model (*grading* the effects of gay parenthood on children) is the wrong model, because differences in the wellness of family members across genders and sexual orientations *per se* tend to be infrequently occurring and the least interesting. We would like to see a better balance of studies on, for example, the covariates of youth's gender repertoires and sexualities, as against the studies on youth's psychometric measures of adjustment ranked high to low. Indeed, if the interest is in how the gender mix and sexual orientations of parents affect children intergenerationally, children's own genderedness and sexual orientations seem like a more theoretically interesting starting point (in part because it is isomorphic to the question) than children's internalizing or acting out. Of course, the same questions should be extended to heterosexual families as well.

Second, this idea of how queer youth emerge into adulthood, and the different pathways they follow in young adulthood, is intriguing. Many queer youth have begun a process of unpacking a secret about self to self and others that can lead to a greater sense of freedom, relief, and joy. They tend to do this in close proximity to entering a life course stage wherein they are somewhat freer than their heterosexual peers from heteronormative time expectations (e.g., of marriage and reproduction). Rindfuss (1991) has shown that the young adult years are a period of multiple transitions; they are *demographically dense*. Fruitful would be to explore how sexual orientation moderates the diversity of sequencing work/school and family transitions, orderly/disorderly transitions, and clear/blurred transitions (Rindfuss, 1991).

Finally, the idea that LGBT family patterns can inform understanding of new form heterosexual families deserves further exploration. For example, among the most striking western demographic trends of the past 50 years is the decline in marriage rates and the rising proportions of women (and men) that remain childless. This means that larger numbers of people will enter old age unmarried and childless. Lesbians and gay men, it turns out, have a lot of experience at this. Exploring how they create families absent legal or biological ties later in life could prove helpful to all kinds of families.

References

Almack, K., Seymour, J. and Bellamy, G. (2010) Exploring the impact of sexual orientation on experiences and concerns about end of life care and on bereavement for lesbian, gay and bisexual older people. *Sociology*, 44 (5), 908–924.

American Academy of Pediatrics. (2002) Coparent or second-parent adoption by same-sex parents. *Pediatrics*, 109, 339–344.

Battle, J. (2012) Methodological issues when conducting research on LGBT people of color. Paper presented at the ASA Sexualities Section Conference of Crossing Boundaries: Workshopping Sexualities, Denver, CO, August 15–16, 2012.

Berger, R. (1982) The unseen minority: older gays and lesbians. *Social Work*, 27 (3), 236–242.

Biblarz, T.J. and Savci, E. (2010) Lesbian, gay, bisexual, and transgender families. *Journal of Marriage Family*,72, 480–497.

Biblarz, T.J. and Stacey, J. (2010) How does the gender of parents matter? *Journal of Marriage and Family*, 72, 3–22.

Black, D., Gates, G., Sanders, S. and Taylor, L. (2000) Demographics of the gay and lesbian population in the United States: evidence from available systematic data sources. *Demography*, 37 (2), 139–154.

Blank, T.O., Asencio, M., Descartes, L. and Griggs, J. (2009) Aging, health, and GLBTQ family and community life. *Journal of GLBT Family Studies*, 5 (1–2), 9–34.

Bilodeau, B.L. and Renn, K.A. (2005) Analysis of LGBT identity development models and implications for practice. *New Directions for Student Services*, 111, 25–39.

Bos, H.M.W., van Balen, F. and van den Boom, D.C. (2003) Planned lesbian families: their desire and motivation to have children. *Human Reproduction*, 18 (10), 2216–2224.

Bos, H.M.W., van Balen, F. and van den Boom, D.C. (2007) Child adjustment and parenting in planned lesbian-parent families. *American Journal of Orthopsychiatry*, 77 (1), 38–48.

Brooks, D. (2013) When Families Fail. *The New York Times* (Feb 14), http://www.nytimes.com/2013/02/15/opinion/brooks-crayons-to-college.html?_r=1&. (accessed May 29, 2013).

Burke, N. (2013) The division of household labor and childcare in gay male partnerships. Working paper, Department of Sociology, University of Southern California.

Brown, M.T. (2009) LGBT aging and rhetorical silence. *Sexuality Research and Social Policy*, 6 (4), 65–78.

Cahill, S. and South, K. (2002) Policy issues affecting lesbian, gay, bisexual, and transgender people in retirement. *Generations*, 26 (2), 49–54.

Carroll, M. (2012) The intersectional collective identity of gay fatherhood. Working paper, Department of Sociology, University of Southern California.

Cass, V.C. (1979) Homosexual identity formation: a theoretical model. *Journal of Homosexuality*, 4, 219–235.

Cherlin, A.J. (2010) Demographic trends in the United States: a review of research in the 2000s. *Journal of Marriage and Family*, 72, 403–419.

D'Augelli, A.R. (1994) Identity development and sexual orientation: toward a model of lesbian, gay, and bisexual development, in *Human Diversity: Perspectives on People in Context* (eds. J.T. Edison, R.J. Watts, and D. Birman), Jossey-Bass, San Francisco, pp. 312–333.

D'Augelli, A.R. (2002) Mental health problems among lesbian, gay, and bisexual youths ages 14 to 21. *Clinical Child Psychology and Psychiatry*, 7 (3), 433–456.

D'Augelli, A.R. and Grossman, A.H. (2001) Disclosure of sexual orientation, victimization, and mental health among lesbian, gay, and bisexual older adults. *Journal of Interpersonal Violence*, 16 (10), 1008–1027.

D'Augelli, A.R., Grossman, A.H., Hershberger, S.L. and O'Connell, T.S. (2001) Aspects of mental health among older lesbian, gay, and bisexual adults. *Aging & Mental Health*, 5 (2), 149–158.

David, S. and Knight, B.G. (2008) Stress and coping among gay men: age and ethnic differences. *Psychology and Aging*, 23 (1), 62–69.

Edelman, L. (2004) *No Future: Queer Theory and the Death Drive*, Duke University Press, Durham.

Eisenberg, M.E. and Resnick, M.D. (2006) Suicidality among gay, lesbian and bisexual youth: the role of protective factors. *Journal of Adolescent Health*, 39 (5), 662–668.

Fields, J. (2001) Normal queers: straight parents respond to their children's "coming out." *Symbolic Interaction*, 24 (2), 165–187.

Floyd, F.J. and Bakeman, R. (2006) Coming-out across the life course: implications of age and historical context. *Archives of Sexual Behavior*, 35 (3), 287–296.

Fox, R.C. (2007) Gay grows up: an interpretive study on aging metaphors and queer identity. *Journal of Homosexuality*, 52 (3–4), 33–61.

Fredriksen-Goldsen, K.I. and Muraco, A. (2010) Aging and sexual orientation: a 25-year review of the literature. *Research on Aging*, 32 (3), 372–413.

Friedman, M.S., Silvestre, A.J., Gold, M.A. *et al.* (2004) Adolescents define sexual orientation and suggest ways to measure it. *Journal of Adolescence*, 27, 303–317.

Friend, R.A. (1989) Older lesbian and gay people: responding to homophobia. *Marriage and Family Review*, 14 (3), 241–263.

Fruhauf, C.A., Orel, N.A. and Jenkins, D.A. (2009) The coming-out process of gay grandfathers: perceptions of their adult children's influence. *Journal of GLBT Family Studies*, 5 (1–2), 99–118.

Gates, G.J. (2011) Family Formation and Raising Children Among Same-Sex Couples. NCFR Report: Family Focus on LGBT Families, http://williamsinstitute.law.ucla.edu/wp-content/uploads/Gates-Badgett-NCFR-LGBT-Families-December-2011.pdf (accessed March 18, 2013).

Gates, G.J. (2013a) LGBT Parenting in the United States. The Williams Institute, http://williamsinstitute.law.ucla.edu/wp-content/uploads/LGBT-Parenting.pdf (accessed March 18, 2013).

Gates, G.J. (2013b) Same-Sex and Different-Sex Couples in the American Community Survey: 2005–2011. The Williams Institute, http://williamsinstitute.law.ucla.edu/wp-content/uploads/ACS-2013.pdf (accessed May 25, 2013).

Goldberg, A.E. (2012) *Gay Dads: Transitions to Adoptive Fatherhood*, New York University Press, New York.

Goldberg, A.E. and Perry-Jenkins, M. (2007) The division of labor and perceptions of parental roles: lesbian couples across the transition to parenthood. *Journal of Social and Personal Relationships*, 24 (2), 297–318.

Goltz, D. (2009) Investigating queer future meanings: destructive perceptions of "The harder path." *Qualitative Inquiry*, 15 (3), 561–586.

Gorman-Murray, A. (2008) Queering the family home: narratives from gay, lesbian and bisexual youth coming out in supportive family homes in Australia. *Gender, Place and Culture*, 15 (1), 31–44.

Gray, M.L. (2009) *Out in Country: Youth, Media, and Queer Visibility in Rural America*, New York University Press, New York.

Green, J. (2013) From "I Do" to "I'm Done": With Newfound Rights, Newfound Fears. The Peculiar Mechanics – and Heartbreak – of Gay Divorce. *New York Magazine* (Feb 24), http://nymag.com/news/features/gay-divorce-2013-3/ (accessed May 29, 2013).

Grossman, A.H., D'Augelli, A.R. and Hershberger, S.L. (2000) Social support networks of lesbian, gay, and bisexual adults 60 years of age and older. *The Journals of Gerontology Series B: Psychological Sciences and Social Sciences*, 55 (3), 171–179.

Grossman, A.H., D'Augelli, A.R. and O'Connell, T.S. (2002) Being lesbian, gay, bisexual, and 60 or older in North America. *Journal of Gay and Lesbian Social Services*, 13 (4), 23–40.

Haber, D. (2009) Gay aging. *Gerontology and Geriatrics Education*, 30 (3), 267–280.

Halberstam, J. (2005) *In a Queer Time and Place: Transgender Bodies, Subcultural Lives*, New York University Press, New York.

Hammack, P.L., Thompson, E.M. and Pilecki, A. (2009) Configurations of identity among sexual minority youth: context, desire, and narrative. *Journal of Youth and Adolescence*, 38, 867–883.

Hash, K. (2006) Caregiving and post-caregiving experiences of midlife and older gay men and lesbians. *Journal of Gerontological Social Work*, 47 (3–4), 121–138.

Heaphy, B. (2007) Sexualities, gender and ageing: resources and social change. *Current Sociology*, 55 (2), 193–210.

Heaphy, B. (2009) The storied, complex lives of older GLBT adults. *Journal of GLBT Family Studies*, 5, 119–138.

Heaphy, B., Yip, A. and Thompson, D. (2003) *Lesbian, Gay and Bisexual Lives Over 50: A Report on the Project "The Social and Policy Implications of Non-Heterosexual Ageing,"* York House Publishing, Nottingham.

Heatherington, L. and Lavner, J.A. (2008) Coming to terms with coming out: review and recommendations for family systems-focused research. *Journal of Family Psychology*, 22 (3), 329–343.

Henrickson, M. and Neville, S. (2012) Identity satisfaction over the life course in sexual minorities. *Journal of Gay and Lesbian Social Services*, 24 (1), 80–95.

Herdt, G., Beeler, J. and Rawls, T.W. (1997) Life course diversity among older lesbians and gay men: a study in Chicago. *International Journal of Sexuality and Gender Studies*, 2 (3), 231–246.

Hochschild, A. (1997) The time bind. *Journal of Labor & Society*, 1 (2), 21–29.

Hochschild, A. and Machung, A. (1989) *The Second Shift: Working Parents and the Revolution at Home*, Viking, New York.

Hostetler, A.J. (2009) Single by choice? Assessing and understanding voluntary singlehood among mature gay men. *Journal of Homosexuality*, 56 (4), 499–531.

Johnson, S.M. and O'Connor, E. (2002) *The Gay Baby Boom: The Psychology of Gay Parenthood*, New York University Press, New York.

Johnson, M.J., Jackson, N.C., Arnette, J.K. and Koffman, S.D. (2005) Gay and lesbian perceptions of discrimination in retirement care facilities. *Journal of Homosexuality*, 49 (2), 83–102.

Jones, R.L. (2011) Imagining bisexual futures: positive, non-normative later life. *Journal of Bisexuality*, 11 (2–3), 245–270.

Kastanis, A. and Badgett, M.V.L. (2013a) Estimating the Economic Boost of Marriage Equality in Illinois. The Williams Institute, http://williamsinstitute.law.ucla.edu/wp-content/uploads/IL-Econ-Impact-Mar-2013.pdf (accessed March 18, 2013).

Kastanis, A. and Badgett, M.V.L. (2013b) Estimating the Economic Boost of Marriage Equality in Rhode Island. The Williams Institute, http://williamsinstitute.law.ucla.edu/wp-content/uploads/RI-Econ-Impact-Mar-2013.pdf (accessed May 16, 2013).

Kastanis, A., Badgett, M.V.L. and Herman, J.L. (2012) The Economic Impact of Extending Marriage to Same-Sex Couples in Washington State. The Williams Institute, http://williams institute.law.ucla.edu/wp-content/uploads/Kastanis-Badgett-Herman-WASalesTaxImpact-Jan-20121.pdf (accessed March 18, 2013).

King Jr., N. (2012) WSJ/NBC Poll: Majority Now Backs Gay Marriage. *Wall Street Journal* (Dec 13), http://blogs.wsj.com/washwire/2012/12/13/wsjnbc-poll-majority-now-backs-gay-marriage (accessed March 18, 2013).

Knauer, N.J. (2011) "Gen Silent": advocating for LGBT elders. *The Elder Law Journal*, 19 (2), 101–161.

Kryzan, C. (2000) OutProud/Oasis Internet survey of queer and questioning youth. Sponsored by *OutProud*, The National Coalition for Gay, Lesbian, Bisexual and Transgender Youth and Oasis Magazine. Contact survey@outproud.org.

LaSala, M.C. (2010) *Coming Out, Coming Home: Helping Families Adjust to a Gay or Lesbian Child*, Columbia University Press, New York.

MacCallum, F. and Golombok, S. (2004) Children raised in fatherless families from infancy: a follow-up of children of lesbian and single heterosexual mothers at early adolescence. *Journal of Psychology and Psychiatry*, 45 (8), 1407–1419.

Marshal, M.P., Friedman, M.S., Stall, R. *et al.* (2008) Sexual orientation and adolescent substance use: a meta-analysis and methodological review. *Addiction*, 103, 546–556.

Masini, B. and Barrett, H. (2008) Social support as a predictor of psychological and physical well-being and lifestyle in lesbian, gay, and bisexual adults aged 50 and over. *Journal of Gay and Lesbian Social Services*, 20 (1–2), 91–110.

Maylor, E.A., Reimers, S., Choi, J. *et al.* (2007) Gender and sexual orientation differences in cognition across adulthood: age is kinder to women than to men regardless of sexual orientation. *Archives of Sexual Behavior*, 36 (2), 235–249.

McFarland, P.L. and Sanders, S. (2003) A pilot study about the needs of older gays and lesbians: what social workers need to know. *Journal of Gerontological Social Work*, 40 (3), 67–80.

Moore, M.R. (2008) Gendered power relations among women: a study of household decision making in black, lesbian stepfamilies. *American Sociological Review*, 73 (2), 335–356.

Moore, M.R. (2011) *Invisible Families: Gay Identities, Relationships, and Motherhood among Black Women*, University of California Press, Berkeley.

Muraco, A. and Fredriksen-Goldsen, K. (2011) "That's what friends do": informal caregiving for chronically ill midlife and older lesbian, gay, and bisexual adults. *Journal of Social and Personal Relationships*, 28 (8), 1073–1092.

Mustanski, B. (2011) Ethical and regulatory issues with conducting sexuality research with LGBT adolescents: a call to action for a scientifically informed approach. *Archives of Sexual Behavior*, 40, 673–686.

Orel, N.A. (2004) Gay, lesbian, and bisexual elders: expressed needs and concerns across focus groups. *Journal of Gerontological Social Work*, 43, 57–77.

Orel, N.A. and Fruhauf, C. (2006) Lesbian and bisexual grandmothers' perceptions of the grandparent-grandchild relationship. *Journal of GLBT Family Studies*, 2 (1), 43–70.

Oswald, R.F. and Lazarevic, V. (2011) "You live *where*?!" Lesbian mothers' attachment to nonmetropolitan communities. *Family Relations*, 60, 373–386.

Oswald, R.F. and Holman, E.G. (2013a) Place matters: LGB families in community context, in *LGBT-Parent Families: Innovations in Research and Implications for Practice* (eds. A. E. Goldberg and K. R. Allen), Springer, New York, pp. 193–208.

Oswald, R.F. and Holman, E.G. (2013b) Rainbow Illinois: How Downstate LGBT Communities Have Changed (2000–2011). Department of Human and Community Development, Urbana-Champaign, Illinois, http://hcd.illinois.edu.libproxy.usc.edu/people/faculty/oswald_ramona_f/documents/rainbowillinoiscommunityreport.pdf (accessed March 18, 2013).

Oswald, R.F., Cuthbertson, C., Lazarevic, V. and Goldberg, A.E. (2010) New developments in the field: measuring community climate. *Journal of GLBT Family Studies*, 6, 214–228.

Pachankis, J.E. and Hatzenbuehler, M.L. (2013) The social development of contingent self-worth in sexual minority young men: an empirical investigation of the "best little boy in the world' hypothesis." *Basic and Applied Social Psychology*, 35 (2), 176–190.

Pappas, S. (2012) Gay Parents Better Than Straight Parents? What Research Says. *Huffington Post* (Apr 16), http://www.huffingtonpost.com/2012/01/16/gay-parents-better-than-straights_n_1208659.html (accessed May 1, 2013).

Patterson, S. (2005) "This is so you know you have options": lesbian grandmothers and the mixed legacies of nonconformity. *Journal of the Motherhood Initiative for Research and Community Involvement*, 7 (2), 38–48.

Perrin, A.J., Cohen, P.N. and Caren, N. (2013) Are children of parents who had same-sex relationships disadvantaged? A scientific evaluation of the no-differences hypothesis. *Journal of Gay and Lesbian Mental Health*, September 2013.

Pilkington, N.W. and D'Augelli, A.R. (1995) Victimization of lesbian, gay, and bisexual youth in community settings. *Journal of Community Psychology*, 23, 33–55.

Pollner, M. and Rosenfeld, D. (2000) The cross-culturing work of gay and lesbian elderly. *Advances in Life Course Research*, 5, 99–117.

Porche, M.V. and Purvin, D.M. (2008) "Never in our lifetime": legal marriage for same-sex couples in long-term relationships. *Family Relations*, 57 (2), 144–159.

Powell, B., Bolzendahl, C., Geist, C. and Steelman, L. (2010) *Counted Out: Same-Sex Relations and Americans' Definitions of Family*, Sage, New York.

Rasmussen, M.L., Rofes, E. and Talburt, S. (2004) *Youth and Sexualities: Pleasure, Subversion, and Insubordination in and out of Schools*, Palgrave Macmillan, New York.

Richard, C.A. and Brown, A.H. (2006) Configurations of informal social support among older lesbians. *Journal of Women & Aging*, 18 (4), 49–65.

Riggle, E.D.B., Whitman, J.S., Olson, A.*et al.* (2008) The positive aspects of being a lesbian or gay man. *Professional Psychology: Research and Practice*, 39 (2), 210–217.

Rindfuss, R.R. (1991) The young adult years: diversity, structural change, and fertility. *Demography*, 28 (4), 493–512.

Rivers, I. and D'Augelli, A.R. (2001) The victimization of lesbian, gay, and bisexual youths, in *Lesbian, Gay, and Bisexual Identities and Youth: Psychological Perspectives* (eds. A.R. D'Augelli and C.J. Patterson), Oxford University Press, New York, pp. 199–223.

Rofes, E. (2004) Martyr-target-victim: interrogating narratives of persecution and suffering among queer youth, in *Youth and Sexualities: Pleasure, Subversion, and Insubordination in and out of Schools* (M.L. Rasmussen, E. Rofes, and S. Talbuet), Palgrave MacMillan, New York, pp. 41–62.

Rosenfeld, D. (1999) Identity work among lesbian and gay elderly. *Journal of Aging Studies*, 13 (2), 121–144.

Rosenfeld, D. (2003) *The Changing of The Guard: Lesbian and Gay Elders, Identity, and Social Change*, Temple University Press, Philadelphia.

Russell, S.T. (2003) Sexual minority youth and suicide risk. *American Behavioral Scientist*, 46, 1241–1257.

Russell, S.T. (2006) Substance use and abuse and mental health among sexual-minority youths: evidence from add health, in *Sexual Orientation and Mental Health: Examining Identity and Development in Lesbian, Gay, and Bisexual People* (eds. A.M. Omoto and H.S. Kurtzman), American Psychological Association, Washington, pp. 13–35.

Rothblum, Esther D., Kimberly F. Balsam and Sondra E. Solomon. (2008) "Comparison of Same-Sex Couples Who Were Married in Massachusetts, Had Domestic Partnerships in California, or Had Civil Unions in Vermont." *Journal of Family Issues* 29:48–78.

Ryan, C., Russell, S.T., Huebner, D. *et al.* (2010) Family acceptance in adolescence and the health of LGBT young adults. *Journal of Child and Adolescent Psychiatric Nursing*, 23 (4), 205–213.

Savin-Williams, R.C. (2001a) A critique of research on sexual-minority youths. *Journal of Adolescence*, 24 (1), 5–13.

Savin-Williams, R.C. (2001b) Suicide attempts among sexual-minority youths: population and measurement issues. *Journal of Consulting and Clinical Psychology*, 69 (6), 983–991.

Shapiro, D.N., Peterson, C. and Stewart, A.J. (2009) Legal and social contexts and mental health among lesbian and heterosexual mothers. *Family Psychology*, 23 (2), 255–262.

Silverstein, L.B., Auerbach, C.F. and Levant, R.F. (2002) Contemporary fathers reconstructing masculinity: clinical implications of gender role strain. *Professional Psychology: Research and Practice*, 33 (4), 361–369.

Slevin, K.F. (2008) Disciplining bodies: the aging experiences of older heterosexual and gay men. *Generations*, 32 (1), 36–42.

Smith, T.W. (2011) Cross-national Differences in Attitudes Towards Homosexuality. The Williams Institute, http://escholarship.org/uc/item/81m7x7kb (accessed May 29, 2013).

Stacey, J. and Biblarz, T.J. (2001) (How) does the sexual orientation of parents matter? *American Sociological Review*, 66 (2), 159–183.

Tasker, F. (2005) Lesbian mothers, gay fathers, and their children: a review. *Developmental and Behavioral Pediatrics*, 26 (3), 224–240.

Tremble, B., Schneider, M. and Appathurai, C. (1989) Growing up gay or lesbian in a multicultural context. *Journal of Homosexuality*, 17, 253–267.

Unks, G. (2003) Thinking about the gay teen," in *The Critical Pedagogy Reader* (eds. A. Darder, M. Baltodano, and R. D. Torres), RoutledgeFalmer, New York, pp. 322–330.

van Wormer, K. and McKinney, R. (2003) What schools can do to help gay/lesbian/bisexual youth: a harm reduction approach. *Adolescence*, 38 (151), 409–420.

Vanfraussen, K., Ponjaert-Kristoffersen, I. and Brewaeys, A. (2003) Family functioning in lesbian families created by donor insemination. *American Journal of Orthopsychiatry*, 73 (1), 78–90.

Whalen, D.M., Bigner, J.J. and Barber, C.E. (2000) The grandmother role as experienced by lesbian women. *Journal of Women and Aging*, 12 (3–4), 39–58.

Whitford, G.S. (1997) Realities and hopes for older gay males. *Journal of Gay and Lesbian Social Services*, 6 (1), 79–95.

7

Family Poverty

Rys Farthing

Poverty is perhaps one of the most extensive and damaging problems faced by families the world over. Poverty is an acute problem in the developing world, where over 1.3 billion people live below the somewhat arbitrarily defined $1.25 per day poverty line (World Bank, 2008), but this suffering is by no means limited to the global south. Amidst the wealth of the global north, in the United Kingdom, for example, 11% of people live below a commonly defined poverty threshold, while in the United States, 17.3% of the population live below this poverty line[1] (OECD, 2012).

But to talk about poverty is somewhat different than talking about other problems families might face; to use the phrase poverty is to implicitly invoke an imperative for action against it (see, e.g., Piachaud, 1981). The very word poverty refers to an "unacceptable state of affairs, which requires some sort of policy response" (Alcock, 2008, p. 131). For this reason, the problem of poverty has always been a key concern for both sociologists and social policy makers. Some of the earliest social science researches were directed toward understanding the experience and causes of poverty, such as Charles Booth's 1880 survey and subsequent typology of poor families in London (Platt, 2005, p. 20). Likewise, some of the earliest social policies were directed toward alleviating the problem of poverty – such as the United Kingdom's 1597 Poor Law (Platt, 2005).

However, despite the widely acknowledged scope of the problem and the centuries of study and policy directed toward it, much debate about the nature and definition of poverty itself remains. Following this breadth of debate, no singular diagnosis or remedy has emerged; different definitions and measures of poverty produce different visions of poor families and call for different policy responses. Different visions of, and policy responses to, poverty can have profoundly different impacts on the lived experiences of families.

This chapter aims to provide an orientation to this debate. It commences by briefly exploring different definitions of poverty across the world, before turning to

The Wiley Blackwell Companion to the Sociology of Families, First Edition.
Edited by Judith Treas, Jacqueline Scott, and Martin Richards.
© 2014 John Wiley & Sons Ltd. Published 2017 by John Wiley & Sons Ltd.

look at the global state of family poverty and which families are "poor". It concludes with an exploration of the lived experience and consequences of poverty for these families, looking at how they "get by" and "get out", specifically in the global north.

Defining Poverty

Defining poverty is not as straightforward as claims of "people living on incomes below $1.25 a day" might make it seem. Definitions have profound implications for both the way we understand poverty and the way we act toward ending or alleviating it.

Sen (1979) argues the poverty analysis starts with a two-stage process of definition. Firstly, the poor are *identified* through the creation of some sort of poverty line which the "poor" fall below, and secondly, information is *aggregated* as these identified "poor" are then counted and measured. Discussions of this sort, around measurement, construct poverty as a distinctly technical concept. However, poverty is more than this technical conceptualization suggests – it is, perhaps firstly, a moral concern. Underneath this technical focus on measurement lies a deeper layer of understanding poverty (Lister, 2004a), where meanings and discourses about being "poor" reside. Lister suggests narrowing our confusion exclusively to technical measures, or indeed starting from measurement first, rather than seeing the broader discourse has the damaging effect of narrowing the sociological focus.

Expanding the focus often requires discussions with "poor" families themselves. Almost by default, technical analysis excludes these families from the process of defining poverty; poverty drastically limits people's opportunity to become social scientists and take part in technical debates. However, such exclusion is not inevitable. Alongside the analysis rooted in conventional, technocratic understandings of poverty often lies sociological research that adopts participatory approaches grounded in the experiences of the "poor" themselves (Lister, 2004a). Each approach stands to highlight a different, but often complementary, aspect of the experience of poverty.

Baulch (1996) visualizes the relationship of these different aspects of poverty as a pyramid (see Figure 7.1). Easy-to-measure and frequently cited manifestations of poverty, such as technical measures of income and consumption, rest on top of a

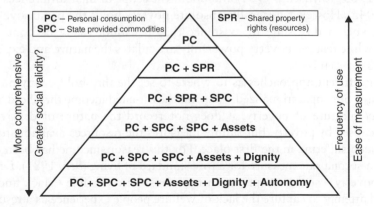

Figure 7.1   The poverty pyramid.
Source: Adapted from Baulch (1996).

realm of other deprivations associated with poverty, such as assets, dignity, and autonomy. Policy interventions are often aimed at different "levels" in the pyramid and can work to either reduce poverty itself or mitigate its impact on people (Lister, 2004a). Both technical and participatory approaches are, however, not oppositional and can work to reinforce each other; however, what becomes apparent is that each sociological understanding of poverty will call for different interventions.

Having established that definitions of poverty are important and expansive, a number of key themes in definitions are notable. Firstly, definitions of poverty can either be *absolute* or *relative*. Absolute poverty, while contested in its own right, tends to refer to poverty as a state of being where people are unable to meet the minimum requirements for their physiological well-being, without references to the prevailing social standards within which they live. The "$1.25 a day" measure tends to be regarded as absolute, as it is widely held that below this threshold, basic human needs for food, water, and warmth cannot be met. The official US poverty line, which is calculated by taking the minimum costs of meeting basic nutritional needs multiplied by three (Fisher, 1992), is also regarded as absolute, as it is intended to reflect the ability of households to meet absolute, basic human needs like food, toiletries, and rent.

In contrast, much sociological research focuses on relative understandings of poverty or understanding that poverty is about not having enough to meet what are socially determined minimum needs:

> individuals, families and groups in the population can be said to be in poverty when they lack the resources to obtain the types of diet, participate in the activities, and have the living conditions and amenities which are customary, or at least widely encouraged and approved, in the societies in which they belong.
>
> (Townsend, 1979, p. 31)

Alternative understandings suggest that poverty within a society is *relative* to normal standards of living. Measures such as those used within the EU, which identifies the poor as those living below 50% or 60% of median income, are considered relative, as they refer to people's ability to meet their needs and participate *within their society*. Debate about the merits of the two approaches exists (see, e.g., Sen, 1985; Townsend, 1985) and about the scope of their differences (see, e.g., Lister, 2004a). However, generally, absolute poverty holds the persuasive power of recording such a dire state of existence that it cannot easily be contested as a problem, while relative poverty powerfully articulates the nature and experience of poverty as a social issue.

Beyond different approaches as to where to set the threshold, many measures of poverty have been operationalized – beyond the oft-cited income threshold. Income is an *indirect* measure of poverty; it does not record the nature of deprivations or suffering caused by poverty, but simply measures the resources available to a family to avoid such suffering in the first place. For this reason, income has been described as at best a second rate measure for a low standard of living (Sen, 1981). *Direct* measures of poverty – such as deprivation measures – are possible (Mack and Lansley, 1985) and attempt to capture the lack of welfare people experience as a result of their poverty. They often measure the material goods and resources available to households, and this alternative focus can lead to policies directed at providing more public resources (such as health care and education) instead of, or in conjunction with, policies designed to improve family incomes. Deprivation measures can be measures of absolute poverty, such as the World Bank's measure of the prevalence of malnutrition in children under 5 years old. Alternatively, they can be relative and capture people's inability to live in way regarded as socially acceptable, such as the ability to replace worn-out furniture or go on holiday for 1 week of the year (DWP, 2011).

While this may seem like an abstract theoretical discussion, how we define poverty drives policy responses to the problem and profoundly impacts the lives of "poor" families. As a powerful example, in the United Kingdom, the idea of "poverty" was undermined within political discourse over the 1980s, with politicians declaring the concept no longer relevant (Alcock, 2008, p. 132). As the Secretary of State for Social Security noted, "when pressure groups say that one-third of the population is living in poverty, they cannot be saying that one-third of people are living below...draconian subsistence levels" (Moore, 1989) and went on to suggest that it was "utterly absurd" to talk of British poverty. According to the then Secretary of State, people who spoke of British poverty should be dismissed because "their motive is not compassion for the less well-off... Their purpose in calling 'poverty' what is in reality simply inequality, is so they can call western capitalism a failure" (Moore, 1989). However, under this government's rule and in the decade prior to his speech, poverty, as measured by the United Kingdom's now preferred relative definition,[2] increased from 7.1 million people or 13.4% of the population in 1979 to 11.8 million or 21.5% in 1989 (IFS, 2010). When "poverty" was accepted by and reintroduced into political discourse in 1999 (Platt, 2005), policies aimed at increasing family incomes, and financial redistribution reduced child poverty figures by 900,000 over 13 years (DWP, 2011). These two approaches, of viewing poverty as an absolute construct akin to the destitution, or as seeing it as a relative problem of low incomes in a time of affluence, produced different policy approaches – such as the provision of minimal, subsistence level support versus a strong redistributive tax and benefit system – which in turn produce two distinctly different lived experiences for families.

While sociological understandings of poverty have evolved even further into complex multidimensional measures or concepts of social exclusion, they are beyond the scope of this chapter.

The State of World Poverty and Consequences for "the Poor"

Some 22.4% of the world's population, or 1.29 billion people, lives on an income of below $1.25 per day (World Bank, 2008). While almost half of these people live in South Asia, sub-Saharan Africa suffers from the highest proportion of poverty (Table 7.1).

People living in these extremely poor families invariably have fewer choices available to them, as much of their limited income needs to be spent on basic sustenance. A survey of 13 low-income countries found that 56–78% of household limited income was spent on providing food for the family (Banerjee and Duflo, 2007). However, while it is tempting to think of the extremely poor as hungry and spending every penny on food, this view denies the, albeit limited, choices these families have. The same survey found

Table 7.1　The number and proportion of people living below the $1.25 poverty threshold by region, 2008

	Number of poor at $1.25 a day (PPP) (millions)	Poverty headcount ratio at $1.25 a day (PPP) (% of population)
East Asia and Pacific (developing only)	284.36	14.34
Europe and Central Asia (developing only)	2.23	0.47
Latin America and Caribbean (developing only)	36.85	6.47
Middle East and North Africa (developing only)	8.64	2.7
Sub-Saharan Africa (developing only)	386.02	47.51
South Asia	570.89	35.98
Low and middle income	1288.99	22.43

Source: Data from World Bank (2008).

that in many places around the world, spending on festivals was a sizeable part of the family budget. For example, in the Udaipur region of India, a median of 10% of the annual household budget was spent on weddings, funerals, or religious festivals (Banerjee and Duflo, 2007, p. 146). The very human needs of extremely poor families are not dissimilar to the needs of the nonpoor; the need for food, shelter, and warmth coexists with the need to participate in the society. Extreme poverty does not necessarily change family needs; rather, it sharply curtails the ability to meet their needs.

Extreme poverty has severe impacts on people's health. For example, the chances of a family's children surviving beyond the age of 5 are, to a large extent, dictated by the poverty of the region they are born into. For example, in 2010, the mortality rate for under 5-year-olds in low-income countries was 107 deaths per 1000 live births but only 6 deaths per 1000 in high-income countries (World Health Organisation, 2012). What causes the deaths of the extremely poor adults also differs, with 58% of deaths in low-income countries attributable to communicable diseases, infections, and nutritional deficiencies compared to 7% in high-income countries (World Health Organisation, 2012).

Beyond limited means and poorer health outcomes, the extremely poor speak of a lack of well-being, a crushing lack of choice, and the overall sense of powerlessness that the lower portion of Baulch's (1996) pyramid conceptualized. The *Voices of the Poor* study (Deepa *et al.*, 2000) captured the thoughts of 40,000 poor people from 50 countries around the world, who spoke of an overall sense of ill-being:

> Poverty is pain; it feels like a disease. It attacks a person not only materially but also morally. It eats away one's dignity and drives one into total despair
>
> 　　　　　　　　　　　　　　　　　　– Moldova (Deepa et al., 2000, p. 6)

> Poverty is lack of freedom, enslaved by crushing daily burden, by depression and fear of what the future will bring
>
> 　　　　　　　　　　　　　　　　　　– Georgia (Deepa et al., 2000, p. 31)

These descriptions are echoed in the global north, where the experience of poverty has been described as "going short materially, socially and emotionally" (Oppenheim and Harker, 1996, p. 5):

> …Living in poverty puts you under constant pressure. It wears you down
> – EU (Czech Presidency of the European Union, 2009, p. 5)

> Living in material poverty means they have stolen our here-and-now. And they are stealing our future by keeping us out of touch with the knowledge-based society
> – EU (Czech Presidency of the European Union, 2009, p. 5)

However, within the global north, the $1.25 absolute poverty line is too acute to accurately capture this experience of families "going short". Instead, a relative income threshold paints a more compelling picture. Using the relative threshold of 50% of median income after taxes and transfers and adjusted to reflect household size, 11% of the population of the OECD live in households that are in poverty (see Table 7.2).

For members of these households, their ability to participate within their society is limited. Direct measures of deprivation available from the United Kingdom, for

Table 7.2   The proportion of the population living below 50% of median household income, equivalized for size, after tax and transfers by selected countries

Country	Poverty rate after taxes and transfers, 50% of current median income	Year
Australia	14.6	2007/2008
Austria	7.9	2008
Canada	12.0	2008
Denmark	6.1	2007
Finland	8.0	2008
France	7.2	2008
Germany	8.9	2008
Greece	10.8	2008
Ireland	9.1	2008
Israel	19.9	2008
Japan	15.7	2006
Korea	15.0	2008
Mexico	20.1	2008
Netherlands	7.2	2008
Norway	7.8	2008
Spain	14.0	2008
Sweden	8.4	2008
Switzerland	9.3	2008
United Kingdom	11.0	2007/2008
United States	17.3	2008
OECD total	**11.1**	

Source: Data from OECD (2012).

example, show that children in lower-income families miss out on activities that could be considered a regular part of growing up in the United Kingdom, such as celebrating special occasions or owning a bicycle (DWP, 2011). While such deprivation seems a long way from the child mortality noted in the developing world, growing up with these relative deprivations limits childhoods:

> I would like to be able to do more things with my friends, when they go out down the town and that. But we can't always afford it. So I got to stay in and that, and just in here it's just boring – I can't do anything.
>
> (Mike 12, in Ridge, 2002)

Which Families are Poor and Why?

Just as the global geography of poverty differs, so too does its demographics. The risk of poverty is not spread evenly, and some families are more at risk of poverty than others. Poverty disproportionately affects families during certain periods of the life course, families headed by women, single-parent families, and families affected by disability.

Families across the life course

One of the earliest sociological studies of poverty conducted by Seebohm Rowntree in 1901 noted that poverty appeared to follow a fairly regular life course. For any individual, the risk of living in poverty increased:

- During childhood, when family incomes were generally lower because most family members were either too young to work or unable to work due to childcare commitments
- Relatedly, when a family had younger children
- In old age, when the ability to earn is often curtailed by poor health.

In between these phases were brief periods of comparative prosperity: during youth when the ability to earn an income was high and later in life when children could provide for themselves but before retirement (Rowntree, 1901).

This cyclical pattern is still notable in many countries. As Figure 7.2 highlights, the poverty rates for both children and the elderly – as marked by grey and dashed lines – tend to be higher than the overall poverty figures – marked by a black line. This is especially true in countries that have overall higher rates of poverty, including the United States and the United Kingdom, where higher risks of poverty exist for children and the elderly.[3] However, some other countries, and especially those that have managed to achieve low levels of overall poverty, appear to have broken the link between poverty and age. For example, child poverty is lower than overall poverty in the Scandinavian nations. This could be the result of universal income maintenance payments to children and highly subsidized childcare. However, rates of poverty among elderly persons in Scandinavia are higher, which may be the result of the failure of earnings-related social insurance schemes to protect those with a history of low wages or intermittent work.

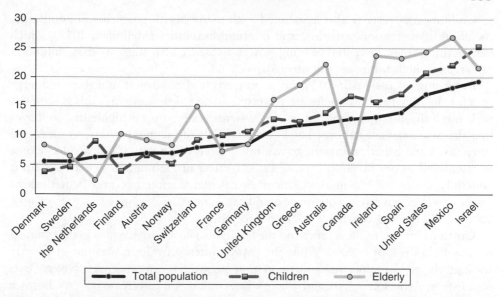

Figure 7.2 Percentages of people living below 50% of median household income, equivalized after tax and transfers by age, mid-2000s.
Source: Data from Luxembourg Income Studies (2012).

Children face a higher risk of poverty than adults partly because of the reasons Rowntree articulated in 1901 and because of changing family demographics including the rise of single-parent families (see discussion later), among other reasons. However, measures of poverty are perhaps inevitably going to record higher levels of child poverty due to their equivalized nature. That is, calculations of household income are "equivalized" to reflect household need by dividing the total income by some sort of denominator reflecting family size. Children will therefore inevitably increase family poverty levels as they increase the denominator.[4]

Child poverty is of particular concern for many families, because of the ability of childhood poverty to scar individuals into adulthood. Poverty during childhood can impact on a child's individual physical, cognitive, and emotional development, reduce educational and health outcomes, and reduce overall well-being long into adulthood. For example, across the global north, there is a negative association between educational outcomes and socioeconomic status (see, e.g., the association between socioeconomic background and reading performance in OECD (2010)), which we could expect to suppress future wages. There are many reasons for this association that suggest that poverty itself might be causal. For example, epidemiologists have shown that the poverty-related stress in early childhood reduced children's cognitive abilities (Duncan and Brooks-Gunn, 1997), and there is much evidence to suggest that poor parents cannot purchase the educational extras, like books and school trips, that richer parents can (Department for Education, 2007). We also know that increasing family incomes can make a difference in children's education outcomes. In the United States in the 1990s, for example, when the Earned Income Tax Credit increased, so too did the poorer children's educational attainment (Dahl and Lochner, 2008).

Childhood poverty is also associated with many health problems in adulthood, including hypertension, arthritis, and limiting disabilities (Melhuish, 2012), which can again decrease potential earning power. Evidence also suggests that childhood poverty can limit future aspirations (Attree, 2006).

Returning to cross-national variation in poverty, data suggest that there is a large role for the state to play in reducing poverty, and one of the key ways this is achieved is through the use of the tax and benefit systems. As Figure 7.3 highlights, countries like the Scandinavian nations that have low levels of income poverty, as measured *after* taxes and benefit transfers, have similar levels of poverty if household income is calculated *before* taxes and transfers. The effect of the tax and benefit system is generally progressive; household incomes calculated after tax and benefit show lower levels of poverty across most countries – the issue becomes a matter of how successfully tax and benefits work to reduce poverty.

Outside of the state, the market and the family also have a role to play in determining a household's risk of poverty. While the market often provides routes out of poverty through the provision of employment, market inequalities can exacerbate poverty (see, e.g., Esping-Anderson, 1990), and where work contracts, it can create poverty. Further, work alone is not a guaranteed route to prosperity (discussed further later). Family structures are equally important in mediating risks of poverty; for example, poverty among the elderly is often reduced by living with extended family (Rendall and Speare, 1995). The role of the family often interacts with the role of the state and the role of the market in shaping the risks of poverty. For example, family composition can compensate for limited state spending on benefits (Tai and Treas, 2009) or impact on parent's ability to work by providing informal childcare (Wheelock and Jones, 2002).

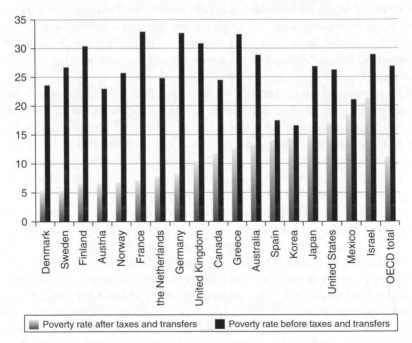

Figure 7.3 Percentage of people, pre tax and transfer and post tax and transfer, living below 50% of median incomes across the developed world, mid-2000s.
Source: Data from OECD (2012).

Women in families

Poverty has a feminine face around the world. Poverty rates across the EU, for example, show that in 2010 women were 9% more likely to be in poverty[5] across all 27 member countries (EUROSTAT, 2012). In the United States, 16.2% of all women live below their poverty threshold compared to 14% of men (2010 data, CPS, 2011). In the developing world, the UNDP estimates that women and girls account for 6 of every 10 of the world's poorest (UNDP, 2011). Women are also more likely to have experienced poverty at some stage of their lives, and are likely to have recurrent or longer spells of poverty (Lister, 2004a, p. 55).

Female poverty reflects the economic marginalization of women. As the UNDP puts it, "women perform 66 percent of the world's work, produce 50 percent of the food, but earn only 10 percent of the income and own only one percent of the property" (UNDP, 2011, p. 1). The reasons behind this are historically and culturally complex but generally include lower levels of employment, lower levels of wages, and higher levels of precarious employment in the informal sector employment (outside of government regulation) (UNIFEM, 2005, p. 2). In the United Kingdom, the gender pay gap was 9.1% (calculated hourly)[6] in 2011 (ONS, 2011b), while in the United States in 2009, it was 19.8% (calculated weekly) (US Bureau of Labor Statistics, 2010).

Female-headed families suffer a greater risk of poverty. Female-headed families can result from the death of a partner (especially in the global south), divorce, or births that occur outside of marriage. While these phenomena could result in either female- or male-headed single-parent families, the vast majority of single-parent families are headed by women; for example, in the United Kingdom in 2011, 92% of single-parent families were headed by women (ONS, 2012), while in the United States, 73% of nonhusband/wife families were headed by women (CPS, 2011). Single-parent households are exposed to greater risks of poverty perhaps because of the inevitable trade-off between earning and child caring. Using the official US poverty measure in 2010, for example, 34.2% of all people in female-headed families without spouses live below the poverty line, compared to 17.3% of people in male- headed households without a spouse and compared to 15.1% of all people (CPS, 2011). This relationship – between gender, single parenthood, and poverty – strongly affects childhood poverty rates (see Figure 7.4).

Poverty also affects women in male-headed households, and this may be somewhat obscured by the way we measure poverty. Poverty counts for *individuals* within households are calculated using *household* income, and rest on the heroic assumption that household income is shared evenly between all members of the household. This may result in "hidden poverty" (Lister, 2004a, p. 56) or people within otherwise non-poor families suffering poverty due to unequal distribution of household resources. Hidden poverty is widely regarded to be a female problem (Glendinning and Millar, 1987). Studies attempting to measure hidden poverty are few and far between, but some authors (such as Lundberg *et al.*, 1997, Ward-Batts, 2008) have found that in small case studies, households do not share money and resources equally, which may make household income an inappropriate way to estimate female poverty levels.

On top of intrahousehold economic marginalization, many studies note that women self-sacrifice, going without food, clothing, and warmth, to meet their families' needs first (Middleton *et al.*, 1994). Kabeer (1995) also found that women in Bangladesh will go without food to feed their husbands. Hidden female poverty therefore reflects

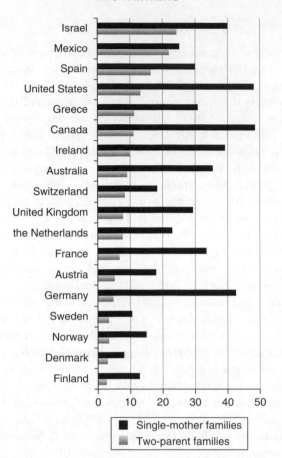

Figure 7.4 The percentage of children growing up in households below the 50% of median household income by family type, mid-2000s.
Source: Data from Luxembourg Income Studies (2012).

two concurrent phenomena: structural issues that reduce women's financial resources and create economic dependence and agentic issues surrounding women's willingness to sacrifice their own needs to meet their families' (Lister, 2004, p. 57).

Families affected by disability

Families affected by disability are more likely to suffer from poverty, and the relationship between the two issues is complex. The "social model" of disability suggests that a disability emerges from the interaction between a person's individual functioning and their social and built environment. For example, someone with mobility issues might not be disabled in a society where transport is made accessible to them, while in a different society the exact same impairment may create a severe disability. Under the social model,

> people are not identified as having a disability based upon a medical condition (rather by their) environment that erects barriers to their participation in the social and economic life of their communities.
>
> (Braithwaite and Mont, 2009, p. 220)

Families affected by disability are too often unable to participate in the economic life of their communities. They suffer from higher risks of poverty the world over, from Europe and Central Asia (Elwan, 1999, Braithwaite and Mont, 2009) to the United Kingdom where 9% of individuals without a disability live below the poverty line, compared to 11% of people with disabilities[7] (DWP, 2011).

The experience of poverty among families affected by disabilities is in part due to the extra costs of impairments and disabilities, such as paying for medication, necessary equipment, and installing adaptations in homes. It "seems obvious" (Braithwaite and Mont, 2009, p. 222) that the costs associated with avoiding deprivation are going to be higher for families affected by disability than those not affected by disability, or as Lister puts it, "an income of 'X' may be adequate for a non-disabled person but may mean a lack of capabilities and poverty for a disabled person" (2004a, p. 65).

But they are also in part due to the opportunity costs associated with the reduced ability to work. Disability can present a barrier to earning an adequate income, for both the person with a disability and the family members who may need to juggle work and caring commitments. People with disabilities are less likely to participate in the labor market; in the United Kingdom in 2001, for example, approximately 48% of the disabled population were economically inactive, compared to 15% of the non-disabled population (Smith and Tworney, 2002, p. 415). But disability also affects the labor market participation of the whole family; the same survey found that 31% of households containing a family member with a disability were workless, compared to 10% of families without a disabled member (Smith and Tworney, 2002, p. 415). Where people with disabilities are able to participate in the labor market, they often have substantially lower wages (Kidd et al., 2000, Schur et. al., 2009). While these lower rates of labor market participation and wages may in part be due to health problems or work-related impairments, there is much evidence to suggest that people with disabilities face very high levels of discrimination within the workplace (Schur et. al., 2009). Disabilities that face higher levels of social stigma are associated with lower levels of pay (Baldwin and Johnson, 2006), and employer discrimination often dictates outcomes for employees with disabilities (Schur et. al., 2009).

Disability-related poverty overlaps with female poverty, as the majority of people with disabilities are female (Lister, 2004, p. 64), and disabled women appear to have even worse labor market outcomes. For example, in the United Kingdom in 2001, 44% of men with disabilities were economically inactive compared to 52% of women with disabilities (Smith and Tworney, 2002, p. 415).

Living in Family Poverty

When a family finds itself in poverty, its experience and responses vary greatly. Lister (2004a) talks about four domains of response to poverty, ranging from the personal to the political and the everyday to the strategic (Figure 7.5). This section sketches out family responses across these domains, outlining how families "get by" and mediate the worst effects of poverty and how families attempt to get out of poverty by boosting family incomes as well as attempt to "get back at" and "get organized" against their situations. For brevity, it will largely use the United States and the United Kingdom as case studies.

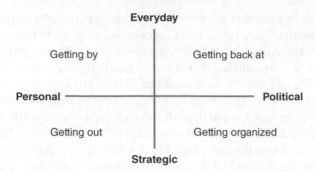

Figure 7.5 Adaptation of Lister's (2004a) model of understanding responses to poverty.

Getting by

The art of "getting by" and making ends meet requires balancing limited resources with family demands. It requires attempts to both increase family resources *and* decrease consumption. This delicate, and often complicated, balancing requires immense financial management and budgeting skills.

Low incomes often mean that family budgets are stretched and meticulously managed. Priorities are determined and money is set aside to meet them, so that wages and benefit payments are often "spent" before they even arrive. Women normally take on the role of managing extremely tight family budgets (Pahl, 1989) and, as discussed earlier, often cut back on their own consumption first. Spending priorities of low-income households generally include meeting housing costs and paying essential bills like electricity, followed by food and other discretionary spending such as clothing (see, e.g., Farrell and O'Connor, 2003). However, unexpected expenditures, like replacing a broken fridge and paying debt, often interfere with such well-ordered priorities (Farrell and O'Connor, 2003).

Food is often purchased on the first day that wages or benefits arrive (Dowler, 1997), and a range of purchasing and consumption strategies are employed to stretch out the pantry. Using discount stores, shopping at many different stores, taking advantage of money-off specials, and purchasing exactly enough of the same few items that you know your family will eat are common approaches (Wiig and Smith, 2009). While buying in bulk might seem sensible to reduce costs, often bulk purchasing is difficult for low-income families; in the United Kingdom, buying a little and often is one tactic to ensure family members do not casually consume what needs to last (Dobson *et al.*, 1995). In the United States, many bulk stores do not accept food stamps (Wiig and Smith, 2009) or require up-front membership fees. While cutting back on food is not the most desired way of coping, food expenditure is often reduced because of necessity, with, for example, "potluck stew" (made with whatever is left in the cupboard), allowing families to pay bills (Dowler, 1997). One study of the dynamics of food expenditure following an increase in disposable income for low-income families found that

> food shopping became more spontaneous, less frequent, as households started to bulk buy, and was bought from better quality outlets. …quantity increased first, followed by quality as households' incomes increased. Meals became healthier and more well-balanced, with the introduction of more meat and fresh fruit and vegetables.
>
> (Farrell and O'Connor, 2003, p. 5)

Budgeting strategies are influenced by the benefit system with which a family lives. In the United States, the monthly "food stamp cycle" can lead to a feast at the beginning of the month and a famine toward the end of the month and can alter family members' metabolisms (Dinour, Bergen, and Yeh, 2007). Food stamps are occasionally traded in order to cover other household expenditure but seldom go unused, while the annual Earned Income Tax Credit payment is frequently used to pay off credit card debts (Duerr, 1995, Leibman, 1999). In the United Kingdom, fortnightly benefit payments mean a more condensed spending cycle; however, the payment of different benefits at different times, especially universal child benefit payments, enables different spending strategies (Walker, Middleton, and Thomas, 1994).

Benefit payments can be the main source of income for families living below the poverty line – however, rarely are they enough to lift families out of poverty. While there have been some arguments suggesting that receipt of benefits creates a culture of dependency, so that "getting by" requires an adaptation to a benefit "lifestyle" (Murray, 1984; Mead, 1993), this belief rests on two assumptions that have not been proven. Firstly, it assumes families respond directly and only to the incentives or disincentives created by benefit regimes, and secondly, it assumes the receipt of benefits, and the poverty that this is said to cause, is persistent (Gordon and Spicker, 1999, p. 36). The evidence that this happens on a large scale is limited and contested (Walker, 1994). Research into poverty dynamics, suggests most spells in poverty tend to be short (Jenkins 2011, Walker 1994) and families respond to competing incentives, such as a desire to avoid the stigma associated with receiving "welfare". This stigma often prevents families claiming benefits where they can possibly scrape by without them. In the United Kingdom, the take-up rates of income support are lower than the take-up of council tax benefits among pensioners partly because of the greater stigma associated with income support (Hernandez, Pudney, and Hancock, 2007). In the United States, stigma reduces the take-up of Medicaid (Stuber and Kronebush, 2004).

Budgeting also involves balancing competing demands from different household members. As discussed earlier, women typically treat their children's and partner's demands as a higher priority than their own. Children's needs regarding education are often regarded as a very high priority (Middleton, Ashworth, and Walker, 1994). Alongside this, children's need not to be singled out as different from their peers, especially when it comes to wearing branded clothing and shoes, can also be prioritized (Hamilton, 2012).

Children themselves are often acutely aware of their family's financial situation and will limit their consumption (and desired consumption) accordingly. They limit on family budgets and often self-exclude, by, for example, not taking home notes about costly school trips (Ridge, 2002) or not asking for gifts on special occasions (Attree, 2006). Children have their own ways of managing within tight budgets, often working part-time jobs, relying on extended family support, or saving up to buy their own consumer goods (Ridge, 2002; Attree, 2006). Regardless, children in low-income families can still place demands on family budgets that cannot be met, causing stress and conflict. Children report a repertoire of techniques, from persistent asking and reframing requests as school related (Ridge, 2002) to more confrontational techniques like tantrums (Walker *et al.*, 1994). Poverty is acutely felt by parents who cannot afford to say "yes" to a child who refuses to take "no" for an answer.

Getting out

Alongside these time-consuming and stressful strategies to get by while living in poverty, families also negotiate the difficult task of "getting out" of poverty. Research from both the United States and the United Kingdom shows that the state of poverty is dynamic and that very few families remain poor forever, challenging the idea of an underclass.

In the United Kingdom, for example, longitudinal data show that between 1991 and 2003, just under half of the British population were affected by poverty at some point,[8] which is almost double the proportion of people affected by poverty in any given year. And the same holds for dependent children in families; around one-half were living in poverty at some stage between 1991 and 2003 (Jenkins, 2011, p. 217), with all of the subsequent implications for their development discussed earlier. This means that there is a fairly large "churn" of poor families, with family incomes moving in and out of poverty in different years. The majority of poverty spells are short, with the length of time in poverty somewhere between 1 and 2 years; however, around one in ten people spends at least 8 out of 10 years poor (Jenkins, 2011, p. 229). Relatively long spells in poverty tend to be experienced by single-parent households and the elderly (Jenkins, 2011, p. 17).

Increased earnings by the head-of-household account for the vast majority of poverty exits, but many poverty exits are also precipitated by income from second earners as well as demographic changes. Changes to household labor earnings accounted for 59% of poverty exits between 1991 and 2004, with other income changes and demographic events making up the rest (Jenkins, 2011, p. 245). On the flip side, demographic changes, like divorce or having children, as well as decreased earnings, accounted for half of all entries to poverty over the same time (Jenkins, 2011, p. 262).

Using data from the Panel Study of Income Dynamics (PSID), Rank and Hirschl (2001) suggest a little over half of American adults will have experienced poverty[9] by the age of 65. As the individual risks of any adult entering poverty were around 3% in the 1980s and 4% in the 1990s (McKernan and Ratcliff, 2002), this suggests poverty in the United States is just as dynamic as it is in the United Kingdom. The risks of entering poverty are higher for women, people in female-headed households, people with lower levels of education, and blacks and Hispanics (McKernan and Ratcliff, 2002).

The duration of poverty in the United States also appears to be short. Bane and Ellwood (1986) and Stevens (1999) estimate that around half of the people who enter poverty remain poor for 1 year, while around three-quarters remain poor for less than 4 years. Again, demographics matter in the duration of poverty; poverty spells for blacks and Hispanics are more often longer than they are for whites and for individuals from female-headed households than couple-headed households (Stevens, 1999). Welfare reform in 1996, however, limited the lifetime receipt of benefits for needy families to 60 months.

Labor market events play a significant role in both entry into and exit from poverty in the United States. Reduced family income, including job loss and reduced earnings, account for about half of all entries to poverty (Bane and Ellwood, 1986). Moving from a couple- to a single-parent-headed household and the birth of a child also play a role (Bane and Ellwood, 1986; McKernan and Ratcliff, 2002) but far less frequently. Relatedly, increases in earnings account for almost two-thirds of exits from poverty (Bane and Ellwood, 1986; McKernan and Ratcliff, 2005), but so too does shifts from female-headed households into a couple and increased educational attainment (Bane and Ellwood, 1986; McKernan and Ratcliff, 2005).

While employment is one of the key routes out of poverty, work is not necessarily a guaranteed route out. In 2004, for example, 83.4% of the UK poor and 62.2% of the US poor lived in households headed by an employed person (LIS, 2012). The issue is not that the poor do not work, rather that the labor market cannot guarantee an income above the poverty line. Low-paid jobs, part-time and insecure employment, and a lack of career progression all combine to produce working poverty. Quite often, people boost their incomes by working simultaneously in a number of low-paying jobs. While some people who gain a foothold in work progress rapidly, low-paid work typically offers little security and few prospects (Holtzer and Lalonde, 2000). Indeed, it is likely that the pattern of recurrent spells of poverty is often shaped by a life spent on the margins of work (Walker, 1994). Aside from low incomes, work can generate other insecurities; waiting a month for the first paycheck without savings to help tide your family over, mounting childcare bills, a lack of certainty about in-work benefits, and, in the United States, the end of health coverage can all make taking low-paid, part-time work a risky business.

Means-tested and out of work benefits can also make taking employment tricky. In the United Kingdom, for example, some benefits are conditional on recipients not working, while others are withdrawn sharply as income increases. This may create a conundrum where some families may not be financially better-off for working (see, e.g., CSJ, 2009). Indeed, after the costs of working, such as transportation, are deducted, families may be financially worse off for taking employment. Claimants are therefore faced with being penalized by very high withdrawal rates and working for very little or no financial gain, or being criminalized for not reporting their earnings or not taking work, thereby confirming to themselves and others that they have joined Mead's (1993) dependency culture.

For low-income, single-parent families, child support from nonresident parents can be a significant source of income (Ha, Cancian, and Meyer, 2007). However, many nonresident parents are themselves affected by poverty; the US evidence shows that the nonresident fathers of children in receipt of benefits often have very low earnings and unstable employment patterns (Cancian and Myer, 2004). These fathers are therefore less able and likely to pay child support (see, e.g., Sorensen and Zibman, 2001). Claiming support from nonresident parents can be fraught with difficulties, particularly where abuse or matters of child custody arise.

Getting back at

The extent to which lower-income families engaged in illicit coping strategies is contested; however, it is indisputable that some do. For some people, the need to support a family means they do not declare income to tax or welfare authorities or they engage in other illegal means of raising income: theft, peddling drugs, prostitution, and robbery (Kempson, 1996; Edin *et al.*, 2000).

There is, however, some debate about how much such illegal activity – and especially "benefit fraud" – is actually an attempt to "get by" and cope. Gilliom (2001), for example, notes that low-income mothers in Appalachia use age-old survival tactics like selling haircuts to get by, and that this has simply continued despite newer welfare regimes which have rendered such activities illegal. They regard their actions necessary to survive. Jordan (1996) talks of benefit fraud in the United Kingdom as a type of everyday resistance, which families choose to engage in as a form of compensation for their social marginalization. The extent to which benefit fraud is an attempt "to get" by or an attempt to "get back" probably depends on the individual family and their circumstances more than either theory could capture.

Likewise, while there is much debate around the relationship between poverty rates and neighborhood crime, the general conclusion is that higher levels of poverty lead to higher levels of neighborhood crime (Hipp and Yates, 2011). According to Wilson (1997), when there are extremely high levels of poverty in an area, crime rates increase exponentially. He posited a downward spiral within deprived communities; once crime becomes rife, a neighborhood acquires a reputation that increases the stigma for law-abiding citizens (Wilson, 1997). Indeed, neighborhoods can acquire negative labels even in the absence of crime merely on account of the fact that they house disproportionate numbers of low-income families (Power and Tunstall, 1995). While there is limited evidence to suggest that such extreme downward spirals are common (Hipp and Yates, 2011), community poverty, crime, and ghettoization may lead to disinvestment, where retailers and employers leave an area, decreasing local property values and employment opportunities. However, it is worth noting that the reverse process – gentrification – common in urban areas the world over, sees cycles of investments that often crowd out low-income families from neighborhoods as prices increase (Atkinson and Bridge, 2005).

Illicit activity may be a symptom of a family's failure to cope under the stress of poverty. People who are financially desperate may be more vulnerable than most to swindles and fraud or to being drawn into criminal activity. Also, a proportion will be further burdened by illiteracy, disability, mental illness, and/or substance abuse and become trapped in a vicious cycle that demands ever-greater coping expertise from people who are the least able to cope (Kempson, 1996; Ramey and Keltner, 2002). Some crimes, such as Medicaid fraud in the United States, can be an institutionalized effort by businesses that exploit the poor to boost revenue.

Getting organized

Collective action against poverty, while necessary to tackle this decidedly *social* problem, is not especially common. This is partly because the collective identity needed to underpin such a movement is lacking. Identifying and collectively organizing as "the poor" is difficult; being "poor" is a stigmatizing and shameful identity actively rejected by many families and, as noted earlier, is often a temporary experience. As Lister (2004b) put it, such collective identity

> is difficult when "poor" represents a shameful economic condition to be endured rather than an individual, never mind collective, identity to be embraced. Disabled people and gays and lesbians have been able to transform a negatively ascribed category into positive affirmation of a collective identity as the basis of a politics of recognition of their own difference. But "proud to be poor" is not a banner under which many want

to march. And the last thing people in poverty want is to be seen as different (http://www.theguardian.com/comment/story/0,,1352913,00.html).

Nonetheless, since there is no singular experience of poverty and people who are poor are heterogeneous in their responses, collective actions by "the poor" against their economic and political marginalization exist and have been successful in many cases.

Firstly, economically speaking, the existence of food cooperatives, credit unions, community banking, and community development initiatives demonstrates that collective agency can emerge spontaneously or be kindled in poorer communities (Holman, 1998). These can both mitigate the consequences of poverty and sometimes work to lift families out of poverty through the provision of resources.

While the collective actions of people living in poverty may not fall "under the banner of poverty", as Lister (2004b) put it, there are a number of examples where people have organized around poverty- and income-related issues. For example, Lister (2004a, p.155) cites the birth of the Welfare Rights movement in the United Kingdom in the 1960s as an example of a grassroots movement of people campaigning for rights to social security and against poverty. In the United States, movements like Justice for Janitors, which campaigns for better wages, better health care, and full-time employment, represent a successful model of collective action against shared economic marginalization (Savage, 2006).

Conclusion

Poverty is best conceptualized as the experience of living on a low income. It is a diverse experience structured by geography, duration, social institutions, and demographics but also shaped by the agency of families themselves. While poverty is often measured through families' incomes, the experience of poverty transcends simple home economics and affects all aspects of their life, from dignity to the ability to maintain life itself.

The geography of poverty matters. Families in poverty in the global south suffer acute deprivations due to a lack of financial resources. They have higher levels of mortality, often from preventable causes, and speak of the soul-crushing burden of living in poverty. In the global north, while the physical consequences of poverty might be different, families speak of similar humiliations, of not being able to participate in the everyday life of their communities and the profound impacts this has on their overall sense of well-being.

The risks of poverty are not shared equally across all families, with institutions and social norms strongly shaping their prospect of poverty. Families with young children and the elderly are more likely to be poor, but to a large extent, this depends on the benefit system of their country and its political willingness to provide a safety net to protect the young and old. Families headed by women are also more likely to be poor, but again, this risk can be shaped by public policy, labor market structures, and gender norms. Families affected by disabilities are also at a higher risk of living below the poverty line, with discrimination and impairments reducing their labor market outcomes.

Poverty often defines the way families live, function, and operate. The art of "getting by" requires meticulous budgeting and balancing family members' needs.

But families are not doomed to forever be "poor". Most spells in poverty are short-lived and families can and do get out. While work is a common route out for many families, it is not guaranteed; low wage, insecure, and temporary employment all conspire against families in poverty. The extent to which families engage in illicit coping behaviors and what to make of them is debateable. Finally, poverty may be a social issue, attempts to mobile as the "poor" for collective action are rare – however, they are often very successful.

Notes

1 Fifty percent of median household income after transfers and tax, equivalized (adjusted to reflect household size).
2 Counted as the number of people living in households earning below 60% of median income, after tax and transfers, adjusted to reflect household size. While most OECD and international data uses a 50% median threshold, within the European Union and the United Kingdom, 60% is the preferred threshold.
3 Canada proves a notable exception, where levels of poverty among the elderly are substantially less, despite comparatively high levels of poverty.
4 The denominator is not a linear reflection of family size, and poverty counts are sensitive to the nonlinear denominator – or equivalization scale – chosen.
5 Defined in the European Union as living in a household with below 60% median income.
6 Calculated as median full-time hourly earnings, excluding overtime.
7 50% median household income, calculated after tax and transfers and before housing costs.
8 Living in households with incomes below 60% of household median, as commonly defined in the United Kingdom, using British Household Panel Survey data.
9 Using the official US Poverty threshold, using PSID data.

References

Alcock, P. (2008) Poverty and social exclusion, in *The Student's Companion to Social Policy* (eds P. Alcock, M. May, and K. Rowlington), Blackwell Publishing, pp.131–138.

Atkinson, R. and Bridge, G. (2005) *Gentrification in a Global Context: The New Urban Colonialism*, Routledge, London.

Attree, P. (2006) The social costs of child poverty: a systematic review of the qualitative evidence. *Children and Society*, 20, 54–66.

Baldwin, M. and Johnson. W. (2006) A critical review of studies of discrimination against workers with disabilities, in *Handbook on the Economics of Discrimination* (ed. W. Rodgers), Edgar Publishing, Northampton, pp. 119–160.

Bane, M. and Ellwood, D. (1986) Slipping into and out of poverty: the dynamics of spells. *Journal of Human Resources*, 21 (1), 1–23.

Banerjee, A. and Duflo, E. (2007) The economic lives of the poor. *Journal of Economic Perspectives*, 21 (1), 141–167.

Baulch, B. (1996) The new poverty agenda: a disputed consensus. *IDS Bulletin*, 27, 1–10.

Braithwaite, J. and Mont, D. (2009) Disability and poverty: A survey of World Bank poverty assessments and implications. *ALTER, European Journal of Disability Research*, 3, 219–232.

Cancian, M. and Meyer, D. (2004) Fathers of children receiving welfare: can they provide more child support? *Social Service Review*, 78, 179–206.

CPS (2011) Annual Social and Economic Supplement, Age and Sex of All People, Family Members and Unrelated Individuals Iterated by Income-to-Poverty Ratio and Race (online), http://www.census.gov/hhes/www/cpstables/032011/pov/new01_100.htm (accessed April 20, 2012).

CSJ (2009) *Dynamic Benefits: Towards Welfare the Works*, Centre for Social Justice, London.

Czech Presidency of the European Union (2009) Where We Live – What We Want: The Report of the 8th European Meeting of People Experiencing Poverty, May 15–16, 2009, Brussels (online), http://www.eapn.eu/images/stories/docs/eapn-report-2009-en-web2-light-version.pdf (accessed April 10, 2012).

Dahl, G. and Lochner, L. (2008) The impact of family income on achievement: evidence from the earned income tax credit. NBER working paper No. 14599, National Bureau of Economic Research, Cambridge, MA.

Deepa, N., Patel, R., Schafft, K. *et al.* (2000) *Voices of the Poor: Can Anyone Hear Us?* Oxford University Press, New York.

Department for Education (2007) *The Costs of Schooling 2007*, DfE, London.

Dinour. L., Bergen, D., and Yeh, M. (2007) The food insecurity–obesity paradox: a review of the literature and the role food stamps may play. *Journal of American Dietetic Association*, 107, 1952–1961.

Dobson, B., Beardsworth, A., Keil, T., and Walker, R. (1995) *Diet, Choice and Poverty*, Family Policy Studies Centre, London.

Dowler, E. (1997) Budgeting for food on a low income in the UK: the case of lone-parent families. *Food Policy*, 22 (5), 405–417.

Duncan, G. and Brooks-Gunn, J. (1997) *Consequences of Growing Up Poor*, Russel Sage Foundation, New York.

Duerr B. (1995) *Faces of Poverty: Portraits of Women and Children on Welfare*, Oxford University Press, New York.

DWP (2011) Households Below Average Income (HBAI) (online), http://research.dwp.gov.uk/asd/index.php?page=hbai (accessed February 10, 2012).

Edin, K. (2001) Hearing on Welfare and Marriage Issues – Testimony Before the Subcommittee on Human Resources of the House Committee on Ways and Means (online), www.gouse.gov/ways_means/humres/107cong/5–22–01/5–22edin.htm (accessed January1, 2002).

Edin, K., Lein, L., Nelson, T., and Clampet-Lundquest, S. (2000) Talking to low-income fathers. *Joint Centre for Poverty Research University of Chicago, Newsletter*, 4 (2).

Ellwood, D. (1988) *Poor Support*, Basic Books, New York.

Elwan, A. (1999) Poverty and disability: a survey of the literature. SP discussion paper No. 9932, The World Bank, December 1999.

Esping-Anderson, G. (1990) *Three Worlds of Welfare Capitalism*, Polity Press, Cambridge.

Eurostat (2012) Income and Living Condition Tables (online), http://epp.eurostat.ec.europa.eu/portal/page/portal/income_social_inclusion_living_conditions/data/main_tables (accessed April 10, 2012).

Farrell, C. and O'Connor, W. (2003) *Low-Income Families and Household Spending: Research Report 192*, Department of Work and Pensions, London.

Fisher, G. (1992) The development and history of poverty thresholds. *Social Security Bulletin*, 55 (40), 3–14.

Gordon, D. and Spicker, P. (1999) *The International Glossary on Poverty*, Zed Books, London.

Gilliom, J. (2001) *Overseers of the Poor*, University of Chicago Press, London.

Glendinning, C. and Millar, J. (1987) *Women and Poverty in Britain*, Wheatsheaf Books, Brighton.

Ha, Y., Cancian, M. and Meyer, D.R. (2007) The Regularity of Child Support and Its Contribution to the Regularity of Income. Report to Wisconsin Department of Workforce Development, University of Wisconsin–Madison, Madison.

Hamilton, K. (2012) Low-income families and coping through brands: inclusion or stigma? *Sociology*, 46 (1), 74–90.

Hernandez, M., Pudney, S. and Hancock, R. (2007) The welfare cost of means-testing: pensioner participation in income support. *Journal of Applied Econometrics*, 22 (3), 581–598.

Hipp, R. and Yates, D. (2011) Ghettos, thresholds, and crime: does concentrated poverty really have an accelerating increasing effect on crime? *Criminology*, 49 (4), 955–990.

Holman, B. (1998) *Faith in the Poor*, Lion Publishing, Oxford.

Holtzer, H. and LaLonde, R.J. (2000) Employment and job stability among less skilled workers, in *Finding Jobs: Work and Welfare Reform* (eds D.E. Card and R.M. Blank), Russell Sage Foundation, New York.

IFS (2010) Poverty and Inequality Data Tables (online), www.ifs.org.uk/bns/bn19figs.zip (accessed February 10, 2012).

Jordan, B. (1996) *A Theory of Poverty and Social Exclusion*, Polity Press, Cambridge.

Jenkins, S. (2011) *Changing Fortunes: Income Mobility and Poverty Dynamics in Britain*, Oxford University Press, Oxford.

Kabeer, N. (1995) *Reversed Realities; Gender Hierarchies and Development Thought*, Verso, London.

Kempson, E. (1996) *Life on a Low Income*, York Publishing Services, York.

Kidd, M., Sloane, P. and Ferko, I. (2000) Disability and the labour market: an analysis of British males. *Journal of Health Economics*, 19 (6), 961–981.

Leibman, J. (1999) *Lessons About Tax-benefit Integration From the US Earned Income Tax Credit Experience*, York Publishing Services, York.

Lister, R. (2004a) *Poverty*, Polity Press, London.

Lister, R. (2004b) No More of "the Poor." *The Guardian* (Nov 17).

Lundberg, S., Pollak, R. and Wales, T. (1997) Do husbands and wives pool their resources? Evidence from the United Kingdom child benefit. *Journal of Human Resources*, 32 (3), 463–480.

Luxembourg Income Studies (2012) (online) http://www.lisdatacenter.org/lis-ikf-webapp/app/search-ikf-figures (accessed May 20, 2012).

Mack, J. and Lansley, S. (1985) *Poor Britain*, George Allen & Unwin, London.

McKernan, S. and Ratcliffe, C. (2002) *Transition Events in the Dynamics of Poverty*, US Department of Health and Human Services, Washington.

McKernan, S. and Ratcliffe, C. (2005) Events that trigger poverty entries and exits. *Social Science Quarterly*, 86 (s1), 1146–1169.

Mead, L. (1993) *The New Politics of Poverty: The Nonworking Poor in America*, Basic Books, New York.

Melhuish, E. (2012) The impact of poverty on child development and adult outcomes: the importance of early years education, in *Ending Child Poverty by 2012: Progress Made and Lessons Learned* (ed. CPAG), CPAG, London.

Middleton, S., Ashworth, K. and Walker, R. (1994) *Family Fortunes*, CPAG, London.

Moore, J. (1989) The end of the line for poverty. Speech to the Greater London Area, CPC, May 11, 1989.

Murray, C. (1984) *Losing Ground: American Social Policy 1950–1980*, Basic Books, New York.

OECD (2010) PISA At a Glance (online), http://www.oecd.org/dataoecd/31/28/46660259.pdf (accessed May 25, 2012).

OECD (2012) OECD.StatExtract (online), http://stats.oecd.org/# (accessed May 25, 2012).

ONS (2011a) Family Spending, 2011 (online), http://www.ons.gov.uk/ons/rel/family-spending/family-spending/family-spending-2011-edition/index.html (accessed May 15, 2012).

ONS (2011b) Annual Survey of Hours and Earnings (online), http://www.ons.gov.uk/ons/publications/re-reference-tables.html?edition=tcm%3A77–235202 (accessed May 10, 2012).

ONS (2012) Families and Households, 2001 to 2011 (online), http://www.ons.gov.uk/ons/dcp171778_251357.pdf (accessed April 19, 2012).

Oppenheim, C. and Harker, L. (1996) *Poverty: The Facts Revised and Updated*, CPAG, London.

Pahl, J. (1989) *Money and Marriage*, Macmillan, Basingstoke.

Piachaud D. (1981) Peter Townsend and the Holy Grail. *New Society* (Sep 10), pp. 419–421.

Platt, L. (2005) *Discovering Child Poverty: The Creation of a Policy Agenda from 1800 to the Present*, Policy Press, Bristol.

Power, A. and Tunstall, R. (1995) *Swimming Against the Tide: Polarisation or Progress on 20 Unpopular Council Estates*, Joseph Rowntree Foundation, York.

Ridge, T. (2002) *Childhood Poverty and Social Exclusion: From a Child's Perspective*, The Policy Press, Bristol.

Ramey, S. and Keltner, B. (2002) Welfare reform and the vulnerability of mothers with intellectual disabilities (mild mental retardation). *Focus*, 22 (1), 82–86.

Rank, M. and Hirschl, T. (2001) The occurrence of poverty across the life cycle: evidence from the PSID. *Journal of Policy Analysis and Management*, 20 (4), 737–755.

Rendall, M. and Speare, A. (1995) Elderly poverty alleviation through living with family. *Journal of Population Economics*, 8 (4), 383–405.

Rowntree, S. (1901) *Poverty: A Study of Town Life*, The Policy Press, Bristol.

Savage, L. (2006) Justice for janitors: scales of organizing and representing workers. *Antipode*, 38 (3), 645–666.

Schur, L., Kruse, D., Blasi, J. and Blank, P. (2009) Is disability disabling in all Workplaces? Workplace disparities and corporate culture. *Industrial Relations*, 48 (3), 381–410.

Sen, A. (1979) Issues in the measurement of poverty. *Scandinavian Journal of Economics*, 81 (2), 287–307.

Sen, A. (1981) *Poverty and Famines: An Essay on Entitlement and Deprivation*, Oxford University Press, Oxford.

Sen, A. (1985) A sociological approach to the measurement of poverty: a reply to Professor Peter Townsend. *Oxford Economic Papers* (37), 669–676.

Smith, A. and Twomey, B. (2002) Labour market experiences of people with disabilities, in *ONS Labour Market Trends*, pp. 415–427.

Sorensen, E. and Zibman, C. (2001) Getting to know poor fathers who do not pay child support. *Social Service Review*, 75, 420–434.

Stevens, A. (1999) Climbing out of poverty, falling back in: measuring the persistence of poverty over multiple spells. *Journal of Human Resources*, 34 (9), 557–588.

Stuber, J. and Kronebusch, K. (2004) Stigma and other determinants of participation in TANF and Medicaid. *Journal of Policy Analysis and Management*, 23 (3), 509–530.

Tai, T. and Treas, J. (2009) Does household composition explain welfare regime poverty risks for older adults and other household members? *Journal of Gerontology: Social Sciences*, 64B (6), 777–787.

Townsend, P. (1979) *Poverty in the United Kingdom*, Allen Lane, Harmondsworth.

Townsend, P. (1985) A sociological approach to the measurement of poverty: a rejoiner to Professor Amartya Sen. *Oxford Economic Papers* (37), 659–668.

UNDP (2011) Fast Facts: Gender Equality and the UNDP (online), http://www.undp.org/content/dam/undp/library/corporate/fast-facts/english/FF-Gender-Equality-and-UNDP.pdf (accessed May 20, 2012).

UNIFEM (2005) *Progress of the World's Women: Women, Work and Poverty*, United Nations Development Fund for Women, New York.

US Department of Labor Statistics (2010) Highlights of Women's Earnings in 2009 (online), http://www.bls.gov/cps/cpswom2009.pdf (accessed February 9, 2012).

Walker, R. (1994) *Poverty Dynamics*, Avebury, Aldershot.

Walker, R., Middleton, S. and Thomas, M. (1994) How mothers use child benefit, in *Family Fortunes: Pressures on Parents and Children in the 1990s* (eds S. Middleton, K. Ashworth, and R. Walker), CPAG, London.

Walker, R., Ashworth, K., Kellard, K. *et al.* (1994) "Pretty, pretty, please" just like a parrot: persuasion strategies used by children and young people, in *Family Fortunes: Pressures on Parents and Children in the 1990s* (eds S. Middleton, K. Ashworth, and R. Walker), CPAG, London.

Ward-Batts, J. (2008) Out of the wallet and into the purse: using microdata to test income pooling. *Journal of Human Resources*, 43 (2), 325–351.

Wheelcock, J. and Jones, K. (2002) "Grandparents are the next best thing": informal childcare for working parents in urban Britain. *Journal of Social Policy*, 31 (3), 441–463.

Wiig, K. and Smith, C. (2009) The art of grocery shopping on a food stamp budget: factors influencing the food choices of low-income women as they try to make ends meet. *Public Health Nutrition*, 12 (10), 1726–1734.

Wilson, W. (1997) *When Work Disappears: The World of the New Urban Poor*, Vintage Books, New York.

World Bank (2006) Malnutrition Prevalence, Weight for age (% of Children under 5) (online), http://data.worldbank.org/indicator/SH.STA.MALN.ZS (accessed May 21, 2012).

World Bank (2008) Povcal (online), http://iresearch.worldbank.org/PovcalNet/index.htm?1 (accessed May 21, 2012).

World Health Organisation (2012) Global World Health Observatory Data Repository (online), http://apps.who.int/ghodata/?vid=180# (accessed May 20, 2012).

8

Transnational Families

LORETTA BALDASSAR, MAJELLA KILKEY, LAURA MERLA
AND RAELENE WILDING

Transnational Families: Introduction and the *Mobility* Turn

The original *Companion to the Sociology of Families*, published a decade ago, did not contain a chapter on transnational families – evidence of the dramatic expansion of this family type. And yet, it would be fairly safe to presume that nearly every reader of this 2014 edition has some direct experience with this kind of family form. Such has been the pace of social change, linked to the intensification of globalization processes that has profoundly influenced family life.

Whether pushed or pulled out of homelands in search of safe asylum, better economic futures, or improved lifestyles and whether chosen or enforced by restrictive migration laws, increasing numbers of people are separated from their families by distance and national borders. Even those family members who *stay behind* become part of social relationships stretched across time and place, though they might never actually move at all. In addition to migrant families, a growing number of other *types* of families are being defined by their experiences of mobility, including commuter, fly-in-fly-out, frequent flyer, expatriate, and even the multilocal families created after divorce and separation.

It must be noted that transnational families are not new. Throughout history, there have been many and varied forms resulting from all types of mobility including emigration and immigration (e.g., of wet nurses and artisans), colonial expansion and exploration, and the separation of family members through entry into religious orders, the custom of apprenticeship, and even the use of boarding schools (Yeates, 2009). Rather, it is the scale of mobility that has been radically transformed as well as the revolution in travel and communication technologies. Whereas in the past transnational family members would stay in touch only by long-awaited letters that traveled by sea, today, people can be *virtually* constantly present in each other's lives.

The Wiley Blackwell Companion to the Sociology of Families, First Edition.
Edited by Judith Treas, Jacqueline Scott, and Martin Richards.
© 2014 John Wiley & Sons Ltd. Published 2017 by John Wiley & Sons Ltd.

Mobility has become such a feature of contemporary life that it has been touted as a new paradigm for the social sciences (Urry, 2000). Traditionally the domain of scholars working on migration and demography, the study of transnational mobility is now increasingly relevant to other areas of study, including family studies. The notion of *transnational families* has been developed as a way of conceptualizing how families are affected by mobility (Bryceson and Vuorela, 2002; Baldassar, Baldock, and Wilding, 2007). This chapter provides an overview of current thinking, incorporating new research results and emerging debates, in this burgeoning field of transnational family research.

We begin with three evocative case studies, from our own research, that capture something of the diversity of experiences of transnational families as well as their interconnections across the globe.

Case studies: Transnational Families and the Global Circulation of Care

Every day during his lunch break at around 1pm, Alberto, who lives in Perth, Australia, phones his 85-year-old father, Angelo, who lives in Rome, Italy. Angelo, who is not in the best of health, is usually sitting at the kitchen table having his morning coffee and bread roll. "It'll only be 6am in Italy, but Dad will always be waiting for my call," Alberto explains. Since Alberto's mother's sudden and unexpected death a year ago, Alberto, an only child, has tried to manage his father's increasing care needs from a distance. He took 6 weeks unpaid leave from work to travel to Italy to arrange the funeral for his mother and put in place care supports for his father. Both Alberto and Angelo see aged care facilities as a last resort option; they are expensive and have a social stigma that reflects badly on families. Angelo wishes to remain living in his own home for as long as he can. Moving to Australia is not an option because of Angelo's failing health; furthermore, aged migration to Australia is costly with prohibitive requirements. Given the aged care regimes in both countries, father and son adopted the commonest solution and hired a domestic worker, Maria, to work from 9 to 5 each day, preparing lunch and dinner, doing the cleaning and shopping and taking Alberto to his medical visits. Maria has agreed to move into the spare room as a live-in carer if Angelo's health deteriorates. A long-time family friend, Nadia, the daughter of Angelo's old friend and neighbor, Nello, sets up a Skype every Sunday when she visits her father (who lives next door). Alberto feels this is the best way to "get a thorough update." Nello has a live-in carer, Stella, who is also on hand at nights if an emergency arises. Alberto plans to spend all his recreation leave in Italy, putting some financial strain on his family in Perth, but fortunately his wife is supportive. Alberto's daughter, Alana, is planning to visit her grandfather while on an exchange student trip to Europe later in the year.

* * * * *

Every Saturday and Sunday, at around 6am, Maria phones her 10-year-old son, Diego, in the Dominican Republic. She arrived in Rome a year ago on a tourist visa to visit her 18-year-old daughter who had traveled to Italy a year earlier. Maria planned to find work as a domestic and help support her daughter to continue studying and also raise enough money to bring Diego to Italy. In the meantime,

Diego lives with his grandmother Lucia, Maria's mother. Twelve people currently live in Lucia's crowded house, including her frail partner Arturo, two of Maria's brothers, their partners and children, and Maria's sister Anna's three children. Anna is a domestic employee in the United States. Maria and Anna call Lucia a few times a week to talk to (and discuss) their children, exchange support with their mother, and talk to other family members present at the time of their call. The two sisters are also in regular contact with their oldest sister, Teresa, who lives in Belgium with her Spanish husband and their three children, and the three women send monthly remittances to their mother. In spite of the distance, Teresa plays a central role in her extended family and is considered by all as the head of the household that is stretched across thousands of kilometers and several countries. Teresa checks with her brothers and sisters-in-law that Arturo, who suffers from diabetes and has lost his sight, takes his medicines and eats properly, and sends emergency remittances when a specific need arises. She visits her family every year, and during these visits she works with her brothers on the renovation of the family house.

* * * * *

Every day after work, Stella calls her 40-year-old daughter and two small grandchildren in Poland. Stella left Poland for Rome in 1999 as an undocumented migrant, before Poland joined the EU (2004). Her move was prompted by the loss of her nursing job in Poland. She had separated from her husband some years earlier. He had been working intermittently in Germany, and they had grown apart during his absences. Stella often reflects on how hard it was to stay in touch back then, even though the distance was not so great. Her two children were grown when she left and really did not need her to be there for them. The money she could send back to them was more useful. Stella quickly found work as a live-in carer for Nello, whose only child Nadia lives in Florence, a 2 h train ride away. Stella is missing seeing her grandchildren grow up and sometimes asks Nadia to help try to Skype with her daughter, but because of the short notice, sometimes, she does not find them at home. It should be easier to visit since her status became regular when Italy lifted its restrictions on Poles' access to the labor market in 2006, but it is difficult to get leave from the job, and she has only been able to go back once or twice a year for only a week at a time. Her daughter wants Stella to return to care for the grandchildren once they start school so that she can return to work. Stella will probably do this – her financial situation has deteriorated during the Eurocrisis – Nello's pension has been cut and the family has reduced Stella's pay. She feels she ought to help her daughter out, and looking after the children part-time will be much less tiring than caring for Nello.

Transnational families: Definitions and key research issues

Members of transnational families maintain a sense of *familyhood* (Bryceson and Vuorela, 2002), in that they continue to feel they *belong* to a family even though they may not see each other or be physically copresent very often or for extended periods of time. As Baldassar, Baldock, and Wilding (2007, p. 13) write, "the result-ing idea of the 'transnational family' is intended to capture the growing awareness that members of families retain their sense of collectivity and kinship in spite of being spread across multiple nations." Angelo, Maria, and Stella have all migrated away from their close family members but sustain their sense of family *belonging* over time through their active involvement in the lives of their parents, children, and grandchildren. As their case studies show, sustaining transnational family life is complex and often difficult, and, as in the case of Stella and her husband, does not always work out. This is because it is influenced by many factors in both the sending and receiving societies, the life stages and characteristics of the family members, as well as by the processes and the timing of the migration and mobility that created it in the first place.

In order to provide a comprehensive overview of the complexities of transnational family life, we have structured this chapter around four central challenges to the analysis and understanding of transnational families:

- The first is the theoretical question of how to conceptualize and define transnational families. Here, we need to draw on insights from both family studies and migration studies to consider their intersections. Of particular relevance to this discussion is the risk of viewing families through a Western-centric lens. For example, it is instructive to consider how in Maria's family it is quite common and acceptable for children to be raised by someone other than their biological parents, a practice which is widespread in certain parts of the world but which is considered quite inappropriate in Western conceptions of *proper* family life.
- The second is the methodological question of how to research such families, whose members by definition are dispersed across different countries, often on separate continents. Do our traditional tools of analysis serve us well? Given the importance of new communication technologies, of particular relevance here is the question of how to adapt our traditional research techniques to study the increasingly important virtual and online dimensions of family life.
- The third is the empirical question of how families actually manage *familyhood* in transnational settings. As the case studies clearly show, access to communication technologies greatly enhances the ability (and obligation) of family members to stay in touch with each other, although access is also differentiated according to factors such as socioeconomic position, age, gender, and geography.
- The fourth is the practical question of how transnational family forms can be supported through relevant policies. Of special importance here is how the standard governing structures of states and nations can meet the needs of families that stretch across borders. Also pertinent is the issue of how migration and other policies generate transnational families in the first place.

Transnational families: Belonging and the centrality of care

These are four very broad fields of enquiry. Our research leads us to argue that a productive way these four challenges can be addressed is by focusing our analysis of transnational families through the lens of caregiving. This is a useful methodological and analytical focus for an analysis of transnational family life because the exchange of care is one of the central processes (practices and performances) that maintains and sustains family relationships.

Our definition of family includes both nuclear and extended types whose members are actively engaged in family survival and maintenance, ranging from those whose involvement is extensive and constant to those whose roles are more marginal. We recognize, too, that these roles and the extent of engagement can change over time and across the life cycle. For this reason, our definition of transnational caregiving includes a wide variety of care exchanges (Baldassar, Baldock, and Wilding, 2007). Drawing on Finch and Mason's (1993) model of family support, five dimensions of care are distinguished: financial and material (including cash remittances or goods such as food, clothing, and paying household and other bills), practical (exchanging advice and assisting with tasks), emotional and moral aimed at improving psychological well-being, personal care (like feeding and bathing), and accommodation (providing shelter and security). This multidimensional definition of care enables distinctions between caring practices that can be exchanged across borders through the use of communication technologies (typically financial and emotional), proximate caring practices that occur during visits, and proxy caring practices, involving the coordination of support provided by others (Wilding, 2006; Baldassar, 2008; Kilkey and Merla, 2013). All these types of care can be exchanged in transnational settings but to varying degrees and subject to a variety of factors, including gender, ethnic, class, and power hierarchies as well as the cultural and structural histories of welfare regimes.

Transnational caregiving, just like caregiving in all families (whether separated by migration or not), binds members together in intergenerational networks of reciprocity and obligation, love, and trust that are simultaneously fraught with tension, contest, and relations of unequal power. Baldassar and Merla (2013) point out how the exchange of care in families is inherently reciprocal and asymmetrical, governed by the *norm of generalized reciprocity* – the *expectation* that the giving of care must ultimately be reciprocated, although it may not always be realized (Finch and Mason, 1993). People give care without measuring exactly the amount they receive, but with the expectation and obligation that care will be returned to them. This said, family members often carefully monitor these exchanges, and they are governed by the multiple and constantly *negotiated family commitments*, intimate and unequal power relations that characterize family life. As this care is given and returned at different times and to varying degrees across the life course, Baldassar and Merla (2013) argue that the care could be described as *circulating* among family members over time as well as distance. This care circulation framework helps to capture all the actors involved in family life as well as the full extent of their care activity, including practical, emotional, and symbolic, that defines their membership in a family. It also helps to avoid the more narrow definition of both family and caregiving that tends to define these processes in dominant Western conceptualizations.

An analysis of transnational caregiving activity must be sensitive to the unevenness of reciprocal exchange, including the withholding and limiting of care. While the circulation of care involves reciprocal exchanges between family members, both the transnational and local care burdens fall most heavily on women, who generally receive less than they give (Ryan, 2007). In this context, care and the ability to exchange it can be considered a form of social capital (or resource) that is unevenly distributed within families subject to cultural notions of gender and other roles, which intersect with and interrelate to the care regimes of the various nation-states and communities in which families reside. The debate in the literature about the transformative potential of migration and transnational processes to reconfigure power relations, in particular of gender, is pertinent here (cf. Mahler and Pessar, 2001). Furthermore, the increasing mobility and profound impact of new communication technologies on abilities to care across distance and manage absence in family life makes an analysis of *the portability of care* (Huang, Thang, and Toyota, 2012, p. 131) a fundamental topic of contemporary lives.

Transnational Families: Conceptual and Theoretical Issues

In Western conceptualizations of family caregiving, *the* family and the nation-state tend to be defined within an interpretive frame that presumes sedentarism and assumes physical copresence as an essential precondition of caregiving (Baldock, 2000; Leira and Saraceno, 2006). These ideas about care and proximity are inherently linked to the notion of *the* family as a private geographical domain represented by a household. The model of the family as featuring a white middle-class heterosexual couple with two children represents family members as bonded together by physical copresence and bounded by the confines of the privately owned land and house that contains them (Morgan, 2011). In these conceptualizations, the structure of the family is viewed as a microcosm and primary reproducer of the nation-state.

This approach to caregiving, families, and states mirrors the way nations and communities were, until recently, largely theorized as inherently connected to a geographical place. Migration was viewed as a process that literally and symbolically breaks away from the norm of sedentarism and therefore results in divided state loyalties, fractured families, and an inability to fulfill obligations to care. The movement out of homeland states, and in particular the resulting distance between family members, was seen to rupture and inhibit continued connections to people and place. Migration was understood as unidirectional – from sending to receiving country – as well as final, culminating in settlement. This view contributed to conceptualizations of the migrant's home and host societies as discrete, homogeneous entities with little in common and few connections between them. Wimmer and Glick Schiller (2002) note how this seemingly unproblematic division of space tended to privilege the straight line theory of assimilation as the end result of migration as well as an either/or approach to home and host allegiances (Alba and Waters, 2010). In this context, it is hardly surprising that the dominant notions about households – and the families they contain – are very much conceived as rooted in static, geographical domains (Stacey, 1998; Hardill, 2004).

As our case studies show, transnational as well as local geographical mobility impacts on increasing numbers of families, both in the *global south* (in developing countries like the Dominican Republic and transitional countries like Poland) and the north (in relatively wealthy countries like Australia and in countries that have been hard hit by the Global Financial Crisis (GFC) like Italy). Transnationalism in this context is defined as "a social process in which migrants establish social fields that cross geographic, cultural, and political borders" (Glick Schiller, Basch, and Szanton-Blanc, 1992, p. ix). What our research examples also reveal is how interconnected these global flows of people and their labor are, both in terms of their contributions to the more *public* economic markets and *private* family domains. Notions like *transnationalism from below* (Gardner and Grillo, 2002) feature the profound impact of these global processes on private and familial lives. A useful way of capturing the extent of these changes is to consider how the processes of social reproduction, which have historically been conceptualized as contained within static and localized notions of families and households, are today more appropriately conceived as (to varying degrees) directly linked to migratory moves, which are expected to provide greater access to the material and financial resources that guarantee family well-being. So, for example, the concept of *global householding* (Douglass, 2006) has been developed to highlight the fact that households themselves become global in all the dimensions that compose them. Marriage and intimate relations, procreation and child-rearing, management of daily life, income generation, caring, and, more generally, the practices of mutual support that guarantee the social reproduction of households increasingly involve, to various degrees, strategies that go beyond local contexts and are affected by global dynamics and phenomena. Kofman (2012) advocates engaging with the concepts of social reproduction and *global householding* in order to "place care work within a wider landscape of activities and sites and to connect supposedly disparate circuits of migration, in particular labour, family, and education, which are usually analysed separately but which are in fact interconnected" (p. 144).

As households have become *transnational* and *global*, so too have the cultural practices and social inequalities that define them. Much like local ones, global households are gendered sites of contestation, negotiation, compromise, and cooperation, articulated around statutory as well as individual differences (Douglass, 2012) and within which emotional, material, and physical support circulates. A particularly compelling example of family inequalities on a global scale is evident in the so-called global care chains (also known as transnational mothering/parenting). The migration of mothers in particular has been a central focus of the care chains literature (Hochschild, 2000; Parreñas, 2001, 2005). Through the framework of global care chains and its elaboration, the delivery of care has been identified as an important, though still relatively underexamined, type of goods and service that circulates in *global scapes* (Appadurai, 1991). This important body of research specifically focuses on the commodification and political economy of care in *south–north* female (domestic) labor flows, along a chain of women that typically includes a carer in the South looking after a child whose mother migrated to the North to look after the child of a woman who works full time. Prior to this research, the literature on care had not taken internationalization into consideration, and women from the South were largely excluded from the study of work–family balance issues (Leira and Saraceno, 2006). A comparable example is provided by the case of Maria, outlined earlier, who left her own children behind in order to care for, not other people's children, but their elderly parents (Alberto's father, Angelo, in Rome). Recent developments in the care chains literature include other types of migrants (such as the highly skilled), caring relations that involve other family members such as men and fathers, as well as regional migration flows such as East to West in the case of Europe and as exemplified by Stella (see, for instance, Lutz and Palenga-Möllenbeck, 2010; Sarti and Scrinzi, 2010; Erel, 2012; Kilkey, Perrons, and Plomien, 2013).

In general, researchers applying a care chains perspective have tended to assume that in order to care for each other effectively, family members must live in close proximity. Because it is largely based on a unidirectional conceptualization of care flows, with *care* being generally equated to *physical* care, the care chains literature tends to reduce the mother's participation in caring exchanges in the family to the sending of remittances. The conceptualization of care flows between the North and the South as unidirectional is linked to the idea that migration involves the *displacement* or *diversion* (Parreñas, 2003) of motherly love: distance makes it impossible for migrant mothers to *love* the children they left behind, and their love is diverted toward their affluent employers' children (or elderly kin). This displacement of love leads Hochschild (2005) to talk of a care drain, "as women who normally care for the young, the old and the sick in their own poor countries move to care for the young, the old, and the sick in rich countries, whether as maids and nannies or as day-care and nursing-home aides" (p. 35). But care drain may not necessarily occur in all transnational families (Sørensen and Guarnizo, 2007), in particular if we extend our understanding of care to include both *embodied* and *disembodied* or *virtual* forms of support and also if we recognize that care can be effectively delivered by extended family members and even friends (other than direct kin).

In analyzing transnational family life, we must be sensitive to the potency of assumptions about family and household that underlie and inform much of our thinking. As explained earlier, the idea that the family and household occupy one locus of residence and the importance placed on the nuclear family type as the ideal configuration for the delivery of care to family members, particularly children, is profoundly influential. Even though members of transnational families increasingly *routinely* live their lives *together across distance* and have developed practices to deal with the challenges posed by absence and separation, there is a general and robust skepticism (Zentgraf and Chinchilla, 2012) about whether transnational families can adequately care for and about each other, that is, how well they can actually *do family*, especially in those families that are separated over long periods of time. The spotlight most often falls on those cases where mothers are separated from young children. It has become clear that transnational mothering challenges a central and deeply held dominant Western notion about the bond between mother and child being biological rather than cultural (Bowlby, 1969) and the associated implications this has for mother and children to be both emotionally and physically close (Chavkin and Maher, 2010; Banfi and Boccagni, 2011; Lutz and Palenga-Möllenbeck, 2012).

The case studies at the start of this chapter provide a glimpse of how families and their members respond to and manage the considerable constraints they face in doing family transnationally. What they also emphasize and critique is the prevailing dominant Western notions about what constitutes *normal* and *healthy* family relationships. The notion of *family* "covers a multitude of senses of relatedness and connections" (Sørensen and Guarnizo, 2007, p.161), both within Western societies and across the globe. This richness is hidden from view in the dominant Western imaginary that identifies family with nuclear households bound up in notions of proximity and intimacy. As Sørensen and Guarnizo (2007) note, migration studies' tendency to identify the family with the domestic group has led researchers to assume that separation automatically leads to family disintegration, particularly when mothers leave husbands and children behind. The argument about the relative absence of anxiety related to physical separation in the African as compared to the Western case is particularly instructive. For instance, Filho (2009) argues that because of the set of imperatives that define migration in the Cape Verdean society, families experience separation as less painful and disruptive than in the West. This is due to "the ethos that emphasizes a lack of anxiety in regard to physical separation between those who stay and those who leave, and the maintenance of a strong feeling of relatedness, acting as a bridge for the physical distance, by means of continuity of material obligations" (p. 525). Similarly, Madianou and Miller (2012) refer to "anthropological accounts of many regions, such as the Caribbean, where the nuclear co-present family has never been the norm" (p. 10). According to Segal (1996), Caribbean migration "should be understood as a form of extended kinship over space and time with frequent rather than one-time movements" (quoted by Nurse, 2004, p. 4). The migration of women from the lower classes in Caribbean societies, for example, has been described as part of a system of circulation of care that is an integral and accepted aspect of family and kinship (Fog Olwig, 2013).

Thus, the way transnational family members experience absence from loved ones is much more dependent on their interpretations of the quality of their relationships and on the socially constructed meanings of mobility than on the actual distance that separates them. This means that we need to revisit normative Western understandings of family, household, migration, and the conceptualization of human mobility more broadly. Transnational migration studies reveal that migratory moves are more likely to result in multiple identities and national belongings, rather than replacing an earlier identity for a new one. Further, recent research on transnational families shows that migration can result in expanded family networks of care as the use of new technologies gives rise to more frequent and complex multidirectional communication flows between members, including across the generations (Baldassar 2011, Madianou and Miller, 2012).

Transnational Families: Research and Methodology across Borders

As Baldassar, Baldock, and Wilding (2007, p. 17) write,

> By its nature, the subject of transnational caregiving demands innovative transnational research methodologies. The experiences and practices we describe in this book are both emotionally intimate and geographically distant, and the need to capture these two experiences simultaneously has meant transforming conventional research tools into different forms.

The reconceptualization of *migrant* families into *transnational families* seeks to take into account the contexts of both receiving and sending societies. By its very nature, research on transnational families thus requires an analysis of family members in different places, and this has been done mainly via the use of multisited qualitative methodologies (Falzon, 2009; Amelina *et al.*, 2012). Comparative cross-national studies are also emerging and require the development of analytical frameworks to *situate* transnationalism within specific institutional contexts and identify relevant parameters for international comparisons (Kilkey and Merla, 2013).

Baldassar, Baldock, and Wilding (2007) point out that multisited and comparative studies tend to take the nation-state as the central unit of analysis and *nation of birth* as a central category for selecting participants. Such uses of *nation* and *national identity* are problematic for a number of reasons. First, they tend to result in the collapsing of the important analytical distinction between the organizational features of the state, on the one hand, and the ideological processes of nation-building, on the other (Blanc, Basch, and Glick Schiller, 1995). Second, the use of national identity terms has the unfortunate and erroneous consequence of reifying perceived ethnic or cultural differences, rather than acknowledging their social construction in specific contexts (Eriksen, 1991). Third, it can result in *methodological nationalism*, the false assumption that particular cultural traits or processes are "unitary and organically related to, and fixed within, [geographic] territories" (Wimmer and Glick Schiller, 2002, p. 305). Finally, national categories tend to homogenize and obscure the diversity of gender, class, regional, and ethnic background within populations (Dilworth-Anderson, Williams, and Gibson, 2002).

Perspectives of social life framed through a focus on social groups and processes that approach mobility as, potentially at least, a sociocultural norm lead to a methodological focus on the individual biography and life course of the people who move to consider how movement impacts on the static structures of the life world, rather than the reverse. In addition to work on transnational families, recent approaches in the sociology of the family, such as the *family practices* approach (Morgan, 2011) or the *configurational approach* (Widmer and Jallinoja, 2008), propose alternative frameworks that move beyond a focus on static, normative constructions of the nuclear family and stress the historical and spatial fluidity of kin relations. Similarly, Kofman (2012) argues for a more processual approach to better account for changes across the family life cycle as well as the full extent of caregiving practices. She adds that "To investigate the different forms, orientations, and directions of care, one would need (...) to adopt an approach that follows longitudinally and spatially the migrant so as to capture care giving and receiving" (p.153). To this end, Baldassar and Merla's (2013) *care circulation framework* offers a way of tracing or mapping the multiple and multidirectional care exchanges that characterize transnational family relations across the life course.

Mapping this caregiving activity requires an examination of the lives of family members in (and between) the various places they reside and so requires a multi-sited methodology (Marcus, 1995; Ortner, 1997; Hage, 2005), as well as posing the challenge of researching social and family life within the virtual world of new technologies (Miller and Slater, 2000). Here, the importance of relations to the material world, of both technologies and *nonhuman actors*, is brought to the forefront. Gille (2012) refers to this as *methodological materialism*, that is, the need to connect *the social with the material*. These factors account for and shape the asymmetries and inequalities, both within and between transnational families, in the capacity to circulate care. As Merla (2012, p. 2) argues, "access to, and use of, these capabilities is strongly influenced by both home- and host-country formal institutional and informal policies" and is shaped by gender, class, and ethnic hierarchies. These policy implications are also taken up in the following text.

Transnational Families: *Doing* Family across Time and Distance

Thus far, we have identified some of the challenges of conceptualizing and researching transnational families. In this section, we turn instead to a discussion of the practices and processes of transnational family caregiving in order to provide a sense of how people actually manage to do this. While the transnational family was not necessarily *produced* out of new communication technologies, it has certainly been transformed by the significant advances in information and communication technologies in recent decades. Numerous scholars have documented the ways in which technologies such as the mobile phone and the Internet and new capacities such as video streaming, social media, and instant financial transfers have transformed the experience of migration and of transnational families. Indeed, given the profound impact new technologies are having on every aspect of social life, we might label this *the virtual age*. In what follows, we briefly describe some of these insights by focusing on a few key studies of specific cases of transnational families. By doing so, we seek to avoid the trap that we identified earlier of assuming that all transnational family forms and practices are the same. Rather, what we aim to highlight is that the existing models and expectations of family of those who migrate intersect with the available technologies and mobilities, in order to create new family practices and expectations that transcend both the destinations and the points of departure. In each of the following examples, what counts as care and what counts as acceptable family formations and practices are socially and culturally specific and negotiated within particular political and economic circumstances.

Baldassar, Baldock, and Wilding (2007) clearly demonstrate that migration does not prevent the exchange of support within families. Indeed, as is evident in the case studies that open this chapter, both aging parents and their adult children are often engaged in intense and complex exchanges of care and support. Emotional support is the most commonly mentioned, perhaps because it is able to be provided through regular letters, telephone calls, and Internet-based communications. But even accommodation support and personal support, generally understood to rely upon physical copresence, are featured in people's experiences. It is important to acknowledge that a family member who delegates caregiving to a third person or institution does not automatically step out of circuits of care but may still be *caring about* (Fisher and Tronto, 1990) the person in need of support, stay informed of the level and quality of care provided, and be ready to *step in* when needed.

Baldassar, Baldock, and Wilding's (2007) research demonstrated that there are cultural specificities in terms of which forms of support are considered more desirable or obligatory, including gendered definitions of familial roles and expectations. For example, Singaporean sons were generally more concerned with providing financial support, and Italian daughters, in contrast, were generally more concerned with providing personal care. This was understood by family members as a function of the cultural expectations regarding family that had been imparted to them as children and of the availability of acceptable caregiving services. Yet, these ideal models of family care were adjusted in response to the situation of living at a distance. Thus, Italian daughters would use their available resources, such as savings and holidays, to return to care for and be with their parents in Italy in order to fulfill the role of *good daughters*. But, when not able to be present physically, this role could and would be displaced onto other siblings or, in some cases, paying for a domestic worker or care worker to take their place in the family home. They would remain closely involved by maintaining persistent contact by phone, letters, and e-mails, seeking to generate a sense of copresence that somewhat ameliorated their physical absence. In those families where daughters were absent, as in the case of Angelo's family, it was sons, like Alberto, often with the support of their wives, who performed these roles. In other cases, such as with the Dutch, regular contact by telephone, fax, or e-mail was considered sufficient to be able to fulfill the obligations and expectations of care. In the Netherlands, it was widely expected and accepted that as people aged, they would enter appropriate supportive accommodation, such that the expectations of sons and daughters remained in the domain of *keeping in touch* rather than being physically copresent. This did not mean that the Dutch perceived their relationships as less caring. Rather, they mobilized available communication technologies to sustain relationships that both aging parents and their children perceived as largely satisfactory, given the limitations of distance.

In part prompted by the arguments about global care chains, a range of studies have focused on women who migrate from the Philippines for work, leaving their children in the care of kin or paid workers (e.g., Parreñas, 2001, 2005; Madianou and Miller, 2012). In these studies, the capacity to sustain family relationships through new information and communication technologies is both asserted and simultaneously identified as inadequate. Unlike relationships between aging parents and adult children, relationships between adults and their dependent children are typically perceived as suffering as a result of geographical distance. An important study by Mirca Madianou and Daniel Miller (2012) indicates that many of the distant mothers perceive their new-found capacity to communicate by mobile phone, Skype, and other forms as enabling them the potential to retain their mothering identities and roles and assert the continuation of the family. However, from the perspective of the left-behind children, these technologies are not always seen in such a positive light. Approximately half of the (now adult) children they interviewed indicated that their mothers' communications were perceived as an unwelcome intrusion. Some denied that communication constituted mothering at all, thereby contesting their mothers' roles as mothers.

The reliance on communication technologies to sustain transnational families highlights the fact that access to such technologies is differential across nations, genders, and age groups (Wilding, 2006). An important part of the dynamics of the relationships between mothers and children in Madianou and Miller's (2012) study was the fact that it was cheaper for mothers to access mobile telephones than it was for their children to do so in the Philippines. Migrants and their family members manage these inequalities in a variety of ways, some using the known expense of communication strategically to avoid contact with particular family members, with others posting sim cards or calling cards to their kin overseas in order to take advantage of cheaper rates from elsewhere. Interestingly, new technologies have tended to increase the direct role and engagement of both men and younger generations in transnational family care exchanges in part because of their general tendency to be more familiar and proficient at using them. While the *kin work* (di Leonardo, 1987) involved in keeping in touch with transnational family members was often the preserve of women, particularly mothers and daughters, who wrote the letters and made the phone calls, it is not uncommon for fathers and sons, as well as grandchildren and cousins, to be directly involved in setting up the e-mail and Skype systems, coordinating and managing their use, and maintaining their upkeep (Baldassar, 2011).

When reflecting on their uses of diverse communication technologies, the participants in the aforementioned studies identify how different modes of communication affect their relationships in different ways. For example, the shift from exchanging letters and cassettes to sharing telephone calls has been associated as both a positive *and* a negative process (Wilding, 2006). The new technology meant that contact could be more frequent, but also meant that the special qualities of the letter, its perceived emotional intensity and insights, were lost. Rather than excitement at the blue airmail envelope, people recalled instead the sense of dread at a telephone call in the middle of the night (has someone died?) or the difficulties of coordinating telephone calls across different time zones and family routines. Nevertheless, gaining access to the *voice* of the distant family members is typically seen as positive, providing a stronger sense of copresence with those who are physically absent. The more recent emergence of e-mails and webcam technologies further transformed what was possible from a distance. In addition to being able to *see* and hear family members, it also became possible to recreate some of the sense of collectivity of family relations and gatherings. Rather than a letter or a telephone receiver being passed around from one person to the next, a family group is able to participate in an online chat or gather around the computer to see and be seen by webcam. Thus, Filipina mothers in Europe are able to help their children in the Philippines with homework, and families are able to share a meal at the same time and within view of each other, albeit not actually sharing the same food in the same room.

These new capacities to hear and be heard, see and be seen create new obligations and expectations for kin separated by distance. It also provides new opportunities for misunderstandings, as not everything can be communicated through a telephone call or webcam image. This helps to explain, for example, why some people choose to turn off their telephones rather than sustain connections. Riak Akuei (2005) describes how the image that many African refugees hold of America as a place *paved in gold* creates unforeseen burdens for those who are resettled in the *land of opportunity*. They are subject to continuing and urgent requests for financial assistance, which are typically managed on minimum wages. Those requesting assistance are unaware of the high costs of living in America and the relatively low levels of income of those from refugee backgrounds. Some of those who have been resettled resort to disconnecting their telephone as one of the few means available to stem the flow of demands. However, the presence of transnational networks of extended kin and community members makes this a risky choice, with the potential for an individual or even an entire family's reputation to be damaged. This example shows that transnational caregiving activity and its circulation wax and wane over the individual and family life course and migration process and members may be *dormant* in some periods and *reactivated* in others (Grillo, 2008). Economically vulnerable family members in particular, including refugees, migrants without legal status, and those with inadequate or unreliable incomes, might break ties when demands for transnational support are too onerous but reactivate them when they are better able to provide support.

The demands for and provision of financial support are themselves a form of receiving and giving care. In Western contexts, the close association of love and money is often denied, disguising the ways in which constructs of family are in large part about "strong bonds of collective welfare" (Huang, Yeoh, and Lam, 2008). In some cases, the provision of money is more important in demonstrating love than is the communication in language of words such as *I love you*. It is from this perspective that Coe (2011) approaches the expression of love within families in which the children remain in Ghana while their parents migrate for work. She explains that, for the children, love between adults and children is present when adults are willing to share their available resources, and a child feels freely able to ask that adult to meet their needs. It is important to recognize that children in Ghana do not necessarily live with their parents, instead being located in those households and with those adults who have a better capacity to provide for their needs. In this context, migrant parents in transnational families are not judged on whether or not they are able to sustain emotional intimacy, as is emphasized in the case of Filipina transnational mothering. Rather, migrant parents who remitted money were typically perceived as good parents, and their absence was not lamented. It was the migrant parents who failed to remit who were typically identified as neglectful and a source of unhappiness. However, children also struggled to retune their *cultural calculus* to a transnational context, not least because they were not always aware of how much of the remittances sent from their parent to their caregiver were being used to support their needs and how much were being withheld or redistributed by the caregiver. Family relationships, expectations, and obligations become more complex as a result of the separation of care into everyday care and financial/material care. In some cases, the caregivers become the focus of everyday frustrations and tensions, while the migrant parents are idealized, safely distant from issues of discipline and management of daily life.

Caregiving provides a window on the emotional intersubjectivities at the heart of all relationships, especially those between family and kin-like friends. In the study of transnational families, the epistemological notion that the self is created through intersubjective relations (shared dialogue and activity) is examined in contexts where people are *living apart together*. A central challenge posed by a mobilities paradigm is how to locate the interdependencies that characterize caring relationships into a transnational context. To this end, the concept of *virtual* and other forms of *copresence* (proxy, imagined, *soft*, *hard*) provides frameworks to explore how people maintain a sense of *being there* for each other, including the special role of visits, remittances, and communications. What then emerges are questions about the implications of these increasingly common practices, of breaching mobility and overcoming distance, on the development of theories of family life. It has become clearer that an assumption of physical copresence and *being there* as the bedrock of family caregiving relationships can no longer be taken for granted. Yet, it remains to be asked just how effective the forms of exchange that are available in transnational contexts can be in approximating or *standing in for* family as a local phenomenon. In addressing these issues, the variability of family practices, expectations, and obligations becomes highlighted in both transnational and local sets of relationships.

Transnational Families: Policy Implications

In this section, we turn to address the fourth and final challenge to the analysis of transnational family forms. This relates to the practical question of how the governing structures of nation-states can meet the needs of families that stretch across borders. Before considering this key issue, it is important to acknowledge that state policies, particularly migration policies, can be implicated in the formation of transnational families in the first place. Many migrants do not *choose* to leave family members behind when they migrate, but are forced to because migration policies create barriers for families to migrate together. This is especially the case for migrants moving from the *global south* to major labor migrant-receiving regions of the world including much of Europe, all of North America and Oceania, and parts of Asia and the Middle East. While migration policies vary significantly across and within those regions, a common trend is to more tightly manage and control immigration flows. The motives for this vary, too, but include a desire to restrict migration to only those persons seen as economically useful, a related desire to prevent *welfare dependency* among immigrants and a desire to limit the long-term settlement of immigrants, especially among groups perceived to be difficult to *integrate* or *assimilate* into the receiving country because of religious or *cultural* differences. One result is that countries may permit the entry of a worker deemed instrumental to the economic needs of the country, but not allow (all) his or her dependants' entry or impose strict conditions on their entry which migrant workers find impossible to meet. In such cases, migrants and their families have little or no choice but to live apart.

For those families separated by borders, a significant issue is whether and how policies facilitate or impede their exchange of care and support. Despite claims that processes such as globalization have led to the *unsettling* of the nation-state, "relocating it in new systems of governance, beyond and within the nation" (Clarke, 2005, p. 408), this remains a relatively recent and challenging question for policy makers who in the main continue to work within social policy environments which are nationally bounded and which assume that *normal* family life is too. Among the first to acknowledge that there was a policy dimension to the practices of transnational families were Baldassar, Baldock, and Wilding (2007) when they argued that transnational caregiving practices are mediated by "a dialectic encompassing the *capacity* of individual members to engage in care-giving and their culturally informed sense of *obligation* to provide care, as well as the particularistic kin relationships and *negotiated family commitments* that people with specific family networks share" (p. 204). Subsequent research has sought to unpack the "capacity" element of the dialectic by identifying firstly the resources required for transnational caregiving and, secondly, the institutions through which those resources are in part derived.

Merla and Baldassar (2011) have identified six interconnected resources needed to underpin transnational caregiving. Firstly, *mobility* refers to the ability to travel to receive or give care. Secondly, *communication* means being able to communicate at a distance and to send items across borders and includes having the physical ability to communicate. Thirdly, *social relations* refers to access to a social network of mutual support in the receiving and home country, which can represent a useful resource for the exchange of information about travel and accommodation and can provide financial and practical support to carers and cared-for. Fourthly, *time allocation* involves having the capacity to take time for exchanging care. Fifthly, *education and knowledge* refer to the possibility to learn how to use communication technologies and to learn the local language. It also includes having one's qualifications recognized, which can influence access to paid work and thus indirectly affect the ability to exchange care. Finally, *paid work* encompasses having access to a satisfying employment position and, if unemployed, to sufficient benefits in order to have the necessary funds to invest in caregiving. Kilkey and Merla (2013) subsequently added a seventh resource – *appropriate housing* – which is crucial for the settlement of immigrant families and can also be a prerequisite for eligibility to family reunification. Moreover, adequate housing is important for family members who travel to provide or receive proximate care, as issues such as lack of space and privacy can create tensions between visitors and their hosts. Appropriate housing, including appropriate institutional care, is also essential for care-receivers who remain in their home country.

The relevance of all seven of these resources to how families care transnationally is captured in the stories of Alberto, Maria, and Stella set out at the beginning of this chapter. Less explicit in those accounts was the set of institutional arrangements, in both the home and the migrant-receiving societies that contribute to realizing these resources. Here, the work of Kilkey and Merla (2013) is instructive. They start with the premise articulated by the concept of *care circulation* (Baldassar and Merla, 2013) discussed earlier that transnational families engage in proximate *and* transnational practices of care, that care flows are multidirectional, and that care relations are multigenerational. They develop the notion of a *situated transnationalism* and draw on *regime* theory, arguing that the capacity to care transnationally is influenced by migrants' and their kin's respective positioning in the migration, welfare, gendered care, and working-time regimes of their societies of origin and destination. By migration regime, they refer to "immigration policies – rules for entrance into a country (quotas and special arrangements), settlement and naturalization rights, as well as employment, social, political and civil rights" (Williams, 2010, p. 390), and which also includes migration cultures in home and host societies. The welfare regime refers to the configuration of social protection for workers (Esping-Andersen, 1990). The gendered care regime aims at capturing who is responsible for care, the nature of state support for nonfamilial care, and provisions for care leave (Williams, 2010), as well as dominant national and local discourses – *care cultures* – on what constitutes appropriate care (Williams and Gavanas, 2008) and gender equality expectations and outcomes associated with care arrangements (Pfau-Effinger, 2000). The working-time regime, finally, includes the set of legal, voluntary, and customary regulations which influence working-time practice (Rubery, Smith, and Fagan, 1998). Kilkey and Merla (2013) also highlight that policies around the regulation of cross-border transport, including its availability and affordability, and around the quality and accessibility of the communications' infrastructure, especially telephone and the Internet, are also important.

Conclusion and Future Directions

It has become necessary to conceptualize transnational families as a growing family form in its own right. To do this, we need to revise and extend definitions and understanding of family practices and processes and the factors that influence them. Households and their members can no longer be conceived as fixed in place, static, and sedentary but must be understood as also potentially extended across space and time. The important work of social reproduction needs to be mapped out across the globe to examine the ways local households and their members are linked into transnational social fields and networks of relationships as well as the global circulation of labor, goods, and services. The policies that govern the well-being of families, so tightly fastened within national frames, need to be loosened and expanded to accommodate the way families and their members increasingly live their lives across national borders. New appreciation and awareness of local, transnational, and global inequalities that impede the ability of family members to sustain family relationships across distance must be factored in to service delivery. We need to imagine into being a future where aged care doctors and nurses regularly schedule Skype or phone meetings with the adult children of their patients living abroad; where images of good mothers include those that are separated from their children; where notions of good parenting encompass the caregiving of extended kin and close friends; where school teachers are prepared to liaise directly with parents based overseas; and where entry and exit visas, basic health cover, and leave from work are provided to ensure family members can give and receive the care they need to and from family members around the globe. In order to support these changes, we need to further develop our understanding of the meanings, actual practices, and obstacles related to *doing* family in a context of increased mobility and geographical distance. Transnational families are as diverse as geographically proximate families, and this variety also needs to be better reflected. This can be done not only by exploring the wide range of transnational families in terms of socioeconomic background, gender, ethnicity, age, etc., but also by including contemporary family forms such as recomposed families and *chosen* families, such as nonheterosexual relationships and friends considered as *family*.

References

Alba, R. and Waters, M. (eds) (2010) *The Next Generation: Immigrant Youth in a Comparative Perspective*, New York University Press, New York.

Amelina, A., Nergiz, D.D., Faist, T. and Glick Schiller, N. (2012) *Beyond Methodological Nationalism:Research Methodologies for Cross-Border Studies*, Routledge, London and New York.

Appadurai, A. (1991) Global ethnoscapes: notes and queries for a transnational anthropology, in *Recapturing Anthropology* (ed. R. Fox), School of American Research Press, Santa Fe, pp. 191–210.

Baldassar, L. (2008) Missing kin and longing to be together: emotions and the construction of co-presence in transnational relationships. *Journal of Intercultural Studies*, 29 (3), 247–266.

Baldassar, L. (2011) Italian migrants in Australia and their relationship to Italy: return visits, transnational caregiving and the second generation, in *Of Home, Belonging and Return: Transnational Links of the Mediterranean-Origin Second Generation* (eds. R. King and A. Christou), Special Issue of *Journal of Mediterranean Studies*, 20 (2), 255–282.

Baldassar, L. and Merla, L. (eds) (2014) *Transnational Families, Migration and the Circulation of Care: Understanding Mobility and Absence in Family Life*, Routledge, London.

Baldassar, L., Baldock, C. and Wilding, R. (2007) *Families Caring Across Borders: Migration, Aging and Transnational Caregiving*, Palgrave Macmillan, Basingstoke.

Baldock, C. (2000). Migrants and their parents: caregiving from a distance. *Journal of Family Studies*, 21 (2), 205–224.

Banfi, L. and Boccagni, P. (2011) Transnational family life and female migration in Italy: one or multiple patterns? in *Gender, Generations and the Family in International Migration* (eds. A. Kraler, E. Kofman, M. Kohli, and C. Schmoll), Amsterdam University Press, Amsterdam, pp. 285–310.

Blanc, C., Basch, L. and Glick Schiller, N. (1995) Transnationalism, nation-states and culture. *Current Anthropology*, 36 (4), 683–686.

Bryceson, D. and Vuorela, U. (2002) *The Transnational Family: New European Frontiers and Global Networks*, Berg, Oxford, New York.

Bowlby, J. (1969) *Attachment and Loss. Vol. I: Attachment*, Hogarth, London.

Chavkin, W. and Maher, J.M. (eds) (2010) *The Globalization of Motherhood. Deconstructions and Reconstructions of Biology and Care*, Routledge, Abingdon, New York.

Clarke, J. (2005) Welfare states as nation states: some conceptual reflections. *Social Policy and Society*, 4 (4), 407–415.

Coe, C. (2011) What is love? The materiality of care in Ghanaian transnational families. *International Migration*, 49 (6), 7–24.

di Leonardo, M. (1987) The female world of cards and holidays: women, families, and the work of kinship. *Signs*, 12 (3), 440–453.

Dilworth-Anderson, P., Williams, I.C. and Gibson, B.E. (2002) Issues of race, ethnicity and culture in caregiving research: a 20-year review (1980–2000). *The Gerontologist*, 42 (3), 237–272.

Douglass, M. (2006) Global householding in Pacific Asia. *International Development Planning Review*, 28 (4), 421–446.

Douglass, M. (2012) Global householding and social reproduction: migration research, dynamics and public policy in East and Southeast Asia. ARI working paper No.188.

Erel, U. (2012) Introduction: transnational care in Europe – changing formations of citizenship, family, and generation. *Social Politics: International Studies in Gender, State & Society*, 19 (1), 1–14.

Eriksen, T.H. (1991) The cultural contexts of ethnic differences. *Man* (N.S.), 26, 127–144.

Esping-Andersen, G. (1990) *The Three Worlds of Welfare Capitalism*, Polity Press, Cambridge.

Falzon, M.-A. (ed) (2009). *Multi-Sited Ethnography: Theory, Praxis and Locality in Contemporary Research*, Ashgate, Farnham.

Filho, W.T. (2009) The conservative aspects of a centripetal diaspora: the case of the cape verdean tabancas. *Africa*, 79 (4), 520–542.

Finch, J. and Mason, J. (1993) *Negotiating Family Responsibilities*, Tavistock, Routledge, London, New York.

Fisher, B. and Tronto, J. (1990) Toward a feminist theory of caring, in *Circles of Care* (eds. E.K. Abel and M.K. Nelson), State University New York Press, Albany, pp. 35–62.

Fog Olwig, K. (2014) Migration and care – intimately related aspects of Caribbean family and kinship, in *Transnational Families, Migration and the Circulation of Care:*

Understanding Mobility and Absence in Family Life (eds. L. Baldassar and L. Merla), Routledge, London.

Gardner, K. and Grillo, R. (2002) Transnational households and ritual: an overview. *Global Networks*, 2 (3), 179–190.

Gille, Z. (2012) Global ethnography 2.0 – from methodological nationalism to methodological materialism, in *Beyond Methodological Nationalism: Research Methodologies for Cross-Border Studies* (eds. A. Amelina, D.D. Nergiz, T. Faist, and N. Glick Schiller), Routledge, London, pp. 91–110.

Glick Schiller, N., Basch, L. and Szanton-Blanc, C. (1992) *Towards a Transnational Perspective on Migration*, New York Academy of Sciences, New York.

Grillo, R. (ed) (2008) *The Family in Question: Immigrant and Ethnic Minorities in Multicultural Europe*, Amsterdam University Press, Amsterdam.

Hage, G. (2005) A not so multi-sited ethnography of a not so imagined community. *Anthropological Theory*, 5 (4), 463–475.

Hardill, I. (2004) Transnational living and moving experiences: intensified mobility and dual-career households. *Population, Space and Place*, 10 (5), 375–389.

Hochschild, A. (2000) Global care chains and emotional surplus value, in *On the Edge: Living with Global Capitalism* (eds. W. Hutton and A. Giddens), Jonathan Cape, London, pp. 130–146.

Hochschild, A. (2005) Love and gold, in *Feminist Politics, Activism and Vision: Local and Global Challenges* (eds. L. Ricciutelli, A. Miles, and M.H. McFadden), Zed/Innana Books, Toronto, pp. 34–46.

Huang, S., Yeoh, B. and Lam, T. (2008) Asian transnational families in transition: the liminality of simultaneity. *International Migration*, 46 (4), 3–13.

Huang, S., Thang, L. and Toyota, M. (2012) Transnational mobilities for care: rethinking the dynamics of care in Asia. *Global Networks*, 12 (2), 129–134.

Kilkey, M. and Merla, L. (2013) Situating transnational families' care-giving arrangements: the role of institutional contexts. *Global Networks*. published online. doi: 10.1111/glob.12034.

Kilkey, M., Perrons, D. and Plomien, A. with Hondagneu-Sotelo, P. and Ramirez, H. (2013) *Gender, Migration and Domestic Work: Masculinities, Male Labour and Fathering in the UK and USA*, Palgrave Macmillan, Basingstoke.

Kofman, E. (2012) Rethinking care through social reproduction: articulating circuits of migration. *Social Politics: International Studies in Gender, State & Society*, 19 (1), 142–162.

Leira, A. and Saraceno, C. (2006) Care: actors, relationships, contexts. *SOSIOLOGI I DAG*, 36 (3), 7–34.

Lutz, H. and Palenga-Möllenbeck, E. (2010) Care work migration in Germany – compliance and complicity. *Social Policy and Society*, 9 (3), 419–430.

Lutz, H. and Palenga-Möllenbeck, E. (2012) Care workers, care drain, and care chains: reflections on care, migration, and citizenship. *Social Politics: International Studies in Gender, State & Society*, 19 (1), 15–37.

Madianou, M. and Miller, D. (2012) *Migration and New Media: Transnational Families and Polymedia*, Routledge, Abingdon and New York.

Mahler, S.J. and Pessar, P.R. (2001) Gendered geographies of power: analyzing gender across transnational spaces. *Identities* 7 (4), 441–459.

Marcus, G.E. (1995) Ethnography in/of the world system: the emergence of multi-sited ethnography. *Annual Review of Anthropology*, 24, 95–117.

Merla, L. (2012) Salvadoran migrants in Australia: an analysis of transnational families' capability to care across borders. *International Migration*, Vol 50, Nov 29 published online. doi: 10.1111/imig.12024.

Merla, L. and Baldassar, L. (2011) Transnational caregiving between Australia, Italy and El Salvador: the impact of institutions on the capability to care at a distance, in *Gender and Well Being: The Role of Institutions* (eds. E. Addis, P.D. Villota, F. Degavre, and J. Eriksen), Ashgate, London, pp. 147–162.

Miller, D. and Slater, D. (2000) *The Internet: An Ethnographic Approach*, Berg, Oxford.

Morgan, D.H.G. (2011) *Rethinking Family Practices*, Basingstoke: Palgrave Macmillan.

Nurse, K. (2004) *Policy Paper: Diaspora, Migration and Development in the Caribbean*, Ottawa: FOCAL–Canadian Foundation for the Americas.

Ortner, S. (1997) Fieldwork in the postcommunity. *Anthropology and Humanism*, 22 (1), 61–80.

Parreñas, R. (2001) Mothering from a distance: emotions, gender, and intergenerational relations in filipino transnational families. *Feminist Studies*, 27 (2), 361–390.

Parreñas, R. (2003) The care crisis in the Philippines: children and transnational families in the new global economy, in *Global Woman: Nannies, Maids, and Sex Workers in the New Economy* (eds. B. Ehrenreich and A.R. Hochschild), Granta Books, London, pp. 39–54.

Parreñas, R. (2005) *Children of Global Migration: Transnational Families and Gendered Woes*, Stanford University Press, Stanford.

Pfau-Effinger, B. (2000) Conclusion: gender cultures, gender arrangements and social changes in the European context, in *Gender, Economy and Culture in the European Union* (eds. S. Duncan and B. Pfau-Effinger), Routledge, London and New York.

Riak Akuei, S. (2005) Remittances as unforeseen burdens: The livelihoods and social obligations of Sudanese refugees, in *Global Migration Perspectives* 18, Global Commission on International Migration, Geneva.

Rubery, J., Smith, M. and Fagan, C. (1998) National working time regimes and equal opportunities. *Feminist Economics*, 4 (1), 71–101.

Ryan, L. (2007) Migrant women, social networks and motherhood: the experiences of Irish nurses in Britain. *Sociology*, 41 (2), 295–312.

Sarti, R. and Scrinzi, F. (2010) Introduction to the special issue: men in a woman's job, male domestic workers, international migration and the globalization of care. *Men and Masculinities*, 13 (1), 4–15.

Segal, A. (1996) Locating the swallows: Caribbean recycling migration. Paper presented at the Caribbean Studies Association Conference, San Juan, Puerto Rico.

Sørensen, N.N. and Guarnizo, L. (2007) Transnational family life across the Atlantic: the experience of Colombian and Dominican migrants in Europe, *Living Across Worlds: Diaspora, Development and Transnational Engagement* (ed. N.N. Sørensen), International Organization for Migration, Geneva, pp. 151–176.

Stacey, J. (1998) *Brave New Families: Stories of Domestic Upheaval in Late Twentieth Century America*, Basic Books, New York.

Urry, J. (2000) *Sociology Beyond Societies: Mobilities for the Twenty-first Century*, Routledge, London.

Widmer, E. and Jallinoja, R. (2008) *Beyond the Nuclear Family: Families in a Configurational Perspective*, Peter Lang, Bern.

Wilding, R. (2006) Virtual intimacies? Families communicating across transnational contexts. *Global Networks*, 6 (2), 125–142.

Williams, F. (2010) Migration and care: themes, concepts and challenges. *Social Policy and Society*, 9 (3), 385–396.

Williams, F. and Gavanas, A. (2008) The intersection of child care regimes and migration regimes: a three-country study, in *Migration and Domestic Work. A European Perspective on a Global Theme* (ed. Helma Lutz), Ashgate, Avebury, pp. 13–28.

Wimmer, A. and Glick Schiller, N. (2002) Methodological nationalism and beyond: nation–state building, migration and the social sciences. *Global Networks*, 2 (4), 301–334.

Yeates, N. (2009) *Globalising Care Economies and Migrant Workers: Explorations in Global Care Chains*, Palgrave, Basingstoke.

Zentgraf, K.M. and Chinchilla, N.S. (2012) Transnational family separation: a framework for analysis. *Journal of Ethnic and Migration Studies*, 38 (2), 345–366.

9

Ethnic Diversity in the United Kingdom: Family Forms and Conjugality

ALISON SHAW

Introduction

For the 2001 Census of the United Kingdom, residents were invited to select their ethnicity from one of four main categories: white, mixed, Asian, or black. The results show an overwhelmingly white majority – 92.1% of the total population of 59 million is white, most of them (85.67% of the total) white British. A minority, at 7.9% of the total, is nonwhite. Nearly half of the nonwhite population is South Asian, comprising 1,053,411 Indians (1.8% of the total), 747,205 Pakistanis (1.3%), and 283,063 Bangladeshis (0.5%). People of black ethnicity make up 2% of the total and comprise black Caribbean (1.0%), black African (0.8%) and black other (0.2%). The mixed category, at 1.2%, of which a third comprises people of white and Caribbean ancestry, had increased significantly since the 1991 Census. The two remaining ethnic categories are Chinese and other Asian (non-Chinese), each at 0.4%.

A question about ethnicity was first introduced into the 1991 Census to help monitor the incorporation of nonwhite immigrant-origin minorities into mainstream British society. In this usage, ethnicity was effectively reduced to a combination of skin color and country of origin, distinguishing nonwhite people of immigrant origin from the white majority, despite a rationale that acknowledges ethnicity as a multifaceted social identity connected with an idea of common ancestry and entailing such elements as kinship, language and religion as well as nationality and physical appearance (Bulmer, 1996). Thus, although an ethnic group can be defined as biologically self-perpetuating, characterized by a particular inventory of cultural traits, and as seen by its members and people of other ethnic groups as distinct (Barth, 1969), the census ethnic group data simply indicate skin color plus country of origin, the latter, moreover, referring to country of ancestral origin, not country of birth. The 2001 Census does distinguish white British, white Irish, and

The Wiley Blackwell Companion to the Sociology of Families, First Edition.
Edited by Judith Treas, Jacqueline Scott, and Martin Richards.
© 2014 John Wiley & Sons Ltd. Published 2017 by John Wiley & Sons Ltd.

white other, but minorities such as Poles and other European labor migrants living and forming families in Britain since EU enlargement are invisible in the census analysis.

The picture of ethnic diversity captured by the census data is largely a consequence of several successive phrases of immigration after World War II. In the 1950s and 1960s, people from Britain's former dependencies in South Asia and the Caribbean entered Britain in significant numbers in response to postwar labor shortages. In the 1970s, British subjects of South Asian origin entered Britain from Africa in response to the Ugandan and Kenyan government's Africanization policies, and there has been black African immigration from the 1980s. More recent nonwhite immigration has been mainly restricted to the dependents or spouses of these earlier immigrants. This immigration and settlement history also explains why Britain's ethnic minority population remains largely concentrated in certain urban areas. Thus, parts of London are strongly associated in academic literature and popular consciousness with particular ethnic groups: Brixton in South London with Afro-Caribbeans (Benson, 1981); Southall – Britain's *South* "Asian capital" – in West London with Punjabi Sikhs (Baumann, 1996); Tower Hamlets in East London with Bangladeshis, the key change noted in a restudy of family and kinship in the East London (Dench, Gavron and Young, 2006) and Waltham Forest in North East London with Pakistanis (Jacobson, 1998). Outside London, Pakistani Muslims are strongly associated with Leeds and Bradford in Yorkshire (Bolognani, 2009), Birmingham in the Midlands, and Manchester in the North (Werbner, 1990).

This chapter will discuss family formation and conjugality among people of African Caribbean and South Asian ancestry, with reference to the transnational networks across which kinship and family are enacted and with a particular focus on South Asians. South Asians comprise nearly a half of Britain's ethnic minority population and have attracted quite substantial academic attention, partly perhaps from an early prejudice that "Asians have culture, West Indians have problems" (Benson, 1996). Both minority groups have been subjected to ethnic stereotyping over the past 50 years on the basis of social and cultural characteristics largely associated with family practices in their countries of ancestral origin. Popular images of young Afro-Caribbeans in the 1970s and 1980s were that they were less law-abiding and more troublesome than South Asians, as evidenced by "race riots" in parts of London and Bristol and perhaps reinforced by the academic identification of an "expressive disreputable orientation" among a group of West Indian youth in Bristol (Pryce, 1979). A distinctively Caribbean pattern of kinship and cohabitation characterized by women-centered single-parent households and originating in patterns of family life in the Caribbean was often cited as the center of unstable and irresponsible child-rearing and as a more important factor than racism or socioeconomic disadvantage underlying wider social problems.

Subsequently, political and academic focus on "troublesome youth" has shifted to Pakistani and Bangladeshi Muslim males. Riots in the former mill towns of Oldham, Burnley, Leeds, and Bradford in May 2001 were reported as the most violent incidences of civil unrest to have occurred in Britain for 20 years. The ensuing public debates over integration and citizenship focused on the persistence of traditional religious and cultural practices, including arranged consanguineous marriages with spouses from the Indian subcontinent, in explaining the apparent nonintegration of

Pakistani and Bangladeshi Muslims, with rather less emphasis given to poverty, unemployment, and religious prejudice. These debates intensified following international crises involving Muslims, including the attacks of September 11, 2001 in the United States and the London bombings of July 7, 2005. Muslims rather than South Asians are often now the focus of debates about integration, but these categories overlap substantially because the majority (86%) of British Muslims are of South Asian origin, and family, marriage and gender continue to be perceived as the main sources of difference from the majority society. Indeed, in the words of one American conservative commentator, the "Muslim kinship structure" – by which he means patrilineal parallel cousin marriage – "is the unexamined key to the war on terror" (Kurtz, 2007).

Such stereotypes are deeply problematic. They obscure differences between and within the South Asian population, in socioeconomic status, in kinship and marriage practices, and in language and religion. In the United Kingdom, significant social change has occurred across all ethnic groups. Moreover, according to the 2001 Census figures, 50% of all Indians, Pakistanis, Bangladeshis, and black Caribbeans are British born. Being in most cases British-raised, these young people are unmistakably British in many respects, despite their maintaining varying degrees of attachment to their parents' or grandparents' countries of origin. Many of them are of childbearing age and in the processes of forming partnerships and having children. It would be reasonable to expect that changes in family and marriage documented for British society in general are also discernable within Britain's ethnic minority population.

In what follows, I begin by outlining the main directions of change in marriage and family formation observed for British society generally and the arguments made in interpreting these trends. Survey data show that these changes are occurring across all ethnic groups, though at different rates for different groups. I suggest that it may be inadequate to assume that identical processes and motivations underpin these changes. Drawing on ethnographic literature, I highlight the importance of extrahousehold and transnational kinship for many Afro-Caribbean and South Asian families. I underline the heterogeneity of the South Asian population with regard to marriage practices, and I note some rather more specific dynamics of change occurring in the patterns of conjugality and family formation among British Pakistani Muslims.

Toward Modern Individualism for All?

It is widely acknowledged in the sociological literature that British society is experiencing major changes in the patterns of household formation and marriage (McRae, 1999; Allen and Crow, 2001; Edwards, 2008). These changes include a rise in cohabitation; lower rates of marriage, with marriage in general occurring later; and an increase in divorce. Currently, around 40% of marriages end in divorce, rates of which have increased significantly since the 1970s (Harper, 2003). There are now more births outside marriage and more single parents; in 2005, around 24% of children were living in lone-parent households (Babb et al 2006:24). There are fewer conventional nuclear families comprising parents plus dependent children and, in part associated with rising divorce, there are more new family groupings – step and reconstituted families – comprising couples with children from previous relationships. There has also been an increase in the number of single-person households, including an increase in the number of elderly living alone (Harper, 2003).

In interpreting these trends, scholars such as Giddens (1992) and Beck and Beck-Gernsheim (1995) have suggested that people are now less materially constrained and thus able to exercise greater individual autonomy in their decisions about how and with whom they live, and so they are choosing alternatives to traditional family life. Beck and Beck-Gernsheim have argued that personal relationships no longer follow set scripts associated with unquestioned roles and obligations, but are now based on the expectation of a mutually satisfying, emotionally fulfilling personal relationship, and if this is not forthcoming, then the relationship can be renegotiated. This is what is meant by modern intimacy: a conjugal relationship that is individualized, gender equal, self-reflective, contingently negotiated, and, consequently, it seems, less stable than traditional marriage (Giddens, 1992). Women's increased participation in the labor force, challenges to traditional gender norms, and greater sexual freedom are usually acknowledged as major reasons for these changes, accompanied by later marriage, less marriage, and fewer births.

Yet the evidence of change in patterns of conjugality and family formation is open to other interpretations (Jamieson, 1998, 1999; Smart and Shipman, 2004). Living singly or in nuclear households tells us little about the nature of the inhabitants' contacts with relatives living in other households, with whom they may retain close ties of extrahousehold kinship. People with extended family networks may be compelled to live separately for socioeconomic reasons rather than because they are driven by modern individualism. Moreover, modern intimacy, in Giddens' sense of the term, may not correspond to what people across different social and cultural contexts perceive as key in constituting their close personal relationships, and other forms of intimacy such as practical caregiving may be more fundamental (Jamieson, 2011). In this respect, intimacy overlaps with the more traditional expectations and negotiations associated with kinship roles and relationships, such as between spouses; between grandparents, parents, and children; or between adult children and elderly parents or grandparents. The shared repertoire of practices entailed in enacting kinship, for example, where older people provide practical care and support to adult children and grandchildren, despite living separately (Harper, 2003), may be as or more important than intimacy in the modern sense of the term.

Questions about the explanatory value of theories of modern individualism and intimacy are especially pertinent when examining the motivations underlying the changes in family formation and marriage observed for Britain's ethnic minorities. In an important paper on ethnic diversity and changing family forms, Berthoud presents three patterns of diversity, represented by Caribbean, white, and South Asian ethnic groups, based on the analysis of large-scale data from the Fourth National Survey of Ethnic Minorities (1993–1994) and combined Labour Force Survey (1985–1995). Berthoud comments that these patterns represent not qualitatively different processes so much as changes in family life along a single scale, from old-fashioned values to modern individualism: "the ethnic groups compared," he writes, "are all moving in the same direction" toward later marriage, or no marriage, accompanied by a wide range of alternative conjugal forms (Berthoud, 2005, p. 249). The three patterns of diversity emerge from the observation that this movement is not occurring at the same rate for all ethnic groups: South Asians are behind in this trajectory, representing traditional family life at the old-fashioned end of the scale, while people of Caribbean origin are "well out in front…moving away from old fashioned family values towards modern individualism" (2005, p. 249).

At the modern end of Berthoud's scale, people of Caribbean ethnicity have the lowest rates of marriage. Data from the Fourth National Survey of Ethnic Minorities (1993–1994) show that just 39% of Caribbeans under the age of 60 are formally married, compared with 60% of whites of the same age group. Caribbean lone mothers are also more likely than mothers of other ethnic groups to be in full-time work (Lindley, Dale, and Dex, 2004, p. 11). People of Caribbean ethnicity also are the most likely to be in mixed ethnicity partnerships: 50% of Caribbean men and 30% of Caribbean women live with white partners. Caribbean women also show the highest rate of lone parenthood, with 50% of Caribbean women being lone mothers. According to a more recent analysis of combined Labour Force survey data sets (2004–2008), mixed ethnic partnerships are more likely among the younger generations and among couples with children. The number of people with a part-Caribbean heritage seems set to increase. Already, the proportion of children living with two Caribbean parents has declined in a decade, from 1 in 4 to 1 in 5 (Platt n.d., p.7).

At the traditional end of Berthoud's scale, nearly all South Asians in partnerships are formally married, and the rate of marriage is high; almost everyone marries sooner or later. South Asians also marry earlier and are less likely to become separated or divorced than whites and Caribbeans. The South Asian rate of divorce or separation was found in 1993–1994 to be 3%, less than half the 7% reported for whites. South Asians are also less likely to have white partners than Caribbeans. South Asian women, especially Pakistani and Bangladeshi women, have more children and are more likely than women of other ethnicities to be housewives without paid extrahousehold employment. The trend away from the nuclear family toward lone parenthood is therefore much less apparent among South Asians, whose households are also the most likely to include elderly relatives typically living with a married son and his wife. Berthoud comments that many characteristics of British South Asian families were evident among white families in the past, adding that "loyalty to their own communities histories and traditions is one of the driving forces behind the preservation of these cultural patterns" (2000, p. 21). This image of British Asians "flying the flag for traditional family life" (Younge, 2000) recurs in academic work and in the self-identity of British South Asians (Yuval-Davis and Werbner, 1997).

At the same time, there are indications of change. There was evidence in the early 1990s that second-generation South Asians are marrying later than their parents, suggesting "some assimilation in marriage patterns…towards those of the white population" (Berrington, 1994, p. 530). There is also evidence of differences between South Asians in this respect, with Indians marrying later and being more likely to cohabit or divorce than Pakistanis and Bangladeshis. An analysis comparing two cohorts, 1992–1995 and 2000–2002, of pooled Labour Force Survey data shows an increase in the proportion of Pakistani and Bangladeshi women in the labor force, the change occurring primarily among childless British-born women aged 19–34 years, underlining the importance of accounting for age, partnership status, and presence of dependent children in analyses of women's labor force participation (Lindley, Dale and Dex, 2004, p. 9). There is also evidence to suggest that the image of the stable traditional South Asian family may now be less widely applicable than it was earlier. Data from the 2001 Census indicate that the percentage of South Asian lone parents has at least doubled since the mid-1990s. According to the Fourth National Survey of Ethnic Minorities (1994–1995), lone-parent families comprised just under 10% of all British Pakistani and Bangladeshi families and 5% of British Indian families (HMSO, 1996, p. 53), but 2001 Census data show this percentage as just under 20% for British Pakistani and Bangladeshi families and over 10% for British Indian families (Babb *et al.*, 2006). The fact that Pakistani and Bangladeshi lone mothers tend not to be single, but to be separated from their husbands, divorced or widowed (Lindley, Dale, and Dex, 2004), signals significant changes in the stability of Pakistani and Bangladeshi marriages.

Can we conclude from these trends that distinctive sociocultural traditions and preferences associated with minority ethnic group identities are becoming less influential than modern cultural influences and socioeconomic pressures in shaping patterns of conjugality, expectations of intimacy, and family formation? The rest of this chapter explores aspects of this question, beginning with a discussion of the Afro-Caribbean experience with reference to recent research on the transnational character of Caribbean kinship. It then considers the significance of socioeconomic background, religion, marriage rules, and gender conventions in accounting for both diversity and change *within* the South Asian population, with particular reference to recent debates and research concerning arranged consanguineous transnational marriages among Pakistani Muslims.

Caribbean Kinship: Transnational Links and Support

Commenting on the greater likelihood that Caribbean lone mothers are in full-time work than lone mothers of other ethnicities, Lindley notes that this may reflect "the independent matriarchal culture prominent among black women" (Lindley, Dale, and Dex, 2004, p. 11). The Afro-Caribbean family pattern, documented for the Caribbean prior to migration to Britain after World War II, is in fact not a single pattern but comprises a variety of household forms, ranging from primarily conjugal to primarily consanguineous and comprising two or three generations of women with often-absent men. Although marriage was an ideal, economic constraints often prevented marriage prior to childbearing, and male monogamy in marriage was not expected. In rural areas, young adults would remain living in the parental household, contributing to the household economy while forming extrahousehold sexual unions, and any children from these nonresidential unions would live with their mothers. Eventually, a man would establish his own household, often cohabiting with the mother of his most recent children for many years before marriage (Foner, 1977). In women-headed (matrifocal) households, a senior woman is the most stable presence and has greater authority than the men. In consanguineal households, which accounted for 40% of households in one field study (Solien, 1965), a woman lives with her children and her daughter's children, the younger mother often being the main wage earner, while her mother, the maternal grandmother, cared for the household and children (Smith, 1988). Solien views this household as an adaptation to an economic system where recurrent male migration is the primary source of cash.

The influence of these patterns following migration to Britain is an intriguing question. Postwar migrants from the Caribbean were primarily from Jamaica. In the 1950s and 1960s, the Jamaican economy was in poor shape, a consequence of colonial rule and the domination of plantation agriculture, and there was high unemployment, a long tradition of emigration, labor migration, and a remittance economy. Those who chose to migrate to Britain in response to the postwar demand for labor were not the most destitute but those who could raise the money for the passage to England, and they tended to be more skilled than the average Jamaican (Phillips and Phillips, 1998). Typically, men migrated first, and wives, common-law wives, or girlfriends followed soon after, while children stayed with their grand-mothers until their parents had saved enough money for the additional fares (Foner, 1979; Olwig, 1999).

Partly as a result of their shocking experiences of racism and of being reminded constantly of racial difference in routine discrimination, half of the adults in Foner's study of pioneer-generation immigrants in London in the 1970s were then planning to return to Jamaica. Foner noticed a degree of conformity to English family patterns in that couples married earlier than in Jamaica, probably as a result of improved economic circumstances that enabled men to be reliable providers. She also noted that couples no longer approved of common-law unions, perhaps in order to avoid the disapproval of local whites. Couples also spent more leisure time together and were more likely to share domestic and child-care responsibilities than was the case in Jamaica (Foner, 1977; see also Driver, 1982). Foner's speculation that this might prove but a short-term adaptation to new conditions and that "there may be a partial return to 'old' patterns of family relations" (1977) seems to have proved accurate. British-born Caribbean women in full-time or part-time work often have close ties with mothers and grandmothers who may do more of the child-rearing and domestic work than their daughters' and granddaughters' male partners. The emerging pattern of cohabitation or later marriage to partners who are not necessarily coethnic may, in part, reflect broader changes in British society but may also reflect a new emphasis on the distinct behavior, lifestyles and identities of black Britons (Alexander, 1996). Here too, age and life-course variables are relevant, as Caribbean single parents with long-term extrahousehold partnerships may eventually marry, in what would be a new form of an older Caribbean pattern.

On the other hand, Berthoud has suggested that "the Caribbean family, in the traditional sense of a Caribbean man married to a Caribbean woman, may be dying out" (2005, p. 249). Marriage within the ethnic group is often viewed as one, if not the single, key to the maintenance of ethnic boundaries (Barth, 1969). With a high rate of interethnic marriage, a growing proportion of children and grandchildren with an only part-Caribbean ancestry, and fewer individuals who have multiple connections to a Caribbean history, Platt wonders if British Caribbeans will be able to effectively sustain distinct cultural and community institutions, "to transmit values and practices associated with their Caribbean heritage, to sustain distinct family histories and to maintain connections with disparately located family members" (Platt, pp. 7–8).

Yet there is evidence indicating that Caribbean patterns of conjugality and family formation in Britain do continue to reflect traditions and changes within the Caribbean itself, where there are high rates of single motherhood and grandmothers and other relatives remain important for providing childcare (Olwig, 2012). Moreover, the ongoing significance of extrahousehold ties and of a strong sense of obligation toward and responsibilities between kin, both within communities in Britain and across transnational networks, challenges the stereotype of Afro-Caribbeans as individualistic in the extreme, with a weak sense of kinship and family (Goulbourne, 1999; Reynolds, 2006; Goulbourne, 2008). Ethnographic research on transnational families details some of the ways in which people create a family identity and a sense of collective welfare across national boundaries (Bryceson and Vuorela, 2002). Chamberlain shows that Caribbean migrants' descriptions of their lives reveal an understanding of migration as connecting rather than severing them from home and an inclusive concept of family and family responsibilities, regardless of geographical location. Periodic family reunions – in the United Kingdom, the United States, or elsewhere – publicly express these family identities. Indeed, the family itself, Chamberlain argues, "has become a statement of cultural and ethnic identity," its structures and values retaining "practical resonance" and being a source of pride for transnationally dispersed Caribbeans, including those born or raised in Britain (Chamberlain, 2005, pp. 182–183). Olwig suggests that to appreciate fully the perspectives on family life held by people living within geographically dispersed networks of kin, it may be necessary for scholars to abandon the national, ethnicity-based frameworks of investigation associated with the countries in which transnational migrants have settled (Olwig, 2007; see also Olwig, 2010).

Diversity of the British South Asian Population

For British South Asians too, links between kin living elsewhere than Britain – in Europe, North America, and the Middle East, for example, as well as in India, Pakistan, and Bangladesh – remain important influences on family formation and patterns of marriage. There are also significant differences within Britain's South Asian population in the nature of these transnational links, as well as in socioeconomic status, marriage rules and gender norms. In this section, after making some preliminary general remarks about continuity and change in South Asian family structures, I describe some dimensions of this diversity relevant for understanding patterns of family formation and marriage before focusing in more detail on British Pakistani Muslims.

The ideal South Asian joint family, to the extent that it can be generalized, is a multigenerational unit (Vatuk, 1972) with external patrilineal links to a local descent group, known variously, according to region and religious identity, as *got* (among Hindus and Sikhs), *patti*, *qaum* (among Muslims), or *zat* (caste) or *biradari* (brotherhood). Marriages are preferentially arranged by families rather than by the couple, take place within the caste, and are motivated in part by concerns to preserve or enhance status. A bride traditionally moves on marriage to her husband's parents' household, lives under the authority of her mother-in-law, and is subordinate to her husband, his elder brothers and their wives. Household relationships are formally governed by gender norms, status, and age. Men are responsible for financial provisioning, with sons handing wages to their father, while women are responsible for the care of any dependent children and elderly relatives. With time, smaller nuclear households may be established as sons marry, have children and move out of the multigenerational household – a process symbolized by a bride's dowry traditionally containing goods necessary for establishing an independent household (Ballard, 1990, p. 235). These smaller households then expand and may in turn divide as the next generation marries and has children. Even so, interhousehold links remain crucial to the formal and informal exchange of goods and services (Vatuk, 1972).

In practice, though, these processes have long been affected by socioeconomic changes within South Asia and by internal and international migration. Migration necessarily separates family members. Households may become women-headed with absent men or become nuclear. Corporate norms may continue to govern relationships between dispersed kin for some, while for others the ideals of joint family living no longer hold the same force. In Britain, household composition is constrained physically by terrace housing, as well as by external pressures to conform to the State's definitions of family that underpin access to welfare. Within the Indian subcontinent, marital practices are changing, toward more young people arranging their own marriages, and with educational status and personal compatibility as key criteria in spouse selection and a new emphasis on companionate marriage (Fuller and Narasimhan, 2008). Research in India also indicates that the conventional contrast between arranged and love marriage is overstated, there is a long-standing and complex relationship between the two, and to prioritize individual emotional fulfillment over filial duty is not necessarily seen simply or solely in terms of "Westernization" (Vatuk, 1972; Donner, 2002; Mody, 2002).

The 2001 Census categories recognize South Asian ethnic diversity as comprising "British" plus "Indian", "Pakistani", or "Bangladeshi", referring to the relatively recent constructions of Pakistan in 1947 and Bangladesh (formerly East Pakistan) in 1971. For British South Asians, however, regional, linguistic, and religious identities are also important. Thus, British Indians include Hindus and Sikhs, with regional origins in Gujarat and the Punjab, and a minority of Muslims, most from North India or Hyderabad in the Deccan. As regards migration history, another distinction concealed by standard ethnicity data can be drawn between direct migrants to the United Kingdom in the 1950s and 1960s from India, Pakistan, or Bangladesh and migrants who came via East Africa. The direct migrants are mostly from rural areas of particular regions. About half of Britain's Pakistani Muslim population is from Mirpur District in Azad Kashmir, with most of the remaining Pakistani population being from the Punjab, Bangladeshi Muslims are mostly from Sylhet district (Gardner, 1995) and Sikhs are mainly from Jullundur district in Indian Punjab. The "twice migrants" (Bhachu, 1985) were largely professionals and business people in Africa who spoke English fluently, of Indian Hindu Sikh and Muslims ancestral origins in pre-Partition India, but whose social links within South Asia are now more attenuated, as is true also of British Hindu Indo-Caribbeans (Vertovec, 1994). These differences help explain why Indians have achieved greater socioeconomic parity with whites (Modood et al., 1997) and are ahead of Bangladeshis and Pakistanis along Berthoud's scale of change in family formation and marriage. East African

Asians are less likely to insist on conventionally arranged marriages, women are more likely to be in the labor force, and young women are more likely to be graduates and to delay marriage and childbearing (Bhachu, 1985).

An "East African effect" on household structure (Blakemore and Boneham, 1994, p. 81) has been noted: one survey found that 71% of a sample of elderly South Asians in Birmingham lived in households of more than six people, while in Coventry, another Midlands city, only 25% of the sample lived in such households and not necessarily because houses in Coventry are smaller. Birmingham's South Asians are mostly direct migrants, whereas Coventry's South Asians are predominantly East African Asians and are more likely to live in nuclear households and to consider that a newly married couple should live independently of the groom's parents. By contrast, Pakistani migrants in Britain seem, in general, to have eventually established joint households, as the independent households established in the 1970s and 1980s with the arrival of wives and children became multigenerational when sons married and were joined by daughters-in-law. Some families creatively adapted cramped British terrace houses to accommodate the extended family; others established ostensibly nuclear households in adjacent properties, in the same street or a short car journey or walk away in the same locality. Yet others purchased the house next door and built a gate into the fence at the back. Classified as nuclear in surveys of household composition, these families may sometimes be joint in intention and use, and wages and household expenses may be paid into, and drawn from, a shared purse (Shaw, 2000). However, degrees of connectedness and the nature of intimate relationships cannot be assumed from surveys of household structure. The reality of life for some elderly South Asian Punjabi, Mirpuri, and Sylheti families may be very different from the stereotype that South Asians look after their own elderly relative (Gardner, 2002; Shaw, 2004; Harriss and Shaw, 2006).

On diversity and change in the conventions and expectations of marriage within Britain's South Asian population, Roger Ballard's (1983, 1990) analysis of the differential impact of marriage rules, gender norms, and the political economies of their regions of origin on the migration pattern of Punjabi Sikhs and Mirpuri Muslims provides a useful starting point. Ballard contrasts the Sikh rules of descent group exogamy, prohibiting marriage into the descent groups (*got*) of each parent and both grandmothers and forbidding the exchange of women between two families, with the Muslim Mirpuri preference for marriages between the children of siblings. In the Sikh pattern, brides usually become geographically separated from their natal kin on marriage and move to families with whom they have no prior kinship links. The Mirpuri pattern implies geographical proximity through overlapping ties of natal and affinal kinship: a bride's mother-in-law is frequently also her aunt. Combined with more restrictive gender conventions and the custom of village burial – which contrasts with the Sikh (and Hindu) practices of cremation – the Mirpuri marriage pattern encourages the creation of more locally focused tight-knit kinship networks centered on their villages or origin, whereas Jullundri Sikhs are less rooted in India. Processes of family reunification whereby wives and children joined men in Britain took place more slowly among Mirpuris than among Sikhs. And although initially pioneer-generation Jullundri Sikhs received and accepted marriage offers for their children from the Punjab, they now tend to arrange marriages within the United Kingdom, the United States, and Canada and allow

British-born adults to choose their marriage partners and live independently of the groom's parents. This, as we will see in the next section, has been much less true of Pakistani Muslims, although there are indications of change. Ballard notes also the part played by the differing political economies of the regions of origin – Jullundur being more prosperous and outward looking than rainfall-dependent, remittance-dependent Mirpur (Ballard, 1983). Jullundri Sikhs in Britain could draw on their business and technical expertise to escape factory work and establish small businesses, and their wives were freer to enter the labor force so were also better protected than Mirpuris from the effects of the recession of the 1970s and 1980s. Aspects of this differential analysis are also helpful for understanding socioeconomic diversity *within* the British Pakistani population – between, for example, families from Mirpur and families from central Punjab – in patterns of marriage and household formation (Shaw, 2001, 2004).

Pakistani Muslim Marriages: Transnationality, Instability, and Consanguinity

This last section discusses the trends in British Pakistani marriages and explores the dynamics associated with the continuing popularity of consanguineous transnational marriages and with the changes in marital stability indicated by survey data.

A conventional justification for arranged marriages is that they are less risky than love marriages with which they are usually contrasted because parents, with their greater experience and knowledge, are better able to judge a good match than young people, and because the responsibility for spouse selection and for the success of marriage is shared among kin. Marrying within the family, typically with first cousins or other consanguineous kin (defined as second cousins or closer, within the category of relatives permitted as spouses by marriage rules), is thought to have further advantages because the potential in-laws are known and trusted relatives and so will not mistreat their daughter-in-law. Such marriages are thus considered safer, particularly for women. Couples who are close kin can expect practical and emotional support from the wider family if they have marital problems, inhibiting separation and divorce. However, unresolved marital conflict involving close kin can result in long-term rifts between families, as in the case of brother–sister exchange (*watta–satta*) marriage, where breakdown in one marriage has serious implications for the other. Divorce is seen as having particularly serious consequences for consanguineous marriage, sometimes resulting in chains of revenge divorce (Werbner, 1990, p. 89).

There is evidence that the rate of consanguineous marriage among British Pakistanis has increased rather than declined and that most of these marriages are transnational (Shaw, 2009). Almost half of British-born Pakistanis aged 19–50 years has a spouse who has migrated to Britain (Dale, 2008). There are socioeconomic advantages for kin in Pakistan in sending a family member to the West, while for relatives in Britain transnational marriage effectively maintains links with and fulfills obligations to kin in Pakistan. Transnational consanguineous marriages, however, have complex motivations and introduce a variety of new risks. In some cases, marriages to which British Pakistani parents and their daughters had agreed were motivated primarily by relatives' desires to gain access to Europe. There is also the danger of brides never being joined by their husbands if entry visas are denied; separating the stages of marriage rituals represents a response to these new risks (Charsley, 2006). New challenges associated with gender and domestic power relations further contribute to the dynamics of marital instability. Marrying husbands from abroad may give British women more equal marital relationships, enabling them to evade the scrutiny of the husbands' kin (Charsley, 2005). This, however, can be problematic for men, since traditionally it is shameful for a man to be a *ghar-damad* (house son-in-law), dependent on his wife's relatives (Charsley, 2008). In such marriages, conflicts also occur over the dynamics of financial provisioning. Wives who have had to demonstrate financial independence and house ownership prior to marriage to enable their husbands' entry permits – an important factor underlying the increase in young childless British-born Pakistani and Bangladeshi women in the labor force – may subsequently resent their husbands remitting money to Pakistan. Wives from abroad, on the other hand, may be more isolated and vulnerable to control by their husbands and in-laws (Charsley, 2008), a vulnerability augmented by the restricted rights of migrant spouses during the probationary 2 years before they can apply for residency.

Arranged consanguineous transnational marriages therefore entail complex risks and benefits, which individuals and families assess and reassess. With greater public recognition of forced marriage, young British-born adults themselves may be concerned to distinguish forced from arranged marriage, emphasizing that the latter requires freely given consent, even as these marriages also meet parental approval (Shaw, 2009). They may also give good reasons for preferring arranged marriages, citing, for example, the Pakistani partner's knowledge of the cultural norms and religious values associated with the country of origin, and they may describe their initial meetings with their partners and aspects of their engagements – such as long-distance phone calls or chaperoned outings – using romantic images that are both modern and distinctly South Asian (Shaw and Charsley, 2006).

Additionally, there has been much debate in the United Kingdom in the past decade about the elevated risk of recessively inherited conditions in the children of consanguineous marriages and whether consanguineous couples should be offered genetic counseling on the basis of their consanguinity (Shaw, 2006, 2009). Such debate is increasingly global, with implications for public health policy in areas of the world where consanguineous marriage is practiced – in the Middle East, parts of South Asia and North Africa, where consanguineous marriage is preferred, and in Europe and America where families practicing consanguineous marriage have settled (Shaw and Raz, forthcoming). Among British Pakistani families with affected children, or with a risk associated with a family history of a genetic condition, responses to risk information need to be understood more broadly in relation to the set of socio-economic and emotional risks and benefits associated with consanguineous marriage (Shaw, 2009, 2011). Although British Pakistani children in school are exposed to the dominant perception of cousin marriage as incest and young adults are exposed to the media discourse and may also have experience of genetic conditions in their families, avoidance of cousin marriage does not necessarily follow (Shaw, 2009). Young Pakistani adults may view cousins in Pakistan as more distant and therefore more acceptable as spouses than local cousins who may be equated with siblings

(Charsley, 2003). Genetic risk may be used to turn down a particular *rishta* (match) with a Pakistani relative that is unacceptable for other reasons (Shaw, 2009). If the marriage pattern changes – given the evidence of instability in transnational cousin marriages – this may be less from concerns about genetic risks and more of a reflection of changing expectations of marriage.

A recent study of the dynamics underlying instability in a small sample of Mirpuri and Punjabi British Pakistani couples (Qureshi, Charsley and Shaw, 2012) takes a longitudinal perspective. It shows that marital difficulties were prominent in the life histories of older Pakistani women, challenging the stereotype of British Pakistanis as stable custodians of old-fashioned values but also showing that divorce was rare. This confirms the findings of earlier studies concerned with domestic violence and forced marriage that show divorce was highly resisted unless in cases of extreme conflict (Samad and Eade, 2002; Gill, 2004; Guru, 2009). Instead, women were expected to endure their hardships (see also Qureshi, 2012). Couples negotiated long-term estrangement, and the extended family sought to reconcile couples, a situation exacerbated by the nonrecognition of Muslim divorces in civil law (Pearl and Menski, 1998), as well as by sometimes strong discouragement from family and from religious authorities toward women seeking divorce (Shah-Kazemi, 2001; Bano, 2011). Qureshi, Charsley and Shaw (2012) distinguish the generic factors underlying marital instability – spousal incompatibility, domestic violence, and infidelity – from factors more specifically associated with British Pakistanis: transnationality, which entails the risks of having insufficient knowledge about a partner, attitudes to parental involvement in arranged marriage, and Islam. Their cases involving young people indicate that the expectation of intimacy in its modern sense of personal fulfillment and companionate marriage is an increasingly important factor in destabilizing marriage. Moreover, Islam in the lives of young British Pakistanis is emerging as a significant resource particularly for young women in asserting their rights, including their rights to divorce (Jacobson, 1997, Brown, 2006). Their analysis points to a shift over time in perceptions of arranged marriage, toward both young people *and* their parents viewing arranged marriages as riskier than love marriages (Qureshi, Charsley, and Shaw, 2012).

Conclusion

Households that are apparently similar in composition may, at any point in time, be the result of quite dissimilar processes of marriage and household formation, with quite different meanings for the participants. Household survey approaches tell us little about relationships within households, between spouses, and between other relatives or about the nature of extrahousehold links with kin and nonkin, including across transnational networks. Such networks may be of enormous practical and emotional importance in the negotiation of care for vulnerable members and in structuring and maintaining marriage and affinal relationships. This may be particularly evident in the narratives of family life associated with Caribbean families and in the practices of South Asian transnational marriage. But what enacting kinship entails across transnational networks may have more general relevance beyond these ethnic groups for geographically dispersed families who nonetheless maintain a sense of family – through using modern communications technologies, for instance. These multisited families can been seen as constituting "global care chains" (Hochschild, 2000, p. 131), shaped by expectations of care and patterns of interdependency that become significant at certain points in the life course (Harriss and Shaw, 2006; Olwig, 2012). Much is at stake in contemporary personal and family relationships beyond the rhetoric of individualism.

As regards British South Asians, particularly the Pakistanis discussed here, there is also evidence of shifts in perceptions of arranged marriage, seen now as potentially more risky than love marriages with which they have long been contrasted, such that if love is not forthcoming in an arranged marriage, then the young people will be supported in divorce and choosing a spouse themselves. This is not, however, to argue that the motivations and pressures underlying these changes are identical to those affecting white families. The increase in marital instability and divorce among British Pakistani families represents not a straightforward cultural convergence with the majority but is the outcome of complex processes that warrant further research including within other British South Asian groups, such as British Bangladeshis, whose patterns of transnational marriage are similar to those of Pakistanis, and British Indians, with their diverse backgrounds and distinct religious affiliations.

References

Alexander, C. (1996) *The Art of Being Black*, Oxford University Press, Oxford.

Allen, G.A. and Crow, G. (eds) (2001) *Families, Households and Society*, Palgrave, London.

Babb, P., Butcher, H., Church, J. and Zealey, L. (eds) (2006) *Social Trends*, No 36, 2006. Office for National Statistics, Palgrave Macmillan, Available at www.statistics.gov.uk.

Ballard, R. (1983) The context and consequences of migration: Jullundur and Mirpur compared. *New Community*, X1 (1–2), 117–136.

Ballard, R. (1990) Migration and kinship: the differential effect of marriage rules on the processes of Punjabi migration to Britain, in *South Asians Overseas: Migration and Ethnicity* (eds C. Clarke, C. Peach, and S. Vertovec), Cambridge University Press, Cambridge.

Bano, S. (2011) Cultural translations and legal conflict: muslim women and the shari'a councils in Britain, in *From Transnational Relations to Transnational Laws: Northern European Laws at the Crossroads* (eds A. Hellum, S. Sardar Ali, and A. Griffith), Ashgate, Aldershot, pp. 165–186.

Barth, F. (1969) Introduction, in *Ethnic groups and Boundaries: The Social Organization of Culture Difference* (ed. Fredrik Barth), George Allen & Unwin, London, pp. 9–38.

Baumann, G. (1996) *Contesting Culture: Discourses of Identity in Multi-ethnic London*, Cambridge University Press, Cambridge.

Beck, U. and Beck-Gernsheim, E. (1995) *Individualisation*, Sage,*The Normal Chaos of Love*. Cambridge. Polity Press, London.

Benson, S. (1981) *Ambiguous Ethnicity*, Cambridge University Press, Cambridge.

Benson, S. (1996) Asians have culture, West Indians have problems: Discourses of race and ethnicity in and out of anthropology, in *Culture, Identity and Politics: Ethnic Minorities in Britain* (eds T.O. Ranger, Y. Samad, and O. Stuart), Avebury, Aldershot, pp. 47–56.

Berrington, A. (1994) Marriage and family formation among the white and ethnic minority populations in Britain. *Ethnic and Racial Studies*, 17 (3), 517–546.

Berthoud, R. (2000) Family formation in multicultural Britain: three patterns of diversity. Working paper, Institute for Social and Economic Research, University of Essex.

Berthoud, R. (2005) Family formation in multi-cultural Britain: diversity and change, in *Ethnicity, Social Mobility and Public Policy: Comparing the US and the UK* (eds G.C. Loury, T. Modood, and S.M. Teles), Cambridge University Press, Cambridge, pp. 222–252.

Bhachu, P. (1985) *Twice Migrants: East African Sikh Settlers in Britain*, Tavistock, London.

Blakemore, K. and Boneham, M. (1994) *Age, Race and Ethnicity: A Comparative Approach*, Open University Press, Milton Keynes.

Bolognani, M. (2009) *Crime and Muslim Britain: Race, Culture and the Politics of Criminology among British Pakistanis*, I B Tauris, London.

Brown, K. (2006) Realising Muslim women's rights: The role of Islamic identity among British Muslim women. *Women's Studies International Forum*, 29, 417–430.

Bryceson, D. and Vuorela, U. (2002) Transnational families in the twenty-first century, in *The Transnational Family: New European Frontiers and Global networks* (eds D. Bryceson and U. Vuorela), Berg, Oxford, pp. 3–30.

Bulmer, M. (1996) *The Ethnic Group Question in the 1991 Census of Population*, HMSO, London.

Chamberlain, M. (2005) Language, identity and Caribbean families: transnational narratives, in *Caribbean Narratives of Belonging: Fields of Relations, Sites of Identity* (eds J. Besson and K.F. Olwig), London: Macmillan CaribbeanWarwick University Caribbean Studies series, pp. 171–188.

Charsley, K. (2005) Unhappy husbands: masculinity and migration in transnational Pakistani marriages. *Journal of the Royal Anthropological Institute*, 11 (1), 85–105.

Charsley, K. (2006) Risk and ritual: the protection of British Pakistani women in transnational marriage. *Journal of Ethnic and Migration Studies*, 32 (7), 1169–1187.

Charsley, K. (2008) Vulnerable brides and transnational ghar damads: gender, risk and "adjustment" among Pakistani marriage migrants to Britain, in *Marriage, Migration and Gender* (eds R. Palriwala and P. Uberoi), Sage, New Delhi.

Charsley, K. 2003. Rishtas: Transnational Pakistani marriages. Unpublished PhD thesis, University of Edinburgh.

Dale, A. (2008) Migration, marriage and employment amongst Indian, Pakistani and Bangladeshi residents in the UK. Working paper 2008-02, University of Manchester, CCSR.

Dench, G., Gavron,K. and Young, M. (2006) *The New East End: Kinship, Race and Conflict*, Profile Books, London.

Donner, H. (2002) "One's own marriage": love marriages in a Calcutta neighbourhood. *South Asia Research*, 22, 79–94.

Driver, G. (1982) West Indian families: an anthropological perspective, in *Families in Britain* (eds R.N. Rapoport, M.P. Fogarty, and R. Rapoport), Routledge and Kegan Paul, London, pp. 205–219.

Edwards, R. (ed.) (2008) *Researching Families and Communities: Social and Generational Change*, Routledge, London and New York.

Foner, N. (1977) The Jamaicans, in *Between Two Cultures* (ed. J. Watson), Blackwell, Oxford.

Foner, N. (1979) *Jamaica Farewell*, University of California Press, Berkeley.

Fuller, C.J. and Narasimhan, H. (2008) Companionate marriage in India: the changing marriage system in a middle-class Brahman subcaste. *Journal of the Royal Anthropological Institute*, 14 (4), 736–754.

Gardner, K. (1995) Global migrants, in *Local Lives: Travel and Transformation in Rural Bangladesh*, Clarendon Press, Oxford.

Gardner, K. (2002) *Age, Narrative and Migration: The Life Course and Life Histories of Bengali Elders in London*, Berg, Oxford.

Giddens, A. (1992) *The Transformation of Intimacy: Sexuality, Love and Eroticism in Modern Societies*, Stanford University Press, Stanford.

Gill, A. (2004) Voicing the silent fear: South Asian women's experiences of domestic violence. *The Howard Journal of Criminal Justice*, 43 (5), 465–483.

Goulbourne, H. (1999) The transnational character of Caribbean kinship in Britain, in *Changing Britain: Families and Households in the 1990s* (ed. S. McRae), Oxford University Press, Oxford.

Goulbourne, H. (2008) Families in black and minority ethnic communities and social capital, in *Researching Families and Communities: Social and Generational Change* (ed. R. Edwards), Routledge, London and New York.

Guru, S. (2009) Divorce: obstacles and opportunities – South Asian women in Britain. *The Sociological Review*, 57 (2), 285–305.

Harper, S. (2003) Changing families as European societies age. *European Journal of Sociology*, 44 (2): 155–184.

Harriss, K. and Shaw, A. (2006) Family care and transnational kinship: British Pakistani experiences, in *Kinship Matters* (eds F. Ebtehaj, B. Lindley, and M. Richards), Hart, Cambridge, pp. 259–274.

HMSO (1996) *Social Trends* No. 26, Her Majesty's Stationery Office (HMSO), London.

Hochschild, A.R. (2000) Global care chains and emotional surplus value, in *On the Edge: Living with Global Capitalism* (eds W. Hutton and A. Giddens), Jonathan Cape, London, pp.130–146.

Jacobson, J. (1997) Religion and ethnicity: dual and alternative sources of identity among young British Pakistanis. *Ethnic and Racial Studies*, 20 (2), 238–256.

Jacobson, J. (1998) *Islam in Transition: Religion and Identity Among British Pakistani Youth*, Routledge, London.

Jamieson, L. (1998) Intimacy: Personal relationships in modern societies. Polity Press, Cambridge.

Jamieson, L. (1999) 'Intimacy Transformed? A Critical Look At The 'Pure Relationship', 33:477–494.

Jamieson, L. (2011) Intimacy as a concept: explaining social change in the context of globalisation or another form of ethnocentrism? *Sociological Research Online*, 16 (4), 15.

Kurtz, S. (2007) Marriage and the terror war. *National Review Online*, http://www.nationalreview.com/articles/219989/marriage-and-terror-war/stanley-kurtz (accessed on December 11, 2013).

Lindley, J., Dale, A. and Dex, S. (2004) Ethnic differences in women's demographic, family characteristics and economic activity profiles, 1992 to 2002: an analysis of family, work, life cycle differences and changes over time among women from different ethnic groups. *Labour Market Trends*, April, 153–165.

McRae, S. (1999) *Changing Britain: Families and Households in the 1990s*, Oxford University Press, Oxford.

Modood, T., Berthoud, R., Lakey, J. *et al.* (1997) *Ethnic Minorities in Britain: Diversity and Disadvantage*, Policy Studies Institute, London.

Mody, P. (2002) Love and the law: love-marriage in Delhi. *Modern Asian Studies*, 36, 223–256.

Olwig, K.F. (1999) Narratives of the children left behind: home and identity in globalized Caribbean families. *Journal of Ethnic and Migration Studies*, 25, 267–284.

Olwig, K.F. (2007) *Caribbean Journeys: An Ethnography of Migration and Home in Three Family Networks*, Durham, N.C.; London: Duke University Press.

Olwig, K.F. (2010) Cosmopolitan traditions: Caribbean perspectives. *Social Anthropology*, 18 (4), 417–424.

Olwig, K.F. (2012) The care chain, children's mobility and the Caribbean migration tradition. *Journal of Ethnic and Migration Studies*, 38 (6), 933–952.

Pearl, D.and Menski, W. (1998) *Muslim Family Law*, Sweet and Maxwell, London.

Phillips, M. and Phillips, T. (1998) *Windrush: The Irresistible Rise of Multi-Racial Britain*, Harper Collins, London.

Platt, L. (n.d.) Ethnicity and Family: Relationships Within and Between Ethnic Groups. An Analysis using the Labour Force Survey, www.equalityhumanrights.com/.../ethnicity_ and_family_report.pdf

Pryce, K. (1979) *Endless Pressure*, Penguin, Harmondsworth.

Qureshi, K. (2013) *Sabar*: body politics among middle-aged migrant Pakistani women. *Journal of the Royal Anthropological Institute*, 19, 120–137.

Qureshi, K., Charsley, K. and Shaw, A. (2014) Marital instability among British Pakistanis: transnationality, changing conjugalities and Islam. *Ethnic and Racial Studies* 37 (2):261–279.

Reynolds, T. (2006) Caribbean families, social capital and young people's disaporic identities. *Ethnic and Racial Studies*, 29 (6), 1087–1103.

Samad, Y. and Eade, J. (2002) *Community Perceptions of Forced Marriage*, Foreign and Commonwealth Office, Community Liaison Unit, London.

Shah-Kazemi, S.N. (2001) *Untying the Knot: Muslim Women, Divorce and the Shariah*, The Nuffield Foundation, London.

Shaw, A. (2000) *Kinship and Continuity: Pakistani Families in Britain*, Routledge/Harwood Academic, London and New York.

Shaw, A. (2001) Kinship, cultural preference and immigration: consanguineous marriage among British Pakistanis. *Journal of the Royal Anthropological Institute*, 7, 315–334.

Shaw, A. (2004) British Pakistani elderly without children: an invisible minority, in *Ageing without Children: European and Asian Perspectives* (eds P. Kreager and E. Schroeder-Butterfill), Berghahn Books, New York, Oxford, pp. 198–221.

Shaw, A. (2006) British Pakistani arranged transnational cousin marriages: critique, dissent and cultural continuity, *Contemporary South Asia, Special Issue: The British South Asian Experience* (eds J. Brown and I. Talbot), pp. 211–222.

Shaw, A. (2009) *Negotiating Risk: British Pakistani Experiences of Genetics*, Berghahn, Oxford and New York.

Shaw, A. (2011) Risk and reproductive decisions: British Pakistani couples' responses to genetic counseling. *Social Science and Medicine*, 73, 111–120.

Shaw, A. and Charsley, K. (2006) Rishtas: adding emotion to strategy in understanding British Pakistani transnational marriages. *Global Networks*, 6 (4), 405–421.

Shaw, A. and Raz, A. (forthcoming) *Cousin Marriages: Between Tradition, Genetic Risk and Cultural Change*, Berghahn Books, London and New York.

Smart, C. and Shipman, B. (2004) Visions in monochrome: families, marriage and the individualization thesis. *British Journal of Sociology*, 55 (4), 491–509.

Smith, R.T. (1988) *Kinship and Class in the West Indies: A Genealogical Study of Jamaica and Guyana*, Cambridge University Press, Cambridge.

Solien, N. L. (1965) The consanguineal household and matrifocality. *American Anthropologist*, 67, 1541–1549.

Vatuk, S. (1972) *Kinship and Urbanization: White Collar Migrants in North India*, University of California Press, Berkeley and Los Angeles.

Vertovec, S. (1994) Caught in an ethnic quandary: Indo-Caribbean Hindus in London, in *Desh Pardesh: The South Asian Presence in Britain* (ed. R. Ballard), Hurst, London.

Werbner, P. (1990) *The Migration Process: Capital, Gifts and Offerings among British Pakistanis*, Berg, Oxford.

Younge, G. 2000. South Asians Fly the Flag for Traditional Family Life. *The Guardian* (Dec 18).

Yuval-Davis, N. and Werbner, P. (1997) Ethnicity, gender relations and multiculturalism, in *Debating Cultural Hybridity: Multicultural Identities and the Politics of Anti-Racism* (eds P. Werbner and T. Modood), Zed, London and New Jersey.

10

Immigrant Families and the Shifting Color Line in the United States

KAREN D. PYKE

A distinctive feature of immigration to the United States is its emphasis on family reunification. Fully two-thirds of US immigration involves family migration unlike most industrialized nations whose immigration is employment driven (Kofman, 2004). So when we talk about American immigrants, we are usually talking about immigrant families.

When families immigrate to the United States, race and racialization in the American context are central to their post-immigrant experience, symbolically as well as materially. As a system of inequality, race shapes immigrant identities, family structures and living arrangements, who marries whom and who is likely not to marry at all, where families reside and children go to school, levels of educational attainment, marital and nonmarital fertility, the kind of jobs people do and how much they earn, exposure to crime, access to healthcare, and how long people live. Understanding the long-term prospects for immigrant and second-generation families requires consideration of the racial structure of the society in which they live out their lives.

Not only does race affect immigrant families but immigrant families affect race. Immigrants are not simply the passive recipients of imposed racial identities and categories in their new homeland. Their mere presence can usher in dramatic changes in the racial–ethnic configuration of the receiving society. Immigrant families also engage racial strategies in forging their identities and social location in the American context with the aim of enhancing their racial status and share of resources in the new society. Over the past decade, scholars have devoted greater attention to how the large influx of racially and ethnically diverse immigrant families is affecting a dramatic demographic transition in the racial order of the United States and, more-over, how that changing system will affect the racial futures of immigrant and second-generation American families. Indeed, the rapidity with which immigration is

The Wiley Blackwell Companion to the Sociology of Families, First Edition.
Edited by Judith Treas, Jacqueline Scott, and Martin Richards.
© 2014 John Wiley & Sons Ltd. Published 2017 by John Wiley & Sons Ltd.

transforming US society and its racial system requires the adaptation of all Americans, not just the newcomers.

This chapter opens with a review of the recent literature on the immigrant-inspired racial transition currently underway as the US population shifts to a majority of racial minorities, complicating the black/white racial paradigm that has dominated the American consciousness for centuries. It next considers how immigrant family trends of interracial marriage and the formation of multiracial families and identities are shaping a US racial order that is both old and new. Finally, this chapter considers how immigration policy affects Hispanic families with undocumented members, potentially affecting downward assimilation for generations and contributing to structural fissures that could cut new racial boundaries along class lines within the Hispanic population. The focus of this chapter is on Hispanics and Asians – the two largest racial categories of US immigrants who, some argue, are achieving proximal whiteness and creating greater distance between black and nonblack/white Americans. As the emphasis is on the racial implications of immigrant family patterns, several aspects of the literature on immigrant families are touched on briefly or not at all, including immigrant family living arrangements, intergenerational relations, and transnational families. These topics are covered in greater depth elsewhere (on transnational families, see Baldassar *et al.*, Chapter 8, this volume, and Treas, 2008; and for more general reviews, see Curran *et al.*, 2006; Pyke, 2007; Clark, Glick, and Bures, 2009; Glick, 2010; and Shaw, Chapter 9, this volume).

A Nation of Immigrant Families, Still

Long perceived as a nation of immigrants, the United States receives more immigrants than any other country, absorbing a fifth of the world's migrant population (Doucet and Hamon, 2007; Rumbaut, 2008, pp. 196–197). Immigration, not fertility, drives the population growth of this industrialized nation – the fastest growing in the world (Fortuny, Hernandez, and Chaudry, 2010). Nearly one-third of the 40 million foreign-born residents in the United States arrived since 2000 (US Census Bureau, 2009). The majority of Asians in the United States are foreign born, and despite the flow of immigrants arriving from Mexico for well over a century, most Mexicans in the United States today are immigrants or the second-generation children of immigrants (Kao and Thompson, 2003). Immigrants are 13% of the US population, slightly less than the peak of 15% in 1890 but significantly higher than in 1970 when their numbers sunk to 5% (Grieco *et al.*, 2012). In contrast to 1890 when the vast majority of immigrants came from Europe, today's US immigrants come primarily from non-Western nations and territories in Latin America, Asia, the Caribbean, and Africa and are more racially, linguistically, and culturally diverse.

The foreign-born and the American-born children of immigrants are the prime movers and shakers of that nation's demographic trends. Immigrants are younger and bear more children than native-born Americans. Overall, one of every four American children lives in an immigrant family, and fully 80% of children of immigrants are native-born Americans (Hernandez, Denton, and Macartney, 2008). Children of immigrants accounted for the entire growth in the number of American children under the age of 9 between 1990 and 2008, given declines in the number of children of native-born parents (Fortuny, Hernandez, and Chaudry, 2010).

In driving the US population growth, the foreign born and their children are generating dramatic changes in the nation's racial composition. Between 1960 and 2010, the percentage of the foreign born from Europe plummeted from 75% to 12%. Meanwhile, the immigrant population from Latin America soared from 6% to 53%, and from Asia grew from 5% to 28% (Schmidley, 2001; Grieco *et al.*, 2012). Although Hispanics are a panethnic and multiracial group, they are considered whites in US official statistics, which divides whites into Hispanics and non-Hispanics. In this chapter, the author joins with race scholars and many Hispanics themselves in regarding them as a distinct racial group. The author uses the terms "Hispanic" and "Latino" interchangeably, at times distinguishing between black and nonblack Latinos. Because they are the largest immigrant group in the United States, the author frequently refers to Mexicans specifically.

Mexico has long been the number one sending country of US immigrants. Thirty percent of all immigrants in the United States today hail from Mexico, and half of them are unauthorized immigrants (Portes and Rumbaut, 2001; Jiménez, 2008; Passel, Cohn, and Gonzalez-Barrera, 2012). There are more immigrants in the United States from Mexico alone (12 million) than the total number of immigrants living in any other country in the world. In 2000, Hispanics surpassed African Americans as the largest racial minority group in the United States (Ramirez and de la Cruz, 2002; Vallejo and Lee, 2009). By 2011, Latinos were 17% and African Americans 14% of the US population (US Census Bureau, 2012).

Immigration flows to the United States continue to take dramatic, often unanticipated, turns in response to ever-dynamic internal and external pressures. Around 2007, immigration from Mexico came to a standstill. For the first time in over two decades, the population of unauthorized Mexican immigrants declined significantly due to several factors in the United States, including tighter border controls, a virulent anti-immigration discourse, a weakened job market, and high rates of deportation. With the slowing of Mexican immigration, Asian immigration to the United States outpaced that of Hispanics for the first time ever (Passel, Cohn, and Gonzalez-Barrera, 2012).

Another dramatic turn has been the rise in black immigration from Africa. While Caribbean black immigrants, including large numbers from Haiti and Jamaica, comprise 70% of black immigrants, there was a 40-fold increase in immigration from Africa between 1960 and 2007, most of which occurred after 1990 when the number of sub-Saharan African immigrants tripled (Massey *et al.*, 2007; Terrazas, 2009). In some major cities like New York, immigrant blacks are over 25% of the black population (Kent, 2007). The largest wave of African immigrants since the importation of slaves was outlawed in 1808 is occurring largely under the radar (Robinson, 2010, p. 164). Black immigrants from Africa and the Caribbean occupy a distinct social location from latter-generation African Americans and are greatly diversifying the population of American blacks. Young native-born African Americans live in an era when being a black American does not mean one is necessarily a descendent of slaves or has a family history confronting white racism.

The influx of immigrants is rapidly transforming the United States to a nonwhite majority–minority nation. The US Census estimates that non-Hispanic whites will be a numeric minority by 2030 (Sanburn, 2011). This transition is occurring faster in some regions of the country, especially around metropolitan gateways of immigration.

In 22 large US cities, racial minorities are now a majority (Sanburn, 2011; US Census Bureau, 2012). And five states have a majority of racial minorities: California and New Mexico are 60% nonwhite; Texas is 55%; Washington, DC, is 65%; and Hawaii is 77%, which is the only state that is majority Asian. At the same time, immigrant groups are spreading out within the interior of the United States, settling in places that have long been primarily white (Waters and Jiménez, 2005).

The demographic shift to a majority–minority has already occurred among the nation's youngest citizens who are the most racially heterogeneous age group. In 2011, racial minorities constituted 50.4% of newborn Americans (US Census Bureau, 2012). As a result, young white Americans are growing up in less racially isolated residential, school, and work settings than did older white cohorts and see race differently than majority-white World War II and baby boomer generations, many of whom grew up in the era of Jim Crow legal segregation. Younger whites and non-whites view racial boundaries as more permeable regarding friendship, dating, and marriage than do older generation Americans (Passel, Wang, and Taylor, 2010; Hochschild, Weaver, and Burch, 2012;). In short, younger Americans are assimilating to the new racial order faster than are their parents and grandparents.

These conditions have prompted a convergence of interest in the race and immigration literatures. While European scholars have long overlapped research on immigration and race (see Shaw, Chapter 9, this volume), this is not the case in the United States where immigration and race have distinct histories, partly due to the fact that not all nonwhites in the United States arrived as immigrants or arrived at all in the case of Native Americans. Hence, race and immigration scholarship pursued divergent lines of inquiry and occupied separate scholarly domains, sometimes to their mutual detriment. Immigration scholars focused on the acculturation and assimilation of immigrant families using models based on European immigrants and thus devoted less attention to racism (Pyke, 2007). This has been changing in recent years, as immigration scholars engage segmented assimilation theory to examine new racialization processes, suggesting that some segments of immigrant groups are downwardly assimilating to the ranks of the black underclass while others enjoy upward assimilation to the white middle class, leading to the formation of racial categories that cut across current racial groups (Zhou, 2004; Lee and Bean, 2007; Hildalgo and Bankston, 2010). At the same time, race scholars, who have long studied racism using a black/white paradigm based in the experience of American descendants of enslaved Africans, now acknowledge the insufficiency of this model for a society whose nonwhite immigrants are generating great racial diversity and complexity (e.g., Bonilla-Silva, 2004; Warren and Twine, 2007; Jiménez, 2008). It is only in recent years that these two intellectual streams are merging around a shared interest in how immigrant families and their descendants are affecting the US racial order and how the US racial order is affecting immigrant families (Burton *et al.*, 2010).

Is the Color Line Shifting?

To evaluate whether contemporary nonwhite immigrant families are merging into whiteness, scholars typically use as a model the process by which earlier European immigrant ethnics became white. Hence, they look to economic, educational, and

marital assimilation into whiteness. Most attention on the shifting racial order
focuses on Asians and Latinos who have dominated the immigrant flows for half a
century, while less scholarly attention has been heaped on African, Afro-Caribbean,
Arab, and Middle Eastern immigrants.

Noting that whites tend to regard Latinos and Asians as more culturally similar
to themselves than blacks, and conversely, Latinos and Asians regard themselves as
closer to whites than blacks, several scholars suggest the category of whiteness is
stretching to incorporate subsets of Latinos and Asians as "honorary whites" (Lee and
Bean, 2007). They argue that a new black/nonblack divide that pivots around the
continued subordination of black Americans is emerging (Yancey, 2003; Lee and
Bean, 2004; Lee and Bean, 2007; Warren and Twine, 2007; Bean *et. al.*, 2009). They
liken this process to that which occurred across the late nineteenth and first half of
the twentieth centuries when the American-born children of Irish, Jewish, Italian,
and Eastern European immigrants racially transitioned from nonwhite ethnics into
whiteness and experienced a concomitant decline in the salience of their ethnic
identity – a social process marked by their movement out of ethnic neighborhoods,
educational and occupational mobility, intermarriage to other white ethnics, and
efforts to assert their superiority to blacks through the adoption of white racist attitudes (Waters, 1990; Ignatiev, 1995; Warren and Twine, 1997; Brodkin, 1998;
Jiménez, 2008). Blacks have long served as the fulcrum for defining whiteness as
well as proximal whiteness for immigrant groups. There are some indications that
native-born Asian-American ethnic groups with a long-term presence in the United
States (e.g., Japanese Americans) have become "honorary whites" and lighter-skinned,
middle-class, latter-generation Mexican Americans have integrated into whiteness
(Foley, 2005).

As the social trends driving a new US racial order are dynamic, complex, contradictory, and vulnerable to unforeseen events, it is impossible to offer more than
educated guesses as to the future of race in the United States. One presumption that
scholars seem to share is whites will remain at the top of the US racial hierarchy
and blacks at the bottom. Everything else, as Hochschild notes, "is up for grabs"
(2005, p. 81). In the following section, the author reviews some of the evidence
regarding the racial prospects of today's US immigrants. The author focuses on
interracial marriage and the birth of biracial and multiracial children among recent
generations of nonwhite immigrant groups and the creation of multiracial families
involving whites and their nonwhite immigrant children who become families
through international transracial adoption.

Interracial dating and outmarriage among immigrant groups

Immigration scholars have long considered the outmarriage of racial/ethnic
immigrants to whites as the final stage of assimilation, while race scholars have
regarded high rates of romantic pairings between nonwhites and whites to be the
harbinger of eroding racial boundaries (Gordon, 1964; Song, 2009; Bean and Lee,
2010). Patterns of cross-racial intimacy and marriage signal a narrowing distance
between groups with the likely merging of distinct racial groupings into a newly
shared racial category. Such patterns also signal a declining commitment among
immigrant groups in maintaining ethnic practices. As the second-generation children

of today's immigrants have entered adulthood, the rate of interracial intimacy has climbed. In the 2010 Census, interracial partnering accounted for 10% of married couples (up from 7% in 2000) and 18% of unmarried cohabitating couples (Lofquist *et. al.*, 2012). Between 2008 and 2010, 22% of all marriages in the western United States were interracial (Wang, 2012). While rates of intermarriage have increased between immigrant groups and whites, interracial marriage with blacks remains relatively low, signaling the distancing of Asians and Latinos from blackness (Passel, Wang, and Taylor, 2010). Children growing up in immigrant families in the United States are part of an American generation that is more open to interracial marriage than any generation before them (Kasinitz *et. al.*, 2008). If left to their own devices, they would likely outmarry at even higher rates than they actually do. But immigrant parents exert great pressure on their children's marital choices.

Immigrant parents from India, the Middle East, and other societies where arranged marriages are common and dating is associated with sexual promiscuity can exert immense control over the marital choices of their children – especially daughters whose failure to conform can bring dishonor to the family. In such communities, marriage traditions are important for the intergenerational maintenance of ethnic and religious identities (Manohar, 2008; Samuel, 2010; see also Shaw, Chapter 9, this volume). Many daughters conform to parental directives so as to maintain their family reputation and connection; others only appear to do so while dating men of their choosing in secret, away from the prying eyes of family and coethnic community members – typically doing so only after they are well into adulthood. This can be very stressful given the deep attachment many feel to their parents and the centrality of marital practices to ethnic identity. Some second-generation members cast a bicultural spin on dating by defining its aim as marriage (Manohar, 2008). Indeed, as more mainstream American youth shun monogamous dating relations, engage in the new "hookup" culture of casual sexual encounters, and delay marriage or opt out altogether (Armstrong, Hamilton, and England, 2010), dating might acquire greater respectability and acceptance as a means to marriage in immigrant communities. Perhaps, US mainstream culture will come to regard dating that leads to marriage as traditional, thus serving up such practices as a way to mark ethnicity. In other words, as new norms replace American dating practices, dating in pursuit of marriage could become associated with immigrant ethnic retention and tradition.

Immigrant parents not from cultures that practice arranged marriages also pressure children's endogamy to preserve family connection, ethnic practices, and a shared ethnic language into the next generation. In part because women are seen as the primary transmitters of culture, parents often exert more pressure for endogamy on their daughters than sons (Kasinitz *et. al.*, 2008; Manohar 2008; Samuel 2010; Morales, 2012). This is not always the case, though. Some immigrant mothers encourage daughters to outmarry as a strategy for avoiding traditional gender arrangements that favor men's interests (Nesteruk and Gramescu, 2012). And many Chinese and Korean immigrant parents, who look to their sons to maintain the blood line and to provide filial care, place more emphasis on sons' than daughters' endogamy (Kibria, 2003), even though a coethnic daughter-in-law is no guarantee she will assume filial duties without resistance (Shih and Pyke, 2010). Some sons might outmarry as a strategy for resisting filial obligations, though much research indicates that children of immigrant parents value parental care as a means of showing love, paying parents back for the sacrifices they endured, and demonstrating their adult status (Pyke, 2000; Kasinitz *et. al.*, 2008). Preferences for endogamous marriage can greatly limit one's marriage pool and encourage transnational marital arrangements (Thai, 2008; see Baldassar *et al.*, Chapter 8, this volume) or contribute to lifelong singlehood, as Ferguson found in her study of never-married Chinese and Japanese American women (2000).

When second-generation children have a difficult time finding a suitable coethnic partner and reach an age when their marital prospects begin to diminish, parents are more likely to accept exogamy. Among nonblack Latino and Asian immigrant parents, there is a clear racial hierarchy in their preferences for exogamy. In general, they prefer coethnics of the same racial group (particularly those seen as culturally similar) or whites, with blacks typically considered unacceptable marriage partners. Many immigrant parents arrive on US shores having already imbibed antiblack racial and skin tone biases in their homeland. They often obscure their racism by basing their opposition to their children's romantic pairing with blacks or dark-skinned Latinos on the grounds of cultural distance or concern that such a union would subject their children and grandchildren to racism (Kibria, 2003; Kasinitz *et. al.*, 2008; Morales, 2012).

Parental racial preferences overlap with children's actual marital practices. Among US-born Hispanics and Asian-Americans, rates of interracial marriage are nearly 40% and 60%, respectively, and fully 92% of interracial marriages are to whites (Qian, 2005). Skin tone and racial identity are extremely important in Hispanic outmarriage with those who identify as black less likely to marry whites (Shin, 2011). Asian-Americans are more likely to outmarry someone who is white than a member of another Asian ethnic group (Chow, 2000). Only 9% of married Asian-Americans born in the United States after 1965 had an Asian-American spouse of a different ethnic group, suggesting that the panethnic Asian identity that some predicted would emerge through interethnic marriage has not come to pass (Kibria, 2003). Structural and cultural assimilation is positively related to outmarriage to whites; it is higher among those who speak English fluently, are college educated, and are US rather than foreign born and among the third and subsequent generations of Americans compared to the second (Stevens, McKillip, and Ishizawa, 2006; Passel, Wang and Taylor, 2010; Shin, 2011; Pew Research Center, 2013).

Some scholars suggest that over time Asian-Americans and Latinos will merge into whiteness or an expanded racial category defined by being not black (Lee and Bean, 2007; Feliciano, Robnett, and Komai, 2009; Hidalgo and Bankston, 2010). However, racial outmarriage is affected not only by attitudes of acceptance for interracial marriage but also by demographic factors such as the size of the immigrant group and the ratio of men to women within that group (Landale, Oropesa, and Bradatan, 2006). Ongoing immigration has been replenishing the Latino and Asian population, thus increasing the numbers available for endogamous marriage. This has contributed to some slowing in outmarriage among second-generation Americans alongside an increase in marriage between native- and foreign-born Asian-Americans and a similar though less dramatic pattern of mixed-nativity marriage among Latinos. These trends signal the possible resurgence in racial/ ethnic identity and a retrenchment of racial boundaries that could contribute a larger number of third-generation Americans who speak the language of their immigrant grandparents and share their racial/ethnic identity (Lichter *et. al.*, 2007; Okamoto, 2007; Jiménez, 2008; Qian and Lichter, 2011; McManus and Apgar, 2012). These marital patterns signal a bifurcated trend with some Asian and Latino Americans integrating into white society and others maintaining a strong ethnic identity and ethnic cultural practices, a pattern noted for years among those who study acculturation of the 1.5- and second-generation American offspring of immigrant parents (Pyke and Dang, 2003). As discussed next, outmarriage to whites can differ substantially across gender, as they do among Asian-Americans, indicating that men and women of the same race might not be accorded the same proximity to whiteness.

Gender patterns of outmarriage among Asian-Americans

Gendered racial stereotypes of Asian men and women contribute to a strong gendered pattern of outmarriage. White men often perceive Asian women as better marriage partners than white women due to stereotypes that cast them as more family-oriented, subservient, and dutiful. Asian men, on the other hand, are stereotyped as threatening, patriarchal, and poor marriage partners relative to white men (Chow, 2000; Kim, 2006; Min and Kim, 2009; Nemoto, 2009; Pyke, 2010). In a study of white racial preferences in online dating, white men were more likely to include Asian women and exclude black women as potential daters, while white women were more likely to exclude Asian men (Feliciano, Robnett, and Komaie, 2009). As noted in this study, whites tend to exercise greater control on racial outmarriage than do nonwhites. Among those married in 2008, 40% of Asian women wed outside their race, mostly to whites, while only 20% of Asian men did so. Meanwhile, Hispanic rates of outmarriage were the same for men and women at 25% (Passel, Wang, and Taylor, 2010). So if outmarriage is an indicator of becoming white or an honorary white, there is evidence that women of Asian descent are more readily accepted into whiteness than Asian men. On the other hand, given the role racial and gendered stereotypes play in intermarriage patterns, it is not certain that intermarriage indicates racial assimilation. While some individuals married to whites might be able to reduce their "otherness" in the eyes of the whites with whom they interact, that is a far cry from all whites viewing all Asian or Latino Americans as white (Zhou, 2004).

That women of Asian descent are more likely to outmarry whites than are men of Asian descent suggests a gendered dynamic to racial incorporation of immigrants that will affect sex ratio imbalances leading to a surplus of single Asian-American men. Such a surplus might encourage Asian-American men to seek Asian brides from abroad. Marriage migration is the largest category of family-sponsored immigration to the United States, and most arrivals in this category are women of the same race as their spouse (Thai, 2008; Monger and Yankay, 2012). Gender imbalances already affect transnational marriages among first-generation Vietnamese American men. With a shortage of Vietnamese immigrant women in the US marriage pool and a corresponding shortage of marriageable men in Vietnam, many Vietnamese American men are seeking wives from Vietnam (Thai, 2008). While the American men regard women in the homeland as more gender traditional than Vietnamese American women, women in Vietnam presume they will find greater gender equity in marriages with Vietnamese men in the United States. These "clashing dreams" can create profound marital conflicts (Thai, 2004, p. 285). While this could contribute to divorce, Thai notes that the stigma associated with divorce in Vietnamese culture and the shame divorce can bring to the couple's parents might mean they will remain married – "for better or worse" (2004, p. 285; see Baldassar *et al.*, Chapter 8, this volume).

Biracial and Multiracial Children

While interracial marriage can signal patterns of assimilation and proximal whiteness among nonwhite immigrant groups, the racial identities of their multi-racial children can provide even greater insight into the long-term effect racial intermarriage will have on the racial order (Lee and Bean, 2004). Most racial outmarriages involve one white partner, and most interracial families – over 85% – contain white and nonwhite individuals (Lee and Edmonston, 2005). Whether children of mixed-race parentage assume a multiracial or monoracial identity, and the extent to which those who identify monoracially self-identify as white or nonwhite, tells us a lot about the salience of racial distinctions." Must have "identify" here or doesn't make sense.

Children born to Asian/white or Latino/white couples are not automatically perceived as monoracially Asian or Latino, and they are less likely to identify as Asian or Latino than those born to monoracial parents (Landale, Oropesa, and Bradatan, 2006). Using data from the 1990 Census that required parents to choose a monoracial identity for mixed-race offspring, Qian (2004) finds that Asian-American/white parents were most likely to identify their children as white and children of African American/white couples least likely. Interestingly, parents were more likely to choose a white racial category for their children when the black parent is foreign born rather than US born. This might indicate a greater desire among immigrant blacks to distance themselves from the latter-generation American descendants of enslaved Africans, as noted elsewhere (Guenther, Pendaz, and Makene, 2011). While some research finds that children of non-white/white parentage are more likely to be identified as nonwhite when their father, rather than mother, is the racial minority parent (Qian, 2004), other research finds fewer consistencies, with children in Asian/white families most likely to share their mother's racial identity regardless of whether she is white or Asian; children of white/black couples more likely to identify with their father's race, especially if he is white; and other mixed-race children (e.g., Latino/white) more likely to identify as white regardless of which parent is white or Latino. Racial context and social class seem to affect the racial identity of multiracial children, with those living in nonwhite neighborhoods or attending nonwhite schools more likely to identify as nonwhite and those of higher socioeconomic status, with the exception of white/black multiracial children, more likely to identify as white (Brunsma, 2005; Bratter and Heard, 2009). Meanwhile, parents who are multiracial are more likely to identify their children as white, indicating a gradual merging into whiteness (Bratter, 2007).

While evidence suggests that children of Asian/white and nonblack Latino/white parentage have more leeway in how they self-identify than children born to black/white couples, the latter are more likely to identify as multiracial or white than in the past (Rockquemore and Brunsma, 2002; Roth, 2005). Unfortunately, this scholarship does not examine the role of phenotype on the racial classification of mixed-race children, a factor that contributes to the confinement of children born to black/white couples to the category of black due to the one drop of black blood rule (e.g., President Barack Obama is biracial but identifies as black and is regarded as black by others). Racial identity also appears to be dynamic across situation and time (Harris and Sim, 2002). Some individuals switch from a white to a black self-identity after experiencing unemployment, impoverishment, or incarceration (Penner and Saperstein, 2008). The importance of class to racial categories might indicate an emerging detachment of race from phenotype in the new racial order.

In response to the growing numbers of children born to interracial couples and pressure from multiracial Americans, the US Census allowed individuals for the first time in 2000 to select all the racial categories to which they feel they belong. Hence, in its official statistics, the United States has moved away from the single-race concept that has defined the racial order for centuries and now allows for and counts multiracial individuals – though to comply with civil rights policies, the Office of Management and Budget also includes multiracials in their component racial categories (Bratter, 2007). The ability to officially identify as multiracial is likely to accelerate the number of multiracial individuals who will do so, not only on official forms but also in their everyday lives. Thus, the racial order in the United States appears to be changing with a synergistic swiftness.

International transracial adoption

Scholarly discussions of immigration tend to overlook the influx of foreign-born children through international adoption even though Americans adopt more children from abroad than any other country. The quiet migration of foreign-born infants and children increased dramatically in the 1990s, after which the US Census added the category "adopted son/daughter" as a family relationship category in 2000 (Selman, 2002; Kreider, 2003). The rate of foreign-born adoption peaked at 23,000 in 2004 and then reversed dramatically in 2012 to its lowest level since 1994 after several top-sending countries put bans or heavy restrictions on international adoptions due to corruption or political tensions with the United States, which, some speculate, might increase the adoption of children from other nonwhite regions, including Africa (Associated Press 2013). The main sending countries of transnational adoptees to the United States have been China, Russia, South Korea, and Guatemala. The majority of immigrant adoptees are nonwhites adopted by white middle-class parents. Even though their numbers are small, they contribute to the growth of multiracial families headed by native-born white Americans (Selman, 2002; Dorow, 2006; Lee *et al.*, 2006).

In a study of the narratives of white adoptive parents of Chinese girls, Dorow finds white adoptive parents regard Asianness as more racially flexible than blackness, which affects their adoption choice. Asians are racially constructed as different, but not too different alongside the "too different" construction of blackness (2006, p. 371). It is easier for a Chinese daughter to be absorbed into the family's whiteness than if she were black. As one adoptive parent notes, "I've gotta admit that if I had a black child, I'd probably think of us as more biracial" (2006, p. 371). Many white adoptive parents emphasize accepting and liking Chinese people and culture as important to raising their daughters with a positive ethnoracial identity. However, they often engage in a kind of "cultural tourism" involving "the selective appropriation and consumption of renovated cultural symbols, artifacts, and events that serve as the source of identity construction" (Quiroz, 2012, p. 527). Such "staged authenticity" contributes to weaker ethnoracial identities among transracially adopted children than found among their American-born ethnoracial counterparts raised by biological immigrant parents (Quiroz, 2012).

It is not simply the identities of transracial immigrant adoptees that are affected by their incorporation into white families. For many adoptive parents, their "white identities are made flexible, potentially transformed through their Chinese children" (Dorow, 2006, p. 371). While the rise in interracial marriage suggests that the category of whiteness might be expanding to include Asians, as well as Latinos, white adoptive parents of nonwhite immigrant children can also experience an expansive transformation of their own white identities by identifying with the race and ethnicity of their adopted children – making them more ethnically interesting and diverse than those whites enmeshed in "bland white culture" (Dorow, 2006, p. 371). The racial flexibility and proximity to whiteness of Chinese children adopted by whites, for example, contribute to the expansive racial flexibility of the parents as well. As the transracial international adoption of children who are Asian unsettles the category of whiteness, it does so by reproducing the distance between whites and blacks (Dorow, 2006).

Segmented Assimilation and the Bifurcation of Racial Groups

The rise of interracial marriage and the birth of multiracial identities are just one pathway by which an immigrant group can experience a bifurcation of its racial identity over time. A plethora of research into patterns of segmented assimilation across various racial/ethnic groups finds the social capital of immigrant parents greatly affects whether children assimilate upwardly through educational attainments and occupational status to the white middle class or experience fewer educational and occupational achievements alongside a downward assimilation to nonwhite lower-class communities (Portes and Rumbaut, 2001; Pyke, 2007; Rumbaut, 2008; Portes, Fernández-Kelly, and Haller, 2009; Glick, 2010; Haller, Portes, and Lynch, 2011). This bifurcation within Asian and Hispanic racial groups is what some refer to as the "Princeton or prison, jail or Yale" phenomenon

(Suárez-Orozco and Gardner, 2003). As described next, recent increases in deportation rates of undocumented Mexicans and Central Americans, many of whom have native-born American children, will affect segmented assimilation of future generations of Latino Americans.

Mixed-status families

Among the undocumented immigrants living in the United States, 76% are Hispanic and 59% are Mexicans. And they tend to live in families. The undocumented are more likely than native-born US citizens to reside with a spouse and children. Nearly half (47%) of all households headed by an undocumented immigrant consist of couples and children, more than double that of households headed by US citizens in which only 21% comprise a couple and children. Three out of every four children living with an undocumented parent were born in the United States, which automatically accords citizenship to all who are native-born, and their numbers doubled between 2000 and 2009 (Passel and Cohn, 2009, 2011). There has recently been a push to end birthright citizenship in the United States, which, if passed, would increase the number of undocumented children (Passel and Cohn, 2011). As these figures indicate, many undocumented immigrants live in mixed-status families – a family whose members have different immigration statuses.

The marginalized status of those who are unauthorized affects the entire family and delays their incorporation into the mainstream society relative to those who are not unauthorized (Abrego and Gonzales, 2010; Bean et al., 2011). As the undocumented live with the constant threat of arrest and deportation, they typically live in the shadows where many social services and community resources are out of reach. Undocumented parents are less likely to access healthcare and police services out of fear of being deported, undermining their own health and well-being as well as that of their children (Menjívar, 2006). Those with citizen children are often uninformed about the public services to which their children have legal access or are too afraid to seek out such services. Hence, citizen children of unauthorized immigrants are denied many of the benefits of citizenship to which they are entitled, and they tend to be the children most in need of those benefits, thus undermining their life chances and access to social citizenship and creating greater inequality among citizen children (Fix and Zimmerman, 2006; Leiter, McDonald, and Jacobson, 2006; Abrego and Gonzales, 2010). Given their vulnerabilities and lack of protections, noncitizen children and the citizen children of undocumented parents are functionally stateless.

At present writing, undocumented Latino children can attend public school through high school but have restricted access as adults to a college education and financial aid. Knowing they are restricted from attaining a higher level of education can weaken their academic motivation and performance, contributing to the high rate of Latino students who drop out before finishing high school. Their undocumented status limits them to an underground economy of low-paying jobs where they are not asked to provide legal documents (Abrego, 2006). Mixed-status families often live in low-income, high-crime neighborhoods with poor, underfunded schools. Some parents, fearing for their children's safety, send them to Mexico or Central

America to live with relatives, often enduring many years without seeing their children (Menjívar, 2006).

In recent years, the United States has implemented stricter and more punitive immigration policies and laws, stepping up worksite raids and border patrols (Capps *et. al.*, 2007) and contributing to the racial profiling of Mexican Americans as undocumented "aliens" (Aguirre, 2004). Deportations more than doubled over the first decade of the new millennium, with more than 70% of deportees being Mexican, including some who had lived in the United States for decades (Passel and Cohen, 2011). Citizen children of undocumented parents as well as undocumented children are at risk of being separated from their parents. For every two adults who are deported through worksite raids, one child is affected (Capps *et al.*, 2007). A US immigrant policy and a public discourse that regards unauthorized immigrants simply as lawbreakers obscure the fact that many of the deported are parents raising citizen children (Yoshikawa, 2011). In contrast to the immigration policies implemented in 1965 that gave special priority to family reunification as a criterion for immigration, both as a means of enhancing family stability and promoting immigrant adaptation, today's policies are splitting families apart (Abrams, 2007). Children in single-parent families or those where both parents are deported are the most vulnerable. Some deported parents just disappear without time to contact family members, adding to their children's emotional trauma (Capps *et al.*, 2007). The loss of a deported parent's presence and earnings creates tremendous financial hardship, psychological stress, vulnerability, and social isolation for the children left behind. And it is not only the young offspring that are vulnerable; the deported often leave behind elderly parents, adult children, and young grandchildren to whom they had been providing care and other kinds of assistance (Treas and Mazumdar, 2004; Treas, 2009; Kanstroom, 2012).

Even when parents are not deported, living with the fear that deportation is a possibility creates stress and hardship for parents and children alike (Yoshikawa, 2011). Children growing up in undocumented families fare worse across many indicators, including cognitive development, than those in immigrant families with documentation (Brabeck and Xu, 2010; Yoshikawa, 2011). The unauthorized status of mothers in particular undermines the educational and class attainments of their second-generation children (Bean *et al.*, 2011).

One of the most important factors determining the incorporation of second- and latter-generation children is the legal status of the first generation. The large number of undocumented Mexicans and Central Americans in the United States today is unlike earlier waves of European immigrants whose pathways to structural incorporation were not legally blocked. Unless legal status is accorded to today's undocumented children, they will grow into English-speaking undocumented adults who are denied access to higher education and economic opportunities. They will thus be forced to live in the social and economic margins of society, where they will raise another generation in lower-income, nonwhite communities who, in turn, will have fewer opportunities for higher education and upward mobility. This segment of the Mexican American population will likely be racialized as nonwhite, while other segments of the Mexican American population, including descendants of legalized residents, will more likely experience upward social mobility to the white middle class and racial outmarriage. These dynamics could bifurcate current racial groups into proximal whites and proximal blacks in the new racial order.

Conclusion

Immigrant families are playing a pivotal role in changing the racial order in the United States. Immigrants' segmented assimilation, high rates of interracial marriage, contribution to multiracial births and identities, as well as the formation of white-headed multiracial families through the transracial adoption of immigrant children highlight structural and attitudinal changes that are shaping dramatic changes in how Americans think about and organize race. While there is much uncertainty about how racial categories will be organized, scholars tend to agree that whites will remain at the top of the racial hierarchy as some nonwhite immigrant segments merge into whiteness or enjoy some racial privilege as proximal whites, with blacks once again confined to the bottom. Due to segmented assimilation, such as occurs among Latinos with documentation and those without, scholars predict that some racial group members who assimilate to the white middle class are more likely to live among and marry whites and enjoy the racial privileges associated with proximal whiteness, while their counterparts who downwardly assimilate and live in nonwhite communities will experience greater racial oppression as proximal blacks. That is, the racial categories we associate with today's immigrant groups can fracture along class lines and thus even along family lines. If that occurs, social class might trump phenotype as the primary mechanism for sorting individuals into racial groups. This could divide families racially. Siblings born to the same parents could be assigned into different racial groups, as occurs in some Latin American societies (Bonilla-Silva, 2004). However, in Latin America, it is phenotype, not class, that racially divides families. The growth of interracial marriages and multiracial births also presents challenges to current monoracial categories. On the other hand, increases in the flows of certain immigrant streams can generate new opportunities for intraracial marriage, a strengthening of racial/ethnic identities, and reinforce the current order marked by distinct monoracial categories. Only time will tell what the new immigrant-driven US racial order will look like, precisely how it will be determined, and how it will affect and be affected by ongoing flows of immigrant families to the United States. Given the rate of change, we will not have to wait very long to find out.

References

Abrams, K. (2007) Immigration law and the regulation of marriage. *Minnesota Law Review*, 91, 1625–1709.

Abrego, L.J. (2006) "I can't go to college because I don't have papers": incorporation patterns of Latino undocumented youth. *Latino Studies*, 4, 212–231.

Abrego, L.J. and Gonzales, R.G. (2010) Blocked paths, uncertain futures: the postsecondary education and labor market prospects of undocumented Latino youth. *Journal of Education for Students Placed at Risk*, 15, 144–157.

Aguirre, Jr., A. (2004) Profiling Mexican American identity: issues and concerns. *American Behavioral Scientist*, 47, 928–942.

Armstrong, E.A., Hamilton, L. and England, P. (2010) Is hooking up bad for young women?" *Contexts*, 9, 22–27.

Bean, F. and Lee, J. (2010) *The Diversity Paradox: Immigration and the Color Line in Twenty-first Century America*, New York, Sage.

Bean, F.D., Feliciano, C., Lee, J. and Van Hook, J. (2009) The new U.S. immigrants: how do they affect our understanding of the African American experience? *The Annals of the American Academy of Political and Social Science*, 621, 202–220.

Bean, F., Leach, M., Brown, S. *et al.* (2011) The educational legacy of unauthorized migration: comparisons across U.S.-immigrant groups in how parents' status affects their offspring. *International Migration Review*, 45, 348–385.

Bonilla-Silva, E. (2004) From bi-racial to tri-racial: towards a new system of racial stratification in the USA. *Ethnic and Racial Studies*, 27, 931–950.

Brabeck, K. and Xu, Q. (2010) The impact of detention and deportation on Latino immigrant children and families: a quantitative exploration. *Hispanic Journal of Behavioral Sciences*, 32, 341–361.

Bratter, J. (2007) Will "multiracial" survive to the next generation? The racial classification of children of multiracial parents. *Social Forces*, 86, 821–849.

Bratter, J. and Holly, H. (2009) Mother's, father's, or both? Parental gender and parent–child interactions in the racial classification of adolescents. *Sociological Forum*, 24, 658–688.

Brodkin, K. (1998) *How Jews Became White Folks and What That Says about Race in America*, Rutgers University Press, New Brunswick.

Brunsma, D.L. (2005) Interracial families and the racial identification of mixed-race children: evidence from the early childhood longitudinal study. *Social Forces*, 84, 1131–115.

Burton, L.M., Bonilla-Silva, E., Ray, V. *et al.* (2010) Critical race theories, colorism, and the decade's research on families of color. *Journal of Marriage and Family*, 72, 440–459.

Capps, R., Castañeda, R.M., Chaudry, A., and Santos, R. (2007) Paying the Price: The Impact of Immigration Raids on America's Children, National Council of La Raza, Washington, DC, http://www.urban.org/UploadedPDF/411566_immigration_raids.pdf (accessed June 15, 2007).

Chow, S. (2000) The significance of race in the private sphere: Asian Americans and spousal preferences. *Sociological Inquiry*, 70, 1–29.

Clark, R.L., Glick, J.E., and Bures, R.M. (2009) Immigrant families over the life course: research directions and needs. *Journal of Family Issues*, 30, 852–872.

Curran, S.R., Shafer, S., Donato, K.M. and Garip, F. (2006) Mapping gender and migration in sociological scholarship: is it segregation or integration? *International Migration Review*, 40, 199–223.

Dorow, S. (2006) Racialized choices: Chinese adoption and the "white noise" of blackness. *Critical Sociology*, 32, 357–377.

Doucet, F. and Hamon, R.R. (2007) A nation of diversity: demographics of the United States of America and their implications for families, in *Cultural Diversity and Families: Expanding Perspectives* (eds B.S. Trask and R.R. Hamon), Sage, Thousand Oaks, pp. 20–43.

Feliciano, C., Robnett, B., and Komaie, G. (2009) Gendered racial exclusion among White Internet daters. *Social Science Research*, 38, 39–54.

Ferguson, S.J. (2000) Challenging traditional marriage: never married Chinese American and Japanese American women. *Gender & Society*, 14, 136–159.

Fix, M. and Zimmermann, W. (2006) All under one roof: mixed-status families in an era of reform. *International Migration Review*, 35, 397–419.

Foley, N. (2005) Becoming Hispanic: Mexican Americans and whiteness, in *White Privilege: Essential Reading on the Other Side of Racism* (ed. P.S. Rothenberg), Worth, New York, pp. 49–57.

Fortuny, K., Hernandez, D., and Chaudry, A. (2010) Young Children of Immigrants: The Leading Edge of America's Future, The Urban Institute, Washington, DC, http://www.eric.ed.gov/PDFS/ED511771.pdf (accessed June 5, 2010).

Glick, J.E. (2010) Connecting complex processes: a decade of research on immigrant families. *Journal of Marriage and Family*, 72, 498–515.

Gordon, M. (1964) *Assimilation in American Life: The Role of Race, Religion, and National Origins*, Oxford University Press, New York.

Grieco, E.M., Acosta, Y.D. G., de la Cruz, P. *et al.* (2012) The Foreign-Born Population in the United States: 2010, U.S. Census Bureau, www.census.gov/prod/2012pubs/acs-19.pdf (accessed June 12, 2012).

Guenther, K., Pendaz, S. and Makene, F. (2011) The impact of intersecting dimensions of inequality and identity on the racial status of eastern African immigrants. *Sociological Forum*, 26, 98–120.

Haller, W., Portes, A. and Lynch, S.M. (2011) Dreams fulfilled, dreams shattered: determinants of segmented assimilation in the second generation. *Social Forces*, 89, 733–762.

Harris, D.R. and Sim, J.J. (2002) Who is multiracial? Assessing the complexity of lived race. *American Sociological Review*, 67, 614–627.

Hernandez, D.J., Denton, N.A. and Macartney, S.E. (2008) Children in immigrant families: looking to America's future. *Social Policy Report*, 23, 3–22.

Hidalgo, D.A. and Bankston, C.L. (2010) Blurring racial and ethnic boundaries in Asian American families: Asian American family patterns, 1980–2005. *Journal of Family Issues*, 31, 280–300.

Hochschild, J. (2005) Looking ahead: racial trends in the United States. *Daedalus*, 134, 70–81.

Hochschild, J., Weaver, V. and Burch, T. (2012) *Creating a New Racial Order*, Princeton University, Princeton.

Ignatiev, N. (1995) *How the Irish Became White*, Routledge, New York.

Jiménez, T.R. (2008) Mexican immigrant replenishment and the continuing significance of ethnicity and race. *American Journal of Sociology*, 113, 1527–567.

Kanstroom, D. (2012) *Aftermath: Deportation Law and the New American Diaspora*, Oxford University Press, New York.

Kao, G. and Thompson, J.S. (2003) Racial and ethnic stratification in educational achievement and attainment. *Annual Review of Sociology*, 29, 417–442.

Kasinitz, P., Mollenkopf, J.H., Waters, M.C. and Holdaway, J. (2008) *Inheriting the City: The Children of Immigrants Come of Age*, Russell Sage Foundation, New York.

Kent, M.M. (2007) Immigration and America's Black Population. *Population Bulletin*, 62, 1–20, http://www.prb.org/pdf07/62.4immigration.pdf (accessed July 20, 2007).

Kibria, N. (2003) *Becoming American: Second-Generation Chinese and Korean American Identities*, Johns Hopkins Press, Baltimore.

Kim, N. (2006) "Patriarchy is so Third World": Korean immigrant women and "migrating" white western masculinity. *Social Problems*, 4, 519–536.

Kofman, E. (2004) Family-related migration: a critical review of European studies. *Journal of Ethnic and Migration Studies*, 30 (2), 243–262.

Kreider, R. (2003) Adopted Children and Stepchildren: 2000, U.S. Census, http://darkwing.uoregon.edu/~adoption/archive/Census2000AC.pdf (accessed February 12, 2003).

Landale, N.S., Oropesa, R.S. and Bradatan, C. (2006) Hispanic families in the United States: family structure and process in an era of family change, in *Hispanics and the Future of America* (eds M. Tienda and F. Mitchell), The National Academic Press, Washington, DC, pp. 138–175.

Lee, J. and Bean, F.D. (2004) America's changing color lines: immigration, race/ethnicity, and multiracial identification. *Annual Review of Sociology*, 30, 221–42.

Lee, S.M. and Edmonston, B. (2005) New marriages, new families: U.S. racial and Hispanic intermarriage. *Population Bulletin*, 60, 3–36.

Lee, J. and Bean, F. (2007) Reinventing the color line: immigration and America's new racial/ethnic divide. *Social Forces*, 86, 561–586.

Lee, R.M., Grotevant, H.D., Hellerstedt, W.L. *et al.* (2006) Cultural socialization in families with internationally adopted children. *Journal of Family Psychology*, 20, 571–580.

Leiter, V., McDonald, J.L. and Jacobson, H.T. (2006) Challenges to children's independent citizenship: immigration, family and the state. *Childhood*, 13, 11–27.

Lichter, D.L., Brown, J.B., Qian, Z. and Carmalt, J.H. (2007) Marital assimilation among Hispanics: evidence of declining cultural and economic incorporation? *Social Science Quarterly*, 88, 745–765.

Lofquist, D., Lugaila, T., O'Connell, M. and Feliz, S. (2012) Households and Families: 2010, Census 2010 Brief # C2010BR-14, U.S. Census Bureau, Washington, DC, pp. 1–22.

McManus, P.A. and Apgar, L. (2012) Marital assimilation and economic outcomes in the second generation. *Population Review*, 51, 102–126.

Manohar, N. (2008) "Sshh…!! don't tell my parents": dating among second-generation Patels in Florida. *Journal of Comparative Family Studies*, 39, 571–588.

Marrow, H.B. (2009) New destinations and immigrant incorporation. *Perspectives on Politics*, 32, 1037–1057.

Massey, D.S., Mooney, M., Torres, K.C. and Charles, C.Z. (2007) Black immigrants and Black natives attending selective colleges and universities in the United States. *American Journal of Education*, 113, 243–271.

Menjívar, C. (2006) Family reorganization in a context of legal uncertainty: Guatemalan and Salvadoran immigrants in the United States. *International Journal of Sociology of the Family*, 32 (2), 223–245.

Min, P.G. and Chigon Kim, C. (2009) Patterns of intermarriages and cross-generational in marriages among native-born Asian Americans. *International Migration Review*, 43, 447–470.

Monger, R. and Yankay, J. (2012) U.S. Legal Permanent Residents: 2011. Annual Flow Report of the Department of Homeland Security Office of Immigration Statistics, http://www.dhs.gov/xlibrary/assets/statistics/publications/lpr_fr_2011.pdf

Morales, E. (2012) Parental messages concerning Latino/Black interracial dating: an exploratory study among Latino/young adults. *Latino Studies*, 10, 314–333.

Nemoto, K. (2009) *Love, Power, and Desire among Asian American/White Couples*, Rutgers University, New Brunswick.

Nesteruk, O. and Gramescu, A. (2012) Dating and mate selection among young adults from immigrant families. *Marriage & Family Review*, 48, 40–58.

Okamoto, D.G. (2007) Marrying out: a boundary approach to understanding the marital integration of Asian Americans. *Social Science Research*, 36, 1391–1414.

Passel, J. and Cohn, D. (2009) A Portrait of Unauthorized Immigrants in the United States, Pew Hispanic Center, Washington, DC, http://www.pewhispanic.org/2009/04/14/a-portrait-of-unauthorized-immigrants-in-the-united-states/ (accessed March 10, 2009).

Passel, J. and Cohn, D. (2011) Unauthorized Immigrant Population: National and State Trends, 2010, Pew Hispanic Center, Washington, DC, http://www.pewhispanic.org/2011/02/01/ii-current-estimates-and-trends/ (accessed March 10, 2011).

Passel, J.S., Wang, W. and Taylor, P. (2010) Marrying Out, Pew Research Center, Washington, DC, June 4, http://pewresearch.org/pubs/1616/american-marriage-interracial-interethnic (accessed June 15, 2010).

Passel, J.S., Cohn, D. and Gonzalez-Barrera, A. (2012). Net Migration from Mexico Falls to Zero – and Perhaps Less, Pew Hispanic Center, Washington, DC, April, http://www.pewhispanic.org/2012/04/23/net-migration-from-mexico-falls-to-zero-and-perhaps-less/ (accessed May 2, 2012).

Penner, A. M. and Saperstein, A. (2008) How social status shapes race. *Proceedings of the National Academy of Sciences of the United States of America*, 105, 19628–19630.

Pew Research Center (2007) Optimism about Black Progress Declines: Blacks See Growing Values Gap between Poor and Middle Class, Nov 13, http://www.pewsocialtrends.org/files/2010/10/Race-2007.pdf (accessed August 1, 2007).

Pew Research Center (2012) The Rise of Asian Americans, Jun 19, http://www.pewsocialtrends.org/2012/06/19/the-rise-of-asian-americans/.

Pew Research Center (2013) Second-Generation Americans: A Portrait of the Adult Children of Immigrants, Feb 7, http://www.pewsocialtrends.org/files/2013/02/FINAL_immigrant_generations_report_2-7-13.pdf.

Portes, A. and Rumbaut, R.G. (2001) *Legacies: The Story of the Immigrant Second Generation*, University of California Press, Berkeley.

Portes, A., Fernández-Kelly, P. and Haller, W. (2009) The adaptation of the immigrant second generation in America: a theoretical overview and recent evidence. *Journal of Ethnic and Migration Studies*, 35, 1077–1104.

Pyke, K. (2000) "The normal American family" as an interpretive structure of family life among grown children of Korean and Vietnamese immigrants. *Journal of Marriage and Family*, 62, 240–255.

Pyke, K. (2007) Immigrant families in the U.S., in *The Blackwell Companion to the Sociology of the Family* (eds J.L. Scott, J. Treas, and M.P.M. Richards), Blackwell Publishers, New York, pp. 253–269.

Pyke, K. (2010) An intersectional approach to resistance and complicity: the case of racialized desire among Asian American women. *Journal of Intercultural Studies*, 31 (1), 81–94.

Pyke, K. and Dang, T. (2003) "FOB" and "whitewashed": identity and internalized racism among 2nd generation Asian Americans. *Qualitative Sociology*, 26, 147–172.

Qian, Z. (2004) Options: racial/ethnic identification of children of intermarried couples. *Social Science Quarterly*, 85, 746–766.

Qian, Z. (2005) Breaking the last taboo: interracial marriage in America. *Contexts*, 4, 33–37.

Qian, Z. and Lichter, D.T. (2011) Changing patterns of interracial marriage in a multiracial society. *Journal of Marriage and Family*, 73, 1065–1084.

Quiroz, P.A. (2012) Cultural tourism in transnational adoption: "staged authenticity" and its implications for adopted children. *Journal of Family Issues*, 33, 527–555.

Ramirez, R.R. and de la Cruz, G.P. (2002) The Hispanic population in the United States: March 2002. Current Population Reports, Series P-20, No. 545, U.S. Census Bureau, Washington, DC, http://www.census.gov/prod/2003pubs/p20-545.pdf (accessed April 5, 2002).

Robinson, E. (2010) *Disintegration: The Splintering of Black America*, Doubleday, New York.

Rockquemore, K.A. and Brunsma, D.L. (2002) *Beyond Black: Biracial Identity in America*, Sage, Thousand Oaks.

Roth, W.D. (2005) The end of the one-drop rule? Labeling of multiracial children in Black intermarriages. *Sociological Forum*, 20, 36–67.

Rumbaut, R.G. (2008) The coming of the second generation: immigration and ethnic mobility in southern California. *The ANNALS of the American Academy of Political and Social Science*, 620, 196–236.

Samuel, L. (2010) Mating, dating and marriage: intergenerational cultural retention and the construction of diasporic identities among South Asian immigrants in Canada. *Journal of Intercultural Studies*, 31, 95–110.

Sanburn, J. (2011) 5 Most Surprising Findings from the 2010 Census. *Time*, Dec 20, http://moneyland.time.com/2011/12/20/5-most-surprising-findings-from-the-2010-census/#ixzz1vEWsrM7x (accessed June 10, 2011).

Schmidley, A.D. (2001) U.S. Census Bureau, Current Population Reports, Series P23–206, Profile of the Foreign-Born Population in the United States: 2000, U.S. Government Printing Office, Washington, DC, http://www.census.gov/prod/2002pubs/p23–206.pdf (accessed 30 May, 2001).

Selman, P. (2002) Intercountry adoption in the new millennium: the "quiet migration." *Population Research and Policy Review*, 21, 205–225.

Shih, K.Y. and Pyke, K. (2010) Power, resistance, and emotional economies in women's relationships with mothers-in-law in Chinese immigrant families. *Journal of Family Issues*, 31, 333–357.

Shin, H.-J. (2011) Intermarriage patterns among the children of Hispanic immigrants. *Journal of Ethnic and Migration Studies*, 37 (9), 1385–1402.

Song, M. (2009) Is intermarriage a good indicator of integration? *Journal of Ethnic and Migration Studies*, 35, 331–348.

Stevens, G., McKillip, M. and Ishizawa, H. (2006) *Intermarriage in the Second Generation: Choosing between Newcomers and Natives*, Migration Policy Institute, Washington, DC.

Suárez-Orozco, M.M. and Gardner, H. (2003) Educating Billy Wang for the world of tomorrow. *Education Week*, 23, 34–44.

Terrazas, A. (2009) African Immigrants in the United States. *Migration Policy Institute*, http://www.migrationinformation.org/ (accessed August 1, 2009).

Thai, H.C. (2004) For better or worse: gender allures in the Vietnamese marriage market, in *Feminist Frontiers* (eds L. Richardson, V. Taylor, and N. Whittier), McGraw Hill, London, pp. 75–86.

Thai, H.C. (2008) *For Better or For Worse: Vietnamese International Marriages in the New Global Economy*, Rutgers University, London.

Treas, J. (2008) Transnational older adults and their families. *Family Relations*, 57, 468–478.

Treas, J. (2009) Four myths about older adults in America's immigrant families. *Generations*, 32, 40–45.

Treas, J. and Mazumdar, S. (2004) Kinkeeping and caregiving: contributions of older people in immigrant families. *Journal of Comparative Family Studies*, 35, 105–122.

U.S. Census Bureau (2009) "Place of Birth by Citizenship Status" and "Year of Entry by Citizenship Status," http://factfinder.census.gov/ (accessed 15 May, 2009).

U.S. Census Bureau (2012) Most Children Younger than Age 1 are Minorities, Census Bureau Reports. Press release CB12–90, http://www.census.gov/newsroom/releases/archives/population/cb12–90.html (accessed June 10, 2012).

Vallejo, J.A. and Lee, J. (2009) Brown picket fences: the immigrant narrative and "giving back" among the Mexican-origin middle class. *Ethnicities*, 9, 5–31.

Wang, W. (2012) The Rise of Intermarriage, Pew Research Center, http://www.pewsocialtrends.org/2012/02/16/the-rise-of-intermarriage/ (accessed March 5, 2012).

Warren, J.W. and Twine, F.W. (1997) White Americans, the new minority? *Journal of Black Studies*, 28, 200–218.

Waters, M. C. (1990) *Ethnic Options: Choosing Identities in America*, University of California Press, Berkeley and Los Angeles.

Waters, M.C. and Jiménez, T. (2005) Assessing immigrant assimilation: new empirical and theoretical challenges. *Annual Review of Sociology*, 31, 105–125.

Yancey, G. (2003) *Who is White? Latinos, Asians and the New Black/Nonblack Divide*, Lynne Rienner, Boulder.

Yoshikawa, H. (2011) *Immigrants Raising Citizens: Undocumented Parents and their Young Children*, Russell Sage Foundation, New York.

Zhou, M. (2004). Are Asian Americans becoming "White"? *Contexts*, 3, 29–37.

Part III
Family Forms and Family Influences

11

Cohabitation: Recent Research and Implications

RHIANNON A. KROEGER AND PAMELA J. SMOCK

Introduction

Cohabitation, or living together in an intimate sexual relationship outside of marriage, has become a normative life event for most population subgroups in the United States as well as in many other countries (Smock, 2000; Lesthaeghe, 2011). While marriage remains desirable and important, with large numbers of adults expressing support for marriage and intentions to marry, recent research demonstrates that cohabitation has unmistakably altered marriage and childbearing processes (Manning, Longmore, and Giordano, 2007; Musick, 2007; Guzzo, 2009). In the United States, the majority of young adults perceive cohabitation as an acceptable arrangement, and by age 25, nearly half have spent some time in a cohabiting relationship (Payne, 2011). Cohabitation has also become common among older adults. Among adults ages 50 and over, the number of cohabitors increased by more than 1.5 million between 2000 and 2010 (Brown, Lee, and Bulanda, 2006; Brown, Bulanda, and Lee, 2012). The incidence of cohabiting partners with children is increasingly widespread, too: nearly 60% of nonmarital births are now to cohabiting parents (Lichter, 2012).

This chapter reviews and evaluates knowledge on cohabitation, with an emphasis on recent research (see Smock, 2000 for a review of earlier research). Our review is not comprehensive. Given the vast amount of research on cohabitation, there are some areas we cover minimally or not at all. As demographers and sociologists, we primarily draw on studies from those disciplines. We also do not address same-sex cohabitation, which is treated elsewhere in this volume (see Biblarz, Chapter 6, this volume). While we incorporate research on cohabitation in other regions of the world, our emphasis is on the United States.

Our chapter is organized into three general sections. First, we present basic cohabitation trends and key patterns in the United States, followed by a review of

The Wiley Blackwell Companion to the Sociology of Families, First Edition.
Edited by Judith Treas, Jacqueline Scott, and Martin Richards.
© 2014 John Wiley & Sons Ltd. Published 2017 by John Wiley & Sons Ltd.

cohabitation patterns in other countries. Next, we identify and summarize the findings of four questions of importance in the extant research on cohabitation. Finally, we draw on recent research to articulate several implications that we believe are important for understanding cohabitation.

Basic Cohabitation Trends and Patterns in the United States

There have been tremendous increases in the prevalence of cohabitation over the past several decades. One way to illustrate such increases is through counts of the number of couples living together. Estimates indicate that approximately 7.6 million heterosexual unmarried couples were living together in the United States as of 2011. This is double the number in 2000, nearly 5 times the number in 1980, and over 17 times the number in 1960 (U.S. Census Bureau, 2011). A clear way to understand why family scholars often term the increase in cohabitation a "revolution" is via data that tell us whether individuals have ever experienced a cohabiting relationship. Approximately 58% of women ages 19–44 have ever cohabited based on data from 2006 to 2008, compared to 45% in 1995 and 33% in 1987. Among 30–34-year-old women, the trend is quite striking: in 2006–2008 roughly 70% had ever lived in a cohabiting relationship (Manning, 2010). Among very young adults, cohabitation is now the most common type of first union, such that nearly half have ever cohabited by age 25 (Kennedy and Bumpass, 2008; Payne, 2011).

Notwithstanding common perceptions that the so-called cohabitation revolution only involves young adults, cohabitation is also common among older adults and the increases have been steep over the last few decades. Estimates from a 1987 survey suggest that 22% of 40–44-year-old women had ever cohabited; data from 2006 to 2008 indicate that nearly 60% had ever done so (Manning, 2010). Moreover, among adults ages 50 and over, the number of cohabitors rose from 1.2 million in 2000 to 2.75 million in 2010 (Brown, Lee, and Bulanda, 2006; Brown, Bulanda, and Lee, 2012). Some research suggests that older generations are "learning" cohabitation from their children. For example, one study found that among parents who were single at their child's 18th birthday, subsequent cohabitation experiences among their adult children increased the likelihood that parents themselves would cohabit rather than marry (McClain, 2011b).

Children in cohabiting unions

Cohabitation is increasingly prominent in children's lives, either by virtue of being born to cohabiting parents or by having a parent, typically the mother, enter into a cohabiting relationship. In fact, cohabiting households are now as likely to include children as married households, with about 40% of cohabiting households including children (Krivickas and Payne, 2010; Cohen, 2011; Lofquist et al., 2012). Up to one half of children born in the early 1990s are expected to live in a cohabiting-parent household at some point in their childhood (Bumpass and Lu, 2000; Kennedy and Bumpass, 2008). The percentage of all US births that were to cohabiting parents increased from 6% in the 1980s to 11% in the 1990s to 20% in 2006–2008 (Bumpass and Lu, 2000; Lichter, 2012). In 2001, 52% of all nonmarital births were to cohabiting parents (Manlove *et al.*, 2010). By 2006–2008, nearly 60% of nonmarital births were to cohabiting parents (Lichter, 2012). Thus, the majority of nonmarital childbearing today occurs not to single women but to couples residing together.

Serial cohabitation

There have also been increases in the number of cohabiting unions that individuals experience. Correspondingly, family scholars have begun to differentiate between single-instance cohabitation and what has been termed "serial" cohabitation. Generally, researchers consider individuals to be serial cohabitors if they have cohabited two or more times. The average number of cohabiting unions increased from 0.44 for women and 0.55 for men in the 1970s to 1.15 for women and 1.36 for men in the early 2000s (Zeng *et al.*, 2012). In 1995, approximately 9% of women ages 15–44 had cohabited with more than one partner. By 2002, this percentage rose to 12% (Lichter, Turner, and Sassler, 2010). Among individuals who have cohabited at least once, between 15% and 25% are estimated to be serial cohabitors (Lichter and Qian, 2008; Cohen and Manning, 2010; Lichter, Turner, and Sassler, 2010; Manning and Cohen, 2012). Serial cohabitation is more prevalent among the young and serial cohabitors enter their first cohabitation 1–2 years earlier than their counterparts who have cohabited only once (Lichter and Qian, 2008; Cohen and Manning, 2010; Lichter, Turner, and Sassler, 2010).

Connections between cohabitation and marriage

Researchers have for some time now been studying the connections between cohabitation and marriage, often driven by the premise that it is not possible to understand the implications of cohabitation without also considering marriage. In addition, the public, and therefore many researchers, have been motivated by whether cohabitation ought to be perceived as a "threat" to marriage. Thus, a central question has been to what extent cohabitation serves as a precursor to marriage rather than a short-lived dating relationship or a long-term alternative to marriage. In the United States, more than 65% of first marriages now begin as cohabitations (Manning, 2010; Copen *et al.*, 2012). This is in sharp contrast to marriages occurring in earlier years. For instance, only about 10% of marriages formed in the 1960s and early 1970s were preceded by cohabitation (Bumpass and Sweet, 1989; Bumpass and Lu, 2000; Manning, 2010).

A somewhat different way to approach the issue about what cohabitation means for the centrality of marriage is to examine the "outcomes" of cohabiting relationships. Some cohabiting couples go on to marry and some do not. In the absence of wedding bells, cohabiting couples either break up or stay together for any number of years. Regardless of whether cohabitating unions end in marriage or dissolution, they are generally short-lived, with most ending within 2 years (Raley and Bumpass, 2003). About half of individuals in their first cohabitations and 16% of those in higher-order cohabitations go on to marry their partners (Lichter and Qian, 2008). Of those remaining, the majority of couples break up within a few years, and only a small percentage continues to cohabit 5 years or longer.

Cohabitation after divorce and prior to, or instead of, remarriage has also become more common. In the 1970s, roughly 24% of women cohabited after divorce, compared to about 46% in the early 2000s (Zeng *et al.*, 2012). Correspondingly, scholars have noted that the likelihood of remarriage after divorce has declined, with cohabitation becoming a much more common route to coupledom.

Who cohabits?

In some sense, given the growing prominence of cohabitation, the question has become "who does not cohabit?" We do know that those with strong religious convictions are less likely to cohabit, as well as individuals living in communities with high levels of religious homogamy (Eggebeen and Dew, 2009; Brown, Bulanda, and Lee, 2012; Gault-Sherman and Draper, 2012).

As with many family patterns, cohabitation patterns are influenced by economic well-being, or what many researchers term "social class." For instance, those who are more advantaged economically are less likely to cohabit than their less advantaged counterparts. Nearly three-quarters (73%) of individuals without a high school degree have ever cohabited compared to less than half (47%) of those with a college degree or more. Congruently, research indicates that serial cohabitation is more prevalent among those at the lower end of the educational spectrum (Lichter and Qian, 2008; Cohen and Manning, 2010; Lichter, Turner, and Sassler, 2010). Further, while many factors influence the likelihood of cohabitation leading to marriage, economic well-being seems to play an important role, with couples remaining reluctant to marry until they have attained economic stability (Smock, Manning, and Porter, 2005). Indeed, cohabitations are less likely to transition to marriage among the economically disadvantaged compared to their more advantaged counterparts (Lichter, Qian, and Mellott, 2006).

Cohabitation patterns also vary by race/ethnicity. Generally, there is little difference across non-Hispanic whites, non-Hispanic blacks, and Hispanics in the likelihood of having ever cohabitated. Statistics on cohabitation rates among Asian-Americans have generally been more difficult to obtain because there are few data sets with sufficient sample sizes to provide solid estimates. However, recent studies utilizing various national data sources suggest that, at least through young adulthood, fewer Asians report having ever cohabited than do their white or black counterparts (Cheng and Landale, 2011; Zeng *et al.*, 2012).

The most striking detail regarding racial/ethnic differences is that fewer cohabitations transition to marriage among non-Hispanic blacks or Hispanics compared to whites (Guzzo, 2009; Zeng *et al.*, 2012). However, it is important to note two distinctions between blacks, whites, and Hispanics. The first is that cohabiting unions among black women are less stable than those among white women (e.g., more likely to break up and less likely to result in marriage). The second is that while relationship stability is similar among whites and Hispanics, Hispanics are more likely to remain in cohabiting unions versus marry than are whites. Scholars generally cite greater cultural acceptance of unmarried cohabitation across various parts of Latin America as being a source of this difference (Landale, Schoen, and Daniels, 2010). Racial/ethnic differences in the number of cohabitations that transition to marriage may in part be related to social class. With whites being more economically advantaged than blacks or Hispanics, one study finds that racial/ethnic differences in women's expectations of marrying their cohabiting partners is narrowed considerably once the male partners' income and earnings are taken into account (Manning and Smock, 2002).

Cohabitation around the Globe

Far from a US-bound phenomenon, cohabitation is prominent across much of the world. While an exhaustive review of cohabitation research in all countries is beyond the scope of this chapter, here we summarize some notable trends in cohabitation around the globe. An important point underlying these trends is that the prevalence of cohabitation in any given country is both motivated by and reflective of national context. In part, scholars have observed that cohabitation is more common in industrialized nations (Lesthaeghe, 2011). Indeed, increases in cohabitation have been observed in conjunction with industrialization in multiple "Western" countries, including Canada, Australia, and many European countries. But the importance of national context is not merely a consequence of industrialization. Indeed, the prevalence of cohabitation is reflective of cultural factors, religious traditions, and politics, and is influenced immensely by social networks (Nazio and Blossfeld, 2003; Heuveline and Timberlake, 2004; Nazio, 2008; Lesthaeghe, 2011).

This complex array of factors influencing cohabitation is apparent across Europe, where cohabitation prevalence varies widely by region. For instance, in Northern Europe, cohabitation is extremely prevalent (Soons and Kalmijn, 2009; Kasearu and Kutsar, 2011). In Sweden, over 60% of 18–45-year-old adults had ever cohabited, and the typical path to marriage is a sequence involving cohabitation, childbearing, and then (maybe) marriage (Kasearu and Kutsar, 2011). In Norway, 75% of the young adult population selects cohabitation (rather than marriage) as their first union and nearly all (90%) of married couples cohabit prior to marriage (Aarskaug Wiik, 2011). Cohabitation is increasingly prevalent in countries such as France, the United Kingdom, Germany, Austria, and Belgium, where between 30% and 50% of the adult population has ever cohabited (Kiernan, 2004;Soons and Kalmijn, 2009; Kasearu and Kutsar, 2011; Ochiai, 2011).

In Central/Eastern Europe, cohabitation levels are more modest. In Russia, recent data suggest that about 20% of the adult population has ever cohabited (Soons and Kalmijn, 2009). Although recent estimates suggest that less than 20% of adults ages 18–45 in Poland have ever cohabited, there has been a striking rise since the early 1990s (Mynarska and Matysiak, 2010; Kasearu and Kutsar, 2011). The spread of cohabitation has been slowest in Southern Europe, although again cohabitation is in upward swing (Munoz-Perez and Recano-Valverde, 2011; Impicciatore and Billari, 2012). In Italy, data from 2008 indicate that less than 11% of the adult population in Italy has ever cohabited (Soons and Kalmijn, 2009). Proportions of individuals with cohabitation experience are not much higher for Portugal (13.3%), Greece (11.4%), or Spain (17.0%).

While the spread of cohabitation has only recently been documented across many Western nations, cohabitation has long existed alongside formal marriage in Latin America, especially among rural and indigenous populations (Gonzalbo Aizpuru,

1998; Castro Martin, 2002; Fussell and Palloni, 2004). Indeed, while cohabitation has gone from negligible to normal over the past several decades in the United States, Canada, Australia, and much of Europe, statistics indicate its persistently high prevalence in Latin America since at least the 1950s (Fussell and Palloni, 2004). Current statistics suggest that more than half of all unions among men and women ages 25–34 in Columbia, Cuba, Panama, Peru, and Venezuela are cohabiting unions (Esteve, Lesthaeghe, and López-Gay, 2012). At the same time, cohabitation's enduring presence in Latin America does not dismiss Latin American countries from the changes in family structure occurring in other parts of the world. For instance, scholars are increasingly examining whether cohabitation patterns in Latin America are becoming more like those observed in industrialized nations like the United States, especially for those in more recent cohorts and for those living in urban areas (Heaton and Forste, 2007).

The importance of national context is especially evident in many Asian countries, where cultural taboos against nonmarital sexual unions have traditionally kept cohabitation prevalence low. While increases in cohabitation have been observed for some industrialized Asian countries, the overall prevalence of cohabitation in these countries remains remarkably low. For instance, in Japan, approximately 15% of adults report having ever been in a cohabiting relationship (Tsuya, 2006; Raymo, Iwasawa, and Bumpass, 2009). In Taiwan, the percentage of women ever having cohabited increased from 11% in the late 1990s to nearly 20% in 2004 (Lesthaeghe, 2011). One exception to the low prevalence of cohabitation across Asia is the Philippines, where cohabitation has been historically important for family formation (Xenos and Kabamalan, 2007). At present, some estimates suggest that approximately 60% of young adults living in the Philippines have ever cohabited (Williams, Kabamalan, and Ogena, 2007).

Major Research Questions about Cohabitation

Family patterns continue to be in flux, even as we write these words. Thus, many scholars are kept busy tracking the changing contours of cohabitation: How long do cohabiting unions last? What percentage of cohabitations break up? What is the percentage of children born to cohabiting couples? How do these patterns vary by subgroups? These are exactly the type of issues we summarize in the previous section. In this section, we identify four research questions as being current and central to the field. The first concerns measurement, the second concerns children, the third concerns comparisons between cohabitation and marriage, and the fourth concerns the relationship between premarital cohabitation and marital instability.

How should cohabitation be measured?

Data and measures available for measuring cohabitation have improved dramatically in recent years. Until the 1990s, many national data sources, such as the US census, did not even directly measure cohabitation. Prior to direct measurement of cohabitation, scholars inferred national cohabitation rates from household composition data

(Glick and Spanier, 1980). Such inferences often led to underestimated cohabitation rates, especially among households with children (Casper and Cohen, 2000).

National surveys began to gather more detailed information about individual experiences with cohabitation in the 1980s. The landmark survey in this regard is the 1987–1988 National Survey of Families and Households (NSFH) (Sweet, Bumpass, and Call, 1988). It obtained complete cohabitation histories from a sample of women and men of all ages and spawned a surge in research on cohabitation. Many national surveys now collect cohabitation histories for each individual interviewed, detailing not only how many cohabitations a person has experienced but also intricate details for each cohabitation reported, including start and end dates, indicators of relationship quality and conflict, and information on partner characteristics such as age, race/ethnicity, gender, etc. Such a potentially vast amount of data for each cohabiting union and the characteristics of individuals, especially in surveys that follow individuals over time, is a treasure trove for family scholars.

There have also recently been significant improvements in cohabitation measurement in existing surveys. The Current Population Survey (CPS), an ongoing survey that is part of the US Bureau of the Census, made major changes in 2007. The structure of the questioning prior to 2007 was such that only cohabitations involving the "reference" person were counted, effectively excluding all cohabitations involving members of the household other than the reference person. Qualitative research had shown that some cohabiting couples reside with others, including roommates, parents, or other relatives, and that this situation was more likely for less economically advantaged couples (Manning and Smock, 1995). In addition, qualitative research indicated that the term used by the CPS ("unmarried partner") did not resonate or make sense to many people (Manning and Smock, 2005). The CPS thus changed their term to "boyfriend/girlfriend/partner." There were also improvements that made it possible to identify the relationship of children in the household to their parent(s). These changes have been important. In 2008, 5% of all cohabiting unions in the CPS were between two household members that did not include the reference person. Moreover, changing the term "unmarried partner" to "boyfriend/girlfriend/ partner" captured 20% more cohabitations (Kennedy and Fitch, 2012).

In addition to the NSFH and CPS, today various nationally representative survey data sources exist that measure cohabitation. The proliferation of such data has allowed family scholars to examine links between cohabitation and a seemingly endless supply of individual-level and relationship-level outcomes. Two data sources that include intricate cohabitation histories are the National Longitudinal Survey of Youth and the National Longitudinal Study of Adolescent Health (Bureau of Labor Statistics, 2002, 2005; Harris, 2009).

At the same time, several factors remain a challenge for accurate measurement of cohabitation. First, cohabitations are often reported inconsistently, depending upon who is asked. For example, among parents and children in cohabiting stepfamily households, only one-third of children whose mothers described their family as a cohabiting stepfamily household did the same. The remainder did not "count" their mothers' cohabiting partner in defining their families (Brown and Manning, 2009). Second, individuals in couples sometimes provide differing responses about whether or not they are cohabiting (Waller and McLanahan, 2005). Third, many individuals are unable to specify an exact start date for their cohabitations, because many cohabiting unions form gradually and often unintentionally over a period of time (Manning and Smock, 2005). A fourth issue is the timing of data collection. For instance, when retrospective cohabitation histories are collected, the accuracy and consistency of the information gathered decreases as the length of time between the interview date and when the cohabitation occurred increases (Hayford and Morgan, 2008). In other words, there is a recall problem. An example is that individuals who had a child together are more likely to describe their relationship status at the time of the birth as "cohabiting" when asked directly after childbirth than when asked 5 years later (Knab and McLanahan, 2007).

How does cohabitation affect child well-being?

Just as numerous studies emerged in the 1980s and 1990s examining the ramification of divorce for children, family scholars are intensively studying the implications of cohabitation for children. In general, research suggests that cohabitation negatively affects child well-being across multiple outcomes. Growing up in a cohabiting household compared to a married household is linked to poorer educational outcomes, more behavioral problems, and poorer health and well-being among children (Willetts and Maroules, 2004; Raley, Frisco, and Wildsmith, 2005; Brown, Lee, and Bulanda, 2006; Apel and Kaukinen, 2008; Bulanda and Manning, 2008; Schmeer, 2011).

More specifically, parental cohabitation is associated with earlier sexual initiation and teen pregnancy among adolescent girls (Bulanda and Manning, 2008). In turn, involvement in nonromantic sexual relationships during adolescence increases the likelihood of involvement in cohabitation during early adulthood, and cohabitations in early adulthood tend to be unstable (Raley, Crissey, and Muller, 2007; Schoen, Landale, and Daniels, 2007). Upon the dissolution of their own cohabiting unions, mothers experience declines in mental health, physical health, and income (Avellar and Smock, 2005; Meadows, McLanahan, and Brooks-Gunn, 2008). These patterns suggest a cycle such that family instability in one generation leads to family instability in the next generation, with negative effects on well-being for both parents and children. Because cohabitation is more prevalent among those who have fewer socioeconomic resources as children, this cycle has implications for the social transmission of well-being from one generation to the next.

The jury is still out, however, about whether it is cohabitation per se that "causes" poorer outcomes for children or whether the issue is really a matter of "selection." That is, children experiencing parental cohabitation are disadvantaged in numerous ways compared to children born and raised by married parents. Economic status or social class is one of those ways. That is, some of the difference in the well-being of children in cohabiting compared to married couple households is explained by differences in the economic situation of the two types of families (Manning and Lamb, 2003; Brown, 2004; Artis, 2007). Consider the following: 47% of children in cohabiting households are living in poverty, compared to 11% of children in married couple households (Williams, 2012a). There is also a stark difference in the percentage of children covered by private health insurance. In cohabiting households, the percentage is 34% compared to 74% for children in married-couple households (Williams, 2012b).

The negative linkage between parental cohabitation and child well-being is also partly explained by family instability. Scholars have known for some time that family structure instability (e.g., divorce) typically does not enhance child well-being. Children born to cohabiting parents are five times more likely to see their parents separate than are children born to married parents (Osborne, Manning, and Smock, 2007). Family instability is associated with worse educational attainment and more behavioral problems during childhood (Cavanagh and Huston, 2006; Cavanagh, Schiller, and Riegle-Crumb, 2006). Moreover, studies suggest that the impact of family instability may endure well into adulthood (Amato *et al.*, 2008; Ryan *et al.*, 2009).

At the same time, there are some nuances that should not be overlooked when making generalizations about cohabitation not being good for children. Relationship quality between cohabiting parents is important and positively related to parental engagement with the child (Carlson *et al.*, 2011). This, in turn, is associated with greater relationship stability among cohabiting parents (Cross Barnet, Cherlin, and Burton, 2011; McClain, 2011a). Further, should cohabiting parents dissolve their unions, high-quality relationships between parents significantly diminish negative effects of union instability on child well-being (Fomby and Osborne, 2010).

Certainly, the influence of cohabitation on child well-being is subject to national context. For example, in countries such as Sweden, where cultural norms and national policy treat cohabitation as more akin to marriage, cohabitation does not adversely affect child well-being (Kalenkoski, Ribar, and Stratton, 2005; Ono and Yeilding, 2009). In this sense, any detrimental effects of cohabitation on child well-being observed in the United States might be caused by government policy that favors marriage. Indeed, prominent US scholars have noted that more marriage-neutral policies may be necessary to foster the well-being of all children, regardless of family structure (Cherlin, 2004).

How does cohabitation compare to marriage?

Much of what we know about cohabiting unions is drawn from comparisons to marital unions. Scholars have been doing this for quite some time. In fact, in Smock's 2000 review chapter, she notes that scholars often "attempt to gauge the meaning of cohabitation by comparing it to marriage" (p. 12). This is understandable given that in order to know what something "is," contrasts with similar categories (in this case living arrangements) can be tremendously useful. In the previous section, we explained that a number of researchers are examining how cohabitation may differ from marriage in terms of implications for child well-being. In this section, we demonstrate that comparisons of cohabitation to marriage characterize a chunk of research much larger than that focused exclusively on effects for children.

Conceptually, cohabitation has been referred to as an "incomplete institution" that lacks the stability found in marital unions (Nock, 1995, 2005), and much research has characterized cohabiting unions as having less commitment and lower relationship quality compared to marital unions (Treas and Giesen, 2000; Stanley, Whitton, and Markman, 2004; Marcussen, 2005;Hamplova and Le Bourdais, 2009; Yabiku and Gager, 2009). In fact, some studies suggest that adults in cohabiting unions experience more depressive symptoms compared to their married counterparts, in part because of such differences in relationship commitment and quality (Brown, 2000; Lamb, Lee, and DeMaris, 2003; Marcussen, 2005).

At the same time, some emerging research contradicts the idea that marriage is inherently "better" than cohabitation, and even suggests that cohabitation may be more beneficial than marriage for some aspects of well-being. Musick and Bumpass (2012) find that marriage is not necessarily more beneficial than cohabitation for physical or psychological well-being. Other studies report no differences in levels of relationship conflict or satisfaction when comparing married individuals and long-term cohabiting couples, with long term defined as 4 years (Willetts, 2006). In addition, a recent study shows that most married individuals who cohabited first are indistinguishable from those who did not in terms of trajectories of wealth accumulation during marriage (Vespa and Painter, 2011). Notably, too, cohabitation seems to be especially stable among older adults ages 50 and over. Older cohabitors report significantly higher levels of relationship quality and satisfaction than younger cohabitors, although they are less likely to have plans to marry their partners (King and Scott, 2005). In addition, older adults report similar levels of relationship quality and commitment across various indicators, regardless of whether they are married or cohabiting (Brown and Kawamura, 2010; Noel-Miller, 2011).

We view this research as important and would add that conclusions about whether marriage is "better" or "worse" across a number of domains may change as cohabitation becomes more normative (e.g., institutionalized) in society and marriage perhaps less so. Indeed, one demographer argues that marriage is becoming "deinstitutionalized" with roles and responsibilities of spouses becoming less clear over time (Cherlin, 2004).

Does premarital cohabitation increase the risk of divorce?

For many years numerous studies found that premarital cohabitation raised the odds of divorce and this became the conventional wisdom: That cohabitation decreases marital stability (Smock, 2000). That is, a couple that cohabits before marriage is at greater risk of eventual divorce.

The reasons? It was posed that either cohabitation changed people in ways leading them to be more likely to end a marriage or that those more prone to divorce were more likely to cohabit in the first place. While not mutually exclusive, the first explanation was that there is something about the experience of cohabitation that raises the odds of divorce (e.g., people learn that relationships can be temporary and that there are alternatives to marriage). The latter is what is termed the "selection" explanation: People who cohabit prior to marriage differ from those who do not across a multitude of factors (e.g., values, attitudes, relationship skills), and these differences increase the likelihood of marital instability.

This conventional wisdom has been overturned with the release of studies using more recent data. One study finds that the positive relationship between premarital cohabitation and marital instability has diminished for more recent birth and marriage cohorts and that cohabitation is not selective of individuals with higher risks of divorce. There is even some evidence that cohabitation may help stabilize remarriages (Reinhold, 2010). Another study finds that for those marrying in the late 1990s and beyond, premarital cohabitation is not associated with marital instability for either women or men (Manning and Cohen, 2012; see also Copen *et al.*, 2012). The declining impact of premarital cohabitation on marital stability observed in the United States is likely related to its increasingly normative presence. Indeed, research focusing on other regions of the world finds that as cohabitation becomes more normative within a country, the effects of premarital cohabitation on subsequent divorce risk decline considerably (Liefbroer and Dourleijn, 2006). This is consistent with research in both the United States and across Europe, demonstrating that peers' direct experiences with cohabitation have influences on individuals' attitudes toward cohabitation and decisions about whether to cohabit themselves (Nazio, 2008; Manning, Cohen, and Smock, 2011).

Concluding Thoughts: Implications

The past several decades have seen sweeping changes in the family. Cohabitation has now become a normative stage in the life course for most population subgroups: young adults, older adults, the well-off, and the working class. In closing, we make five observations about current knowledge on cohabitation.

The first is that while cohabitation has become a normative life event for nearly all population subgroups, we wish to underscore that its role varies considerably by social class. For economically advantaged adults, cohabitation is more of a step toward marriage; they are substantially more likely to see their cohabitations "end" in marriage versus dissolution. In contrast, individuals in the most disadvantaged groups are more likely to see their cohabitations end, rather than serve as a step to marriage, and are more likely to enter a number of cohabiting unions throughout the life course. This instability has ramifications for their children as well; children born to cohabiting parents are much more likely to see their marriages end than those born to married parents (Manning, Smock, and Majumdar, 2004).

A second observation is that the complex and dynamic nature of cohabitation and marriage – of family life – has important implications for how scholars craft their research questions. As noted earlier, much research attempts to understand cohabitation by comparing it to marriage. Going forward, it is clear that this is not necessarily the most useful way to study cohabitation, and families more broadly. If we continue to build our knowledge of cohabitation based on how it compares to marriage, we will miss some crucial insights. We encourage more research that is acknowledging other forms of coupledom such as Living Apart Together and even Living Together Apart; these may well provide considerable traction for understanding what may, or may not be, unique about cohabitation (Regnier-Loilier, Beaujouan, and Villeneuve-Gokalp, 2009; Cross Barnet, Cherlin, and Burton, 2011).

A third observation concerns what is missing from our review. We did not fully address scholarship on the reasons for the increase in cohabitation in the United States or elsewhere, beyond noting the importance of national context for the prevalence of cohabitation in any given country. At present, many scholars examining cohabitation in the United States are engaged in qualitative studies that focus on motives to cohabit among individuals or couples. These studies find that some young adults perceive living together as a chance to evaluate their potential success as marital partners, while others have no intentions to someday marry their partners

(Edin, Kefalas, and Reed, 2004; Manning and Smock, 2005; Huang *et al.*, 2011). For the latter, reasons for cohabiting often include finances, convenience, and housing needs (Sassler, 2004). This is consistent with research indicating that individuals from more disadvantaged backgrounds frequently cohabit due to financial necessity, while holding marriage as a union that can only be entered once one is established financially (Cherlin, 2004; Cherlin and Fomby, 2004; Gibson-Davis, Edin, and McLanahan, 2005; Smock, Manning, and Porter, 2005). Such research is consistent with the pattern of working-class couples moving from dating to cohabitation more quickly than middle-class couples while at the same time being less likely to be engaged than their more advantaged counterparts (Sassler and Miller, 2011a).

Our fourth observation stems from a review on cohabitation a dozen years ago undertaken by the second author (Smock, 2000). In that review, Smock noted that while early research and popular opinion was that cohabitation was more gender egalitarian than marriage, there was other research to suggest that this distinction was overstated. She concluded that cohabitation is gendered in much the same way that marriage continues to be, focusing on studies showing an unequal division of housework in both cohabiting and marital unions and that men's economic characteristics appear to have more influence on whether cohabiting couples marry (Smock and Manning, 1997; Gupta, 1999). As she wrote, "That these findings emerge even among cohabitors, a subgroup less traditional in terms of attitudes toward gender roles, suggests the intractability of a division of labor that assigns breadwinning to men and homemaking to women" (Smock, 2000, p. 15).

Has research suggested a different conclusion more than a decade later? In large part, research conducted over the past dozen years has reinforced Smock's conclusions. For instance, research using recent data suggests that women experience more severe economic consequences when exiting cohabiting relationships than do their male counterparts (Avellar and Smock, 2005). Further, qualitative research is suggestive of gendered views and dynamics of cohabitation. One study indicates that women perceive cohabitation more as a step in the marriage process than do men. In addition, women appear to be more concerned that cohabitation may delay marriage and reduce chances of a marriage proposal, whereas men express views that the downside of cohabitation is that it constrains their freedom (Huang *et al.*, 2011). Another study finds that women in cohabiting relationships often feel that the man is in control of the progression of the relationship (Sassler and Miller, 2011b). At the same time, some recent studies suggest that although cohabiting women do more housework than cohabiting men, both decisions about housework and the division of housework are more egalitarian among cohabiting couples compared to married couples, with cohabiting women spending between 5 and 7 fewer hours on housework per week than their married counterparts (Batalova and Cohen, 2002; Baxter, 2005; Cunningham, 2005; Davis, Greenstein, and Gerteisen Marks, 2007).

Our fifth and final observation is that cohabitation has brought challenges to the study and our understanding of families. What we mean is that families today are characterized by considerable flux, complexity, and ambiguity, and probably more so for the less advantaged in our society. As we noted earlier in this chapter, a substantial proportion of adolescents and their mothers do not even agree about who is in their family. Families are increasingly likely to be characterized by part-time residents; these may include half-siblings or children of cohabiting partners. And even when a cohabiting relationship ends, ties between members who once lived together may remain, even between a child and his or her mother's former cohabiting partner, to give just one example. Thus, what constitutes a "family" is changing and is increasingly changing over the lifetimes of members of families themselves. Surveys are trying to grapple with how to measure families, acknowledging this complexity and that families increasingly stretch over two or more households. This is a challenge for survey research, which has tended to sample households and many surveys have been based on the assumption that all family members live in the same household. It is likely to be an ongoing challenge. Arguably, cohabitation (and marriage and families) will continue to change as they have throughout history.

Acknowledgments

Rhiannon A. Kroeger acknowledges support by an F32 NICHD Ruth L. Kirschstein National Research Service Award (F32 HD072616), as well as an NICHD center grant to the Population Research Center at The University of Texas at Austin (R24 HD042849). The second author acknowledges support by an NICHD center grant to the Population Studies Center at the University of Michigan (R24 HD041028).

References

Aarskaug Wiik, K. (2011) Socioeconomic differentials in the transition to first cohabitation in Norway. *International Review of Sociology*, 21 (3), 533–548.

Amato, P.R., Landale, N.S., Havasevich-Brooks, T.C. *et al.* (2008) Precursors of young women's family formation pathways. *Journal of Marriage and Family*, 70 (5), 1271–1286.

Apel, R. and Kaukinen, C. (2008) On the relationship between family structure and antisocial behavior: parental cohabitation and blended households. *Criminology*, 46 (1), 35–70.

Artis, J.E. (2007) Maternal cohabitation and child well-being among kindergarten children. *Journal of Marriage and Family*, 69 (1), 222–236.

Avellar, S. and Smock, P.J. (2005) The economic consequences of the dissolution of cohabiting unions. *Journal of Marriage and Family*, 67 (2), 315–327.

Batalova, J.A. and Cohen, P.N. (2002) Premarital cohabitation and housework: couples in cross-national perspective. *Journal of Marriage and Family*, 64 (3), 743–755.

Baxter, J. (2005) To marry or not to marry: marital status and the household division of labor. *Journal of Family Issues*, 26 (3), 300–321.

Brown, S.L. (2000) The effect of union type on psychological well-being: depression among cohabitors versus marrieds. *Journal of Health and Social Behavior*, 41 (3), 241–255.

Brown, S.L. (2004) Family structure and child well-being: the significance of parental cohabitation. *Journal of Marriage and Family*, 66 (2), 351–367.

Brown, S.L. and Manning, W.D. (2009) Family boundary ambiguity and the measurement of family structure: the significance of cohabitation. *Demography*, 46 (1), 85–101.

Brown, S.L. and Kawamura, S. (2010) Relationship quality among cohabitors and marrieds in older adulthood. *Social Science Research*, 39 (5), 777–786.

Brown, S.L., Lee, G.R. and Bulanda, J.R. (2006) Cohabitation among older adults: a national portrait. *The Journals of Gerontology Series B: Psychological Sciences and Social Sciences*, 61 (2), S71–S79.

Brown, S.L., Bulanda, J.R., and Lee, G.R. (2012) Transitions into and out of cohabitation in later life. *Journal of Marriage and Family*, 74 (4), 774–793.

Bulanda, J.R. and Manning, W.D. (2008) Parental cohabitation experiences and adolescent behavioral outcomes. *Population Research and Policy Review*, 27 (5), 593.

Bumpass, L. and Sweet, J. (1989) National estimates of cohabitation. *Demography*, 26, 615–625.

Bumpass, L. and Lu, H.-H. (2000) Trends in cohabitation and implications for children's family contexts in the United States. *Population Studies – A Journal of Demography*, 54 (1), 29–41.

Bureau of Labor Statistics, U.S. Department of Labor (2002) National Longitudinal Survey of Youth 1979 Cohort, 1979–2002 (Rounds 1–20) [computer file]. Edited by The Ohio State University Center for Human Resource Research. Center for Human Resource Research, The Ohio State University, Columbus.

Bureau of Labor Statistics, U.S. Department of Labor (2005) National Longitudinal Survey of Youth 1997 Cohort, 1997–2003 (Rounds 1–7) [computer file]. Edited by the University of Chicago National Opinion Research Center. Center for Human Resource Research, The Ohio State University, Columbus.

Carlson, M.J., Pilkauskas, N., McLanahan, S., and Brooks-Gunn, J. (2011) Couples as partners and parents over children's early years. *Journal of Marriage and Family*, 73 (2), 317.

Casper, L.M. and Cohen, P.N. (2000) How does POSSLQ measure up? Historical estimates of cohabitation. *Demography*, 37 (2), 237–245.

Castro Martin, T. (2002) Consensual unions in Latin America: persistence of a dual nuptiality system. *Journal of Comparative Family Studies*, 33 (1), 35–55.

Cavanagh, S. and Huston, C. (2006) Family instability and children's early problem behavior. *Social Forces*, 85 (1), 551–581.

Cavanagh, S., Schiller, K.S., and Riegle-Crumb, C. (2006) Marital transitions, parenting, and schooling: exploring the link between family-structure history and adolescents' academic status. *Sociology of Education*, 79 (4), 329–354.

Cheng, Y.-H.A. and Landale, N.S. (2011). Adolescent precursors of early union formation among Asian American and white young adults. *Journal of Family Issues*, 32 (2), 209–236.

Cherlin, A.J. (2004) The deinstitutionalization of American marriage. *Journal of Marriage and Family*, 66 (4), 848–861.

Cherlin, A.J. and Fomby, P. (2004) Welfare, work, and changes in mothers' living arrangements in low-income families. *Population Research and Policy Review*, 23 (5–6), 543–565.

Cohen, J.A. (2011) Children in Cohabiting Unions. FP-11-07. National Center for Family & Marriage Research, Bowling Green State University, Bowling Green.

Cohen, J.A. and Manning, W.D. (2010) The relationship context of premarital serial cohabitation. *Social Science Research*, 39 (5), 766–776.

Copen, C.E., Daniels, K., Vespa, J., and Mosher, W.D. (2012) First Marriages in the United States: Data from the 2006–2010 National Survey of Family Growth. U.S. Department of Health and Human Services, *National Health Statistics Reports*, 49.

Cross Barnet, C., Cherlin, A.J. and Burton, L. (2011) Bound by children: intermittent cohabitation and living together apart. *Family Relations*, 60 (5), 633–647.

Cunningham, M. (2005) Gender in cohabitation and marriage: the influence of gender ideology on housework allocation over the life course. *Journal of Family Issues*, 26 (8), 1037–1061.

Davis, S.N., Greenstein, T.N., and Gerteisen Marks, J.P. (2007) Effects of union type on division of household labor: do cohabiting men really perform more housework?" *Journal of Family Issues*, 28 (9), 1246–1272.

Edin, K., Kefalas, M.J., and Reed, J.M. (2004) A peek inside the black box: what marriage means for poor unmarried parents. *Journal of Marriage and Family*, 66 (4), 1007.

Eggebeen, D.J. and Dew, J. (2009) The role of religion in adolescence for family formation in young adulthood. *Journal of Marriage and Family*, 71 (1), 108–121.

Esteve, A., Lesthaeghe, R., and López-Gay, A. (2012) The Latin American cohabitation boom, 1970–2007. *Population & Development Review*, 38 (1), 55–81.

Fomby, P. and Osborne, C. (2010) The influence of union instability and union quality on children's aggressive behavior. *Social Science Research*, 39 (6), 912–924.

Fussell, E. and Palloni, A. (2004) Persistent marriage regimes in changing times. *Journal of Marriage and Family*, 66, 1201–1213.

Gault-Sherman, M. and Draper, S. (2012) What will the neighbors think? The effect of moral communities on cohabitation. *Review of Religious Research*, 54 (1), 45–67.

Gibson-Davis, C.M., Edin, K., and McLanahan, S. (2005) High hopes but even higher expectations: the retreat from marriage among low-income couples. *Journal of Marriage and Family*, 67 (5), 1301–1312.

Glick, P.C. and Spanier, G.B. (1980) Married and unmarried cohabitation in the United States. *Journal of Marriage and Family*, 42, 19–30.

Gonzalbo Aizpuru, P. (1998) *Familia y orden colonial*, el Colegio de MÈxico, Centro de estudios histÙricos, Mexico.

Gupta, S. (1999) The effects of marital status transitions on men's housework performance. *Journal of Marriage & Family*, 61, 700–711.

Guzzo, K.B. (2009) Marital intentions and the stability of first cohabitations. *Journal of Family Issues*, 30 (2), 179–205.

Hamplova, D. and Le Bourdais, C. (2009) One pot or two pot strategies? Income pooling in married and unmarried households in comparative perspective. *Journal of Comparative Family Studies*, 40 (3), 355–385.

Harris, K.M. (2009) The National Longitudinal Study of Adolescent Health (Add Health), Waves I & II, 1994–1996; Wave III, 2001–2002; Wave IV, 2007–2009 [machine-readable data file and documentation]. Carolina Population Center, University of North Carolina at Chapel Hill, Chapel Hill.

Hayford, S.R. and Morgan, S.P. (2008) The quality of retrospective data on cohabitation. *Demography*, 45 (1), 129–141.

Heaton, T.B. and Forste, R. (2007) Informal unions in Mexico and the United States. *Journal of Comparative Family Studies*, 38 (1), 55–69.

Heuveline, P. and Timberlake, M.J. (2004) The role of cohabitation in family formation: the United States in comparative perspective. *Journal of Marriage and Family*, 66 (5), 1214.

Huang, P.M., Smock, P.J., Manning, W.D. and Bergstrom-Lynch, C.A. (2011) He says, she says: gender and cohabitation. *Journal of Family Issues*, 32 (7), 876–905.

Impicciatore, R. and Billari, F. (2012) Secularization, union formation practices, and marital stability: evidence from Italy. *Sécularisation, Pratiques de Mise en Union et Stabilité des Mariages: Le Cas de l'Italie*, 28 (2), 119–138.

Kalenkoski, C.M., Ribar, D.C., and L.S. Stratton. (2005) Parental child care in single-parent, cohabiting, and married-couple families: time-diary evidence from the United Kingdom. *The American Economic Review*, 95 (2), 194–198.

Kasearu, K. and Kutsar, D. (2011). Patterns behind unmarried cohabitation trends in Europe. *European Societies*, 13 (2), 307–325.

Kennedy, S. and Bumpass, L. (2008) Cohabitation and children's living arrangements: new estimates from the United States. *Demographic Research*, 19, 1663–1692.

Kennedy, S. and Fitch, C.A. (2012) Measuring cohabitation and family structure in the United States: assessing the impact of new data from the current population survey. *Demography*, 49 (4), 1479–1498.

Kiernan, K. (2004) Redrawing the boundaries of marriage. *Journal of Marriage and Family*, 66 (4), 980.

King, V. and Scott, M.E. (2005) A comparison of cohabiting relationships among older and younger adults. *Journal of Marriage and Family*, 67 (2), 271–285.

Knab, J.T. and McLanahan, S. (2007) Measuring cohabitation: does how, when, and who you ask matter? in *Handbook of Measurement Issues in Family Research*, (eds. S.L. Hofferth and L.M. Casper), Lawrence Erlbaum Associates, Mahwah.

Krivickas, K. and Payne, K.K. (2010) Cohabitation in the US, 2006–2008. FP-10-02. National Center for Family & Marriage Research, Bowling Green State University, Bowling Green.

Lamb, K.A., Lee, G.R., and DeMaris, A. (2003) Union formation and depression: selection and relationship effects. *Journal of Marriage and Family*, 65 (4), 953.

Landale, N.S., Schoen, R. and Daniels, K. (2010) Early family formation among white, black, and Mexican American women. *Journal of Family Issues*, 31 (4), 445–474.

Lesthaeghe, R. (2011) The "second demographic transition": a conceptual map for the understanding of late modern demographic developments in fertility and family formation. *Der "zweite demographische Übergang": Ein Orientierungskonzept zum Verständnis spätmoderner demographischer Entwicklungen von Fertilität und Familienbildung*, 36 (2), 179–218.

Lichter, D.T. (2012) Childbearing among cohabiting women: race, pregnancy, and union transitions, in *Early Adulthood in a Family Context* (eds. A. Booth, S.L. Brown, N.S. Landale *et al.*), Springer, New York, pp. 209–219.

Lichter, D.T. and Qian, Z. (2008) Serial cohabitation and the marital life course. *Journal of Marriage and Family*, 70 (4), 861–878.

Lichter, D.T., Qian, Z., and Mellott, L.M. (2006) Marriage or dissolution? Union transitions among poor cohabiting women. *Demography*, 43 (2), 223–240.

Lichter, D.T., Turner, R.N., and Sassler, S. (2010) National estimates of the rise in serial cohabitation. *Social Science Research*, 39 (5), 754–765.

Liefbroer, A.C. and Dourleijn, E. (2006) Unmarried cohabitation and union stability: testing the role of diffusion using data from 16 European countries. *Demography*, 43 (2), 203–221.

Lofquist, D., Lugalla, T., O'Connell, M., and Feliz, S. (2012) Households and Families: 2010. United States Census Bureau, 2010 Census Briefs, no. 14, U.S. Department of Commerce, Economics and Statistics, Washington, DC.

Manlove, J., Ryan, S., Wildsmith, E., and Franzetta, K. (2010) The relationship context of nonmarital childbearing in the U.S.. *Demographic Research*, 23, 615–653.

Manning, W.D. (2010). Trends in Cohabitation: Twenty Years of Change, 1987–2008. FP-10-07. National Center for Family & Marriage Research, Bowling Green State University, Bowling Green.

Manning, W.D. and Smock, P.J. (1995) Why marry? Race and the transition to marriage among cohabitors. *Demography*, 32, 509–520.

Manning, W.D. and Smock, P.J. (2002) First comes cohabitation and then comes marriage? *Journal of Family Issues*, 23 (8), 1065–1087.

Manning, W.D. and Lamb, K.A. (2003) Adolescent well-being in cohabiting, married, and single-parent families. *Journal of Marriage and the Family*, 65 (4), 876–893.

Manning, W.D. and Smock, P.J. (2005) Measuring and modeling cohabitation: new perspectives from qualitative data. *Journal of Marriage and the Family*, 67 (4), 989–1002.

Manning, W.D. and Cohen, J.A. (2012) Premarital cohabitation and marital dissolution: an examination of recent marriages. *Journal of Marriage and Family*, 74 (2), 377–387.

Manning, W.D., Smock, P.J., and Majumdar, D. (2004) The relative stability of cohabiting and marital unions for children. *Population Research and Policy Review*, 23 (2), 135–159.

Manning, W.D., Longmore, M.A., and Giordano, P.C. (2007) The changing institution of marriage: adolescents' expectations to cohabit and to marry. *Journal of Marriage and Family*, 69 (3), 559–575.

Manning, W.D., Cohen, J.A., and Smock, P.J. (2011) The role of romantic partners, family, and peer networks in dating couples' views about cohabitation. *Journal of Adolescent Research*, 26 (1), 115–149.

Marcussen, K. (2005) Explaining differences in mental health between married and cohabiting individuals. *Social Psychology Quarterly*, 68 (3), 239–257.

McClain, L.R. (2011a) Better parents, more stable partners: union transitions among cohabiting parents. *Journal of Marriage and Family*, 73 (5), 889–901.

McClain, L.R. (2011b) Cohabitation: parents following in their children's footsteps? *Sociological Inquiry*, 81 (2), 260–271.

Meadows, S.O., McLanahan, S.S., and Brooks-Gunn, J. (2008) Stability and change in family structure and maternal health trajectories. *American Sociological Review*, 73 (2), 314–334.

Munoz-Perez, F. and Recano-Valverde, J. (2011) A century of nuptiality in Spain, 1900–2007. *European Journal of Population-Revue Europeenne De Demographie*, 27 (4), 487–515.

Musick, K. (2007) Cohabitation, nonmarital childbearing, and the marriage process. *Demographic Research*, 16, 249–286.

Musick, K. and Bumpass, L. (2012) Reexamining the case for marriage: union formation and changes in well-being. *Journal of Marriage and Family*, 74 (1), 1–18.

Mynarska, M. and Matysiak, A. (2010) Diffusion of cohabitation in Poland. *Studia Demograficzne*, 1–2 (157–158), 11–25.

Nazio, T. (2008) *Cohabitation, Family and Society*, Routledge, New York.

Nazio, T. and Blossfeld, H.-P. (2003) The diffusion of cohabitation among young women in West Germany, East Germany and Italy. *European Journal of Population/Revue européenne de Démographie*, 19 (1), 47–82.

Nock, S.L. (1995) A comparison of marriages and cohabiting relationships. *Journal of Family Issues*, 16, 53–76.

Nock, S.L. (2005) Marriage as a public issue. *The Future of Children*, 15 (2), 13–32.

Noel-Miller, C. (2011) Partner caregiving in older cohabiting couples. *The Journals of Gerontology*, 66B (3), 341–353.

Ochiai, E. (2011) Unsustainable societies: the failure of familialism in East Asia's compressed modernity. *Gesellschaften ohne Nachhaltigkeit: Das Versagen des Familialismus in der komprimierten Moderne Ostasiens*, 36 (2), 219–245.

Ono, H. and Yeilding, R. (2009) Marriage, cohabitation and childcare: the US and Sweden. *Social Indicators Research*, 93 (1), 137–140.

Osborne, C., Manning, W.D., and Smock, P. (2007) Married and cohabiting parents' relationship stability: a focus on race and ethnicity. *Journal of Marriage and Family*, 69 (5), 1345–1366.

Payne, K.K. (2011) On the Road to Adulthood: Forming Families. FP-11-08. National Center for Family & Marriage Research, Bowling Green State University, Bowling Green.

Raley, R.K. and Bumpass, L.L. (2003) The topography of the plateau in divorce: levels and trends in union stability after 1980. *Demographic Research*, 8, 246–258.

Raley, R.K., Frisco, M.L., and Wildsmith, E. (2005) Maternal cohabitation and educational success. *Sociology of Education*, 78 (2), 144–164.

Raley, R.K., Crissey, S. and Muller, C. (2007) Of sex and romance: late adolescent relationships and young adult union formation. *Journal of Marriage and Family*, 69 (5), 1210–1226.

Raymo, J., Iwasawa, M. and Bumpass, L. (2009) Cohabitation and family formation in Japan. *Demography*, 46 (4), 785–803.

Regnier-Loilier, A., Beaujouan, E., and Villeneuve-Gokalp, C. (2009) Neither single, nor in a couple. A study of living apart together in France. *Demographic Research*, 21, 75–108.

Reinhold, S. (2010) Reassessing the link between premarital cohabitation and marital instability. *Demography*, 47 (3), 719–733.

Ryan, S., Franzetta, K., Schelar, E., and Manlove, J. (2009) Family structure history: links to relationship formation behaviors in young adulthood. *Journal of Marriage and Family*, 71 (4), 935–953.

Sassler, S. (2004) The process of entering into cohabiting unions. *Journal of Marriage and the Family*, 66 (2), 491–505.

Sassler, S. and Miller, A.J. (2011a) Class differences in cohabitation processes. *Family Relations*, 60 (2), 163–177.

Sassler, S. and Miller, A.J. (2011b). Waiting to be asked: gender, power, and relationship progression among cohabiting couples. *Journal of Family Issues*, 32 (4), 482–506.

Schmeer, K.K. (2011) The child health disadvantage of parental cohabitation. *Journal of Marriage and Family*, 73 (1), 181–193.

Schoen, R., Landale, N., and Daniels, K. (2007) Family transitions in young adulthood. *Demography*, 44 (4), 807–820.

Smock, P.J. (2000) Cohabitation in the United States: an appraisal of research themes, findings, and implications. *Annual Review of Sociology*, 26, 1–20.

Smock, P.J. and Manning, W.D. (1997). Cohabiting partners' economic circumstances and marriage. *Demography*, 34, 331–341.

Smock, P.J., Manning, W.D., and Porter, M. (2005) "Everything's there except money": how money shapes decisions to marry among cohabitors. *Journal of Marriage and Family*, 67 (3), 680–696.

Soons, J.P.M. and Kalmijn, M. (2009) Is marriage more than cohabitation? Well-being differences in 30 European countries. *Journal of Marriage and Family*, 71 (5), 1141–1157.

Stanley, S.M., Whitton, S.W., and Markman, H.J. (2004) Maybe I do: interpersonal commitment and premarital or nonmarital cohabitation. *Journal of Family Issues*, 25 (4), 496–519.

Sweet, J.A., Bumpass, L.L., and Call, V. (1988) *The Design and Content of the National Survey of Families and Households*. University of Wisconsin, Center for Demography and Ecology, Madison.

Treas, J. and Giesen, D. (2000) Sexual infidelity among married and cohabiting Americans. *Journal of Marriage and the Family*, 62 (1), 48–60.

Tsuya, N.O. (2006) Patterns and correlates of partnership formation in Japan. *Journal of Population Problems*, 621.

U.S. Census Bureau. (2011) Table UC1. Unmarried Partners of the Opposite Sex, by Presence of Children: 1960 to Present 2011, http://www.census.gov/hhes/families/data/cps2011.html (accessed October 31, 2013).

Vespa, J. and Painter, M.A. (2011) Cohabitation history, marriage, and wealth accumulation. *Demography*, 48 (3), 983–1004.

Waller, M.R. and McLanahan, S. (2005) "His" and "Her" marriage expectations: determinants and consequences. *Journal of Marriage and Family*, 67, 53–67.

Willetts, M.C. (2006) Union quality comparisons between long-term heterosexual cohabitation and legal marriage. *Journal of Family Issues*, 27 (1), 110–127.

Willetts, M.C. and Maroules, N.G. (2004) Does remarriage matter? The well-being of adolescents living with cohabitating versus remarried mothers. *Journal of Divorce & Remarriage*, 41 (3/4), 115–133.

Williams, S. (2012a) Child Poverty in the United States, 2010. FP-12-17. National Center for Family & Marriage Research, Bowling Green State University, Bowling Green.

Williams, S. (2012b) Health Insurance Coverage of U.S. Children, 2010. FP-12-16. National Center for Family & Marriage Research, Bowling Green State University, Bowling Green.

Williams, L., Kabamalan, M., and Ogena, N. (2007) Cohabitation in the Philippines: attitudes and behaviors among young women and men. *Journal of Marriage and Family*, 69 (5), 1244–1256.

Xenos, P. and Kabamalan, M.M.M. (2007) Emerging forms of union formation in the Philippines. *Asian Population Studies*, 3 (3), 263–286.

Yabiku, S. and Gager, C. (2009) Sexual frequency and the stability of marital and cohabiting unions. *Journal of Marriage and Family*, 71 (4), 983–1000.

Zeng, Y.I, Morgan, S.P., Wang, Z. *et al.* (2012) A multistate life table analysis of union regimes in the United States: trends and racial differentials, 1970–2002. *Population Research and Policy Review*, 31 (2), 207–234.

12

Partnerships, Family, and Personal Configurations

Eric D. Widmer

Work presented in this chapter was supported by great 100015-122413 and by the NCCR Lives (overcoming vulnerability: Life course perspectives) of the Swiss National Science Foundation. Various recent authors have stressed the usefulness of considering family and personal networks as factors shaping couples' interactions, projects, and behavior. Several dimensions of the relational context of partnerships have proved to be important for couples. Researchers have provided evidence in the last decade that the processes shaping such dyads can be better explained as pieces and parcels of larger chains of relationships. Following recent trends in family sociology (Widmer and Jallinoja, 2008; Jallinoja and Widmer, 2010), this chapter reconsiders this evidence by conceptualizing families and personal networks as configurations. The configurational perspective proposes a set of processes and explanations that somewhat modify and renew the understanding of family relationships in late modernity. I first present the main features of the configurational perspective on families and personal networks, and then, I turn to a series of studies concerning couples and their configurations that exemplify this perspective.

Family Configurations and Interdependences

Family members often have strong feelings and concerns about what happens to each other. The configurational perspective focuses on the interdependencies between key family dyads, such as the parent–child dyads or conjugal partnerships, and larger sets of family ties (Widmer and Jallinoja, 2008; Widmer, 2010). With the decline of the nuclear family and the pluralization of life trajectories, the number and the complexity of family contexts have grown. Indeed, family members that matter cannot be defined a priori, using the household as a natural boundary of the family. The number of meaningful family relationships to be taken into account in order to understand contemporary families is much greater than that between partners or

---

between parents and their resident children. In sum, the family should not be theorized as a small group with obvious boundaries but as a rather large and unbounded personal configuration of interdependences (Widmer, 2010).

The configurational perspective on families and personal relationships traces complex patterns of emotional, cognitive, financial, and practical interdependencies among large numbers of individuals beyond the nuclear family. It focuses on the interdependencies of partners, children, and other individuals such as relatives and friends (Widmer, 2006; Widmer and Jallinoja, 2008). Its main assumption is that partnerships and parent–child relationships are embedded in a larger set of family relationships that account for how they may develop. Accordingly, the configurational perspective is based on the assumption that each individual is the center of a complex set of relationships that are interconnected. It focuses on the influence of the configuration of relationships in which each individual is included on key dyads and the development of self-identity.

These relationships are defined as interdependencies, that is, relationships that respond to important personal needs such as social recognition, emotional connection, financial survival, or maintenance of functional autonomy in everyday life (Widmer et al., 2009). If practical services and money transfers clearly constitute a set of interdependencies within families, they are not the only or even the most significant ones. Although the literature on family support stresses the importance of financial and practical interdependences, emotions and cognitions concerning family members should not be underestimated as interdependencies. Various contingencies from late modernity may increase or decrease financial and practical interdependencies depending on personal or collective circumstances. The cognitive and emotional interdependencies between parents and children remain however strong in most cases across the lifespan (Antonucci and Akiyama, 1995). People may not receive money from their parents or they may not see them regularly because they do not need the provision of money or because they live far away from them. Despite that, they are in most cases still emotionally and cognitively interdependent with them. Psychological networks, that is, those that have an emotional significance, have a major importance for interdependencies (Milardo, 1989; Surra and Milardo, 1991; Widmer, 2010). Feeling loved and cared for is a central element for the development and maintenance of self-identity (Giddens, 1991). Emotional support and communication are prime features of relationships of individuals with their parents and siblings in adulthood (Coenen-Huther et al., 1994). Once established, the persistence of such interdependency does not require frequent, recent, long, or even positive interactions (Widmer, 2010).

The configurational approach is close to social network analysis, although different in its purpose. Both share a common interest for large sets of relationships, which cannot be defined on the basis of institutional criteria. However, social network analysis is most of all a methodological tool used by scholars from various theoretical backgrounds on a variety of relationships and social settings. In distinction, the configurational approach features a set of theoretical assumptions and explanatory mechanisms about relationships which can be empirically operationalized in a variety of ways, which do not necessarily relate to social network methods. The focus on relationships fulfilling basic individual needs, be they material or psychological, means that configurational researchers focus on relationships servicing social identity, with an emphasis on social mechanisms involving support and conflict.

The boundaries of family configurations

Family structures refer to institutional criteria related to families, such as household membership, marriage, custody rights, or support obligations for a child. At first sight, these criteria may appear valid enough for defining significant family contexts; they however lead researchers to disregard some of the relational complexities of families. Indeed, family boundaries should not be defined by institutional criteria, but rather by interdependencies. So what each individual needs from others is given prime importance (Widmer, 2010).

Stepfamilies are a good case to illustrate the importance of empirically addressing the composition of family configurations. Researchers have underlined that their boundaries are ambiguous because divorce and remarriage create ties among different households and extend the set of family roles (for instance, Cherlin and Furstenberg, 1994). This diversity stems from a variety of changes following family recomposition. First, the size of configurations is in some circumstances increased. A common source of expansion is the paternal grandmother who retains relationships with her former daughter-in-law and her relatives while at the same time adds new relatives with her son's remarriage (Johnson and Barer, 1987). Adding new sets of ties to surviving ones increases the inclusivity of such configurations. Second, the connectedness of configurations after remarriage is lower than those of the configurations in first marriages. Researchers have emphasized that relationships among stepparents and stepchildren differ in strength from those of parents and children (Ferri, 1984; Hobart, 1987; Coleman and Ganong, 1990). Because relationships among stepparents and stepchildren are less intimate and less supportive and are associated with more conflicts than relationships between parents and children (Coleman and Ganong, 1990), they tend to create low-density family configurations (Widmer *et al.*, 2012). That is, each remarried spouse is likely to have a larger proportion of unshared family members than for first marriage couples. Third, the matrifocality of family configurations tends to be reinforced as a solidarity unit develops with mothers and children while ties between fathers and children may weaken after divorce and remarriage (Furstenberg and Winquist Nord, 1985; Cherlin and Furstenberg, 1994). Finally, achievement may in many cases take precedence over ascription in configurations of remarried couples. In her research on US middle-class suburban divorced families, Johnson (1988, 2000) found that about one-third of couples were involved in configurations where family members from their serial marriages were blurred and where distance from or closeness to kin was established on the basis of liking, rather than from a sense of responsibility.

Although stepfamilies present a good case for stressing the diversity of family configurations, this diversity is also relevant for first-time families (Widmer, 2010). Much of the recent research shows that these are not homogeneous, and scholars have stressed the uncertainty associated with many family roles in adulthood, including sibships (Cicirelli, 1995), aunts and uncles (Milardo, 2010), parents, and grandparents (Silverstein and Marenco, 2001; Mueller, Wilhelm, and Elder, 2002). Some individuals develop or maintain strong relationships with them in adulthood, while others disengage from them (Carroll, Olson, and Buckmiller, 2007). In some cases, pseudokinship ties, such as friends, may be considered as family members and play a significant role, as in other cases they do not (Weston, 1997). Therefore, the composition and boundaries of family configurations vary greatly from one person to the next according to a series of factors related with their biography of family relationships. In late modernity, who belongs to the family and who does not has become an open question, not only for stepfamilies but also all other family forms (Widmer, 2010).

In a Swiss study based on a sample of 300 women with a child aged between 5 and 12, half with a stepfamilies structure and half with first-time partners, we found no less than 9 types of family configurations (Widmer et al., 2012). Friend configurations focused on friends who were considered to be family members, as respondents in this group included on average three female friends in their family configurations. In-law configurations had a strong orientation toward the partner and the in-laws. The partner and the partner's mother were overrepresented, as well as other in-law relationships. Brother and sister configurations included the respondent's siblings and their children and current partners. Kinship configurations included a variety of individuals related by blood and marriage, such as partners, parents, children, uncles, aunts, nieces, nephews, cousins, and grandparents. Beanpole configurations focused on blood relatives, with the inclusion of members of various generations, such as respondents' parents and grandparents. These were vertically rather than horizontally oriented, contrary to the brother and sister configurations. Nuclear family configurations were almost exclusively centered around the partner and the children and corresponded to a definition of the family as a coresident unit. Without-partner and postdivorce configurations were only found in the stepfamily subsample. Without-partner configurations did not include the present partner as a significant family member, although, as in all other cases, he lived within the same household as the respondent and her child. This was in contrast to postdivorce configurations which had two simultaneous orientations: one toward the former partner and his relatives and the other toward the new partner and his relatives (including his children and, in some cases, his ex-partner).

Similar family configurations are also present in other life stages. Beanpole, friendship, postdivorce, conjugal, kinship (either on the father's or mother's side), and sibling family configurations set the boundaries of family configurations of young adults (Widmer, 2010). Each type features a well-defined logic, with an emphasis on kinship or friendship ties, on parents, in-laws, or stepfamily members. Individuals focus on either male or female members and invest in their father's side or in their mother's side of their kinship networks. They may reinforce blood ties by maintaining strong interdependencies with their biological parents and siblings. But in contrast, they sometimes make the links with their in-laws prominent. They may choose to maintain or develop interdependencies with steprelatives. They may develop interdependences beyond the realm of blood and marriage by investing in friendship ties defined by them as family ties; they may follow a logic of genealogical proximity by promoting interdependencies with the closest blood or marriage ties or rather pick more distant relatives in genealogical terms as significant family members. Interestingly, those configurations exhibit a remarkable consistency throughout life stages, as they make generational shifts rather than truly change in older cohorts. For instance, in a sibling configuration, young adults build their configurations on their mother and their mother's sisters, whereas older adults focus on their own sisters and their brothers-in-law, their nephews, and their nieces. The logic is the same, although the generations involved are different because their uncles and their aunts have passed away.

By asking individuals to define their family configurations, it becomes clear that the variability of family contexts matters rather than the institutional criteria traditionally used to define the family, such as the composition of the household. In this respect, family configurations are distinct from family structures, which have received so far much more research attention. Contrasting first-time families and stepfamilies as two highly distinct but homogeneous family structures, as is often done in empirical research, disregards the various configurations of inter-dependencies which are present in both of them and the interdependencies that they share.

Social capital and family configurations

Interdependencies within a configuration provide resources. So, the importance of family relationships as social capital has been stressed by researchers (Furstenberg and Hughes, 1995; Furstenberg and Kaplan, 2004; Widmer, 2004). Social capital is defined as resources stemming from the possession of a durable network of acquaintance or recognition (Bourdieu, 1986). Traditionally, the concept focuses on the benefits accruing to individuals by virtue of participation in associations (Portes, 2000; Putnam, 2000). Social capital has however also been measured in configurations of interpersonal ties. Family-based social capital in the form of family interdependences has positive consequences, such as promoting physical and psychological health or increasing individual resilience for adverse life course events (Furstenberg and Hughes, 1995; Furstenberg and Kaplan, 2004; Widmer, 2004; Widmer, Kellerhals, and Levy, 2004).

Much of this work uses a definition of social capital based on network closure, that is, a high density of relationships (Coleman, 1988). In dense configurations, most, if not all, individuals are interconnected. Such high interconnection enhances expectations, claims, obligations, and trust because of the collective nature of normative control. If a configuration member violates some shared norms or expec-tations, several other configuration members may jointly react. Dense configurations also facilitate communication by multiplying the number of information channels and by reducing the number of intermediaries between any two configuration members. Finally, in dense configurations, support is collective, as individuals are likely to coordinate their efforts in helping each other. From this perspective, social capital is found in family configurations in which most persons are interconnected by highly significant relationships.

Bridging social capital is an alternative to bonding social capital based on brokerage opportunities that some individuals develop in more heterogeneous family and personal configurations (Putnam, 2000; Burt, 2002). The absence of some connections and the diversity of the family circles present create "holes" in the configuration that provide some persons, known as brokers, with opportunities to mediate the flow of resources among members and, therefore, control and influence others. Such persons benefit from being intermediaries between other individuals, otherwise not directly connected to each other, by increasing their decisional autonomy and the variety of their resources. Bridging social capital proved to have positive consequences in a variety of domains as it stimulates the ability of individuals to innovate and to adjust to a complex and changing environment (Putnam, 2000; Davidsson and Honig, 2003; Szreter and Woolcock, 2004).

Families are generally assumed to be mostly producing bonding social capital, as they are considered small groups of densely connected individuals (Granovetter, 1973). This assumption, however, is challenged by some research, for instance, that on stepfamilies. Here, relationships among stepparents and stepchildren are more likely to be characterized as weaker ties than parent–child relationships (Ferri, 1984; Hobart, 1987; Coleman and Ganong, 1990; Ganong and Coleman, 2004). Although some children keep strong connections with both divorced parents, former spouses often see their relationships rapidly decrease in intensity. Therefore, many children of separated parents become the primary, if not the only, connecting persons between their divorced biological parents (Ganong and Coleman, 2004). Relationships with in-laws are also associated with relational or the so-called structural holes. Although the relationship between partners is usually a strong one, relationships with the spouse's parents are frequently far from straightforward, and conflict, open or otherwise, is frequent (Fischer, 1983; Coleman, Ganong, Cable, 1997). Therefore, two spouses often have quite distinct family members (Stein *et al.*, 1992). Research on friends considered as family members shows similar patterns (Weston, 1997).

These observations on different types of family relationships suggest that family configurations may sometimes promote a bridging type of family social capital, associated with a low density of connections among family members and a higher centrality of the individual in his or her family configuration. In various studies, a direct link was indeed found between the composition of family configurations and the type of social capital that they make available to their members (Widmer, 2006, 2010; Widmer *et al.*, 2012). In beanpole and nuclear family configurations, there is a strong emphasis on bonding social capital. Here, individuals are embedded in a dense set of interdependencies; they are under the care and scrutiny of a large number of interconnected family members from older generations. In contrast, bridging social capital is dominant in friendship family configurations where both friends and blood relatives are considered family members but are often kept separate. Therefore, respondents benefit from a large structural autonomy. The investment in time, energy, and sociability necessary to maintain discrepant family connections may however overshadow the advantages provided by having an intermediary position in the family configuration. Postdivorce family configurations are representative of bridging social capital as well. Respondents' centrality is high. Individuals in such family configurations have relatively few direct connections and their supportive alters are not densely connected. This is likely to be a peculiar situation for respondents as they have an intermediary position between family members who also have an intermediary position between their own family members. For instance, mothers have a central position between their child and their new partner (who is not the father of the child), and the new partner mediate the relationship of the mother with his own children. Therefore, postdivorce family configurations are chains of individualized interdependencies. This explains why much more active work is required in "doing family" to create and maintain interdependences in stepfamilies (Schneider, 1980; Cherlin and Furstenberg, 1994).

Conflict and ambivalence

Because individuals are interdependent in families, family configurations face power issues. Family resources are scarce and individuals, while cooperating, may also struggle for them (Widmer et al., 2009). Family members compete for each other's time, love, money, support, and social recognition. The unequal distribution of such resources within family configurations is subject to power and control attempts that make family configurations shift from one state of balance to another state over time. The patterns of interdependencies that characterize family configurations, therefore, are commonly unintended as no individual can fully control their distribution among such a large number of partly cooperating, partly competing family members. Such patterns, in turn, shape the cooperation strategies and the conflicts that occur in each dyad belonging to each configuration. The complex and often ambivalent mix of negative and positive emotions that characterize many personal relationships, especially in the family realm, is of central interest for the development of key dyads and self-identity.

In this perspective, conflict and ambivalences stem from the chains of positive interdependences linking family members and friends (Widmer and Lüscher, 2011). Consider, for instance, the story told by individuals facing divergent religious affiliations within their family configurations (Pillemer and Lüscher, 2004). The difficulty of developing a set of religious beliefs conflicting with those of parents is linked with the fear of endangering the emotional link with them. Parents may overact negatively because their own self-identity to some extent depends on their childhood religious affiliations. An open conflict with parents is costly as it means a decrease in exchange of support and self-validation. In such situations, a frail and shifting balance of power between the individual, the parents, and the partner develop, in which the needs of all four people compete and partly adjust to each other. A prioritization of one dyad over the others may follow to stabilize the configuration. As self-identity depends on the balance of interdependencies, this kind of shift is strongly intertwined with the development of new personal identities.

In the study of women with a child between 5 and 12 (Widmer et al., 2012), it was found that vertical and nuclear family configurations had a much higher density of conflict than postdivorce or friendship family configurations. As those configurations had the highest density of support, the dyads were very often characterized by simultaneous conflict and support. In those configurations, dyadic ambivalence was therefore dominant. In postdivorce and friendship configurations, conflict and cooperation more often concerned relationships with different family members. For instance, a child might receive emotional and practical support from her mother who is supported by her new partner, but the child and the new partner may develop a conflicted relationship, with very little exchange of support. In this case, ambivalence is triadic rather than dyadic: the individuals develop interdependencies that contradict each other as the child and the stepfather have other investments to prioritize over their relationship, but they are joined by strong interdependences with their mother/partner as a third person. Such individuals belong to an ambivalent triad, which is likely to produce oscillations in relationships and self-identity, with a greater need for reflexivity.

The configurational perspective stresses the importance of larger configurations of interdependences for understanding family conflict. This collective structuration of ambivalences is difficult to control by any one person, as the number of competing individuals that contribute to it is likely to be large.

Conjugal Dyads

Overall, the resources and conflicts created by members of personal configurations beyond the nuclear family should be stressed when dealing with partnerships. Conjugal dyads are embedded in configurations of family ties and friends. The variety of such family contexts is high as one's family configuration originates not only from one's life trajectory but also from the social convoy of ties that each family member develops throughout the life course (Widmer, 2010). The organization of ties in family configurations has consequences for processes occurring in conjugal dyads. I now present evidence to show how various transitions and relational issues associated with intimate partnerships depend on the configuration of ties to which partners belong. As predicted by the configurational approach, the distribution of resources among a large number of family members and friends becomes key for the understanding of conjugal dyads (Widmer, 2010).

Courtship

Interpersonal attraction develops in relational contexts where family configurations and friends play an important role as go-between, facilitators, or hindrances in the courtship process. Family members and friends' approval is one important factor in couples going successfully through the courtship process and one explanation of the prevalence of the high rates of endogamy and homogamy characterizing contemporary couples, as family and personal configurations feature a high rate of social homogeneity (Clark-Ibanez and Felmlee, 2004). The emotional reaction of friends and family members to a partnership influences the likelihood that it develops and stabilizes. Positive social reactions of friends strengthen a pair's sense of identity as a couple and increase partners' ability to withstand threats to relationship viability (Felmlee, 2001). Interpersonal attraction and courtship happen in social contexts where personal configurations play an important role. Individuals tend to foster a state of balance or "transitivity" within configurations (Milardo, 1986). Typically, this state is achieved when friends and family members of both partners become acquainted. Transitivity in configurations helps couples develop because third parties are less likely to entice partners into other commitments and the social capital lost by both partners following a breakup is higher. Thus, a powerful collective and often unacknowledged influence is exerted by configurations on personal choices concerning the development of intimate relationships, including initiation of conjugal relationships.

The concern of family members for each other's intimate relationships is explained by the important consequences for family configurations of developing a partnership.

The strengthening of interdependencies between partners means the loosening of other ties and the decrease in size of each of the partners' personal configuration, a process referred to as "dyadic withdrawal" (Parks and Eggert, 1991; Kalmijn, 2003). Partners become less active with others as courtship progresses (Surra, 1985). In the later stages of courtship, dating individuals interact with fewer people, less often, and for shorter periods (Milardo, Johnson, and Huston, 1983). Some ties are severed in order for the couple to be able to affirm its primacy over other relationships: ex-lovers, formerly intimate relationships that might endanger couple intimacy, need to be put into a new perspective. Relationships with parents and siblings are recast. Accordingly, family configurations may slow down the development of a new partnership. The influence of configurations may not always be a positive one for couples. For instance, configuration members may disapprove of a romantic relationship and speed its demise (Johnson and Milardo, 1984; Felmlee, 2001).

Usually, however, as two persons become closer, the overlap between their personal configurations increases. Among dating couples, the absolute number of mutual contacts and the ratio of mutual to separate contacts increases as couples get more involved: one study, for example (Milardo, 1982), found that couples in the later stages of courtship had roughly twice as many mutual contacts in their configurations as couples in the earlier stages of courtship. Transitions such as living together and marriage are crucial transitions that make partners' configurations became more interdependent (Kearns and Leonard, 2004). Thus, courtship and marriage restructures various relationships in making new connections in response to the functional necessity for couples to have a large number of shared configuration members as well as in reducing older interdependencies which may endanger conjugal privacy and conjugal primacy. The development of interpersonal attraction and courtship shows the duality of couples and family configurations. On the one hand, family members and friends play a major role for the initiation of a new couple, in making joint interactions possible, in imposing social expectations toward pairing, in providing support and information, and in imposing barriers (Parks and Eggert, 1991). On the other hand, the emergence of a partnership implies profound changes in the interdependencies characterizing each family configuration.

The division of household tasks

The process of dyadic withdrawal extends beyond courtship into other family stages, making the personal configurations of spouses or partners smaller and more overlapping (Kalmijn, 2003). The consequences of such a development are drawn from several studies on personal networks. The issue was first empirically addressed by the seminal work of Elisabeth Bott, which paved the way to a series of empirical studies. Briefly, Bott (1955, 1957) found that the segregation of conjugal roles was related to the extent of network connectedness. Couples with a high degree of segregation in the relationship between husbands and wives had highly connected configurations. Expressed differently, couples where husband and wife had an equal division of labor (i.e., no role segregation) had low network density. Because it is not self-evident, this finding has attracted the attention of scholars. As underlined by Milardo and Allan (1997), Bott explained this correlation between role differentiation and network density in two ways: First, dense configurations are more apt, because of their interconnectedness, to impose norms concerning conjugal roles compared with loosely connected configurations. Second, in dense configurations, mutual assistance among members is high, and as a consequence, spouses will have less need for one another's collaboration and companionship. Thus, segregated marital roles have a greater chance to emerge.

Although the Bott's hypothesis has triggered considerable interest, there is only sparse empirical evidence to support it. Milardo and Allan (1997) suggest that one problem lies in the fact that Bott equated a high density of interdependencies with traditionalist views of configuration members concerning conjugal roles. This assumption was never tested and might be problematic. Highly interconnected configurations might well be associated with weaker segregation of conjugal roles if their members hold progressive views about gender and the division of labor. In other words, structural features of conjugal configurations may only make a difference when the content of values or norms that they support is also considered, that is, when functional and structural features of groups are considered at the same time. Also, it was recently proposed that influence of kin on gender inequality in domestic tasks is likely to stem less from normative control and more from the kin exchanges that make a spouse's assistance unnecessary (Treas, 2011). Data collected in various countries indeed showed that relationships in marriage are associated with characteristics of family configurations. Tight-knit configurations display gender-segregated marital relationships, as evidenced by the womens' replacement of their male partner's involvement in domestic chores and emotional support by configuration members (Treas, 2011). To summarize, because personal resources in time, money, and love are limited, various mechanisms balance out investments done in the dyads constituting family configurations.

The transition to parenthood

With regard to the understanding of couples' division of household and paid work, the transition to parenthood is a crucial moment. Research stressed how parenthood pushes couples to enter a male breadwinner model by the combined effect of traditional gender-based norms and structural constraints (Krüger and Levy, 2001). Once parents, men tend to assume the majority of professional and economic responsibilities, and women to reduce considerably their time of employment in order to assume household and child-related tasks.

Among the resources that play a role in the differentiation of individual trajectories, personal configurations represent a capital that exercises multiple effects on the employment of individuals once they become parents. Personal configurations of individuals undergoing the transition to parenthood are not well known (Bost *et al.*, 2002). However, there is some evidence that personal configurations and the transition to parenthood are interrelated. Support from family members represents a resource allowing new parents to continue to work full time and have a more equal division of labor (Treas, 2011). The effects of personal configurations may also, as suggested by Milardo and Allan (1997), be caused by the normative pressure stemming from highly dense configurations of interrelated family members and friends.

Following a cohort of couples becoming first-time parents throughout the transition, we considered the impact of several properties of configurations on men and women's intentions regarding future work participation and on real changes occurring during the transition (Le Goff, J.-M. and Levy R., 2011; Sapin and Widmer, 2009). Size, density, and overlaps between partner's personal configurations were considered. In line with Bott's hypothesis, results showed that the density of personal configurations was significantly correlated with the intentions of employment for the near future and the actual changes of employment. Women with a dense personal configuration more often intended to reduce their occupational time; as for men, the opposite was true. Those with a dense configuration had a higher chance of maintaining or even increasing their occupational time. Dense personal and family configurations actually promote a situation where women invest in mixed solutions of full-employment and the homemaker status.

In the transition to parenthood, two mechanisms derived from Bott's perspective are at work. Couples with dense social configurations adopt a more unequal division of labor once they become parents, as women can more easily adjust to the demand of parenthood without institutional support (Treas, 2011), which paradoxically makes full-time employment less easy. Second, the informal social control exercised by denser personal configurations is stronger, which makes it easier for women to hold to prevalent social norms such as the benefits for young children of having their mothers at home with them.

Interestingly, in the transition to parenthood, configurations become on average denser, as the birth of the child creates a new focus point which changes the ways in which relationships between the parents are organized (Sapin and Widmer, 2009). The care for the new child activates a set of joint activities and coordination among individuals, such as indivudual's grandparents, uncles, and aunts, from both paternal and maternal sides of the family. Therefore, having a child creates new activities and new connections both for parents and grandparents. Therefore, an increase of bonding social capital follows the transition to parenthood which has a cumulative effect of decreasing the labor force participation of women. Dense family configurations entice women to reduce their paid work participation, and the decrease of paid work makes their likelihood of developing bridging social capital less likely. This may be especially true in countries with liberal or conservative welfare state regimes (Korpi, 2000) where various institutional structures (such as the differences between women's and men's parental leaves, a strong gender segregation in the labor market, and the lack of childcare institutions) push couples to adopt an unequal division of tasks once they become parents (Krüger and Levy, 2001; Giudici and Gauthier, 2009).

Conjugal satisfaction

The interest raised by Bott's hypothesis also transferred to the issue of conjugal satisfaction. Spouses with denser and more overlapping personal configurations report greater conjugal satisfaction, more spouse support, and more marital stability (Stein *et al.*, 1992; Kearns and Leonard, 2004; Cornwell, 2012). Network support is associated with greater conjugal quality (Burger and Milardo, 1995; Bryant and Conger, 1999; Felmlee, 2001). There is however a curvilinear effect of involvement of configuration members (Holman, 1981; Johnson and Milardo, 1984; Widmer,

2009). One major problem of couple embeddedness in configurations has been termed network interference, that is, interdependencies with configuration members being considered as threatening the integrity of the couple. For instance, in a study on couples and their personal configurations, 22% of women and 18% of men felt that their couple was controlled by their family (Widmer *et al.*, 2009). When configuration members are too involved in partnerships, partners may see them as interfering in their functioning. As such, support from them becomes counterproductive in terms of conjugal quality. Members of personal configurations and partners actually compete sometimes (Johnson and Milardo, 1984; Julien *et al.*, 1994). Developing a relationship creates anxiety in configurations by challenging time and energy previously devoted to other relationships. Thus, configuration members may try to hold or regain some influence by interfering in partnerships. In this respect, configurations with a high level of bonding social capital do not buffer the effects of conjugal conflict, but actually increase it, because the emergence of conjugal problems opens doors to further interference from the configuration members in the couple's relationships. Those problems stimulate and contribute to conflict between spouses, especially when interdependences among relatives are strong. Dense configurations, in which members feud with each other, become destructive for partnerships. For instance, intervention of third parties in an existing conjugal conflict reinforces partners' self-legitimacy (Klein and Milardo, 2000), thus making a consensual solution less likely. The fact that social support is not linearly associated with conjugal satisfaction reveals the power struggles that stem from family cooperation.

Some studies on couples and their configurations (Widmer, Kellerhals, and Levy, 2004; Widmer *et al.*, 2009) found that family and personal configurations matter for conjugal quality. Based on a cluster analysis, six types of configurations were found. Couples with bicentric configurations were characterized by frequent contacts with relatives and friends. Financial, domestic, and emotional support from relatives and friends was available for both partners. Relationships with relatives were frequent and warm, and relatives were seen as never interfering in the couples' decisions. Couples with patricentric configurations reported significantly higher support from the men's personal configurations compared with the women's personal configurations. We described such configurations as asymmetrical or unicentric, for example, when one partner's friends and relatives are predominant. In this case, relatives and friends of the male partner were perceived as much more supportive than relatives and friends of the female partner. Couples with matricentric configurations were defined symmetrically by the greater support provided by the women's personal configurations. Overall, these three clusters were characterized by a low level of interference. The next three types of configurations were characterized by interference. Couples with interfering configurations felt controlled by relatives of both partners, while for couples with patri-interfering, it was the men's relatives, and couples with matri-interfering configurations felt more controlled by the women's relatives. Note that these configurations provided as much support to couples as noninterfering configurations. Couples with sparse configurations were characterized by no support and no interference from their friends and relatives and reported little contact with them. Such couples were to a large extent isolated. Personal configurations and conflict management strategies of couples were significantly correlated. Overall, couples in which both partners had good conflict management strategies were underrepresented in interfering and sparse configurations and were over-represented in bicentric configurations. As a consequence, the level of conjugal satisfaction was higher in bicentric configurations than in others. The positive effect of bicentric configurations was mostly an indirect effect, as such configurations increased the partners' likelihood of having fewer conjugal problems and conjugal disagreements and poor coping strategies, which positively affect their overall positive feeling toward the conjugal bond. This result suggests that configurations prevent the occurrence of poor conjugal quality in a variety of ways, such as emotional support, alternate social ties, and social comparison.

Separation and remarriage

When the process of divorcing begins, family configurations face many important changes (Milardo, 1987; Feld and Carter, 1998). The community dimension of divorce – that is, splitting friends, dismantling ties with former in-laws, and learning to live as a single person again – is a necessary stage in the process of divorcing (Bohannan, 1970). Typically, relationships with in-laws do not survive the dissolution of the marital dyad, especially when there are no children (Spicer and Hampe, 1975; Ambert, 1988). Divorce, therefore, decreases the size of family configurations, as relationships with in-laws are often severed (Widmer *et al.*, 2012). But at the same time, divorce is sometimes an opportunity to invest in friendship (Albeck and Kaydar, 2002) and intensify relationships with other family members (Terhell, Broese van Groenou, and van Tilburg, 2004, 2007). Differences between men and women are significant in this regard. For men, personal friendships are key in dealing with divorce effects. For women, bonds with kin remain central after marriage, while bonds with friends are only secondary (Milardo, 1988).

In these circumstances, family configurations get a prime importance after divorce and are high in interdependences related with both social support and interference (Hurlbert and Acock, 1990). They indeed have consequences for the ways in which intimate partnerships in remarriage are worked out. In the study of 300 female respondents with a biological child referenced earlier, we found that parent–child dyads and conjugal dyads were related in distinct ways in first-time families and stepfamilies (Widmer *et al.*, 2012). In stepfamilies, conjugal satisfaction depended to a large extent on the composition of the family configuration. Respondents who were embedded in a nuclear family configuration developed a much higher satisfaction in the relationship with their new partner than respondents who developed a postdivorce configuration or a without-partner configuration, which underplayed the current partner in favor of the previous partner. In those cases, the previous partner was still considered a central family member, as the biological father of the child. Accordingly, there is some form of trade-off between two competing interdependences in such configurations. The new conjugal partnership and the coparenting relationship between the custodian parent and her previous partner (the father of her child) compete for time, attention, and emotional involvement, as well as, in some cases, financial and practical support. In such family configurations, the interdependencies with the previous partner created by the joint parenthood should be taken into account for understanding conjugal satisfaction in the current partnership.

Conclusion

This chapter has stressed the importance of family and personal configurations for the understanding of partnerships at various stages of their development. Partnerships belong to chains of interdependencies of various kinds, emotional, practical, and financial, embedded in configurations of family members and friends. Such interdependencies have been shown to have consequences for couples.

The boundaries and composition of personal and family configurations is one meaningful dimension. The ways in which individuals set up the boundaries of their family and personal configurations have direct consequences for their partnership. For instance, family configurations which give space to in-laws or focus on household members while excluding ties from other origins are associated with a higher conjugal satisfaction than those in which ex-partners are more prominent. In stepfamilies, acknowledging the current partner as a family member is obviously associated with a more profound integration of the conjugal partnership in the family context. In contrast, keeping strong connections with the former partner in the coparenting process is likely to make the integration of the new partner more difficult. Individual strategies are developed for the composition and boundaries of family contexts and proved to be interrelated with the ways in which partnerships develop.

Relational resources and their distribution among a large number of family members and friends are a second key for the understanding of conjugal dyads in a configurational perspective (Widmer, 2010). Overall, couples embedded in dense configurations of interdependencies face a normative and supportive context which is more effective than for couples in family configurations with a lower density of interdependencies. Bonding social capital is strengthened by the transition to parenthood and has consequences for the distribution of household labor between partners. As the evidence shows, it promotes collective forms of support for the couple while increasing the pressure toward the performance of gendered roles within the partnership. An alternative to bonding social capital, bridging social capital is where individuals benefit from connecting otherwise unrelated people. Several sets of family members are not directly connected because they do not know each other or because they have weakened their ties after life events such as a divorce, a conflict, or the death of a family member. In those cases, some intermediaries become prominent in the configuration. Those individuals can draw resources and information from a variety of heterogeneous social circles within their family and personal configurations. Some family configurations, such as friendships or postdivorce family configurations, include members from various circles of sociability with gaps between them. This alternate form of organization of interdependencies may have positive consequences for social integration in complex societies. Indeed, developing bridging social capital in their family and personal configurations helps individuals to learn how to play intermediary roles in heterogeneous social circles (Wellman, 1999; Putnam, 2000; DiPrete et al., 2011).

Family interdependencies however also create power struggles because of the limitations of the resources that they convey. Cooperation in configurations triggers unexpected tensions and conflicts because it is associated with various constraints that individuals enforce on each other by their interdependencies. Resources are scarce and their unequal distribution within family configurations is subject to control attempts. Interference is a process associated with such unintended consequences of cooperation in personal and family configurations. While some configuration members try to actively help couples by providing emotional and practical support and information, there are various possibilities that such support creates additional tensions in partnerships. The inequality between the given and the received decreases the feeling of partners to be self-supportive while increasing the likelihood of having third parties tapping into the emotional exchanges usually shared only by partners. Imbalance between personal networks of partners may twist the interdependence between partners in favor of the one with the larger personal configuration in case of conjugal conflict. There are a large number of situations in which family and personal configurations create interference or conflicts in partnerships. Therefore, ambivalence is a main feature of configurations.

Overall, stressing the importance of personal and family configurations makes it easier to grasp how the relational context of partners intermingles and shapes a reality that becomes a resource as well as a source of conflicts for couples. By stressing the set of interdependences that link each individual with a relatively large number of significant others, we understand partnerships as parcels of larger chains of interdependences facing conflicting priorities in their line of solidarity. The pluralization of personal life courses made such configurations more complex, diverse, and individualized. And, while being influenced by them, partnerships actively contribute to build up such configurations.

References

Albeck, S. and Kaydar, D. (2002) Divorced mothers: their network of friends pre- and post-divorce. *Journal of Divorce and Remarriage*, 36, 111–138.

Ambert, A.M. (1988) Relationships with former in-laws after divorce: a research note. *Journal of Marriage and the Family*, 50, 679–686.

Antonucci, T.C. and Akiyama, H. (1995) Convoys of social relations: family and friendships within a life span context, in *Handbook of Aging and the Family* (eds. R. Blieszner and V.H. Bedford), Greenwood Press, Westport, pp. 355–372.

Bohannan, P. (1970) *Divorce and After: An Analysis of the Emotional and Social Problems of Divorce*, Anchor, Garden City.

Bost, K.K., Cox, M.J., Burchinal, M.R. and Payne, C. (2002) Structural and supportive changes in couples' family and friendship networks across the transition to parenthood. *Journal of Marriage and the Family*, 64 (2), 517–531.

Bott, E. (1955) Urban families: conjugal roles and social networks. *Human Relations*, 8, 345–350.

Bott, E. (1957) *Family and Social Networks*, Tavistock, London.

Bourdieu, P. (1986) The forms of capital, in *Handbook of Theory and Research for the Sociology of Education* (ed. J. G. Richardson), Greenwood Press, New York, pp. 241–258.

Bryant, C.M. and Conger, R.D. (1999) Marital success and domains of social support in long-term relationships: does the influence of network members ever end? *Journal of Marriage and the Family*, 2, 437–450.

Burger, E. and Milardo, R.M. (1995) Marital interdependence and social networks. *Journal of Social and Personal Relationships*, 12 (3), 403–415.

Burt, R.S. (2002) The social capital of structural holes, in *The New Economic Sociology: Developments in an Emerging Field* (eds. M.F. Guillén, R. Collins, P. England and M. Meyer), Russell Sage Foundation, New York, pp. 148–190.

Carroll, J.S., Olson, C.D. and Buckmiller, N. (2007) Family boundary ambiguity: a 30-year review of theory, research, and measurement. *Family Relations*, 56 (2), 210–230.

Cherlin, A.J. and Furstenberg, F.F. (1994) Stepfamilies in the US: a reconsideration. *Annual Review of Sociology*, 20, 359–381.

Cicirelli, V.G. (1995) *Sibling Relationships Across the Life Span*, Plenum Press, New York.

Clark-Ibanez, M. and Felmlee, D. (2004) Interethnic relationships: the role of social network diversity. *Journal of Marriage and Family*, 66 (2), 293–305.

Coenen-Huther, J., Kellerhals, J., von Allmen, M. *et al.* (1994) *Les réseaux de solidarité dans la famille*, Réalités sociales, Lausanne.

Coleman, J. (1988) Social capital and the creation of human capital. *American Journal of Sociology*, 94, 95–121.

Coleman, M. and Ganong, L.H. (1990) Remarriage and stepfamily research in the 1980s: increased interest in an old family form. *Journal of Marriage and the Family*, 52, 925–940.

Coleman, M., Ganong, L. and Cable, S.M. (1997) Beliefs about women's intergenerational family obligations to provide support before and after divorce and remarriage. *Journal of Marriage and Family*, 59 (1), 165–176.

Cornwell, B. (2012) Spousal network overlap as a basis for spousal support. *Journal of Marriage and the Family*, 74 (2), 229–238.

Davidsson, P. and Honig, B. (2003) The role of social and human capital among nascent entrepreneurs. *Journal of Business Venturing*, 18 (3), 301–331.

DiPrete, T.A., Gelman, A., McCormick, T. *et al.* (2011) Segregation in social networks based on acquaintanceship and trust. *American Journal of Sociology*, 116 (4), 1234–1283.

Feld, F. and Carter, W. C. (1998) Foci of activity as changing contexts for friendship, in *Placing Friendship in Context* (eds. R.G. Adamsand and G. Allan), Cambridge University Press, Cambridge, pp. 136–152.

Felmlee, D.H. (2001) No couple is an island: a social network perspective on dyadic stability. *Social Forces*, 79 (4), 1259–1287.

Ferri, E. (1984) *Stepchildren: A National Study*, Humanities, Atlantic Highlands.

Fischer, L.R. (1983) Mothers and mothers-in-law. *Journal of Marriage and the Family*, 45, 187–192.

Furstenberg, F.F. and Winquist Nord, C. (1985) Parenting apart: patterns of childrearing after marital disruption. *Journal of Marriage and the Family*, 47, 893–904.

Furstenberg, F.F. and Hughes, M.E. (1995) Social capital and successful development among at-risk youth. *Journal of Marriage and Family*, 57 (3), 580–592.

Furstenberg, F.F. and Kaplan, S.B. (2004) Social capital and the family, in *The Blackwell Companion to the Sociology of Families*, 1st edn (eds. J. Scott, J. Treas and M. Richards), Wiley Blackwell, London, pp. 218–232.

Ganong, L.H. and Coleman, M. (2004) *Stepfamily Relationships: Development, Dynamics, and Interventions*, Kluwer Academic/Plenum Publishers, New York.

Giddens, A. (1991) *Modernity and Self-Identity: Self and Society in the Late Modern Age*, Stanford University Press, Stanford.

Giudici, F. and Gauthier, J.-A. (2009) Différenciation des trajectoires professionnelles liée à la transition à la parentalité en Suisse. *Swiss Journal of Sociology*, 35 (2), 253–278.

Granovetter, M.S. (1973) The strength of weak ties. *American Journal of Sociology*, 78 (6), 1360–1380.

Hobart, C. (1987) Parent-child relations in remarried families. *Journal of Family Issues*, 3, 259–277.

Holman, T.B. (1981) The influence of community involvement on marital quality. *Journal of Marriage and the Family*, 143 (1), 43–149.

Hurlbert, J.S. and Acock, A. (1990) The effects of marital status on the form and composition of social networks. *Social Science Quarterly*, 71 (1), 163–174.

Jallinoja, R. and Widmer, E.D. (eds) (2010) *Families and Kinship in Contemporary Europe: Rules and Practices of Relatedness*, Palgrave Macmillan Studies in Family and Intimate Life, Basingstoke.

Johnson, C.L. (1988) *Ex-Familia: Grandparents, Parents and Children Adjust to Divorce*, Rutgers University Press, New Brunswick.

Johnson, C.L. (2000) Perspectives on American kinship in the later 1990s. *Journal of Marriage and the Family*, 62 (3), 623–639.

Johnson, M.J. and Milardo, R.M. (1984) Network interference in pair relationships: a social psychological recasting of Slater's theory of social regression. *Journal of Marriage and the Family*, 46 (4), 893–899.

Johnson, C.L. and Barer B.M. (1987) Marital instability and changing kinship networks of grandparents. *The Gerontologist*, 27, 330–335.

Julien, D., Markman, H.J., Leveille, S. *et al.* (1994) Networks'support and interference with regard to marriage: disclosure of marital problems to confidants. *Journal of Family Psychology*, 8, 16–31.

Kalmijn, M. (2003) Shared friendship networks and the life course: an analysis of survey data on married and cohabiting couples. *Social Networks*, 25 (3), 231–249.

Kearns, J.N. and Leonard, K.E. (2004) Social networks, structural interdependence, and marital quality over the transition to marriage: a prospective analysis. *Journal of Family Psychology*, 18 (2), 383–395.

Klein, R.C.A. and Milardo, R.M. (2000) The social context of couple conflict: support and criticism from informal third parties. *Journal of Social and Personal Relationships*, 17 (4–5), 618–637.

Korpi, W. (2000) Faces of inequality: gender, class, and patterns of inequalities in different types of welfare states. *Social Politics*, 7 (2), 127–191.

Krüger, H. and Levy, R. (2001) Linking life courses, work and the family: theorizing a not so visible nexus between women and men. *Canadian Journal of Sociology*, 26 (2), 145–166.

Le Goff, J.-M. and Levy R. (2011) Devenir parent. Rapport technique sur la réalisation des enquêtes quantitative et qualitative. Lines working papers no. 8, Lausanne.

Milardo, R.M. (1982) Friendship networks in developing relationships: converging and diverging social environments. *Social Psychology Quarterly*, 45, 162–172.

Milardo, R.M. (1986) Personal choice and social constraint in close relationships: applications of network analysis, in *Friendship and Social Interaction* (eds. V.J. Derlega and B.A. Winstead), Springer, New York, pp. 145–166.

Milardo, R.M. (1987) Changes in social networks of women and men following divorce. *Journal of Family Issues*, 8 (1), 78–96.

Milardo, R.M. (1989) Theoretical and methodological issues in the identification of the social networks of spouses. *Journal of Marriage and the Family*, 51, 165–174.

Milardo, R.M. (2010) *The Forgotten Kin: Aunts and Uncles*, 1st edn, Cambridge University Press, New York.

Milardo, R. and Allan, G. (1997) Social networks and marital relationships, in *Handbook of Personal Relationships* (ed. S. Duck), Wiley, Chichester, pp. 505–523.

Milardo, R.M., Johnson, M.P. and Huston, T.L. (1983) Developing close relationships: changing patterns of interaction between pair members and social networks. *Journal of Personality and Social Psychology*, 44 (5), 964–976.

Mueller, M.M., Wilhelm, B. and Elder, G.H. (2002) Variations in grandparenting. *Research on Aging*, 24 (3), 360–388.

Parks, M.R. and Eggert, L.L (1991) The role of social context in the dynamics of personal relationships. *Advances in Personal Relationships*, 2, 1–34.

Pillemer, K.A. and Lüscher, K. (2004) *Intergenerational Ambivalences: New Perspectives on Parent-Child Relations in Later Life*, Elsevier/JAI, Boston.

Portes, A. (2000) The two meanings of social capital. *Sociological Forum*, 15 (1), 1–12.

Putnam, R.D. (2000) *Bowling Alone: The Collapse and Revival of American Community*, Simon and Schuster, New York.

Sapin M. and Widmer E.D. (2009) Changes in personal networks during the transition to parenthood. An empirical assessment in Switzerland. Paper presented at the European Sociological Association, held in Lisbon, September 2–5, 2009.

Schneider, D.M. (1980) *American Kinship. A Cultural Account*. The University of Chicago Press, Chicago/London.

Silverstein, M. and Marenco, A. (2001) How Americans enact the grandparent role across the family life course. *Journal of Family Issues*, 22 (4), 493–522.

Spicer, J.W. and Hampe, G.D. (1975) Kinship interaction after divorce. *Journal of Marriage and the Family*, 37 (1), 113–119.

Stein, C.H., Bush, E.G., Ross, R.R. and Ward M. (1992) Mine, yours and ours: a configural analysis of the networks of married couples in relation to marital satisfaction and individual well-being. *Journal of Personal Relationships*, 9, 365–383.

Surra, C.A. (1985) Courtship types: variations in interdependence between partners and social networks. *Journal of Personality and Social Psychology*, 49 (2), 357–375.

Surra, C.A. and Milardo, R.M. (1991) The social psychological context of developing relationships: interactive and psychological networks, in *Advances in Personal Relationships*, 3rd edn (ed. J. Kingsley), Jessica Kingsley, London, (3) pp. 1–36.

Szreter, S. and Woolcock, M. (2004) Health by association? Social capital, social theory, and the political economy of public health. *International Journal of Epidemiology*, 33 (4), 650–667.

Terhell, E.L., Broese van Groenou, M.I. and van Tilburg, T. (2004) Network dynamics in the long-term period after divorce. *Journal of Social and Personal Relationships*, 21 (6), 719–738.

Terhell, E.L., Broese van Groenou, M.I. and van Tilburg, T. (2007) Network contact changes in early and later postseparation years. *Social Networks*, 29 (1), 11–24.

Treas, J. (2011) Revisiting the Bott thesis on kin networks and marriage. *Social Science Research*, 40 (3), 716–726.

Wellman, B. (1999) *Networks in the Global Village*, Westview Press, Boulder.

Weston, K. (1997) *Families We Choose: Lesbian, Gays, Kinship*, Columbia University Press, New York.

Widmer, E.D. (2004) Couples and their networks, in *Blackwell Companion to the Sociology of Families* (eds. J. Scott, J. Treas and M. Richards), Blackwell Publisher, London, pp. 356–373.

Widmer, E.D. (2006) Who are my family members? Bridging and binding social capital in family configurations. *Journal of Personal and Social Relationships*, 23 (6), 979–998.

Widmer E., D., Giudici, F., Le Goff J.-M. and Pollien, A. (2009) From Support to Control. A Configurational Perspective on Conjugal Quality. *Journal of Marriage and Family*. Retrieved from http://onlinelibrary.wiley.com/doi/10.1111/j.1741-3737.2009.00611.x/full

Widmer, E.D. (2010) *Family Configurations: A Structural Approach to Family Diversity* (ed. L. Ashgate), Ashgate Publishing, London, p. 155.

Widmer, E.D., Jallinoja, R. (eds) (2008) *Beyond the Nuclear Family. Families in a Configurational Perspective*, Peter Lang, Berlin.

Widmer, E.D. and Lüscher, K. (2011) Les relations intergénérationnelles au prisme de l'ambivalence et des configurations familiales. *Recherches Familiales*, 8, 49–60.

Widmer, E.D., Kellerhals, J. and Levy, R. (2004) Types of conjugal networks, conjugal conflict and conjugal quality. *European Sociological Review*, 20 (1), 63–77.

Widmer, E.D., Giudici, F., Le Goff, J.-M. and Pollien, A. (2009) From support to control. A configurational perspective on conjugal quality. *Journal of Marriage and Family*, 71 (13), 437–448.

Widmer, E.D., Favez, N., Aeby, G. *et al.* (2012) *Capital social et coparentage dans les familles recomposees et de premiere union* (Sociograph., p. 209). Department of Sociology, Geneva, http://www.unige.ch/ses/socio/publications/dernierespublications/sociograph13.html (accessed October 30, 2013).

13

Health and Families

DEBORAH CARR, KRISTEN W. SPRINGER AND
KRISTI WILLIAMS

Introduction

Health is the single most important indicator of the overall well-being of a society. The World Health Organization (2006) defines health as "complete physical, mental, and social well-being and not merely the absence of disease or infirmity." Family is among the most powerful influences on health, as it provides economic, social, and psychological resources (and strains) that protect (or threaten) the health of its members. One of the most important developments in recent decades is that contemporary scholars have moved beyond the question does family structure affect health, and instead explore *under what conditions*, *for which outcomes*, *for whom*, and *through which pathways* do family structure, context, and process affect health?

In this chapter, we synthesize contemporary theories and empirical research that explore how families affect physical and mental health over the life course. We also highlight gender, race, socioeconomic status (SES), and cross-national differences in the distinctive ways that families shape health.

We begin by describing core concepts in the study of families and health. Second, we explore how family structures and processes affect the health and well-being of children and adolescents. Third, we document how marital roles, relations, and transitions affect adult health, with attention to the competing perspectives of social selection versus social causation. Fourth, we investigate how parenthood and its structural context affect adult health. We conclude by suggesting directions for future research on families and health.

The Wiley Blackwell Companion to the Sociology of Families, First Edition.
Edited by Judith Treas, Jacqueline Scott, and Martin Richards.
© 2014 John Wiley & Sons Ltd. Published 2017 by John Wiley & Sons Ltd.

Core Concepts and Measures in the Study of Families and Health

Measuring health

Research on families and health typically focuses on physical and mental health conditions and symptoms, and health behaviors. Many researchers rely on large-scale sample survey data sets that include detailed measures of family structures and processes as well as self-reported indicators of physical health (e.g., symptom and illness checklists, self-rated health, functional limitations), mental health (e.g., depression, anxiety), and health behaviors (e.g., smoking, drinking, and exercise patterns). A growing number of population-based surveys now obtain biological indicators of health (or "biomarkers"), allowing studies to examine the physiological and social responses to stress that may contribute to physical and mental health (McEwen, 1998).

Stress perspectives
Conceptual models of stress provide a useful framework for understanding how health is affected by family structures (e.g., the composition of one's family), relationship quality, and family transitions, (e.g., divorce or the death of a spouse). *Stress* refers to any environmental, social, biological, or psychological demand that requires a person to adjust his or her usual patterns of behavior or emotional responses. Stressors may be *chronic* and persistent, such as strained marital quality or abusive parenting practices, or *acute events*, such as a parent's death or a residential relocation. Although stressors often exact a toll on physical and mental health, the adverse effects depend on the nature of the stressor and characteristics of the individual, including the availability of social, economic, and psychological resources (Thoits, 1995).

Social support and control frameworks

Although stress models emphasize health disadvantages associated with family strain and distressing transitions, social support and social control models emphasize the health benefits provided by families. Social support and control models propose that persons with high-quality close relationships are more likely than those with tenuous or strained ties to engage in health-enhancing behaviors and to enjoy better health (House, Landis, and Umberson, 1988). Social support perspectives emphasize that those who have meaningful social ties receive emotional and instrumental supports that are health enhancing (House *et al.*, 1988; Thoits, 1995). Social control perspectives, by contrast, focus on the role of significant others in directly regulating and encouraging positive health behaviors (Lewis and Rook, 1999), which, in turn, enhance health.

Social selection versus causation perspectives

Both stress and social support and control models argue that family affects health (social causation). However, scholars also recognize that a statistical association between aspects of family life and health may reflect *social selection* processes in which, for example, healthy and financially secure people are more likely to marry and remain married, relative to their less well-off counterparts. In other words, married people are healthier than single people because they were better-off even prior to marrying. Taken together, each of these perspectives provides an important framework for interpreting empirical findings.

Families and Child Health: Core Concepts and Measures

Measuring child health

Families play a critical role in shaping children's health and well-being. Because most children do not have major illnesses or health conditions, many researchers instead examine behaviors or temperaments conceptualized as either correlates of, or precursors to, compromised physical and mental health. Many studies focus on "externalizing" behaviors and "internalizing" problems. Externalizing behaviors encompass antisocial, delinquent, and/or aggressive behaviors such as acting impulsively, disobeying at home, and having a bad temper (King and Sobolewski, 2006). More extreme instances include violent behaviors (e.g., fighting and using weapons) and/ or drug use (Hawkins, Amato, and King, 2007). Internalizing problems refer to symptoms of psychological distress including depression, anxiety, and low self-esteem (King and Sobolewski, 2006; Hawkins *et al.*, 2007).

Conceptualizing family of origin

A child's *family of origin*, or the family (or families) in which he or she grew up, may have powerful consequences for health. *Family structure* refers to the composition of a child's coresidential family – including whether parents and children are related by blood (e.g., biological parent), marriage (e.g., stepparent), or neither (e.g., a "social" father, such as the cohabiting boyfriend of child's biological mother). *Family transitions* that affect child health include residential and relational (e.g., divorce) family changes. *Family processes and characteristics* encompass dynamics and attributes that exist within any type of family, such as parenting style, parent–child closeness, or economic hardship. The following sections describe how each of these aspects of family life affects child and adolescent health.

Families and Child Health: Empirical Research

Family structure

The assumption that children's health is best served by living with two biological parents has provided the foundation for much empirical work over the past half century. However, contemporary research foci have changed in response to dramatic shifts in family structures. For example, children living in two-parent households may reside with legally married parents, stepparents, cohabiting parents, or same-sex parents; each such context may have distinctive implications for child well-being (Brown, 2010; Carr and Springer, 2010). Similarly, single-parent households vary widely, encompassing nonmarital births as well as two-parent households that end in divorce or, in rare cases, widowhood (Kreider, 2008).

In the United States and much of western and northern Europe, the two-parent family is no longer as ubiquitous as it was in prior decades. In the United States in 2011, only 65% of children resided with two parents (Child Trends, 2011). Even more pronounced patterns are evidenced outside the United States. For example, in 2008 in Sweden and Estonia, almost 50% of children under 18 years of age lived in households not headed by two married parents (Iacovou and Skew, 2011). Although the two-parent biological family may no longer be the statistical norm, the arrangement arguably persists as a *cultural norm* of what families should be. This cultural idealization of the two-parent biological family may explain, in part, why this arrangement is more protective for children's health than other family forms (Brown, 2010).

Scholars increasingly recognize that a narrow focus on legal and biological ties is insufficient to capture the complexity of family structures and contexts that shape child health. For example, such an approach would categorize many children in gay and lesbian families as living with an unmarried biological parent, and thus hypothesize that they have poorer health than children in two married-parent families. However, recent studies suggest that children living with two same-sex parents have health outcomes similar to children living with two heterosexual married parents, despite experiencing some stigma associated with their parents' sexual orientation (Stacey and Biblarz, 2001). Scholars also challenge the assumption that it is "best" for children to reside with one mother and one father; a synthesis of recent empirical studies found that children raised by a mother and father fared no better than children raised by two mothers (Biblarz and Stacey, 2010).

Important questions persist regarding why and how family structure matters for child health. The protective effects of the two-parent biological family are particularly strong for adolescent mental health (Barrett and Turner, 2005), behavioral outcomes such as drug use (Hoffman, 2002), and early sexual behavior (Upchurch *et al.*, 2001). The latter patterns may reflect the social control function provided by two coresidential parents. The advantaged economic position of two-parent families is another important mechanism, but economic factors alone cannot fully explain the child health benefits of residing with married parents (relative to single parents) as such effects persist even in generous welfare states such as Sweden (Ringbäck *et al.*, 2003). Further, the benefits of residing in a two-parent household are not due solely to the stability of the parents' relationship, as 5-year-old children living with continually married parents have better health than those residing with equally stable cohabiting parents (Schmeer, 2011). Other potential explanatory pathways considered include cultural context, such as the stigmatization of "nontraditional" family forms; psychosocial influences, such as the greater parental attention given to children with two coresidential parents; evolutionary explanations, which highlight parents' motivation to provide more support to biological versus nonbiological children (Brown, 2010); and social selection processes in which socioeconomic resources and emotional stability are positively associated with forming and remaining in two-parent biological households (Amato, 2005).

Family transitions

Simple indicators of a child's family structure may capture both enduring and changing aspects of family life. Whereas a single-parent household captures the enduring experience of a child living with one adult, it also may represent a transition in the parent's life, which in turn affects child well-being. Key family transitions that affect child well-being – by either adding or subtracting a parent or caregiver from the family home – include parental divorce, separation, remarriage, or death. Transitions, even transitions that may be desirable such as a parent's remarriage, are a potential source of health-depleting stress (Sweeney, 2007).

Parental divorce adversely affects mental health of young children (Strohschein *et al.*, 2005), adolescents (Oldehinkel *et al.*, 2008), and even subsequent generations including grandchildren (Amato and Cheadle, 2005). The magnitude and time course of these effects vary by child gender (Oldehinkel *et al.*, 2008); the number, types, and timing of transitions; and parenting quality (Osborne and McLanahan, 2007). For example, Oldehinkel *et al.* (2008) found that Dutch boys and girls of divorced parents had similar rates of depression when they were 10 years old, but these gender gaps widened over time, as the daughters developed more depressive symptoms throughout adolescence.

The recent proliferation of longitudinal panels that include multiple observations over time on a single study participant has allowed researchers to identify the distinctive health effects of the event of parental divorce, the chronic strains that preceded (and gave rise to) the transition, and secondary stressors that resulted from the transition. For example, studies examining the effects of parental divorce on teens have found that such teens faced considerable stress even prior to the parents' divorce, including psychological and behavioral problems, problem drinking, and lower SES (Furstenberg and Kiernan, 2001).

A single transition, such as parental divorce, also may be part of a trajectory of several transitions that jointly influence child health. Many children from divorced families become members of a stepfamily when their parent remarries. Although this transition may carry independent effects on child health, the magnitude may depend on prior family context. For example, children entering a stepfather family after a parental divorce experience fewer depressive symptoms than children entering a stepfather family after a nonmarital birth, underscoring the importance of the specific nature of family trajectories (Sweeney, 2007).

Family processes and characteristics

Family *processes* such as parental child-rearing practices, father involvement, and adaptations to stressors like poverty each have direct implications for child well-being. The association between family processes and health may be reciprocal, where child health may affect processes including parents' marital quality and employment experiences, further complicating research on family effects.

Parenting practices

Problematic parent–child relations and parents' strained marital relations generally have deleterious effects on child well-being. A cross-national meta-analysis revealed that parental rejection is associated with children's "psychological maladjustment" (Khaleque and Rohner, 2002). Parental conflict is associated with adverse outcomes ranging from adolescent antisocial behavior (Feinberg, Kan, and Hetherington 2007) to infant emotion dysregulation (Du Rocher Schudlich *et al.*, 2011). Parental substance use and mental health problems also have harmful effects on children's mental health and behavioral outcomes, operating via diminished parenting practices (Meadows, McLanahan, and Brooks-Gunn, 2007).

More severe forms of domestic conflict take a harsh toll on child health. Cross-national studies have focused on the most dire outcome, child death. According to a World Health Organization (2002) report, in 2000, there were an estimated 57,000 homicides among children under age 15 across the world, with children ages 0–4 at the greatest risk. Most of these murders are perpetrated by parents. Rates of violence against children, even some culturally approved forms of violence, are staggering. Childhood psychological, physical, and sexual abuse also has long-term implications for adult health (Springer, 2009).

Father involvement
Research on families and child health historically focused on maternal behaviors, as mothers traditionally have been primary caregivers. However, an emerging area of study is the ways that fathers affect children, with an emphasis on the distinctive effects of father–child legal, biological, and residential ties. An exciting new area of inquiry is the role of "social" fathers, or men who coreside with a child yet are not a biological parent. Half of all children in the United States are expected to reside with a biological mother and social father at some point during childhood (Kennedy and Bumpass, 2008).

Most studies concur that high-quality involvement, support, and communication from *any type* of father predict better health for children (Bzostek, 2008), including less smoking and drinking (Coley and Medeiros, 2007), and fewer internalizing and externalizing unhealthy behaviors (King and Sobolewski, 2006). Some research even suggests that children fare best when they maintain positive ties with *multiple* fathers, such as a stepfather and nonresident biological father (King, 2006). However, the child–father tie that is most closely linked to child well-being is typically the one marked by coresident status and the most frequent and regular interaction (King, 2006).

Parental socioeconomic status (SES)
The association between family SES and child health is well established across the globe. Family poverty is linked with children's poorer health, low birth weight, lead poisoning, emotional problems, injuries from accidents or abuse, undernourishment, infectious diseases, and death (Brooks-Gunn and Duncan, 1997). Similar patterns are found whether SES is measured as income, poverty status, parental occupation, or parental education. SES is not static and therefore recent studies emphasize the importance of studying a family's economic trajectory. Living in poverty for multiple years during childhood is worse for children's health than a single or short stint of poverty (Brooks-Gunn and Duncan, 1997). Poverty during adolescence is particularly damaging, as its deleterious effects may persist through adulthood (Sobolewski and Amato, 2005).

In sum, child well-being is shaped by one's family of origin structures, transitions, and processes. As families further diversify, researchers must continue to expand the meaning of family effects; explore how family structures, transitions, and processes interact to shape health outcomes in complex ways; and examine the reciprocal effects of family factors and childhood health to better understand their causal ordering.

Marital Status, Transitions, and Processes: Implications for Adult Health

Research on family relationships and adult health has its conceptual roots in Durkheim's (1897) *Suicide*. Close relationships provide emotional, social, economic, and instrumental supports that can be protective for physical and emotional health. Although social relationships encompass ties to relatives, friends, and colleagues, most studies of adult health focus on the protective effects of marriage, which is assumed to be the most salient relationship for most adults.

The assumption that marriage (or a long-term marriage-like relationship) is protective for all persons and all health outcomes has been challenged in the past decade. Four discoveries are particularly influential. First, the health benefits of being in a romantic partnership vary based on *structural* aspects of one's union; legal marriage is more protective than cohabitation or a long-term same-sex union, and first marriage is more protective than remarriage (Carr and Springer, 2010). However, scientists have yet to explicate *why* all unions are not equal in their consequences. Second, not all marriages are "good" marriages; health benefits are contingent upon processes and interactions within a marriage. Mounting research based on survey, biomarker, qualitative, and experimental data reveals the specific processes that affect adult health, with most concurring that negative processes (e.g., conflict) are stronger predictors than positive interactions (e.g., feeling loved and cared for). Third, longitudinal surveys that track individual-level health changes in response to marital transitions have allowed researchers to better distinguish social causation versus selection processes in understanding the association between marital status and health.

Finally, scholars increasingly recognize the diversity of the unmarried population, which includes those in nonmarital unions as well as never-married, divorced/ separated, and widowed persons. Even within one unmarried category, individuals differ with respect to their duration and pathway into that status. Yet because married persons continue to serve as the benchmark against which other relationship statuses are compared, scholars have not adequately explored the ways that unmarried categories differ from one another. Further, scholars are only beginning to document sources of heterogeneity *within* each unmarried category, with respect to health outcomes, health-depleting stressors, and health-enhancing resources.

These new research foci have been motivated, in part, by dramatic changes in family structure over the past five decades including delayed age at first marriage, rising rates of nonmarital cohabitation, rising and then stabilizing rates of divorce and remarriage, and greater cultural acceptance of "nontraditional" family forms such as lifelong singlehood and same-sex partnerships. In this section, we synthesize contemporary research on the consequences of family structures and processes for adult health, with attention to sources of within- and between-group differences.

The "marriage benefit"

Empirical studies in the United States, Europe, and most developed nations consistently document protective effects of marriage on health outcomes including lower levels of disability (Schoenborn, 2004; Hughes and Waite, 2009), morbidity (Lorenz et al., 2006), and mortality (Gardner and Oswald 2004; Manzoli et al., 2007) and better self-assessed mental (Johnson and Wu, 2002; Williams, 2003) and physical health (Williams and Umberson, 2004). The few studies that distinguish first marriage from remarriage generally concur that the health benefits of remarriage are more modest and short-lived than those of first marriage (Barrett, 2000; Williams and Umberson, 2004).

Marriage improves individual health through economic, psychosocial, and behavioral mechanisms. The psychosocial benefits of marriage have received the most attention, given the well-established centrality of social support, social integration, and behavior modification via social control for health (House et al., 1988). The benefits of marriage for economies of scale and spousal specialization (Waite, 2009) translate to greater wealth that can be used to access health insurance and quality care (Jovanovic, Lin, and Change, 2004). The extent to which spouses garner such benefits varies widely across marital contexts, however.

Heterogeneity in the marriage benefit

Mounting evidence indicates that the health benefits of marriage are not universal but are limited to particular outcomes and vary substantially by aspects of the individual, the marital dyad, and the larger social context. Gender differences in the marriage benefit have been a traditional focus. Recent studies focused on physical health support the early claims of feminist scholar Jessie Bernard (1972) that marriage benefits men more than women (Johnson et al., 2000; Gardner and Oswald, 2004, but see Manzoli et al., 2007). However, studies focused on mental health generally find that men and women manifest different symptoms, where marriage protects against women's depressive symptoms and men's problematic alcohol use (Williams 2003; Strohschein et al., 2005).

Scholars have only recently begun to explore the ways that SES and race condition the marriage–health relationship. For example, Choi and Marks (2008) find that among men only, the mortality benefit associated with marriage is limited to those with low incomes. Studies of race differences are few and inconclusive. Some show that marriage is equally protective for blacks and whites (Johnson et al., 2000; Schoenborn, 2004), yet others suggest that marriage is less protective for blacks because the psychological, economic, and instrumental benefits received in marriage vis-à-vis other social relationships (e.g., extended family, religious community) are less pronounced for blacks (Kroeger-D'Souza, 2012). This remains an important avenue for future research. Blacks' low rates of marriage may contribute to their elevated risk of mortality and morbidity, especially if marriage provides significant health benefits for blacks.

Marital quality

Recent studies underscore that the marriage benefit is limited to those who enjoy supportive, high-quality unions (Hawkins and Booth, 2005; Proulx, Helms, and Buehler, 2007). Some studies even conclude that unmarried persons report better mental health than married persons in unhappy or high-conflict marriages (Williams 2003; Hawkins and Booth, 2005).

Gender differences in the health impact of marital quality are inconsistent, with some studies suggesting that marital quality is more important to women than men (Proulx, Helms, and Buehler, 2007) and others revealing no differences (Williams, 2003). However, as Umberson and Williams (2005) argue, even if marital quality similarly affects men and women, women experience consistently lower levels of marital quality over their lives than men; thus, this gender gap in marital quality may place married women at a health disadvantage compared to men.

Cohabitation

Cohabitation is now the dominant pathway to family formation in the United States and many European countries (Kennedy and Bumpass, 2008). Most research finds that cohabitants fare better than unmarried persons but less favorably than married persons with respect to health outcomes including depressive symptoms (Brown, 2000), mortality (Koskinen *et al.*, 2007), and self-rated physical health (Wu *et al.*, 2003). Differences in relationship quality and union stability may contribute to this disparity, as fewer than half of all cohabiting relationships in the United States last longer than 2 years (Kennedy and Bumpass, 2008). Selection processes also are an important consideration. Studies based on data from the United States (Musick and Bumpass, 2012), Sweden (Drefahl, 2012), and several other European nations show that a considerable proportion of the married–cohabiting health disparity is due to factors such as lower SES, weaker religiosity, and lower employment rates among cohabiting persons.

The relative health benefits of cohabitation vis-à-vis marriage vary cross-nationally; the gap is typically narrowest in nations where cohabitation is most prevalent. An analysis of 28 European countries finds substantially smaller disparities in countries where cohabitation is a legally recognized family status (Soons and Kalmijn, 2009). An important question for future study is whether the health consequences of cohabitation vary based on one's reason for cohabiting. In the United States, approximately half of cohabitors eventually marry their partners (Bumpass and Lu, 2000), whereas others view cohabitation as a long-term alternative to marriage, a convenience, or an economic necessity (Manning and Smock, 2005). Further, the health consequences of serial cohabitation – a growing pattern in the United States (Cohen and Manning, 2010) – deserve attention. Taken together, these patterns suggest that as cohabitation becomes increasingly normative and a less select form of union formation, its health benefits may approximate those gained in marriage.

Gay and lesbian relationships

Little is known about the health of men and women in same-sex unions, although a recent report by the Institute of Medicine (2011) suggests that chronic stress associated with sexual minority status may undermine the benefits of being in a stable partnership. Until very recently, population-based US studies of the health consequences of same-sex unions have been limited by data availability, requiring researchers to merge data from multiple sources. One such study found few differences in self-assessed health between partnered gay and lesbian adults and their married or straight cohabiting counterparts (Wienke and Hill, 2009). However, a more recent analysis of national data challenges this conclusion by showing that at similar levels of SES, being in a same-sex cohabiting relationship is associated with worse self-assessed health than being in a different-sex marriage (Liu, Reczek, and Brown, 2013). An important question for future research is whether legal recognition of same-sex unions confers greater health benefits. Although direct comparative evidence is unavailable, research in Denmark where same-sex unions have legal status as registered unions suggests few benefits (Drefhal, 2012). However, the evidence is currently too limited to suggest clear conclusions.

Divorce

Divorce, or the legal dissolution of marriage, is a stressful life event that typically follows a period of chronic strain (e.g., marital conflict) and precedes a period of chronic secondary strains (e.g., poverty). As such, decades of research indicate that divorced individuals have poorer physical and mental health than their married counterparts, yet mounting evidence suggests that divorce represents a temporary crisis from which adult mental health eventually rebounds (Gardner and Oswald, 2004; Strohschein et al., 2005; Lorenz et al., 2006). The long-term consequences for physical health are not well understood, however, with some studies showing persistent long-term decrements (Williams and Umberson, 2004; Hughes and Waite, 2009), others showing short-term effects only (Dupre and Meadows, 2007), and other showing lagged effects that do not appear until roughly 10 years after the divorce due to the multiple secondary stressors that follow divorce (Lorenz et al., 2006).

Another important focus is documenting heterogeneity in divorce consequences, particularly by gender, race, and prior marital quality. Some longitudinal studies have found that divorce is associated with steeper declines in psychological well-being for women than men (Kalmijn and Monden, 2006) and greater declines in physical health for men than women (Dupre and Meadows, 2007), yet others find no gender differences (Williams, 2003; Strohschein et al., 2005; Manzoli et al., 2007). The processes through which marital dissolution influence health also may differ by gender, triggering risky health behaviors among men, yet socioeconomic disadvantage for women (Dupre, Beck, and Meadows, 2009). Race and class differences in divorce consequences have received less attention but the evidence available indicates few differences (Barrett, 2003).

The impact of divorce also varies based on the quality of the marriage being exited. Studies generally concur that exiting a problematic marriage may be beneficial; longitudinal analyses show that persons who dissolved stressful marriages reported long-term gains in self-rated health, relative to persons who remained in troubled marriages (Williams and Umberson, 2004; Hawkins and Booth, 2005). Limited evidence suggests, however, that distress may persist even after a troubled marriage ends. Kalmijn and Monden (2006) found that persons who exited marriages marked by verbal and physical aggression showed a subsequent increase in depressive symptoms, perhaps reflecting ongoing custody or child support battles.

Two important questions remain unresolved. First, we do not know precisely how the stress of divorce affects physical health. Laboratory-based research offers promising new findings: divorce-related stressors may affect blood pressure reactivity which, if persistent, could impede health (Sbarra *et al.*, 2009). Second, studies fail to consider that divorce occurs within a larger family context, and its consequences could vary based on other concurrent family roles and obligations such as caring for parents or children.

Widowhood

Widowhood, like divorce, is a stressful transition that can compromise health. Also like divorce, the health consequences of widowhood vary based on characteristics of the individual, the marriage, and the transition. Widowhood is distinct from divorce, however, in that it disproportionately affects older adults; two-thirds of the two million deaths occurring in the United States each year befall persons aged 65 and older (Federal Interagency Forum on Aging-Related Statistics, 2012). As such, the health-depleting effects of marital loss may be compounded by preexisting health complications that accompany the processes of aging.

The death of one's spouse is associated with elevated risk of mortality (Manzoli *et al.*, 2007), functional limitations (Schoenborn, 2004), and depressive symptoms (Carr *et al.*, 2000), with effects strongest during the first 2 years postloss. Common wisdom attributes the widowhood–mortality link to the survivor's "dying of a broken heart," yet empirical evidence points to spouses' shared health-promoting (or health-depleting) environment; the strains of caregiving for a dying spouse; poor health behaviors postloss (especially for men), including erratic sleep, compromised diet, and poor compliance with medication regimens; and social selection, where the healthiest widow(er)s are most likely to remarry, thus leaving less health widowed persons at elevated risk of mortality (Elwert and Christakis, 2008).

The health decrements associated with widowhood are more severe for men than women, because wives are more likely than husbands to monitor their husbands' health behaviors. Consistent with social control perspectives, one study based on a sample of more than 150,000 persons in Finland found that widowers are more likely than married men to die of accidents, alcohol-related deaths, lung cancer, and heart disease during the first 6 months after their loss, but not from other causes that are less closely linked to health behaviors (Martikainen and Valkonen, 1996). Women also fare better than men because they typically maintain closer ties with children and friends over the life course, and thus receive more instrumental and emotional support as they cope with loss (Ha, 2008).

The well-being of older widow(er)s also is linked to the emotional climate of the late marriage and the context of the death. The loss of high-quality marriages is more distressing than the loss of conflictual marriages (Carr *et al.*, 2000). Anticipated deaths tend to be less distressing than sudden or unanticipated ones, yet for older adults the former often are preceded by stressful spousal caregiving and neglect of one's own symptoms – which may harm one's own health (Carr *et al.*, 2001). Thus, the health effects of widowhood are contingent upon the nature of the stressful event, as well as one's resources to cope with the death, and its stressful precursor and consequences.

Never-married persons

Little is known about the factors that influence the health of never-married persons. This lack of knowledge largely reflects methodological constraints. The population of "never-married" persons is small and difficult to define; most young and midlife persons identified as "never married" in cross-sectional surveys will marry eventually. Among persons aged 65+ in the United States, only 3–4% of men and women have never married (Spraggins, 2005). This small number limits researchers' ability to conduct adequately powered analyses using data from nationally representative health surveys.

Mortality is one of the few physical health outcomes studied among never-married persons because mortality and marital status data are available on large administrative data sets and vital registries, especially in Europe. However, these data include limited demographic measures, so investigators cannot adequately identify the pathways through which singlehood affects health. Analyses show that never-married persons are at elevated risk of overall and some cause-specific (e.g., heart disease, suicide) mortality risks yet they do not explicate *why* (Johnson *et al.*, 2000; Manzoli *et al.*, 2007).

A handful of survey-based studies provide preliminary insights into how singlehood affects health in later life (because "never-married" persons in younger samples may still ultimately marry). Older (age 65+) never-married women enjoy mental health (Pudrovska, Schieman, and Carr, 2006) and physical health (Cwikel, Gramotnev, and Lee, 2006) equal to their married peers and superior to their formerly married counterparts. These patterns partly reflect social selection, where older cohorts of never-married women are more educated than their married and formerly married peers, and have higher levels of economic stability than their divorced or widowed peers. Both studies conclude that never-married women adjust to their status over time; they choose relationships that provide socioemotional support (Pudrovska *et al.*, 2006) and rely on formal services such as meal preparation services to help manage age-related health declines (Cwikel *et al.*, 2006).

In sum, research suggests that never-married women are not disadvantaged with respect to mental health, yet unmarried men and women have an elevated – and unexplained – mortality risk relative to their married peers. Psychologists' recent strides in conceptualizing and operationalizing "loneliness" (i.e., a discrepancy between one's desired and actual relationships) may help scholars to explicate the linkage between singlehood and physical health. Loneliness is linked to sleep problems, poor cardiovascular health, and elevated blood pressure, each of which carries long-term consequences for mortality risk (Luo *et al.*, 2012).

Implications of Parenthood for Adult Health

Parenthood is a common yet pivotal experience in the adult life course and its consequences for health have long been of interest to family scholars and the general public. Until recently, most empirical studies indicate that the strains associated with parenthood undermine well-being more than the benefits of parenthood protect it (Umberson, Pudrovska, and Reczek, 2010). Implicit in the study of parenthood is a comparison to the childless – a topic of increasing interest as rates of childlessness approach or exceed 20% in the United States and Western Europe (Dykstra, 2009; U.S. Census Bureau, 2010). Despite long-standing norms that stigmatize childlessness, there is little evidence that it is accompanied by psychological distress (Nomaguchi and Milkie, 2003; Evenson and Simon, 2005) or poor physical health (Mastekaasa, 2000). In fact, most studies find that childless persons have fewer depressive symptoms than parents of young children (Nomaguchi and Milkie, 2003; Evenson and Simon, 2005). An exception is research indicating that childless adults have higher rates of mortality than parents (Grundy and Tomassini, 2005), but this may partly reflect differential selection due to the influence of health on infertility.

Contemporary scholars recognize that the social context of childbearing has changed dramatically in recent decades, and these new contexts have implications for parental health. Parenthood is delayed until later ages, and is increasingly decoupled from marriage. The median percentage of births to unmarried women throughout the world has risen from 7.1% in the 1970s to 33.8% in the first decade of the twenty-first century (United Nations, 2011). In the United States, 40% of all births in 2009 were to unmarried women, but nearly 60% of those nonmarital births occurred in cohabiting unions (Child Trends, 2013). These percentages are higher in much of Western Europe (Kiernan, 2001).

Recognizing the shifting and diversifying contexts of childbearing, scholars are now investigating the health consequences of these new family forms, and sources of heterogeneity therein. We summarize recent research on the health consequences of nonmarital and Multipartner Fertility (MPF) and the extent to which the health consequences of parenthood vary by birth timing.

Nonmarital fertility

Nonmarital fertility is considered an important social problem among many researchers and policy makers, because it is consistently associated with poorer health and increased mortality risk among women in the United States (Williams *et al.*, 2011), Great Britain (Whitehead, Burstro, and Diderichsen, 2000), Norway (Elstad, 1996), Finland (Martikainen, 1995), and Sweden (Whitehead *et al.*, 2000). However, most scholars concur that nonmarital fertility does not necessarily have direct harmful effects on health. Rather, unmarried women face a host of other adversities that place them at risk of health problems, including poverty (Johnson and Favreault, 2004), and chronic strain and psychological distress (Barrett and Turner, 2005), relative to married mothers.

The strength of the association between nonmarital childbearing and health varies widely across contexts and demographic subgroups. A particularly important contextual factor is whether the birth occurred in a cohabiting union. Most studies show that unmarried cohabiting mothers and fathers have more mental health problems (DeKlyen *et al.*, 2006) than their married counterparts, but fewer problems than those who are no longer romantically involved with the other parent. It is unknown whether this association persists over time, for physical health outcomes, or beyond the United States.

The magnitude of the association between nonmarital fertility and maternal health also varies by race and ethnicity, reflecting differential access to health-enhancing resources. For example, Williams *et al.* (2011) found that nonmarital fertility is linked to poorer long-term health outcomes for black and white, but not Hispanic women. However, scholars are only beginning to identify the mechanisms through which nonmarital fertility affects women's health, or how these patterns might differ by race/ethnicity and international context. Researchers also know little about the ways that nonmarital fertility affects the health of men, particularly those who are involved in their children's lives and who father children with multiple partners (Guzzo and Furstenberg, 2007). These are important avenues for future research.

Multipartner fertility (MPF)

MPF – having biological children with more than one partner – is an increasingly common context of parenthood. In the United States, roughly one-fifth of women who have completed their childbearing have had children with more than one partner (Dorius, 2012), although this proportion is considerably higher among unmarried versus currently married women (Carlson and Furstenberg, 2006). Rates of MPF are lower in European countries where cohabiting unions are more stable and enduring (Lappegård and Rønsen, 2011).

MPF is increasingly experienced in the context of nonmarital fertility rather than remarriage following divorce or widowhood (Guzzo and Furstenberg, 2007). Scholars have hypothesized that strains and role ambiguity associated with child-rearing across households may undermine health, although little research has yet been done here. Research in this area is nascent and much remains to be investigated about the potential effect of MPF on physical health and, whether it varies across race/ethnic, class, and international contexts.

Birth timing

The health effects of parenthood also vary based on the age at which one becomes a parent. US studies indicate that, at least up until about age 30, earlier ages at first birth are associated with worse health outcomes including mental health (Mirowsky and Ross, 2002), mortality (Mirowsky, 2002), and indices of health problems (including self-assessed health) (Mirowsky, 2002). Research on European populations shows consistent and similar patterns (Grundy and Tomassini, 2005).

Although the teen birthrate in the United States has declined in recent years, approximately 8.4% of all births and 21% of first births in 2011 occurred to women aged 19 or younger – a higher rate than in any other developed country (Hamilton,

Martin, and Ventura, 2012). However, most studies show that teenage and young adult mothers do not typically fare worse than other women with respect to depressive symptoms after social selection factors are adjusted (Mollborn and Morningstar, 2009). It is important to note, though, that a focus on the immediate consequences of teen childbearing may obscure long-term causal effects that accumulate over the life course – a factor that may be especially relevant for research predicting physical health consequences of teen childbearing because chronic conditions linked to stress may take decades to emerge (Lynch and Smith, 2005).

Conclusion and Future Directions

The health implications of one's family statuses vary based on structural, processual, and contextual aspects of the relationship; the nature and timing of family transitions; and other resources and relationships prior to, during, and after that transition. Recent studies also identify specific aspects of interpersonal interactions that affect child and adult health. This is an important line of inquiry, because relationship dynamics are potentially modifiable factors. Although public policy initiatives in the early twenty-first century encouraged *marriage*, current programs have the more realistic goal of encouraging *healthy relationships*. Such programs include parent education, conflict resolution, communication, health behaviors, and financial literacy modules (Halford, Markman, and Stanley, 2008). Although these programs cannot ameliorate a root cause of unhealthy relationships – economic adversity – they may provide at least some benefits for child and adult health.

Directions for future research

We expect that scholars will make even further advances in the study of families and health by using cutting-edge quantitative research methods (*dyadic- and family-level analyses* and *behavioral genetics approaches*) and relying on *qualitative methods* to investigate in depth the distinctive ways that families affect health in underresearched subpopulations. We highlight what we see as the most promising avenues for researchers in the coming decade.

Dyadic- and family-level analyses. One of the most ironic limitations of studies on "families" and health is that most focus on *one individual* within the larger family network. This limitation is due, in part, to traditional models of data collection in which one person answers survey questions on his or her own union and parental statuses, relationship quality, and own health as well as the health of one's spouse or a child. Such studies cannot adequately capture the complexities of family life – including the possibility that two romantic partners, siblings, or coparents experience their relationship (and its health consequences) in very different ways.

Dyadic data analysis enables researchers to use data from multiple reporters within a family to estimate how much each person's outcome is associated with both own and partner characteristics. This approach enables researchers to explore, for example, how both spouses' reports of marital conflict are associated with each spouse's health behaviors (Sandberg *et al.*, 2009). We suspect that these pathbreaking studies and methods will set the stage for further family-level explorations in the coming decade.

Behavioral genetics approaches. Researchers have long attempted to understand the relative contributions of genetic versus social influences on health. In the last decade, scientific knowledge and available data have become sufficiently sophisticated to accurately identify specific gene/environment interactions that affect health. A promising development is the identification of specific genetic polymorphisms (i.e., genetic variations that produce different outcomes within the same species) that affect health risks both directly and in conjunction with family process and structure indicators. For example, Guo, Roettger, and Cai (2008) found that specific polymorphisms predicted adolescent delinquency net of confounding variables, but not among adolescents who shared daily meals with their parents. These provocative findings suggest that family processes may limit (or facilitate) the extent to which a genetic propensity for a particular condition is expressed. Future studies of genetics and environment may reveal both those individuals at greatest genetic risk of health problems, as well as the family processes that protect against or exacerbate these risks.

Qualitative methods to study underresearched population. Social scientists have made important strides in documenting population-level relationships between family characteristics and child and adult health outcomes. However, we are only beginning to discover whether such population-level patterns hold in ethnic communities, among recent immigrants, and among same-sex couples. Qualitative studies provide insights into the ways that the cultural views and practices of ethnic families affect health and health behaviors. For example, gendered cultural views such as "machismo" (i.e., men's adherence to traditionally masculine, high-risk behaviors) and "marianismo" (i.e., women's self-sacrifice for spouse and children) in Latino families affect both family relations and health practices (Cianelli, Ferrer, and McElmurry, 2008). We are optimistic that future research blending qualitative and quantitative research will better illuminate the ways that cultural context shapes the relationship between family and health, broadly defined.

References

Amato, P.R. (2005) The impact of family formation change on the cognitive, social, and emotional well-being of the next generation. *The Future of Children*, 15, 75–96.

Amato, P.R. and Cheadle, J. (2005) The long reach of divorce: divorce and child well-being across three generations. *Journal of Marriage and Family*, 67, 191–206.

Barrett, A.E. (2000) Marital trajectories and mental health. *Journal of Health and Social Behavior*, 41 (4), 451–464.

Barrett, A.E. (2003) Race differences in the mental health effects of divorce. *Journal of Family Issues*, 24 (8), 995–1019.

Barrett, A.E. and Turner, R.J. (2005) Family structure and mental health: the mediating effects of socioeconomic status, family process, and social stress. *Journal of Health and Social Behavior*, 46 (2), 156–69.

Bernard, J. (1972) *The Future of Marriage*, Yale University Press, New Haven.

Biblarz, T.J. and Stacey, J. (2010) How does the gender of parents matter? *Journal of Marriage and the Family*, 72, 3–22.

Brooks-Gunn, J. and Duncan, G.J. (1997) The effects of poverty on children. *The Future of Children*, 7, 55–71, http://futureofchildren.org/publications/journals/article/index.xml?journalid=53&articleid=287 (accessed October 30, 2013).

Brown, S.L. (2000) The effect of union type on psychological well-being: depression among cohabitors versus marrieds. *Journal of Health and Social Behavior*, 41 (3), 241–255.

Brown, S.L. (2010) Marriage and child well-being: research and policy perspectives. *Journal of Marriage and Family*, 72, 1059–1077.

Bumpass, L. and Lu, H-H. (2000) Trends in cohabitation and implications for children's family contexts in the United States. *Population Studies*, 54 (1), 29–41, http://www.jstor.org/stable/2584631 (accessed October 30, 2013).

Bzostek, S.H. (2008) Social fathers and child well-being. *Journal of Marriage and Family*, 70, 950–961.

Carlson, M.J. and Furstenberg, F.F., Jr. (2006) The prevalence and correlates of multipartnered fertility among urban US parents. *Journal of Marriage and Family*, 68 (3), 718–732.

Carr, D. and Springer, K.W. (2010) Advances in families and health research in the 21st century. *Journal of Marriage and Family*, 72, 744–761.

Carr, D., House, J.S., Kessler, R.C., *et al.* (2000) Marital quality and psychological adjustment to widowhood among older adults: a longitudinal analysis. *Journal of Gerontology: Social Sciences*, 55B (4), S197–S207.

Carr, D., House, J.S., Wortman, C.B. *et al.* (2001) Psychological adjustment to sudden and anticipated spousal death among the older widowed. *Journal of Gerontology: Social Sciences*, 56B (4), S237–S248.

Child Trends (2012) *Births to Unmarried Women: Indicators on Children and Youth*, Child Trends Data Bank, Washington, DC, http://www.childtrendsdatabank.org/sites/default/files/59_Family_Structure_December.pdf (accessed November 20, 2013).

Choi, H. and Marks, N.F. (2008) Marital conflict, depressive symptoms, and functional impairment. *Journal of Marriage & Family*, 70 (2), 377–390.

Cianelli, R., Ferrer, L. and McElmurry, B.J. (2008) HIV prevention and low-income Chilean women: machismo, marianismo, and HIV misconceptions. *Culture, Health & Sexuality: An International Journal for Research, Intervention, and Care*, 10, 297–306.

Cohen, J. and Manning, W. (2010) The relationship context of premarital serial cohabitation. *Social Science Research*, 39 (5), 766–776.

Coley, R.L. and Medeiros, B.L. (2007) Reciprocal longitudinal relations between nonresident father involvement and adolescent delinquency. *Child Development*, 78, 132–147.

Cwikel, J., Gramotnev, H. and Lee, C. (2006) Never-married childless women: health and social circumstances in older age. *Social Science & Medicine*, 62, 991–2001.

DeKlyen, M., Brooks-Gunn, J., McLanahan, S. and Knab, J. (2006) The mental health of married, cohabiting, and non-coresident parents with infants. *American Journal of Public Health*, 96 (10), 1836–1841.

Dorius, C. (2012) Does MPF Put Women at Risk? Theories of Multipartnered Fertility and Health. PSC Research Report 12-770. Population Studies Center, University of Michigan.

Drefahl, S. (2012) Do the married really live longer? The role of cohabitation and socioeconomic status. *Journal of Marriage and Family*, 74 (3), 462–475.

Dupre, M.E. and Meadows, S.O. (2007) Disaggregating the effects on health. *Journal of Family Issues*, 28 (5), 623–652.

Dupre, M.E., Beck, A.N. and Meadows, S.O. (2009) Marital trajectories and mortality among US adults. *American Journal of Epidemiology*, 170 (5), 546–555.

Durkheim, É. (1966 [1897]) *Suicide*, Free Press, New York.

Du Rocher Schudlich, T.D., White, C.R., Fleischhauer, E.A. and Fitzgerald, K.A. (2011) Observed infant reactions during live interparental conflict. *Journal of Marriage and Family*, 73, 1741–3737.

Dykstra, P.A. (2009) Childless old age, in *International Handbook of Population Aging* (ed P. Uhlenberg), Springer, Dordrecht, pp. 671–690.

Elstad, J.I. (1996) Inequalities in health related to women's marital, parental, and employment status: a comparison between the early 70s and the late 80s, Norway. *Social Science & Medicine*, 42 (1), 75–89.

Elwert, F. and Christakis, N.A. (2008) Variation in the effect of widowhood on mortality by the causes of death of both spouses. *American Journal of Public Health*, 98, 2092–2098.

Evenson, R.J. and Simon, R.W. (2005) Clarifying the relationship between parenthood and depression. *Journal of Health and Social Behavior*, 46 (4), 341–358.

Federal Interagency Forum on Aging-Related Statistics (2012) *Older Americans 2012: Key Indicators of Well-Being*. Federal Interagency Forum on Aging-Related Statistics, U.S. Government Printing Office, Washington, DC, http://www.agingstats.gov/agingstatsdotnet/main_site/default.aspx (accessed November 8, 2012).

Feinberg, M.E., Kan, M.L. and Hetherington, E. M. (2007) The longitudinal influence of coparenting conflict on parental negativity and adolescent maladjustment. *Journal of Marriage and Family*, 69, 687–702.

Furstenberg, F.F. and Kiernan, K.E. (2001) Delayed parental divorce: how much do children benefit? *Journal of Marriage and Family*, 63, 446–457.

Gardner, J. and Oswald, A.J. (2004) How is mortality affected by money, marriage, and stress? *Journal of Health Economics*, 23, 1181–1207, http://dx.doi.org/10.1016/j.jhealeco.2004.03.002 (accessed October 30, 2013).

Grundy, E. and Tomassini, C. (2005) Fertility history and health in later life: a record linkage study in England and Wales. *Social Science & Medicine*, 61 (1), 217–228.

Guo, G., Roettger, M.E. and Cai, T. (2008) The integration of genetic propensities into social-control models of delinquency and violence among male youths. *American Sociological Review*, 73, 543–568.

Guzzo, K.B. and Furstenberg, F.F. (2007) Multipartnered fertility among young women with a nonmarital first birth: prevalence and risk factors. *Perspectives on Sexual & Reproductive Health*, 39 (1), 29–38.

Ha, J.-H. (2008) Changes in support from confidantes, children, and friends following widowhood. *Journal of Marriage and Family*, 70, 306–318.

Halford, W.K., Markman, H.J. and Stanley, S. (2008) Strengthening couples' relationships with education: social policy and public health perspectives. *Journal of Family Psychology*, 22, 497–505.

Hamilton, B.E., Martin, J.A. and Ventura, S.J. (2012) Births: preliminary data for 2011. *National Vital Statistics Report*. Hyattsville.

Hawkins, D.N. and Booth, A. (2005) Unhappily ever after: effects of long-term, low-quality marriages on well-being. *Social Forces*, 4, 445–465.

Hawkins, D.N., Amato, P.R. and King, V. (2007) Nonresident father involvement and adolescent well-being: father effects or child effects? *American Sociological Review*, 72, 990–1010.

Hoffman, J.P. (2002) The community context of family structure and adolescent drug use. *Journal of Marriage and Family*, 64, 314–330.

House, J.S., Landis, K.R. and Umberson, D. (1988) Social relationships and health. *Science*, 241 (4865), 540–545.

Hughes, M.E. and Waite, L.J. (2009) Marital biography and health at midlife. *Journal of Health and Social Behavior*, 50, 344–358.

Iacovou, M. and Skew, A. (2011) *Population and Social Conditions*. Statistics in Focus, 52/2011, Eurostat, http://epp.eurostat.ec.europa.eu/cache/ITY_OFFPUB/KS-SF-11-052/EN/KS-SF-11-052-EN.PDF (accessed October 30, 2013).

Institute of Medicine (IOM) (2011) *The Health of Lesbian, Gay, Bisexual and Transgender People: Building a Foundation for Better Understanding*, National Academies Press, Washington, DC.

Johnson, D.R. and Wu, J. (2002) An empirical test of crisis, social selection, and role explanations of the relationship between marital disruption and psychological distress: a pooled time-series analysis of four-wave panel data. *Journal of Marriage and Family*, 64 (1), 211–224.

Johnson, R.W. and Favreault, M.M. (2004) Economic status in later life among women who raised children outside of marriage. *Social Sciences*, 59 (6), 315–323.

Johnson, N.J., Backlund, E., Sorlie, P.D. and Loveless, C.A. (2000) Marital status and mortality. *Annals of Epidemiology*, 10 (4), 224–238.

Jovanovic, Z., Lin, C.J. and Change, C.H. (2004) Uninsured vs. insured population: variations among nonelderly Americans. *Journal of Health and Social Policy*, 17, 71–85.

Kalmijn, M. and Monden, C. (2006) Are the negative effects of divorce on well-being dependent on marital quality? *Journal of Marriage and Family*, 68, 1197–1213.

Kennedy, S. and Bumpass, L. (2008) Cohabitation and children's living arrangements: new estimates from the United States. *Demographic Research*, 19, 1663–1692.

Khaleque, A. and Rohner, R.P. (2002) Perceived parental acceptance-rejection and psychological adjustment: a meta-analysis of cross-cultural and intracultural studies. *Journal of Marriage and Family*, 64, 54–64.

Kiernan, K. (2001) The rise of cohabitation and childbearing outside marriage in Western Europe. *International Journal of Law, Policy, and the Family*, 15, 1–21.

King, V. (2006) The antecedents and consequences of adolescents' relationships with stepfathers and nonresident fathers. *Journal of Marriage and Family*, 68, 910–928.

King, V. and Sobolewski, J.M. (2006) Nonresident fathers' contributions to adolescent well-being. *Journal of Marriage and Family*, 68, 537–557.

Koskinen, S., Joutsenniemi, K., Martelin, T. and Martikainen, P. (2007) Mortality differences according to living arrangements. *International Journal of Epidemiology*, 36 (6), 1255–1264.

Kreider, R.M. (2008) *Living Arrangements of Children: 2004*. Current Population Reports, P70–114. U.S. Census Bureau, Washington, DC, http://www.census.gov/prod/2008pubs/p70-114.pdf (accessed October 30, 2013).

Kroeger-D'Souza, R.A. (2012) Union formation, parenthood, and health risk indicators among the socially disadvantaged. PhD dissertation. The Ohio State University.

Lappegård, T. and Rønsen, M. (2011) Socioeconomic differentials in multi-partner fertility among men. *Statistics Norway discussion paper* no. 653, Statistics Norway.

Lewis, M.A. and Rook, K.S. (1999) Social control in personal relationships: impact on health behaviors and psychological distress. *Health Psychology*, 18, 63–71.

Liu, H., Reczek, C. and Brown, D. (2013) Same-sex couples and self-rated health. *Journal of Health and Social Behavior*, 54, 25–45.

Lorenz, F.O., Wickrama, K.A.S., Conger, R.D. and Elder, G.H. (2006) The short-term and decade-long effects of divorce on women's midlife health. *Journal of Health and Social Behavior*, 47, 111–125.

Luo, Y., Hawkley, L., Waite, L.J. and Cacioppo, J. (2012) Loneliness, health, and mortality in old age: a national longitudinal study. *Social Science and Medicine*, 704, 907–914.

Lynch, J. and Smith, G.D. (2005) A life course approach to chronic disease epidemiology. *Annual Review of Public Health*, 26, 1–35.

Manning, W.D. and Smock, P.J. (2005) Measuring and modeling cohabitation: new perspectives from qualitative data. *Journal of Marriage and Family*, 67 (4), 989–1002.

Manzoli, L., Villari, P., Pirone, G.M. and Boccia, A. (2007) Marital status and mortality in the elderly: a systematic review and meta-analysis. *Social Science & Medicine*, 64 (1), 77–94.

Martikainen, P.T. (1995) Women's employment, marriage, motherhood and morality: a test of the multiple role and role accumulation hypotheses. *Social Science & Medicine*, 40, 199–212.

Martikainen, P. and Valkonen, T. (1996). Mortality after the death of a spouse: rates and causes of death in a large Finnish cohort. *American Journal of Public Health*, 86,1087–1093.

Mastekaasa, A. (2000) Parenthood, gender and sickness absence. *Social Science & Medicine*, 50 (12), 1827–1842.

McEwen, B.S. (1998) Stress, adaptation, and disease: allostasis and allostatic load. *Annals of the New York Academy of Science*, 33–44.

Meadows, S.O., McLanahan, S.S. and Brooks-Gunn, J. (2007) Parental depression and anxiety and early childhood behavior problems across family types. *Journal of Marriage and Family*, 69, 1162–1177.

Mirowsky, J. (2002) Parenthood and health: the pivotal and optimal age at first birth. *Social Forces*, 81 (1), 315–349.

Mirowsky, J. and Ross, C.E. (2002) Depression, parenthood, and age at first birth. *Social Science and Medicine*, 54, 1281–1298.

Mollborn, S. and Morningstar, E. (2009) Investigating the relationship between teenage childbearing and psychological distress using longitudinal evidence. *Journal of Health and Social Behavior*, 50 (3), 310–326.

Musick, K. and Bumpass, L. (2012) Re-examining the case for marriage: union formation and changes in well-being. *Journal of Marriage and Family*, 74 (1), 1–18.

Nomaguchi, K.M. and Milkie, M.A. (2003) Costs and rewards of children: the effects of becoming a parent on adults' lives. *Journal of Marriage and Family*, 65 (2), 356–374.

Oldehinkel, A.J., Ormel, J., Veenstra, R. *et al.* (2008) Parental divorce and offspring depressive symptoms: Dutch developmental trends during early adolescence. *Journal of Marriage and Family*, 70, 284–293.

Osborne, C. and McLanahan, S. (2007) Partnership instability and child well-being. *Journal of Marriage and Family*, 69, 1065–1083.

Proulx, C., Helms, H.M. and Buehler, C. (2007) Marital quality and personal well-being: a meta-analysis. *Human Development*, 69, 576–593.

Pudrovska, T., Schieman, S. and Carr, D. (2006) The strains of singlehood in later life: do race and gender matter? *Journal of Gerontology: Social Sciences*, 61,315–322.

Ringbäck Weitoft, G., Hjern, A., Haglund, B. and Rosén, M. (2003) Mortality, severe morbidity, and injury in children living with single parents in Sweden: a population-based study. *The Lancet*, 361, 289–295.

Sandberg, J.G., Harper, J.M., Miller, R. *et al.* (2009) The impact of marital conflict on health and health care utilization in older couples. *Journal of Health Psychology*, 14, 9–17.

Sbarra, D., Law, R.W. Lee, L.A. and Mason, A.E. (2009) Marital dissolution and blood pressure reactivity: evidence for the specificity of emotional intrusion-hyperarousal and task-rated emotional difficulty. *Psychosomatic Medicine*, 71, 532–540.

Schmeer, K.K. (2011) The child health disadvantage of parental cohabitation. *Journal of Marriage and Family*, 73, 181–193.

Schoenborn, C. (2004) Marital status and health: United States, 1999–2002. *U.S. National Center for Health Statistics. Advance Data from Vital and Health Statistics.* pp. 1–32.

Sobolewski, J.M., and Amato, P.R. (2005) Economic hardship in the family of origin and children's psychological well-being in adulthood. *Journal of Marriage and Family*, 67, 141–156.

Soons, J.P.M. and Kalmijn, M. (2009) Is marriage more than cohabitation? Well-being differences in 30 European Countries. *Journal of Marriage and Family*, 71 (5), 1141–1157.

Spraggins, R. (2005) *We the People: Women and Men in the United States, Census 2000 Special Report*. U.S. Census Bureau, Washington, DC.

Springer, K.W. (2009) Childhood physical abuse and mid-life physical health: testing a multi-pathway life course model. *Social Science & Medicine*, 69, 138–146.

Stacey, J. and Biblarz, T.J. (2001) (How) Does the sexual orientation of parents matter? *American Sociological Review*, 66, 159–183, http://www.jstor.org/stable/2657413 (accessed October 24, 2012).

Strohschein, L., McDonough, P., Monette, G. and Shao, Q. (2005) Marital transitions and mental health: are there gender differences in the short-term effects of marital status change? *Social Science & Medicine*, 61 (11), 2293–2303.

Sweeney, M.M. (2007) Stepfather families and the emotional well-being of adolescents. *Journal of Health and Social Behavior*, 48, 33–49.

Thoits, P.A. (1995) Stress, coping, and social support processes: where are we? What next? *Journal of Health and Social Behavior*, (Extra Issue), 53–79.

Umberson, D. and Williams, K. (2005) Marital quality, health, and aging: gender equity? *Journals of Gerontology Series B*, 60B (Special Issue II), 109–112.

Umberson, D., Pudrovska, T. and Reczek, C. (2010) Parenthood, childlessness, and well-being: a life course perspective. *Journal of Marriage and Family*, 72 (3), 612–629.

United Nations, Department of Economic and Social Affairs, Population Division (2011) World Fertility Report 2009, United Nations Publication.

Upchurch, D.M., Aneshensel, C.S., Nudgal, J. and McNeely, C.S. (2001) Sociocultural contexts of time to first sex among hispanic adolescents. *Journal of Marriage and Family*, 63, 1158–1169.

U.S. Census Bureau (2010) Fertility of American Women: June 2010, Table 1. Washington, DC, http://www.census.gov/hhes/fertility/data/cps/2010.html (accessed October 22, 2012).

Waite, L.J. (2009) Marital history and well-being in later life, in *International Handbook of Population Aging* (ed P. Uhlenberg), Springer, Dordrecht, pp. 691–704.

Whitehead, M., Burstro, B. and Diderichsen, F. (2000) Social policies and the pathways to inequalities in health: a comparative analysis of lone mothers in Britain and Sweden. *Social Science & Medicine*, 50, 255–270.

Wienke, C. and Hill, G.J. (2009) Does the "marriage benefit" expect to partners in Gay and Lesbian relationships? Evidence from a random sample of sexually active adults. *Journal of Family Issues*, 30, 259–289.

Williams, K. (2003) Has the future of marriage arrived? A contemporary examination of gender, marriage, and psychological well-being. *Journal of Health and Social Behavior*, 44 (4), 470–487.

Williams, K. and Umberson, D. (2004) Marital status, marital transitions, and health: a gendered life course perspective. *Journal of Health and Social Behavior*, 45 (1), 81–98.

Williams, K., Sassler, S., Frech, A., *et al.* (2011) Nonmarital childbearing, union history, and women's health at midlife. *American Sociological Review*, 76 (3), 465–486.

World Health Organization (WHO) (2002) *World Report on Violence and Health: Summary*. World Health Organization, Geneva, http://www.who.int/violence_injury_prevention/violence/world_report/en/summary_en.pdf (accessed October 30, 2013).

World Health Organization (WHO) (2006) *Constitution of the WHO*, World Health Organization, New York.

Wu, Z., Penning, M.J., Pollard, M.S., and Hart, R. (2003) In sickness and in health: does cohabitation count? *Journal of Family Issues*, 24, 811–838.

14

Religion and Families

CHRISTOPHER G. ELLISON AND XIAOHE XU

Introduction

Social scientists are once again actively interested in the connections between religion and family, two institutions that have enjoyed a long and complementary relationship (Wilcox, 2004; Edgell, 2006). This interest can be observed in the increased number of works on this topic that have appeared in recent years in major peer-reviewed outlets in sociology, family studies, psychology, religious studies, and allied fields and the significant volumes now published on prominent university and trade presses. In this chapter, we will review the existing theoretical and empirical literature linking multiple dimensions of religion with various facets of family life.

Several caveats are in order. First, because much of the work on this topic has been conducted about and within the United States, our review will necessarily concentrate on this context, and we will return to this as a limitation in the concluding section. Second, most studies on religion and family in the United States and other Western societies center on the Judeo-Christian tradition, and consequently, our work will emphasize this theme as well. Third, although there are important literatures on religious variations toward family-related issues (e.g., women's roles, equal rights for gay, lesbian, bisexual, and transgender persons), due to space limitations, we will focus primarily on specific family-related behaviors.

The remainder of this chapter is organized as follows. First, we will briefly review key patterns and trends in religion and spirituality in the United States over the past 25 years. Then, we will review recent theory and research linking religion with the following areas of family life, organized primarily by life course stage: (i) premarital interactions, (ii) cohabitation and timing of marriage, (iii) relationship dynamics and quality, (iv) childbearing, (v) child-rearing, and (vi) intergenerational

The Wiley Blackwell Companion to the Sociology of Families, First Edition.
Edited by Judith Treas, Jacqueline Scott, and Martin Richards.
© 2014 John Wiley & Sons Ltd. Published 2017 by John Wiley & Sons Ltd.

relations. Finally, we will call attention to substantive and methodological issues and gaps in religion–family research. We will underscore the importance of research in non-Western contexts, where attention to religion has often been consigned to studies of fertility and related issues.

The American Religious Landscape: A Brief Overview

Because much of the research on religion and family has been conducted in US context, it is appropriate to begin with a very brief glimpse of the contemporary American religious scene. Although much of the developed West has been heavily influenced by secularization – manifested by diminished public role of religious institutions and values and in many settings by reduced individual religious commitment and belief – for the most part, the United States has been regarded as a stubborn outlier (Norris and Inglehart, 2004). The United States is also characterized by substantial religious diversity; it has been estimated that more than 2000 religious groups and faith traditions are active in the United States. Despite the absence of any single official source of data on religion in the United States, it is possible to combine data from a number of nationwide surveys of individuals and congregations to reach several broad conclusions (Chaves, 2011; Ellison and McFarland, 2013).

First, when asked, most American adults report an affinity (but not necessarily affiliation) with a Christian religious group or tradition. Specifically, approximately 30% of Americans associate themselves with conservative (evangelical, fundamentalist, or charismatic) Protestant groups (e.g., Southern Baptist, Assemblies of God, many smaller denominations and independent churches, as well as many nondenominational groups, including many of the rapidly growing megachurches). Significant proportions of African Americans, as well as increasing numbers of Latinos and Asian Americans, belong to such conservative faith communities. These groups and many of their members tend to affirm the inerrancy and authority of the Bible as well as beliefs about Original Sin, the imperative of salvation through grace, and others (Hempel and Bartkowski, 2008). Around 12% of Americans are affiliated with moderate and liberal Protestant groups (e.g., Episcopal, Methodist, most Presbyterian churches, etc.). In general, the more conservative groups have gained membership and social influence over the past 30–50 years, while the more moderate and liberal groups have declined. Approximately 25% of US adults self-identify as Roman Catholics. The percentage of US adults reporting *no religion* on surveys has climbed to roughly 20%. The remainder (13%) of the American public consists of members of non-Christian faiths (e.g., Judaism, Islam), sectarian groups (e.g., Mormons, or Latter-Day Saints), and a myriad others. One of the fastest growing segments of the US population self-identifies as *spiritual but not religious*. This group – now approximately 25% of the adult population and higher among younger cohorts – includes some individuals who retain tenuous denominational identities, as well as many who have rejected organized religion entirely.

Second, religious affiliation, practice, and belief are socially patterned. For example, scholars have long referred to the *social sources* of American religious affiliation, especially region and socioeconomic status (Ellison and McFarland, 2013). Conservative Protestants have been historically concentrated in the Southeast and lower Midwest, while Catholics have long maintained cultural strongholds in the Northeast, upper Midwest, and Southwest. Liberal Protestants have been concentrated in the Northeast, while Jews have typically resided in coastal urban contexts. Mormons have long dominated Utah, and now maintain majorities or pluralities in many other parts of the Mountain West. With respect to education and SES, conservative Protestants have historically lagged behind most other groups in education, income, and wealth. This has also been true of Catholics, although they have experienced considerable upward mobility across generations. Liberal Protestants and Jews have traditionally enjoyed comparatively high levels of education and social and economic standing. Although many of these *social sources* remain influential, specific patterns are shifting under the weight of geographical mobility, assimilation, intermarriage, and other factors. Moreover, during the past few decades, a number of factors have shifted the focus of many Americans' religious attentions and loyalties away from denominations and toward local congregations (Chaves, 2011).

It has proven to be difficult to estimate levels of religious attendance with precision, due to the biases inherent in self reports of behavior in general, and especially this particular behavior (Chaves, 2011). Observers cautiously estimate that perhaps 25% of US adults attend some type of religious service in a given week. Large majorities of Americans pray weekly or more, while the frequency of meditation is much lower. Two-thirds or more of US adults say that religion is *very important* to them. In terms of core doctrine, levels of support for the concepts of Heaven and Hell (especially the latter) have declined over the past few decades, while beliefs in some type of God and some type of afterlife have remained strong and stable (Schwadel, 2011).

By most indicators of personal religiosity (e.g., attendance at services, prayer, religious salience), women are more religious than men. Comparatively high levels of religiousness are found among racial and ethnic minorities, married people (especially those with children), and older adults. Contrary to many popular impressions, the associations between religious involvement and socioeconomic status are uneven. For example, income and education are positively associated with the frequency of attendance and the occupation of church leadership positions. On the other hand, less educated and less affluent persons tend to engage in more frequent devotional activities (e.g., prayer, scriptural study) and to hold more conservative or orthodox religious beliefs (Ellison and McFarland, 2013).

In recent years, social scientists have assessed trends in American religion by decomposing age, period, and cohort influences. Overall, most forms of religious practice and belief increase modestly with age. Controlling for these age-related patterns, recent studies have revealed significant cohort-based declines in the likelihood of regular attendance, weekly prayer, and belief in biblical inerrancy, which have accelerated for those born after the mid-1940s (Schwadel, 2011). It is also important to note that Americans' confidence in organized religion has been on the decline for some time, and is plummeting even more rapidly than their confidence in most other social institutions (Chaves, 2011). Thus, although the

United States clearly remains one of the most conventionally religious nations in the developed West, there are also signs of change and possible secularization on the American religious scene.

Religious Influences and Family Life

At the broadest level, can religion be said to influence family life? If so, how might this occur? First, denominations and faith traditions may embrace distinctive religious teachings regarding the family or aspects thereof. For example, conservative Protestants tend to believe that the Bible is the inerrant Word of God and that it is the authoritative source of guidance in all human affairs; that is, levels of support for these core doctrines are significantly higher in conservative Protestant denominations than in other religious groups. In practice, however, not all parts of the Bible receive equal emphasis among self-described inerrantists. Given their beliefs about the doctrine of original sin and the primacy of the (heterosexual) family unit, conservative Protestant readings of the Bible often stress passages about human sexuality (e.g., fornication, adultery, homosexuality), marital and gender roles, and other family-related themes (Hempel and Bartkowski, 2008). Mormons (Latter-Day Saints) have strong beliefs about marriage, sexuality, and procreation as well, all of which are intertwined with a very distinctive view of the family as an eternal unit. These and other faith communities may constitute subcultures within which specific understandings of family life are socialized.

In addition, religious participation and salience may also have implications for family attitudes and behaviors. Although certain denominations and traditions hold particularly distinctive ideologies, most religious groups attempt, to varying degrees and with varying levels of effectiveness, to guide the morality and behaviors of their members. This may be especially true in certain areas, such as sexuality and other family matters. The frequency of attendance at services may reflect one's level of religious commitment, because attendance requires the expenditure of scarce resources such as time and energy (and may involve financial contributions as well). This form of religious involvement may also reflect the degree of one's immersion in religious teachings about the family, which may be communicated formally (via sermons and religious education classes) and informally (via social network ties).

Compliance with religious teachings about family-related matters may result from the threat of shame due to the actual or prospective violation of internalized norms, among persons for whom religion is important, a significant component of their personal identity. In addition, for those enmeshed in networks of coreligionists, deviance may be deterred by social sanctions, or rewards for desirable conduct, or diminished opportunities within religious networks for certain types of deviant behavior, such as illicit sexual conduct (Hoffmann and Bahr, 2005). Of course, it is also possible that apparent religious *effects* may partly reflect the role of selectivity, as individuals who do not wish to adhere to the guidelines of a particular faith (or any religion) may switch denominations or abandon organized religion altogether.

Dating and premarital sex

Dating is an extremely important element of the lives of adolescents. In contrast to the patterns observed among previous cohorts of youth, who tended to transition into marriage and childbearing at much earlier ages, today's adolescents and young adults engage in a succession of premarital romantic relationships. Although the nature of these relationships can vary widely, they are often characterized by emotional attachment and physical (and sometimes sexual) attraction, and they meet a number of needs and desires, ranging from companionship, personal discovery, and anticipatory socialization. Researchers have linked dating experiences with subsequent family and life course transitions as well as adolescent mental health and well-being. Although investigators have explored a number of influences on dating behavior, with few exceptions, the role of religion has received short shrift.

Recent research suggests that this has been a significant oversight. Work by Bartkowski, Xu, and Fondren (2011) revealed a number of noteworthy links between teen and family religion and dating behavior. For example, they have shown that members of conservative Protestant and sectarian groups tend to date more often than others and do so primarily with coreligionist partners. Jewish teens date less often, on average, but tend to engage in comparatively high levels of interfaith dating. Teen beliefs in the religious exclusivity, that is, the superiority of their own faith, are associated with less frequent dating and lower levels of interfaith dating. Although teens' organizational religious involvement and family religious engagement are weakly and inconsistently associated with the frequency of overall dating and interfaith dating, more religiously devoted teens are less inclined to date persons from other faiths.

Over the years, a much larger body of work has explored the links between religious factors and adolescent sex, with a particular focus on the timing of coital debut and to a lesser extent the frequency of sexual activity and the number of sexual partners (e.g., Hardy and Raffaelli, 2003; Meier, 2003). Most researchers have concluded that religious teens hold more conservative attitudes about premarital sex, due partly to parental religious socialization (Pearce and Thornton, 2007), tend to delay their sexual debut, and to have sex less often and with fewer partners than other adolescents. However, investigators have differed over the precise nature of these patterns, as well as denominational variations in adolescent sexual behavior, due to differences in data sources and analytic strategies.

Perhaps, the most exhaustive project in this area has been executed by Regnerus (2007), who combined the data from multiple nationwide surveys with the data from a large number of in-depth interviews with a representative sample of teens. Although his results were complex and defy easy summary, his key results showed that, despite their distinctive sexual scripts, for example, strong beliefs and rhetoric regarding teen chastity, conservative Protestant sexual behavior does not differ greatly from that of other religious groups. Mormon (Latter-Day Saint) youths are more consistent in their conservative beliefs and practices. Jewish youth combine liberal attitudes with relatively conservative sexual behaviors in most areas. In addition, consistent with much previous research, religiosity, defined as the frequency of religious attendance and the degree of religious salience, is a much stronger predictor of most sexual attitudes and behaviors than denominational identification.

Regnerus also showed that the virginity pledge movement, started by conservative Protestants and exemplified by such groups as True Love Waits, has involved only a small minority of adolescents (Bearman and Bruckner, 2001). While not entirely curtailing premarital sex even among pledgers, the movement has nevertheless had several notable effects. On average, pledgers delay first sex longer, have fewer sexual partners prior to marriage, and choose partners who themselves have had fewer sexual partners.

Finally, and somewhat paradoxically, Regnerus showed that new forms and rationales of sexual restraint are emerging among youths who come from those religious groups with comparatively relaxed sexual mores, especially Jews and liberal Protestants. Adolescents from these religious backgrounds (and especially males) appear to be comparatively likely to engage in oral sex, masturbation, and pornography (especially from the Internet) as substitutes for vaginal intercourse. According to Regnerus, the motivations for these patterns may be largely strategic, and may reflect the social class composition of these religious denominations. This *new middle-class sexual morality*, as he labeled it, is aimed at avoiding the risks associated with early sexual activity in order to enhance the likelihood of educational completion and the formation of rewarding nuclear families.

One important topic that has received recent attention in the literature is the phenomenon of *hooking up* among young adults, particularly on college campuses. *Hookups* are loosely defined as casual, unplanned physical liaisons, often sexual in nature, with no expectation of any future relationship. A number of scholars have observed that such encounters have largely supplanted more formal dating among college students and young adults. Although some commentators view these practices as relatively benign, critics have expressed concern over the potential negative consequences for social, emotional, and physical well-being, especially for women (Freitas, 2009). Researchers have identified religious variations in hooking up using both quantitative and qualitative data. For example, in one sample of 1000 college women, Burdette *et al.* (2009) found that (i) Catholic women were more likely to have hooked up than others; (ii) conservative Protestant women were less likely to have hooked up, largely due to their higher levels of religious attendance; and (iii) women attending Catholic institutions were especially prone to have hooked up, over and above the estimated net effects of individual affiliation. Although there were limitations to their data, the results dovetailed with the findings of other research on hooking up (Freitas, 2009), and with broader observations that the depth of religious and moral socialization of young Catholics may be declining (Smith and Denton, 2005). It has been suggested that conservative Protestant colleges, by contrast, are relatively successful in deterring *the hookup culture*.

Marriage and cohabitation

A significant body of theoretical and empirical work has demonstrated that more religious individuals, and especially those with conservative Protestant affiliations and beliefs, were more likely to oppose cohabitation and to embrace promarriage attitudes (e.g., Pearce and Thornton, 2007; Ellison, Acevedo, and Ramos-Wada, 2013). Although numerous studies document associations between multiple dimensions of religiousness and family-related attitudes, does religious involvement actually shape patterns of cohabitation and marriage? The available evidence suggests an affirmative answer to this question. Young adults with low rates of religious salience were much more likely to cohabit than others, and less likely to marry. Parental religiosity also influenced these behaviors, largely (but not entirely) by shaping their religiosity. Religious affiliation effects on cohabitation and marriage were weak and inconsistent (Thornton, Axinn, and Hill, 1992). Fine-grained analyses of religious effects on marriage and cohabitation have generally yielded several conclusions. Conservative Protestants, especially those with high levels of personal religiosity, and Mormons were particularly unlikely to cohabit. Individuals from these religious backgrounds also tended to marry earlier than other persons. Moderate Protestants and Catholics tended to marry at roughly similar ages, and thus occupied a middle ground in terms of age at (first) marriage. Liberal Protestants, Jews (except for Hasidim), and nonreligious persons married significantly later than other persons (Xu, Hudspeth, and Bartkowski, 2005; Lehrer, 2011).

Another important issue involves the choice of marital partners. Specifically, a long tradition of theory and research addresses causes, patterns, and trends in religious homogamy and intermarriage, with religion typically measured via denominational affiliation. Researchers have been interested in the probability of intermarriage and the distance of intermarriage if it occurs (Sherkat, 2004; Lehrer, 2011). Several key findings have emerged from this literature. First, in the United States, although religious homogamy remains an important phenomenon, rates of interfaith marriage have increased significantly among younger cohorts (Sherkat, 2004). This overall pattern may reflect declining theological differences and degrees of social distance among many religious groups, as well as reduced ability of many religious groups to sanction marital decisions. Educational upgrading, especially among women, geographical mobility, the growth of mass media and culture, and perhaps other factors are also thought to influence the general trend toward greater intermarriage. Second, although interfaith marriage is clearly on the rise, the trend toward greater exogamy in the United States has occurred more slowly among Catholics, conservative Protestants, and Mormons, as compared with more liberal denominations; however, the relative ordering of distances between Catholics and conservative Protestants stands out as a particularly formidable barrier to intermarriage (Sherkat, 2004). Third, the study of religious homogamy and interfaith marriage has long been complicated by the issue of religious switching; many partners who married outside the faith tended to convert to the religion of their spouse, resulting in higher apparent levels of religious homogamy. However, such tendencies toward conversion for marital reasons are waning among younger cohorts (Waite and Lewin, 2010).

In the United States and most Western European societies, Catholics have generally remained more endogamous than Protestants, and the more conservative Protestant groups (e.g., the conservative Reformed Protestants in the Netherlands) have maintained comparatively low rates of interfaith marriage (Kalmijn, 1998). However, the prevailing trends point to increasing rates of exogamy among most religious groups throughout Europe. Although many studies on this topic have omitted Jews due to their small numbers in most datasets, it has been widely assumed that rates of interfaith marriage have been quite low (Kalmijn, 1998). However, at least among non-Orthodox Jews in the United States, rates of exogamy have increased significantly, raising concerns about the intergenerational transmission of Judaism (Lazerwitz, 1995).

Childbearing

A number of distinguished scholars have explored religious differentials in fertility and fertility-related behaviors. According to one well-cited formulation, religion should be expected to make a difference when three important conditions are met: (i) religious groups and traditions hold distinctive theological beliefs regarding ideal family size, contraception, and other relevant factors; (ii) these religious groups have sufficient cultural and organizational strength to enforce these norms and to sanction violators; and (iii) religion is an important component of individuals' identities, such that they would be deterred from violating these norms (McQuillan, 2004). To this list, one might also add the importance of parental religion in the intergenerational transmission of attitudes and preferences regarding ideal family size and other fertility-related matters (Pearce, 2002). For several decades, most research conducted in the United States focused on Catholic–Protestant fertility differences; Catholics tended to have significantly higher fertility rates, due to lower levels of contraceptive use as well as the higher percentage of European American immigrants in the Catholic population. However, these differences declined with rising rates of contraceptive use by Catholic women, and increases in assimilation and upward mobility by most European American ethnic groups (Westoff and Jones, 1979). Indeed, with the exception of specific groups such as Hispanic immigrants to the United States, evidence of Catholic distinctiveness in fertility rates has virtually disappeared in the United States and much of Europe (Frejka and Westoff, 2008).

By the early 1990s, investigators in the United States redirected their gaze toward the comparatively high fertility rates of three other groups (Mosher, Williams, and Johnson, 1992). First, although their Total Fertility Rates (TFRs) have declined over time and across cohorts, Mormons (Latter-Day Saints) still outpace nearly all other religio-ethnic groups in the United States. Second, although most Protestant denominations across the theological spectrum had reached broad agreement in support of family planning by the 1970s, some segments of conservative Protestantism began to reconsider this view 10–15 years later. Thus, as a group, conservative (i.e., fundamentalist, evangelical, and charismatic) Protestants now tend to have TFRs that surpass most other segments of the US population (Mosher, Williams, and Johnson, 1992). These patterns stand in marked contrast to the relatively low (below replacement value) TFRs of members of liberal Protestant groups and religiously unaffiliated persons. Third, although most segments of the Jewish population (Reform, secular, and even Conservative) have TFRs well below replacement level (i.e., below 2.0), Orthodox, and especially Hasidic, Jews have extremely high TFRs (over 3.0 for Orthodox and well over 6.0 for Hasidim). This high level of reproduction, accompanied by exceptionally low rates of intermarriage, has led some observers to conclude that they will dominate the US Jewish population in scarcely more than a generation (Stark, 2012).

In addition to these subgroup variations in fertility, several scholars have emphasized the role of religious commitment in general (e.g., frequency of attendance at services, religious salience) in predicting fertility intentions and behavior. According to one exhaustive set of analyses, both attendance and salience bear independent associations with the likelihood of having two or more children among women ages 18–44 in the United States (Frejka and Westoff, 2008). Another study in the United States revealed broadly consistent findings and also showed that a substantial portion of the link between religious salience (especially high salience) and fertility intentions was linked with a broader complex of traditional value orientations with respect to gender roles, marriage, and sexuality (Hayford and Morgan, 2008).

Religious attendance and salience are linked with fertility patterns in various European nations, albeit less strongly and less consistently than in the United States. After noting considerable regional variation in fertility patterns across Europe, Frejka and Westoff (2008) concluded that "if Europeans were as religious as Americans one might theoretically expect a small fertility increase for Europe as a whole, but considerably more for Western Europe." Indeed, other scholars have gone much further, even suggesting that the low fertility rates among the least religious segments of the European population may imply that secularization (now widely heralded in many parts of Europe) may be a demographically self-limiting process, and that the differential fertility rates now observed between more and less (or non-) religious subgroups could lead to a de facto religious revival in Europe (Kaufmann, 2010).

Finally, one noteworthy recent contribution has explored religious differences in the timing of first births (Pearce, 2010). Briefly, and perhaps surprisingly, conservative Protestant and Catholic affiliations were positively associated with, while religious attendance was inversely related to, the likelihood of having a premaritally conceived first birth. The denominational patterns may reflect a combination of the focus on abstinence-based sex education and lack of contraception in some quarters and the greater cultural pressure to legitimize childbearing through marriage. Although there were no meaningful denominational differences, religious attendance was associated with faster rate of maritally conceived first births.

Child-rearing values

For several decades, scholars have investigated adult and parental child-rearing values, or the traits that are most preferred in children. Much of this attention has centered on two such values: obedience to authority and intellectual autonomy (or thinking for oneself). Studies have shown that the preference for autonomy in children increased steadily throughout much of the twentieth century, while the emphasis on obedience has declined (Alwin and Felson, 2010).

Early studies focused on Catholic–Protestant differences in child-rearing orientations, showing that Catholics expressed greater enthusiasm for obedience and less support for intellectual autonomy. However, by the 1980s, such differences had all but disappeared (Alwin and Felson, 2010), and the gaze of researchers has shifted to conservative Protestants, whose preferences for obedience in children have now been well established in the literature (Ellison and Sherkat, 1993a; Starks and Robinson, 2005). One trend analysis using NORC General Social Survey Data from 1986 to 2002 revealed no change in the valuation of obedience among Catholics, but an increase in support for obedience among frequently attending conservative Protestants over the 16-year study period (Starks and Robinson, 2005). One notable finding in some of these studies is that while early research on religion and child-rearing values presumed that obedience and autonomy were antithetical preferences, contemporary research suggests that conservative Protestants tend to value both of these traits highly, perhaps because they want children to obey parental and religious authority figures but also want them to exercise independent judgment in sifting through secular information and cultural messages that may be incompatible with their religious worldviews (Ellison and Sherkat, 1993a).

Although most work on religion and child-rearing values has been conducted in the United States, a handful of studies have explored these issues in other contexts. For example, research among Turkish Muslims has linked higher levels of religious-ness (orthodox belief, frequency of prayer, religious salience) with greater preference for the traits of obedience and good manners in children while also showing that more religious adults are less supportive of intellectual autonomy and creativity (Acevedo, Ellison, and Yilmaz, 2013). A comparative study of child-rearing values in 11 European nations reported that adults in societies with higher proportions of Protestants were more prone to value imagination and creativity in children than those persons in predominantly Catholic countries. However, religious cultural tra-dition was unrelated to the valuation of obedience and religious faith in children (Fjellvag, 2011).

Child-rearing practices and child discipline

Beginning in the 1990s, an expanding body of research in the United States has focused on the distinctive parenting philosophies of conservative Protestants. One study of advice manuals produced for parents revealed sharp differences between materials generated within these religious circles and those written by secular child-rearing experts. According to this work, conservative Protestants are distinctive with regard to long-term parenting objectives (authority-mindedness in preparation for spiritual salvation, as opposed to emotional health and social skills), structure of parent–child relations (hierarchal rather than egalitarian), definition of parental roles (preference for clearly defined and gendered parental roles), and firm child discipline, including corporal punishment (Alwin and Felson, 2010).

Building on this research, subsequent scholarly inquiry has focused on religious variations in approaches to child discipline, including corporal punishment of chil-dren. Those who initiated research in this area found that members of conservative Protestant groups were more prone to support, and to use, mild-to-moderate forms of corporal punishment (i.e., spanking and slapping) to discipline children than persons from other (or no) religious backgrounds (Ellison and Sherkat, 1993b;

Ellison, Bartkowski, and Segal, 1996). These patterns have been traced to several specific theological tenets that are disproportionately embraced by conservative Protestants, including the belief that the Bible is without error and is the authoritative guide for human behavior, the belief in original sin, the belief that God is judgmental as well as loving, and the belief in a literal Hell. To achieve spiritual salvation, conservative Protestant theology holds that individuals must repent of their sinful ways, submit to divine authority, and accept salvation through God's grace (Hempel and Bartkowski, 2008). These core conservative Protestant beliefs help to explain the high premium placed on obedience, as parents believe they have a duty to *shape the will* of children, making them more submissive and setting the stage for their salvation (Ellison and Sherkat, 1993b). Moreover, corporal punishment (*the rod*) is prescribed as the appropriate punishment for willful disobedience and rebellion against parental authority (Ellison, Bartkowski, and Segal, 1996). Research has shown that conservative Protestant mothers tend to employ corporal punishment as part of a coherent parenting strategy, rather than a spontaneous expression of anger or frustration, and that these mothers are unconvinced by the arguments of secular experts about the harm that this practice might do (Gershoff, Miller, and Holden, 1999).

In recent years, investigators have also explored religious differentials in other aspects of parental – and especially paternal – involvement in the lives of children. Here, as in many other domains of family life, some scholars have been particularly interested in the potential distinctiveness of conservative Protestantism. Some observers in this area have conceptualized paternal involvement as a three-dimensional construct, comprising paternal supervision, affective fathering, and father–child interaction. Contrary to some popular assumptions, this work found that conservative Protestant fathers tended to engage in greater supervision and affective fathering than other fathers; the contrast with their nonreligious counterparts was especially marked (Bartkowski and Xu, 2000). Other studies have explored the association between the overall religiousness of parents (fathers and mothers) and their involvement in the lives of their children. For example, one study using data from a nationwide probability sample of parents linked the frequency of attendance with paternal supervision, affective parenting, father–child interaction, and several specific paternal behaviors with school-age children, including one-on-one activities, having dinner together, and youth-related activities such as school or community activities, and scouting (Bartkowski and Xu, 2000; Wilcox, 2002). An important alternative hypothesis – that these associations stemmed from a broader set of values, mores, and practices, termed *middle-class conventionalism* – received no empirical support (Wilcox, 2002).

Although most of this research has been conducted using probability samples drawn from the general population, a parallel set of studies have explored similar issues among fragile families, that is, samples of urban, lower SES, disproportionately minority, and mostly unmarried parents of young children. Several findings are noteworthy. First, paternal religious attendance was positively associated with a summary measure of paternal engagement with children ages 1–5, and this pattern was especially strong for fathers who increased their attendance immediately following the birth of a new child (Petts, 2007). Second, in contrast to findings in the general population, conservative Protestant affiliation was inversely associated with an omnibus measure of paternal engagement (Wildeman, 2008). After examining associations between parental (and especially maternal) religious attendance and paternal and child well-being in fragile families, one researcher concluded that religious practices and communities offer valuable resources for single mothers, in particular. Such resources could conceivably encompass formal programs and ministries, informal support networks, and norms of successful, spiritually grounded child-rearing (Petts, 2012).

Child outcomes

In addition to parental values and child-rearing practices, researchers have increasingly focused on religious differences in child outcomes. One area of interest has involved corporal punishment, which is widely presumed to foster externalizing behavior problems (aggression, antisocial conduct) and internalizing problems (emotional distress), as well as other developmental issues for children. An emerging body of work has suggested that mild-to-moderate forms of corporal punishment (i.e., spanking and slapping) may bear fewer (or no) negative associations on children from conservative Protestant families, as compared with those from other backgrounds (Gunnoe, Hetherington, and Reiss, 2006; Ellison, Musick, and Holden, 2011). Indeed, in one longitudinal study, children of conservative Protestant mothers who were spanked at the initial data collection point (when the children were ages 2–4) but were no longer spanked 5 years later exhibited particularly low levels of antisocial behavior and emotional problems compared with other children. Several factors could mitigate any deleterious effects of corporal punishment for this specific subgroup. These may include (i) distinctive modes of administering corporal punishment, about which much advice has been offered by conservative Protestant leaders and writers, and (ii) a cultural climate within this religious community – clergy, peers, relatives, and others – that may normalize and support corporal punishment as an appropriate disciplinary response to certain types of childish misbehavior (Ellison, Musick, and Holden, 2011). In addition, any harmful effects of this type of discipline may be mitigated by the lower levels of yelling and verbal abuse (Bartkowski and Wilcox, 2000) and the higher levels of parental warmth and nurturance (Wilcox, 1998), which are exhibited by conservative Protestant parents. Clearly, this is a topic that begs for additional investigation in the future.

In addition to the research summarized earlier, many studies have explored relationships between facets of parental, child, and/or adolescent religiousness and a range of other child and adolescent outcomes, often reporting salutary patterns in the samples of the general population as well as major subgroups (Regnerus, 2003). For example, studies have demonstrated that children (school-age children and adolescents) from more religiously active backgrounds have often exhibited fewer internalizing and externalizing behaviors. In several studies, they achieved better academic outcomes and interpersonal relationships and tended to follow instructions and avoid disciplinary problems more than those from less religious backgrounds (Muller and Ellison, 2001; Bartkowski, Xu, and Levin, 2008). Many other studies – too numerous to review here – have linked aspects of religiousness (on the part of parents and children or adolescents) with a host of outcomes, ranging from reduced delinquency to increased levels of volunteering and civic involvement (Regnerus, 2003). There is evidence that these links between parental religiousness and child outcomes may be due to higher levels of parental supervision and expectations, as well as greater intergenerational closure within religious families and networks (Smith, 2003).

One important area of research involves the role of religious similarity or dissimilarity (in terms of denominational affiliation, attendance patterns, or theological beliefs) among family members in shaping child outcomes. For example, couples with highly dissonant affiliation patterns have reported increased marital conflict and reduced religious participation compared to those couples with similar religious affiliations; according to one study, the adolescent children of these unions were more likely than others to engage in marijuana use and underage drinking (Pearce and Haynie, 2004). Other research has revealed that the more religious mothers and adolescents were, the less likely adolescents were to engage in acts of delinquency; however, significant religious discord between mothers and adolescents – especially when mothers valued religion much more than their children did – was associated with elevated levels of delinquent behavior (Stokes and Regnerus, 2009). Nor are these patterns restricted to the quality of relationships between parents and adolescents. Similar findings have surfaced in research on the associations between the religious congruence between mothers and their adult children and positive perceptions of their relationships by both parties (Pearce and Axinn, 1998). Finally, one recent study of mothers' perceptions in late life revealed that their perceptions of religious value similarity to their adult children predicted assessments of greater affection and lower levels of conflict. These patterns were especially pronounced in African American families (Sechrist *et al.*, 2011).

Studies of general parental religiousness highlight its possible role in shaping relationship quality between parents and older adult children. Some of these works have focused on paternal religiousness and relationship quality among fathers and older adult children. In the work by King (2010), father's religious salience predicted positive assessments of father–child relationship quality (measured in terms of understanding, trust, fairness, and affection) as reported by older adult offspring. It is striking that these patterns persisted despite statistical adjustments for parental involvement during the teen years, offspring reports of antisocial behavior during adolescence, and multiple indicators of marital quality. Maternal religiousness (attendance, salience) has also been linked with positive relationships with adult children (Pearce and Axinn, 1998). Further, more religious grandparents tend to be more active in the lives of their grandchildren than their less religious counterparts, partly because they are more enmeshed in family relationships of many types (King and Elder, 1999). Such findings clearly underscore the need to understand the role of religion in shaping family relationships across generations.

Marital functioning and marital dissolution

A long tradition of theory and research has linked religion and spirituality with marital quality. However, over the past 10–15 years, there have been several innovations in this literature, such as the emergence of new measures in the domain of religion and spirituality, the development of fresh ways of conceptualizing and modeling the links between religion and marital quality, and attention to an expanded array of marital outcomes, including satisfaction and happiness, dependence, conflict and conflict resolution, domestic violence, and risk of marital dissolution.

A wealth of studies has centered on the association between religious factors – primarily affiliation, attendance, and salience or commitment – and positive indicators of marital quality, such as marital happiness and satisfaction. With only a few notable exceptions, the vast majority of work in this area has reported salutary associations between religious involvement and positive indicators of marital quality. Although many studies in this area have used generic measures of religiosity such as religious attendance and salience, as reported by one partner, more recent works have focused on dyadic information, with particular attention to the couple's joint religious activities, such as devotional activities (e.g., prayer, scriptural study) in the home (Lichter and Carmalt, 2009; Ellison, Burdette, and Wilcox, 2010).

Why might we expect a connection between the institutions of religion and marriage? One conceptual scheme points to three elements: norms, networks, and nomos (Wilcox and Wolfinger, 2008). Briefly, most religious groups and traditions promote norms that can facilitate happy and stable relationships. These may be general norms, involving kindness, generosity, forgiveness, and *Golden Rule* ethics. However, religious norms regarding marriage may be more specific. Religious groups often embrace certain expectations about appropriate marital roles (i.e., what it means to be a *good* husband, a *good* wife), as well as particular types of behaviors to be avoided. Both types of norms are typically grounded in scripture and theology, and they may be communicated through written materials and sermons. In addition to these two types of norms, religious communities consist of networks that can also foster positive marital outcomes. This may occur through informal mechanisms, such as relationships among individuals and couples within the congregation, or through formal mechanisms such as premarital counseling, couples' ministries and marital enrichment programs, and religious education classes. Finally, the term *nomos* refers to a religious interpretive framework, through which the marital bond takes on added spiritual significance. Such a religious perspective, a version of which is discussed more fully later, may foster a shared understanding between partners that the union is more covenantal than contractual in nature.

Family researchers influenced by developments in psychology have increasingly conceptualized the links between religion and marital quality in terms of a *relational spirituality* approach, which often distinguishes between *distal* and *proximal* religious constructs. Examples of the former include religious practice and commitment, while examples of the latter include interconnected relational virtues such as forgiveness and sanctification, among others (Mahoney, 2010). The latter has become a particularly important construct in this literature. Briefly, sanctification refers to the extent to which individuals ascribe sacred characteristics to the relationship or to one's partner, or view the relationship having sacred meaning or significance. Researchers have linked sanctification with a range of desirable outcomes, including greater marital satisfaction, happiness, and bonding, as well as lower levels of negative interaction and conflict, and improved communication and conflict resolution skills (Mahoney *et al.*, 1999; Mahoney, 2010). In addition, controls for sanctification often eliminate the associations between religious practice or commitment and these marital outcomes, sometimes even reversing the signs of the coefficients. Sanctification has also been shown to moderate the deleterious effects of general relationship stress, financial strain, and marital inequity on relationship quality (Ellison *et al.*, 2011).

Several additional factors have been advanced to account for the links between religiousness and intimate relationship quality. Among the most prominent explanations are forgiveness (Fincham, Hall, and Beach, 2006), joint communication, especially around religious or spiritual matters (Mahoney *et al.*, 1999), self-sacrifice, and the expression of love and affection in the form of compliments, emotional supportiveness, and gratitude (Wilcox and Wolfinger, 2008; Wolfinger and Wilcox, 2008). To date, however, the precise nature of these associations remains unclear (Stafford, David, and McPherson, 2013), and additional research is needed to establish their role in marital and relationship quality.

Another important topic involves the association between religious homogamy, or religious similarity of partners, and marital quality. Although investigators focused on denominational homogamy, the importance of denomination as a marker of same-faith (or mixed-faith) unions appears to have declined over the past several decades (Myers, 2006). Thus, in more recent studies, investigators have tended to focus on other facets of religious similarity among partners. Some researchers have emphasized the importance of shared religious commitment, often measured in terms of similar or joint attendance at worship services (Wilcox and Wolfinger, 2008). In a recent study that considered multiple aspects of couples' religion, shared religious and spiritual values – along with joint family religious activities – strongly predicted relationship quality among working-age couples (Ellison, Burdette, and Wilcox, 2010).

In addition to marital happiness and satisfaction, social scientists have also examined several additional facets of marital quality, and we turn to those briefly. One such dimension is marital dependency, or the extent to which either spouse believes that the quality of his or her life (in terms of money, companionship, sex, or various other factors) would decline should the marriage end. This gauges the extent to which marital partners depend upon the union for various types of resources. One study of a large sample of US adults has explored the associations between spouses' religiosity and dependency using dyadic data. This work found that conservative Protestants (especially non-Baptists), members of *quasiethnic* religions (e.g., Lutherans, Mormons), regular churchgoers, and persons in same-faith unions expressed greater marital dependency than others, although those patterns varied somewhat by gender (Wilson and Musick, 1996).

Studies have also addressed religious variations in marital conflict. For example, various forms of religious similarity and dissimilarity have been shown to be linked with the levels and types of arguments in a large sample of US married couples (Curtis and Ellison, 2002). The estimated effects of denominational heterogamy on marital conflict were modest and inconsistent; however, spousal differences in attendance patterns, and especially differences in core theological beliefs (e.g., the belief that the Bible is the inerrant Word of God), were linked with more frequent arguments. In addition to the frequency of such conflicts, research has also provided information on religious differences in the risk of specific types of conflicts. For example, sexual infidelity is a key source of marital strife, and studies have shown that regular churchgoers, persons who believe that the Bible is error-free, and conservative Protestants with high religious commitment and inerrantist beliefs are especially unlikely to engage in extramarital sex (Burdette *et al.*, 2007). Theological dissimilarity among partners has been associated with more frequent conflicts in two specific areas: finances and household labor. One possible explanation for housework conflicts between very conservative and very liberal partners involves the tendency of the former to embrace separate spheres ideology, according to which household labor is divided fairly rigidly along gender lines, with women primarily responsible for daily domestic chores (e.g., cooking, cleaning) and men responsible for sporadic tasks (e.g., repairs). Among couples in which both partners share conservative beliefs about the inerrancy and authority of the Bible, women perform more housework than their counterparts from other backgrounds, and in those households, domestic tasks are also more gender segregated (Ellison and Bartkowski, 2002).

Turning to the issue of more severe forms of conflict, a modest body of research has also examined the connections between religion and intimate partner violence. Briefly, nationwide survey data indicate that frequency of religious attendance is strongly inversely associated with the perpetration of acts of violence by men and women. This pattern among men was stronger for African Americans than men from other ethnic backgrounds, due largely to elevated rates of perpetration among nonattending African American men. In addition, dissimilarities of theological conservatism were associated with violence; specifically, the risk of violence was elevated among couples in which the man held much more conservative beliefs about the Bible than the woman (Ellison, Bartkowski, and Anderson, 1999). A parallel literature has explored partner violence within religious communities in more detail (Nason-Clark, 1997). Although the findings defy easy summary, this line of work has suggested that many congregations and (male) clergy members may be poorly informed and ill-suited to address women's victimization by intimate partners. For example, some clergy dismiss the possibility of violence within the church community, while others can give inappropriate advice (e.g., counseling abused women to remain in violent relationships for religious or other reasons). On the other hand, informal networks (primarily fellow churchwomen) can be valuable sources of solace and assistance (Nason-Clark, 1997).

Finally, a number of studies have explored the role of religious factors in shaping the risk of divorce or marital dissolution. Clearly, religious groups have differed sharply on their views regarding marriage and divorce. For example, in recent nationwide studies, conservative Protestants have expressed particular discomfort with the phenomenon of divorce, and greater enthusiasm for restricting divorce, than other Americans (Stokes and Ellison, 2010; Ellison, Wolfinger, and Ramos-Wada, 2013). Indeed, religious conservatives were the key force behind the phenomenon of covenant marriage, a specific, legally recognized form of marriage in some parts of the United States, in which couples agree to premarital counseling and a more restricted set of conditions for divorce (Nock, Sanchez, and Wright, 2008). Although the goals of this movement included reducing divorce rates and strengthening individual marriages (and strengthening marriage as a social institution), recent research has cast doubt on the effectiveness of covenant marriage in at least one state (DeMaris, Sanchez, and Krivickas, 2012). Despite the deep concerns in religious circles about the current state of the institution of marriage, it is interesting to note that conservative Protestant congregations have been no more likely than others to offer marital counseling or other marital support programs (Wilcox, Chaves, and Franz, 2004).

Early research centered on whether mixed-faith unions, that is, those in which partners belonged to disparate denominations or faith traditions, faced heightened risk of divorce. This was a reasonable line of inquiry to the extent that denominational differences were also indicative of broader differences in lifestyles, cultural preferences, and social networks. However, most recent studies have reported only modest links between denominational homogamy and marital stability, with a few caveats (Lehrer, 2011). In particular, certain patterns of mixed-faith marriage, especially those in which one partner belonged to an *exclusivist* (or conservative) denomination and the other belonged to an *ecumenical* (or more liberal) denomination, were at particularly high risk of dissolution. In addition, specific types of homogamy (e.g., among Mormons) appeared to be more insulated from dissolution than other unions. Finally, although there is no evidence of a protective effect for conservative Protestants overall, homogamous conservative Protestant couples in which both partners attended services regularly had lower rates of marital dissolution than other types of unions (Vaaler, Ellison, and Powers, 2009).

Many investigators have turned their focus to other facets of religion that may influence marital stability. Some observers argued that religious participation, especially attendance at services, was more closely linked with marital stability, due to shared networks and activities, as well as common religious socialization among partners. However, religious homogamy remains a topic of interest; several researchers have concluded that spousal differences in attendance patterns and core theological beliefs are linked with heightened risk of marital dissolution (Call and Heaton, 1997; Vaaler, Ellison, and Powers, 2009). These findings may track broader changes in American religion (e.g., restructuring along conservative–liberal or religious–secular lines), as religious beliefs such as biblical inerrancy increasingly cross denominational boundaries. One study has reported gendered patterns, indicating that unions in which the men attend much more often than the women, and those in which the women are much more conservative than the men, may face elevated risk of dissolution than others (Vaaler, Ellison, and Powers, 2009), although this finding needs additional replication and investigation.

Conclusion

In this chapter, we have reviewed a large and growing body of empirical research on the associations between multiple aspects of religion and a wide array of family-related attitudes and behaviors. As we noted at the outset, space limitations required that we focus on a limited set of outcomes, and the structure of scholarly literature dictated that much of our review centered on (Judeo-)Christian religion and on studies conducted primarily in the United States. We conclude the chapter with several general observations about the limitations of the literature in this area, as well as broad suggestions for future work.

First, we have dealt solely with studies that have treated religion as an independent variable, demonstrating or suggesting *effects* on family-related outcomes. However, it is also important to remember that the religion–family connection is bidirectional, that is, that family structures and relations can shape religious affiliations, practices, and beliefs. This is particularly evident in the research on religious socialization among adolescents and young adults. For example, adults may alter their religious participation when they marry or have children, at least partly with the needs of partners and offspring in mind. In addition, parental marital discord and divorce can alter or impair the intergenerational transmission of faith. There are many additional examples of this *other* religion–family connection.

Second, the religion–family literature has focused almost exclusively on heterosexual families. At one level, this may not be surprising, given the widespread derogation and exclusion of GLBT persons and same-sex couples within many religious communities. However, new religious denominations (e.g., the Metropolitan Community Church) with a focus on the GLBT population are flourishing, existing denominations (e.g., the United Methodist Church) are reevaluating their positions with respect to homosexuality and same-sex unions, and new expressions of GLBT spirituality are emerging beyond the bounds of organized religion. Limited evidence has linked religiosity with positive relationship functioning among same-sex couples as well (Oswald *et al.*, 2008). The role of religion and spirituality among GLBT couples and families clearly warrants further research.

Third, expanding on the previous point, *nontraditional* families (not just GLBT but also divorced, cohabiting, and single-parent families) are becoming increasingly common in the United States and other Western societies. Most religious institutions have been heavily invested in the traditional model of the two-parent heterosexual family for both theological and institutional reasons. Others have not always been well served by existing religious institutions, in terms of formal programming or informal social climates. In a very real sense, however, the long-term viability of organized religion in the United States may well depend upon how quickly and successfully existing religious structures adapt to changing family definitions and realities (Edgell, 2006).

Although we have focused heavily on general population samples, we note an important paradox: some of the most highly religious segments of the US population, notably African Americans, also face some of the greatest obstacles to marriage and family stability. A few studies have used data on a large sample of fragile families, which includes a disproportionate share of ethnic minority parents (e.g., Wolfinger and Wilcox, 2008), and a small number of studies have compared the associations between religion and family among multiple ethnic groups (Brown, Orbuch, and Bauermeister, 2008; Ellison, Burdette, and Wilcox, 2010). But there are few studies on African Americans specifically, and there remains a dearth of information on the role of religion in the family lives of Latinos, Asian Americans, and other minority populations. Remedying this defect should be an urgent priority for future investigators.

Finally, with the exception of fertility-related attitudes and behaviors, to our reading, there is a significant shortage of systematic empirical research on the links between religion and family life outside the United States and especially in non-Western contexts. (Our search was necessarily limited to English language materials.) Thus, additional comparative research on varied religions and family life should be strongly encouraged. It is hoped that future inquiry along the lines sketched earlier will further illuminate the continuing, and changing, associations between the social institutions of religion and family.

References

Acevedo, G., Ellison, C.G. and Yilmaz, M. (2013) Religion and child-rearing values in Turkey. *Journal of Family Issues*. doi.10.1177/0192513X13504921.

Alwin, D. and Felson, J. (2010) Religion and child-rearing, in *Religion, Families, and Health: Population-based Research in the United States* (eds C.G. Ellison and R.A. Hummer), Rutgers University Press, New Brunswick, pp. 40–60.

Bartkowski, J.P. and Wilcox, W.B. (2000) Conservative protestant child discipline: the case of parental yelling. *Social Forces*, 79, 265–290.

Bartkowski, J.P. and Xu, X. (2000) Distant patriarchs or expressive dads? The discourse and practice of fathering in conservative protestant families. *The Sociological Quarterly*, 41, 865–885.

Bartkowski, J.P., Xu, X. and Levin, M.L. (2008) The impact of religion on child development: evidence from the early childhood longitudinal study. *Social Science Research*, 37, 18–36.

Bartkowski, J.P., Xu, X. and Fondren, K.E. (2011) Faith, family, and teen dating: examining the effects of personal and household religiosity on adolescent romantic relationships. *Review of Religious Research*, 52, 248–265.

Bearman, P.S. and Bruckner, H. (2001) Promising the future: virginity pledges and first intercourse. *American Journal of Sociology*, 106, 859–912.

Brown, E., Orbuch, T. and Bauermeister, J. (2008) Religiosity and marital stability among black American and white American couples. *Family Relations*, 57, 185–196.

Burdette, A.M., Ellison, C.G., Sherkat, D.E. and Gore, K. (2007) Are there religious variations in marital infidelity? *Journal of Family Issues*, 28, 1553–1581.

Burdette, A.M., Ellison, C.G., Hill, T.D and Glenn, N.D. (2009) "Hooking up" at college: does religion make a difference? *Journal for the Scientific Study of Religion*, 48, 535–551.

Call, V.R.A. and Heaton, T.B. (1997) Religious influence on marital stability. *Journal for the Scientific Study of Religion*, 36, 382–392.

Chaves, M. (2011) *American Religion: Contemporary Trends*, Princeton University Press, Princeton.

Curtis, K.T. and Ellison, C.G. (2002) Religious heterogamy and marital conflict: findings from the national survey of families and households. *Journal of Family Issues*, 23, 551–576.

DeMaris, A., Sanchez, L.A. and Krivickas, K. (2012) Developmental patterns in marital satisfaction: another look at covenant marriage. *Journal of Marriage and Family*, 74, 989–1004.

Edgell, P.A. (2006) *Religion and Family in a Changing Society*, Princeton University Press, Princeton.

Ellison, C.G. and Sherkat, D.E. (1993a) Obedience and autonomy: religion and parental values reconsidered. *Journal for the Scientific Study of Religion*, 32, 313–329.

Ellison, C.G. and Sherkat, D.E. (1993b) Conservative protestantism and support for corporal punishment. *American Sociological Review*, 58, 131–144.

Ellison, C.G. and Bartkowski, J.P. (2002) Conservative protestantism and the division of household labor among married couples. *Journal of Family Issues*, 23, 950–985.

Ellison, C.G. and McFarland, M.J. (2013) The social context of religion and spirituality in the United States, in *Handbook of the Psychology of Religion and Spirituality*, vol. 1 (eds K. Pargament, J. Jones, and J. Exline), American Psychological Association, pp. 21–50.

Ellison, C.G., Bartkowski, J.P. and Segal, M.L. (1996) Conservative protestantism and the parental use of corporal punishment. *Social Forces*, 74, 1003–1028.

Ellison, C.G., Bartkowski, J.P. and Anderson, K.L. (1999) Are there religious variations in domestic violence? *Journal of Family Issues*, 20, 87–113.

Ellison, C.G., Burdette, A.M. and Wilcox, W.B. (2010) "The couple that prays together": couples' religion, race, ethnicity, and relationship quality among working-age couples. *Journal of Marriage and Family*, 72, 963–975.

Ellison, C.G., Musick, M.A. and Holden, G.W. (2011) Does conservative protestantism moderate the association between corporal punishment and child outcomes? *Journal of Marriage and Family*, 73, 946–961.

Ellison, C.G., Wolfinger, N.H. and Ramos-Wada, A. (2013) Attitudes toward marriage, divorce, cohabitation, and casual sex among working-age Latinos: does religion matter? *Journal of Family Issues*, 34, 295–322.

Ellison, C.G., Henderson, A.K., Glenn, N.D. and Harkrider, K. (2011) Sanctification, stress, and marital quality. *Family Relations*, 60, 404–420.

Fincham, F.D., Hall, J. and Beach, S.R.H. (2006) Forgiveness in marriage: current status and future directions. *Family Relations*, 55, 415–427.

Fjellvag, T. (2011) Socialization values, cultural-religious zones, and modernization theory. *European Sociological Review*, 27, 196–211.

Freitas, D. (2009) *Sex and the Soul: Spirituality, Sexuality, Romance, and Religion on America's College Campuses*, Oxford University Press, New York.

Frejka, T. and Westoff, C.F. (2008) Religion, religiousness, and fertility in the U.S. and in Europe. *European Journal of Population*, 24, 5–31.

Gershoff, E.T., Miller, P.C. and Holden, G.W. (1999) Parenting influences from the pulpit: religious affiliation as a determinant of parental corporal punishment. *Journal of Family Psychology*, 13, 307–320.

Gunnoe, M.L., Hetherington, E. and Reiss, D. (2006) Differential impact of fathers' authoritarian parenting on early adolescent adjustment in conservative protestant versus other families. *Journal of Family Psychology*, 4, 589–596.

Hardy, S.A. and Raffaelli, M. (2003) Adolescent religiosity and sexuality: an investigation of reciprocal influences. *Journal of Adolescence*, 26, 731–739.

Hayford, S.R. and Morgan, S.P. (2008) Religiosity and fertility in the United States: the role of fertility intentions. *Social Forces*, 86, 1163–1188.

Hempel, L.M. and Bartkowski, J.P. (2008) Scripture, sin, and salvation: theological conservatism reconsidered. *Social Forces*, 86, 1647–1674.

Hoffmann, J.P. and Bahr, S.M. (2005) Crime and deviance, in *Handbook of Religion and Social Institutions* (ed. H.R. Ebaugh), Springer, New York, pp. 241–263.

Kalmijn, M. (1998) Intermarriage and homogamy: causes, patterns, and trends. *Annual Review of Sociology*, 24, 395–421.

Kaufmann, E. (2010) *Shall the Religious Inherit the Earth? Demography and Politics in the Twenty-first Century*, Profile Books, London.

King, V. (2010) The influence of religion on ties between the generations, in *Religion, Families, and Health: Population-based Research in the United States*, (eds C.G. Ellison and R.A. Hummer), Rutgers University Press, New Brunswick, pp. 86–105.

King, V. and Elder, G.H. Jr. (1999) Are religious grandparents more involved grandparents? *Journal of Gerontology: Social Sciences*, 54B, S317–S328.

Lazerwitz, B. (1995) Jewish-Christian marriages and conversions 1971 and 1990. *Sociology of Religion*, 56, 433–443.

Lehrer, E.L. (2011) *Religion, Economics, and Demography: The Effects of Religion on Education, Work, and Family*, Routledge, New York.

Lichter, D.T. and Carmalt, J.H. (2009) Religion and marital quality among low-income couples. *Social Science Research*, 38, 168–187.

Mahoney, A. (2010) Religion and families, 1999–2009: a relational spirituality framework. *Journal of Marriage and Family*, 72, 805–827.

Mahoney, A., Pargament, K.I., Jewell, T. *et al.* (1999) Marriage and the spiritual realm: the role of proximal and distal religious constructs in marital functioning. *Journal of Family Psychology*, 13, 321–338.

McQuillan, K. (2004) When does religion influence fertility? *Population and Development Review*, 30, 25–56.

Meier, A.M. (2003) Adolescents' transition to first intercourse, religiosity, and attitudes about sex. *Social Forces*, 81, 1031–1052.

Mosher, W.D., Williams, L.B. and Johnson, D.P. (1992) Religion and fertility in the United States: new patterns. *Demography*, 29, 199–214.

Muller, C. and Ellison, C.G. (2001) Religious involvement, social capital, and adolescent academic progress: evidence from the national educational longitudinal study of 1988. *Sociological Focus*, 34, 155–183.

Myers, S.M. (2006) Religious homogamy and marital quality: historical and generational patterns, 1980–1997. *Journal of Marriage and Family*, 68, 292–304.

Nason-Clark, N. (1997) *The Battered Wife: How Christians Confront Family Violence*, Westminster John Knox Press, Louisville.

Nock, S.L., Sanchez, L.A. and Wright, J.D. (2008) *Covenant Marriage: The Movement to Reclaim Tradition in America*, Rutgers University Press, New Brunswick.

Norris, P. and Inglehart, R. (2004) *Sacred and Secular: Religion and Politics Worldwide*, Cambridge University Press, New York.

Oswald, R.F., Goldberg, A., Kuvalanka, K. and Clausell, E. (2008) Structural and moral commitment among same-sex couples: relationship duration, religiosity, and parental status. *Journal of Family Psychology*, 22, 411–419.

Pearce, L.D. (2002) The influence of early life course religious exposure on young adults' dispositions toward childbearing. *Journal for the Scientific Study of Religion*, 41, 325–340.

Pearce, L.D. (2010) Religion and the timing of first births in the United States, in Religion, Families, and Health: Population-Based Research in the United States (eds C. G. Ellison and R.A. Hummer), Rutgers University Press, pp. 19–39.

Pearce, L.D. and Axinn, W.G. (1998) The impact of family religious life on the quality of mother-child relationships. *American Sociological Review*, 63, 810–828.

Pearce, L.D. and Haynie, D. (2004) Intergenerational religious dynamics and adolescent delinquency. *Social Forces*, 82, 1553–1571.

Pearce, L.D. and Thornton, A. (2007) Religious identity and family ideologies in the transition to adulthood. *Journal of Marriage and Family*, 69, 1227–1243.

Petts, R.J. (2007) Religious participation, religious affiliation, and engagement with children among fathers experiencing the birth of a new child. *Journal of Family Issues*, 28, 1139–1161.

Petts, R.J. (2012) Single mothers' religious involvement and early childhood behavior. *Journal of Marriage and Family*, 74, 251–268.

Regnerus, M.D. (2003) Religion and positive adolescent outcomes: a review of theory and research. *Review of Religious Research*, 44, 394–413.

Regnerus, M.D. (2007) *Forbidden Fruit: Sex and Religion in the Lives of American Teenagers*, Oxford University Press, New York.

Schwadel, P. (2011) Age, period, and cohort effects on religious activities and beliefs. *Social Science Research*, 40, 181–192.

Sechrist, J., Suitor, J.J., Vargas, N. and Pillemer, K. (2011) The role of perceived religious similarity in the quality of mother-child relations in later life: differences within families and between races. *Research on Aging*, 33, 3–27.

Sherkat, D.E. (2004) Religious intermarriage in the United States: trends, patterns, and predictors. *Social Science Research*, 33, 606–625.

Smith, C. (2003) Religious participation and network closure among american adolescents. *Journal for the Scientific Study of Religion*, 42, 259–267.

Smith, C., with Denton, M.L. (2005) *Soul Searching: The Religious and Spiritual Lives of American Teenagers*, Oxford University Press, New York.

Stafford, L., David, P. and McPherson, S. (2013) Sanctity of marriage and marital quality. *Journal of Social and Personal Relationships*. doi.10.1177/0265407513486975.

Stark, R. (2012) *America's Blessings: How Religion Benefits Everyone, Including Atheists*, Templeton Press, West Conshohocken.

Starks, B. and Robinson, R.V. (2005) Who values the obedient child now? The religious factor in adult values for children, 1986–2002. *Social Forces*, 84, 343–359.

Stokes, C.E. and Regnerus, M.D. (2009) When faith divides family: religious discord and adolescent reports of parent-child relations. *Social Science Research*, 38, 155–167.

Stokes, C.E. and Ellison, C.G. (2010) Religion and attitudes toward divorce laws among U.S. adults. *Journal of Family Issues*, 31, 1279–1304.

Thornton, A., Axinn, W.G. and Hill, D.H. (1992) Reciprocal effects of religiosity, cohabitation, and marriage. *American Journal of Sociology*, 98, 628–651.

Vaaler, M.L., Ellison, C.G. and Powers, D.A. (2009) Religious influences on the risk of marital dissolution. *Journal of Marriage and Family*, 71, 917–934.

Waite, L.J. and Lewin, A.C. (2010) Religious intermarriage and conversion in the United States: patterns and changes over time, in *Religion, Families, and Health: Population-based Research in the United States* (eds C.G. Ellison and R.A. Hummer), Rutgers University Press, New Brunswick, pp. 148–163.

Westoff, C.B. and Jones, E.F. (1979) The end of "catholic" fertility. *Demography*, 16, 209–217.

Wilcox, W.B. (1998) Conservative protestant childrearing: authoritarian or authoritative? *American Sociological Review*, 63, 786–809.

Wilcox, W.B. (2002) Religion, convention, and paternal involvement. *Journal of Marriage and Family*, 64, 780–792.

Wilcox, W.B. (2004) *Soft Patriarchs, New Men: How Christianity Shapes Fathers and Husbands*, University of Chicago Press, Chicago.

Wilcox, W.B., Chaves, M. and Franz, D. (2004) Focused on the family? Religious traditions, family discourse, and pastoral practice. *Journal for the Scientific Study of Religion*, 43, 491–504.

Wilcox, W.B. and Wolfinger, N.H. (2008) Living and loving "decent": religion and relationship quality among urban parents. *Social Science Research*, 37, 828–843.

Wildeman, C. (2008) Conservative protestantism and paternal engagement in fragile families. *Sociological Forum*, 23, 556–574.

Wolfinger, N.H. and Wilcox, W.B. (2008) Happily ever after? Religion, marital status, gender, and relationship quality in urban families. *Social Forces*, 86, 1311–1337.

Wilson, J. and Musick, M.A. (1996) Religion and marital dependency. *Journal for the Scientific Study of Religion*, 35, 30–40.

Xu, X., Hudspeth, C.H. and Bartkowski, J.P. (2005) The timing of first marriage: are there religious variations? *Journal of Family Issues*, 26, 584–618.

Part IV
Family Processes

15

Divorce: Trends, Patterns, Causes, and Consequences

Juho Härkönen

Introduction

The increases in divorce rates have been among the most visible features of the recent decades of family change. Some have seen this as a sign of social and moral disruption with a potential to shatter the family institution and the foundations of society itself. Others have celebrated these trends as signaling increased individual liberty and the loosening of suffocating social mores. Divorce is one of the most often mentioned major life events (Gähler, 1998), and can cause major stress and upheaval for many, and a sense of relief and opportunity for personal growth for others. It is no wonder that divorce and family instability have attracted wide attention among social scientists.

This chapter provides an overview to what is known about divorce, its trends, cross-national variation, predictors, and consequences. Geographically, the focus is on Europe and North America, and the author follows the trend in research and focuses on divorce, that is, the ending of a marital union. In most cases, the event of significance is the end of marital cohabitation. The legal procedures that end the marriage may, in many cases, continue well past the separation of the couple. Other forms of union or marital dissolution, such as permanent separation, desertion, and annulment (marriage declared not valid) have received less research attention.

However, acknowledging the changing family landscape, in which much cohabitation and family life occur outside marriage, a growing number of studies have looked into the dissolution of unmarried cohabitations. There is still active debate on whether, when, and in which countries cohabitation is like marriage, or not (Heuveline and Timberlake, 2004). Many cohabiting unions either split up or are transformed into marriages relatively quickly, even in countries in which cohabitation is common (Jalovaara, 2012). In general, cohabiting unions are less stable than marriages (Andersson, 2002). There are many similarities in the factors that promote or undermine the stability of marriage and cohabitation, as they are in the consequences of their dissolution. However, some important differences can be found which are generally linked to the weaker institutionalization of unmarried cohabitation (Brines and Joyner, 1999).

Furthermore, almost all of the literature has focused on heterosexual couples. Recent years have seen a wave of legal recognition of same-sex partnerships, which has consequently raised scholars' interest in their demography. But, information concerning the dissolution of same-sex couples remains relatively limited. Research suggests that although same-sex partnerships are in general less stable than hetero-sexual marriages, the predictors of their instability are in many respects similar (Andersson *et al.*, 2006; Lau, 2012).

Theoretical perspectives on divorce have ranged from macrosociological theories of the role of divorce in the family system to microlevel perspectives on the processes conducive to marital instability (Kitson and Raschke, 1981). Many scholars begin from a least implicit account of divorce in which partners remain in their marriages, as long as the benefits of doing so exceed the sum of the costs of dissolving them and the benefits of other options (Levinger, 1976; Brines and Joyner, 1999). This rationalistic perspective is most explicit in economic approaches to marriage and divorce (Becker, Landes, and Michael, 1977; Becker, 1981). The benefits and costs include emotional rewards, mutual support and commitment, economic and moral considerations, social sanctions and approval, legal issues, children, and new part-ners. Divorces can be analyzed as events, that is, the decision to leave a partnership and the ending of the marriage. However, they are often preceded by a long process of ending the relationship, which can include estragement from the spouse, stress, conflicts, and even violence (Amato, 2000), and, as mentioned, the legal procedures dissolving the marriage may last well after both spouses consider the marriage ended. Thus, defining and measuring divorce – when it starts and when it ends – can be difficult. Despite the conflicts surrounding many divorces, many seemingly functional marriages end in divorce (Amato and Hohmann-Marriott, 2007), and on the other hand, not all troubled marriages break up. This underlines the hetero-geneity of divorces, the importance of factors that act as barriers to divorce or the possible options beyond it, and the need for looking beyond marital quality and satisfaction as determinants. Divorce, in other words, is a multifaceted event (Gähler, 1998).

Trends and Cross-National Differences in Divorce

Consider Figure 15.1 which shows the trends in the crude divorce rate for selected countries. Before proceeding to a discussion of these trends, it is important to under-stand what these numbers tell us. The crude divorce rate shows the number of divorces per 1000 individuals in the population. It is not a perfect measure of under-lying marital instability and, particularly, does not tell how many couples eventually divorce (Preston and McDonald, 1979; Schoen and Canudas-Romo, 2006). Crude rates are known to fluctuate over time, and a sudden increase, for example, can indi-cate that many couples divorce sooner than they otherwise would have. As it is not

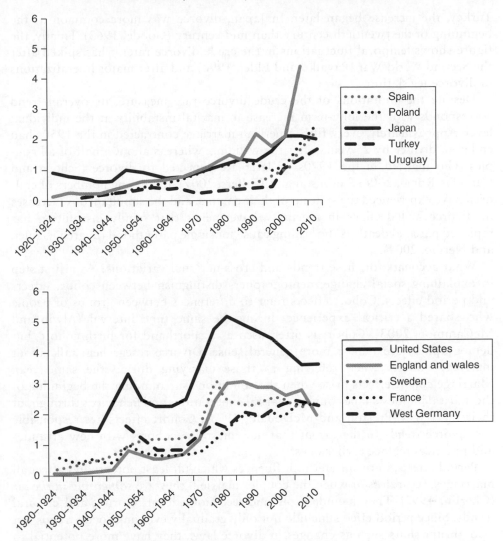

Figure 15.1   Crude divorce rates in selected countries, 1920–2010.
Sources: United Nations (various years); National Center for Health Statistics (various years).

adjusted for the number of married couples, the crude rate can also be affected by
changes in the popularity of marriage. Despite these limitations, the crude divorce
rate correlates strongly with better measures (Amato, 2010). It is available for long
time periods and for several countries, and is thus suitable for describing long-term
cross-national trends.

   Divorce rates were higher in all the countries represented in Figure 15.1 at the
beginning of the new millennium than just after the First World War. Yet, there
are major cross-national differences. The United States has traditionally been a
high-divorce society, whereas in Spain, divorce was not possible until 1981. The
1960s saw the beginning of a sharp increase in divorce rates in many countries,
but they have stabilized, or even decreased since. In others, such as Spain and

Turkey, the increase began later. In Japan, divorce was more common at the beginning of the twentieth century than mid-century (Goode, 1963). Finally, the figure shows temporal fluctuations in the crude divorce rate: it has spiked after the Second World War (Pavalko and Elder, 1990) and after major liberalizations in divorce legislation.

Despite the limitations of the crude divorce rate measure, its overall trend corresponds with the long-term increase in marital instability at the individual level. Approximately, every fifth American marriage contracted in the 1950s had ended in divorce by 25 years after the wedding, whereas about a half of all couples who married in the 1970s or later are expected to divorce (Schoen and Canudas-Romo, 2006; Stevenson and Wolfers, 2007). Increasing numbers of children have experienced the split-up of their parents, and the simultaneous increases in divorce and declines in mortality have meant that family dissolution has replaced parental death as the leading cause for single parenthood (Bygren, Gähler, and Nermo, 2004).

What accounts for these trends and cross-national variations? As a first step in explaining social change, demographers distinguish between cohort effects and period effects. Cohort effects refer to differences between groups of people who shared a critical experience during the same time interval (Alwin and McCammon, 2003). Cohort is often used as a shorthand for birth cohort, but demographers use it in a more general sense. Divorce researchers talk about marriage cohorts when referring to those marrying during the same year. Marriage cohort effects arise when the conditions surrounding the beginning of the marital journey shape couples' marital expectations and behaviors throughout their marriages (Preston and McDonald, 1979). Cohort effects are responsible for divorce trends to the extent that new marriage cohorts with new attitudes and practices replace earlier ones.

Period effects, in turn, refer to influences which (at least potentially) affect all marriages, regardless of when the couples married; they are *something in the air* (Cherlin, 1992). They include economic recessions, legal reforms, and cultural trends. Since period effects include not only gradually evolving social trends but also abrupt shifts such as changes in divorce laws, they have more potential to cause sudden increases or decreases in divorce. Divorce researchers generally agree that period effects dominate over cohort effects (Thornton and Rodgers, 1987; Cherlin, 1992; Lyngstad and Jalovaara, 2010). Therefore, to understand divorce trends, we must look into the factors that at least potentially affect all marriages.

The initial increases in divorce took social scientists by surprise (Cherlin, 1992), and even now, there is no single explanation of why divorce rates have increased, or vary cross-nationally. Suggested explanations range from economic trends to cultural shifts and legal changes. Many explanations point to the change in gender roles – from gender asymmetry to increasing gender symmetry and equality – and, in particular, to the dramatic increases in married women's labor market activity. Indeed, the trends in female employment and in divorce rates have closely followed one another (Cherlin, 1992; Ruggles, 1997), and a positive relationship between the two is also visible across countries (Kalmijn, 2007). Most researchers have interpreted the causality to run from female employment to divorce. A problem with this interpretation is that, as will be discussed in the next section, the microlevel evidence regarding this link is not conclusive (Özcan and Breen, 2012). Other economic explanations have focused on the relative deterioration of men's economic fortunes in many countries, but neither of these can explain the big picture (Stevenson and Wolfers, 2007).

Other theories emphasize cultural changes (Lesthaeghe, 1995; Coontz, 2005; Cherlin, 2009). A popular account is provided by the second demographic transition thesis (Lesthaeghe, 1995), which links the changes in family behavior to the increases in individualism and other postmaterial values. There has been a shift in family attitudes toward more gender equality, personal fulfillment, and acceptance of nontraditional family behaviors such as divorce (Thornton and Young-De Marco, 2001). This shift has been very uneven across the Western world and major cross-national variation in the acceptance of divorce remains (Gelissen, 2003).

These new ideas fit squarely with the traditional views of marriage and family life, which were based on rigid roles and sharp gender inequalities, and emphasized the married couple as a single unit, rather than a partnership of two individuals (Coontz, 2005). However, as with explanations having to do with attitudes more generally, there is a chicken-and-egg problem of which came first, attitudes or behavior? Divorce attitudes often seemed to adjust to changing realities, instead of providing the initial push to increased divorce (even though liberalized attitudes may have made later divorces easier and more common) (Cherlin, 1992). More generally, testing these explanations is often difficult and constrained by the availability of relevant cross-national data over long periods of time. Some scholars have used religiosity as a measure of cultural acceptance of divorce and found secularization to correlate positively with divorce rates (Kalmijn, 2010). In an interesting study in Brazil, Chong and La Ferrera (2009) found that the spread of *telenovelas* in that country was followed by increases in divorce, presumably as couples became increasingly exposed to new ideas about family life. Even though the explanatory power of cultural influences on divorce is difficult to assess, the spread of new ideas and attitudes is likely to have contributed to the increases in family instability.

Divorce laws have changed markedly through the twentieth century and the beginning of the twenty-first century. Divorce was prohibited until recently in several Western countries (e.g., Italy legalized divorce in 1974, Spain in 1981, Ireland in 1997, and Malta in 2011), and is still difficult to obtain in others. Often, divorces could be granted on the basis of serious faults (such as adultery, violence, or mental illness), or possibly, by the mutual consent of the spouses (Härkönen and Dronkers, 2006). Even then, the process was usually expensive and lengthy. Major liberalization of divorce laws began during the 1960s and 1970s, and in 1970, California was the first US state to implement unilateral '*no fault*' divorce, in which either spouse could exit the marriage without having to provide specific reasons. Sweden followed suit in 1974, and by the turn of the millennium, most Western countries had liberalized their divorce legislation (Gonzalez and Viitanen, 2009).

Do these legislative changes affect divorce rates, or do they merely reflect the rising acceptance of and demand for divorce? Recent research has generally concluded that liberalization of divorce laws did cause short-term spikes in divorce rates (see, e.g., Sweden in 1974 in Figure 15.1), presumably as spouses in ill-functioning marriages took advantage of the better opportunities for exiting their marriages (Wolfers, 2006; Stevenson and Wolfers, 2007; González and Viitanen, 2009). According to many, these effects were not lasting, and the long-term effect of the liberalization of divorce laws was, at most, a small increase in divorce rates (however, see González and Viitanen, 2009). Loosening of official control over marriages and divorces did, however, change the divorce process and the dynamics of marriages. Unilateral divorce – the possibility of exiting a marriage without the consent of one's spouse – shifted the power balance to the spouse more willing to exit, while the shortening of the legal process and the weakening need to show fault or irreconcilability have made divorce processes faster and possibly less conflict-ridden (Stevenson and Wolfers, 2007).

All in all, social scientists have had difficulties in explaining the increases in divorce. All available explanations have limitations. An interpretation of the trends is that values have changed and reorientations provide the social opportunities and subjective motives for divorce, whereas increases in women's economic independence have been among the factors providing the means for doing so (Cherlin, 2009). Together, these changes meant that people were more ready, willing, and able to divorce (Coale, 1973; Sandström, 2012).

If social scientists were unable to foresee an increase in divorce, they were equally unable to predict the recent stabilization of marriages in many countries. These developments – see Figure 15.1 – are not merely due to the limitations of crude divorce measures. There has been a corresponding leveling and even decrease in underlying marital instability. This has been clear in the United States since the 1980s (Goldstein, 1999; Schoen and Canudas-Romo, 2006; Stevenson and Wolfers, 2007), and also found in other countries, such as Sweden (Andersson and Kolk, 2011). Marriages, of course, must take place for there to be divorce, and thus many scholars have looked at the characteristics of marrying couples for clues regarding recent stabilization in divorce rates. One of the issues here has been the increase in the age at marriage. As will be discussed later, older age at marriage is associated with lower divorce risk, and this has been found to contribute to the stabilization of marriage in the United States (Heaton, 2002). Increases in educational levels are another contributing factor. Additionally, increases in nonmarital cohabitations (which are more likely to dissolve) can mask the overall instability of couple relationships (Raley and Bumpass, 2003).

Who Divorces? The Predictors of Divorce

Earlier in this chapter, I discussed findings regarding trends in divorce over time and cross-national variation in divorce rates. Divorce trends were seen to be primarily caused by period effects, by something that *is in the air* as Andrew Cherlin (1992, p. 31) has described it. However, just as everyone does not get rich during an economic boom or does not get the flu during an epidemic, not all marriages end in divorce, and there are systematic differences in which do and which do not.

When asked why Mrs. and Mr. Jones divorced, many would give reasons such as growing apart; they were never suited to each other; they were always arguing; or perhaps infidelity. A large body of research has investigated the proximate and psychological factors that may lead to divorce (Bradbury, Finchman, and Beach, 2000). Unsurprisingly, low marital satisfaction is a strong predictor of divorce and infidelity, while incompatibility, and behavioral and relationship problems rank high among the reasons people give for their divorces (Amato and Rogers, 1997; Amato and Previti, 2003; De Graaf and Kalmijn, 2006). Interestingly, De Graaf and Kalmijn (2006) observed that in the Netherlands, strong reasons for divorce, such as infidelity or violence, have become less often cited, whereas psychological and relational problems, and reasons to do with the division of housework, have increased in importance. These findings are in line with ideas of marital change toward a partnership between equal individuals respecting their personal needs (Coontz, 2005; Cherlin, 2009). Despite its interest, the author does not discuss further the psychological literature on divorce, but instead turns to the importance of more sociological factors.

We know a good deal about the socioeconomic and demographic predictors of divorce (for recent reviews, see Amato, 2000, 2010; Amato and James, 2010; Lyngstad and Jalovaara, 2010). Even though the strength of the different predictors may vary from one country and time period to the next (Wagner and Weiß, 2006), many point in similar directions, regardless of the context (Amato and James, 2010; Lyngstad and Jalovaara, 2010).

Whether a couple divorces or not is related to the life-course stages and prior experiences of the partners. Young couples, for instance, have been consistently shown to have higher divorce rates due to their lower (psychological and socioeconomic) maturity, potentially unreasonable expectations, and a shorter search that led to making an unstable match or overlooking better outside options (alternative partners) (Booth and Edwards, 1985; Lyngstad and Jalovaara, 2010).

Having been previously married also predicts divorce, and generally, the more prior partnerships one has accumulated, the higher the divorce risk is (Castro Martin and Bumpass, 1989; Teachman, 2008). This finding has been commonly explained by selection into further marriage: one has to divorce before marrying for the second time, and those who divorced once would be more likely to do it again (Poortman and Lyngstad, 2007). A similar *selection* explanation has been used to explain why couples who cohabited before marrying are more likely to divorce, even though one might expect the opposite, given that such couples have more experience and information about each other and life together (Axinn and Thorton, 1992; Amato, 2010; Lyngstad and Jalovaara, 2010). According to this explanation, couples who cohabited are less traditional and may have different ideals and expectations of marriage. Some scholars, however, have proposed that experience of cohabitation may actually increase divorce risk by undermining the commitment to marriage as the context for sexual relationships and childbearing (Thomson and Collella, 1992), or through relationship inertia by which relatively incompatible cohabiting couples drift into marriage, as the barriers to ending the relationship accumulate (e.g., shared possessions and, possibly, children) (Stanley, Rhoades, and Markman, 2006).

Divorce risk is not constant through the course of marriage. While few marriages dissolve soon after the wedding, the likelihood of it happening increases through the first years. Marital satisfaction generally declines over the course of marital life (Umberson et al., 2005), and couples have the highest risk of divorcing between the fourth and the seventh year after the wedding. After this, divorce risk begins to decline gradually as couples accumulate investments in their marriage which increase the barriers for leaving it (Lyngstad and Jalovaara, 2010).

One such barrier is children. Theoretically, children can be regarded as shared investments (Becker, Landes, and Michael, 1977; Brines and Joyner, 1999), and parents can forgo, or at least postpone their divorce, if they are concerned with its adverse effects on their children. Indeed, couples with children, especially small ones, have lower divorce risks than childless couples (Lyngstad and Jalovaara, 2010). Again, this may reflect the characteristics of the couples who do not have children, as they might have lower trust in their marriages to begin with. Whether having children actually stabilizes marriages seems, on the other hand, to depend on the country and the time period (Lyngstad and Jalovaara, 2010). Some research even suggests that having boys can have a stronger stabilizing effect (Morgan, Lye, and Condran, 1988), presumably due to fathers' increased involvement in child-care. However, this finding remains contested. Having children can also destabilize marriages if it means less time for fostering the relationship (Twenge, Campbell, and Foster, 2004), which, as discussed, has become increasingly important in modern marriages.

Socioeconomic factors related to divorce have been widely discussed in the litera-ture. The starting point for practically all research is that husbands' and wives' socio-economic resources have different influences. This assumption is often based on an economic approach to family life, which sees economic resources as an exchange for unpaid domestic work and in which husbands' and wives' roles are complementary (Becker, Landes, and Michael, 1977; Becker, 1981). In practice, this perspective predicts that mens' socioeconomic resources – such as education, employment, and earnings – stabilize marriages, whereas wives' resources destabilize them. While this prediction has found general support in research in regard to men's resources (Lyngstad and Jalovaara, 2010), findings are less consistent when it comes to the influence of wives' resources. The relationship between female education and marital stability is a case in point. In the United States, women with higher levels of educa-tion have had lower rates of divorce for a long time and this gap has grown (Martin, 2006). In many other countries, highly educated women used to have higher divorce rates. But, over time, less educated women have seen their divorce risks increase at a faster rate, and currently, they are as, or more, likely to divorce in several countries (Härkönen and Dronkers, 2006). These developments are in line with the Goode hypothesis, which maintains that the initially high social, legal, and economic bar-riers to divorce kept it the privilege of those with high enough resources to overcome them (Goode, 1962). As these barriers have declined, divorce has become accessible to those with fewer resources, who are often those under more economic and other marital stress. Similar discrepancies can be seen in the research on female employment and marital instability (Amato, 2010; Amato and James, 2010; Lyngstad and Jalovaara, 2010; Özcan and Breen, 2012). Earlier predictions were that female employment would destabilize marriages, as it weakened the benefits from a household division of labor (Becker, Landes, and Michael, 1977; Becker, 1981), improved opportunities for maintaining independent households (England and Farkas, 1986), and increased the chances to meet new partners (South and Lloyd, 1995). Many empirical findings supported this.

Predictions of the destabilizing effect of female employment and earnings have, however, been increasingly questioned. Many have argued that female employment can stabilize partnerships by strengthening families' economic security and balancing the spouses' roles and responsibilities (Oppenheimer, 1997). Others claimed that the expectation of divorce may actually lead to increases in wives' employment, rather than the opposite (Özcan and Breen, 2012). Furthermore, wives' employment and earnings may help them exit dysfunctional marriages rather than destabilizing all marriages (Sayer and Bianchi, 2000; Sayer *et al.*, 2011), or have destabilizing effects only if they do not adhere to the values of the couple (Amato *et al.*, 2007) or the surrounding society (Cooke, 2006). An additional modifier of these effects is public policy. Female employment can stabilize marriages in countries with policies that support work–family balance (Cooke *et al.*, Forthcoming). Overall, then, the effects of female economic activity are much more contingent than previously thought.

Women, however, have practically always and everywhere been more likely to file for divorce and start the process leading to divorce. This remarkably stable finding seems to be found for every society where such statistics exist, Western and non-Western alike (Mignot, 2009). Exceptions have been during major wars and their aftermaths. Many findings furthermore suggest that women's divorce filings are more closely related to socioeconomic factors (Kalmijn and Poortman, 2006; Sayer *et al.*, 2011; Boertien, 2012), and women are more likely to name relational and psychological motives for their divorces (De Graaf and Kalmijn, 2006). Men, on the other hand, appear less likely to initiate divorce when the couple has young children (Kalmijn and Poortman, 2006; Hewitt, 2009), possibly reflecting an anticipation of weaker postdivorce contact with their children.

Increases in international migration have spurred interest into the family lives of migrant groups. Migration as a major life event can itself have a divorce-inducing effect, especially since one of the spouses may benefit from the move more than the other (Lyngstad and Jalovaara, 2010). Migrant groups can find themselves landing in a society in which marital mores and divorce rates differ noticeably from those in their country of origin. In particular, much of the migration flows to the Western countries are from societies with less divorce, and exposure to the new environment can entail increases in divorce rates of these groups (Landale and Ogena, 1995; Qureshi, Charsley, and Shaw, 2012). At the same time, these groups may keep features of their countries of origin, and in general, one finds major differences in marital stability between different groups (Kalmijn, 2011; Qureshi, Charsley, and Shaw, 2012). Increased immigration has led to an increase in the number and share of marriages between migrant groups and the native population, and between migrant groups themselves. While intermarriage is commonly regarded as a sign of integration, such exogamous marriages face higher dissolution rates; the further apart the spouses are culturally, the higher the dissolution rates are (Dribe and Lundh, 2012).

Consequences of Divorce

One of the main concerns with the increase in divorce has been its effects on the well-being of children and adults. These questions have aroused major interest among social and psychological scientists, and many conclusions have been remarkably conflicting (McLanahan and Sandefur, 1994; Cherlin, 1999). What can we say about the effects of divorce and family dissolution on adults and children?

Most studies conclude that divorced adults and their children fare worse according to several indicators of psychological, physical, and socioeconomic well-being, compared to those who did not experience divorce (Amato, 2000, 2010; Garriga and Härkönen, 2009; Amato and James, 2010). Findings of these effects range from heightened poverty levels (Callens and Croux, 2009) and lower educational performance of the children of divorce (Garriga and Härkönen, 2009; Amato and James, 2010) to increased occurrence of psychological distress (Amato and Keith, 1991) and many physical health conditions (Amato and James, 2010).

Does the experience of divorce itself cause these differences? Couples who break up differ from those remaining together in many respects. They are generally less happy and often more conflictual, and they also differ in terms of socioeconomic resources and many demographic characteristics. All these can themselves affect well-being, and divorcing couples and their children might have fared worse even without the divorce. Indeed, those who remain in unhappy marriages fare worse in terms of life satisfaction than those who dissolved their unhappy marriages (Hawkins and Booth, 2005).

Since the golden tool for addressing causality – the randomized experiment – is for obvious reasons out of the question when assessing the effects of divorce, researchers are left to various second-best alternatives. Furthermore, since divorce is not simply a snapshot event but rather a (potentially long-lasting) process, it can be conceptually challenging even to separate divorce effects (i.e., divorce-as-event-effects) from the effects of the preceding process (Amato, 2000, 2010), as discussed in the Introduction section.

Despite the difficulties, several scholars have used various sophisticated methods to assess this issue. A common conclusion is that divorce can indeed affect the well-being and performance of adults and children alike, even though the effects are neither necessarily large nor long-lasting, and tend to show a great deal of heterogeneity (Amato, 2000, 2010; Garriga and Härkönen, 2009).

Take the example of the effects on the well-being of adults. Despite the sadness, upset, and feelings of loss associated with divorce, it can also be a relief to at least one of the partners, often for the one who has most wanted to separate (Wang and Amato, 2004). In many instances, psychological well-being tends to decrease already years prior to the divorce itself, stressing the processual nature of marital dissolution (Mastekaasa, 1994; Amato, 2000). In general, the adjustment of divorced persons shows major variation, with some individuals managing to adjust to the new situation relatively fast, while for others, divorce represents a long-term chronic problem from which they might never fully recover (Amato, 2000, 2010; Amato and James, 2010).

Whether divorce leads to declines in well-being depends on the nature of the marriage which the partners are leaving. Divorced persons who end a high-conflict marriage often experience less decline and even an increase in well-being, whereas those whose marriage was characterized by low conflict and relatively high satisfaction often experience more loss in well-being (Kalmijn and Monden, 2006; Amato and Hohmann-Marriott, 2007). Furthermore, adjustment to divorce depends on various socioeconomic and interpersonal resources, such as employment, income, social support, and whether one has a new partner (Gähler, 1998; Wang and Amato, 2004). It also depends on the broader societal context, and divorce effects are weaker in countries in which family support is stronger and in which divorce is more common (Kalmijn, 2010). Finally, there are no consistent gender differences in the subjective well-being consequences of divorce (even though men seem to suffer greater physical health declines) (Amato and James, 2010).

Divorce can have important economic consequences, especially for women (DiPrete and McManus, 2000; McManus and DiPrete, 2001; Uunk, 2004). Economic dependency in the marriage tends to lead to larger economic losses following divorce, whereas the sole or main economic providers may even gain economically (McManus and DiPrete, 2001). On the other hand, welfare state arrangements that provide income and support the employment of divorced mothers ameliorate the negative economic consequences of family dissolution (DiPrete and McManus, 2000; Uunk, 2004). Despite the variation in the economic consequences of divorce, it is among the main life events that can lead to poverty (Callens and Croux, 2009).

There has been even more concern on the effects of family dissolution on children. Over time, views have ranged from assumptions of major long-term negative effects on children's emotional and socioeconomic well-being to claims of no effects at all (McLanahan and Sandefur, 1994; Cherlin, 1999). Empirical findings support neither view. Children of divorce generally fare worse in terms of emotional and educational outcomes, but the effects are, on average, small or modest (Amato and Keith, 1991; Amato and Booth, 1997; Cherlin, 1999; Amato, 2000, 2010; Garriga and Härkönen, 2009; Amato and James, 2010).

These negative outcomes are already present some while before the parental divorce (Cherlin et al., 1991; Sanz-de-Galdeano and Vuri, 2007; Kim, 2011), underlining the earlier-mentioned difficulty in separating the effects of divorce from the processes leading to it. Growing up in a high-conflict family can in itself have negative effects on children's well-being and socioeconomic outcomes, and in such cases, parental divorce may actually have positive effects (Amato, Loomis, and Booth, 1995; Amato and Booth, 1997; Cherlin, 1999; Dronkers, 1999; Booth and Amato, 2004). However, children whose parents ended a low-conflict marriage fare generally worse than those whose parents remained together. The effects of parental divorce on children's outcomes thus vary in the same ways as the effects on divorcing adults, and small or modest average effects hide considerable underlying variation.

The effects of parental divorce depend on the immediate economic consequences and the general instability surrounding family dissolutions, which can have repercussions particularly on academic achievement (McLanahan and Sandefur, 1994; Thomson, Hanson, and McLanahan, 1994; Amato, 2000). Major drops in economic well-being, frequent residential moves, changes in the social environment, and other instability-generating factors have the potential to undermine children's outcomes. Some similar effects have been found for parental repartnering, which often can lead to new separations (Amato, 2010; Sweeney, 2010). Economic resources do not explain all of the effects of parental divorce, and psychological and relationship factors play an important role in explaining the effects of parental divorce. The adjustment of the parents themselves and their parenting practices during and after the divorce process contribute to the adjustment of their children, as does the overall quality of the relationships the children maintain with both of their parents. For these reasons, parental divorce can affect child outcomes even in well-developed welfare states (Gähler, 1998; Garriga and Härkönen, 2009; Amato and James, 2010).

Parental divorce often causes increased levels of anxiety during the divorce process, which can be exacerbated by the stress it lays on parents and their capability to engage in effective parenting. For many children, however, these effects are relatively short-lived, as many adjust to the new situation reasonably well over time (Amato and Keith, 1991; Cherlin, 1999; Amato, 2000, 2010; Pryor and Rodgers, 2001). For others, it may present a source of more chronic strain from which they never fully recover. One of the avenues through which parental divorce can have long-term effects on children's life courses is through educational attainment. If parental divorce disturbs the child's educational career – for example, through affecting their economic or psychological well-being or relationships with his/her parents, teachers, or friends – this disturbance may translate into lower levels of socioeconomic attainment and physical and psychological well-being in adulthood (Garriga and Härkönen, 2009; Amato and James, 2010).

Another long-term effect of parental divorce concerns the family life experiences of the children themselves. A well-documented finding is the intergenerational transmission of divorce: children of divorce are more prone to divorce themselves, as they may lack interpersonal skills that are conducive to marital stability or are more likely to perceive divorce as a viable solution to marital problems (Wolfinger, 2005; Dronkers and Härkönen, 2008). Parental divorce can also weaken contacts between children, their parents, and their grandparents (Aquilino, 1994; Garriga and Härkönen, 2009; Albertini and Garriga, 2011). These negative effects are particularly likely for the relationships between children and their fathers and the fathers' kin. This is not surprising, given the still-prevalent custody arrangements and women's role as kin-keepers. Finally, even if parental divorce generally has weak long-term effects on clinical indicators of psycho-emotional well-being, such as depression and anxiety disorders, many children of divorce still experience feelings of sadness and loss, even long after the parental separation (Amato, 2010).

One might expect that the effects of parental divorce have weakened as divorce rates have increased, its stigma decreased, and parents and societies have developed strategies to cope with its consequences. Maybe surprisingly, there is no strong evidence to support this belief (Ely et al., 1999; Amato, 2001; Garriga and Härkönen, 2009). However, one noticeable change in children's postdivorce conditions concerns their custody arrangements. In many countries, legal and practical joint custody arrangements have become more common, and in some cases even the norm. The limited number of studies on the topic does not permit strong conclusions, but existing findings suggest that joint custody can have positive effects on several well-being outcomes. Increasing joint custody can also weaken the negative effects of divorce on father–child relationships (Bauserman, 2002; Bjarnarson and Arnarsson, 2011).

Summing up, divorce has the potential to cause major disruption in the lives of adults and children, and the effects can be long-lasting. However, not everyone experiences long-lasting negative effects; most people adjust well over time, and for some, divorce may be beneficial (Cherlin, 1999; Amato, 2000). Regarding children's adjustment, Amato and James (2010, p. 9) summarized that "children function reasonably well after divorce if their standard of living does not decline dramatically, their resident mothers are psychologically well adjusted and engage in high-quality parenting, they maintain close ties to fathers, and their parents avoid conflict and engage in at least a minimal level of cooperation in the postdivorce years."

The discussion thus far has concerned effects of divorce on those individuals who experience it. Rising divorce rates can also affect those who did not experience divorce: living in a high-divorce (risk) society may itself affect behavior and well-being. Lower obstacles for leaving partnerships improve the chances of doing so and can empower partners – especially the weaker partner – to bargain for a better deal. Liberalization of divorce laws (the adoption of unilateral divorce) has decreased rates of female suicide, domestic violence, and women murdered by their spouses (Stevenson and Wolfers, 2006). These new laws gave partners, and women especially, the chance to improve their relationship or optionally leave a potentially disruptive (and even lethal) one. Facing the prospect of divorce can encourage partners to protect against its consequences, for example, by improving one's position in the labor market (Özcan and Breen, 2012) or by saving more (Gonzalez and Özcan, 2008). Children may also be affected. Those who grew up under a liberal divorce regime had weaker well-being outcomes according to various indicators (Gruber, 2004), and children exposed to peers with divorced parents have been found to fare poorer in school (Pong, Dronkers, and Hampden-Thomson, 2003).

Discussion

Divorce rates have increased among Western countries and beyond during the last decades, and these trends are considered key components of family change. Yet, these developments have been uneven and occurred at different times in different countries; furthermore, in many countries, divorce rates have stabilized and even decreased in more recent years. Divorce has become a part of the family institution and a realistic possibility, which spouses need to take into consideration when marrying. Though less stigmatized than before, divorce can still cause major distress and disruption to the adults and children who experience it. The possibility of experiencing divorce, and contact with people who have, can in themselves shape behaviors and experiences.

What will the future look like? As discussed earlier, the initial increases in divorce rates took many social scientists by surprise, as have the recent trends toward marital stability in some countries. Therefore, it is clearly difficult to foresee in which countries divorce rates will continue to increase and in which marriages will become more stable. The increases in unmarried cohabitation pose another challenge, as divorce rates have become an ever weaker indicator of couple relationship instability. Despite some indications that the retreat from marriage may have stalled in some of the countries where it started first (Ohlsson-Wijk, 2011), it seems unlikely that marriage will recover the same centrality in family life as it had in the previous decades.

Overall, there are considerable uncertainties in attempts to predict future rates of divorce and couple relationship instability. To the extent that the increases in divorce and instability reflected incompatibilities between prevailing family institutions and changing society, it is possible that divorce rates will stabilize and decline if social practices and institutions adapt to the changing circumstances. Such declines in divorce have occurred before. As briefly mentioned earlier, divorce in Japan was more common at the beginning of the twentieth century than some decades later, which was interpreted as reflecting adaptation of family life to broader societal changes (Goode, 1963). In the Western countries, an important candidate for change is gender roles. The changes in gender roles were to a large extent driven by changes in women's roles and activities, whereas men have been much slower in taking up what were previously female tasks. An increase in men's willingness to do their share in the household may thus lead to increased family stability, as this would fit better with the increasingly prevailing egalitarian ideals of partnerships and marriage as a union of two equals with their individual needs (cf. Esping-Andersen and Billari, 2012). However, even if rates of divorce and family instability were to decline, it is likely that the previous era of stable marriages and nuclear families will not return in the near future.

Can policies affect family instability and help adults and children who experience it adjust to it better? Earlier, it was pointed out that many of the findings regarding the effects of divorce legislation on divorce do not suggest that such laws have major long-term effects on divorce rates. Thus, a shift toward stricter regulation of marriages may not have the desired effect, especially since much of modern family life occurs outside the institution of marriage. How effective can policies be in helping adults and children adjust successfully to the divorce experience? Many traditional social policies, such as income transfers and policies aimed at helping (single) mothers find and keep employment, can be effective in combating the financial consequences of divorce, which are generally reduced in the generous welfare states such as the Nordic countries (Uunk, 2004). This can itself be an important policy goal and help divorced persons and their children adjust by decreasing the importance of one of the stressors which often follow divorce. However, they may not be enough, as many of the influences of divorce function through psychological stressors and their effects on parenting and other social relationships. To target these factors, counseling programs aimed at easing such stressors and helping with parenting can be effective (Pryor and Rodgers, 2001).

References

Albertini, M. and Garriga, A. (2011) The effect of divorce on parent-child contacts: evidence on two declining effect hypotheses. *European Societies*, 13 (2), 257–278.

Alwin, D.F. and McCammon, R.J. (2003) Generations, cohorts, and social change, in *Handbook of the Life Course* (eds. J.T. Mortimer and M.J. Shanahan), Springer, New York, pp. 23–50.

Amato, P.R. (2000) The consequences of divorce for adults and children. *Journal of Marriage and the Family*, 62 (6), 1269–1287.

Amato, P.R. (2001) Children of divorce in the 1990s: an update of the Amato-Keith (1991) meta-analysis. *Journal of Family Psychology*, 15 (3), 355–370.

Amato, P.R. (2010) Research on divorce: continuing developments and new trends. *Journal of Marriage and Family*, 72 (3), 650–666.

Amato, P.R. and Keith, B. (1991) Parental divorce and the well-being of children: a meta-analysis. *Psychological Bulletin*, 110 (1), 26–46.

Amato, P.R. and Booth, A. (1997) *A Generation at Risk: Growing Up in an Era of Family Upheaval*, Harvard University Press, Cambridge.

Amato, P.R. and Rogers, S.J. (1997) A longitudinal study of marital problems and subsequent divorce. *Journal of Marriage and the Family*, 59 (3), 612–624.

Amato, P.R. and Previti, D. (2003) People's reasons for divorcing: gender, social class, the life course, and adjustment. *Journal of Family Issues*, 24 (5), 602–626.

Amato, P.R. and Hohmann-Marriott, B. (2007) A comparison of high- and low-distress marriages that end in divorce. *Journal of Marriage and Family*, 69 (3), 621–638.

Amato, P.R. and James, S. (2010) Divorce in Europe and the United States: commonalities and differences across nations. *Family Science*, 1 (1), 2–13.

Amato, P.R., Loomis, L.S. and Booth, A. (1995) Parental divorce, marital conflict, and offspring well-being during early adulthood. *Social Forces*, 73 (3), 895–915.

Amato, P.R., Booth, A., Johnson, D.R. and Rogers, S.J. (2007) *Alone Together: How Marriage in America is Changing*, Harvard University Press, Cambridge.

Andersson, G. (2002) Dissolution of unions in Europe: a comparative overview. *Zeitschrift für Bevölkerungswissenschaft*, 27, 493–504.

Andersson, G. and Kolk, M. (2011) Trends in childbearing and nuptiality in Sweden: an update with data up to 2007. *Finnish Yearbook of Population Research*, XLVI, 21–29.

Andersson, G., Noack, T., Seierstad, A. and Weedon-Fekjær, H. (2006) The demographics of same-sex marriages in Norway and Sweden. *Demography*, 43 (1), 79–98.

Aquilino, W.S. (1994) Later life parental divorce and widowhood: impact on young adults' assessment of parent-child relations. *Journal of Marriage and Family*, 56 (4), 908–922.

Axinn, W.G. and Thornton, A. (1992) The relationship between cohabitation and divorce – selectivity or causal influence. *Demography*, 29 (3), 357–374.

Bauserman, R. (2002) Child adjustment in joint-custody versus sole-custody arrangements: a meta-analytic review. *Journal of Family Psychology*, 16 (1), 91–101.

Becker, G.S. (1981) *A Treatise on the Family*, Harvard University Press, Cambridge.

Becker, G.S., Landes, E.M. and Michael, R.T. (1977) An economic analysis of marital instability. *Journal of Political Economy*, 85 (6), 1141–1187.

Bjarnason, T. and Arnarsson, A.M. (2011) Joint physical custody and communication with parents: a cross-national study of children in 36 Western countries. *Journal of Comparative Family Studies*, 42, 871–890.

Boertien, D. (2012) Jackpot? Gender difference in the effects of lottery wins on separation. *Journal of Marriage and Family*, 74 (5), 1038–1053.

Booth, A. and Edwards, J.N. (1985) Age at marriage and marital instability. *Journal of Marriage and the Family*, 47 (1), 67–75.

Booth, A. and Amato, P.R. (2004) Parental predivorce relations and offspring postdivorce wellbeing. *Journal of Marriage and the Family*, 63 (1), 197–212.

Bradbury, T.N., Finchman, F.D. and Beach, S.R.H. (2000) Research on the nature and determinants of marital satisfaction: a decade in review. *Journal of Marriage and Family*, 62 (4), 964–980.

Brines, J. and Joyner, K. (1999) The ties that bind: principles of cohesion in cohabitation and marriage. *American Sociological Review*, 64 (3), 333–355.

Bygren, M., Gähler, M. and Nermo, M. (2004) Familj och arbete – vardagsliv i förändring, in *Familj och Arbete – Vardagsliv i Förändring* (eds. M. Bygren, M. Gähler and M. Nermo), SNS Förlag, Stockholm, pp. 11–55.

Callens, M. and Croux, C. (2009) Poverty dynamics in Europe: a multilevel recurrent discrete-time hazard analysis. *International Sociology*, 24 (3), 368–396.

Castro Martin, T. and Bumpass, L.L. (1989) Recent trends in marital disruption. *Demography*, 26 (1), 37–51.

Cherlin, A.J. (1992) *Marriage, Divorce, Remarriage*, 2nd edn, Harvard University Press, Cambridge.

Cherlin, A.J. (1999) Going to extremes: family change, children's well-being, and social science. *Demography*, 36 (4), 421–428.

Cherlin, A.J. (2009) *The Marriage-Go-Round. The State of Marriage and Family in America Today*, Knopf, New York.

Cherlin, A.J., Furstenberg, F.F., Jr., Chase-Lindsale, L. *et al.* (1991) Longitudinal studies of the effects of divorce on children in Great Britain and the United States. *Science*, 525 (5011), 1386–1389.

Chong, A. and La Ferrera, E. (2009) Television and divorce: evidence from Brazilian novelas. *Journal of the European Economic Association*, 7 (2–3), 458–468.

Coale, A. (1973) The demographic transition reconsidered, in *International Population Conference: Liége 1973 – Congres International de la Population: Liége 1973*, vol. 1, IUSSP, Liége.

Cooke, L.P. (2006) "Doing" gender in context: household bargaining and the risk of divorce in Germany and the United States. *American Journal of Sociology*, 112 (2), 442–472.

Cooke, L.P., with Erola, J., Evertsson, M. *et al.* (forthcoming) Labor and love: wives' employment and divorce risk in its sociopolitical context. *Social Politics*

Coontz, S. (2005) *A History of Marriage: From Obedience to Intimacy, or How Love Conquered Marriage*, Viking, New York.

De Graaf, P.M. and Kalmijn, M. (2006) Divorce motives in a period of rising divorce: evidence from a Dutch life-history survey. *Journal of Family Issues*, 27 (4), 483–505.

DiPrete, T.A. and McManus, P.A. (2000) Family change, employment transitions, and the welfare state: household income dynamics in the United States and Germany. *American Sociological Review*, 65 (3), 343–370.

Dribe, M. and Lundh, C. (2012) Intermarriage, value context and union dissolution: Sweden 1990–2005. *European Journal of Population*, 28, 139–158.

Dronkers, J. (1999) The effects of parental conflicts and divorce on the well-being of pupils in Dutch secondary education. *European Sociological Review*, 15 (2), 195–212.

Dronkers, J. and Härkönen, J. (2008) The intergenerational transmission of divorce in cross-national perspective: results from Fertility and Families Surveys. *Population Studies*, 62 (3), 273–288.

Ely, M., Richards, M., Wadsworth, M. and Elliott, B.J. (1999) Secular changes in the association of parental divorce and children's educational attainment – evidence from three British cohorts. *Journal of Social Policy*, 28 (3), 437–455.

England, P.G.F. (1986) *Households, Employment and Gender: A Social, Economic and Demographic View*, Aldine, Hawthorne.

Esping-Andersen, G. and Billari, F. (2012) Demographic theory revisited. Working paper, Pompeu Fabra University and University of Oxford.

Gähler, M. (1998) *Life After Divorce: Economic, Social and Psychological Well-Being Among Swedish Adults and Children Following Family Dissolution*. Swedish Institute for Social Research Reports No 32, Swedish Institute for Social Research, Stockholm.

Garriga, A. and Härkönen, J. (2009) The Effects of Marital Instability on Children's Well-Being and Intergenerational Relations. EQUALSOC state-of-the-art report. Universitat Pompeu Fabra and Stockholm University.

Gelissen, J. (2003) Cross-national differences in public consent to divorce: Effects of cultural, structural, and compositional factors, in *The Cultural Diversity of European Unity: Findings, Explanations and Reflections from the European Values Study* (eds. W.A. Arts, J.A.P. Hagenaars and L.C.J.M. Halman), Brill, Leiden, pp. 24–58.

Goldstein, J. (1999) The leveling of divorce in the United States. *Demography*, 36 (3), 409–414.

González, L. and Özcan, B. (2008) The risk of divorce and household savings behavior. Discussion paper no. 3726, IZA, Bonn.

González, L. and Viitanen, T. (2009) The effect of divorce laws on divorce rates in Europe. *European Economic Review*, 53 (2), 127–138.

Goode, W.J. (1962) Marital satisfaction and instability. A cross-cultural class analysis of divorce rates, in *Class, Status, and Power. Social Stratification in Comparative Perspective* (eds. R. Bendix and S.M. Lipset), The Free Press, New York, pp. 377–383.

Goode, W.J. (1963) *World Revolution and Family Patterns*, Free Press, New York.

Gruber, J. (2004) Is making divorce easier bad for children? The long-run implications of unilateral divorce. *Journal of Labor Economics*, 22 (4), 799–833.

Hawkins, D.N. and Booth, A. (2005) Unhappily ever after: effects of long-term, low-quality marriages on well-being. *Social Forces*, 84 (1), 451–471.

Heaton, T.B. (2002) Factors contributing to increasing marital stability in the United States. *Journal of Family Issues*, 23 (3), 392–409.

Heuveline, P. and Timberlake, J.M. (2004) The role of cohabitation in family formation: the United States in comparative perspective. *Journal of Marriage and Family*, 66 (5), 1214–1230.

Hewitt, B. (2009) Which spouse initiates marital separation when there are children involved? *Journal of Marriage and the Family*, 71 (2), 362–372.

Härkönen, J. and Dronkers, J. (2006) Stability and change in the educational gradients of divorce: a comparison of 17 countries. *European Sociological Review*, 22 (5), 501–517.

Jalovaara, M. (2012) Socioeconomic resources and first-union formation in Finland, cohorts born 1969–81. *Population Studies*, 66 (1), 69–85.

Kalmijn, M. (2007) Explaining cross-national differences in marriage, divorce, and cohabitation in Europe. *Population Studies*, 61 (3), 243–263.

Kalmijn, M. (2010) Country differences in the effects of divorce on well-being: the role of norms, support, and selectivity. *European Sociological Review*, 26 (4), 475–490.

Kalmijn, M. (2011) Racial differences in the effects of parental divorce and separation on children: generalizing the evidence to a European case. *Social Science Research*, 39 (5), 845–856.

Kalmijn, M. and Monden, C.W.S. (2006) Are the negative effects of divorce on well-being dependent on marital quality? *Journal of Marriage and Family*, 68 (5), 1197–1213.

Kalmijn, M. and Poortman, A.-R. (2006) His or her divorce? The gendered nature of divorce and its determinants. *European Sociological Review*, 22 (2), 201–214.

Kim, H.S. (2011) Consequences of parental divorce for child development. *American Sociological Review*, 76 (3), 487–511.

Kitson, G.C. and Raschke, H.J. (1981) Divorce research: what we know; what we need to know. *Journal of Divorce*, 4 (3), 1–37.

Landale, N.S. and Ogena, N.B. (1995) Migration and union dissolution among Puerto-Rican women. *International Migration Review*, 29 (3), 671–692.

Lau, C.Q. (2012) The stability of same-sex cohabitation, different-sex cohabitation, and same-sex marriage. *Journal of Marriage and Family*, 74 (5), 973–988.

Lesthaeghe, R. (1995) The second demographic transition in Western countries: an interpretation, in *Gender and Family Change in Industrialized Countries* (eds. K.O. Mason and A.-M. Jensen), Clarendon Press, Oxford, pp. 17–62.

Levinger, G. (1976) A social psychological perspective on marital dissolution. *Journal of Social Issues*, 32 (1), 21–47.

Lyngstad, T.H. and Jalovaara, M. (2010) A review of the antecedents of union dissolution. *Demographic Research*, 23, 255–292.

Martin, S.P. (2006) Trends in marital dissolution by women's education in the United States. *Demographic Research*, 15, 537–560.

Mastekaasa, A. (1994) Psychological well-being and marital dissolution. *Journal of Family Issues*, 15 (2), 208–228.

McLanahan, S.S. and Sandefur, G. (1994) *Growing Up with a Single Parent: What Hurts, What Helps?* Harvard University Press, Cambridge.

McManus, P.A. and DiPrete, T.A. (2001) Losers and winners: the financial consequences of separation for men. *American Sociological Review*, 66 (2), 246–268.

Mignot, J.-F. (2009) *Formation et dissolution des couples en France dans la seconde moitié du XXe siècle. Une évaluation empirique du pouvoir explicatif de la théorie du choix rationnel*, Sciences Po, Paris.

Morgan, S.P., Lye, D.N. and Condran, G.A. (1988) Sons, daughters and the risk of marital disruption. *American Journal of Sociology*, 94 (1), 110–129.

National Center for Health Statistics (various years) *Marriages and Divorces*, Centers for Disease Control and Prevention, Washington, D.C.

Ohlsson-Wijk, S. (2011) Sweden's marriage revival: an analysis of the new-millennium switch from long-term decline to increasing popularity. *Population Studies*, 65 (2), 183–200.

Oppenheimer, V.K. (1997) Women's employment and the gain to marriage: the specialization and trading model. *Annual Review of Sociology*, 23, 431–453.

Özcan, B. and Breen, R. (2012) Marital instability and female labor supply. *Annual Review of Sociology*, 38, 463–481.

Pavalko, E.K. and Elder, G.H., Jr. (1990) World War II and divorce: a life-course perspective. *American Journal of Sociology*, 95 (5), 1213–1234.

Pong, S.-L., Dronkers, J. and Hampden-Thompson, G. (2003) Family policies and children's school achievement in single- versus two-parent families. *Journal of Marriage and the Family*, 65 (3), 681–699.

Poortman, A.-R. and Lyngstad, T.H. (2007) Dissolution risks in first and higher order marital and cohabiting unions. *Social Science Research*, 36 (4), 1431–1446.

Preston, S.H. and McDonald, J. (1979) The incidence of divorce within cohorts of American marriages contracted since the Civil War. *Demography*, 16 (1), 1–25.

Pryor, J., Rodgers, B. (2001) *Children in Changing Families: Life After Parental Separation*, Blackwell, Oxford.

Qureshi, K., Charsley, K. and Shaw, A. (2012) Marital instability among British Pakistanis: transnationalities, conjugalities, and Islam. *Ethnic and Racial Studies*, 35, 1–19.

Raley, R.K. and Bumpass, L. (2003) The topography of the divorce plateau: levels and trends in union stability in the United States after 1980. *Demographic Research*, 8, 245–260.

Ruggles, S. (1997) The rise of divorce and separation in the United States. *Demography*, 34 (4), 455–466.

Sandström, G. (2012) *Ready, Willing, and Able: The Divorce Transition in Sweden 1915–1974.* Report No. 32 from the Demographic Database, Umeå University, Umeå.

Sanz-de-Galdeano, A. and Vuri, D. (2007) Parental divorce and students' performance: evidence from longitudinal data. *Oxford Bulletin of Economics and Statistics*, 69 (3), 321–338.

Sayer, L.C. and Bianchi, S.M. (2000) Women's economic independence and the probability of divorce: a review and re-examination. *Journal of Family Issues*, 21, 906–943.

Sayer, L.C., England, P., Allison, P. and Kangas, N. (2011) She left, he left: how employment and satisfaction affect men's and women's decisions to leave marriages. *American Journal of Sociology*, 116 (6), 1982–2018.

Schoen, R. and Canudas-Romo, V. (2006) Timing effects on divorce: 20th century experience in the United States. *Journal of Marriage and Family*, 68 (3), 749–758.

South, S.J. and Lloyd, K.M. (1995) Spousal alternatives and marital dissolution. *American Sociological Review*, 60 (1), 21–35.

Stanley, S.M., Rhoades, G.K. and Markman, H.J. (2006) Sliding versus deciding: inertia and the premarital cohabitation effect. *Family Relations*, 55 (4), 499–509.

Stevenson, B. and Wolfers, J. (2006) Bargaining in the shadow of divorce: divorce laws and family distress. *Quarterly Journal of Economics*, 121, 267–288.

Stevenson, B. and Wolfers, J. (2007) Marriage and divorce: changes and their driving forces. *Journal of Economic Perspectives*, 21 (2), 27–52.

Sweeney, M. (2010) Remarriage and stepfamilies: strategic sites for family scholarship in the 21st century. *Journal of Marriage and Family*, 72 (3), 667–684.

Teachman, J.D. (2008) Complex life course patterns and the risk of divorce in second marriages. *Journal of Marriage and the Family*, 70 (2), 294–305.

Thomson, E. and Collella, U. (1992) Cohabitation and marital stability—quality or commitment. *Journal of Marriage and the Family*, 54 (2), 259–267.

Thomson, E., Hanson, T.L. and McLanahan, S.S. (1994) Family structure and child well-being: economic resources vs. parental behaviors. *Social Forces*, 73 (1), 221–242.

Thornton, A. and Rodgers, W.L. (1987) The influence of individual and historical time on marital dissolution. *Demography*, 24 (1), 1–22.

Thornton, A. and Young-De Marco, L. (2001) Four decades of trends in attitudes toward family issues in the United States: the 1960s through the 1990s. *Journal of Marriage and the Family*, 63 (4), 1009–1037.

Twenge, J.M., Campbell, W.K. and Foster, C.A. (2004) Parenthood and marital satisfaction: a meta-analytic review. *Journal of Marriage and the Family*, 65 (3), 574–583.

Umberson, D., Williams, K., Powers, D.A. *et al.* (2005) As good as it gets? A life course perspective on marital quality. *Social Forces*, 84, 493–511.

United Nations (various years) *Demographic Yearbook*, United Nations, New York.

Uunk, W. (2004) The economic consequences of divorce for women in the European Union: the impact of welfare state arrangements. *European Journal of Population*, 20 (3), 251–285.

Wagner, M. and Weiß, B. (2006) On the variation in divorce risks in Europe: findings from a meta-analysis of European longitudinal studies. *European Sociological Review*, 22 (5), 483–500.

Wang, H. and Amato, P.R. (2004) Predictors of divorce adjustment: stressors, resources, and definitions. *Journal of Marriage and the Family*, 62 (3), 655–668.

Wolfers, J. (2006) Did unilateral divorce raise divorce rates? A reconciliation and new results. *American Economic Review*, 96 (5), 1802–1820.

Wolfinger, N.H. (2005) *Understanding the Divorce Cycle: The Children of Divorce in Their Own Marriages*, Harvard University Press, Cambridge.

16

Partner Violence in World Perspective

EMILY M. DOUGLAS, DENISE A. HINES AND
MURRAY A. STRAUS

Defining and Measuring Partner Violence

Definitions

The World Health Organization (WHO) (WHO, 2010) draws on work by Heise and Garcia-Moreno (2002) to define PV as acts within an intimate relationship that cause physical, sexual, or psychological harm; this could include physical aggression, sexual coercion, psychological abuse, and controlling behavior. The US Centers for Disease Control and Prevention (n.d.) takes their definition of PV from the work of Saltzman, Holden, and Holahan (2005) and describes four types of PV: (i) physical violence, the intentional use of force that could cause injury or harm; (ii) sexual violence, which involves using physical force to engage in sexual acts against a person's will, attempting/completing sexual acts without the victims comprehension or consent to participation, or abusive sexual acts; (iii) threats of physical or sexual violence; and (iv) emotional/psychological violence, which includes humiliating, embarrassing, or controlling the victim.

Measuring partner violence

The most widely used tool to measure and assess PV is the *Conflict Tactics Scale (CTS)*, which was developed in the 1970s and is a behavioral checklist that asks research participants to indicate the methods or *tactics* that they have used to resolve a difference with an intimate partner – dating, married, or otherwise (Straus, 1979). A revised version of the CTS was developed in the 1990s (Straus *et al.*, 1996), which continues to be used today. The CTS has been used in hundreds of studies, translated into dozens of languages (Straus, 2005), and administered on diverse populations (Straus, 2004, 2008a; Anderson and Leigh, 2010); at one point, it was estimated that

The Wiley Blackwell Companion to the Sociology of Families, First Edition.
Edited by Judith Treas, Jacqueline Scott, and Martin Richards.
© 2014 John Wiley & Sons Ltd. Published 2017 by John Wiley & Sons Ltd.

the CTS was featured in six new family violence publications each month (Straus, 2005). The CTS that is used today measures five different tactics: (i) negotiation, (ii) psychological aggression (minor and severe), (iii) physical assault (minor and severe), (iv) physical injury (minor and severe), and (v) sexual coercion. Participants rate the extent to which they perpetrated or sustained any of the behaviors measured in the CTS within a specified time period, usually 12 months or lifetime experiences. Examples of behaviors that are measured include (i) negotiation – listening to a partner's side of the story; (ii) psychological aggression – threatening to hurt a loved one or calling a partner names; (iii) physical assault – hitting/slapping a partner or beating up a partner; (iv) physical injury – leaving a small bruise or cut on a partner or needing medical attention; and (v) sexual coercion – using force or threats to make partner have sex (Straus *et al.*, 1996).

Prevalence

The United States leads the world on the study of PV; however, well over 200 studies have been conducted on PV in countries outside the United States. The majority of these studies assess only female rather than male victimization (Esquivel-Santovena, Lambert, and Hamel, 2013). We focus on the prevalence rates established from two relatively recent, major, worldwide studies of PV: (i) WHO's Multi-Country Study on Women's Health and Domestic Violence Against Women, a 10-country study on PV against women (WHO, 2005a), and (ii) the International Dating Violence Study (IDVS), a 32-nation study of primarily heterosexual college student dating relationships, the only large-scale, cross-national study that assessed both men and women as potential perpetrators and victims of PV (Straus, 2008a, b). In addition, we discuss a major literature review on PV worldwide (Esquivel-Santovena, Lambert, and Hamel, 2013) to highlight key issues in assessing prevalence.

   WHO collected data from 24,000 women in 10 countries with varied geographical, cultural, and regional setting (Bangladesh, Brazil, Ethiopia, Japan, Peru, Namibia, Samoa, Serbia and Montenegro, Thailand, and the United Republic of Tanzania). The underlying theoretical perspective guiding this study was that "violence against women is both a consequence and a cause of gender inequality" (WHO, 2005a, p. viii). Thus, only victimization of women was assessed. They found that the prevalence of lifetime physical PV ranged from a low of 13% in Japan to a high of 61% in Peru, with most cites ranging from 23% to 49%. For severe PV victimization (e.g., hit with a fist, kicked, dragged, choked, burned, having a weapon used against her), the prevalence ranged from 4% in Japan to 49% in Peru. For sexual PV, lifetime prevalence ranged from 6% in Japan and Serbia to 59% in Ethiopia, with most cites falling between 10% and 50%. Finally, for emotionally abusive or controlling acts (e.g., being insulted/made to feel bad about oneself, humiliated, intimidated, threatened, restricting access to family or friends), between 20% and 75% of women experienced one or more of these in the previous year (WHO, 2005a).

   The WHO study examined only female victimization; the IDVS, however, assessed perpetration and victimization of both men and women. This is important because in both the United States (Langhinrichsen-Rohling *et al.*, 2012) and other nations (Esquivel-Santovena, Lambert, and Hamel, 2013), bidirectional PV, when both partners are violence with each other, is the dominant pattern. Population-based studies show that PV is predominantly bidirectional in 15 countries (China, Hong Kong, Philippines, Thailand, Botswana, Namibia, Swaziland, Zimbabwe, Barbados, Brazil, Jamaica, Trinidad and Tobago, Portugal, the Ukraine, and the United States); in 11 countries, female victimization/male perpetration is the dominant pattern (Esquivel-Santovena, Lambert, and Hamel, 2013).

The IDVS represents over 136,000 university students in 32 nations; rates of any physical PV perpetration for men ranged from a low of 10% in Singapore to a high of 95.5% in Iran; for women, perpetration rates ranged from 15.8% in Malta to 71.4% in Iran. For severe PV perpetration, rates for men ranged from 0% in Malta and Singapore to 42.9% in South Africa; for women, perpetration rates ranged from 2% in Sweden to 25.7% in the Netherlands (Straus, 2008a). Additionally, at least 50% or more of the violent couples in 31 of the 32 nations examined showed some level of bidirectionality. Moreover, if just severe physical PV is assessed, data from 22 nations show that at least half of the severely violent couples were bidirectionally violent.

Contextual and Causal Mechanisms

There are several major theoretical perspectives that guide the field's understanding of PV. We review the most dominant of these theories here, but this discussion is not exhaustive of all theoretical perspectives.

Patriarchy theory

Patriarchy theory is the dominant perspective on PV, both within Western nations (Dutton and Corvo, 2006) and around the world (WHO, 2005b). Patriarchal theorists hold that *the* cause of PV is the gendered structure of world societies. In all nations of the world, men have economic, political, social, and occupational power over women, and this power structure is reflected in heterosexual intimate relationships. This theory purports that men strategically use violence to maintain their dominant status over women (Dobash and Dobash, 1979). WHO (2005b) argues that "the abuse of women and girls, regardless of where it occurs, should be considered as 'gender-based violence,' as it largely stems from women's subordinate status in society with regard to men" (p. 11).

There is limited empirical support for this theoretical perspective. A meta-analysis of studies addressing PV against women and the male partner's patriarchal ideology (Sugarman and Frankel, 1996) provided little support for patriarchal theory. A more recent meta-analysis (Stith *et al.*, 2004) found that traditional sex role ideology and PV against women were moderately associated. A cross-national literature review by WHO (2010) showed that "traditional gender norms and social norms supportive of violence" was not a consistent or strong predictor of PV against women. Moreover, there is an abundance of evidence that contradicts patriarchy theory: the consistent findings that women physically assault their partners at rates comparable to men (Archer, 2000) – including the large majority of nations assessed in the IDVS (Straus, 2008a); and, rates of PV in gay and lesbian couples are at least as high as in heterosexual couples (Hines, Malley-Morrison, and Dutton, 2013).

The IDVS assessed both men and women as potential PV perpetrators and victims; thus, it provides a more nuanced understanding of how dominance, subordination, and attitudes toward women and men are related to PV on a world-wide level. For example, Straus (2008a) found that the predominant pattern of physical PV in all nations was bidirectional; the next most common form of PV was female-only perpetrated. According to the participants' self-reports, in 24 of 32 nations, women were more dominant on average than men within their romantic relationships, with little gender difference overall in dominance. Furthermore, dominance *by either partner* was associated with an increased probability of bidi-rectional PV, female-only PV, and male-only PV. Also using the IDVS, Hines (2007a) found that rates of sexual PV by intimate partners within nations were influenced by both the status of women in that nation (a composite measure of women's political, educational, and workforce participation) and general levels of hostility toward members of the opposite sex, providing little evidence to support the patri-archy theory.

Intergenerational transmission

One of the most consistent findings in the research is that PV passes through the generations; children who are exposed to aggression in their families of origin are more likely to perpetrate or be victimized by aggression in their relationships as adults than children who are never exposed to familial aggression (Stith *et al.*, 2000; Ehrensaft *et al.*, 2003). This has been supported by a meta-analysis of 39 studies, which found a significant association between both the witnessing of interparental aggression and the experience of child abuse, with PV in adulthood among both genders in Western nations (Stith *et al.*, 2000). WHO (2005a) reports on studies from other world regions, stating that exposure to violence during childhood increases men's perpetration of PV by – three to four times (Gil-González *et al.*, 2008); exposure to childhood sexual abuse triples men's perpe-tration of sexual violence toward women (Jespersen, Lalumiere, and Seto, 2009); and childhood exposure to violence increases women's victimization from both PV and sexual violence (Söchting, Fairbrother, and Koch, 2004; Martin, Taft, and Resick, 2007; Vung and Krantz, 2009). Further, using the IDVS data, researchers found that violence socialization in childhood was related to both victimization and perpetration of aggression in adulthood for both men and women (Douglas and Straus, 2006; Hines, 2007b; Gamez-Guadix, Straus, and Hershberger, in press).

The most often cited theory to explain the intergenerational transmission of PV is social learning theory (Bandura, 1979), which posits that when children witness individuals in their family rewarded for using aggression, they learn to resolve frustrations and conflicts with family members through the use of their own aggression (Eron, 1997). There is some evidence to support this theory, but not necessarily as the sole *cause* of the intergenerational transmission of IPV (Straus and Yodanis, 1996). Instead, attachment theorists claim that aggression witnessed in childhood may create an avoidant–ambivalent bonding style that persists into adulthood romantic relationships and leads to overly demanding and angry behavior with their partners (Dutton, 2007). Bowlby (1988) states that the attachment bond formed in infancy becomes the internal working model for all later significant relationships. Empirical studies show that individuals who are most at risk for expressing anger are those who are anxiously attached to their partners; these individuals usually experienced violence in their families of origin (Dutton, 2007). Attachment theory has been well established in Western nations, but there is debate about the applicability of this theory in other cultures (van Ijzendoorn and Sagi-Schwartz, 2008; Jin *et al.*, 2012). Nevertheless, multinational data from the IDVS shows that higher rates of neglect during childhood are related to physical PV perpetration against dating partners (Straus and Savage, 2005).

Alcohol abuse

A consistent predictor of PV is alcohol abuse. This link has been primarily demonstrated among samples in the United States, including male batterers (Fals-Stewart, 2003), community samples of men (Leonard, 1993), and population-based samples (Caetano, Schafer, and Cunradi, 2001). When male alcoholics remit from using alcohol through the administration of empirically based alcohol treatment programs, their rates of PV perpetration decrease significantly (O'Farrell *et al.*, 2003). This finding demonstrates the importance of screening for and treating alcoholism in male batterers.

Alcohol abuse has been shown to predict PV perpetration on a multinational level as well. WHO (2010) reports that alcohol use is strongly associated with the perpetration of PV, including low- and middle-income countries. Overall, these studies show that the abuse of alcohol is associated with a 1.6–4.8 times greater likelihood of men perpetrating PV. The IDVS showed that across nations, there are no gender differences in the prediction of PV perpetration from alcohol abuse (Hines and Straus, 2007), showing that alcohol abuse equally predicts PV perpetration for both men and women.

Personality dysfunction

There is also empirical support for the relationship between PV perpetration and personality disorders. For example, Dutton *et al.* (1994) found that several personality problems – borderline personality, antisocial personality, aggressive-sadistic personality, and passive-aggressive personality – are related to PV perpetration by men. It is argued that men with such mental health concerns have a *fearful-angry* attachment style, which results in them lashing out violently toward their female partners during confrontations and perceived separations. The relationship between attachment, personality dysfunction, and PV has been confirmed by others as well (Holtzworth-Munroe and Stuart, 1994).

WHO (2010) also identified antisocial personality as a contributor of male perpetration of both sexual violence and PV. It cites studies (two from high and one from middle-income countries) that provide support for this association. The IDVS provides evidence of associations between both antisocial personality (Hines and Straus, 2007) and borderline personality (Hines, 2008) with PV perpetration across all sites with similar strength of correlations for men and women.

Ecological model

Increasingly, researchers are using an ecological model to understand PV (Dutton, 1985; Gelles, 1998; Hines and Malley-Morrison, 2005). In this perspective, PV researchers tend to focus on four levels of influences, all of which have their roots in Bronfenbrenner's (1979) work: (i) the individual's unique bio-psycho-social characteristics that exist even before birth and that individuals bring to every interaction, (ii) the *microsystem*, which consists of the individual's immediate settings (e.g., the home), (iii) the *exosystem*, which includes the larger neighborhood, mass media, and state agencies, and (iv) the *macrosystem*, which consists of broad cultural factors.

An ecological perspective conveys the notion that in order to understand how someone may commit PV, we need to understand the genetic endowments of that individual, the microsystem in which he/she was raised, the microsystem in which he/she is currently embedded, characteristics of the neighborhood within which he/she functions (including the availability of social services and the criminal justice system), and the larger society that either condones or condemns PV (Hines, Malley-Morrison, and Dutton, 2013). WHO (2010) also promotes an ecological model; however, it maintains its focus on female victims of male-perpetrated violence, and therefore, only focuses on elements of the patriarchal perspective at each level of the model (WHO, 2005b).

Correlates of and Potential Impact of Partner Violence

Since research on family violence was developed in the early 1970s (Steinmetz and Straus, 1974; Straus, 1976; Carroll, 1977; Steinmetz, 1977), researchers have documented a range of negative factors that are correlates of, or the potential consequence of, PV – including mental and physical health problems of victims, the well-being of children who witness PV, as well as the costs to society.

Mental health concerns of victims

Community studies of female victims of PV show that they have poorer mental health than nonvictims (Coker *et al.*, 2000; Weinbaum *et al.*, 2001), and are at an increased risk for panic, depression, anxiety, sleep problems, posttraumatic stress disorder, and suicidal ideation (Leserman *et al.*, 1998; Golding, 1999; Hathaway *et al.*, 2000). They are also more likely to abuse alcohol and illegal and prescription drugs (Golding, 1999; Black and Breiding, 2008). Most of this research has been conducted on populations in Western nations, but WHO (2010) cites similar problems for women throughout the world; the research also references a lack of fertility control and the increased risk of HIV/AIDS to women who experience sexual assault at the hands of their male partners.

A small, but growing, body of research concerning males' experiences with PV victimization and mental health concerns; results are similar to what has been found for females. Males from community samples who have experienced PV are more at risk for posttraumatic stress symptoms/disorder, alcohol abuse, substance abuse, depression, and anxiety (WHO, 2005a; Hines, 2007a; Kaura and Lohman, 2007;

Romito and Grassi, 2007; Sabina and Straus, 2008; Hines and Douglas, 2011b; Hines and Douglas, 2012). Results from the IDVS found that male victims across nations experience suicidal ideation, and self-harm (Chan *et al.*, 2008).

Some research has also compared the outcomes of men and women who have experienced PV victimization. US-based research has found that both women and men who experience physical PV report higher levels of psychological distress (Fortin *et al.*, 2012), depressive symptoms, chronic mental illness, and illegal and prescription drug abuse (Coker *et al.*, 2002; Carbone-Lopez, Kruttschnitt, and MacMillan, 2006). Further, research has shown that after controlling for lifetime exposure to aggression, there were no gender differences in the influence of PV on these mental health outcomes (Pimlott-Kubiak and Cortina, 2003). Similar results were found among a cohort study in New Zealand (Fergusson, Horwood, and Ridder, 2005). The IDVS has found that across the globe, men and women do not always have parallel correlates of victimization and mental health concerns, but that in general, victimization raises the likelihood of mental health concerns for all men and women (Chan *et al.*, 2007; Sabina and Straus, 2008).

As a cautionary note, we remind readers that the research which has been conducted on health and mental health problems associated with PV victimization has been correlational in nature and has not established causal links between PV victimization and health concerns. It is possible that individuals who have poorer mental health are more likely to become engaged in violent relationships.

Children's exposure to PV

The study of children's exposure to PV is a developing field. Most research focuses on child witnesses of male-to-female PV (Levendosky *et al.*, 2003, 2006; Stover, Horn, and Lieberman, 2006; Heugten and Wilson, 2008; Spilsbury *et al.*, 2008) using small program or community-based samples in Western nations (Lang and Stover, 2008; Owen *et al.*, 2009), although a small body of research exists on non-Western nations/ cultures (Speizer, 2010; Vameghi *et al.*, 2010; Chan, 2011). Exposure to PV between one's parents can include a wide range of behaviors, such as hearing PV, seeing it, calling for emergency services, being caught in the middle, seeing the destruction/injuries resulting from PV, or becoming a victim of PV (Fantuzzo, Mohr, and Noone, 2000; Martiny, 2006). Research has shown that being exposed to PV between parents can have a direct effect on children's mental health (Sternberg *et al.*, 2006), including externalizing problems such as disobedience, defiance, and aggressiveness (Kalil, 2003), and, internalizing problems such as depression, anxiety, (Clements, Oxtoby, and Ogle, 2008; Heugten and Wilson, 2008), and posttraumatic stress symptoms. (Kilpatrick and Williams, 1998; Lang and Stover, 2008). Other research has documented physical health problems in child witnesses, including maladaptive brain development (Gunnar and Barr, 1998), and increased heart rates and cortisol levels, which place children at risk for memory and attention problems (Saltzman, Holden, and Holahan, 2005). Differences in children's responses to witnessing PV based on parental gender are inconclusive (Stover, Horn, and Lieberman, 2006; Clements, Oxtoby, and Ogle, 2008), but suggest that child witnesses of female-to-male PV may be at an increased risk for emotional and behavioral problems (Leisring, Dowd, and Rosenbaum, 2002) and be more aggressive toward romantic partners and peers in adolescence (Moretti *et al.*, 2006).

Services for Victims

Sources of help

Since the 1970s, a number of different types of services have been developed to help victims of PV (Higgins, 1978). Today, there are a number of ways in which victims seek help, including domestic violence shelters (sometimes called *battered women's shelters*) (Bowker and Maurer, 1985) and hotlines/helplines specializing in domestic violence issues and concerns; these are common in most countries and can be one of the first *low-cost* steps taken to address PV (Mršević and Hughes, 1997; Bennett *et al.*, 2004; Sun-Hee Park, 2005; Hines, Brown, and Dunning, 2007). The passage of the 1994 Violence Against Women Act in the United States helped to formally criminalize domestic violence (Crais, 2005), which means that victims in the United States commonly seek help from law enforcement officers (Buzawa and Austin, 1993; Shannon *et al.*, 2006; Johnson, 2007), as they do in other countries (Stanko, 2000). Victims also often contact attorneys for advice on how to leave a violent relationship, how to document the abuse, and how to protect children in the process (Bowker, 1983; Erez and King, 2000; Stanko, 2000). PV victims seek help from health professionals, such as in emergency rooms, mental health professionals (Leone, Johnson, and Cohan, 2007; McNamara, Tamanini, and Pelletier-Walker, 2008), and members of the clergy (El-Khoury *et al.*, 2004). Victims also use more informal sources of support, such as on the Internet (Web sites for information about PV, forums, LISTSERV, e-mail groups, etc.) (Douglas and Hines, 2011), and seek assistance from family and friends (Leone, Johnson, and Cohan, 2007; Douglas and Hines, 2011). WHO (2005a) states that many women tell family and friends about their experiences, but they rarely seek help from agencies, police, or other providers.

Help-seeking experiences

Women in Western nations have relatively positive experiences when seeking help for PV victimization. A study of women who sought services from a domestic violence shelter found that 89% of the clients believed that they were helped by the services that they received and a high proportion reported that they felt better because of these services (McNamara, Tamanini, and Pelletier-Walker, 2008). These findings are similar to a study which examined women's impressions of a hospital-based DV support group (Norton and Schauer, 1997). These findings are consistent with other literature which states that women are often very satisfied with the services that they received for PV (Bowker and Maurer, 1985; Molina *et al.*, 2009). Battered women also report being satisfied with the assistance that they receive from the police. One study of female PV victims indicated that the female victims found the police to be very helpful and the majority would contact the police again for assistance (Apsler, Cummins, and Carl, 2003). WHO (2010) reports that many similar efforts have or are being tried in less developed countries, but that women do not seek help very often. There are multiple barriers to seeking help for PV victimization, including cultural attitudes, not knowing where to obtain help, economic constraints, personal and family shame, and being revictimized when seeking help (Mason, 2009; Shen, 2011; Ogunsiji *et al.*, 2012).

Men in Western nations report more difficulty in obtaining services. One study of men's help-seeking experiences found that family and friends were overwhelmingly the most helpful resource to them in coping with their PV victimization (Douglas and Hines, 2011). Mental health and medical professionals were rated as being the most helpful formal resources; they took the male victims seriously and inquired about the origin of the men's injuries. The resources providing the least support to men were those at the core of the DV service system: DV agencies, DV hotlines, and the police. Many men reported being turned away. This research is consistent with Cook (2009) who found that some DV hotline workers say that they only help women, infer/state that the men must be the actual instigators of the violence, ridicule them, or refer them to batterers' programs. Some men report that when they call the police they sometimes fail to respond, ridicule them, or the men are incorrectly arrested as the primary aggressor. Other research has found that male victims do not feel that the police take their concerns seriously and are significantly less satisfied with the police response than female victims of PV (Buzawa and Austin, 1993). Other populations in Western nations which cite difficulty in obtaining assistance include gay men, lesbians, and older women; these populations report that services are not available for them or are not tailored to meet their specific needs (Renzetti, 1989; Donnelly, Cook, and Wilson, 1999; McClennen, Summers, and Vaughan, 2002; Beaulaurier et al., 2007). This research is consistent with the analyses of US DV agencies, which report being less able to support older men and women, adolescents, and gays and lesbians (Hines and Douglas, 2011a).

Costs to society

A small body of research has estimated the costs to society (other than children) associated with PV, such as within the health care, social service, and criminal justice systems (Max et al., 2004; Rivara et al., 2007; Chan and Cho, 2010; Fishman et al., 2010; Logan, Walker, and Hoyt, 2012). Several studies have demonstrated the increased costs within the health-care system to individuals, health insurance companies, government-sponsored insurance, and health-care facilities. For example, the utilization and cost of US women who experience PV victimization is 1.6–2.3 times higher than women who do not experience PV victimization (Ulrich et al., 2003). One study estimated these costs to be $1700 higher over a 3-year period of time, per individual female victim (Jones et al., 2006); another study estimated the total cost of PV against all female victims to be between 2.3 and 7.0 billion dollars – depending on how it is calculated (Brown, Finkelstein, and Mercy, 2008). Similar results have been found in other countries as well. A Danish study found higher rates of health-care use and costs for both men and women who had experienced PV victimization (Helweg-Larsen et al., 2011).

PV has additional costs to society. Women who experience PV are more likely to miss days at work and to be distracted when they are at work, than women who have not experienced PV victimization (Reeves and O'Leary-Kelly, 2007). There are also significant tolls on the criminal justice system, as they process and enforce restraining orders, investigate and prosecute cases of assault, stalking, rape, and murder. These costs have estimated to be around $8.3 billion a year in the United

States (Max *et al.*, 2004). Another US study estimated the combined costs of PV to women and society in a 6-month period of time to be $17,497. This calculation included health and mental health services, victim services, lost time from work, family, etc., lost property and transportation, health-related quality of life costs, and legal/criminal justice system costs (Logan, Walker, and Hoyt, 2012). A British study concerning the combined costs of PV to society, including productivity, the criminal justice system, health care, social services, housing, and legal fees, amounted to £23 billion (~38 billion US dollars) in 2008 (Walby, 2009). A similar study of costs to the Australian society estimated the total costs of health, productivity, consumption, administration, and costs to children to be about 15.6 million Australian dollars (~14 million US dollars) a year (Commonwealth of Australia, 2009). Most of the research concerning the costs to society have focused on female victimization in Western nations; WHO (2004) comes to similar conclusions, although it does not cite research from non-Western nations.

Policy, Primary Prevention, and Offender Treatment

On a worldwide level, the theory that has the strongest influence on policy, prevention, and offender treatment is patriarchal theory. Both the United Nations and WHO have issued recommendations for policy review and development, primary prevention programming, and treatment protocols that are consistent with this theory. They state that violence against women is rooted in gender biases, stereotypes, and socializations, and the United Nations calls upon all nations to adopt national action plans to prevent violence against women (WHO, 2005b; United Nations Women, 2012).

An initial problem with the framing of PV as a form of violence against women is that PV is perpetrated by both men and women toward both men and women; therefore, it is not an accurate or encompassing definition of the problem of PV. Second, lumping all forms of violence that can be perpetrated against women into the catchall phrase, *violence against women*, is misguided because it assumes that PV has similar etiologies and can be remediated with similar tactics; yet, there is no evidence for this assumption (Dutton, 2012).

Policy

Both the United Nations and WHO have had considerable influence on the development of policies throughout the world. The United Nations Women (2012) has called upon all countries to review and revise their existing legislation to conform to international law. At least 115 governments have revised or adopted laws to address violence against women or PV specifically (Ortiz-Barreda, Vives-Cases, and Gil-González, 2011). These include the Violence Against Women Act in the United States, the Law on the Protection of Women's Rights and Interests in China (Zhang, 2009), and the Protection of Women from Domestic Violence Act in India (Germain, 2007). Moreover, the African Charter on Human and People's Rights on the Rights of Women, the Council of Europe, the European Parliament of the European Union, and the Inter-American Convention on the Prevention, Punishment, and Eradication of Violence Against Women have urged all member states to take necessary action to protect women and eradicate violence against women (United Nations Women, 2012).

Although the revision and development of policy to prevent violence is good practice, the legislation has been developed under the misleading premise that PV only happens to women in heterosexual relationships. There is a danger to forming policy that protects only women from PV. Such policy "may implicitly encourage a lack of understanding and relaxed response to other types of physical assault towards intimate partners, such as same sex, female to male, or reciprocal PV" (Dixon and Graham-Kevan, 2011, p. 1152). In addition, without acknowledging that same-sex, female-to-male, and reciprocal violence occurs, a nation is not protecting a substantial portion of PV victims.

Prevention programming

As part of national action plans, the United Nations Women (2012) urges that all nations develop prevention strategies. They explicitly state that the prevention of and response to violence against women "will necessarily be distinct to other forms of violence" (p. 12), despite overwhelming evidence that PV is linked to other forms of violence (Malone, Tyree, and O'Leary, 1989; Giordano et al., 1999; Felson, 2002; Ehrensaft, Moffitt, and Caspi, 2004; WHO, 2005b; Medeiros and Straus, 2006). Both the United Nations and WHO call for prevention plans to address the root causes of violence against women, which they say are "gender inequality, gendered social constructions, and inadequacies in education" (United Nations Women, 2012, p. 32). Thus, a crucial element in the prevention of PV is increasing the status of women in employment, education, political participation, and legal rights. All such prevention programming should take place both universally and in targeted groups, such as primary and secondary educational institutions, workplaces, the military, faith-based and cultural institutions, and all professionals who may have contact with women victims (WHO, 2005b; United Nations Women, 2012).

One could argue that such widespread calls for this type of prevention programming are premature, as there is little evidence that prevention programs that take these strategies work to reduce PV, particularly all forms of PV. For example, evaluations of programs that take a patriarchal perspective, such as Skills for Violence-Free Relationships (Levy, 1984), show that they do not work in changing attitudes or knowledge regarding PV, either in the short- or long term (Avery-Leaf and Cascardi, 2002). One large-scale review of PV prevention studies between the years 1993 and 2012 found that there were 19 experimental or quasi-experimental studies, only 9 of which were methodologically sound (Whitaker et al., 2013). They found that the Safe Dates program in schools was one of the only prevention programs that reduced PV perpetration and victimization over 4 years. It was also equally effective for boys and girls, across races/ethnicities, and for adolescents who had previously experienced PV and those who had not. The Safe Dates program is a gender-neutral, mixed-gender program that includes a theater production, a 10-session curriculum, and a poster contest (Foshee and Langwick, 2004).

Another consideration with the United Nations and WHO mandates is that they overlook a major portion of PV that is experienced by people worldwide. Prevention programming should accurately reflect what the majority of any population experiences; "otherwise the message may not be internalized by the majority as something that applies to them" (Dixon and Graham-Kevan, 2011, p. 1151). When prevention campaigns contain messages that PV is severe, unidirectional violence that men perpetrate toward women, then victims who experience other forms of PV might think that their experiences do not fall under the rubric of PV (Dixon and Graham-Kevan, 2011). Thus, we argue for public education which states that all forms of violence are unacceptable, so that we reduce the rates, severity, and frequency of all forms of PV.

Treatment

The United Nations Women (2012) says that intervention programs for male batterers should be part of every nation's national action plan. Such programs should have minimum standards and be reviewed by women's NGOs and female survivors. The minimum standards include "a programme commitment to work within a gendered structural analysis of violence against women" (p. 59), despite the evidence that programs with such an orientation have been shown to be ineffective (Davis, Taylor, and Maxwell, 1998; Babcock, Green, and Robie, 2004).

Nevertheless, Batterer Intervention Programs (BIPs) that are built around this gender paradigm are the main treatment programs mandated by law in many nations. In the United States, BIPs are the primary diversionary programs for batterers and are mandated by most state laws. In Great Britain, PV is considered a special case, unrelated to other forms of violence, and thus, general violence programs are unavailable to or explicitly exclude PV perpetrators; perpetrators are routed to BIPs there as well (Dixon, Archer, and Graham-Kevan, 2012). Because of the strict adherence to programs that do not work, some researchers have argued that the primary goal of these programs is not to change perpetrator's behavior or keep victims safe, but rather to deconstruct male privilege in an effort to reeducate the male participants (Corvo, Dutton, and Chen, 2009). BIPs assume that PV is the result of underlying gender biases, stereotypes, and socialization. This assumption may be one of the reasons why BIPs are ineffective. We argue that PV perpetrators – both men and women – need to be assessed for the wide range of potential risk factors we have already discussed, including alcohol abuse, impulsivity, personality disorders, history of trauma and abuse, poor emotional regulation, coping skills, hostility, etc. (Dixon, Archer, and Graham-Kevan, 2012), in order to design/select treatment programs that will be most suitable to perpetrators. We also support assessing the behavior of both partners, which is consistent with systems theory (Dixon, Archer, and Graham-Kevan, 2012). Given that there is little evidence of any substantial sex differences in the risk factors or motivations for PV (Moffitt et al., 2001), it is likely that programs can be developed for both male and female perpetrators. Current evidence suggests that the best programs focus on constructs such as readiness to change and motivational enhancement (Eckhardt et al., 2013).

Future and Concluding Remarks

As noted throughout this chapter, we disagree with and do not think that there is evidence to support the *dominant story* of PV, that it is something which only men do to women. Thus, we maintain the need for a broader and more comprehensive understanding of PV, and one that is based in evidence. In this regard, we encourage researchers to examine victimization and perpetration among both men and women; for public education campaigns to acknowledge the bidirectionality of PV as a way for victims and perpetrators to accurately name and identify their experiences; for human service providers to reach out and to serve all individuals who seek assistance; and for policy on all levels – from agency policy to national policy – to be gender-inclusive and to be based in research and evidence, so that we as a global society maximize our potential to reduce PV regardless of gender, class, sexual orientation, race/ethnicity, or nationality.

References

Anderson, M.L. and Leigh, I.W. (2010) Internal consistency and factor structure of the revised conflict tactics scales in a sample of deaf female college students. *Journal of Family Violence*, 25 (5), 475–483.

Apsler, R., Cummins, M. R. and Carl, S. (2003) Perceptions of the police by female victims of domestic partner violence. *Violence Against Women*, 9 (11), 1318–1335.

Archer, J. (2000) Sex differences in aggression between heterosexual couples: a meta-analytic review. *Psychological Bulletin*, 126, 651–680.

Avery-Leaf, S. and Cascardi, M. (2002) Dating violence education: prevention and early intervention strategies, in *Preventing Violence in Relationships: Interventions Across the Life Span* (ed. P.A. Schewe), American Psychological Association, Washington, DC, pp. 79–105.

Babcock, J.C., Green, C.E. and Robie, C. (2004) Does batterers' treatment work? A meta-analytic review of domestic violence treatment outcome research. *Clinical Psychology Review*, 23, 1023–1053.

Bandura, A. (1979) The social learning perspective: mechanisms of aggression, in *Psychology of Crime and Criminal Justice* (ed. H. Toch), Holt, Rinehart, & Winston, New York, pp. 198–236.

Beaulaurier, R., Seff, L., Newman, F. and Dunlop, B. (2007) External barriers to help seeking for older women who experience intimate partner violence. *Journal of Family Violence*, 22 (8), 747–755.

Bennett, L., Riger, S., Schewe, P. *et al.* (2004) Effectiveness of hotline, advocacy, counseling, and shelter services for victims of domestic violence. *Journal of Interpersonal Violence*, 19 (7), 815–829.

Black, M.C. and Breiding, M.J. (2008) Adverse health conditions and health risk behaviors associated with intimate partner violence – United States, 2005. *Morbidity and Mortality Weekly Report*, 57 (5), 113–117.

Bowker, L.H. (1983) Battered wives, lawyers, and district attorneys: an examination of law in action. *Journal of Criminal Justice*, 11 (5), 403–412.

Bowker, L.H. and Maurer, L. (1985) The importance of sheltering in the lives of battered women. *Response to the Victimization of Women & Children*, 8 (1), 2–8.

Bowlby, J. (1988) *A Secure Base: Parent-Child Attachment and Healthy Human Development*, Basic Books, New York.

Bronfenbrenner, U. (1979) *The Ecology of Human Development: Experiments by Nature and Design*, Harvard University Press, Cambridge.

Brown, D.S., Finkelstein, E.A. and Mercy, J.A. (2008) Methods for estimating medical expenditures attributable to intimate partner violence. *Journal of Interpersonal Violence*, 23 (12), 1747–1766.

Buzawa, E.S. and Austin, T. (1993) Determining police response to domestic violence victims: the role of victim preference. *American Behavioral Scientist*, 36 (5), 610–623.

Caetano, R., Schafer, J. and Cunradi, C.B. (2001) Alcohol-related intimate partner violence among white, black, and Hispanic couples in the United States. *Alcohol Research and Health*, 25, 58–65.

Carbone-Lopez, K., Kruttschnitt, C. and MacMillan, R. (2006) Patterns of intimate partner violence and their associations with physical health, psychological distress, and substance use. *Public Health Reports*, 121, 382–392.

Carroll, J.C. (1977) The intergenerational transmission of family violence: the long-term effects of aggressive behavior. *Aggressive Behavior*, 3 (3), 289–299.

Chan, K.L. (2011) Association between childhood sexual abuse and adult sexual victimization in a representative sample in Hong Kong Chinese. *Child Abuse & Neglect*, 35 (3), 220–229.

Chan, K.L. and Cho, E.Y.-N. (2010) A review of cost measures for the economic impact of domestic violence. *Trauma, Violence, & Abuse*, 11 (3), 129–143.

Chan, K.L., Tiwari, A., Leung, W.C. *et al.* (2007) Common correlates of suicidal ideation and physical assault among male and female university students in Hong Kong. *Violence and Victims*, 22 (3), 290–303.

Chan, K.L., Straus, M.A., Brownridge, D.A. *et al.* (2008) Prevalence of dating partner violence and suicidal ideation among male and female university students worldwide. *Journal of Midwifery and Women's Health*, 53, 529–537.

Clements, C.M., Oxtoby, C. and Ogle, R.L. (2008) Methodological issues in assessing psychological adjustment in child witnesses of intimate partner violence. *Trauma, Violence & Abuse*, 9 (2), 114–127.

Coker, A.L., Smith, P.H., Bethea, L. *et al.* (2000) Physical health consequences of physical and psychological intimate partner violence. *Archives of Family Medicine*, 9, 451–457.

Coker, A.L., Davis, K.E., Arias, I. *et al.* (2002) Physical and mental health effects of intimate partner violence for men and women. *American Journal of Preventive Medicine*, 23 (4), 260–268.

Cook, P.W. (2009) *Abused Men: The Hidden Side of Domestic Violence*, 2nd edn. Praeger, Westport.

Commonwealth of Australia (2009) *The Costs of Violence Against Women and their Children*, Department of Families, Housing, Community Services and Indigenous Affairs; The National Council to Reduce Violence Against Women and their Children, Greenway ACT.

Corvo, K., Dutton, D.G. and Chen, W.Y. (2009) Do duluth model interventions with perpetrators of domestic violence violate mental health professional ethics? *Ethics and Behavior*, 19 (4), 323–340.

Crais, L.E. (2005) Domestic violence and the federal government. *Georgetown Journal of Gender & the Law*, 6 (3), 405–430.

Davis, R.C., Taylor, B.G. and Maxwell, C.D. (1998) Does batterer treatment reduce violence? A randomized experiment in Brooklyn. *Justice Quarterly*, 18, 171–201.

Dixon, L. and Graham-Kevan, N. (2011) Understanding the nature and etiology of intimate partner violence and implications for practice and policy. *Clinical Psychology Review*, 31, 1145–1155.

Dixon, L., Archer, J. and Graham-Kevan, N. (2012) Perpetrator programmes for partner violence: are they based on ideology or evidence? *Legal and Criminological Psychology*, 17, 196–215.

Dobash, R.E. and Dobash, R.P. (1979) *Violence Against Wives: A Case Against the Patriarchy*, Free Press, New York.

Donnelly, D.A., Cook, K.J. and Wilson, L. (1999) Provision and exclusion: the dual face of services to battered women in three Deep South states. *Violence Against Women*, 5 (7), 710–741.

Douglas, E.M. and Straus, M.A. (2006) Assault and injury of dating partners by university students in 19 countries and its relation to corporal punishment experienced as a child. *European Journal of Criminology*, 3 (3), 293–318.

Douglas, E.M. and Hines, D.A. (2011) The helpseeking experiences of men who sustain intimate partner violence: an overlooked population and implications for prace. *Journal of Family Violence*, 26 (6), 473–485.

Dutton, D.G. (1985) An ecologically nested theory of male violence towards intimates. *International Journal of Women's Studies*, 8 (4), 404–413.

Dutton, D.G. (2007) *The Abusive Personality: Violence and Control in Intimate Relationships*, 2nd edn, Guilford, New York.

Dutton, D. (2012) The case against the role of gender in intimate partner violence. *Aggression & Violent Behavior*, 17 (1), 99–104.

Dutton, D.G. and Corvo, K. (2006) Transforming a flawed policy: a call to revive psychology and science in domestic violence research and practice. *Aggression and Violent Behavior*, 11, 457–483.

Dutton, D.G., Saunders, K., Starzomski, A.J. and Bartholomew, K. (1994) Intimacy anger and insecure attachment as precursors of abuse in intimate relationships. *Journal of Applied Social Psychology*, 24 (15), 1367–1386.

Eckhardt, C.I., Murphy, C.M., Whitaker, D.J., *et al.* (2013). The effectiveness of intervention programs for perpetrators and victims of intimate partner violence. *Partner Abuse*, 4 (2), 196–231.

Ehrensaft, M.K., Moffitt, T.E. and Caspi, A. (2004) Clinically abusive relationships in an unselected birth cohort: men's and women's participation and developmental antecedents. *Journal of Abnormal Psychology*, 113 (2), 258–271.

Ehrensaft, M.K., Cohen, P., Brown, J. *et al.* (2003) Intergenerational transmission of partner violence: a 20-year prospective study. *Journal of Consulting and Clinical Psychology*, 71, 741–753.

El-Khoury, M.Y., Dutton, M.A., Goodman, L.A. *et al.* (2004) Ethnic differences in battered women's formal help-seeking strategies: a focus on health, mental health, and spirituality. *Cultural Diversity and Ethnic Minority Psychology*, 10 (4), 383–393.

Erez, E. and King, T.A. (2000) Patriarchal terrorism or common couple violence: attorneys' views of prosecuting and defending woman batterers. *International Review of Victimology*, 7 (1–3), 207–226.

Eron, L.D. (1997) The development of antisocial behavior from a learning perspective, in *Handbook of Antisocial Behavior* (eds. D.M. Stoff, J. Breiling and J.D. Maser), John Wiley and Sons, New York, pp. 140–147.

Esquivel-Santovena, E.E., Lambert, T. and Hamel, J. (2013) Partner abuse worldwide. *Partner Abuse*, 4 (1), 6–75.

Fals-Stewart, W. (2003) The occurrence of partner physical aggression on days of alcohol consumption: a longitudinal diary study. *Journal of Consulting and Clinical Psychology*, 71, 41–52.

Fantuzzo, J.W., Mohr, W.K. and Noone, M.J. (2000) Making the invisible victims of violence against women visible through university/community partnerships. *Journal of Aggression, Maltreatment & Trauma*, 3 (1), 9–23.

Felson, R.B. (2002) *Violence and Gender Reexamined*, American Psychological Association, Washington, DC.

Fergusson, D.M., Horwood, L.J. and Ridder, E.M. (2005) Partner violence and mental health outcomes in a New Zealand birth cohort. *Journal of Marriage & Family*, 67 (5), 1103–1119.

Fishman, P.A., Bonomi, A.E., Anderson, M.L. *et al.* (2010) Changes in health care costs over time following the cessation of intimate partner violence. *Journal of General Internal Medicine*, 25 (9), 920–925.

Fortin, I., Guay, S., Lavoie, V. *et al.* (2012) Intimate partner violence and psychological distress among young couples: analysis of the moderating effect of social support. *Journal of Family Violence*, 27 (1), 63–73.

Foshee, V.A. and Langwick, S.A. (2004) *Safe Dates: An Adolescent Dating Abuse Prevention Curriculum [Program Manual]*, Hezelden Publishing and Educational Services, Center City.

Gamez-Guadix, M., Straus, M.A. and Hershberger, S. (in press) Childhood and adolescent victimization and perpetration of sexual coercion by male and female university students. *Deviant Behavior*, 32 (8), 712–742.

Gelles, R.J. (1998) Family violence, in *The Handbook of Crime and Punishment* (ed. M. Tonry), Oxford University Press, New York, pp. 178–206.

Germain, A. (2007) Violence against women and children. *Lancet*, 369, 24.

Gil-González, D., Vives-Cases, C., Teresa Ruiz, M. *et al.* (2008) Childhood experiences of violence in perpetrators as a risk factor of intimate partner violence: a systematic review. *Journal of Public Health*, 30 (1), 14–22.

Giordano, P.C., Millhollin, T.J., Cernkovich, S.A. *et al.* (1999) Delinquency, identity, and women's involvement in relationship violence. *Criminology*, 37 (1), 17–40.

Golding, J.M. (1999) Intimate partner violence as a risk factor for mental disorders: a meta-analysis. *Journal of Family Violence*, 14 (2), 99–132.

Gunnar, M.R. and Barr, R.G. (1998) Stress, early brain development, and behavior. *Infants & Young Children: An Interdisciplinary Journal of Special Care Practices*, 11 (1), 1–14.

Hathaway, J.E., Mucci, L.A., Silverman, J.G. *et al.* (2000) Health status and health care use of Massachusetts women reporting partner abuse. *American Journal of Preventive Medicine*, 19 (4), 302–307.

Heise, L. and Garcia-Moreno, C. (2002) Violence by intimate partners, in *World Report on Violence and Health* (eds. E.G. Krug, L.L. Dahlber, J.A. Mercy *et al.*), World Health Organization, Geneva, pp. 87–121.

Helweg-Larsen, K., Sørensen, J., Brønnum-Hansen, H. and Kruse, M. (2011) Risk factors for violence exposure and attributable healthcare costs: results from the Danish national health interview surveys. *Scandinavian Journal of Public Health*, 39 (1), 10–16.

Heugten, K.V. and Wilson, E. (2008) Witnessing intimate partner violence: review of the literature on coping in young persons. *Social Work Review*, 20 (3), 52–62.

Higgins, J.G. (1978) Social services for abused wives. *Social Casework*, 59 (5), 266–271.

Hines, D.A. (2007a) Posttraumatic stress symptoms among men who sustain partner violence: an international multisite study of university students. *Psychology of Men & Masculinity*, 8 (4), 225–239.

Hines, D.A. (2007b) Predictors of sexual coercion against women and men: a multilevel, multinational study of university students. *Archives of Sexual Behavior*, 36, 402–422.

Hines, D.A. (2008) Borderline personality and intimate partner aggression: an international multi-site, cross-gender analysis. *Psychology of Women Quarterly*, 32, 290–302.

Hines, D.A. and Malley-Morrison, K. (2005) *Family Violence in the United States: Defining, Understanding, and Combating Abuse*, Sage, Thousand Oaks.

Hines, D.A. and Douglas, E.M. (2011a) The reported availability of U.S. domestic violence services to victims who vary by age, sexual orientation, and gender. *Partner Abuse*, 2 (1), 3–28.

Hines, D.A. and Douglas, E.M. (2011b) Symptoms of post-traumatic stress disorder in men who sustain intimate partner violence: a study of helpseeking and community samples. *Psychology of Men & Masculinity*, 12 (2), 112–127.

Hines, D.A. and Douglas, E.M. (2012) Alcohol and drug abuse in men who sustain intimate partner violence. *Aggressive Behavior*, 38, 31–46.

Hines, D.A. and Straus, M.A. (2007) Binge drinking and violence against dating partners: the mediating effect of antisocial traits and behaviors in a multinational perspective. *Aggressive Behavior*, 33 (5), 441–457.

Hines, D.A., Brown, J. and Dunning, E. (2007) Characteristics of callers to the domestic abuse helpline for men. *Journal of Family Violence*, 22 (2), 63–72.

Hines, D.A., Malley-Morrison, K. and Dutton, L.B. (2013) *Family Violence in the United States: Defining, Understanding, and Combating Abuse*, 2nd edn, Sage, Thousand Oaks.

Holtzworth-Munroe, A. and Stuart, G.L. (1994) Typologies of male batterers: three subtypes and the differences among them. *Psychological Bulletin*, 116, 476–497.

Jespersen, A.F., Lalumiere, M.L. and Seto, M.C. (2009) Sexual abuse history among adult sex offenders and non-sex offenders: a meta-analysis. *Child Abuse and Neglect*, 33 (3), 179–192.

Jin, M.K., Jacobvitz, D., Hazen, N. and Jung, S.H. (2012) Maternal sensitivity and infant attachment security in Korea: cross-cultural validation of the strange situation. *Attachment & Human Development*, 14 (1), 33–44.

Johnson, I.M. (2007) Victims' perceptions of police response to domestic violence incidents. *Journal of Criminal Justice*, 35 (5), 498–510.

Jones, A.S., Dienemann, J., Schollenberger, J. *et al.* (2006) Long-term costs of intimate partner violence in a sample of female HMO enrollees. *Women's Health Issues*, 16 (5), 252–261.

Kalil, A. (2003) Domestic violence and children's behavior in low-income families. *Journal of Emotional Abuse*, 3 (1/2), 75–101.

Kaura, S.A. and Lohman, B.J. (2007) Dating violence victimization, relationship satisfaction, mental health problems, and acceptability of violence: a comparison of men and women. *Journal of Family Violence*, 22, 367–381.

Kilpatrick, K.L. and Williams, L.M. (1998) Potential mediators of post-traumatic stress disorder in child witnesses to domestic violence. *Child Abuse & Neglect*, 22 (4), 319–330.

Lang, J.M. and Stover, C.S. (2008) Symptom patterns among youth exposed to intimate partner violence. *Journal of Family Violence*, 23 (7), 619–629.

Langhinrichsen-Rohling, J., Misra, T.A., Selwyn, C. and Rohling, M. (2012) Rates of bi-directional versus uni-directional intimate partner violence across samples, sexual orientations, and race/ethnicities: a comprehensive review. *Partner Abuse*, 3 (2), 199–230.

Leisring, P.A., Dowd, L and Rosenbaum, A. (2002) Treatment of partner aggressive women. *Journal of Aggression, Maltreatment & Trauma*, 7 (1/2), 257–277.

Leonard, K.E. (1993) Drinking patterns and intoxication in marital violence: review, critique, and future directions for research, in *Research Monograph 24: Alcohol and Interpersonal Violence: Fostering Multidisciplinary Perspectives*. U.S. Department of Health and Human Services, National Institutes of Health, Rockville, pp. 253–280.

Leone, J.M., Johnson, M.P. and Cohan, C.L. (2007) Victim help seeking: differences between intimate terrorism and situational couple violence. *Family Relations: An Interdisciplinary Journal of Applied Family Studies*, 56 (5), 427–439.

Leserman, J., Li, Z., Drossman, D.A. and Hu, Y.J. (1998) Selected symptoms associated with sexual and physical abuse history among female patients with gastrointestinal disorders: the impact on subsequent health care visits. *Psychological Medicine*, 28 (2), 417–425.

Levendosky, A.A., Huth-Bocks, A.C., Shapiro, D.L. and Semel, M.A. (2003) The impact of domestic violence on the maternal-child relationship and preschool-age children's functioning. *Journal of Family Psychology*, 17 (3), 275–287.

Levendosky, A.A., Leahy, K.L., Bogat, G.A. *et al.* (2006) Domestic violence, maternal parenting, maternal mental health, and infant externalizing behavior. *Journal of Family Psychology*, 20 (4), 544–552.

Levy, B. (1984) *Skills for Violence-Free Relationships*, Southern California Coalition on Battered Women, Santa Monica.

Logan, T.K., Walker, R. and Hoyt, W. (2012) The economic costs of partner violence and the cost-benefit of civil protective orders. *Journal of Interpersonal Violence*, 27 (6), 1137–1154.

Malone, J., Tyree, A. and O'Leary, K.D. (1989) Generalization and containment: different effects of past aggression for wives and husbands. *Journal of Marriage and the Family*, 51, 687–697.

Martin, E.K., Taft, C.T. and Resick, P.A. (2007) A review of marital rape. *Aggression and Violent Behavior*, 12 (3), 329–347.

Martiny, C. (2006) When adults lose it, do children catch it? What to say to children who witness interadult violence, in *Talking to Children About Responsibility and Control of Emotions* (eds. M. Schleifer and C. Martiny), Detselig Enterprises, Calgary, pp. 71–91.

Mason, G.E. (2009) Help-Seeking Behavior of Jamaican Women in Abusive Relationships, 69, ProQuest Information & Learning, US. Retrieved from http://search.ebscohost.com/login. aspx?direct=true&db=psyh&AN=2009-99060-143&site=ehost-live. Available from EBSCO host psyh database (accessed November 1, 2013).

Max, W., Rice, D.P., Finkelstein, E. *et al.* (2004) The economic toll of intimate partner violence against women in the United States. *Violence and Victims*, 19 (3), 259–272.

McClennen, J.C., Summers, A.B. and Vaughan, C. (2002) Gay men's domestic violence: dynamics, help-seeking behaviors, and correlates. *Journal of Gay & Lesbian Social Services*, 14 (1), 23–49.

McNamara, J.R., Tamanini, K. and Pelletier-Walker, S. (2008) The impact of short-term counseling at a domestic violence shelter. *Research on Social Work Practice*, 18 (2), 132–136.

Medeiros, R.A. and Straus, M.A. (2006) Risk factors for physical violence between dating partners: implications for gender-inclusive prevention and treatment of family violence, in *Family Interventions in Domestic Violence: A Handbook of Gender-Inclusive Theory and Treatment* (eds. J. Hamel and T. Nicholls), Springer, New York, pp. 59–85.

Moffitt, T.E., Caspi, A., Rutter, M. and Silva, P.A. (2001) *Sex Differences in Antisocial Behaviour: Conduct Disorder, Delinquency and Violence in the Dunedin Longitudinal Study*, Cambridge University Press, Cambridge.

Molina, O., Lawrence, S.A., Azhar-Miller, A. and Rivera, M. (2009) Divorcing abused latina immigrant women's experiences with domestic violence support groups. *Journal of Divorce & Remarriage*, 50 (7), 459–471.

Moretti, M.M., Obsuth, I., Odgers, C.L. and Reebye, P. (2006) Exposure to maternal vs. paternal partner violence, ptsd, and aggression in adolescent girls and boys. *Aggressive Behavior*, 32 (4), 385–395.

Mršević, Z. and Hughes, D.M. (1997) Violence against women in Belgrade, Serbia: SOS hotline 1990–1993. *Violence Against Women*, 3 (2), 101–128.

Norton, I.M. and Schauer, J. (1997) A hospital-based domestic violence group. *Psychiatric Services*, 48 (9), 1186–1190.

O'Farrell, T.J., Fals-Stewart, W., Murphy, M. and Murphy, C.M. (2003) Partner violence before and after individually based alcoholism treatment for male alcoholic patients. *Journal of Consulting and Clinical Psychology*, 71, 92–102.

Ogunsiji, O., Wilkes, L., Jackson, D. and Peters, K. (2012) Suffering and smiling: West African immigrant women's experience of intimate partner violence. *Journal of Clinical Nursing*, 21 (11–12), 1659–1665.

Ortiz-Barreda, G., Vives-Cases, C. and Gil-González, D. (2011) Worldwide violence against women legislation: an equity approach. *Health Policy*, 100, 125–133.

Owen, A., Thompson, M., Shaffer, A. *et al.* (2009) Family variables that mediate the relation between intimate partner violence (IPV) and child adjustment. *Journal of Family Violence*, 24 (7), 433–445.

Pimlott-Kubiak, S. and Cortina, L.M. (2003) Gender, victimization, and outcomes: reconceptualizing risk. *Journal of Consulting and Clinical Psychology*, 71 (3), 528–539.

Reeves, C. and O'Leary-Kelly, A.M. (2007) The effects and costs of intimate partner violence for work organizations. *Journal of Interpersonal Violence*, 22 (3), 327–344.

Renzetti, C.M. (1989) Building a second closet: third party responses to victims of lesbian partner abuse. *Family Relations*, 38 (2), 157–163.

Rivara, F.P., Anderson, M.L., Fishman, P. *et al.* (2007) Intimate partner violence and health care costs and utilization for children living in the home. *Pediatrics*, 120 (6), 1270–1277.

Romito, P. and Grassi, M. (2007) Does violence affect one gender more than the other? The mental health impact of violence among male and female university students. *Social Science & Medicine*, 65, 1222–1234.

Sabina, C. and Straus, M.A. (2008) Polyvictimization by dating partners and mental health among U.S. college students. *Violence and Victims*, 23 (6), 667–682.

Saltzman, K.M., Holden, G.W. and Holahan, C.J. (2005) The psychobiology of children exposed to marital violence. *Journal of Clinical Child and Adolescent Psychology*, 34 (1), 129–139.

Shannon, L., Logan, T.K., Cole, J. and Medley, K. (2006) Help-seeking and coping strategies for intimate partner violence in rural and urban women. *Violence and Victims*, 21 (2), 167–181.

Shen, A.C.-T. (2011) Cultural barriers to help-seeking among Taiwanese female victims of dating violence. *Journal of Interpersonal Violence*, 26 (7), 1343–1365.

Söchting, I., Fairbrother, N. and Koch, W.J. (2004) Sexual assault of women: prevention efforts and risk factors. *Violence Against Women*, 10 (1), 73–93.

Speizer, I.S. (2010) Intimate partner violence attitudes and experience among women and men in Uganda. *Journal of Interpersonal Violence*, 25 (7), 1224–1241.

Spilsbury, J.C., Kahana, S., Drotar, D. *et al.* (2008) Profiles of behavioral problems in children who witness domestic violence. *Violence & Victims*, 23 (1), 3–17.

Stanko, E.A. (2000) Unmasking what should be seen: a study of the prevalence of domestic violence in the London Borough of Hackney. *International Review of Victimology*, 7 (1–3), 227–242.

Steinmetz, S.K. (1977) *The Cycle of Violence: Assertive, Aggressive, and Abusive Family Interaction*, Praeger, Oxford.

Steinmetz, S.K. and Straus, M.A. (1974) *Violence in the Family*, Dodd, Mead, Oxford.

Sternberg, K.J., Baradaran, L.P., Abbott, C.B. *et al.* (2006) Type of violence, age, and gender differences in the effects of family violence on children's behavior problems: a mega-analysis. *Developmental Review*, 26 (1), 89–112.

Stith, S.M., Rosen, K.H., Middleton, K.L. *et al.* (2000) The intergenerational transmission of spouse abuse: a meta-analysis. *Journal of Marriage and the Family*, 62, 640–654.

Stith, S.M., Smith, D.B., Penn, C.E. *et al.* (2004) Intimate partner physical abuse perpetration and victimization risk factors: a meta-analysis review. *Aggression and Violent Behavior*, 10 (1), 65–98.

Stover, C., Horn, P. and Lieberman, A. (2006) Parental representations in the play of preschool aged witnesses of marital violence. *Journal of Family Violence*, 21 (6), 417–424.

Straus, M.A. (1976) Sexual inequality, cultural norms, and wife-beating. *Victimology*, 1 (1), 54–70.

Straus, M.A. (1979) Measuring intrafamily conflict and violence: the conflict tactics scales. *Journal of Marriage & Family*, 41, 75–88.

Straus, M.A. (2004) Cross-cultural reliability and validity of the revised conflict tactics scales: a study of university student dating couples in 17 nations. *Cross-Cultural Research: The Journal of Comparative Social Science*, 38 (4), 407–432.

Straus, M.A. (2005) Reflections on "measuring intrafamily conflict and violence," in *Violence Against Women: Classic Papers* (eds. R.K. Bergen, J.L. Edleson and C.M. Renzetti), Pearson Education, Inc., Boston, pp. 195–197.

Straus, M.A. (2008a) Dominance and symmetry in partner violence by male and female university students in 32 nations. *Children and Youth Services Review*, 30 (3), 252–275.

Straus, M.A. (2008b) Prevalence and effects of mutuality in physical and psychological aggression against dating partners by university students in 32 nations. Paper presented at the International Family Aggression Society Conference, University of Central Lancashire, http://pubpages.unh.edu/~mas2/ID64B-PR64%20IFAS.pdf (accessed November 1, 2013).

Straus, M.A. and Yodanis, C.L. (1996) Corporal punishment in adolescence and physical assaults on spouses in later life: what accounts for the link? *Journal of Marriage & the Family*, 58 (4), 825–841.

Straus, M.A. and Savage, S.A. (2005) Neglectful behavior by parents in the life history of university students in 17 countries and its relation to violence against dating partners. *Child Maltreatment*, 10 (2), 124–135.

Straus, M.A., Hamby, S.L., Boney-McCoy, S. and Sugarman, D. (1996) The revised conflict tactics scales (CTS-2): development and preliminary psychometric data. *Journal of Family Issues*, 17, 283–316.

Sugarman, D.B. and Frankel, S.L. (1996) Patriarchal ideology and wife assault: a meta-analytic review. *Journal of Family Violence*, 11, 13–40.

Sun-Hee Park, L. (2005) Navigating the anti-immigrant wave: the Korean women's hotline and the politics of community, in *Domestic Violence at the Margins: Readings on Race, Class, Gender, and Culture* (eds. N.J. Sokoloff and C. Pratt), Rutgers University Press, Piscataway, pp. 350–368.

Ulrich, Y.C., Cain, K.C., Sugg, N.K. *et al.* (2003) Medical care utilization patterns in women with diagnosed domestic violence. *American Journal of Preventive Medicine*, 24 (1), 9–15.

United Nations Women (2012) Handbook for National Action Plans on Violence Against Women. Retrieved from http://www.un.org/womenwatch/daw/vaw/handbook-for-nap-on-vaw1.pdf (accessed November 1, 2013).

US Centers for Disease Control and Prevention (n.d.) Intimate Partner Violence: Definitions, http://www.cdc.gov/ViolencePrevention/intimatepartnerviolence/definitions.html (accessed November 1, 2013).

Vameghi, M., Feizzadeh, A., Mirabzadeh, A. and Feizzadeh, G. (2010) Exposure to domestic violence between parents: a perspective from Tehran, Iran. *Journal of Interpersonal Violence*, 25 (6), 1006–1021.

van Ijzendoorn, M.H. and Sagi-Schwartz, A. (2008) Cross-cultural patterns of attachment: universal and contextual dimensions, in *Handbook of Attachment: Theory, Research, and Clinical Applications*, 2nd edn (eds. J. Cassidy and P.R. Shaver), Guilford Press, New York, pp. 880–905.

Vung, N.D. and Krantz, G. (2009) Childhood experiences of interparental violence as a risk factor for intimate partner violence: a population-based study from northern Vietnam. *Journal of Epidemiology and Community Health*, 63, 708–714.

Walby, S. (2009) *The Cost of Domestic Violence: up-date 2009*, Lancaster University, Lancaster.

Weinbaum, Z., Stratton, T.L., Chavez, G. *et al.* (2001) Female victims of intimate partner physical domestic violence (IPP-DV), California 1998. *American Journal of Preventive Medicine*, 21 (4), 313–319.

Whitaker, D.J., Murphy, C.M., Eckhardt, C.I. *et al.* (2013) Effectiveness of primary prevention efforts of intimate partner violence. *Partner Abuse*, 4 (2), 1–28.

World Health Organization (2004) The economic dimensions of interpersonal violence. Geneva, Switzerland, Department of Injuries and Violence Prevention, World Health Organization, http://whqlibdoc.who.int/publications/2004/9241591609.pdf.

World Health Organization (2005a) *Multi-Country Study on Women's Health and Domestic Violence Against Women*, World Health Organization, Geneva.

World Health Organization (2005b) Researching Violence Against Women: A Practical Guide for Researchers and Activists, Retrieved from http://www.path.org/publications/detail.php?i=1524 (accessed November 1, 2013).

World Health Organization (2010) Preventing Intimate Partner and Sexual Violence Against Women: Taking Action and Generating Evidence, Retrieved from http://whqlibdoc.who.int/publications/2010/9789241564007_eng.pdf (accessed November 1, 2013).

Zhang, L. (2009) Domestic violence network in China: translating the transnational concept of violence against women into local action. *Women's Studies International Forum*, 32, 227–239.

17

Money Management, Gender, and Households

Sean R. Lauer and Carrie Yodanis

When couples share a household, they must settle on an approach to managing money in order to meet their individual and shared needs and desires. How money in households is managed goes beyond these practical arrangements, however. Embedded in these arrangements are questions central to social science including efficiency, trust, inequality, gender, social rules and expectations, cultural variation, and social change. As a result, money management has been a long-time interest of social scientists. Most often, this interest lies with the family and the dynamics between husbands and wives in households.

Two themes are prominent in the social science research on money management within couples: (i) the choice of integrating resources over keeping money separate and (ii) the equality of relationships associated with different money management strategies. Much of this research examines money management at the level of couples. After reviewing this research, we place the study of money management and couple-level analysis into a larger institutional-level analysis. We show that the dynamics of money in households are rooted in social arrangements larger than individual couples (Zelizer, 1989; Singh, 1997). The larger context shapes how spouses manage their money. Institutional arrangements, in particular the rules and expectations of marriage and gender, shape the variation in money management strategies over time and across cultures. With this perspective, the strategies for managing money in marriage become indicators of how both the institution of marriage and gender dynamics have or have not changed. The study of money management, gender, and households allows us to understand complex aspects of social institutions, culture, and social change. Our goal is not to suggest that all

Parts of this entry were adapted from Yodanis, Carrie and Sean R. Lauer. 2007b. "Managing Money in Marriage: Multilevel and Cross-national Effects of the Breadwinner Role." *Journal of Marriage and Family*, 69: 1307–1325, and Lauer, Sean R., and Carrie Yodanis. 2011. "Individualized Marriage and the Integration of Resources." *Journal of Marriage and Family*, 73: 669–683.

research on money management in marriage should focus on institutional contexts. Rather, we hope our review will draw attention to the important ways that couple-level and institutional-level analyses complement one another.

Managing Money at the Couple Level

Sociologists have documented a number of management approaches within couples. For instance, married couples can choose to keep two separate pools of money. Treas (1993) describes this as keeping separate purses: his and her accounts, so to speak. Pahl (1983, 1995) calls this the independent management system. In Britain, Vogler, Brockmann, and Wiggins (2006) have seen this approach increasing slightly at the beginning of the twenty-first century to around 10% of British couples. Couples that kept at least some, if not all, money in separate purses made up 17% of those couples (Vogler, Brockmann, and Wiggins, 2006).

Despite these trends, most married couples across countries choose to pool their money in a common pot rather than maintain separate purses (Treas, 1993; Heimdal and Houseknecht, 2003; Pahl, 2008). The integration of money in marriage symbolizes, legally and practically, two individuals have become a single unit. Spouses move into the same home, open a joint bank account, file taxes together, and, in some places, have rights to half of all that is acquired throughout the marriage. Based on interviews with couples in Australia, Singh (1997) found that pooling money has grown to mean togetherness, commitment, and trust in marriage and thus be considered an essential foundation for a couple. As she writes, "When people speak of jointness and pooling, sharing, togetherness, trust and commitment, they express not only what they think is happening with money in their marriage, but what they expect to happen..." (Singh, 1997, p. 56). Vogler, Brockman, and Wiggins (2006) find nearly three-quarters of British couples choosing some form of pooling. Looking across 31 countries, Lauer and Yodanis (2011) find that over 80% of couples pool resources. For some couples, the decision to pool their money begins right away, while for others they slide toward pooling over the course of their relationship. For many married couples who start off with separate accounts, the slide toward some form of pooling can come quite quickly (Burgoyne *et al.*, 2007, 2010). Similarly, cohabitors are more likely to pool resources the longer they have been together. When cohabitors have plans to marry or to have children, they are more likely to pool their money than cohabitors who do not see marriage or children in their future (Lyngstad, Noack, and Tufte, 2011).

Among the explanations for why couples pool their money, couple-level approaches remain prominent. Treas (1993), for example, provides the classic couple-level explanation for the pooling of resources. She follows transaction costs economic arguments and finds that when couples expect the relationship to last, when they have sunk costs in the relationship, and when monitoring of contributions is difficult, couples pool resources. When couples make long-term investments in the relationship such as marriage, raising children, or specialization in market versus household work, pooling resources reduces transaction costs, making it a more efficient management strategy. Her findings have been supported in research on cohabitation, divorce, and across country contexts (Burgoyne and Morison, 1997; Elizabeth, 2001; Heimdal and

Houseknecht, 2003; Oropesa, Landale, and Kenkre, 2003). Comparisons of married and cohabiting couples are common here. For instance, Heimdal and Houseknecht (2003) compare married and cohabiting couples in the United States and Sweden and find that cohabiting couples are more likely to keep separate accounts, even when accounting for differences in socioeconomic status and gender ideology. Oropesa, Landale, and Kenkre (2003) find a similar pattern among married and cohabiting couples in Puerto Rico. In a follow-up study, Oropesa and Landale (2005) find more relationship stability among cohabitors that pool resources compared to those who keep separate accounts.

Building on the work of economists such as Pollak (1985), Treas (1993, p. 724) suggests that maintaining separate accounts introduces market-like exchange and bargaining between husbands and wives. While this can allow couples to maintain individual interests within the relationship, it also can increase day-to-day hassles of managing, coordinating, and haggling over financial decisions.

This is not to suggest that all couples act with consensus about the spending of money when collective strategies of money management are adopted. When money is pooled in a common pot, it can become a significant source of conflict within couples. Papp, Cummings, and Goeke-Morey (2009) find that conflicts about money are particularly intense and hard to resolve compared to more mundane conflicts over issues such as child care and chores. Using diaries completed over 15 days by both husbands and wives, they found conflicts surrounding children, chores, communication, and leisure more common than conflicts surrounding money. Though slightly less common, money conflicts were considered the hardest issue to work through by husbands and second hardest by wives.

Recognizing these conflicts, sociologists have focused their attention on the unique gendered dynamics of money management in couples. Within the collectivized approaches to family money management, Pahl (1983, 1995) makes further distinctions in management strategy including shared management, whole wage, and housekeeping allowance systems. When couples use a shared management system, they each have access to pooled assets, and each partner takes monies as needed. Whole wage approaches take two forms. In a male whole wage approach, the husband takes sole responsibility for managing household finances. A female whole wage approach sees a husband handing over a portion of his wages to his wife so that she can manage the household finances. The housekeeping allowance approach follows separate, gendered spheres of responsibility. In this arrangement, the husband manages the family money and provides an allowance to the wife for certain household expenditures.

As these different management approaches show, the decisions of household allocation can often reflect gendered preferences and power differences within the household. The management of assets is often examined as an indication of the equality of relationships with a shared management approach deemed ideal (Blumstein and Schwartz, 1991; Vogler and Pahl, 1993, 1994; Pahl, 1995; Elizabeth, 2001). When resources are jointly managed, both partners are more likely to have equal access to pooled monies. If one spouse manages the assets, however, there is more likely to be an imbalance in control over money, say, in how it is spent, and access to personal spending money or experiences of deprivation (Pahl, 1995).

Restricted access to assets is bundled with a number of other indicators of inequality, including a disproportionate share of the unpaid housework and less power and influence in decision making (Blumstein and Schwartz, 1985, 1991). Tichenor (2005), for example, links men's say over money, veto power in spending decisions, other decision-making authority, and lack of responsibility for unpaid work at home as dimensions of male power in relationships. An imbalance in access and control over financial resources can have serious consequences, including economic dependence of one spouse on the other and barriers to leaving unhealthy and unsafe relationships (Barnett and LaViolette, 1993). Research on abuse within marriage finds a link between the controlling behavior associated with abuse and control of financial resources. Known as economic abuse, abusive men often control wives' access to bank accounts and their ability to earn and control their own money (Johnson, 1995).

Blood and Wolfe (1960) provide the classic couple-level explanation for marital inequality stemming from money management. Using resource theory, they suggest that the relative resource contribution of spouses is the key factor promoting more or less equal arrangements. When relative resource contributions – income in particular – approach equality, there is a corresponding equality in management and access to money. Conversely, when one spouse is the sole or dominant provider, that spouse maintains an economic advantage and has better alternatives to the relationship, making them likely to be the sole money manager (Blood and Wolfe, 1960). While income contribution is important, Blumberg's (1988) theory of gender stratification draws attention to control of resources. With a particular concern for inequality experienced by women in relationships, Blumberg (1988) points out that even when women contribute income or own property, they remain unequal with their spouses if they do not control the resources. This distinction between contribution and controlling of resources remains important in the sociological literature on money management in marriage (see Pahl, 1995; Schmeer, 2005).

For a long time, economists made the sociologically naïve assumption that couples shared interests, and therefore, they treated couples as a single decision-making agent (see Lundberg and Pollak, 1996). Within-couple dynamics were ignored in favor of the assumption of consensus within couples or of an altruistic leader making decisions in the best interest of the family. This began to change with the work of Manser and Brown (1980) and McElroy and Horney (1981) who broke up the couple into separate units with sometimes competing interests. These bargaining models draw on game theory to examine the competing interests of husbands and wives and threats to exit or withdraw. Husbands and wives can threaten divorce in the bargaining process. The more credible threat based on options available upon exiting the relationship determines advantage in the bargaining process. Lundberg and Pollak (1993) have proposed a model that uses the threat of withdrawn contributions to the couple's shared goods. Here, husbands and wives only contribute the minimum to the couple in order to make the shared relationship better than divorce. The outcome is collectively worse as each pursue their singular interest rather than the benefits following from a shared agreement to cooperate. Income contributions again take an important place in the bargaining of husbands and wives.

The insights following from bargaining models have been used to study inequality in marriage in the United Kingdom (Lundberg, Pollak, and Wales, 1997), Canada

(Phipps and Burton, 1998) and in developing countries such as South Africa (Gummerson and Schneider, 2012). Lundberg, Pollak, and Wales (1997) took advantage of a change in the UK Child Benefit in the late 1970s to examine bargaining dynamics between husbands and wives. Prior to 1977, a family and child tax deduction was available to households with children. This was discontinued and replaced with a Child Benefit payment made weekly to mothers. Lundberg, Pollak, and Wales (1997) found that with this change, there was a corresponding change in family expenditures toward wives' and children's goods, suggesting wives' increased bargaining advantage.

Gummerson and Schneider (2012) have shown that the research in developing countries raises interesting questions about bargaining models. Typically, these models assume two-person, husband and wife, bargaining contexts. In many developing countries, however, households commonly include sets of adults who make income contributions and have interests on household expenditures. Examining data from South Africa, Gummerson and Schneider (2012) show that these more complicated household structures influence the bargaining dynamics. First, as the number of adults in a household increases, the influence of wives' relative income contribution decreases. Second, they find that gendered bargaining dynamics still persist in larger households, with more female adults influencing household expenditures toward wives' interests. The finding raises questions about household financial contributions coming from adults other than husbands and wives. While the research focuses on intrahousehold contributions, contributions from outside the household in the form of transfers or remittances may also be important (see Guzman, Morison, and Sjoblom, 2008).

Institutional Approaches to Managing Money

Our own work (Yodanis and Lauer, 2007a, b; Lauer and Yodanis, 2011), which we draw on here, has built on Treas's initial observation that "family financial practices exist in a context of cultural values and societal ideologies" (Treas, 1993, p. 727). The notion that institutionalized practices and norms shape couples' options and their assumptions about possible action is rooted in new institutional approaches in sociology (Cherlin, 1978). The approach suggests that the institutional context within which couples are embedded provides tools that shape and limit possibilities for action (Swidler, 1986). Following Nee (2005, p. 55), we define institutions as "a dominant system of interrelated informal and formal elements – customs, shared beliefs, conventions, norms, and rules – which actors orient their actions to when they pursue their interests." When couples decide a course of action, they do not act solely as a couple or as individuals, but as members of a larger social context, and they refer and defer to established rules for, practices of, and thinking about how to act. This approach provides an important complement to the couple level of analysis discussed earlier. An institutional approach, for instance, finds that decisions to integrate resources or to manage pooled resources equally are modified by the existing institutions in which they are embedded. In the following text, we first examine how an institutional approach can provide insights into a couple's practice of integrating resources in a common pot or maintaining separate purses. Following this, we examine how an institutional approach can provide key understanding of inequality of money management in marriage.

Institutional approaches to integrating resources

As sociologists and historians have previously documented, marriage as an institution evolves over time (Burgess and Locke, 1945; Cherlin, 2004; Coontz, 2004, 2005). Originally, the focus of marriage was connecting families to advance and maintain their political and economic interests. The individuals getting married were largely irrelevant to this goal and had little say in the arrangement, which was used to build family networks in order to consolidate socioeconomic standing and power or secure economic survival (Coontz, 2005). Households did the work that other social institutions, including the economy and legal and political systems, do today (Mintz and Kellogg, 1988). These institutional arrangements were patriarchal, with a male head of the family having the legal and social authority to have control over the behavior and resources of family members, including the wife (Coontz, 2005). This patriarchy was reflected in male domination of money management. Zelizer (1989) has shown that patriarchal marriage was characterized by men controlling all of the household money, giving women only a certain amount to spend on household needs.

With larger societal and economic shifts, the state, economy, and other social institutions took over much of the production and power that had rested within the family (Mintz and Kellogg, 1988). In this context, marriage changed to what Burgess and Locke (1945) called a companionate marriage characterized by an integrated partnership between spouses. The focus of the companionate marriage is love and the feelings between the husband and wife as two people become *one* after marriage. The marriage symbolizes an integrated unit with each spouse specializing in a socially defined role – typically the husband as the income earner and the wife as a housekeeper and caregiver.

Fulfilling these traditional family roles took precedence over fulfilling one's personal interests and desires. This interdependence between spouses was of relatively low risk because it was legally, economically, and socially difficult to end a marriage. Marriage, despite constraining personal freedoms, served as an institutional guarantee for the partners (Becker, 1981). As the institution of marriage shifted to companionate marriages, characterized by a greater integrated partnership between spouses, pooling money became the dominant arrangement for managing money (Zelizer, 1989).

Many contemporary sociologists and historians consider our current period a new stage in the institution of marriage (Giddens, 1992; Beck and Beck-Gernsheim, 2002; Amato *et al.*, 2007). Lauer and Yodanis (2010) suggest that there are two separate propositions following from these current discussions of marriage that are often conflated. First, they find that these arguments suggest that marriage in many modern societies is one option among others, and the marital unit is no longer the only or most prominent coupling arrangement (Cherlin, 2004). They call this the alternatives to marriage proposition (Lauer and Yodanis, 2010, 2011). Second, they find a proposal that marriage is itself becoming more individualized (Amato *et al.*, 2007; Cherlin, 2009). Individualized marriage includes new understandings of entering and exiting marriage. According to this proposal, relationships are being entered for their own sake and for the intimacy and emotional support that the relationship provides (Giddens, 1992). When partners no longer receive these benefits, they are free to leave the relationship to manage on their own or to find support in another relationship (Cherlin, 2009). As a result, even when in relationships, partners maintain their individuality and ability to leave the relationship and avoid arrangements that would make it difficult to end the relationship when it is no longer satisfying (Giddens, 1992). Within individualized marriage, the two individuals are less likely to become one interdependent unit or to sacrifice their own individuality for socially defined roles. They pursue their own interests and goals and remain two individuals within the context of a relationship. This leads to less specialization in tasks, with husbands and wives both contributing to the family income and unpaid care work. Roles are negotiated through a democratic process rather than by externally prescribed rules, with each partner having competencies in a wider range of roles and thereby being able to care and provide for him- or herself (Giddens, 1992). As with other institutional changes in marriage, these new rules and practices should be associated with different accepted practices for managing money. In particular, as we develop later, pooling money in a common pot runs counter to the practice of individualized marriages. Under individualized marriage, we should see each partner managing their own money.

There is an important symmetry to the research on transaction costs, individualized marriage, and decisions to pool or not to pool money in marriage. Treas (1993), as we noted earlier, first recognized the relevance of transaction costs arguments to the management of money in married couples. When relationship-specific investments are made, such as couple's investments in their relationship through having children or specializing in market work, collective money management is more likely because of the efficiency gained through reduced transaction costs. Important to our institutional interest here, we argue that the relationship characteristics that transaction cost arguments attribute to forming collective arrangements are the inverse of factors attributed to institutional changes toward the individualization of marriage. Couples with individualized understandings of marriage seek to maintain independent identities and independence, including the ability to easily leave a relationship if they choose (Cherlin, 2009). Therefore, they avoid relationship-specific investments in an effort to maintain individual autonomy and the ease of ending relationships. As a result, within the context of individualized marriage, couples should be less likely to pool their money in a common pot and be more likely to keep and manage their money separately.

Supporting this, Treas and Widmer (2000) examined how characteristics of individualized marriage found in postmaterialist societies shape the management of money. Their work suggests that increased rates of cohabitation and declining beliefs that the purpose or outcome of marriage lies in relationship-specific investments (such as having children) increased the prevalence of couples who kept their money separate. Lauer and Yodanis (2011) looked at money management arrangements across 31 country contexts and found that keeping money separate was quite rare. Overall, only 6% of couples kept all of their money separate. There was variation across contexts. In Hungary and Spain, less than 1% of couples kept money separate, but in the United States, nearly 8% did. In Finland, just over half of couples pooled resources, but over 25% kept all of their money separate. Looking to explain this variation, Lauer and Yodanis (2011) find that when couples approached their marriage with individualized understandings, they were more likely to keep their money separate.

If the current institutional context of marriage tends toward individualization, the most surprising finding of this research may be the persistence of the practice of pooling money. Lauer and Yodanis (2011) find that keeping money completely separate is rare, and keeping even some money separate is uncommon. Even married couples who start off with individualized, separate money management systems move quite quickly toward some form of pooled money management (Burgoyne, Reibstein, Edmunds, and Dolman, 2007; Burgoyne, Reibstein, Edmunds, and Routh, 2010).

It can be valuable to compare married and cohabiting couples surrounding the decision to pool income. Cohabiting relationships are an alternative to marriage that appear to be more individualized and can relax some expectations for long-term commitment. Heimdal and Houseknecht (2003), for instance, find that cohabitors in both the United States and Sweden are more likely to keep their money in separate accounts than are married couples. This difference persists even when holding socio-economic status and gender ideology constant. Even here, however, most cohabiting couples pool their incomes. In Sweden, where cohabiting is quite common, 52.1% of couples pooled resources, and in the United States, 54.3% pooled (Heimdal and Houseknecht, 2003, p. 532). In a study of Norwegian couples, Lyngstad, Noack, and Tufte (2011) find that, like married couples, cohabiting couples are more likely to pool resources when their relationships are long term.

A current debate in Canada regarding rights to money and financial assets in cohabiting couples highlights interesting questions from an institutional perspective. In Canada, couples in cohabiting relationships have been granted most of the same legal rights and responsibilities as married couples. The one exception has been financial rights, and this is currently also changing. In the province of British Columbia, for example, with the new Family Law Act, cohabiting couples who live together for 2 years will have joint legal access to money and property. Following the model of joint property rights in divorce law, these changes are meant to equalize partners' access to money and property in the relationship. Yet in Quebec, where cohabiting is very common like in Sweden, there is opposition to requiring cohabiting couples to view their money as joint property. This, it is argued, would make cohabitation too much like marriage (LeBourdais and Lapierre-Adamcyk, 2004). Cohabiting, they have argued, should not have the same institutional rules as marriage because people choosing to cohabit instead of marrying are doing so because they want an alternative.

There are a few possible explanations for persistence of pooling resources in a common pot. First, there may remain some efficiency in pooling resources like those first addressed by Treas (1993), particularly when couples develop long-term conti-nuity expectations or make relationship-specific investments. Second, Vogler, Brockmann, and Wiggins (2006) suggest that keeping money separate may promote more inequality in relationships, especially when spouses have unequal incomes (Kenney, 2006), an outcome that would not be appealing to couples in individual-ized contexts. Third, it may be that, even in contexts where marriage is becoming individualized, integrating resources remains an important symbol of commitment between partners (Singh 1997; Burgoyne *et al.*, 2010). Finally, and perhaps most simply, the persistence of integrating resources may reflect the lack of individualization in the institution of marriage (Jamieson, 1999; Lauer and Yodanis, 2011). Indeed, there is evidence that many practices continue in marriage that are not indicators of individualized marriage, including wives taking their husbands' last names in the United States, couples sharing friendship networks and spending large amounts of time together in leisure activities in the Netherlands, and a rigid gendered division of labor across countries (Kalmijn and Bernasco, 2001; Gooding and Kreider, 2010; Treas and Drobnic, 2010; Yodanis and Lauer, 2014).

One interesting development in the integration of resources involves what Ashby and Burgoyne (2008) call partial-pooling strategies. Partial-pooling includes couples who pool money while also keeping at least some money separate. Partial-pooling may capture the unique dynamics of individualization processes, as it allows couples to handle the practical aspects of coupling while maintaining some individual autonomy in the relationship. Looking across-country contexts, Lauer and Yodanis (2011) found that within countries where marriages were more individualized, couples were more likely to keep at least some money separate. Partial-pooling strategies may be an important area for future research on the decision to pool or not to pool resources.

Institutional approaches to gender inequality in money management

As gender theorists have long argued, gender involves individual actions and beliefs and also becomes institutionalized in patterned ideology and expectations for behavior that rigidly shape and constrain possible actions (Ferree, 1990; Martin, 2004; Risman, 2004). As with the institution of marriage, gender structures shape couples' management of money. Zelizer (1989, p. 368), for example, takes a historical look at money in marriage at the turn of the nineteenth century finding that "regardless of its sources, once money had entered the household, its allocation, calculation, and uses were subject to a set of domestic rules distinct from the rules of the market." Rather than its typical instrumental designation as a means of exchange, money takes on meaning in the context of the household and the people who control it. This may vary by gender, class, and even age. Zelizer (1989) finds children's money a subject of debate at the time, for instance. Allowances emerged as a proper allocation for children, but it was considered as educational money. It is wives' money that particularly interested Zelizer (1989) – the means, timing, and amount allocated, along with its primary use as housekeeping money. She finds the allocation of housekeeping money followed cultural expectations, varying by class, rather than a universal logic of the market. In the domestic realm, the meaning of income earned by spouses and the arrangements for managing and spending money are tied to dominant beliefs and practices regarding men and women's *acceptable* roles in marriage, in particular who is expected to be the breadwinner and who is expected to provide care (Blumstein and Schwartz, 1985). These institutionalized rules for gendered marital behavior evolve and change over time yet continually shape the role of money in marriage.

Gendered rules shape the dynamics of pooled money, including who and how spouses benefit from it. Returning to Pahl's (1983, 1995) distinctions between shared management, whole wage, and housekeeping allowance systems, these various strategies for managing collective assets highlight that pooling assets can be an equal or unequal arrangement depending on who is in charge of the collective pot. An equal distribution of money means partners have equal access to assets; inequality exists when one spouse is in charge of the pooled assets. Although shared management can include unique inequalities (see Singh, 1997), Pahl (1995) has found that shared management is more equal than one spouse managing the pooled income (see also Vogler and Pahl, 1993, 1994; Nyman, 1999). Interestingly, shared management approaches are more equal for women than approaches that give them sole responsibility for the management of household finances. The gender of the spouse who is the sole manager of the money impacts spouses' access to money and how they spend it. Research has found that, in general, women are disadvantaged if one spouse, either the wife or the husband, manages their pooled assets (Pahl, 1995; Nyman, 1999). Male management systems are associated with male dominance in the relationship and personal spending (Pahl, 2000). Yet, often women's management is not related to their advantage in the relationship. Perhaps, surprisingly, women can experience more financial deprivation and less personal spending when they manage assets than if men do (Pahl, 1995; Nyman, 1999). Vogler and Pahl (1994), in a sample of British households, found that wives' control of finances increased decision-making power but also resulted in greater financial deprivation for wives.

When a household has limited money and, thereby, the task of managing money and making ends meet is particularly difficult, women are more likely to have the job. Evidence from national and cross-national surveys shows that men are more likely to manage the money when the family income is high and women are more likely to manage the money when the family income is low (Pahl, 1983, 1995). When money is short and women are in control of finances, they deprive themselves of needs and desires rather than require the same sacrifices from other family members. Nyman (1999) captures this dynamic in her interviews of Swedish couples. In all couples, the wife had primary responsibility for day-to-day family expenditures. The wives in her study were often burdened with expenditures dealing with day-to-day management of the household. These expenditures often led them to take from their own discretionary money in order to meet these needs. In many cases, both husbands and wives agree that more of their household money is spent on the husband's interests, but it was not acknowledged by the couples as unfair. Overall, men's income and management of the couple's pooled assets often translates into power, whereas women's income and management can become another household task (Vogler and Pahl, 1994; Nyman, 1999).

These complexities are also apparent in Japan. In comparison to other countries, Japan is more traditional in terms of gender ideology and gendered divisions of labor (Yodanis and Lauer, 2007b). Despite this, Yodanis and Lauer (2007b), in a comparison of 21 countries, found Japanese women are far more likely to report that they, not their husbands, manage the household money. It seems that for Japanese women, money management might simply be part of household work. There is also evidence that Japanese women are not powerless in their money management position. Data from an insurance company survey in Japan found that a majority of Japanese women kept secret bank accounts that their husbands did not know about. They used this as security for the family and in case the relationship would end (Tanikawa, 2006).

The gendered aspects of household expenditures and the different interests and pressures associated with husbands and wives when spending money are an important demonstration of how the gendered household and gendered preferences are institutionalized. Wives' spending of money is shaped by gendered expectations that women's spending, not men's, is directed toward the collective care of children and the family. This has consequences for child welfare (Pahl, 2000). Kenney (2008) points out that research in developing countries has often led the way here, noting that women's control of income was associated with improvements in child health in Brazil (Thomas, 1990); increased spending on nutrients, health, and housing in Mexico (Djebbari, 2005); and increased spending on food and decreased spending on clothing, alcohol, and cigarettes in Ivory Coast (Hoddinott and Haddad, 1995). These dynamics are not limited to developing countries, however. In their classic study, Lundberg, Pollak, and Wales (1997) found increases in the ratio of children's to men's clothing expenditures with the initiation of the Child Benefit payment that went to mothers in the United Kingdom. In Canada, Phipps and Burton (1998) have also found women's income associated with increased food expenditures. In the United States, Kenney (2008) finds that fathers' control of money is associated with greater food insecurity for children in the low- and moderate-income households she examined.

Kenney's research highlights the importance of control of household money, which is not always explicitly addressed in research on spending. Schmeer (2005) addresses income contribution and control separately in her research on expenditures in the Philippines. Her research examines weekly food expenditures and measures separately relative income contribution, control over pooled money spending, receipt of a spousal income transfer, or control of household food money. Schmeer (2005) finds that control of income by women in poor households is particularly important for directing resources toward purchases of food for children. Notably, this benefit is seen when women both contribute *and* control money and not when they only contribute or control money. This raises a question about the value of keeping separate accounts for gender equality in marriages. It seems clear that when wives have control of separate accounts, they are able to direct resources toward expenditures they deem valuable. Often, this improves the welfare of children in the household but may overlook the potential inequality stemming from keeping separate accounts. Wives on average earn less than husbands, so keeping separate accounts can create a default disadvantage. Nyman (1999) captures this in her research on Swedish couples, many of whom kept separate accounts. These couples held a strong orientation toward equality, but by keeping separate accounts, wives often deprived themselves of their own needs and desires in order to satisfy their children's. Discussing the difficulties of balancing family needs, one respondent says, "...I think it would be really good if we had a joint account...where our paychecks could be deposited, we could pay all our bills from there..." (Nyman, 1999, p. 780). This desire captures the potential downside of separate accounts.

Gendered rules also shape how each spouse's income translates into control over pooled resources. Institutionalized breadwinning roles, that is, expectations about who should be the primary income provider in couples, are a particularly important part of the money management context. In contexts with strong expectations that men, and not women, should be the primary providers within families, husbands have more access to and control over family income. Women with little or no income are less likely to have equal management arrangements with their husbands, while women with more equal income contributions are more likely to have control over the money (Kenney, 2006). Still, husbands' control over the household money continues regardless of the true value of the income earned by each spouse (Blumstein and Schwartz, 1985; Vogler and Pahl, 1993; Vogler, 1998). Tichenor (1999) finds that when women earn more than men, the opposite of what resource theory and rational actor models would predict occurs. Women do not use their higher earnings to gain authority over financial assets and spending as men may do when they earn more. Instead, there is evidence that inequality again increases, with women often giving final veto power to their husbands when they provide more income to the relationship than their spouse. Tichenor, like Brines (1994) and Blumstein and Schwartz (1991), suggests that this occurs because of institutionalized rules for appropriate gender behavior that override the effect of resource contribution. When women make more than men, it is counternormative, as the socially defined expectations for the breadwinner role are violated. For women to control the income would further violate these rules. When women have access to the resources, they could use these to their advantage, as resource theory would predict, but they do not. Instead, gendered rules for behavior take precedence (Blumstein and Schwartz, 1985; Tichenor, 1999).

Recently, one of the more interesting developments in marriage research has questioned the potential of gendered rules of married life to override the importance of financial contributions to a household. This challenge has focused particularly on domestic labor (Gupta, 2006, 2007; Sullivan, 2011a). Gupta (2007) has proposed an autonomy hypothesis that suggests a wife's absolute income is the most important factor influencing the amount of housework she engages in, with higher incomes leading to less housework. He finds support for this hypothesis, and importantly, this effect rules out the influence of relative resource contribution and overcompensation in gendered displays of housework. This work highlights the need to consider other social rules and practices, in addition to gendered inequalities, that can impact inequality in money management within households. Yodanis and Lauer (2007a), for example, find that the level of economic inequality overall in a society can influence the likelihood of having equal or unequal money management arrangements. High levels of income inequality, low levels of social expenditures, and ideological support of inequality in a country can trickle down into households, making unequal money management arrangements in households within those countries more likely.

Key to our discussion here, however, the argument in support of an autonomous effect of income on housework does not challenge a gendered household (see Gupta, 2007, Sullivan, 2011b). While surplus income can allow wives to purchase some freedom from housework, this dynamic assumes an institutionalized gendered household. In fact, Gupta (2007) points to the research on household expenditures coming from the money management field as an inspiration for the autonomous approach to domestic labor. The importance of these expectations is particularly clear when we look across contexts at the management of money. Treas and Tai (2012) found that, cross-nationally, women's higher income relative to their husbands does translate into women having more say in major purchases, but it also translates into their making decisions about the children and weekend activities. In other words, women, especially if they have a higher income, do more of the household management. As Treas and Tai (2012, pp. 22–23) suggest, "traditionally responsible for family and household, women may feel a greater stake than men in household outcomes, or women may simply take on household management to validate a feminine identity by 'doing gender.'"

Yodanis and Lauer (2007b) also use a comparative approach to study unequal versus equal money management arrangements across multiple country contexts. Gendered ideologies and practices that vary across countries, particularly related to breadwinner roles, are also an important influence on money management arrangements. Within contexts where shared breadwinning ideologies are dominant either ideologically or in practice, couples are less likely to report the unequal money management arrangement of one person controlling all the household income. Institutionalized gendered rules shape how women's income is related to the management of money, the influence on the control of money, and the direction of household expenditures.

Conclusions

The management of money in marriage has proven to be a rich source of research for sociologists. Cross-national surveys comparing dozens of countries and country-specific studies from across the globe, including Canada, the United Kingdom, the United States, Puerto Rico, the Philippines, Japan, South Africa, Sweden, Norway, and Australia, have provided important insights to a daily practice, interaction, source of conflict, and inequality within households.

Day to day, couples manage household income through couple-level interaction. Yet the rules for these interactions are rooted in institutionalized rules and practices that shape how it is done and the consequences of it. As sociologists, we take a step back from the interactions to understand the institutional arrangements that shape the variation in money management strategies over time and across cultures. Through these analyses, the study of money management helps us understand how both the institution of marriage and gender dynamics have changed (or how much they have not changed). From recent studies, we know that pooling money remains common in marriage and that women manage money when resources are tight and prioritize the needs and desires of other family members over their own. The study of money management in households can thus lead us to question the extent to which marriage is actually individualized and the extent to which gendered rules within marriage have actually become weaker or more equal. The study of money management is complex, because money in households is a lot more than its use in financial exchanges (Zelizer, 1989; Singh, 1997). How money is managed has symbolic meaning in marriage. The same system of management can have different meanings and outcomes depending on the gender of the person in charge. Income contribution is different from money management, and management is not the same as control or power. Money is not simply money. Rather, it symbolizes and is a window into complex social dynamics and institutions. As such, the management of money in households holds continuing interest and promise within sociology.

References

Amato, P., Booth, A., Johnson, D. and Rogers, S. (2007) *Alone Together: How Marriage in America is Changing*, Harvard University Press, Cambridge, MA.

Ashby, K. and Burgoyne, C. (2008) Separate financial entities? Beyond categories of money management. *Journal of Socio-Economics*, 37, 458–480.

Barnett, O. and LaViolette, A. (1993) *It Could Happen to Anyone: Why Battered Women Stay*, Sage, Newbury Park.

Beck, U. and Beck-Gernsheim, E. (2002). *Individualization: Institutionalized Individualism and its Social and Political Consequences*, Sage, London.

Becker, G. (1981). *A Treatise on the Family*, Harvard University Press, Cambridge, MA.

Blood, R. and Wolfe, D. (1960) *Husbands and Wives: The Dynamics of Married Living*, Free Press, New York.

Blumberg, R.L. (1988) Income under female versus male control: hypotheses from a theory of gender stratification and data from the third world. *Journal of Family Issues*, 9, 51–84.

Blumstein, P. and Schwartz, P. (1985) *American Couples: Money, Work, and Sex*, Pocket Books, New York.

Blumstein, P. and Schwartz, P. (1991) Money and ideology: their impact on power and the division of household labor, in *Gender, Family, and Economy: The Triple Overlap* (ed. R.L. Blumberg), Sage, Newbury Park, pp. 261–288.

Brines, J. (1994) Economic dependency, gender, and the division of labor at home. *American Journal of Sociology*, 100, 652–688.

Burgess, E. and Locke, H. (1945) *The Family: From Institution to Companionship*, American, Book Co., New York.

Burgoyne, C. and Morison, V. (1997) Money in remarriage: keeping things simple—and separate. *Sociological Review*, 45, 363–395.

Burgoyne, C.B., Reibstein, J., Edmunds, A. and Dolman, V. (2007) Money management systems in early marriage: factors influencing change and stability. *Journal of Economic Psychology*, 28, 214–228.

Burgoyne, C.B., Reibstein, J., Edmunds, A. and Routh, D. (2010) Marital commitment, money and marriage preparation. What changes after the wedding? *Journal of Community and Applied Social Psychology*, 20, 390–403.

Cherlin, A. (1978) Remarriage as an incomplete institution. *American Journal of Sociology*, 84, 634–650.

Cherlin, A.J. (2004) The deinstitutionalization of American marriage. *Journal of Marriage and Family*, 66, 848–861.

Cherlin, A.J. (2009) *The Marriage-Go-Round: The State of Marriage and the Family in America Today*, Knopf, New York.

Coontz, S. (2004) The world historical transformation of marriage. *Journal of Marriage and Family*, 66, 974–979.

Coontz, S. (2005) *Marriage, a History: From Obedience to Intimacy or How Love Conquered Marriage*, Viking, New York.

Djebbari, H. (2005) *The Impact on Nutrition of the Intrahousehold Distribution of Power*. IZA Discussion Paper 1701, Institute for the Study of Labor, Bonn Germany.

Elizabeth, V. (2001) Managing money, managing coupledom: a critical examination of cohabitants' money management practices. *Sociological Review*, 49, 389–411.

Ferree, M.M. (1990) Beyond separate spheres: feminism and family research. *Journal of Marriage and the Family*, 52, 866–884.

Giddens, A. (1992) *The Transformation of Intimacy: Sexuality, Love and Eroticism in Modern Societies*, Stanford University Press, Stanford.

Gooding, G. and Kreider, R. (2010) Women's marital naming choices in a nationally representative sample. *Journal of Family Issues*, 31, 681–701.

Gummerson, E. and Schneider, D. (2012) Eat, drink, man, woman: gender, income share and household expenditures in South Africa. *Social Forces*, 91, 813–836.

Gupta, S. (2006) Her money, her time: women's earnings and their housework time. *Social Science Research*, 35, 975–999.

Gupta, S. (2007) Autonomy, dependence, or display? The relationship between married women's earnings and housework. *Journal of Marriage and Family*, 69, 399–417.

Guzman, J.C., Morison, A. and Sjoblom, M. (2008) The impact of remittances and gender on household expenditure patterns: evidence from Ghana, in *The International Migration of Women* (ed. A.R. Morrison, M. Schiff, and M. Sjoblom), Palgrave Macmillian, New York, NY, pp. 125–152.

Heimdal, K.R. and Houseknecht, S.K. (2003) Cohabiting and married couples' income organization: approaches in Sweden and the United States. *Journal of Marriage and Family*, 65, 525–538.

Hoddinott, J. and Haddad, L. (1995) Does female income share influence household expenditures? Evidence from Cote D'Ivoire. *Oxford Bulletin of Economic Statistics*, 57, 77–96.

Jamieson, L. (1999) Intimacy transformed? A critical look at the 'pure relationship'. *Sociology*, 33, 477–494.

Johnson, M. (1995) Patriarchal terrorism and common couple violence. *Journal of Marriage and Family*, 57, 283–294.

Kalmijn, M. and Bernasco, W. (2001) Joint and separated lifestyles in couple relationships. *Journal of Marriage and Family*, 63, 639–654.

Kenney, C.T. (2006) The power of the purse: allocative systems and inequality in couple households. *Gender & Society*, 20, 354–381.

Kenney, C.T. (2008) Father doesn't know best? Parents' control of money and children's food insecurity. *Journal of Marriage and Family*, 70, 654–669.

Lauer, S.R. and Yodanis, C. (2010) A reconsideration of the deinstitutionalization of marriage: a new institutional approach to changes in marriage. *Journal of Family Theory and Review*, 2, 58–72.

Lauer, S.R. and Yodanis, C. (2011) Individualized marriage and the integration of resources. *Journal of Marriage and Family*, 73, 669–683.

LeBourdais, C. and Lapierre-Adamcyk, E. (2004) Changes in conjugal life in Canada: is cohabitation progressively replacing marriage? *Journal of Marriage and Family*, 66, 929–942.

Lundberg, S. and Pollak, R. (1993) Separate spheres bargaining in the marriage market. *Journal of Political Economy*, 101, 988–1010.

Lundberg, S. and Pollak, R. (1996) Bargaining and distribution in marriage. *Journal of Economic Perspectives*, 10, 139–158.

Lundberg, S., Pollak, R. and Wales, T. (1997) Do husbands and wives pool their resources? Evidence from the United Kingdom child benefit. *Journal of Human Resources*, 32, 463–480.

Lyngstad, T.H., Noack, T. and Tufte, P.A. (2011) Pooling of economic resources: a comparison of Norwegian married and cohabiting couples. *European Sociological Review*, 27, 624–635.

Manser, M. and Brown, M. (1980) Marriage and household decision making: a bargaining analysis. *International Economic Review*, 21, 31–44.

Martin, P.Y. (2004) Gender as social institution. *Social Forces*, 82, 1249–1273.

McElroy, M.B. and Horney, M.J. (1981) Nash bargaining household decisions. *International Economic Review*, 22, 333–349.

Mintz, S. and Kellogg, S. (1988) *Domestic Revolutions: A Social History of American Family*, Free Press, New York.

Nee, V. (2005) The new institutionalism in economics and sociology, in *Handbook of Economic Sociology* (eds N. Smelser and R. Swedberg), Princeton University Press, Princeton, pp. 49–70.

Nyman, C. (1999) Gender equality in 'the most equal country in the World'?: money and marriage in Sweden. *Sociological Review*, 47, 766–793.

Oropesa, R.S. and Landale, N. (2005) Equal access to income and union dissolution among mainland Puerto Ricans. *Journal of Marriage and Family*, 67, 173–190.

Oropesa, R.S., Landale, N. and Kenkre, T.S. (2003) Income allocation in marital and cohabiting unions. *Journal of Marriage and Family*, 65, 910–926.

Pahl, J. (1983) The allocation of money and the structuring of inequality within marriage. *Sociological Review*, 31, 237–262.

Pahl, J. (1995) His money, her money: recent research on financial organization in marriage. *Journal of Economic Psychology*, 16, 361–376.

Pahl, J. (2000) The gendering of spending within households. *Radical Statistics*, 75, 38–48.

Pahl, J. (2005) Individualism in couple finances: who pays for the children? *Social Policy & Society*, 4, 381–391.

Pahl, J. (2008) Family finances, individualization, spending patterns, and access to credit. *Journal of Socio-Economics*, 37, 577–591.

Papp, L.M., Cummings, M.E. and Goeke-Morey, M.C. (2009) For richer or poorer: money as a topic of marital conflict in the home. *Family Relations*, 58, 91–103.

Phipps, S. and Burton, P. (1998) What's mine is yours? The influence of male and female incomes on patterns of household expenditure. *Economica*, 65, 599–613.

Pollak, R.A. (1985) A transaction cost approach to families and households. *Journal of Economic Literature*, 23, 581–608.

Risman, B. (2004) Gender as a social structure: theory wrestling with activism. *Gender & Society*, 18, 429–450.

Schmeer, K. (2005) Women's resource position and household food expenditures in Cebu, Philippines. *Journal of Marriage and Family*, 67, 399–409.

Singh, S. (1997). *Marriage Money: The Social Shaping of Money in Marriage and Banking*, Allen & Unwin, St. Leonards.

Sullivan, O. (2011a) An end to gender display through the performance of housework? A review and reassessment of the quantitative literature using insights from the qualitative literature. *Journal of Family Theory and Review*, 3, 1–13.

Sullivan, O. (2011b) Gender deviance neutralization through housework: where does it fit in the bigger picture? Response to England, Kluwer, and Risman. *Journal of Family Theory and Review*, 3, 27–31.

Swidler, A. (1986) Culture in action: symbols and strategies. *American Sociological Review*, 51, 273–286.

Tanikawa, M. (2006) Out of the Dresser and into the Bank. *The New York Times* (Aug 4). http://www.nytimes.com/2006/08/04/your-money/04iht-mmanage05.2390040.html?_r=1& (accessed November 22, 2013).

Thomas, D. (1990) Intra-household resource allocation: an inferential approach. *The Journal of Human Resources*, 25, 635–664.

Tichenor, V.J. (1999) Status and income as gendered resources: the case of marital power. *Journal of Marriage and the Family*, 61, 638–650.

Tichenor, V.J. (2005) *Earning More and Getting Less: Why Successful Wives Can't Buy Equality*, Rutgers University Press, New Brunswick.

Treas, J. (1993) Money in the bank: transaction costs and the economic organization of marriage. *American Sociological Review*, 58, 723–734.

Treas, J. and Drobnic, S. (eds) (2010) *Dividing the Domestic: Men, Women, and Household Work in Cross-National Perspective*, Stanford University Press, Palo Alto, CA.

Treas, J. and Tai, T. (2012) How couples manage the household: work and power in cross-national perspective. *Journal of Family Issues*, 32, 1–29.

Treas, J. and Widmer, E. (2000) Whose money? A multi-level analysis of financial management in marriage for 23 countries, in *The Management of Durable Relations: Theoretical Models and Empirical Studies of Households and Organizations* (eds J. Weesie and W. Raub), ThelaThesis, Amsterdam, pp. 44–58.

Vogler, C. (1998) Money in the household: some underlying issues of power. *Sociological Review*, 46, 687–713.

Vogler, C. and Pahl, J. (1993) Social and economic change and the organization of money within marriage. *Work, Employment, & Society*, 7, 71–95.

Vogler, C. and Pahl, J. (1994) Money, power and inequality within marriage. *Sociological Review*, 42, 263–288.

Vogler, C., Brockmann, M. and Wiggins, R.D. (2006) Intimate relationships and changing patterns of money management at the beginning of the twenty first century. *British Journal of Sociology*, 57, 455–482.

Yodanis, C. and Lauer, S.R. (2007a) Economic inequality in and outside of marriage: individual resources and institutional context. *European Sociological Review*, 23, 573–583.

Yodanis, C. and Lauer, S.R. (2007b) Managing money in marriage: multilevel and cross-national effects of the breadwinner role. *Journal of Marriage and Family*, 69, 1307–1325.

Yodanis, C. and Lauer, S.R. (2014) Is marriage individualized? What couples actually do. *Journal of Family Theory and Review*, 6, 2.

Zelizer, V.A. (1989) The social meaning of money: 'special monies'. *American Journal of Sociology*, 95, 342–377.

18

Family Transmission of Social and Cultural Capital

TOBY L. PARCEL AND JOSHUA A. HENDRIX

Scholars agree that inequality begins early in life. The families into which children are born provide resources children access beginning in infancy; families have unequal resources, and these differences influence the extent to which parents invest in their children as well as which investments they choose. We focus on two forms of investment – social and cultural capital. We believe that investments in these forms of capital play a major role in the unequal learning and social outcomes that children display as they move into adolescence and subsequent adulthood.

Our review is organized as follows. First, we offer a theoretical approach featuring social and cultural capital to unify what otherwise might seem to be unrelated perspectives on child and adolescent outcomes. We review literature that shows how social and cultural capital affects academic and social well-being. Referring to social well-being, we assume that delinquency is an indicator of poor social adjustment and so include a discussion of the effects of social and cultural capital on delinquency in our review. Second, we use a life course approach to summarize additional literature that takes either social or cultural capital, or both, seriously in determining several aspects of child and adolescent academic and social well-being. We devote particular attention to social class differences in patterns of investment. We conclude with discussion of unanswered questions and directions for future research.

In adopting this approach, we largely neglect the roles of human and financial capital, also important resources transmitted through families (Bradley and Corwyn, 2002; Conger and Donnellan, 2007). In addition, we omit much of the literature that discusses peers and adolescent networks as social capital (Haynie, 2001). Our review also precludes literature suggesting that children themselves can generate social capital useful in their own development (Offer and Schneider, 2007). While most of the empirical studies we cite focus on US populations, we set our review in international context through initial coverage of parental investment in several societies.

The Wiley Blackwell Companion to the Sociology of Families, First Edition.
Edited by Judith Treas, Jacqueline Scott, and Martin Richards.
© 2014 John Wiley & Sons Ltd. Published 2017 by John Wiley & Sons Ltd.

We selectively note findings from non-US studies in subsequent sections and in our review of cultural capital theory. Most of the studies we include are quantitative.

A major function of the family is to produce and socialize children, something that has occurred throughout human history. Precisely, what is transmitted to children, however, is historically bound. Originally, parents socialized children for survival and to become productive accepted adults within their cultures. Thus, the transmission of social and cultural capital occurred within the context of daily life. In the United States, settlers in New England adopted this approach with strong emphasis on religious indoctrination and preparing children for sex-typed, productive, and reproductive roles in adulthood (Mintz and Kellogg, 1988). They also had clear traditions involving the transmission of financial capital across generations, which included giving land to first-born sons and providing dowries for daughters upon marriage. It was not until the late eighteenth century that families began to show increased concern for child development as we understand it, and by the early nineteenth century, childhood began to be viewed as a distinct phase of life (Mintz and Kellogg, 1988; see also Ariès, 1962). Adolescence was not a term used until the early twentieth century (Crosnoe and Johnson, 2011). Thus, modern notions of families transmitting social and cultural capital to children and adolescents are recent ones, and, as we develop later, are class bound.

Theoretical Framework: Investment in Children and Adolescents

Social capital

Following Coleman (1988, 1990), by social capital, we understand resources that inhere in the relationships between and among actors and facilitate a range of social outcomes. Family social capital refers to the bonds between parents and children useful in promoting child socialization and, as such, includes the time and attention parents spend in interaction with children and in monitoring their activities and promoting child well-being (Kim and Schneider, 2005; Dufur, Parcel, and McKune, 2008). Furstenberg's (2005, p. 810) definition of social capital as a "stock of social goodwill created through shared social norms and a sense of common membership" is compatible with our view; integration in a family system typically includes shared norms and feelings of belonging, as well as social support and increased connections. Noting Putnam's (2000) distinction between *bonding* and *bridging* social capital, these intrafamily connections refer to *bonding* social capital, and these bonds are presumed to facilitate the positive growth of children and adolescents. Coleman also identifies *time closure* as a resource that encourages family bonding, because when parents are committed to one another and to children over an extended period of time, parental investments are likely to be greater and potentially more effective in socialization.

In addition, children benefit from the social connections that parents have with others such as neighbors, school personnel, and work colleagues (Johnson, Crosnoe, and Elder, 2001; Parcel and Dufur, 2001a, b; Crosnoe, 2004). *Intergenerational closure*, which Coleman defines as occurring when parents know their children's friends' parents, enables parents to pool resources in establishing and enforcing norms for children. Such connections beyond the family illustrate *bridging* social capital; the stronger these connections, the greater are the resources to which children have access. Critics of social capital theory contend that it fails to specify how families and individuals "generate, accumulate, manage, and deploy" social capital (Portes, 2000; Furstenberg, 2005, p. 809); this is not a debate we can fully adjudicate, although our review does speak to the deployment of social capital in the context of child and adolescent socialization.

Cultural capital

Bourdieu (1973) posits that advantaged families equip their children with high-status cultural symbols that facilitate social selection into high-status domains; he developed this perspective within the context of European societies. More privileged families teach their children to cultivate certain preferences, behaviors, and attitudes that institutions, such as schools and organizations, value and reward (see Lamont and Lareau, 1988; Lareau and Weinberg, 2003). As a result, academic and economic discrepancies form between the children of families who can and cannot provide the resources necessary to cultivate these behaviors in their children. Thus, cultural capital is exclusionary and contributes to social reproduction (Kingston, 2001). Bourdieu treats cultural capital as *highbrow competence* and measures possession of capital as participation in and consumption of elite art, such as trips to museums and classical concerts (Jæger, 2009; Yamamoto and Brinton, 2010).

Other researchers conceptualize cultural capital differently, while still maintaining that early differences in cultural capital reproduce social class. Farkas's (1996) approach to cultural capital emphasizes active parental investment in "skills, habits, and styles," arguing that elite arts participation is irrelevant in the social context of the United States. Class-based investments that parents make via regular social interaction with their children lead middle- and upper-class children to be differentially prepared to navigate institutional settings, to be perceived favorably by teachers, and to see their own place in the status hierarchy as privileged (Wildhagen, 2009; Lareau, 2011). Some of these investments reflect different norms that middle- and upper-class parents inculcate in children, particularly with reference to valuing schooling as a vehicle for upward mobility or, at minimum, for status inheritance. Lareau's work (2011), which we treat in more detail later, stresses the connections between childhood socialization strategies and activities in both childhood and adolescence. These several literatures combined suggest that parents are active and important agents who invest both social and cultural capital in their children, with the expectations that these investments will pay off in terms of future child and adolescent well-being.

Forms of Family Capital Diluted, Diffused, or Intertwined

This investment framework is also useful because, in addition to identifying family resources helpful to children, it also helps explain how resources can be *diluted* or *diffused*. For example, when there are more children in a family, all parental resources – social, financial, and cultural – are more finely spread across children

(Downey, 2001; Sun and Li, 2009). In addition, as Coleman argues, when there are not two adults in the household or when maternal work takes mothers out of the home, investment in children may suffer. In a classic work, McLanahan and Sandefur (1994) provide strong support in the United States for Coleman's assertion that children from single-parent families are worse off than those who grow up with both biological parents when it comes to school graduation, early parenthood, and occupational attainment. Although Coleman's idea that there are dangers to long maternal work hours has received some support, the overall notion that maternal work outside the home hinders child development has been overgeneralized (Parcel and Menaghan, 1994a, b; Goldberg *et al.*, 2008; see also Sayer, Bianchi, and Robinson, 2004). Comparative studies that assess children's outcomes across nations provide additional support for the notion that maternal work is generally not harmful to children (Cooksey, Joshi, and Verropoulou, 2009). Still, the idea that family capital can be diluted persists, in part, because the greater the amount of time that mothers and fathers work would seem to limit the time they can spend investing in child well-being.

Another possibility, however, is that social and cultural resources *interact* in their effects on academic and social outcomes. Bronfenbrenner (1979, 1989) argues that child genetic potential interacts with institutional characteristics beginning with family characteristics, but also with the characteristics of the successively nested systems in which the child is embedded, including the school, neighborhood, and the larger economy. This conceptualization suggests considerable complexity to the processes through which parental investment is accomplished, in part because parents often influence the other contexts that children experience. In addition, given the potential for each context to affect children both additively and interactively, there are a multitude of pathways through which parental investment may operate. Similarly, Coleman (1988, 1990) argues that parental human capital, no matter how high, will not automatically result in improved child outcomes unless there is sufficient family social capital to allow children access to parental resources. For example, higher levels of maternal mental ability may be more consequential if mothers are more engaged with children's schoolwork, thus supporting child intellectual development.

That these conditions are prevalent is widely believed in the social sciences because they reflect the idea that children who are favored in one context are often favored in another, thus leading to institutions that reinforce or exacerbate one another's effects, either for good or for ill. These effects are *resource boosters* (Parcel and Dufur, 2001a) or complementary resources. For example, Crosnoe (2004) identifies interaction between family and school resources as part of Bronfenbrenner's (1979, 1989) mesosystem and finds resource boosters operative in his study of adolescent US academic achievement. If resource boosters are pervasive, inequality increases. As Haveman *et al.* (2004) and Bianchi *et al.* (2004) argue, as family income inequality has increased, variation in family ability to invest in children has increased, the fates of youth have become more sharply differentiated, and groups of the advantaged and disadvantaged have diverged (see also Heckman, 2008). Alternatively, some effects may interact and reach a limit, producing *threshold* or *ceiling/floor* effects. For example, perhaps a combination of strong parental social networks outside the home and strong parental bonding with children both promote child achievement, but in combination have more modest effects than the strictly additive models would suggest (Parcel and Dufur, 2001a). Thus, the joint effects of investments do not automatically boost or hinder children; under these conditions, the *matching* of resources across contexts becomes less consequential and, presumably, inequality is ameliorated, not exacerbated. We return to these ideas later.

Parental Investment in International Context

The idea that parents can invest in children in ways that will benefit them later in life has received global support. Jæger and Holm (2007) decompose parental social class effects on the educational outcomes of Danish children and find that parental social and cultural capital operate as resources for children's educational attainment. Specifically, parental access to cultural capital importantly explains child attainment of upper secondary education; social and economic capital are important in child completion of vocational education. Taken together, these three forms of capital substantially explain the *raw* effect of social class of children educational attainment. Pensiero (2011) investigates children's reading ability and their locus of control in Great Britain. She finds that it is child engagement in cognitively stimulating activities, rather than participation in organized activities as such, that predicts these two outcomes. In addition, parental expectations, direct stimulation, parental interactions with the school, and children's engagement in cognitively stimulating activities mediate more than half of the Socioeconomic Status (SES) effect, even in the presence of strong controls.

In a study of Netherlands families, De Graaf, De Graaf, and Kraaykamp (2000) demonstrate that parental reading behavior has a stronger effect than parental beaux arts participation on children's educational attainment, particularly when the parents themselves have low levels of education. Also in the Netherlands, Notten, and Kraaykamp (2010) find that parental reading pays off for children, while parental television viewing is disadvantageous. Parents who select highbrow literature for their own reading promote educational success, while parental viewing of more popular television programs is disadvantageous. In addition, active parental investment in children's reading, such as giving children books for holiday gifts and reading to young children and discussing books with them, has a positive effect on children's educational attainment. Alternatively, Katsillis and Rubinson (1990) study Greece and find that although paternal social class and family SES influence student cultural capital, this form of capital itself does not translate into educational achievement; student ability and effort are much more consequential.

Studies of Asian samples take a somewhat different approach. Park, Byun, and Kim (2011) find that Korean parents invest considerable resources in locating and monitoring private tutors for their children. Those who do so invest have children with improved math and English test scores. Lee and Shouse (2011) find that such *shadow education* is tied to students' desires to attend prestigious higher educational institutions. Yamamoto and Brinton (2010) argue that objectified cultural capital (family possession of a piano, antiques, or complete works of literature/encyclopedias) and embodied cultural capital (e.g., being read to by parents when young) are differently implicated in attainment at different points in the educational process in Japan and that these findings vary for male and females students. These investments are surely tied to parental financial capital in ways that are beyond the scope of this chapter but, more generally, suggest considerable interest in parental investment strategies contextualized within Asian as well as European societies. In particular, studies of parental investment in cultural capital in non-US societies provide welcome tests of social theory as well as findings specific to those countries.

Social Capital and Academic Outcomes

A large body of US-based research links social capital to academic achievement and attainment among adolescents. Close ties to parents and high levels of intergenerational closure increase the likelihood of college attendance (Kim and Schneider, 2005), reduce school dropout rates (Carbonaro, 1998), and improve grades (Crosnoe, 2004). Furthermore, Kim and Schneider (2005) contend that social capital aligns adolescents' and parents' educational expectations, thus promoting academic achievement, even when parental financial capital is limited (see also Hao and Bonstead-Bruns, 1998). In this perspective, social capital promotes achievement by both heightening adolescents' expectations for academic performance and mobilizing other types of resources that contribute positively to educational outcomes. In partial contrast, Morgan and Todd (2009) find that intergenerational closure is a modest contributor to adolescent achievement in Catholic schools, but comparable relationships in US public schools can be entirely explained by family background.

Both theory and research support the notion that forms of family capital may interact in their effects on youth outcomes. The existing literature on academic outcomes demonstrates that adolescents may only benefit from other types of capital (e.g., human capital, cultural capital) when family-based social capital is high (Parcel and Dufur, 2001a; Domina, 2005). Thus, while social and cultural capital represent distinct types of assets upon which young people can draw, they can condition one another's utility (Vandewater and Lansford, 2005).

Cultural Capital and Academic Outcomes

Overall, despite divergence in conceptualization and measurement of cultural capital, existing research indicates that cultural capital – whether tapped with measures of elite arts consumption or Cultural Extracurricular Activities (EAs) – improves educational outcomes (e.g., Dumais, 2002 for the United States; Jæger, 2009 for Denmark). More recently, Jæger (2011) finds modest effects of cultural capital on students' reading and math achievement in the United States, with indicators reflecting highbrow culture and reading habits more consequential for upper SES students and concerted cultivation EAs more consequential for lower SES students. Roksa and Potter (2011) attribute some of the relationship between cultural capital and student achievement in the United States to parenting practices, thus speaking directly to issues of parental investment. Covay and Carbonaro (2010) study US elementary school children and find that the notable relationship between extracurricular academic activities and academic achievement is a function of the effect of these activities on noncognitive skill acquisition. We return to this issue later when we focus on social class differences in parenting practices.

Social Capital and Social Adjustment

Much of the literature covered earlier ties family investment in social and cultural capital to child academic outcomes. However, such investments also have major implications for child social adjustment, and its inverse, child behavior problems and juvenile delinquency. Although not always explicitly recognized, the underlying logic of many criminological theories is based on various forms of capital accumulation or capital scarcity. The attachment component of Hirschi's (1969) social control theory emphasizes the strength of parent–child relationships, one form of social capital, as a precipitating factor for understanding delinquency. Specifically, when parent–child bonds are weak, children are more likely to engage in delinquency. Hirschi's emphasis on the internalization of norms among children mirrors that of intergenerational closure because internalization of norms refers to the investments that parents make in their children. Although internalization of norms is largely achieved through direct parental supervision, the ultimate goal is to establish indirect control. Hirschi's *virtual supervision* suggests that children who have internalized parental norms bring these norms with them even when outside of direct parental control; in the presence of a delinquent opportunity, they will ask themselves "what will my parents think?"

Sampson and Laub (1993) use social capital as a central concept in their age-graded theory of informal social control, suggesting that relationships marked by social capital produce obligation and mutual reciprocity among individuals and are thus a strong source of informal social control against criminal and deviant behaviors. Accordingly, institutional involvements, and especially familial involvement, are central for understanding individuals that drift in and out of criminal behavior over the life course. According to Gottfredson and Hirschi's (1990) self-control theory, parental socialization strategies (monitoring children, recognizing deviant behavior when it occurs, and correcting deviant behavior) produce the capacity for self-regulation in children. This quality enables children to delay gratification and to consider long-term consequences of their actions, thus providing the necessary skills for future success in important societal institutions. In addition, Sampson, Raudenbush, and Earls (1997) underscore the importance of collective efficacy for understanding variation in neighborhood crime rates, with collective efficacy reflecting a version of social capital tapping the willingness of individuals in a neighborhood to work together toward goals such as crime control.

Social capital and behavior problems in young children

Parcel and Menaghan (1993, 1994a, b) demonstrate that parental investment in family social capital reduces the risk of children's behavior problems. Stronger home environments lower the risk of behavior problems, as does stronger maternal self-concept and the mother being married (Parcel and Menaghan, 1994b). Parental overtime work is a risk factor if additional children are recently born into the family. Parcel and Menaghan (1994a) demonstrate that low paternal working hours during early childhood is associated with elevated child behavior problems at ages 3–6, but that maternal work hours do not have comparable effects. In addition, Dufur, Parcel, and McKune (2008) demonstrate that social capital at home is more consequential than social capital at school in reducing the risk of children's behavior problems.

Social capital and delinquency

Many studies find general support for the notion that parent–child attachment is a significant buffer against delinquent or risky behavior for adolescents (Rankin and Kerns, 1994; Dornbusch *et al.*, 2001). Criminologists posit that children who have strong attachments to their parents avoid engaging in delinquency because they perceive that such behaviors will damage relationships with parents (Hirschi, 1969). Wright and Fitzpatrick (2006) find that significant parental involvement and strong parent–child attachment reduce violent behavior and enhance emotional and social skills. Wright, Cullen, and Miller (2001) find that children with high levels of family capital internalize prosocial norms, are successful in school, and are less likely to associate with delinquent friends and to engage in delinquency. As Salmi and Kivivuori (2006) report, weak parental support is associated with delinquent behavior irrespective of structural and individual level controls.

As some authors argue, close parent–child relationships are important for curbing delinquent behaviors among children, but direct parental control strategies such as monitoring and supervision have a stronger effect (Loeber and Stouthamer-Loeber, 1986). Criminologists contend that parental supervision plays a central role in the development of self-control in children (Gottfredson and Hirschi, 1990) and reduces children's time spent in unstructured socializing with peers (Osgood and Anderson, 2004). Indeed, research suggests that children who spend significant amounts of time outside of parental control are more likely to engage in delinquent behavior than more sufficiently controlled children (Demuth and Brown, 2004). The findings of these studies align well with Coleman's argument that parents must be physically available for children in order to transmit social capital. As Hoffmann and Dufur (2008) note, many studies that predict delinquency focus on family structure as a key explanatory variable; it can act as a proxy for social capital because single-mother families are not typically capable of providing as much social capital to children compared to two-parent families (see also Demuth and Brown, 2004).

As Gauthier and DeGusti (2012) suggest, parental investment in children in the form of shared activities and positive parenting has important influence on children's well-being, but the time that parents devote to their children varies considerably across countries. Cross-national variations in parental investment are affected by the countries' level of economic development, the structure of the labor market, work–family support, and societal norms. For example, they argue that Nordic countries, which are characterized by relatively low hours of paid work among workers, a general view toward work as necessary for survival more so than self-expression, and high gender equality, are also characterized by high levels of father–child time. Contrastingly, Eastern European countries are characterized by low levels of maternal and paternal time with children, possibly explained by these countries having lower levels of economic development, higher hours of paid work, and lower levels of gender equality. In France, parents spend comparatively little time in childcare, and this may be a function of the low level of gender equality and the preference for public childcare (see also Sayer and Gornick, 2011).

Parenting styles and delinquency

Other literature suggests that different parenting styles can have unique effects on parent–child investments. Baumrind's (1971) classic taxonomy (later extended by Maccoby and Martin, 1983) describes four parenting styles: authoritative (high support, high control), authoritarian (low support, high control), overly permissive (high support, low control), and neglectful (low support, low control). US and UK contexts have generally touted authoritative parenting as the most optimal strategy, as it fosters autonomous decision-making among children and is linked to academic achievement and fewer behavioral problems (Steinberg, Elmen, and Mounts, 1989; Grolnick *et al.*, 2000).

However, within the United States, this classification system may not adequately characterize the parenting styles of racial minority groups. Some African American parents employ more control and less warmth than Caucasian parents as a means of enabling children to manage ethnic and racial barriers (Garcia-Coll, 1990). Latino families may be more likely to exhibit warm parenting practices but with less control over their children as a function of the shared extended-kin responsibility for child-rearing (Baca Zinn, 1994). Preferences for authoritative parenting in the United States and United Kingdom may not accurately depict preferred parenting styles across the globe. Whereas many American parents worry that overstressing academic success is unhealthy for their children's emotional development, many parents in China and Korea believe that academic achievement is a reflection of effective parenting (Chao and Tseng, 2002). French parents wait longer periods before responding to their children's cries in order to teach their children that the world does not revolve around them. Additionally, French parents are less likely to embrace the view that children need access to choices as a means of promoting autonomous decision-making (Druckerman, 2012). Studies in Egypt (von der Lippe, 1999) and China (Chen, Dong, and Zhou, 1997) suggest that parenting strategies are heavily influenced by social class, with more educated parents preferring authoritative parenting styles.

Cultural capital and delinquency

EAs represent one avenue through which parents invest in adolescents. Research finds that children who participate in EAs are less likely to engage in delinquency and other risky behaviors than children who are uninvolved in such activities (Mahoney and Cairns, 1997; Mahoney, 2000). Why is this? One view is that children who participate in EAs have significantly less time to spend in unstructured and unsupervised activities, which are more likely to produce environments conducive to delinquency (Osgood *et al.*, 1996). Others suggest that EAs give children access to conventional role models (i.e., coaches and teachers) who promote conventional values (Csikszentmihalyi, Rathunde, and Whalen, 1993).

Alternatively, such activities may affect delinquency indirectly, because they culti-vate in children a number of culturally and socially valued traits that enhance their prosocial opportunities. EAs may enhance children's sense of competitiveness and their ability to work well with peers and adults (Danish and Gullotta, 2000), in addition to improving their confidence levels and psychological well-being (Mahoney and Cairns, 1997). Accordingly, children who accumulate these traits are likely to succeed in institutional settings such as school and thus have more to lose by engaging in various forms of misconduct (Hirschi, 1969).

These positive effects may not operate uniformly under all conditions. Some research finds that participation in nonathletic activities such as school clubs and student government, and in organizations formed for students who have high academic achievements (known as *honor societies* in the United States), buffer chil-dren's delinquent trajectories more so than participation in school sports (Hoffmann, 2006). Some studies link athletic participation to increased opportunities for sexual experimentation (Miller *et al.*, 1998) and increased use of alcohol (Eccles *et al.*, 2003). Athletics may indirectly encourage delinquency by promoting aggressiveness (Burton and Marshall, 2005) and also by significantly reducing the time that chil-dren spend with family members (Mahoney, Cairns, and Farmer, 2003).

EAs may also have different effects depending on the child's gender. Hoffman (2006) shows that athletic participation protects against sexual behavior and alcohol use among girls but not among boys, possibly because these behaviors may enhance social status for males but not for females. Also, the relationship between EAs and delinquency depends on the SES of the school in which the activities are available (Hoffmann and Xu, 2002). Together, these findings indicate that the relationship between EA participation and behavioral outcomes is contingent upon individual and contextual-level factors.

Additional literature suggests that children's participation in community-oriented activities may also act as an important means for children to achieve cultural capital and to abstain from participation in delinquency and other risky behaviors (Hoffmann, 2006). Involvement in community activities may instill in children civic-minded values (Youniss and Yates, 1997), enhance their social networks (Hanks and Eckland, 1978), and encourage a broader and more compassionate worldview (Wuthnow, 1991). However, the socioeconomic context of the community condi-tions the extent to which community involvement benefits children's educational and behavioral outcomes (see Hoffmann and Xu, 2002 for a review).

Transmission of Social and Cultural Capital across the Life Course

Young children's educational environments

As noted earlier, scholars have become increasingly attuned to the inequality of family resources as they impact young children's development and have argued that by the time children reach school age, their educational environments have already prepared them either well or poorly for formal schooling (Heckman, 2008). Over time, initial disadvantages may be compounded, not ameliorated, by unequal environments else-where, so that *boosting* is cumulatively negative instead of positive, thus exacerbating inequality. Alternatively, if higher levels of resources in one context can compensate for lower levels in another (threshold effects), inequality will be (somewhat) ameliorated. We have a poor understanding of the extent to which parental resources combine with resources from other contexts to boost or compensate in the socialization of children and youth.

Parents are their children's first teachers, and the resources they use at home have important implications for child well-being. An important early resource is the sheer quantity of verbal interaction children experience with adults. In a U.S study, Hart and Risley (1995) find that there is considerable variation by social class in the quantity of words and types of sentences that very young children experience. Children in welfare households experience less verbal interaction with adults than do children in working-class households; children who have professional parents experience even more verbal interaction than working-class children. Also, children in professional households are exposed to more complex sentences and questions that encourage their verbal responsiveness, while children in welfare households experience simpler sentences and more frequent direct commands. These differences are associated with predictable differences in children's verbal capabilities by age 3. Thus, parents' verbal interactions with children are a form of investment that has implications for children's verbal facility several years later.

Children's home environments

Researchers in the United States have also demonstrated that other dimensions of children's home environments are consequential for their future well-being (Bradley and Caldwell, 1987). Children are advantaged when their home environments are reasonably clean, uncluttered, and free of obvious hazards and when parents express verbal affection, introduce children to visitors, speak pleasantly to them, and typically avoid physical punishment and harsh verbal rebukes. Children also are advantaged when their homes contain age-appropriate intellectual resources that can encourage cognitive development. For the youngest children, resources would include age-appropriate books and toys, and someone who reads to them. For older children, key resources would include being encouraged to pursue hobbies or create collections. For children 10 years of age and older, an additional relevant resource is whether children manage their own time. A combination of a safe home, a warm affective environment, and a stimulating cognitive environment constitutes a better home environment, which is a strong predictor of both child academic success and positive child social behavior (Parcel and Menaghan, 1994b).

Children with more educated mothers and with mothers whose jobs have more autonomy and complexity will also experience stronger home environments (Parcel and Menaghan, 1994b). Although some have argued that better home environments may not be strongly associated with parental financial resources (Bradley *et al.*, 1989), some of the markers of cognitive enrichment, which we associate with cultural capital, such as music lessons or visiting museums, require household funds. More recently Schaub (2010) argues that US households of varying financial means are reading to their young children, while earlier such enrichment was associated with higher levels of social class. Children who have access to computers at home may experience an educational advantage over those who do not (Espinosa *et al.*, 2006).

Social class and socialization

Sociologists have studied the relationship between parental social class and child socialization practices. Kohn (1977) and Kohn and Schooler (1982) link occupational working conditions and adult psychological functioning by arguing that the working conditions parents face on the job influence their child-rearing values. Blue-collar work tends to be standardized and is often closely supervised, while white-collar work often involves use and/or manipulation of symbols or ideas, as well as interpersonal interaction; it may be complex and is often performed under indirect supervision, permitting greater autonomy and self-direction. The values parents use in socializing children reflect these occupational conditions, with parents implicitly assuming that their children will inherit the types of jobs the parents occupy. As a result, white-collar parents emphasize self-direction and internalization of norms for their children, while blue-collar parents stress conformity to externally imposed rules. In addition, blue-collar work, which is routinized, low in autonomy, and provides little opportunity for creative thought, will erode intellectual flexibility and promote psychological distress, which in turn promotes less attentive and responsive parenting. The more intellectually complex work that white-collar parents perform can act as a positive resource for children, because it encourages parents to set high expectations for child self-direction and intellectual flexibility, qualities that children can use to further their own educational and socioeconomic outcomes as they mature. Parcel and Menaghan (1994a, b) provide direct empirical evidence for these ideas using longitudinal data that link parental working conditions to children's home environments, as well as to child cognition and social adjustment. Interestingly, Kohn (1989) also develops his ideas referencing cross-national data.

Annette Lareau's (2011) work reinforces the connection between social class and differentiated childhood socialization. Using in-depth case studies of 12 nine- and 10-year-old US children and their families, she finds that middle-class children are advantaged because their parents engage in *concerted cultivation*. These parents identify their children's special talents and abilities and encourage their children to develop them. Also, they use language instrumentally in order to foster their children's abilities to articulate their opinions, to make special requests of figures in positions of power, and to effectively challenge authority when individual needs are not being met. These parents intervene to ensure that their children are able to *maximize* their opportunities in ways that would best prepare them for the future (e.g., enrolling them in prep courses for standardized college admission tests, encouraging rigorous curricula, etc.). Her 10-year follow-up shows that the children who received the most deliberate cultivation from their parents went on to have positive educational and occupational experiences, as they had internalized important middle-class values and skills, such as time management, competition, and cooperation, and had become comfortable with performance-based evaluations.

In contrast, lower-income parents provide fewer of these adult-led extracurricular opportunities and instead encourage free play and relationships with extended family members, which Lareau terms *the accomplishment of natural growth*. These children develop fewer skills in dealing with adults outside the family. This limits their ability to negotiate adult-led environments at school and outside the home generally. These working class and poor children had not accrued the same institutional advantages at the 10-year follow-up. It is notable that Lareau (2011) finds strong continuity in the differentiated parenting practices across time, so that early advantage and disadvantage are amplified 10 years later. While the small numbers of cases precludes making definitive causal inferences, these findings are highly suggestive of social class differentiation in parental investment strategies and imply that such differentiation has long-term consequences. Her scholarship has been very influential, in part because she was able to differentiate race from class in parenting practices. For example, both black and white middle-class parents practiced concerted cultivation.

At the same time, others provide contrasting evidence. Chin and Phillips (2004) study how several forms of capital affect children's participation in organized summer activities. They find that class differences in participation are a function of differential financial resources, differences in parental knowledge about nurturing children's interests, and differences in information about activity availability. Covay and Carbonaro (2010) find that working-class children do participate in more EAs than one might infer from Lareau. Similarly, Bennett, Lutz, and Jayaram (2012) find overlap by social class in parental considerations regarding participation in structured activity that focus on keeping children active, socializing and fostering their personal development. However, they also find differences in that working-class parents are more concerned with ensuring child safety and social mobility. Middle-class parents are especially attuned to the fit between the child's interests and the opportunities for participation. Overall, it seems unlikely that middle-class parents are indifferent to the role that such activities play in social mobility. These disagreements and differing emphases suggest this is a very fertile area for future research that has sparked the imagination of numerous sociologists.

Parental work schedules

Literature also suggests that the timing of parental work schedules can influence the ways in which parents invest in their children. A growing proportion of Americans are required to work evening, night, rotating, irregular, weekend, and split-shift work schedules, collectively referred to as *nonstandard work schedules* (Presser, 2000). Parents who work nonstandard schedules are likely to be absent during evening hours and weekends, when parents traditionally invest social and cultural capital in their children. These parents often miss eating meals together, helping with homework, and spending quality recreational time together; additionally, they may not be available to participate in events that researchers consider essential for concerted cultivation, such as parent–teacher conferences, child sporting events, and school ceremonies or recitals (Wight, Raley, and Bianchi, 2008).

In addition, nonstandard schedules may cause higher levels of adult stress (Perry-Jenkins *et al.*, 2006), exhaustion (Wight, Raley, and Bianchi, 2008), and marital instability (Presser, 2000), which may limit positive and capital-rich interactions with their children. Nonstandard schedules are linked to complications in cognitive development among young children (Han, 2005), behavioral problems and academic disengagement among middle-stage children (Strazdins *et al.*, 2004; Hsueh and Yoshikawa, 2007), and delinquency and psychological problems among adolescents (Han and Miller, 2009; Han, Miller, and Waldfogel, 2010).

Other research, however, suggests that nonstandard work schedules can actually *enhance* parents' abilities to invest in their children. Some parents may deliberately juxtapose their work schedules to achieve *tag-team parenting*, in which work schedules are nonoverlapping and thus allow one parent to be available to the child at all times (Hattery, 2001). Such a strategy may be especially useful for covering the *high-risk* hours after school (Snyder and Sickmund, 1999) and for allowing parents to spend more one-on-one time with children, thus establishing stronger bonds (Wight, Raley, and Bianchi, 2008). Nonstandard schedules are not as likely to enhance parent–child interactions in single-parent families, however (Han and Waldfogel, 2007).

Household location and school choice

Parents can also influence children's social and cultural capital via where they choose to live. Pettit and McLanahan (2003) find that although moving is disruptive for children, the less advantaged who move have difficulty establishing new social ties because of their initial disadvantages, whereas the more advantaged who move to middle-class neighborhoods experience only minor disruptive effects. Mouw (2006) notes that, given the tendency for individuals to place themselves in contexts with others who are socially similar, it can be difficult to untangle the effects of such selection from the capital investment itself; for example, DeLuca and Dayton (2009) find that moving to better neighborhoods does not translate into measurable and sustained gains in educational outcomes, perhaps because among families that do move, most characteristics of those families remain the same.

When parents choose where they and their children live, they are often simultaneously choosing the schools their children will attend (Logan, Minca, and Adar, 2012). Neighborhoods that are characterized by high levels of racial residential segregation will typically also have schools whose racial distributions reflect neighborhood characteristics. The same can be said for social class. Given the well-documented tendency for lower SES and minority schools to contain less favorable learning environments than higher SES and majority schools, residential choice may compound the advantage or disadvantage present in the neighborhood. In addition, Ream (2005) finds that household mobility may reduce the social capital that Mexican American adolescents build with peers, with negative implications for their academic achievement. College choice is consequential for older adolescents. Turley (2009) demonstrates that student locale has a substantial impact on where students decide to go to college. Thus, parental decisions regarding family location can have long-term consequences.

Unanswered Questions and Future Directions for Research

A key unanswered question concerns whether specific empirical indicators reflect parental investment in social capital, cultural capital, or both. For example, Bradley's treatment of home environments includes items such as whether parents are reading to young children and whether older children have access to musical instruments in the home. While several researchers argue these reflect social capital, Yamamoto and Brinton (2010) use very similar items to reflect cultural capital. Concerns expressed by Kingston (2001) regarding how cultural capital is measured and by Furstenberg (2005) and Portes (2000) regarding social capital provide corroborating considerations.

Clearly, differentiating cultural capital from social capital for very young children may not yield much benefit. At this stage of the life course, parents are the primary actors who invest *all* forms of capital in their children. As children reach adolescence, however, such differentiation may be more consequential. For older children, we need more research that takes as problematic whether given measures more closely align with what we consider to be some form of social capital (e.g., bonding or bridging); whether they more accurately reflect one of several conceptualizations of cultural capital; or whether they reflect both forms of capital. Such studies will be important precursors to determining whether social or cultural capital is more influential in predicting particular academic and social outcomes, or whether these effects vary in strength depending on particular conditions and child characteristics.

Second, we remain relatively ignorant of how combinations of social and cultural capital investment either exacerbate inequality or ameliorate it. Studies often neglect to test for the interactive effects of social and cultural capital with reference to academic and social adjustment (see Parcel, Dufur, and Zito, 2010 for one review). Thus, although scholars have argued that inequality among children is increasing, the mechanisms through which parental investment is implicated are poorly understood.

In addition, we understand relatively little regarding how parental investment in children may be changed. Furstenberg (2011) reviews evidence suggesting that lower SES parents may not easily alter their investment patterns to facilitate child educational outcomes, while collective interventions such as preschool education may be more successful. *Where* investment in children should take place for optimal effect is a question that forces us to consider whether parental transmission of capital is always sufficient, or whether such investment operates to selectively advantage those children who have access to more parental resources (Dufur, Parcel, and Troutman, 2013).

Finally, we need more systematic inquiry that allows us to compare how similar and different these parental investment processes are by culture. Some relevant studies focus on one society at a time, possibly owing to data limitations and the challenge of doing comparative work generally. However, we should seek opportunities to engage in research with comparable data sets across more than one society so that we can make sharper comparisons (Campbell and Parcel, 2010; Parcel, Campbell, and Zhong, 2012). Such studies will lend greater precision to our inferences and provide a firmer basis on which to understand the important patterns through which parents transmit social and cultural capital to their children.

References

Ariès, P. (1962) *Centuries of Childhood: A Social History of Family Life*, Alfred A. Knopf, New York.

Baca Zinn, M. (1994) Adaptation and continuity in Mexican-origin families, in *Minority Families in the United States: A Multicultural Perspective* (ed. R.L. Taylor), Prentice-Hall, Englewood Cliffs, pp. 64–81.

Baumrind, D. (1971) Current patterns of parental authority. *Developmental Psychology*, 4, 99–102.

Bennett, P.R., Lutz, A. and Jayaram, L. (2012) Beyond the school yard: the role of parenting logics, financial resources, and social institutions to the social class gap in structured activity participation. *Sociology of Education*, 85, 131–157.

Bianchi, S., Cohen, P.N., Raley, S. and Nomaguchi, K. (2004) Inequality in parental investments in child-rearing: expenditures, time, and health, in *Social Inequality* (ed. K.M. Neckerman), Russell Sage, New York, pp. 189–219.

Bourdieu, P. (1973) Cultural reproduction and social reproduction, in *Knowledge, Education, and Cultural Change: Papers in the Sociology of Education* (ed. R. Brown), Tavistock Publications, London, pp. 71–112.

Bradley, R.H. and Caldwell, B.M. (1987) Early environment and cognitive competence: the little rock study. *Early Child Development and Care*, 27, 307–341.

Bradley, R.H. and Corwyn, R.F. (2002) Socioeconomic status and child development. *Annual Review of Psychology*, 53, 371–399.

Bradley, R.H., Caldwell, B.M., Rock, S.L. *et al.* (1989) Home environment and cognitive development in the first 3 years of life: a collaborative study involving six sites and three ethnic groups in North America. *Developmental Psychology*, 25, 217–235.

Bronfenbrenner, U. (1979) *The Ecology of Human Development: Experiments by Nature and Design*, Harvard University Press, Cambridge.

Bronfenbrenner, U. (1989) Ecological systems theory, in *Six Theories of Child Development: Revised Formulations and Current Issues* (ed. R. Vesta), JAI Press, Greenwich, pp. 187–249.

Burton, J.M. and Marshall, L.A. (2005) Protective factors for youth considered at risk of criminal behaviour: does participation in EAs help? *Criminal Behavior and Mental Health*, 15, 46–64.

Campbell, L.A. and Parcel, T.L. (2010) Children's home environments in Great Britain and the United States. *Journal of Family Issues*, 31, 559–584.

Carbonaro, W.J. (1998) A little help from my friends' parents: intergenerational closure and educational outcomes. *Sociology of Education*, 71, 295–313.

Chao, R.K. and Tseng, V. (2002) Parenting of Asians, in *Handbook of Parenting: Vol. 4. Social Conditions and Applied Parenting*, 2nd edn (ed. M.H. Bornstein), Lawrence Erlbaum, Mahwah, pp. 59–93.

Chen, X., Dong, Q. and Zhou, H. (1997) Authoritative and authoritarian parenting practices and social and school adjustment in Chinese children: a cross-cultural perspective. *International Journal of Behavioural Development*, 20, 855–873.

Chin, T. and Phillips, M. (2004) Social reproduction and childrearing practices: social class, children's agency, and the summer activity gap. *Sociology of Education*, 77, 185–210.

Coleman, J.S. (1988) Social capital in the creation of human capital. *American Journal of Sociology*, 94, 95–120.

Coleman, J.S. (1990) *Foundations of Social Theory*, Harvard University Press, Cambridge.

Conger, R.D. and Donnellan, M.B. (2007) An interactionist perspective on the socioeconomic context of human development. *Annual Review of Psychology*, 58, 175–199.

Cooksey, E., Joshi, H. and Verropoulou, G. (2009) Does mothers' employment affect children's development? Evidence from the children of the British 1970 birth cohort and the American NLSY79. *Journal of Longitudinal and Life Course Studies*, 1, 95–115.

Covay, E. and Carbonaro, W. (2010) After the bell: participation in EAs, classroom behavior, and academic achievement. *Sociology of Education*, 83, 20–45.

Crosnoe, R. (2004) Social capital and the interplay of families and schools. *Journal of Marriage and Family*, 66, 267–280.

Crosnoe, R. and Johnson, M.K. (2011) Research on adolescence in the 21st century. *Annual Review of Sociology*, 37, 439–460.

Csikszentmihalyi, M., Rathunde, K. and Whalen, S. (1993) *Talented Teenagers: The Roots of Success and Failure*. Cambridge University Press, New York.

Danish, S.J. and Gullotta, T.P. (2000) *Developing Competent Youth and Strong Communities Through After-School Programming*. Child Welfare League of America, Inc., Washington, DC.

De Graaf, N.D., De Graaf, P.M. and Kraaykamp, G. (2000) Parental cultural capital and educational attainment in the Netherlands: a refinement of the cultural capital perspective. *Sociology of Education*, 73, 92–111.

DeLuca, S. and Dayton, E. (2009) Switching social contexts: the effects of housing mobility and school choice programs on youth outcomes. *Annual Review of Sociology*, 35, 457–491.

Demuth, S. and Brown, S.L. (2004) Family structure, family processes, and adolescent delinquency: the significance of parental absence versus parental gender. *Journal of Research in Crime and Delinquency*, 41, 58–81.

Domina, T. (2005) Leveling the home advantage: assessing the effectiveness of parental involvement in elementary school. *Sociology of Education*, 78, 233–249.

Dornbusch, S.M., Erickson, K.G., Laird, J. and Wong, C.A. (2001) The relation of family and school attachment to adolescent deviance in diverse groups and communities. *Journal of Adolescent Research*, 16, 396–422.

Downey, D.B. (2001) Number of siblings and intellectual development: the resource dilution explanation. *American Psychologist*, 56, 497–504.

Druckerman, P. (2012) *Bringing Up Bebe: One American Mother Discovers the Wisdom of French Parenting*, Penguin Group, London.

Dufur, M., Parcel, T.L. and McKune, B.A. (2008) Capital and context: using social capital at home and at school to predict child social adjustment. *Journal of Health and Social Behavior*, 49, 146–161.

Dufur, M.J., Parcel, T.L. and Troutman, K. (2013) Does capital at home matter more than capital at school? Social capital effects on academic achievement. *Research in Social Stratification and Mobility*, 31, 1–21.

Dumais, S.A. (2002) Cultural capital, gender, and school success: the role of habitus. *Sociology of Education*, 75, 44–68.

Eccles, J.S., Barber, B.L., Stone, M. and Hunt, J. (2003) EAs and adolescent development. *Journal of Social Issues*, 59, 865–889.

Espinosa, L.M., Laffey, J.M., Whittaker, T. and Sheng, Y. (2006) Technology in the home and the achievement of young children: findings from the early childhood longitudinal study. *Early Education and Development*, 17, 421–441.

Farkas, G. (1996) *Human Capital or Cultural Capital? Ethnicity and Poverty Groups in an Urban School District*, Aldine de Gruyter, New York.

Furstenberg, F.F. (2005) Banking on families: how families generate and distribute social capital. *Journal of Marriage and Family*, 67, 809–821.

Furstenberg, F.F. (2011) The challenges of finding causal links between family educational practices and schooling outcomes, in *Whither Opportunity? Rising Inequality, Schools, and Children's Life Chances* (eds. G.J. Duncan and R.J. Murnane), Russell Sage Foundation, New York, pp. 465–482.

Garcia-Coll, C.T. (1990) Developmental outcome of minority infants: a process-oriented look into our beginnings. *Child Development*, 61, 270–289.

Gauthier, A. and DeGusti, B. (2012) The time allocation to children by parents in Europe. *International Sociology*, Online, 1–17. doi:10.1177/0268580912443576.

Goldberg, W.A., Prause, J.A., Lucas-Thompson, R. and Himsel, A. (2008) Maternal employment and children's achievement in context: a meta-analysis of four decades of research. *Psychological Bulletin*, 134, 77–108.

Gottfredson, M.R. and Hirschi, T. (1990) *A General Theory of Crime*. Stanford University Press, Stanford.

Grolnick, W.S., Kurowski, C.O., Dunlap, K.G. and Hevey, C. (2000) Parental resources and the transition to junior high. *Journal of Research on Adolescence*, 10, 465–480.

Han, W.J. (2005) Maternal nonstandard work schedules and child cognitive outcomes. *Child Development*, 76, 137–154.

Han, W.J. and Waldfogel, J. (2007) Parental work schedules, family process, and early adolescents' risky behavior. *Children and Youth Services Review*, 29, 1249–1266.

Han, W.J. and Miller, D.P. (2009) Parental work schedules and adolescent depression. *Health Sociology Review*, 18, 36–49.

Han, W.J., Miller, D.P. and Waldfogel, J. (2010) Parental work schedules and adolescent risky behaviors. *Developmental Psychology*, 46, 1245–1267.

Hanks, M. and Eckland, B.K. (1978) Adult voluntary associations and adolescent socialization. *Sociological Quarterly*, 19, 481–490.

Hao, L. and Bonstead-Bruns, M. (1998) Parent–child difference in educational expectations and the academic achievement of immigrant and native students. *Sociology of Education*, 71, 175–198.

Hart, B. and Risley, T.R. (1995) *Meaningful Differences in the Everyday Experience of Young American Children*, Paul H. Brookes Publishing Company, Baltimore.

Hattery, A.J. (2001) Tag-team parenting: costs and benefits of utilizing nonoverlapping shift work in families with young children. *Families in Society: Journal of Contemporary Human Services*, 82, 419–427.

Haveman, R., Sandefur, G., Wolfe, B. and Voyer, A. (2004) Trends in children's attainments and their determinants as family income has increased, in *Social Inequality* (ed. K.M. Neckerman), Russell Sage Foundation, New York, pp. 149–188.

Haynie, D.L. (2001) Delinquent peers revisited: does network structure matter? *American Journal of Sociology*, 106, 1013–1057.

Heckman, J.J. (2008) Schools, skills, and synapses. *Economic Inquiry*, 46, 289–324.

Hirschi, T. (1969) *Causes of Delinquency*. University of California Press, Berkeley.

Hoffmann, J.P. (2006) Family structure, community context, and adolescent problem behaviors. *Journal of Youth and Adolescence*, 35, 867–880.

Hoffmann, J.P. and Xu, J. (2002) School activities, community service, and delinquency. *Crime and Delinquency*, 48, 568–591.

Hoffmann, J.P. and Dufur, M.J. (2008) Family and school capital effects on delinquency: substitutes or complements? *Sociological Perspectives*, 51, 29–62.

Hsueh, J.A. and Yoshikawa, H. (2007) Working nonstandard schedules and variable shifts in low-income families: associations with parental psychological well-being, family functioning, and child well-being. *Developmental Psychology*, 43, 620–632.

Jæger, M.M. (2009) Equal access but unequal outcomes: cultural capital and educational choice in a meritocratic society. *Social Forces*, 87, 1943–1971.

Jæger, M.M. (2011) Does cultural capital really affect academic achievement? New evidence from combined sibling and panel data. *Sociology of Education*, 84, 281–298.

Jæger, M.M. and Holm, A. (2007) Does parents' economic, cultural, and social capital explain the social class effect on educational attainment in the Scandinavian mobility regime? *Social Science Research*, 36, 719–744.

Johnson, M.K., Crosnoe, R. and Elder, G.H. (2001) Students' attachment and academic engagement: the role of race and ethnicity. *Sociology of Education*, 74, 318–340.

Katsillis, J. and Rubinson, R. (1990) Cultural capital, student achievement, and educational reproduction: the case of Greece. *American Sociological Review*, 55, 270–279.

Kim, D.H. and Schneider, B. (2005) Social capital in action: alignment of parental support in adolescents' transition to postsecondary education. *Social Forces*, 84, 1181–1206.

Kingston, P.W. (2001) The unfulfilled promise of cultural capital theory. *Sociology of Education*, 74, 88–99.

Kohn, M.L. (1977) Reassessment 1977, in *Class and Conformity: A Study in Values*, 2nd edn, University of Chicago Press, Chicago.

Kohn, M.L. (1989) *Cross-National Research in Sociology*, Sage, Newberry Park.

Kohn, M.L. and Schooler, C. (1982) Job conditions and personality: a longitudinal assessment of their reciprocal effects. *American Journal of Sociology*, 87, 1257–1286.

Lamont, M. and Lareau, A. (1988) Cultural capital: allusions, gaps and glissandos in recent theoretical developments. *Sociological Theory*, 6, 153–168.

Lareau, A. (2011). *Unequal Childhoods: Class, Race, and Family Life, Second Edition with an Update a Decade Later*, University of California Press, Berkeley.

Lareau, A. and Weinberg, E.B. (2003) Cultural capital in educational research: a critical assessment. *Theory and Society*, 32, 567–606.

Lee, S. and Shouse, R.C. (2011) The impact of prestige orientation on shadow education in South Korea. *Sociology of Education*, 84, 212–224.

Loeber, R. and Stouthamer-Loeber, M. (1986) Family factors as correlates and predictors of juvenile conduct problems and delinquency, in *Crime and Justice: An Annual Review of Research*, vol. 7 (eds. M.H. Tonry and N. Morris), University of Chicago Press, Chicago, pp. 29–149.

Logan, J.R., Minca, E. and Adar, S. (2012) The geography of inequality: why separate means unequal in American public schools. *Sociology of Education*, 85, 1–15.

Maccoby, E. and Martin, J.A. (1983) Socialization in the context of the family: parent-child interaction, in *Handbook of Child Psychology: Volume 4. Socialization, Personality, and Social Development*, 4th edn, Wiley, New York, pp. 1–101.

Mahoney, J.L. (2000) School extracurricular activity participation as a moderator in the development of antisocial patterns. *Child Development*, 71, 502–516.

Mahoney, J.L. and Cairns, R.B. (1997) Do EAs protect against early school dropout? *Developmental Psychology*, 33, 241–253.

Mahoney, J.L., Cairns, B.C. and Farmer, T. (2003) Promoting interpersonal competence and educational success through extracurricular activity participation. *Journal of Educational Psychology*, 95, 409–418.

McLanahan, S. and Sandefur, G.D. (1994) *Growing Up with a Single Parent: What Hurts, What Helps*, Harvard University Press, Cambridge.

Miller, K.E., Sabo, D.F., Farrell, M.P. *et al.* (1998) Athletic participation and sexual behavior in adolescents: the different worlds of boys and girls. *Journal of Health and Social Behavior*, 39, 108–123.

Mintz, S. and Kellogg, S. (1988) *Domestic Revolutions: A Social History of American Family Life*, Free Press, New York.

Morgan, S.L. and Todd, J.J. (2009) Intergenerational closure and academic achievement in high school: a new evaluation of Coleman's conjecture. *Sociology of Education*, 82, 267–286.

Mouw, T. (2006) Estimating the causal effects of social capital: a review of recent research. *Annual Review of Sociology*, 32, 79–102.

Notten, N. and Kraaykamp, G. (2010) Parental media socialization and educational attainment: resource or disadvantage? *Research in Social Stratification and Mobility*, 28, 453–464.

Offer, S. and Schneider, B. (2007) Children's role in generating social capital." *Social Forces*, 85, 1125–1142.

Osgood, D.W. and Anderson, A. (2004) Unstructured socializing and rates of delinquency. *Criminology*, 42, 519–549.

Osgood, D.W., Wilson, J.K., O'Malley, P.M. *et al.* (1996) Routine activities and individual deviant behavior. *American Sociological Review*, 61, 635–655.

Parcel, T.L. and Menaghan, E.G. (1993) Family social capital and children's behavior problems. *Social Psychology Quarterly*, 56, 120–135.

Parcel, T.L. and Menaghan, E.G. (1994a) Early parental work, family social capital, and early childhood outcomes. *American Journal of Sociology*, 99, 972–1009.

Parcel, T.L. and Menaghan, E.G. (1994b) *Parents' Jobs and Children's Lives*. Aldine de Gruyter, New York.

Parcel, T.L. and Dufur, M.J. (2001a) Capital at home and at school: effects on child social adjustment. *Journal of Marriage and Family*, 63, 32–47.

Parcel, T.L. and Dufur, M.J. (2001b) Capital at home and at school: effects on student achievement. *Social Forces*, 79, 881–912.

Parcel, T.L., Dufur, M.J. and Zito, R.C. (2010) Capital at home and at school: a review and synthesis. *Journal of Marriage and Family*, 72, 828–846.

Parcel, T.L., Campbell, L.A. and Zhong, W. (2012) Children's behavior problems in the United States and Great Britain. *Journal of Health and Social Behavior*, 53, 165–182.

Park, H., Byun, S. and Kim, K. (2011) Parental Involvement and Students' cognitive outcomes in Korea: focusing on private tutoring. *Sociology of Education*, 82, 3–22.

Pensiero, N. (2011) Parent-child cultivation and children's cognitive and attitudinal outcomes from a longitudinal perspective. *Child Indicators Research*, 4, 413–437.

Perry-Jenkins, M., Goldberg, A.E., Pierce, C.P. and Sayer, A.G. (2006) Shift work, role overload, and the transition to parenthood. *Journal of Marriage and Family*, 69, 123–138.

Pettit, B. and McLanahan, S. (2003) Residential mobility and children's social capital: evidence from an experiment. *Social Science Quarterly*, 84, 632–649.

Portes, A. (2000) The two meanings of social capital. *Sociological Forum*, 15, 1–12.

Presser, H.B. (2000) Nonstandard work schedules and marital instability. *Journal of Marriage and the Family*, 62, 93–110.

Putnam, R.D. (2000) *Bowling Alone*, Simon and Schuster, New York.

Rankin, J.H. and Kerns, R.M. (1994) Parental attachments and delinquency. *Criminology*, 32, 495–515.

Ream, R.K. (2005) *Uprooting Children: Mobility, Social Capital, and Mexican American Underachievement*, LFB Scholarly Publishing LLC, New York.

Roksa, J. and Potter, D. (2011) Parenting and academic achievement: intergenerational transmission of educational advantage. *Sociology of Education*, 84, 299–321.

Salmi, V. and Kivivuori, J. (2006) The association between social capital and juvenile crime: the role of individual and structural factors. *European Journal of Criminology*, 3, 123–148.

Sampson, R.J. and Laub, J.H. (1993) *Crime in the Making Pathways and Turning Points Through Life*, Harvard University Press, Cambridge.

Sampson, R.J., Raudenbush, S.W. and Earls, F. (1997) Neighborhoods and violent crime: a multilevel study of collective efficacy. *Science*, 227, 918–924.

Sayer, L.C. and Gornick, J. (2011) Cross-national variation in the influence of employment hours on child care time. *European Sociological Review*, 28, 421–442.

Sayer, L.C., Bianchi, S.M. and Robinson, J.P. (2004) Are parents investing less in children? Trends in mothers' and fathers' time with children. *American Journal of Sociology*, 110, 1–43.

Schaub, M. (2010) Parenting for cognitive development from 1950 to 2000: the institutionalization of mass education and the social construction of parenting in the United States. *Sociology of Education*, 83, 46–66.

Snyder, H.N. and Sickmund, M. (1999) *Juvenile Offenders and Victims: 1999 National Report*. Office of Juvenile Justice and Delinquency Prevention, Washington, DC.

Steinberg, L., Elmen, J.D. and Mounts, N.S. (1989) Authoritative parenting, psychosocial maturity, and academic success among adolescents. *Child Development*, 60, 1424–1436.

Strazdins, L., Korda, R.J., Lim, L.L. *et al.* (2004) Around-the-clock: parent work schedules and children's well-being in a 24-h economy. *Social Science and Medicine*, 59, 1517–1527.

Sun, Y. and Li, Y. (2009) Parental divorce, sibship size, family resources, and children's academic performance. *Social Science Research*, 38, 622–634.

Turley, R.N. (2009) College proximity: mapping access to opportunity. *Sociology of Education*, 82, 126–146.

Vandewater, E.A. and Lansford, J.E. (2005) A family process model of problem behaviors in adolescents. *Journal of Marriage and Family*, 67, 100–109.

von der Lippe, A.L. (1999) The impact of maternal schooling and occupation on child-rearing attitudes and behaviours in low income neighborhoods in Cairo, Egypt. *International Journal of Behavioral Development*, 23, 703–729.

Wight, V.R., Raley, S.B. and Bianchi, S.M. (2008) Time for children, one's spouse and oneself among parents who work nonstandard hours. *Journal of Marriage and Family*, 87, 243–271.

Wildhagen, T. (2009) Why does cultural capital matter for high school performance? An empirical assessment of teacher-selection and self-selection mechanisms as explanations of the cultural capital effect. *The Sociological Quarterly*, 50, 173–200.

Wright, D.R. and Fitzpatrick, K.M. (2006) Social capital and adolescent violent behavior: correlates of fighting and weapon use among secondary school students. *Social Forces*, 84, 1435–1453.

Wright, J.P., Cullen, F.T. and Miller, J.T. (2001). Family social capital and delinquent involvement. *Journal of Criminal Justice*, 29, 1–9.

Wuthnow, R. (1991) *Acts of Compassion: Caring for Others and Helping Ourselves*, Princeton University Press, Princeton.

Yamamoto, Y. and Brinton, M.C. (2010) Cultural capital in East Asian educational systems – the case of Japan. *Sociology of Education*, 83, 67–83.

Youniss, J. and Yates, M. (1997) *Community Service and Social Responsibility in Youth*. University of Chicago Press, Chicago.

Part V
Life Course Perspectives

19

Adult Intergenerational Relationships

Matthijs Kalmijn

Introduction

This chapter is concerned with the relationships between parents and their adult, grown-up children. Traditionally, interest in intergenerational ties came from functionalist perspectives in sociology, which argued that the process of modernization – and in particular the growing rates of social and geographical mobility – had undermined the extended family. Empirically, this hypothesis was quickly rejected, however (Litwak, 1960), and more recent historical research showed that the extended family, at least in terms of residence, was not that prevalent before the modernization process to begin with (Ruggles, 2011). More recently, interest in intergenerational ties has increased again as a result of the aging of Western societies. Life expectancy beyond the retirement age has increased considerably, which has implied increasing shared lifetime of the generations. This not only leads to more demand for personal and physical care in times of illness, it also creates a need for social and emotional support from adult children. While this development may have increased the importance of adult intergenerational relationships, other societal trends may hinder such a (re)strengthening of family ties. Women have been the primary kinkeepers; hence, the increase in women's employment has reduced the amount of time adult children have available for their parents. The increase in divorce has resulted in a growing number of older parents, especially fathers, who are estranged from their children. Finally, both children and parents have been influenced by individualization. For children, normative obligations to support their parents are replaced by considerations of affection. At the same time, older parents increasingly emphasize the wish to be independent of children for practical support and personal care. These conflicting developments make the study of intergenerational ties both more interesting and more relevant.

The Wiley Blackwell Companion to the Sociology of Families, First Edition.
Edited by Judith Treas, Jacqueline Scott, and Martin Richards.
© 2014 John Wiley & Sons Ltd. Published 2017 by John Wiley & Sons Ltd.

The Solidarity Perspective

Adult intergenerational relations have frequently been studied from the perspective of intergenerational solidarity (Rossi and Rossi, 1990; Roberts, Richards, and Bengtson, 1991). In classic sociological writings, the term *solidarity* was used to explain the cohesion of social groups or societies more generally. Solidarity referred to a tendency to do or mean something for each other and for the collective, while avoiding the pursuit of pure self-interest that would lead to a disintegration of the group. This more general concept was applied to family relations in two ways (Roberts, Richards, and Bengtson, 1991). From classic sociological theories, the idea was borrowed that cohesion in the family would depend on functional dependencies on the one hand (mechanical solidarity) and normative motivations on the other hand (organic solidarity). From classic microsociological work, especially the work by Homans, the idea was borrowed that family cohesion would further depend on levels of interaction and affection. By using the concept of solidarity, authors also placed intergenerational relations in the debate about aging: how and to what extent is a society able to support the elderly, and what is the ideal division of labor between intergenerational solidarity inside the family and solidarity between (age) generations outside of the family (Kohli, 1999)?

The theoretical developments provided earlier resulted in the idea that intergenerational solidarity can be distinguished into six dimensions (Silverstein and Bengtson, 1997): (i) associational solidarity (contact), (ii) functional solidarity (support giving), (iii) structural solidarity (opportunities for contact), (iv) affective solidarity (positive feelings for each other), (v) consensual solidarity (agreement on values), and (vi) normative solidarity (normative obligations to support each other). Some of these dimensions are behavioral or have underlying behavioral choices (i–iii), whereas others are concerned with mental and cognitive aspects of intergenerational relationships (iv–vi).

Most studies, especially those written from an aging perspective, have focused on functional solidarity. Functional solidarity, or support, occurs in both *directions*, from adult children to parents (upward stream) and from parents to adult children (downward stream). Support is usually distinguished into instrumental (or practical) support, emotional support, and financial support. Instrumental support covers a variety of behaviors, such as help with household work, taking care of grandchildren, mending the house, shopping, running errands, administrative work, and personal care. These forms of support almost always involve face-to-face contact and can be time consuming, especially when recurrent personal care is involved. Personal care is more directly related to health problems, whereas other practical forms of support are driven by a more heterogeneous set of needs and life events (e.g., moving, unemployment). Daughters provide more support than sons, and consequently, they are often depicted as the main kinkeepers, just as they tend to be the main providers of care to children in the home (Hagestad, 1988). Social stratification plays a role too: in low-status families, there is more informal support exchange between parents and children than in high-status families (Van Groenou *et al.*, 2006).

Even if there is not a high level of support exchanged between the generations at any specific point in time, the family does seem to function as a safety net: in times of crises, or when there are specific needs and problems, the family is mobilized for support (Hogan and Eggebeen, 1995). Because such needs and problems vary over the life course, support exchange is also highly dependent on age and other life course factors (Rossi and Rossi, 1990). For example, parents can support adult children by grandparenting, but this is often limited to the stage in which the grandchildren are preschool and primary school age (Hank and Buber, 2009). The notion of the family as a safety net is an element in the so-called convoy model in gerontology, which argues that people have networks that can be called upon for support if needed, that networks members are hierarchically ordered in terms of support potential, and that parents and children form the inner circle of the potential support network (Antonucci and Akiyama, 1987). There has been debate, however, about the *degree* to which children respond to parental needs (see also later) and the degree to which structural constraints such as proximity complicate this (Hogan and Eggebeen, 1995). Moreover, for personal and physical care, either the spouse or more formal means of support are still more important than the children (Brandt, Haberkern, and Szydlik, 2009; Pinquart and Sörensen, 2011).

Financial support includes transfers of money, the giving of consumer durables, giving money to pay for college, and helping a child buying a home and setting up a new household (Hochguertel and Ohlsson, 2009). Most financial transfers are downward (Kohli, 1999), but among non-Western migrants, upward financial transfers are common as well (Sana and Massey, 2005). Inheritances are also studied as a form of intergenerational transfers (Szydlik, 2004). Economists use the terms *inter vivos* transfers and testamentary transfers to distinguish the two forms of giving.

Associational solidarity has also been studied frequently, in part because questions on contact have often been included in large national surveys. Contact is frequent in most Western societies. In a comparative study of Austria, (former) West Germany, Great Britain, and the United States, Kalmijn and De Vries showed that about 40%–60% of the children had at least weekly *face-to-face* contact with their parents (Kalmijn and De Vries, 2009). When combining face-to-face contact and telephone contact, 80%–90% of older adults in Europe have at least weekly contact with their adult children (Hank, 2007). There is no clear trend in contact frequency with the mother; for fathers, there seems to be a decline, probably as a result of divorce (Kalmijn and De Vries, 2009; Treas and Gubernskaya, 2012). Daughters have more frequent contact than sons, and mothers have more contact than fathers (Rossi and Rossi, 1990; Kalmijn, 2007). Higher educated persons have less frequent contact with their parents than lower educated persons, in part because they tend to live further away from their parents (Kalmijn, 2006).

Research on the subjective dimensions of intergenerational solidarity suggests that both parents and children, although parents more than children, evaluate their relationship generally in a positive way (Mandemakers and Dykstra, 2008). It is not well known if intergenerational relationships have become more or less positive over time. There are good theoretical reasons, however, to expect that the trend has been in a positive direction. First, generational differences in values at the macro level have declined due to the slowing down of cultural trends (Inglehart, 1997). This is likely to have affected generational differences within the family as well, although that remains an empirical question. Other possible contributors to a positive trend are the decline in the number of siblings and the shift from an authoritarian to a liberal child-rearing style (Alwin, 1988). Descriptive research further suggests that normative solidarity is strong (Ganong and Coleman, 2005). Interesting is that older persons emphasize filial norms less strongly than do younger persons, especially when it comes down to personal and physical care (Gans and Silverstein, 2006). One explanation for this is that older persons in many cultures have a desire for autonomy.

Intergenerational solidarity was not only a classificatory scheme for various aspects of intergenerational relations; it was also a theory about how different indicators of solidarity were causally related (Roberts, Richards, and Bengtson, 1991). Consequently, much research has been devoted to assessing the causal relationships between the different dimensions of intergenerational solidarity (Bengtson and Roberts, 1991). In many cases, causal connections can go in both ways. For example, contact is a condition for giving support, but when there is much contact, it is easier to detect a need for support so that support exchange becomes more likely. Similarly, when there is affection, contact is more pleasant, but social-psychological theories also argue that contact itself can lead to more affection. Finally, filial norms can motivate support, but the reports of norms can be affected by support exchange. People tend to avoid cognitive dissonance so that they may weaken their support for the norm of filial obligations when they offer little support to their parents.

Initially, the causal relationships were examined with cross-sectional data, using statistical models that allow for mutual causality (Bengtson and Roberts, 1991; Klein *et al.*, 1999). To study such effects in a more convincing fashion, authors increasingly used longitudinal data. For example, Silverstein, Parrott, and Bengtson (1995) showed that contact and affection at one point in time positively affected support giving to older parents at a later point in time while filial norms did not predict later support (Silverstein, Parrott, and Bengtson, 1995). Other studies showed that norms at one point in time do affect later support but only when the need for support increases (Silverstein, Gans, and Yang, 2006). Because causal arrows can go both ways, and because there are six dimensions of solidarity, the theory became more and more complex. A recent attempt to link seven dimensions of solidarity in a panel design with each other yielded 42 crossdimensional effects ((7 × 7) − 7), of which only 13 were significant (Hogerbrugge and Komter, 2012). This does not provide strong support for the causal implications of the solidarity model, but the length of the panel in this study – and hence the degree of change in solidarity – was rather limited.

The structural dimension of solidarity is quite influential empirically. For example, proximity has a strong positive effect on contact and support. Even for this structural factor, however, the causality can go in both ways. Silverstein, for instance, documented that (the demand for) support exchange can lead to moving closer to one's parents or not moving further away from parents (Silverstein, 1995). Hence, distance is not a pure *restriction* and should thus not be included routinely as a *control* variable. Another structural variable is the number of siblings. The more siblings one has, the less contact there is at the level of the parent–child dyad (Eggebeen, 1992). This effect probably reflects real-time constraints from the parents' perspective. At the level of the parent, however, the effect is different. Here, there is some advantage for parents who have more children: The more children parents have, the more likely it is that there is contact with or support from at least one child (Grundy and Read, 2012).

To bypass the complexities of the model while retaining the notion of underlying dimensions of solidarity, some authors have resorted to the study of typologies (Silverstein and Bengtson, 1997; Van Gaalen and Dykstra, 2006). Using statistical techniques for clustering cases, groups of children or parents are formed on the basis of a specific combination of scores on multiple dimensions of solidarity. What these analyses reveal is that not all dimensions coincide. For example, there are quite a few parents and children who have frequent contact without feeling very positively about the relationship. The assumption is that for these persons, contact is driven by normative obligations rather than by affection. Moreover, there are also the opposite types of relationships, where parents and children are fond of each other without having much contact or providing much support. This type has been called *intimacy at a distance*.

Conflict, Tension, and Ambivalence

A criticism of the solidarity perspective is that it has neglected conflict in families (Luescher, 2002). Whether conflict is incompatible with the solidarity theory remains debated, but the criticism is fair: There are more studies on support, contact, proximity, and affection than there are studies that explicitly examine conflict. Although both everyday observations and popular movies and novels suggest that family conflict is prevalent, descriptive studies do not confirm this: a fair number of people report occasional conflict, but only a small minority of people report frequent conflict (Bengtson *et al.*, 2002; Szydlik, 2008). Several authors have argued that even though overt conflict may be rare, the experience of tensions in the intergenerational relationship is common (Cichy, Fingerman, and Lefkowitz, 2003). It is possible that norms of family solidarity prevent conflicts from escalating. Because avoidance is more difficult in ascribed relationships such as relationships with children or parents, interpersonal tensions may then increase.

There are several sources of conflict (Clarke *et al.*, 1999). Conflicts can first be about differences in taste and values, but this is now less likely than it was in 1960s and 1970s, when the generation gap in norms and values was often severe (Inglehart, 1997). Probably a more important cause of conflict lies in the relationship itself (Clarke *et al.*, 1999). One hypothesis here is the generational stake hypothesis, which argues that children are more important to parents than parents are to children (Rossi and Rossi, 1990). Related to this is the developmental schism hypothesis, which argues that parents and children have different needs because they are in different parts of the life course (Fingerman, 1996). For example, the child may be investing in the start of the career and building a family, with little time left for social contacts, while the parents may just be retiring and in need of social and emotional support. Conflict about the relationship itself is probably especially common for the so-called sandwich generation, parents who are taking care of young children at home and older parents at the same time (Grundy and Henretta, 2006). These types of conflicts have also been an issue in immigrant families where expectations and ideals about intergenerational relationships are often different for migrant parents than for their native born children (Treas and Mazumdar, 2002).

Criticisms of the solidarity perspective have argued that conflict and tensions are not merely the negative poles of solidarity, but to some extent orthogonal dimensions. In other words, high levels of contact and support can go hand in hand with conflict. This argument has been made most strongly in the emerging literature on intergenerational ambivalence (Luescher, 2002; Pillemer and Suitor, 2002; Fingerman *et al.*, 2008). There continues to be debate about what ambivalence means, and various conceptualizations are now being used next to each other. One view is that ambivalence is the combination of positive and negative *feelings* about one's parents or children. Such feelings occur when the relationship is intimate but also characterized by conflict. Another view is that ambivalence is a conflict between *roles*. For example, adult children may desire to be autonomous, while they still receive support from parents, for instance, when setting up their own household. This is a conflict between the role of child and the role of adult, and this can lead to intrapersonal feelings of ambivalence. Sometimes, ambivalence refers to feelings of guilt, for example, when children are not supporting their parents while they feel normatively obliged to do so. This is a conflict between *norm and behavior*. There can also be conflicts between different norms about family ties, for instance, the norm for parents to treat children equally and the norm to help the neediest child the most.

Papers from several different countries show that some parent–child dyads are indeed characterized by high levels of contact, support, and intimacy on the one hand, and frequent conflict on the other hand (Bengtson *et al.*, 2002; Van Gaalen and Dykstra, 2006; Steinbach, 2008; Szydlik, 2008). Although this is in line with the notion of ambivalence, the prevalence of these types of relationships is low, varying from 5% to 15%. Other authors have measured ambivalence by asking people directly about such feelings (Luescher and Pillemer, 1998) or by looking at sum scores of positive and negative *feelings* (Fingerman *et al.*, 2008). These studies suggest that adult children often feel ambivalent toward parents, whereas ambivalent feelings among parents are less common (Kiecolt, Blieszner, and Savla, 2011). Moreover, young adults experience more ambivalence than older adults (Fingerman, Hay, and Birditt, 2004). These findings suggest that ambivalence is a developmental phenomenon that has to do with the tensions between autonomy and dependence that adults experience when they move through the life course.

Exchange and/or Altruism

Much of the literature has been devoted to testing theories about why parents and children provide each other with support. Two theoretical perspectives have been used, one based on altruism and one based on exchange. The exchange approach is based on the rational egoistic model of man, as used in economics and parts of sociology. The starting point of this approach is, first, that there are costs and benefits involved in engaging in personal relationships and, second, that the balance of these costs and benefits is the main motivation for what people do in a relationship. The interesting point of this theory is the counterintuitive idea that even in intimate and affective relationships, people are rational and selfish. The application of this general idea to intergenerational relationships comes from exchange theory, which basically argues that the costs of supporting someone else – in terms of time and energy – are compensated by the benefits of receiving support in return. Two forms of exchange exist.

First, there is immediate or direct exchange. In this case, parents may support their children in one way while the children support the parents in another way. For example, parents help children with the painting of their house, and subsequently, children have their parents over for dinner at the end of the day. Instrumental and socioemotional support are exchanged. Second, there is intertemporal exchange, which means that parents give something to their children at a young age in the hope that they will be supported by their children when they are old. In other words, exchange is embedded in the life course. What parents give at an early age can be seen as an investment in children. Investments not only take place when the children are living at home, but also when children are making the transition to adulthood. In this stage, parents can support their children in setting up a new household, for example. Intertemporal exchange is made possible by the norm of reciprocity, which reduces the uncertainty that people would have about whether or not they would receive something back. Because there are norms against selfishness in personal relationships, exchange in parent–child relationships is believed to work in a somewhat subtle, implicit, and possibly hidden way (Batson, 1993).

Exchange theory has often been tested by showing that the support that older parents receive is positively affected by the support that parents give to adult children (Klein Ikkink, van Tilburg, and Knipscheer, 1999; Grundy, 2005). Other studies have pointed to the reverse effect: the support children receive is positively affected by the support children give to elderly parents (Leopold and Raab, 2011). These cross-sectional designs point to instantaneous exchange, but they are not clear about the direction of the exchange. Moreover, upward and downward streams may be correlated due to common causes, such as familialistic norms. Within-family comparisons are better able to rule out such common family causes, and these have provided positive evidence as well: mothers give more support to the child from whom they received more support or from whom they expect more support in the future (Suitor, Pillemer, and Sechrist, 2006; Kalmijn, 2013).

Life course research has tried to test the idea of intertemporal exchange. Authors have pointed to the effects of aging on the balance of support exchange. The theory would suggest that at a certain age, the balance of support would reverse. This is often true in non-Western societies (Cong and Silverstein, 2011), but less so in Western societies where even at quite old ages, parents continue to support their adult children more than children support parents (Kohli, 1999). Longitudinal studies of parent–child dyads have shown that the support children received from parents at an earlier point in the life course has significant effects on the support children later give to parents (Silverstein et al., 2002). This is more direct evidence of intertemporal exchange, but the effects were small in magnitude. Moreover, this finding leaves open the question of whether parents are motivated by exchange; it primarily shows that children reciprocate. In one recent study, it is shown that parents give more money to children when, at an earlier point in time, they received more visits from these children, suggesting that parents also engage in intertemporal exchange (Lennartsson, Silverstein, and Fritzell, 2010).

A different theoretical perspective on intergenerational relationships is altruism. There are many definitions of altruism, but a common one is that people take the well-being of others into account as a *benefit* in their own utility (Schroeder et al., 1994). Like exchange theory, the perspective of altruism is rational in the sense that people weight the costs and benefits of engaging in intergenerational relationships.

A difference between altruism and exchange is that altruism requires empathy: one needs to understand what the costs and benefits are for someone else. Altruism is also used as a framework in economic research (Arrondel and Masson, 2006), but it has been used on a larger scale and for a longer period in (social) psychological research (Schroeder *et al.*, 1994). Social psychologists do not argue against egoism; they argue instead that the frame people use depends on the type of relationship: personal relationships are governed by altruism, while instrumental relationships are governed by exchange (Batson, 1993).

The theory of altruism seems incomplete without an explanation of where altruism comes from. One explanation focuses on the biological nature of altruism. If there are altruistic genes, these are more likely to survive since the children of altruists will have a better chance of reaching the reproductive ages. This explanation of altruism applies to parents and not to children. Another explanation of altruism is that there are side benefits of helping, such as more self-esteem, a sense of meaning, and perhaps a general increase in well-being. These considerations have been summarized with the phrase *doing well by doing good* (Piliavin and Siegl, 2007). That there are side benefits to helping others is plausible, but because they are basically selfish motivations, the explanation blurs the distinction between altruism and exchange.

The theory has been tested indirectly by focusing on the needs of parents and children. The underlying assumption is that meeting another person's need makes that other person happier, an assumption that is plausible in most cases. Empirical research has provided considerable evidence in favor of this hypothesis when the focus is on what children give to parents. Virtually all indicators of parental need – for example, living alone, health problems – increase the support that children give (Grundy, 2005). An exception appears to lie in financial transfers. Few children give money to their parents, even when parents are living in poverty (Hogan and Eggebeen, 1995). Parents also respond to the needs of children (Bucx, van Wel, and Knijn, 2012). Especially convincing here is evidence coming from multiactor studies. These within-family comparisons show that children who were single, who were lower educated, and who had health or other personal problems received more support than their married, higher educated siblings who had no problems (Suitor, Pillemer, and Sechrist, 2006; Fingerman *et al.*, 2009; Kalmijn, 2013).

Economists have tested exchange and altruism by studying *inter vivos* transfers (money donations to children) and inheritances. Research has shown that after controlling for parental income, the income level of a child has a negative effect on the chance to receive a financial transfer from parents (Hochguertel and Ohlsson, 2009). Because children with low incomes are more in need of support, this finding is consistent with altruism and shows that parents compensate for economic inequality within the family. The study of inheritances was motivated by the strategic bequest hypothesis, which argued, on the basis of exchange theory, that parents would strategically use their bequest to secure support from their children (Bernheim, Shleifer, and Summers, 1985). Although originally supported by Bernheim, later studies found no evidence that children provide more support to parents when they expect to inherit a larger amount of money or property (Wilhelm, 1996; Sloan, Picone, and Hoerger, 1997).

The study of inheritances does not seem to support altruism either. Despite income differences among children within families, the large majority of parents give all children the same part of the inheritance (Finch and Mason, 2000; Behrman and Rosenzweig, 2004). This evidence is in contrast to the research on *intra vivos* transfers, which shows that poorer children receive more financial support from parents. Economists have resolved this discrepancy by arguing that parents can conceal financial gifts but not inheritances (Arrondel and Masson, 2006). Sociologists have argued that parents hardly think about the option of not giving equal shares to the children, in other words, equal division is part of the normative frame that parents use (Finch and Mason, 2000). Qualitative interviews suggest that parents do sometimes differentiate by passing on personal items to specific children to express their preferences (Finch and Mason, 2000). Inheritances thus have an expressive, more symbolic meaning that is suggested by either the altruistic or the exchange perspective.

Marriage, Divorce, and Remarriage

Marriage and divorce have important effects on adult intergenerational relations, in particular for fathers. All studies find that fathers who divorced have a weaker relationship with their adult children (from the dissolved marriage) than fathers who remained married. These effects occur for a number of dimensions, including contact frequency, support exchange, affection, and conflict (De Graaf and Fokkema, 2007; Albertini and Garriga, 2011). Effects are much stronger when the father divorced while the children were still at home, but there are also small negative effects for later divorces (Aquilino, 1994). There is some tendency that negative effects for one parent do not coincide with negative effects for the other parent; hence, there is some compensation (Kalmijn, 2012). This can be explained by the fact that children are often faced with loyalty conflicts after divorce – they feel caught in the middle – which makes them draw closer to one parent (Amato and Afifi, 2006). The findings for fathers are worrisome, not only for children who miss a father figure in their adult life, but also for fathers. Fathers who do not repartner may miss the support they need when they are old and frail. The divorce revolution has not yet *hit* the elderly, but this will change as the baby boom enters old age.

A common explanation of these findings lies in the notion of investments and hence, in exchange theory. Fathers rarely get custody, and although many divorced fathers remain involved in the lives of their children, this involvement will typically be less intensive than it was before the divorce. An early decline in involvement can be seen as a decline in investment in children, which, according to principles of reciprocity, will lead to less frequent support from and contact with children when children are older. Fewer investments in children during marriage may also lead to lower-quality ties when the children are older. One piece of evidence for this lies in the effects of the age at divorce. The older the children are when they experience the divorce of their parents, the shorter the period during which fathers are faced with visitation arrangements, and the more they have been able to invest at normal levels in their children. Several studies confirm that there are positive effects of the child's age at divorce on father–child relationships (Aquilino, 2006; Kalmijn, 2012).

A different type of argument is that fathers maintain ties with adult children through marriage. Mothers are generally the kinkeepers at home; for example, they make arrangements for visits, they call more often, they buy the birthday presents, and so forth. When married, fathers benefit from these investments, but when they divorce, they not only lose a spouse, they also lose a kinkeeper. As a result, outside of marriage, fathers may be less able to maintain ties with their children when the children are adult, and the fathers are living on their own. In other words, marriage and children are often a package deal for men, or to put it more positively, marriage *protects* men (Kalmijn, 2007; Clark and Kenney, 2010). Direct evidence for this marriage protection effect is scarce, but studies do find that widowed fathers also have less frequent contact with their children than married fathers, suggesting that even without the decline in investment opportunities after divorce, there is a negative effect (Ha *et al.*, 2006; Kalmijn, 2007).

Most theoretical arguments have addressed the role of the father, and there is less attention for how the mother's ties to the children are affected by a divorce. Adult children with married parents can visit their parents together or can give support to them simultaneously. For children of divorced parents, such economies of scale do not exist. Hence, unless the children of divorce decide to make extra time for their parents, one would expect that they spend less time with their father and their mother, compared to the children of married parents. A divorce may also lead to emotional problems for the parent, which in turn can affect the relationship with the adult child negatively. This applies to mothers and fathers. Studies sometimes find negative effects of divorce on relationships between adult children and mothers, especially for the degree of conflict between mother and child (Kalmijn, 2012).

The role of repartnering for intergenerational relationships has also been studied. One line of inquiry examines how the formation of new unions affects relationships with young children, either children in one's own home (mostly for mothers who repartner), or for relations to children in the home of the ex-partner (mostly for fathers who repartner). How repartnering affects ties to adult children has been studied less frequently, but there are some studies suggesting that for fathers, repartnering may have cumulative negative effects (Clark and Kenney, 2010). This finding is in line with the notion that marriage and children are a package deal for men. When a new marriage is formed, and possibly new children are born, ties to prior children may become weaker. A more recent strand of research further suggests that relationships to adult stepchildren are somewhat weaker than relationships to adult biological children from the current marriage (van der Pas and van Tilburg, 2010). These effects also depend on the length of time the stepchild was living with the parent. Ties to stepchildren who never shared residence with the father will probably be weaker still. Moreover, it is not yet clear if divorced fathers have more contact with adult stepchildren than with the biological children they had from a prior marriage, although studies on sequential parenthood among fathers do suggest this (Manning and Smock, 2000).

Consequences for Individual Well-Being

An underlying assumption in the solidarity literature is that adult intergenerational relations, and especially support, are important for individual parents and children.

A number of studies have explicitly tested this assumption by relating various solidarity dimensions to measures of well-being. Three theoretical perspectives have been formulated. The first, most basic theory argues in terms of the costs and benefits of support and expects positive effects of receiving support on well-being and negative effects of giving support. The second and slightly different theory argues in terms of equity by stating that the balance of support is crucial (Davey and Eggebeen, 1998). Giving too much support may lead to a decline in well-being because parents or children feel exploited, which may lead to anger and, as a consequence, reduced well-being. Receiving too much support may lead to a decline in well-being as well because it enhances feelings of guilt and helplessness. Especially this last prediction distinguishes the equity perspective from the cost–benefit perspective. The third perspective starts from notions of altruism and argues that helping others may improve well-being. Helping others in need may provide meaning in one's life, may improve self-esteem, and may lead to normative approval of others. Rather than seeing help to others as a cost, this perspective sees helping others as a benefit.

What has the research shown for various perspectives? Some studies focus only on the main effects of giving and receiving support. These studies generally provide inconsistent results for the hypotheses. Sometimes there is no effect of receiving help on well-being, sometimes there is a positive effect (Ingersoll-Dayton, Morgan, and Antonucci, 1997), and more often, there is a negative effect on well-being (Liang, Krause, and Bennett, 2001). Those who examine equity find that older adults who receive more support than they give have the lowest level of life satisfaction (Davey and Eggebeen, 1998). Overbenefiting thus appears to be negative, seemingly in support of the equity theory.

Selection bias is a serious empirical problem in this area. Older adults who are ill or depressed may have a greater need for support. This will lead to a negative association between support received and well-being, which in turn suppresses the potential positive causal effect of support received. A different reasoning applies to the effect of overbenefiting. Older adults who are very ill will receive much support and will not be able to give support. This leads to a negative association between overbenefiting and equity, and, hence, the observed effect in cross-sections may be spurious. Solving the problem of selection bias in this literature is difficult, in part because adjustments for health problems do not help. After all, health problems are part of the dependent variable and should not be controlled for.

A better solution is to use longitudinal data and to estimate effects of *changes* in support exchange on *changes* in well-being. A longitudinal study on children's well-being finds no effects of support exchange with parents on the well-being of adult children (Merz, Schuengel, and Schulze, 2009). Longitudinal analyses for parents in Southern California show that parents who gave instrumental support to their adult children had fewer depressive symptoms at a later age (Byers *et al.*, 2008). Similar results were found in the European SHARE data: starting to give support to an adult child appeared to improve well-being, whereas starting to give support to an elderly parent did not improve well-being (Opree and Kalmijn, 2011). This asymmetry in well-being effects for parents and children seems in line with the generational stake theory as well as with biological altruism – parents feel good if they help their children. It is less consistent with the notion of self-esteem enhancement since children do not seem to benefit from helping parents, at least not in terms of well-being.

While the evidence for support exchange and well-being is still developing now that more and more longitudinal surveys have become available, there is clearer evidence for the consequences of other aspects of intergenerational relations. Many authors find that intergenerational relationship quality is strongly associated with well-being for both parents and children (Umberson, 1992; Merz *et al.*, 2009). Moreover, intergenerational conflict is associated with a decline in well-being, and ambivalence is associated with poorer well-being of both generations as well (Fingerman *et al.*, 2008). Hence, of all the dimensions of intergenerational solidarity, the affective dimension is probably the most important for well-being.

Country Differences and Institutional Effects

There are large differences among societies in the degree of intergenerational solidarity. Due to the development of multinational surveys in Europe, country differences have primarily been studied in the European context. The major line of comparison here is North–South, contrasting family-oriented catholic countries in Southern Europe with individualized protestant countries in the North and West. East–West differences are important as well, with earlier marriage and more intergenerational coresidence to the East of the Hajnal line than to the West. Esping-Andersen's welfare regime typology has also played a role in these comparisons.

The main reason to compare intergenerational relationships among countries lies in institutional effects. One interpretation of institutions focuses on the policies that countries have installed to deal with intergenerational relationships, and especially policies about care for the elderly (Daatland, Herlofson, and Lima, 2011). Another interpretation focuses on the cultural climate that can emphasize or de-emphasize the solidarity of the extended family (Reher, 1998). Important elements of this value climate are norms about intergenerational coresidence, older adult's preferences for autonomy, and beliefs about the legitimacy of state intervention in personal affairs. There is quite some variation in the strength of intergenerational norms, with stronger norms in Southern and Eastern European countries than in Northern and Western European countries (Kalmijn and Saraceno, 2008; Daatland, Herlofson, and Lima, 2011).

An important theme in this literature has been the crowding-out hypothesis, which argues that generous policies toward elderly care reduce the strength of intergenerational relationships or, in other words, that public transfers crowd out private transfers (Kunemund and Rein, 1999). The crowding-out hypothesis has been examined in a number of studies. First, there are descriptive studies that show that there is more intergenerational contact in Southern European countries than in Northern and Western European countries (Attias-Donfut, Ogg, and Wolff, 2005; Börsch-Supan, *et al.*, 2005; Hank, 2007). For support exchange, descriptive studies have not been entirely supportive. Some comparative analyses suggest that differences in the level of support are small and less systematic (Daatland and Lowenstein, 2005; Ogg and Renaut, 2006) or even absent when controlled for compositional differences in the elderly population (Motel-Klingebiel, Tesch-Römer, and von Kondratowitz, 2005). Results have been less convincing for the 5-nation OASIS study than for the 11-nation SHARE study, suggesting that more variation among countries leads to a better test of the hypothesis.

The descriptive studies do not measure policies and thus leave open the question of the underlying causes. In this sense, they provide a weak test of the crowding-out hypothesis. Cultural values and policies are highly correlated because in democratic countries, policies often reflect underlying values. As a result, the descriptive findings can also be due to cultural differences, that is, different norms and values about family responsibilities. More convincing tests come from studies that operationalize institutional differences with macrolevel variables. In an innovative study, Brandt et al. (2009) use the share of employees working in the service sector as an indicator of policies. They find that in countries where this share is high, children provide more practical help to parents but less personal care (Brandt, Haberkern, and Szydlik, 2009). This suggests that crowding-out refers only to personal care, thereby leaving more room for other types of care, which are not negatively affected. In other words, elderly in more generous welfare states more often receive a mixture of formal and informal care than elderly in less generous welfare states (Motel-Klingebiel, Tesch-Römer, and von Kondratowitz, 2005). Kalmijn and Saraceno (2009) use norms about care to older parents, norms about coresidence, and norms about financial support to measure familialism in a cultural sense. They find that the more familialistic the values in a country, the stronger the *effect* of the needs of the parents on the degree to which adult children provide support (Kalmijn and Saraceno, 2008). So far, the evidence does support the importance of institutional effects, but the question remains whether these come from policies or from values. Moreover, since it also depends on the type of care we look at, the linear substitution model of crowding-out is not generally confirmed, and a model of specialization appears more fitting.

Conclusion

The literature on adult intergenerational relationships is both theoretically and empirically rich. Due to the aging of modern societies, the relevance of this topic will only be growing. It is difficult to summarize the main conclusions from the research; the research is still developing, and several issues remain undecided. The solidarity perspective has shown that intergenerational relationships are generally strong. There is much contact and support exchange between parents and adult children, but this is highly dependent on the setting (e.g., country differences, ethnic differences), on life course factors (e.g., divorce, remarriage, aging), and on social stratification (e.g., education). Very intensive and time-consuming forms of support of parents by adult children – that is, personal care – are not common, however; for these, the spouse or formal means of support are more dominant (Börsch-Supan *et al.*, 2005). Moreover, parents continue to support children when parents are quite old, in contrast to the traditional exchange model in which there would be an intergenerational reversal in the flow of support exchanged during the life course. Especially for the way parents behave, there is considerable support for altruistic theories. For both parents and children, elements of exchange are also involved. Normative concerns play an important role as well, especially in the degree to which children respond to parental needs.

There is evidence that some intergenerational relationships are characterized by tension and conflict. Because this has been a more recent strand of research than the solidarity research, less is known about this more negative side of inter-generational relationships. Tension and conflict do not seem very common, but social desirability and perhaps selective nonresponse as well may lead to underes-timates of such problems. What is clear is that positive and negative aspects of parent–child relationships can go hand in hand. In this sense, the literature on intergenerational ambivalence has added an element to the literature without necessarily contradicting the solidarity perspective. Conclusions about the conse-quences of intergenerational relationships are least certain, in part because the design to study these issues is demanding. This nonetheless appears an important area for continued study. After all, the claim that "families (still) matter" needs an empirical test, and such a test requires a renewed focus on individual conse-quences. Consequences can be examined for health and well-being, but outcomes for social stratification seem relevant here as well (e.g., children's schooling, employment, income, and so forth). Links between the literature on intergenera-tional relationships and the literature on social stratification and mobility could be strengthened.

Several newer themes have been suggested by the literature as well. Authors have pointed out that solidarity and conflict in (im)migrant families will become increas-ingly important to study. This is an interesting field because of the many conflicting pressures that are going on in such families, that is, the potentially disruptive force of immigration, the difficulty of maintaining international ties, and the generation gap in traditional family norms and values (Treas and Mazumdar, 2002). There are also large ethnic differences in children's living arrangements (Landale, Thomas, and Van Hook, 2011), and these may have important repercussions for adult intergenerational relationships. Second, grandparenting, although not a new theme, is becoming more common as more and more mothers are entering the labor force. Grandparenting is not simply another form of instrumental support that parents provide to children; the embeddedness of this support in a three-generational relationship is theoretically challenging as well (Hagestad, 2006). Third, the themes of diversity and complexity will become more important. Much is known about the effects of parental divorce, but this is only one *complication* in the life course that affects intergenerational ties. Due to remarriage, fertility in remarriage, and second union dissolution, parents can now have many different types of children. For example, a father can have children from a previous union (*old* children), children from his new and current union (*new* children), and nonbiological children from his current union (stepchildren). How the ties of these children will develop into adulthood is not well known. Theoretically, this is interesting because it raises important questions about the role of biology, marriage, and shared residence for understanding the development of parent–child ties (King, 2009). Finally, it can be expected that inheritances will become a more important issue in the literature. Pension systems have become more vulnerable due to aging, on the one hand, and risks in the financial sector, on the other hand. At the same time, however, current generations of elderly have accumulated much wealth, in particular in housing. As a result, there is more to pass on than before, but there is also pressure on older adults to consume their wealth when retirement benefits are lower than expected (Szydlik, 2004).

References

Albertini, M. and Garriga, A. (2011) The effect of divorce on parent-child contacts: evidence on two declining effect hypotheses. *European Societies*, 13, 257–278.

Alwin, D.F. (1988) From obedience to autonomy: changes in traits desired in children, 1924–1978. *Public Opinion Quarterly*, 52, 33–52.

Amato, P.R. and Afifi, T.D. (2006) Feeling caught between parents: adult children's relations with parents and subjective well-being. *Journal of Marriage and the Family*, 68, 222–235.

Antonucci, T.C. and Akiyama, H. (1987) Social networks in adult life and a preliminary examination of the convoy model. *Journals of Gerontology*, 42, 519–527.

Aquilino, W.S. (1994) Later life parental divorce and widowhood: impact on young adults' assessment of parent-child relations. *Journal of Marriage and the Family*, 56, 908–922.

Aquilino, W.S. (2006) Noncustodial father-child relationship from adolescence into young adulthood. *Journal of Marriage and Family*, 68, 929–946.

Arrondel, L. and Masson, A. (2006) Altruism, exchange or indirect reciprocity: what do the data on family transfers show? In *Handbook of the Economics of Giving, Altruism and Reciprocity: Applications*, vol. 2 (eds S.-C. Kolm and J.M. Ythier), Elsevier, Amsterdam, pp. 971–1054.

Attias-Donfut, C., Ogg, J. and Wolff, F.-C. (2005) European patterns of financial and time transfers. *European Journal on Aging*, 2, 161–173.

Batson, C.D. (1993) Communal and exchange relationships: what is the difference. *Personality and Social Psychology Bulletin*, 19, 677–683.

Behrman, J.P. and Rosenzweig, M.R. (2004) Parental allocations to children: new evidence on bequest differences among siblings. *The Review of Economics and Statistics*, 86, 637–640.

Bengtson, V., Giarrusso, R., Mabry, J.B. and Silverstein, M. (2002) Solidarity, conflict, and ambivalence: complementary or competing perspectives on intergenerational relationships? *Journal of Marriage and Family*, 64, 568–576.

Bengtson, V.L. and Roberts, Robert E.L. (1991) Intergenerational solidarity in aging families – an example of formal theory construction. *Journal of Marriage and the Family*, 53, 856–870.

Bernheim, B.D., Shleifer, A. and Summers, L. (1985) The strategic bequest motive. *Journal of Political Economy*, 93, 1045–1076.

Börsch-Supan, A., Brugiavini, A., Jürges, H. *et al.* (2005) *Health, Ageing and Retirement in Europe: First Results from the Survey of Health, Ageing and Retirement in Europe*. MEA, Mannheim.

Brandt, M., Haberkern, K. and Szydlik, M. (2009) Intergenerational help and care in Europe. *European Sociological Review*, 25, 585–601.

Bucx, F., van Wel, F. and Knijn, T. (2012) Life course status and exchanges of support between young adults and parents. *Journal of Marriage and Family*, 74, 101–115.

Byers, A.L., Levy, B.R., Allore, H.G. *et al.* (2008) When parents matter to their adult children: filial reliance associated with parents' depressive symptoms. *Journals of Gerontology Series B-Psychological Sciences and Social Sciences*, 63, P33–P40.

Cichy, K., Fingerman, K. and Lefkowitz, E. (2003) Age and gender differences in topics of interpersonal tensions. *Gerontologist*, 43, 387.

Clark, S. and Kenney, C. (2010) Is the United States experiencing a "matrilineal tilt?" Gender, family structures and financial transfers to adult children. *Social Forces*, 88, 1753–1776.

Clarke, E.J., Preston, M., Raksin, J. and Bengtson, V.L. (1999) Types of conflicts and tensions between older parents and adult children. *Gerontologist*, 39, 261–270.

Cong, Z. and Silverstein, M. (2011) Intergenerational exchange between parents and migrant and nonmigrant sons in rural China. *Journal of Marriage and Family*, 73, 93–104.

Daatland, S.O. and Lowenstein, A. (2005) Intergenerational solidarity and the family-welfare state balance. *European Journal of Ageing*, 2, 174–182.

Daatland, S.O., Herlofson, K. and Lima, I.A. (2011) Balancing generations: on the strength and character of family norms in the west and east of Europe. *Ageing & Society*, 31, 1159–1179.

Davey, A. and Eggebeen, D.J. (1998) Patterns of intergenerational exchange and mental health. *Journal of Gerontology: Psychological Sciences*, 53B, P86–P95.

De Graaf, P.M. and Fokkema, T. (2007) Contacts between divorced and non-divorced parents and their adult children in The Netherlands: an investment perspective. *European Sociological Review*, 23, 263–277.

Eggebeen, D.J. (1992) Family structure and intergenerational exchanges. *Research on Aging*, 14, 427–447.

Finch, J. and Mason, J. (2000) *Passing On: Kinship and Inheritance in England*. Routledge, London.

Fingerman, K.L. (1996) Sources of tension in the aging mother and adult daughter relationship. *Psychology and Aging*, 11, 591–606.

Fingerman, K.L., Hay, E.L. and Birditt, K.S. (2004) The best of ties, the worst of ties: close, problematic, and ambivalent social relationships. *Journal of Marriage and Family*, 66, 792–808.

Fingerman, K.L., Pitzer, L., Lefkowitz, E.S. *et al.* (2008) Ambivalent relationship qualities between adults and their parents: implications for the well-being of both parties. *Journals of Gerontology Series B-Psychological Sciences and Social Sciences*, 63, P362–P371.

Fingerman, K.L., Miller, L., Birditt, K.S. and Zarit, S. (2009) Giving to the good and the needy: parental support of grown children. *Journal of Marriage and the Family*, 71, 1220–1233.

Ganong, L. and Coleman, M. (2005) Measuring intergenerational obligations. *Journal of Marriage and Family*, 67, 1003–1011.

Gans, D. and Silverstein, M. (2006) Norms of filial responsibility for aging parents across time and generations. *Journal of Marriage and Family*, 68, 961–976.

Grundy, E. (2005) Reciprocity in relationships: socio-economic and health influences on intergenerational exchanges between third age parents and their adult children in Great Britain. *British Journal of Sociology*, 56, 233–255.

Grundy, E. and Henretta, J.C. (2006) Between elderly parents and adult children: a new look at the intergenerational care provided by the "Sandwich Gencration". *Ageing & Society*, 26, 707–722.

Grundy, E. and Read, S. (2012) Social contacts and receipt of help among older people in England: are there benefits of having more children? *Journals of Gerontology Series B-Psychological Sciences and Social Sciences*, 67, 742–754.

Ha, J., Carr, D., Utz, R.L. and Nesse, R. (2006) Older adults' perceptions of intergenerational support after widowhood: how do men and women differ? *Journal of Family Issues*, 27, 3–30.

Hagestad, G.O. (1988) Demographic change and the life course: some emerging trends in the family realm. *Family Relations*, 37, 405–410.

Hagestad, G.O. (2006) Transfers between grandparents and grandchildren: the importance of taking a three-generation perspective. *Zeitschrift für Familienforschung*, 3, 315–333.

Hank, K. (2007) Proximity and contacts between older parents and their children: a European comparison. *Journal of Marriage and Family*, 69, 157–173.

Hank, K. and Buber, I. (2009) Grandparents caring for their grandchildren: findings from the 2004 survey of health, ageing and retirement in Europe. *Journal of Family Issues*, 30, 53–73.

Hochguertel, S. and Ohlsson, H. (2009) Compensatory inter vivos gifts. *Journal of Applied Econometrics*, 24, 993–1023.

Hogan, D.P. and Eggebeen, D.J. (1995) Sources of emergency help and routine Assistance in old-age. *Social Forces*, 73, 917–936.

Hogerbrugge, M.J.A. and Komter, A.E. (2012) Solidarity and ambivalence: comparing two perspectives on intergenerational relations using longitudinal panel data. *Journals of Gerontology Series B-Psychological Sciences and Social Sciences*, 67, 372–383.

Ingersoll-Dayton, B., Morgan, D. and Antonucci, T. (1997) The effects of positive and negative social exchanges on aging adults. *Journals of Gerontology Series B-Psychological Sciences and Social Sciences*, 52, S190–S199.

Inglehart, R. (1997) *Modernization and Postmodernization: Cultural, Economic and Political Change in 43 Societies*. Princeton University Press, Princeton.

Kalmijn, M. (2006) Educational inequality and family relationships: influences on contact and proximity. *European Sociological Review*, 22, 1–16.

Kalmijn, M. (2007) Gender differences in the effects of divorce, widowhood and remarriage on intergenerational support: does marriage protect fathers? *Social Forces*, 85, 1079–1104.

Kalmijn, M. and Saraceno, C. (2008) A comparative perspective on intergenerational support-Responsiveness to parental needs in individualistic and familialistic countries. *European Societies*, 10, 479–508.

Kalmijn, M. (2013) Long-term effects of divorce on parent-child relationships: within-family comparisons of fathers and mothers. *European Sociological Review*, 29 (5), 888–898.

Kalmijn, M. (2013) How mothers allocate support among adult children: evidence from a multiactor survey. *The Journals of Gerontology Series B: Psychological Sciences and Social Sciences*, 68 (2), 268–277.

Kalmijn, M. and Saraceno, C. (2008) A comparative perspective on intergenerational support - responsiveness to parental needs in individualistic and familialistic countries. *European Societies*, 10, 479–508.

Kalmijn, M. and De Vries, J. (2009) Change and stability in parent-child contact in five western countries. *European Journal of Population-Revue Europeenne De Demographie*, 25, 257–276.

Kiecolt, K.J., Blieszner, R. and Savla, J. (2011) Long-term influences of intergenerational ambivalence on midlife parents' psychological well-being. *Journal of Marriage and Family*, 73, 369–382.

King, V. (2009) Stepfamily formation: implications for adolescent ties to mothers, nonresident fathers, and stepfathers. *Journal of Marriage and the Family*, 71, 954–968.

Klein Ikkink, K., van Tilburg, T. and Knipscheer, K.C.P.M. (1999) Perceived instrumental support exchanges in relationships between elderly parents and their adult children: normative and structural explanations. *Journal of Marriage and the Family*, 4, 831–844.

Kohli, M. (1999) Private and public transfers between generations: linking the family and the State. *European Societies*, 1, 81–104.

Kunemund, H. and Rein, M. (1999) There is more to receiving than needing: theoretical arguments and empirical explorations of crowding in and crowding out. *Ageing & Society*, 19, 93–121.

Landale, N.S., Thomas, K. and Van Hook, J. (2011) The living arrangements of children of immigrants. *Future of Children*, 21, 43–70.

Lennartsson, C., Silverstein, M. and Fritzell, J. (2010) Time-for-money exchanges between older and younger generations in Swedish families. *Journal of Family Issues*, 31, 189–210.

Leopold, T. and Raab, M. (2011) Short-term reciprocity in late parent-child relationships. *Journal of Marriage and the Family*, 73, 105–119.

Liang, J., Krause, N.M. and Bennett, J.M. (2001) Social exchange and well-being: is giving better than receiving? *Psychology and Aging*, 16, 511–523.

Litwak, E. (1960) Occupational mobility and extended family cohesion. *American Sociological Review*, 25, 9–21.

Luescher, K. (2002) Intergenerational ambivalence: further steps in theory and research. *Journal of Marriage and Family*, 64, 585–593.

Luescher, K. and Pillemer, K. (1998) Intergenerational ambivalence: a new approach to the study of parent-child relations in later life. *Journal of Marriage and the Family*, 60, 413–425.

Mandemakers, J.J. and Dykstra, P.A. (2008) Discrepancies in parent's and adult child's reports of support and contact. *Journal of Marriage and the Family*, 70, 495–506.

Manning, W.D. and Smock, P.J. (2000) "Swapping" families: serial parenting and economic support for children. *Journal of Marriage and the Family*, 62, 111–122.

Merz, E.-M., Schuengel, C. and Schulze, H.-J. (2009) Intergenerational relations across 4 years: well-being is affected by quality, not by support exchange. *Gerontologist*, 49, 536–548.

Merz, E.-M., Consedine, N. S., Schulze, H.-J. and Schuengel, C. (2009) Wellbeing of adult children and ageing parents: associations with intergenerational support and relationship quality. *Ageing & Society*, 29, 783–802.

Motel-Klingebiel, A., Tesch-Römer, C. and von Kondratowitz, H.-J. (2005) Welfare States do not crowd out the family: evidence for mixed responsibility from comparative analyses. *Ageing & Society*, 25, 863–882.

Ogg, J. and Renaut, S. (2006) The support of parents in old age by those born during 1945–1954: a European perspective. *Ageing & Society*, 26, 723–743.

Opree, S.J. and Kalmijn, M. (2011) Exploring causal effects of combining work and intergenerational support on depressive symptoms among middle-aged women. *Ageing & Society*, 32, 130–146.

Piliavin, J.A. and Siegl, E. (2007) Health benefits of volunteering in the Wisconsin longitudinal study. *Journal of Health and Social Behavior*, 48, 450–464.

Pillemer, K. and Suitor, J.J. (2002) Explaining mothers' ambivalence toward Their adult children. *Journal of Marriage and the Family*, 64, 602–613.

Pinquart, M. and Sörensen, S. (2011) Spouses, adult children, and children-in-law as caregivers of older adults: a meta-analytic comparison. *Psychology and Aging*, 26, 1–14.

Reher, D.S. (1998) family ties in western Europe: persistent contrasts. *Population and Development Review*, 24, 203–234.

Roberts, R.E.L., Richards, L.N. and Bengtson, V. (1991) Intergenerational solidarity in families. *Marriage and Family Review*, 16, 11–46.

Rossi, A.S. and Rossi, P.H. (1990) *Of Human Bonding: Parent-child Relations Across the Life Course*. Aldine de Gruyter, New York.

Ruggles, S. (2011) Intergenerational coresidence and family transitions in the United States, 1850–1880. *Journal of Marriage and Family*, 73, 136–148.

Sana, M. and Massey, D.S. (2005) Household composition, family migration, and community context: migrant remittances in four countries. *Social Science Quarterly*, 86, 509–528.

Schroeder, D.A., Dovidio, J.F., Penner, L.A. and Piliavin, J.A. (1994) *The Social Psychology of Helping And Altruism*. McGraw-Hill, New York.

Silverstein, M. (1995) Stability and change in temporal distance between the elderly and their children. *Demography*, 32, 29–46.

Silverstein, M. and Bengtson, V.L. (1997) Intergenerational solidarity and the structure of adult child-parent relationships in American families. *American Journal of Sociology*, 103, 429–460.

Silverstein, M., Parrott, T.M. and Bengtson, V.L. (1995) Factors that predispose middle-aged sons and daughters to provide social support to older parents. *Journal of Marriage and the Family*, 57, 465–475.

Silverstein, M., Gans, D. and Yang, F.M. (2006) Intergenerational support to aging parents: the role of norms and needs. *Journal of Family Issues*, 27, 1068–1084.

Silverstein, M., Conroy, S.J., Wang, H. *et al.* (2002) Reciprocity in parent-child relations over the adult life course. *Journals of Gerontology Series B: Psychological Sciences and Social Sciences*, 57B, S3–13.

Sloan, F.A., Picone, G. and Hoerger, T.J. (1997) The supply of children's time to Disabled elderly parents. *Economic Inquiry*, 35, 295–308.

Steinbach, A. (2008) Intergenerational solidarity and ambivalence: types of Relationships in German families. *Journal of Comparative Family Studies*, 39, 115–127.

Suitor, J.J., Pillemer, K. and Sechrist, J. (2006) Within-family differences in mothers' support to adult children. *Journals of Gerontology Series B-Psychological Sciences and Social Sciences*, 61, S10–S17.

Szydlik, M. (2004) Inheritance and inequality: theoretical reasoning and empirical evidence. *European Sociological Review*, 20, 31–45.

Szydlik, M. (2008) Intergenerational solidarity and conflict. *Journal of Comparative Family Studies*, 39, 97–114.

Treas, J. and Mazumdar, S. (2002) Older people in America's immigrant families - dilemmas of dependence, integration, and isolation. *Journal of Aging Studies*, 16, 243–258.

Treas, J. and Gubernskaya, Z. (2012) Farewell to moms? Maternal contact for seven countries in 1986 and 2001. *Journal of Marriage and Family*, 74, 297–311.

Umberson, D. (1992) Relationships between adult children and their parents - psychological consequences for both generations. *Journal of Marriage and the Family*, 54, 664–674.

van der Pas, S. and van Tilburg, T.G. (2010) The influence of family structure on the contact between older parents and their adult biological children and stepchildren in the Netherlands. *Journals of Gerontology Series B-Psychological Sciences and Social Sciences*, 65, 236–245.

Van Gaalen, R.I. and Dykstra, P.A. (2006) Solidarity and conflict between adult children and parents: a latent class approach. *Journal of Marriage and Family*, 68, 947–960.

Van Groenou, M., Glaser, K., Tomassini, C. and Jacobs, T. (2006) Socio-economic status differences in older people's use of informal and formal help: a comparison of four European countries. *Ageing & Society*, 26, 745–766.

Wilhelm, M.O. (1996) Bequest behavior and the effect of heirs' earnings: testing the altruistic model of bequests. *American Economic Review*, 86, 874–892.

20

Children's Families: A Child-Centered Perspective

Jacqueline Scott

Introduction

The focus of this chapter is on children's families in the context of rapid social change. In the literature, terms like *modern childhood* and *children of postmodernity* are used. The societal changes that have altered the shape of adult lives – secularization, urbanization, industrialization, globalization, individualization, and the like – also affect the lives of children. For children, many of the effects of social changes are played out in the context of family life. Families themselves have, as this volume shows, changed markedly in the modern era. The greater diversity of families associated with the increases in childbirth outside of marriage and the high rates of divorce is well known in Western societies and beyond. Changes in maternal work patterns and the changing work–family balance have had consequences for the culture of care, in which children are both recipients and providers. Falling birthrates have resulted in smaller families with fewer siblings. Increased longevity has changed intergenerational relations in ways that are little short of revolutionary. Transnational mobility and international migration have altered the context of family relations in ways that can introduce new tensions for both children and parents. All these changes to the structure of family life have important implications for what, from the child's point of view, is his or her own particular family.

We all tend to take our families for granted while, at the same time, regarding them as unique. When we fall in love, have kids, get divorced, we are bowled over by experiences that are intensely personal. Yet, as sociologists, we are all too aware of how even something as private as having a baby is a highly structured experience. The declining rate of childbirth in Europe, in one sense, is the sum of many individual choices. However, those choices are made in the context of socioeconomic opportunities and constraints which have led to the postponement and reduction of childbearing. Similarly, children's lives are structured in ways that reflect socioeconomic

The Wiley Blackwell Companion to the Sociology of Families, First Edition.
Edited by Judith Treas, Jacqueline Scott, and Martin Richards.
© 2014 John Wiley & Sons Ltd. Published 2017 by John Wiley & Sons Ltd.

events and changes. Many of these changes are mediated through families because children's lives are codependent on parents and other family members (see chapter by Parcel and Hendrix, Chapter 18, this volume). Yet children's own preferences and actions are also crucial. The study of children's families involves understanding the structure of childhood, the experiences and agency of children, and the dynamic processes that are associated with children's unfolding lives across time and place.

It is now taken as a given that *childhood* is a social construction. In 1962, the now classic book *Centuries of Childhood* by Philippe Ariès set the tone for the new sociological interest in children and childhood. The questions he addressed revolved around the origin of modern ideas about the family and about childhood. Ariès argued that before the seventeenth century, a child was regarded as a small and inadequate adult; the concept of *the child* as something distinct from adults is a creation of the modern world. The change involved far-reaching implications for the family, for education, and for children themselves. "The concept of the family…is inseparable from the concept of childhood. The interest taken in childhood…is only one form, one particular expression of this more general concept – that of family" (Ariès, 1962, p. 353). Ariès' work has had many critics, but, for our purposes, it does not matter whether Ariès historical interpretation is right or wrong. What Ariès succeeded in, beyond doubt, was demonstrating that childhood and family are social constructs that are rooted in time and place.

In the nineteenth-century America, the increasing differentiation between economic production and the home transformed the basis of family cohesion. According to Zelizer (1985), between the late nineteenth century and early twentieth century, there emerged the *economically worthless* but *emotionally priceless* child. Children are expensive and contribute relatively little to the household income or even to household chores. From the hard-nosed perspective of rational choice, "As soon as men and women…acquire the habit of weighing the individual advantages and disadvantages of any prospective course of action, they cannot fail to become aware of the heavy personal sacrifices that family ties and especially parenthood entails under modern conditions" (Schumpeter, [1942] 1988, pp. 501–502). The below-replacement population levels of fertility in many Western societies suggest that the wish for parenthood may indeed erode further under the pressures of competing opportunities for men and women.

However, the relationship between price and value is far from straightforward as Zelizer shows. There is a curious paradox in that the market price of an economically useless child far exceeds the money value of a nineteenth-century *useful* child. The very notion of a market price is an uncomfortable one, when applied to children. But people pay huge sums for black market babies. And childless women (and their partners) may expend enormous amounts of money, time, and suffering in new fertility treatments to assuage their mounting "baby hunger" as the biological clock ticks by Hewlitt (2002). The value of children is not something that can be inferred, simply, from economic and demographic trends.

As Gillis (2009) points out, developed societies have become extraordinarily child centered even as children have become an ever smaller part of the population. In 1870, the proportion of American households without children was 27%; by 1983, it has reached 64% (Coleman, 1990, p. 590). Gillis claims that it is more common for households to have pets (80%) than children, in part because of falling birthrates and increased voluntary childlessness but also because of the greater longevity of adults who are far more likely to live apart from children in old age. Yet child images pervade modern politics, commerce, and culture. Thus, there is a paradox in that childhood is ever more celebrated in family life even if the actual presence of children has diminished.

Zelizer (2002) argues that by shifting our attention to children's experiences, we discover that the creation of an ostensibly useless child never segregated children from economic life. She urges that a new agenda for research on children's economic relations should move in three directions: (i) toward the variable and unequal experience of children within high-income capitalist countries, (ii) toward the enormous variety of children's circumstances in the lower-income regions where most of the world's children actually live, and (iii) toward the historical changes that are transforming children's economic relations (inside and outside their family and household) in rich and poor countries alike.

It is not just children's economic activities that can take very different forms in the rich minority world and the developing majority world, but there is also a new agenda of research opening up concerning the very different forms that children and young people's family relationships can take. For example, Jamieson and Milne (2012) focus on the forms of intergenerational and familial disruption precipitated by parents and experienced by many children. In parts of the developing world, the absence of a parent or parents because of premature death or economic migration is common, leaving significant proportions of children and young people brought up by a lone parent or carer stand-in for migrant parents. In contrast, for a significant proportion of children and young people in parts of the developed world, the main disruption to their family households and access to their parents is the upheaval of parental divorce or separation. Such comparisons across space and time can be valuable for exploring the different economic, political, and cultural systems that express the socially constructed conventional *generational social order* between children, young people, and adults (Alanen, 2009) and the *family–sex–power* nexus (see Introductory chapter of this volume, and Therborn, 2004).

The sociology of children's families has come a long way since the 1980s when a variety of authors bemoaned the lack of research on children. Ambert (1986), for example, identified a near absence of children in North American sociological research and argued that this reflected the continuing influence of founding theorists whose preoccupations were shaped by the patriarchal values of the societies in which they lived and the nature of rewards in a discipline which favors research on *big issues* such as class, bureaucracies, or the political system. Feminist work challenging such patriarchal preconceptions was well under way, when Thorne (1987) raised the question "Where are the children?" The notion that children or childhood should be accorded the same conceptual autonomy as other groups in society was novel. As Qvortrup notes (1990), "Children are 'human beings', not only 'human becomings', they have not only needs, a fact which is recognized, they also have interests, that may or may not be compatible with the interests of other social groups or categories."

Thirty years on, Qvortrup, Corsaro, and Honig (2009) look back at the *new* sociology of childhood and suggest that hindsight allows us to distinguish five characteristics that marked the *new childhood paradigm*: (i) the aim to study normal childhood and issues concerning the development of prosperous and healthy surroundings for children; (ii) a critique of the conventional socialization perspective, which under-played the importance of children's lives as children; (iii) the emphasis on children's agency and the recognition of the active role children played in constructing rela-tionships and affecting their environment; (iv) the importance of understanding the various structural contexts of childhood across time and place, including common features such as the representation of generational ordering in terms of how children were perceived in relationship to adults; and (v) the extension of common social sci-ence methodologies to include research with children. These five characteristics have helped shape subsequent research concerning children's families in a global world. The emergence of new sociological thinking about childhood and children has gone hand in hand with new political and policy concerns about children's rights and well-being. Policy interests have inevitably helped shape research agendas in the Western world – if only because the public purse is an important funder of social research. There are several major interrelated public concerns about children and families, at national and international levels (Brannen, 1999; Bühler-Niederberger, 2010). The first theme relates to concerns about the "breakup" of the family life, parental responsibilities when marriage and childbirth are separated, and how children fare in the face of marital instability and family change. A second theme relates to concerns about growing levels of child poverty and its consequences. Other concerns involve changing *work–life balance* that has put a time squeeze on families and has led to increasing pressures on family care and demographic shifts that have changed the balance of generations and the ratio of children to elderly, with all that entails for the future of welfare. Encompassing these themes is the focus on chil-dren's rights and how they should be translated in law and practice in an increasingly globalized world.

These areas of policy concern are all bound up with the changing context of children's family lives. Childhood experience is inextricably linked to changes in the lives of women and the shifting boundaries of the public and private spheres. In the early twentieth century, the creation of a *family wage* cemented the notion of women and children as dependents. The traditional gender division of labor was taken as a given. *Family* meant a male breadwinner and a female carer who would look after the household needs and be responsible for the care of the children.

How times have changed. There is a worldwide increase in the number of children living with single mothers. Single-mother families are disproportionately represented in lower-income households. The "feminization of poverty" (Garfinkel and McLanahan, 1985) is therefore something of a misnomer. The women who are overrepresented among the poor are women with children. It is the feminization and pauperization of childhood that go hand in hand. This is particularly marked in the United States, and, according to the Luxembourg Income Study data, 55% of all American children living in a household headed by a single female with no other adult present live in poverty (Heuveline and Weinshenker, 2008). This is the highest rate among the 15 high-income nations examined in their study. A recent report on single mothers and poverty in Europe points to how a well-designed and generous system of child benefits can do much to reduce poverty, but such benefits need to be accompanied by policies that enable single mothers to engage in paid employment (Van Lancker *et al.*, 2012). The prospects for reduction of child poverty in the richest countries of the world are not looking good as welfare retrenchment becomes a plank of deficit reduction strategies in much of Europe and the United States.

Another change is the increasing diversity among children's families. In the United States, as we enter the twenty-first century, even for the white middle class, family structure has become increasingly diverse. Not only are mothers more likely to be employed outside the home, but among married couples, dual-earner couples are now the modal family type. Families with same-sex parents have become more visible. Nearly 40% of all births in the United States were to unmarried women in 2007. In 1980, that rate was only 18.4% (Ventura, 2009). While the majority of children currently live with married parents (including stepparents), divorce and single parenthood have changed the family experiences of many children. Children experience family diversity from a very different vantage point from that of their parents. This applies not just to family composition but also to the different childhood experiences associated with gender, class, and ethnicity.

In this chapter, we review some of the findings of the new sociological approach to children that takes the viewpoint of the child. We also examine studies that use the life course perspective to investigate how children's experiences are shaped by historical time and place and how childhood experience, in turn, shapes their various pathways through to adult life. One of the central arguments that we make is that the two perspectives are both needed. It is not a case of *either* approaching children as *beings or* approaching children as *becoming*. It must be both.

In the next section, we examine the new sociological perspective which views children as social actors. We show how social constructions of childhood have helped render aspects of children's activities invisible. One example concerns the *time bind syndrome* (Hochschild, 1997) where the long work-hour culture changes children's experiences of family time and family care. Another example which, in some instances, may be a consequence of the time bind is *children's work*. In the industrial West, the domestic work and informal labor of children have often been ignored because work has been defined as *paid work*. The subsequent section explores the implications of childhood as a *social category*. Following Qvortrup (1990), we show why it is so important to make children visible, rather than being subsumed as part of the family or household, as is often the case. We examine what is known and what is lacking in current knowledge about the social economic conditions of *childhood* in general and children's families, in particular. This *structural* approach to childhood is illustrated by reference to family structure, child poverty, and well-being. The final section reviews what the life course perspective has revealed about children and families in time and place. The life course perspective is concerned with the way societal change impinges on individual lives. It also offers a dynamic view of how the codependencies of children and family members are changing, in a rapidly changing world. In the conclusion, we suggest that the sociological understanding of children and families has made rapid progress in the past few decades, but there are some glaring deficiencies in our knowledge. These reflect not only conceptual limitations in our understanding of children's families but also ongoing divisions of methodologies. In addition, we suggest that research on children's families is hindered by the ideological baggage associated with *ideals* of childhood and family and value judgments concerning *family change* and *family decline*.

Children as Social Actors

The United Nations Convention on the Rights of the Child (1989) has had a wide-ranging impact on the way children are treated by the state and their entitlement to representation in the judicial and administrative procedures that affect their lives. This includes their family relationships, in the wake of divorce. The interest in children's rights has provided a receptive climate for social research that puts children at the center of focus. The *new* sociological perspective on children takes seriously the notion that childhood and children's social relationships and cultures are worthy of study in their own right and not just in respect to their social construction by adults. This new paradigm asserts that children should be seen as actively involved in the construction of their own social lives, the lives of those around them, and the societies in which they live.

There has been a wealth of research in the last few decades that belongs to this emerging paradigm. Strangely, there was some initial reluctance to study children in the context of family lives. For example, James and Prout (1996) recount how researchers working toward establishing the independent intellectual integrity of a sociology of childhood have wanted to wrestle the study of children out of the familial context of socialization where it was traditionally located. This was because while children were seen within family sociology under headings such as child-rearing and other adult-centric activities, children were certainly not heard. Just as women had to be liberated from their families (conceptually speaking) in order to be seen and heard, this same consideration applied to children (Oakley, 1994). But the position that studying children in their family settings is inappropriate was clearly untenable. Families are the key context in which children's identities are formed. Moreover, changes that affect the life world of parents, such as the long work-hour culture, have far-reaching implications for the experience of the child. Families are also the key context in which states intervene to modify childhood and parental practices and influence generational relations (Mayall, 2009). Things like childcare provision and parental leave entitlement vary hugely across countries (Moss, 2011) and have important ramifications, for the children's lives.

Children's take on the time bind

How do children view the complex "culture of care" that is necessitated when parents work long hours? Even when only 4 years old, children can learn a great deal through eavesdropping on parental conversations. Hochschild (2001) points to how two children have very different *takes* on their care situations. One child clearly resented the parents' absence and was angry and difficult at dinnertime, which made it all the harder for the parents to come home (the time bind syndrome). The other child did not seem to feel any resentment, had ceased to look to the parents as exclusive caregivers, and made it less hard for the parents to reenter family life.

What explains the difference? Hochschild suggests that children are themselves sophisticated observers of their social worlds. They pick up on what their parents never say to them directly. From overheard conversations, they learn about the *problems* parents experience in finding care, the conflicts that result from different expectations of care, and whether the carers are doing the work for love, money, or both. Children know the difference between care done by Granny or Grandpa and by the paid care worker. They know, in other words, if the care culture is one that draws on an integrated community of neighbors and kin who are involved in the child's life, or whether it draws on a market economy, where carers are "good with children," but in relation to *any* child. The former, Hochschild suggests, is getting rarer but may work better from the child's point of view.

There is an ongoing and highly charged debate about the consequences of maternal employment for children. Recent studies have claimed that there has been surprising continuity in the amount of time children spend with their mothers, despite the dramatic changes in mothers' labor market commitment (Bianchi, 2000). Yet, although mothers may be quite successful at juggling time to ensure that children's well-being is not adversely affected, children from a very young age are exposed to diverse forms of care that may be more or less beneficial, in terms of child outcomes.

The point is worth reiterating that what is "good care" from the adult perspective may not appear the same to the eyes of a child. Children's interests, mother's interests, and societal interests do not necessarily coincide. The change in maternal labor force participation and the long work-hour culture is one example of the relation between social change and family life. Since family is not a monolith, it is necessary to differentiate between the different family members, whose acceptance, responses, and contributions to change will vary. Children's perspectives and contributions to family life are beginning to be taken seriously, but the long tradition of pervasive adult-centric bias in sociology means that there is a long way to go.

Children's work

Childhood research has traditionally been located in sociology of family. By contrast, studies of "work" and children, until quite recently, focused almost exclusively on the impact of children on the labor force participation of adults, mothers in particular. Of course, many children do work – in formal part-time employment, in casual informal work, in their family businesses, and in domestic labor. Yet children's labor outside school has been rendered relatively invisible by conceptions of children as dependent and nonproductive (Morrow, 1996). In both Europe and the United States, there is mounting evidence that children do contribute to household labor in the form of routine daily tasks and childcare. The characterization of children as "priceless but useless" may understate their continuing contributions to the domestic economy, the division of labor, and family care. It may be the case that, because of exposure to family disruption and family diversity, children perform more emotional labor – for instance, in supportive roles such as parental confidante – at quite young ages. Certainly, the children of immigrants are often called on, in both routine and emergency situations, to act as "language brokers," on their parents' behalf.

In the United States, nearly all adolescents do paid work at some point during high school, and, perhaps for that reason, there has been a longer tradition of US research on adolescents' work than in Britain. An interesting study that contrasts the family and work relations of youth in a rural and urban community found that young people in rural communities are more likely than their urban counterparts to suggest that parents construe their work as "adultlike" (Shanahan *et al.*, 1996).

The researchers suggest that the rural–urban difference is because urban work opportunities are highly variable, whereas much of the available work in the rural community is integral to the shared agricultural way of life. These findings echo a study of the involvement of Norwegian children in the fishing industry, where children worked alongside adults in baiting fishing lines (Solberg, 1994). Children's temporary position as workers meant that restrictions associated with the status of *child* were frequently overridden.

Similarly, in a study of "homestaying" children in Norway (children who spend a good deal of time at home, unsupervised, while parents are at work), Solberg (1990) notes how, by "looking after themselves" and by contributing to "home care," children are able to negotiate an enhanced "social age." Solberg puts a positive spin on children spending more time by themselves, suggesting that children can benefit from parental acknowledgment of their autonomy. Hochschild, in her study of the time bind of work and family in corporate America, sees "home-alone" children in a less positive light. She suggests that rationalizing parental absence in the name of children's "independence" is yet another twist on the varied ways of evading the "time bind." Children, in this instance, are being asked in essence to "save time" by growing up fast (Hochschild, 1997, p. 229)

Children the world over help shoulder responsibilities toward their families and contribute in different ways to the family economy. Building on her study of children's work in fishing and coir making in the South Western Indian state of Kerala, Nieuwenhuys (1994, 2009) challenges the current restrictive approaches to child labor for the developing world and defends the potential of the working children's movements to participate in the fight to achieve dignity for working children. It is possible however to acknowledge both the importance of children's agency *and* the need for protective labor laws, albeit recognizing that some working children view any restriction as potential threats to their livelihoods.

The child-focused research, described in this section, looks at children as "beings in the present." Viewing children as prospective adults – workers, parents, citizens, or dropouts of the future – can inadvertently diminish the importance of children as children. Yet, rejecting *developmental* perspectives on childhood makes no sense, given that children's actions, family life, and the social and economic processes which are integral to family structure and change unfold over time. This is why the study of children's families also requires a life course approach. Before examining the insights that can be gained from adopting a life course perspective, we first consider what it means to examine childhood as a social category and why an understanding of children's families is not the same as the study of families with children.

The Social Structure of Childhood

There is a case for arguing that childhood is a structural concept that is a permanent form, even if its members change continuously and even if it varies considerably across historical time and place. This assumption is necessary for a comparative framework that examines conditions of childhood (e.g., poverty rates of "dependent children") across different societies, across different groups within societies, and across time. In this section, we examine how childhood has been affected by the revolutionary demographic shifts in family life in the West, in the latter part of the twentieth century. One of the consequences of these changes is the increase in single-parent families, the vast majority being headed by women, and the related increase in child poverty.

Children's family structures

Changes in demographic behavior have been so dramatic that they have been termed by some the *second demographic transition* (Lesthaeghe, 1995). This term contrasts the changes that have occurred since 1960 with those in the first half of the century. Underlying the more recent demographic shifts is an increased value placed on individual autonomy and the associated shifts in ideas concerning gender equality. These changes have been the subject of heated debate, with traditionalists believing that the family is collapsing, while modernists welcome the new opportunities for women and the wider choices for both sexes. However, among both camps, there are those who suggest that the greater choice for parents and equality gains for women may be at the expense of their children (Clarke, 1996; Parreñas, 2005). Whatever the truth in the judgments about the relative benefits for adults and children, these changes are unlikely to be reversed.

Patterns of family formation and dissolution have become markedly more frequent, less strictly patterned, and more complex, since the 1960s. But, to a great extent, it is adults not children who trigger these family changes. The evidence is beginning to be assembled on the relative (in)stability of different household forms, the frequency of household compositional change, and the amount of time, contact, and resources that flow between different family members, as they form, leave, and reform household groups. But what has happened to the children?

By the turn of the twenty-first century, children in Northern Europe and the United States were more likely to be born into populations where increasing numbers choose not to have children. Children were also more likely to be born outside marriage, to experience family shifts, to have few siblings, and to live in either a dual-earner or one-parent family (Jensen, 2009). An unmarried mother used to be synonymous with a single mother. This is no longer the case. Many children are born to mothers in consensual unions, and this proportion is increasing. As Jensen suggests, the lost monopoly of marriage for childbirth was a first step on the road to pluralization of children's family forms.

However, it is not just that family forms are plural but they are also more fragile and children are more likely to spend part of their childhood in different family arrangements and living apart from one of their biological parents (usually the father). Figure 20.1 shows the percentage of young adolescents (11–15) currently living in either a stepfamily or single-parent household. The majority of children still live with both parents, but as the figure shows, substantial numbers of children in some countries do not. The ramifications of the greater diversity and fragility of family forms for children include the enhanced risk of material deprivation in single-parent families, the potential loss of contact with fathers, and the greater likelihood of children having to move between parental homes, as a result of parental splits.

Does it matter that an increasing proportion of children experience a variety of family settings as they pass through childhood and adolescence? Current consensus

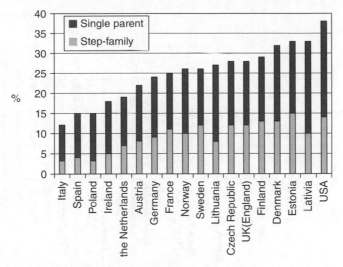

Figure 20.1 Living arrangements of young adolescents (11–15) in Europe, 2005–2006.
Source: data from Health Behaviour in School-aged Children Survey 2005/2006 in Chapple (2009).

is that it does. As we shall see, the evidence is more complex to evaluate than the media headlines acknowledge. To understand the very different experiences of children as they negotiate the complex family settings that can follow family disruption, qualitative methods can be invaluable. However, large-scale longitudinal surveys are also crucial for following the lives of children over time and unpacking the complex relationship between family structure and process and between the antecedents and consequences of children's attributes and actions. We review some of the survey findings in the section on the life course perspective.

Child poverty and children's well-being

The size and structure of children's families are important in determining child poverty. In Britain, despite a fall in the number of families with children and declining family size, the number of children living in households with below half the average income had risen rapidly in the last decades of the twentieth century. By the end of the 1990s, about one-fifth of all children were living in such households; this represented a threefold increase over just two decades between 1979 and 1999 (Department for Work and Pensions, 2012). This rise in child poverty reflected a growth in the number of children living in families without work. Sixty-one percent of all poor children lived in a household with no one employed. Half of all poor children lived in a lone-parent household. Three-quarters of poor children were white, but the risk of child poverty was higher in all minority ethnic groups, especially households of Bangladeshi or Pakistani origin (Bradshaw, 2002). According to OECD statistics (OECD, 2009a), there is some evidence that the policy targets set by the New Labour government to reduce child poverty had some effect.

As can be seen in Figure 20.2, by the mid-2000s, child poverty in the United Kingdom was slightly below the OECD average with one-tenth of children living in households with below 50% of the median equivalized income (the OECD average

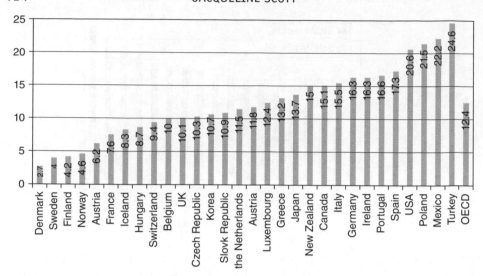

Figure 20.2 Percentage of children (aged 0–17 years) living in poor households (below 50% of median equivalized income), circa 2005.
Source: OECD, *Doing Better for Children* (2009), Fig. 2.2; data from OECD *Income Distribution database*, developed for OECD (2008b), *Growing Unequal: Income Distribution and Poverty in OECD Countries*.

being 12.4%). According to the OECD 2011 Report, "Doing better for families," before the financial crisis, child poverty in the United Kingdom fell by the largest proportion out of all OECD countries. However, the report also notes that progress in child poverty reduction has stalled and is now predicted to increase. One area of concern that the report highlights is the relatively high childcare costs in the United Kingdom, which remains a barrier to work for both low-earning families and those higher up the income scale.

By contrast, child poverty rates remain very high in the United States with one-fifth of children in the mid-2000s living in poor households with less than half the median equivalized income. With the continuing financial crisis, child poverty is fore-cast to increase still further. The OECD analysis suggests that the United States could do much to reduce children's poverty rates by strengthening early year's services and benefits, including legislating for paid parental leave, and building on the successes of child education and care services, such as the Headstart program. The United States is the only OECD country without a national paid parental leave policy, although some states provide leave payments.

In both the United States and Britain, there has been an extraordinary output of work on the causes and consequences of child poverty. While much of the research is directly relevant to policy interventions and is couched in terms of "What works for children?" (e.g., Chase-Lansdale and Brooks-Gunn, 1995; Waldfogel, 2006), it must be recognized that children's interests, family interests, and societal interests may well be different (Glass, 2001). For example, policies aimed to reduce poverty by raising family income through paid work may not necessarily be consistent with the desire to strengthen family ties or to prioritize parental care of young children. While sociological research can usefully inform policy initiatives, the role of sociology is not in constructing societal engineering blueprints. Rather, it consists of "careful analyses of social processes, awareness of their concealed and unintended manifestations, and sustained efforts to understand the participants' own reactions to their situation" (Portes, 2000).

There has been a great deal of work analyzing the complexity of social processes involved in *growing up poor*. As family structure, parental characteristics and household poverty are so interlinked, sorting out what is causing what, and with what consequences is no easy task (Duncan *et al.*, 1998; Mayer, 2010). There has been much less work devoted to understanding children's own reactions to their family's poverty. Child poverty is measured in terms of household income, but we know from a number of influential feminist studies that the household allocation of resources is often structured on gender and generational lines. The "black box" of household finances is very difficult to prize open. One of the few studies to look at household income from the child's perspective suggests that children, as young as seven, are good tacticians in persuading parents to buy them the things they want. Nevertheless, although parents are often willing to make financial sacrifices to protect children from some of the more visible aspects of poverty, children, like adults, suffer from relative deprivation. Children's consumption ideas are shaped by affluent images portrayed in the media and comparisons with more fortunate peers (Middelton *et al.*, 1994; Cook, 2009).

Children's Families: A Life Course Perspective

One thing life course research has demonstrated convincingly is that children's lives are not *determined* by historical circumstances, economic change, or family structures. Nevertheless, some children grow up in much more disadvantaged circumstances than others, which has clear knock-on effects for children's subsequent behaviors and achievements. A great deal of research has been devoted to understanding why some children's life courses are blighted by disadvantage, while others "beat the odds" and make a success of their lives, despite the risks. Fundamental to the idea of risk is the predictability of life chances from earlier circumstances (Bynner, 2001). There are clear patterns and associations between earlier circumstances and later outcomes. For example, persistent child poverty has a well-known detrimental effect on educational attainment. However, there is also considerable individual variation in children's developmental pathways. To understand children's life chances, we need to take seriously the way children act to select, shape, and respond to the great number of choices, available in contemporary societies.

Studying children's lives in times of extreme social, economic, or cultural upheaval can be a useful way of revealing the processes by which an external risk affects the vulnerability and resilience of children. It can also help identify factors that minimize or accentuate the risk. "Children of the Depression" was one of the first of this mold (Elder, [1974] 1999). The study examined archival data on children born in Oakland California in 1920–1921. It showed that the impact of economic deprivation during the Depression was felt mainly through children's changing family experiences, including altered family relationships, different division of labor, and enhanced social strain.

Elder also undertook a comparison study, using a group of children from Berkeley, born just 8 years later in 1928–1929. This showed marked differences between the ways economic deprivation affected the children of the two birth cohorts. The Oakland children encountered the Depression hardships after a relatively secure phase of early childhood in the 1920s. By contrast, the Berkeley group spent their early childhood years in families which were under extraordinary stress and instability. The adverse effects of the Depression were far more severe for the Berkeley group, particularly the boys. The Oakland cohorts were old enough to take on jobs outside the home, and, as we saw in the last section, children, by working, can enhance their status within families. This would have been particularly true under conditions of economic hardship, when children's earning money could be vital to their families' welfare.

The study underlines the need to recognize children as agents of their own family experience and the need to take account of the multiple relationships which define patterns of family adaptation in hard times. Such insights have helped shape the four principles that underpin the life course perspective (Elder, 2001). First, the historical time and place of childhood leaves a lasting imprint on people's lives. Second, the timing of events, life transitions, and behavioral choices are critically important. Third, individual lives are inseparably linked to the lives of significant others, especially family members. Fourth, human agency, including children's agency, must be recognized. We illustrate, in turn, how these insights have contributed to more recent studies of the interrelation of social change, families, and children's lives. These studies predate the publication of the research projects that have been commissioned by various funding bodies in Europe and the United States to examine how the ongoing "great recession" affects family life and children's well-being.

The imprint of changing historical time

One way of looking at the imprint of historical time on children lives is to compare children's experiences across different societies or different sociohistorical contexts (Wadsworth, 1991; Elder, Modell, and Parke, 1993). With the increasing availability of longitudinal samples, it is possible to compare the diverse pathways from childhood to early adulthood, of children born at different points in time. One such study, comparing children born in 1958 and 1970 in Britain, found that the material circumstances of families had improved for the more recent cohort. The study also found that the accumulative disadvantages associated with children's socioeconomic background have become more marked over time (Schoon *et al.*, 2002; Schoon, 2006). This result brings little comfort to politicians who hoped that by raising the standard of living, without tackling inequality, they would improve children's life chances. Subjective assessments of economic well-being are not usually based on comparisons with the past, but on existing expectations for life. Children, whose families are left behind in the overall improvement of standards of living, continue to be at a disadvantage.

The timing of events and interlinked lives

Research in both Britain and the United States has shown that family economic conditions in early childhood are more important, than those of later childhood, for predicting children's cognitive ability and educational achievement (Duncan and

Brooks-Gunn, 1997; Schoon *et al.*, 2002). It is also worth noting that family economic resources seem to matter far more than family structure in terms of children's cognitive development (Duncan and Brooks-Gunn, 1997; Joshi *et al.*, 1999). Still, most research, to date, suggests that children experiencing lone parenthood or family disruption or both have, on average, tougher lives, more limited options, and less desirable outcomes than those who do not (Rodgers and Pryor, 1998; McCulloch *et al.*, 2000).

Using British birth cohort data from 1946, 1958, and 1970, Ely *et al.* (1999) examined the secular trends in the overall association of parental divorce or separation and children's educational attainment at school-leaving age, during the period spanning a quarter of a century since the World War II in Britain. The results refute the commonly held opinion that the effects of divorce on children have attenuated with the increasing prevalence of divorce. These results were indeed surprising as divorce has become less stigmatized than it was for earlier generations, and, in addition, the selection hypothesis would suggest that as divorce increases, the average child of divorce would come from a less troubled family. A different study using more varied measures of disadvantage but with the same 1958 and 1970 British birth cohort studies, results confirmed that the association between parental divorce and subsequent disadvantage has remained remarkably stable over time (Sigel-Rushton *et al.*, 2005). Disadvantage was measured both by children's temperament and academic success at age 11, and also by lack of educational qualifications, receipt of means-tested benefits, and mental health at age 30. The robustness of this negative association between parental divorce, children's well-being at 11, and subsequent adult disadvantage raises the most intriguing question for future research: why is it that the associations are so stable across a time period that saw such dramatic change in the frequency of divorce and the acceptance of alternative family structures?

In order to begin to answer this question, researchers need to unpack what really matters about parental divorce for children. Is it a fall in economic status? A loss of a father figure? An erosion of social contacts? A reduction in parental care? Do all of them matter? And is what matters different for different children? We can glean some evidence from studies that go into greater detail about the context of childhood experiences and the process through to later outcomes. For example, an intriguing qualitative study by of Scottish children unpacks the complex perspectives and choices that accompany parental splits, as well as other family changes such as repartnering and family migration (Highet and Jamieson, 2007). Their findings suggest that even relatively commonplace family changes do not feel ordinary to the child. From the child's perspective, such upheavals disrupt what they regard as normal life.

Until quite recently, survey researchers, when investigating aspects of childhood, have preferred to ask adult respondents such as parents or teachers to report on children's lives, rather than to ask children themselves. In part, this has been because of concerns about the cognitive ability of children to process and respond to structured questions about behavior, perceptions, opinions, and beliefs. Yet by including children as respondents in longitudinal surveys, social scientists can improve the theoretical understanding and empirical knowledge of the dynamics of social inclusion and exclusion as they affect childhood experiences and children's life course trajectories.

Interviewing children does pose distinctive methodological problems that could impinge on the quality of data (Scott, 2008). In particular, survey techniques might not be appropriate for younger children because of cognitive and language limitations. However, by preadolescence (as young as 10), children are quite capable of providing meaningful and insightful information. Research on children as respondents lags behind research on adult respondents. Although child respondents do pose some special concerns (e.g., issues of power and ethics), when children are asked questions they are able and willing to answer, young age is no barrier to data quality.

Children's agency. Children have an active role in shaping their own life course. Of course, many childhood experiences, including poverty and family disruption, are not in the child's control. However, the process that links childhood experience and adult outcomes involves many chains of action that the child, himself or herself, initiates.

One chain of links was traced in a British study that followed a group of young people from age 10, through to their choice of first partner. The study demonstrated that childhood behavioral problems exacerbated the risk of young people choosing a first partner who was *deviant*, in terms of antisocial behavior, persistent drug or alcohol misuse, or marked problems in interpersonal relations (Rutter *et al.*, 1995). Women were much more likely to have a deviant partner than were men. However, the things that helped reduce the risk were similar for both girls and boys. Children who showed forethought in planning life choices were at less risk, and those who had a nondelinquent peer group were less likely to form a "problem" partnership. A harmonious family environment also helped.

Children make choices among options that become building blocks of their evolving life courses. Often, choices amplify tendencies already present. Problem peer groups enhance the chances of a child with deviant leanings going off the rails, whereas high-achieving friends further motivate children's efforts to succeed. There is considerable individual variation in outcomes. Although family advantage, adversity, genes, and environment all tilt the odds, children's lives are their own and, to a great degree, are of their own making.

Children and Families: Looking Back and Looking Forward

In this chapter, we have taken it as a given that childhood, like family, is a social construct. The way childhood is conceived, in a particular time and place, frames our knowledge and understanding. In sociology, until quite recently, children were subsumed under family and households and not considered as actors in their own right. The *new* sociology of childhood rightly emphasizes that children are agents. Children are not passive victims of circumstance, they act and exert influence on the lives of others around them, and they make choices, within the opportunities and constraints that contemporary life brings. Those opportunities and constraints are closely bound with the social positions that are reproduced and transmitted from one generation, to the next, within the family context. Yet children's fates are in no way determined. There is great variation in outcomes, with some children beating the odds and thriving despite childhood adversities, including poverty and family disruption.

We have insisted that family context is crucial for understanding children's contemporary well-being and future pathways. Children are agents, but agency is not individual, it is relational. Children's actions and choices are codependent on the lives of others, particularly their family members. Parents' lives are also codependent on the lives of their children. There are, of course, important power differences that age statuses bestow. However, as we saw both from examples of children's work and from children's responses to the time bind syndrome, children, from a very early age, actively shape their family environment.

The study of children's families crosses the disciplinary divides and necessitates different methodologies for different purposes. In an early statement about "a new paradigm for the sociology of childhood," it was asserted that there was a need to break with the traditions of developmental psychology (Prout and James, 1990). It was also stated that ethnography is a particularly useful methodology for the study of childhood. Both claims are unfortunate. There is an ongoing divide between the mainly quantitative studies of children's families that use the developmentally informed life course perspective, on the one hand, and the mainly qualitative research exploring children's perspectives, on the other. This divide needs to be broken down. It is not a matter of understanding children as beings or as becomings. We need both.

We have insisted that children must not be marginalized through seeing them only in terms of their family or household. This obscures the position of children. By making children visible in statistics, it becomes evident that children's interests can differ from those of women, parents, or other groups in society. The potential interest clash between children and other societal groups is clear when there are scarce resources to be distributed (e.g., in the case of child poverty). There may also be a clash between children's need for family stability and adults' desire for greater individual freedom and family choice.

The thorny issue of family change or family decline poses a particular challenge to the future study of children's families. Research on effects for children of family disruption, family diversity, changing work–family balance, and different care cultures is often contentious. Ideology frequently colors interpretations and claims far exceed knowledge. Examples of ideology masking interpretation come from both liberal and conservative viewpoints. To use currently fashionable jargon, we need to "deconstruct" the literature on children's families to examine how ideals of childhood and family shape not only what questions are asked but also what answers are found.

References

Alanen, L. (2009) Generational order, in *The Palgrave Handbook of Childhood Studies* (eds. J. Qvortrup, W.A. Corsaro and M.-S. Honig), Palgrave MacMillan, London, pp. 159–174.

Ambert, A. (1986) The place of children in North American sociology. *Sociological Studies in Child Development*, 1, 11–31.

Ariès, P. (1962) *Centuries of Childhood*, Penguin, Harmondsworth.

Bianchi, S. (2000) Maternal employment and time with children: dramatic change or surprising continuity? *Demography*, 37, 401–414.

Bradshaw, J. (2002) Child poverty and child outcomes. *Children and Society*, 16, 131–140.

Brannen, J. (1999) Reconsidering children and childhood: sociological and policy perspectives, in *The New Family?* (eds. E. Silva and C. Smart), Sage, London, pp. 143–158.

Bühler-Niederberger, D. (2010) Introduction: childhood sociology – defining the state of the art and ensuring reflection, *Current Sociology*, 58,155–164.

Bynner, J. (2001) Childhood risks and protective factors in social exclusion. *Children and Society*, 15, 285–301.

Chapple, S. (2009) Child Well-Being and Sole-Parent Family Structure in the OECD: an Analysis. *OECD social, employment and migration working paper, no. 82*, OECD, Paris.

Chase-Lansdale, P.L. and Brooks-Gunn, J. (1995) *Escape from Poverty: What Makes a Difference for Children?* Cambridge University Press, Cambridge.

Clarke, L. (1996) Demographic change and the family situation of children, in *Children in Families: Research and Policy* (eds. J. Brannen and M. O'Brien), The Falmer Press, London, pp. 66–83.

Coleman, J.S. (1990) *Foundations of Social Theory*, Harvard University Press, Cambridge.

Cook, D. (2009) Children as Consumers, in *The Palgrave Handbook of Childhood, Studies* (eds. Q. Qvortrop, W.A. Corsaro and M.-S. Honig), Palgrave MacMillan, London, pp. 332–346.

Department for Work and Pensions (2012) *Households Below Average Income*, http://statistics.dwp.gov.uk/asd/index.php?page=hbai (accessed January 4, 2013).

Duncan, G. and Brooks-Gunn, J. (1997) Income effects across the life span: integration and interpretation, in *Consequences of Growing Up Poor* (eds. G. Duncan and J. Brooks-Gunn), Russell Sage, New York.

Duncan, G., Yeung, W.J., Brooks-Gunn, J. and Smith, J. (1998) The effects of childhood poverty on the life chances of children. *American Sociological Review*, 63, 406–423.

Elder, G.H., Jr. (1999) [1974] *Children of the Great Depression*, Westview Press, Boulder.

Elder, G.H., Jr. (2001) Families, social change and individual lives. *Marriage and Family Review*, 31, 177–192.

Elder, G.H., Jr., Modell, J.M. and Parke, R.D. (1993) *Children in Time and Place*, Cambridge University Press, New York.

Ely, M., Richards, M.P.M, Wadsworth, M.E.J and Elliott, B.J (1999) Secular changes in the association of parental divorce and children's educational attainment – evidence from three British birth cohorts. *International Journal of Social Policy*, 28 (3), 437–455.

Garfinkel, I. and McLanahan, S. (1985) The Nature, Causes and Cures of the Feminization of Poverty. Paper at Annual Meeting, Population Association of America, Boston.

Gillis, J. (2009) Transitions to Modernity, in *The Palgrave Handbook of Childhood Studies* (eds. J. Qvortrup, W.A. Corsaro and H.-S. Honig), Palgrave MacMillan, London, pp. 114–126.

Glass, N. (2001) What works for children? The political issues. *Children and Society*, 15, 14–20.

Heuveline, P. and Weinshenker, M. (2008) The international child poverty gap: does demography matter? *Demography*, 45 (1), 173–191.

Hewlitt, S.A. (2002) *Baby Hunger: The New Battle for Motherhood*, Atlantic Books, London.

Highet, G. and Jamieson, L. (2007) *Cool with Change: Young People and Family Change*, http://www.crfr.ac.uk/reports/CWC%20final%20report%202007.pdf (accessed January 7, 2013).

Hochschild, A. (1997) *The Time Bind: When Work Becomes Home and Home Becomes Work*. Metropolitan Books, New York.

Hochschild, A. (2001) Eavesdropping children, adult deals, and cultures of care, in *Working Families* (eds. R. Hertz and N. Marshall), University of California Press, Berkeley, pp. 340–353.

James, A. and Prout, A. (1996) Strategies and structures: towards a new perspective on children's experiences of family life, in *Children in Families: Research and Policy* (eds. J. Brannen and M. O'Brien), The Falmer Press, London, pp. 41–52.

Jamieson, L. and Milne, S. (2012) Children and young people's relationships, relational processes and social change: reading across worlds. *Children's Geographies*, 10 (3), 265–278.

Jensen, A.-M. (2009) Pluralisation of family forms, in *The Palgrave Handbook of Childhood Studies* (eds. J. Qvortrup, W.A. Corsaro and M.-S. Honig), Palgrave MacMillan, London, pp. 140–156.

Joshi, H., Cooksey, E., Wiggins, R. *et al.* (1999) Diverse family living situations and child development: a multi-level analysis comparing longitudinal information from Britain and the United States. *International Journal of Law and Social Policy*, 13, 293–314.

Lesthaeghe, R. (1995) The second demographic transition in western countries: an interpretation, in *Gender and Family Change in Industrialized Countries*, (eds. K. Mason and A.-M. Jensen), Clarendon, Oxford, pp. 17–62.

Mayall, B. (2009) Generational relations at family level, in *The Palgrave Handbook of Childhood Studies* (eds. J. Qvortrup, W.A. Corsaro, and M.-S. Honig), Palgrave MacMillan, London, pp. 175–187.

Mayer, S. (2010) Revisiting an old question: how much does parental income affect child outcomes? *Focus*, 27 (2), 21–26.

McCulloch, A., Wiggens, R., Joshi, H. and Sachdev, D. (2000) Internalising and externalising children's behaviour problems in Britain and the US: relationships to family resources. *Children and Society*, 14, 368–383.

Middelton, S., Ashworth, K. and Walker, R. (1994) *Small Fortunes: Pressures on Parents and Children in the 1990s*, CPAG Ltd, London.

Morrow, V. (1996) Rethinking childhood dependency: children's contributions to the domestic economy. *Sociological Review*, 44, 58–77.

Moss, P. (ed) (2011) *International Review of Leave Policies and Related Research 2011*. http://www.leavenetwork.org/fileadmin/Leavenetwork/Annual_reviews/Complete_review_2011.pdf (accessed November 19,January 2013).

Nieuwenhuys (1994) *Children's Lifeworlds: Gender, Welfare and Labour in the Developing World*, Routledge, London.

Nieuwenhuys (2009) From child labour to working children's movements, in *The Palgrave Handbook of Childhood Studies* (eds. J. Qvortrup, W.A. Corsaro and M.-S. Honig), Palgrave MacMillan, London, pp. 289–300.

Oakley, A. (1994) Women and children first and last: parallels and differences between children's and women's studies, in *Children's Childhood Observed and Experienced* (ed. B. Mayall), The Falmer Press, London, pp. 114–127.

OECD (2009a) Doing Better for Children, http://www.oecd.org/els/familiesandchildren/doingbetterforchildren.htm (accessed January 7, 2013).

OECD (2009b) Family Database, http://www.oecd.org/els/familiesandchildren/41919559.pdf (accessed November 27, 2013).

OECD (2011) Doing Better for Families, http://www.oecd.org/els/familiesandchildren/doingbetterforfamilies.htm (accessed January 7, 2013).

Parreñas (2005) *Children of Global Migration*, Stanford Press, Stanford.

Prout, A. and James, A. (eds) (1990) A new paradigm for the sociology of children? Provenance, promise and problems, in *Constructing and Reconstructing Childhood*. The Falmer Press, London, pp. 7–43.

Portes, A. (2000) The hidden abode: sociology as analysis of the unexpected, *American Sociological Review*, 65, 1–18.

Qvortrup, J. (1990) A voice for children in statistical and social accounting: a plea for children's rights to be heard, in *Childhood: Constructing and Reconstructing Childhood: Contemporary Issues in the Sociological Study of Childhood* (eds. A. James and A. Prout), The Falmer Press, London, pp. 78–98.

Qvortrup, J. Corsaro, W. and Honig, M.-S. (2009) *The Palgrave Handbook of Childhood Studies*, Palgrave MacMillan, London.

Rodgers, B. and Pryor, J. (1998) *Divorce and Separation. The Outcomes for Children*, The Joseph Rowntree Foundation, New York.

Rutter, M., Champion, L., Quinton, D. *et al.* (1995) Understanding individual differences in environmental risk exposure, in *Examining Lives in Context: Perspectives on the Ecology of Human Development* (eds. P. Moen, G.H. Elder Jr. and K. Lüscher), American Psychological Association, Washington, DC, pp. 61–93.

Schoon, I. (2006) *Risk and Resilience, Adaptations in Changing Times*, Cambridge University Press, Cambridge.

Schoon, I., Bynner, J., Joshi, H. *et al.* (2002) The influence of context, timing and duration of risk experiences for the passage from childhood to early adulthood. *Child Development*, 73 (5), 1486–1504.

Schumpeter, J.A. (1988) [1942] Decomposition. *Population and Development Review*, 14, 499–506.

Scott, J. (2008) Children as respondents: the challenge for quantitative methods, in *Research with Children*, (eds. P. Christensen and A. James), 2nd edn, Falmer Press, London, pp. 87–108.

Shanahan, M., Elder, G. H., Jr., Burchinal, M. and Conger, R. (1996) Adolescent earnings and relationships with parents: the work-family nexus in urban and rural ecologies, in *Adolescents, Work and Family* (eds. J. Mortimer and M. Finch), Sage, London.

Sigel-Rushton, W., Hobcraft, J. and Kiernan, K. (2005) Parental divorce and subsequent disadvantage, *Demography*, 42 (3), 427–446.

Solberg, A. (1990) Negotiating childhood: changing constructions of age for Norwegian children, in *Constructing and Reconstructing Childhood* (eds. A. James and A. Prout), Falmer Press, Basingstoke, pp. 118–137.

Solberg, A. (1994) *Negotiating Childhood: Empirical Investigations and Textual Representations of Children's Work and Everyday Lives*. Nordic Institute for Studies in Urban and Regional Planning, Stockholm.

Therborn, G. (2004) *Between Sex and Power: Family in the World 1900–2000*. Routledge, London.

Thorne, B. (1987) Revisioning women and social change: where are the children? *Gender and Society*, 1, 85–109.

Van Lancker, W., Ghysels, J. and Cantillon, B. (2012) An international comparison of the impact of child benefits on poverty outcomes for single mothers. CSB working paper, no. 12, 03, http://www.centrumvoorsociaalbeleid.be/sites/default/files/CSB%20Working%20Paper%2012%2003_Maart%202012.pdf (accessed January 07, 2013).

Ventura, S. (2009) *Changing Patterns of Non-Marital Childbearing in the United States*, National Center for Health Statistics, Hyattsville, Data Brief, Number 18. http://www.cdc.gov/nchs/data/databriefs/db18.pdf (accessed November 19, 2013).

Wadsworth, M. (1991) *The Imprint of Time: Childhood, History and Adult Life*, Clarendon Press, Oxford.

Waldfogel, J. (2006) *What Children Need*, Harvard University Press, Cambridge.

Zelizer, V. (1985) *Pricing the Priceless Child: The Changing Social Value of Children*, Basic Books, New York.

Zelizer, V. (2002) Kids and commerce. *Childhood*, 9, 375–396.

21

Fathers and Fatherhood

Kevin M. Roy

Are we living through the "end of men" (Rosin, 2010)? Is this a time to reimagine men's roles at work and in families (Romano and Dokoupil, 2010)? Popular media in the United States suggests that this may be the case, and men's daily experiences and social science research show that fatherhood has likely undergone important shifts in recent decades. The traditional assumption that fathers are defined by their ability to provide financially for their families has grown into the requirement that men obtain the package deal – a good job, home ownership, marriage, and fatherhood (Townsend, 2002). This configuration of residence, relationships, and employment increasingly becomes the line that divides "good fathers" and "bad fathers."

These two types of fathers seem to reflect the increasing inequality that we recognize in contemporary societies. Fatherhood research has tended toward basic distinctions between provider fathering in families where men are married, coresidential, and employed and have a substantial amount of resources or capital, and nonprovider fathering of men who move in and out of families as nonresidential, sporadically employed, cohabiting or unmarried, and lacking resources or capital (Marsiglio and Roy, 2012). But more importantly, these categories are too simplistic to capture the vast diversity of men's experiences in contemporary society. As we discover more about men's roles as parents, questions have continued to multiply about what we still do not understand.

In this review of the literature, I focus on over 300 studies (2004–2012) primarily from the United States to provide an up-to-date perspective on fatherhood. I introduce new debates, reopen ongoing discussions, and mark critical shifts in the ways that fathers work, play, and strive – and in the ways that we frame their lives. Due to the wide range of emergent changes in family life over the past 30 years, our approach to fatherhood has become more attuned to diverse ecological contexts and to many textures of parenting processes.

The Wiley Blackwell Companion to the Sociology of Families, First Edition.
Edited by Judith Treas, Jacqueline Scott, and Martin Richards.

The chapter is divided into four sections. First, I examine changing expectations for men in families, as fathers who once strived to be breadwinners/providers now also embrace nurturance and caregiving reflected in a "new fatherhood" that is commonplace in modern societies such as the United States. I also review research on coparenting and partnering processes between fathers and mothers. Research on coresidence and household division of labor continues to illuminate under-standing of family life, and studies of what happens after these relationships end – in separation and divorce, and through child support – add new dimensions. Third, I focus on men's nurturance of children over time and take special note of how father involvement has been demonstrated to influence children's well-being, from childhood through adulthood. Finally, I explore challenges to new father-hood in a review of emerging findings on incarceration, immigration, mental health concerns, and broad social consequences of inequality that reshape fathering on a daily basis.

Expectations for New Fatherhood

In contrast to strict provider roles, men in the United States are more involved as fathers than in previous decades, as measured in terms of the amount of time they spend each week caring for their children, including play, monitoring, physical care such as hygiene and feeding, transportation, and household duties (Sayer, Bianchi, and Robinson, 2004). These patterns of increased father involvement suggest a kind of nurturance among fathers, a term that defines who men are and what they do as fathers, both in conduct and consequences for children's development (Marsiglio and Roy, 2012). Responsiveness is another concept that recognizes men's active interaction with children and speculates on how that engagement can influence chil-dren and men themselves (Holmes and Huston, 2010; Ashbourne, Daly, and Brown, 2011). Fathers are key players in complex patterns of play and talk, which are shaped as well by race, culture, and interaction with mothers (Cabrera *et al.*, 2004).

Child care is still portrayed largely as women's work, but recent evidence shows that fathers are not only more involved but more highly value their involvement (Pleck and Masciadrelli, 2004). Mothers and fathers are both attentive to how men gain skills as caregivers, and fathers feel more effective as parents as they do more with children (Barry *et al.*, 2011). However, becoming a "new father" who success-fully provides and cares for children is not an easy transition. The majority of men and women think that being a father today is more challenging than in the 1970s and 1980s (Parker, 2007).

Some men are better positioned to be new fathers than are others. Men in professional occupations may have more time, money, or status to recraft their iden-tities as involved caregivers and providers (Plantin, 2007). Compared to men in non-marital relationships, married men gather more social capital (Ravanera, 2007). These extensive resources may enable some fathers to rework traditional expecta-tions of work commitments, gendered parenting, power dynamics, and emotional trade-offs in daily family interaction (Matta and Knudson-Martin, 2006). Resources acquired as providers may enable some men to be more successful than others as nurturing new fathers.

The economic fortunes of fathers have diverged dramatically since the 1970s, especially for young men without high school degrees who do not live with their children (Sum *et al.*, 2011). Recent economic crises have hit men in families hard, and a renewed focus on provision may tell us more about challenges for new fathers. What was once routine for many American men – a good wage to support a family, down payment on a house, medical benefits – is no longer taken for granted (Henwood, Shirani, and Coltart, 2010). Changing labor markets and rising inequality have bifurcated populations of young fathers, not only by income, but by social class and across races (Furstenberg, 2011; Murray, 2012).

In countries challenged by extreme economic transitions, men may aspire to be caregivers but are confined by the limitations of their providing roles. Korean and Japanese fathers began to move toward greater involvement as caregivers, supported by government policies, but retrenched into traditional provider roles during recent fiscal crises (Kwon and Roy, 2007; Yamato, 2008). Perhaps the greatest caution to the new father model is from Russian fathers, who often simply reject the new father ideal as too ambitious, too unattainable given the limited economic opportunities afforded to them (Utrata, 2008).

Shifts in Coparenting and Partnering

Fatherhood research has become more dynamic with a shift away from a focus on family structure – which coparents are "in" a family? – to family process – what do coparents "do"? Fathers and mothers simultaneously negotiate expectations as partners and as coparents. Men are better able to set aside conflict if they can understand how these two roles – partner and coparent – are different from each other (Hardesty *et al.*, 2008). Fathers and mothers also respond in complex ways to each other's involvement as coparents. For example, mother involvement is critical for children's school readiness, but fathers serve mainly as buffers, enhancing school readiness when mothers are uninvolved (Martin, Ryan, and Brooks Gunn, 2010). Both parents perform a complex cluster of responsibilities with children and household duties, but mothers multitask more frequently than fathers. For mothers, this mix of work conflicts more often (Offer and Schneider, 2011) and is often time spent alone, on a tight timetable, and in more physical activities than for fathers (Craig, 2006).

Gender role ideology plays an important part in determining how coparents make decisions on father involvement. Men and women's educational status and work contexts consistently relate to choices about shares of child care, even when these relationships vary slightly across different countries (Craig and Mullan, 2011). Fathers with higher educational attainment cared more frequently for their children in Denmark and Australia, but not in France and Italy, where these fathers were more traditionally masculine. These ideologies can be passed over generations, from parents to children and particularly adolescents (Davis and Wills, 2010). In some contexts, however, a shared parenting ethos may fade and be framed less as a social duty than as a personal choice (Vuori, 2009). In some cases, personal choice may lead to shared coparenting. Couples who committed to childbirth before marriage showed greater father involvement and more shared coparenting decisions (Hohmann-Marriott, 2011).

In the midst of global economic recession, renegotiation of men's roles in families occurs at the edge of public and private debates around work and family life. Men tend to spend more time in care for children when mothers work, including more solo time with children, more routine care, and more activities that reflect enhanced responsibility (Raley, Bianchi, and Wang, 2012). However, both mothers and fathers are reluctant to give up time with children. Despite the continuing importance of the provider norm, parental and child development can take priority over career concerns. In Norway, men trim their work hours during their children's preschool years but extend work hours when they reach school age (Dommermuth and Kitterod, 2009). These concerns may be specific to different social contexts and national policies, however. Biggart and O'Brien (2010) argue that being a father – and not one's career stage – best predicts longer work hours for men in the United Kingdom.

Coparenting in low-income families

Much of what we know about fathers has been based on the experience of white, middle- and working-class, married men. In the case of the United States, where couple unions are less stable (Cherlin, 2010) and socioeconomic inequality is greater, public safety net less generous, and incarceration higher, this inattention to lower-class fathers is a serious omission. Low-income fathers are more likely to show complex patterns of family formation and child-rearing that occur outside of marriage, across households, or within contexts of multiple-partner fertility (Furstenberg, 2011). For example, over one-third of children in the United States live apart from their biological fathers, with higher proportions of poor children and children of color (DeBell, 2008).

These social demographic changes are reflected in research on fathers, with most journal articles still concerned with two-parent families but an increasing number focused on men in unmarried, nonresidential, cohabiting, single, or stepfather contexts. The availability of new longitudinal data, particularly from the Fragile Families and Child Well-Being project, has transformed the study of men and coparenting in low-income families. This study recruited a cohort of over 4,700 parents of newborns and their children, across hospitals in 20 cities in the United States, with follow-up interviews planned up through childhood to age 15. It focused on non-marital childbearing, welfare reform, and low-income fathers.

Among fathers in Fragile Families data, half displayed low involvement and a quarter displayed high involvement with children. A key to increasing father involvement was quality relations with mothers and with maternal and paternal kin (Ryan, Kalil, and Ziol-Guest, 2008). Roy and Burton (2007) examined how mothers recruit biological fathers, as well as social fathers (usually nonbiologically related boyfriends or male maternal kin), in search of an ideal model for their children, but are cautious about implications for intimacy and for the safety of their children. Relationship histories of young mothers can be important for understanding dynamics in subsequent partnering relationships. Sheftall *et al.* (2010) suggest that higher-quality coparenting results from mothers having histories of low attachment avoidance, more trust and less conflict with partners, and strong parenting alliance. Moreover, fathers often respond and adjust their involvement in relation to mothers' decisions. Low-income nonresidential men are likely to end contact with their children if mothers find new partners (Guzzo, 2009), but not if fathers themselves find new partners.

Although marriage and residence may be transitory for low-income couples, they clearly influence men's coparenting and children's well-being. Fragile Families data indicate that married and cohabiting African American fathers report similar levels of father involvement (Perry, Harmon, and Leeper, 2012). Bzostek (2008) confirms that involvement with a social father or a nonresidential biological father has similar effects and that contact with a biological father who lives apart does not diminish the positive effects of social fathers on child well-being. Choi (2010) notes that non-residential fathering may lead to problems with children's behavior and cognitive development, not simply through absence of fathers but rather in terms of how that absence shapes the parenting of single mothers.

Over many years, the commitment of low-income parents to raise children by remaining together as coparents may take priority over a commitment to being *together* in a committed marital relationship (Roy, Buckmiller, and McDowell, 2008). The Fragile Families study suggests that maternal support for father involvement in the first year after birth leads to more father engagement with children at age 3 (Fagan and Palkovitz, 2011). Regardless of the romantic status of these relationships, communication across households and coparenting quality remains a strong predictor of future involvement for nonresidential fathers (Carlson, McLanahan, and Brooks-Gunn, 2008).

Distinct from coparenting support is the perception about support and paternal involvement. If couples do not believe that men's caregiving is important, they are less likely to marry and more likely to end their union (Hohmann-Marriott, 2009). Men are less likely to perceive support from the mother of their children if they are incarcerated or have a new partner or more than one child or either of the parents has limited education (Bronte-Tinkew and Horowitz, 2010). Mothers' perceptions of support are central to their parenting as well. Their perceived emotional parenting support from fathers influences how stressed they are about parenting (Harmon and Perry, 2011).

Fathers' social capital extends beyond support of children's mothers into investment by extended family members. The involvement of younger fathers in particular depends heavily on grandparent support, maternal gatekeeping efforts, and shifting romantic status of coparents, even as it declines and stabilizes in the first few years of children's lives (Herzog *et al.*, 2007). But support from extended kin is not always beneficial for involvement. Support from paternal kin tends to increase men's involvement, whereas support from maternal kin may decrease involvement (Perry, 2009).

Postdivorce coparenting and child support

Research on coparenting after divorce and remarriage, blended families and new partners, and complex family configurations offers new insights into fatherhood. Joint custody, higher socioeconomic status, and better coparenting dynamics also predict more contact and nurturance from fathers over time (Peters and Ehrenberg, 2008). When mothers remarry, stepfather involvement may become more influential for child outcomes than involvement of nonresidential fathers (King, 2006). Fathers may be warmer and yet more controlling than stepfathers (Claxton-Oldfield, Garber, and Gillcrist, 2006), and the unique nature of these relationships may leave room for contributions from stepfathers in alliances between male parents (Marsiglio and Hinojosa, 2007).

Changes in families can also reconfigure expectations of the child support system for fathers to pay support. Fathers are less likely to pay child support if mothers find new partners (Meyer and Cancian, 2012). Almost 20 years after extensive reform, the economic child support system in the United States is more effective in securing contributions from parents in postdivorce relationships. Child support systems have been reconfigured to provide training, enhance communication, and reshape coparenting relationships in challenging family contexts. Formal payments from fathers lead to more contact with children in later years (Nepomnyaschy, 2007).

From 2000 to 2010, child support and visitation increased for never-married-mother families (Huang, 2009). However, for Fragile Families participants, informal and overall support dropped off in the first year of a child support order, and formal support increased only slightly after 3 years (Nepomnyaschy and Garfinkel, 2010). If obligation rates are lowered for disadvantaged fathers, mothers who receive welfare may lose up to 30% of their income, and those who do not receive welfare over 40% of their income (Huang, Mincy, and Garfinkel, 2005). Moreover, if studies do not take into account multiple children of fathers, they overestimate amounts that could be paid by 33–60% (Sinkewicz and Garfinkel, 2009). Ongoing reforms of the child support system emphasize services to enable disadvantaged fathers to work and to pay for their children (Cancian, Meyer, and Han, 2011), which could transform their capacity to provide for children and their relationships with mothers of their children.

Nurturance of Children over Time

For three decades, there have been debates about the similarity, or otherwise, of men and women's parenting and about the quality versus quantity of father involvement. Lamb *et al.*'s (1985) three-dimensional definition of father involvement (interaction, accessibility, responsibility) transformed how we think about what fathers do in families. Pleck (2010) draws on this research to redirect researchers primarily to positive engagement, warmth and responsiveness, and control – and secondarily to indirect care and process responsibility, such as scheduling of doctor appointments or transportation. His recommendations echo work on nurturance (Marsiglio and Roy, 2012) and on male caregivers' discomfort and negotiation of physical presence with female caregivers, with other men, and with children themselves in "estrogen-filled" environments (Doucet, 2006).

In addition to these concepts for measuring involvement, studies of family structure have compared the involvement of resident fathers with the involvement of nonresident fathers. Numerous negative child outcomes are associated with nonresidence, including aggression, antisocial behavior, depression, anxiety, and low self-esteem (Carlson, 2006). However, it remains a challenge to pinpoint the processes by which lack of coresidence for fathers and children lead to these outcomes. Hofferth (2007) found that children's academic successes were related to demographic and economic factors, whereas their problematic internalizing and externalizing behaviors were more closely related to fathers' residence and family structure.

Research with the Fragile Families study has identified clear predictors of low-income men's involvement, often linked to child outcomes. If men care for pregnant partners and provide resources and support prenatally, they are more likely to be engaged fathers up to 3 years later (Cabrera, Fagan, and Farrie, 2008). Bronte-Tinkew *et al.* (2007a, b) also find that prenatal intentions are a vital aspect in predicting involvement for low-income fathers. Men who did not want their partners to carry pregnancies to term were less likely to show paternal warmth to their children. Cabrera *et al.* (2011) show that the quality of a father's relationship with his child in fifth grade predicted children's behavioral problems and peer relationship quality. Residence with children, however, had no long-term links to social development. We often expect gender of children to play a critical role in relationship dynamics. Fathers who marry at a child's birth live more often with sons than daughters. By the end of the first year, however, no evidence in Fragile Families data relates child gender to living arrangements, time, or financial investment of fathers (Lundberg, McLanahan, and Rose, 2007).

Paternal leave

Paternal leave policies are motivated by the belief that even a short period of child care early on will result in bonding that translates into continued involvement as the child grows older. Although fathers who take leave in the United States may give the impression that they are less dedicated to their workplace, other perceptions of these fathers – including recent cohorts of young adults – can be very positive, although it is assumed that these men sacrifice career success by taking leave (Coleman and Franiuk, 2011).

Progressive policies and experiments to promote gender equity in Scandinavian countries have set the tone for a broad public approach to paternal leave. To encourage uptake, the Scandinavian Daddy Leave cannot be transferred to mothers, thus signaling that child care by fathers is acceptable and desirable. This policy, with Sweden at the forefront, has shown that more days of paternal leave result in more child care and more satisfaction with child contact (Haas and Hwang, 2008). Data from Sweden suggests that men who take more paternal leave time even have lower mortality rates and are likely to be more stable, more fit, and healthier (Månsdotter and Lundin, 2010).

In the United States, the lack of a federal parental leave policy has left it up to individual employers. Mechanisms such as Employee Assistance Programs (EAP) craft flexible and tailored options, if they exist at all (Bocchicchio, 2006). In the United States and the United Kingdom, fathers who take more time on leave tend to be more involved in care of their children (Nepomnyaschy and Waldfogel, 2007). In the United Kingdom, fathers have taken shorter periods of leave (1 week) compared to the United States (longer time by relying on vacation days) (Kaufman, Lyonette, and Crompton, 2010).

The larger question may be how policies can promote men's caregiving as well as better opportunities for women in the workforce (Perlesz, 2006). Flexible leave policies may only be effective when backed by formal rights and statutory work–life balance measures to allow for change in the division of household labor (Gregory and Milner, 2008). In Canada, fathers' take up of leave is shaped by mothers' personal preferences as well as public policies, such as eligibility of mothers for paid leave (McKay and Doucet, 2010). Alternatively, if mothers are afforded paid leave and employment security, as in Australia, fathers may be rendered invisible through state initiatives that neglect to recognize men's potential contributions as caregivers (Ainsworth and Cutcher, 2008).

Adolescents, young adults, and divorce

As with childhood outcomes, fathers' residence matters for adolescent health and feeling of closeness (Booth, Scott, and King, 2010). Men's connection and involvement are negatively related to internalizing and externalizing behaviors of adolescents (Day and Padilla-Walker, 2009). And later in life, if children lived with their fathers during adolescence, chances of being teen fathers or living apart from their own children are diminished (Forste and Jarvis, 2007).

In addition to father effects, we need to consider bidirectional influences and transactional models of child effects. For example, Hawkins, Amato, and King (2007) recognize how adolescent well-being is a primary driver of the involvement of nonresident fathers. Decisions that adolescents make about their own health encourages responses from fathers as well. Adolescent sexual risk taking can promote fathers to seek more information about their children and to create more family activities, in an effort to deter their children's risky activities (Coley, Votruba-Drzal, and Schindler, 2009).

The long course of father–child relations is defined by unpredictability, particularly when it is marked by separation or divorce among provider fathers (Wallerstein and Lewis, 2008). Children from previously intact and coresidential families have better relationships with their fathers after divorce than children with nonresidential fathers. Men's relationships with their daughters may be more damaged after divorce than those with sons (Nielsen, 2011). Efforts to repair and maintain communication and closeness may take many years and can influence daughters' own intimate relationships (Miller, 2010). Sons may weather divorce differently. Kenyon and Koerner (2008) find that maternal disclosure about fathers most directly affects boys with low emotional maturity.

Looking at postdivorce relationships over a 14-year period, Cheadle, Amato, and King (2010) used longitudinal data to find that two-thirds of divorced fathers in the United States have unchanging relationships with their children (either high involvement or complete noninvolvement). In contrast, upward of 23% have declining contact and 8% show increasing contact over time. Just over one-third (36%) of nonresidential fathers never see their children (Huang, 2009). This contemporary snapshot compares favorably with relationships in the 1970s; nonresidential fathers have more frequent contact with their children today, especially if they pay child support or if they were married when their children were born (Amato, Meyers, and Emery, 2009).

We have learned more about how adult children manage relationships with their nonresidential fathers. When children have good relations with their mothers, they are able to stay in contact with their fathers as well, and these relationships grow closer when young adult children get married or have children of their own (Scott et al., 2007). Aquilino's research (Aquilino, 2006) confirms that fathers' relations with their young adult children remain strong if they were strong during adolescence. Young adult fathers may seek out close relations with their own fathers to gather support and advice in the struggle with limited job options and the pressure to provide for their children (Roy *et al.*, 2010). However, men whose fathers lived apart from them are more likely to be absent from their own children, and women are more likely than men to have children with partners who are absent (Pougnet *et al.*, 2012). And much later in life, older fathers may receive less social support from family or others in the wake of divorce, widowhood, and remarriage (Kalmijn, 2007).

An emphasis on process and contexts has led to research on fathers' transitions in involvement with children across the life course. The transition to fatherhood for new parents in general may enhance well-being and lead to more work hours (Knoester, Petts, and Eggebeen, 2007), but new fathers experience this in distinct ways. Complex postpartum partnering dynamics can demand negotiation of marital satisfaction, attitudes about men's involvement, and commitment to men's and women's employment (Lee, 2007). Young fathers may feel conflicted about choices between finding a job, equated with being a good provider and father, and finishing school, which is reflective of being a good parent more generally (Futris, Nielsen, and Olmstead, 2010).

A life course perspective urges us to consider the longer view, that men remain fathers for their entire lives, and the lives of their children. Men change their behavior and perspectives across multiple transitions *within* fatherhood, and not just *to* fatherhood (Palkovitz and Palm, 2009). The challenge is capturing such transitions, and longitudinal data and new statistical techniques, such as latent class analyses, may hold the greatest promise to explore transitions in men's lives over many years (Dariotis *et al.*, 2011).

Challenges and Inequality in New Fatherhood

One of the most salient issues in men's pursuit of new fatherhood expectations of provision and caregiving are the substantial challenges that most men face in achieving these expectations. With increasing income inequality and larger gaps between those with education and employment and those without, successful new fathers are difficult to find (Smeeding, Garfinkel, & Mincy, 2011). What are some of the key challenges to new fatherhood?

New fatherhood itself reflects a hegemonic masculinity that fits with a global economy and shifting gender roles in families, but it is a version of masculinity that is not appropriate for all fathers. Gay fathers and stay-at-home fathers have crafted different expectations for men, in terms of expressions of care, alternative family values, and even the proper physical location of fathers in homes and in public settings (Doucet, 2006; Goldberg, 2012; Merla, 2008). Low-income African American fathers integrate these mainstream versions of manhood with street versions of manhood that emphasize independence, respect, and risk taking that may run counter to what we associate with "good fathering" (Roy and Dyson, 2010). In effect, the heterogeneity of the population of disadvantaged fathers, in their divergent experiences as parents and partners, contradicts widely held assumptions that all have failed as fathers. Through commitment to fathering that does not fit with mainstream expectations, these men dissemble stereotypes of the nonessential father, the deadbeat dad, and the "player" who runs in fear from commitment or marriage (Tamis-LeMonda and McFadden, 2010).

For many fathers, multiple-partner fertility raises real challenges to father involvement. Such higher-order births are more likely for disadvantaged urban men, men with depression, men with limited educational attainment, and unmarried or minority men (Bronte-Tinkew *et al.*, 2009). About one-third of men who have multiple children with multiple partners are involved in nonmarital relationships, and that pattern is increasing. These men also tend to be younger at their first sexual activity or their first birth (Manlove *et al.*, 2008). Fathers with low conflict and high relationship satisfaction stay with current partners for the next child, but men in unstable relationships are more likely to have children with a new partner (Scott *et al.*, 2010). However, multiple-partner fertility is not primarily a problematic father behavior. Mothers in low-income families are more likely to have a second child than unmarried fathers (Guzzo and Hayford, 2010). For mothers or fathers, higher-order births are associated with negative child outcomes across these studies.

Incarceration as a risk to father involvement

Research has begun to demystify how risks of incarceration, substance abuse, or domestic violence can become barriers to low-income fathers' involvement with children. In the Fragile Families sample, half of all fathers had such a risk, which was negatively associated with men's involvement with mothers and children, although men's relationships with mothers often mediated the impact of risks on involvement with children (Waller and Swisher, 2006). Fatherhood also presents low-income men in particular with an opportunity for second chances to rebuild their identities and daily routines around generative behavior, and to turn away from risky behavior (Roy and Lucas, 2006). Social institutions can foster a context in which fathers can recover from risks. School attendance is a protective factor for young fathers who stayed in school. They exhibited lower rates of risky behavior than dropouts or even graduates no longer in school (Weinman *et al.*, 2007). For men who are unemployed and homeless, shelters provide behavioral and psychological boundaries within which fathers can build new parenting roles (Schindler and Coley, 2007).

Correctional facilities prove to be institutional settings that can curtail men's efforts to be involved with their children. Research on mass incarceration of low-income and men of color has expanded dramatically (see review by Raphael, 2011). Again, among the Fragile Families sample, half of all African American fathers were incarcerated by their child's fifth birthday (Perry and Bright, 2012). These men fared worse in employment, earning less and working fewer hours in underground and off the books jobs compared with never incarcerated fathers (Lewis, Garfinkel, and Gao, 2007). Incarceration forced men to confront starkly different expectations for being an inmate and being a father (Dyer, Pleck, and McBride, 2012). Fathering while doing prison time could be productive and generative, and men were confident in their commitment to involvement and value of contact with their children (Lee *et al.*, 2012). However, it was often not feasible to meet their expectations upon release. Families facilitated formal and informal networks of support for men (Walker, 2010) who could not easily deliver on their promises of engagement with children during reentry (Yocum and Nath, 2011).

The impacts of paternal incarceration are extensive. Children of incarcerated fathers show increased attention problems and aggressive behavior. Paternal incarceration has even stronger effects than father absence for children (Geller *et al.*, 2012). Moreover, in some European countries, children of offenders are more likely to be convicted themselves (Besemer and Farrington, 2012). At the very least, the process of prisonization can lead African American fathers to practice more restrictive and harsh parenting upon release (Modecki and Wilson, 2009) and can result in high levels of parenting stress (Loper *et al.*, 2009).

Stress and depression

Poor working conditions and lower social class have subtle associations with the quality of fathers' parenting. In the United States, fathers who reported less supportive work environments, more work stress, and nonstandard work schedules (as well as fewer work hours) also provided poor linguistic stimulation and relatively negative effect in interaction with their children (Goodman *et al.*, 2011). Further, fathers in workplaces with low self-direction and high stress – likely to be working-class jobs – showed less engaged and sensitive parenting (Goodman *et al.*, 2008). These contexts may also be associated with depression, marital conflict, role overload, and low levels of intimacy with children (Ransford, Crouter, and McHale, 2008).

Stress and conflict over work and family life decisions play out differently in distinct contexts. For example, mothers in dual-earner families may appreciate fathers' contributions more, as they were less likely to undermine fathers' play and caregiving than in single-earner families. Perhaps mothers appreciate men's contributions as active new fathers (Buckley and Schoppe Sullivan, 2010). Race factors – as evident in structural inequalities and possibly differences in values – also shape men's work or care options. White men worked more when they became fathers, but those with traditional values were twice as likely to work more when they became fathers, compared with white men with egalitarian attitudes. In contrast, black men – regardless of traditional or egalitarian attitudes – did not work more hours when they became fathers (Glauber and Gosjolko, 2011).

Schindler (2010) found that men's parenting engagement and financial contributions were positively related to their psychological well-being – but such well-being did not necessarily lead fathers into engagement and financial contribution. As in the case of mothers, fathers' depression appears to have strong impacts on children and on parental involvement. Depression among nonresidential fathers often results in low levels of father involvement (Paulson, Dauber, and Leiferman, 2011). Kane and Garber (2009) suggest that father depression leads to children's externalizing behavior, although this may depend on levels of conflict in father–child relationships.

Significant focus has been dedicated to the effects of depression, which is likely the most common mental health problem for fathers. Depression is shaped not only by education and age but by race, marital status, employment, drug use, and incarceration history. It is related to parenting stress, and it decreases engagement with children, relationship quality with partners, and coparenting support (Bronte-Tinkew *et al.*, 2007). Low-income African American men have a much higher rate of depression than men in the general population (Sinkewicz and Lee, 2011). One possible strategy to ameliorate depression for these men may be more active engagement with sons, including monitoring their safety and teaching them how to survive as young black men in America, which increase personal mastery

(Caldwell *et al.*, 2011). Fathering programs may also be a site in which to offer mental health interventions for depression, alongside parenting and employment services (Fitzgerald *et al.*, 2012).

In the broader context of health challenges for men, Fragile Families data confirms that unmarried fathers' health does improve upon marriage due to benefits from mothers' health insurance (Haldane, Mincy, and Miller, 2010). With the advent of affordable health care in the United States, disadvantaged fathers are likely to see better health outcomes. Improved children's health may impact outcomes for fathers as well, because poor child health decreases employment for fathers, especially for cohabiting low-income fathers (Noonan, Reichman, and Corman, 2005).

Immigration

The process of immigration to the United States presents a stressful and crucial transition for family relationships, as many families are divided and reunited across time and place (Strier and Roer-Strier, 2010). Immigration continues to present substantial challenges to the involvement of even highly committed fathers (see Behnke, Taylor, and Parra-Cardona, 2008, for discussion of Mexican fathers). Some families carry more traditional values and beliefs and utilize them effectively in these dramatic shifts in residence and culture.

However, immigrant families have undergone important shifts in expectations for men's parenting and in consequences of men's involvement with children (Chuang and Moreno, 2008). Some recent immigrant parents shift child-rearing techniques to permit youth more choice and power, but they make sure to retain positions of authority and discipline (Nesteruk and Marks, 2011). Mothers have greater knowledge of children's daily routines than fathers, and the parent/adolescent relationship and youth adjustment is shaped by their parents' division of paid labor (Updegraff, Delgado, and Wheeler, 2009). If mothers and fathers both work, conflictual negotiation of work/family responsibilities is more likely to spill over and bring stress into relationships with children.

Some fathers leave their children behind in a home country when they seek better jobs and more income elsewhere. Mexican children may interact more frequently with fathers who have migrated than with those who divorced; this may be an outgrowth of men's remittances and investment in their children's schooling (Nobles, 2011). However, children left behind may themselves feel that their families are incomplete (Thomas, 2010) and may suffer from a higher chance of illness (Schmeer, 2009). Latino adolescents in particular struggle with the impact of fathers who do not reside with them. Lopez and Corona (2012) present qualitative evidence of high-risk adolescents' anger, longing, and indifference as they navigate early childhood memories and mothers' interpretations of fathers' reduced involvement.

The long arm of immigrant men's jobs shapes family relationships and circumstances. Crouter *et al.* (2006) found that Mexican fathers' income in the United States was negatively associated with depression among highly acculturated families – but it did not buffer depression among less acculturated families. Likewise, racism at men's place of employment was associated with depression in these less acculturated families, but not in families that were more acculturated. Other aspects of immigrant incorporation have complex and sometimes contradictory results. For example, citizenship in the United States is negatively associated with warmth for Chinese fathers, yet the use of English language skills is positively associated with physical care and nurturing for Mexican fathers (Capps, Bronte-Tinkew, and Horowitz, 2010).

Conclusion

In this chapter, I took an explicitly multidisciplinary approach to capture a wide range of recent research on fathering and fatherhood. As we study more about how fathers play a critical role in contemporary family life, we must situate these insights within dramatic demographic, policy, economic, and social changes that run throughout a globalized community. I suggest that fatherhood – especially in the past decade – has been indelibly marked by a diversification of fathering experiences and perspectives, as well as an emergent inequality that goes beyond differences in income.

Future research on fathers should be attuned to the forces of diversity and inequality as they remake the context in which men care and provide for their children. And on a more individual level, how do families and fathers themselves reframe, reequip, and reposition men as fathers who face numerous challenges, particularly as they strive to become new fathers who both care and provide for their children? Studies cited in this chapter suggest that innovative methodological designs and insightful, original concepts will help to push our understanding of men's parenting forward in coming years. In this way, it may be that we are witnessing "the end of men" in a traditional sense – as well as acknowledging the beginning of contemporary fatherhood, as a broad, diverse, and full range of expressions and behaviors for men with varying resources and from divergent life experiences.

References

Ainsworth, S. and Cutcher, L. (2008) Expectant mothers and absent fathers: Paid maternity leave in Australia. *Gender, Work & Organization*, 15, 375–393.

Amato, P., Meyers, C. and Emery, R. (2009) Changes in nonresident father-child contact from 1976 to 2002. *Family Relations*, 58, 41–53.

Aquilino, W. (2006) The noncustodial father–child relationship from adolescence into young adulthood. *Journal of Marriage & Family*, 68, 929–946.

Ashbourne, L., Daly, K. and Brown, J. (2011) Responsiveness in father-child relationships: The experience of fathers. *Fathering*, 9, 69–86.

Barry, A., Smith, J., Deutsch, F. and Perry-Jenkins, M. (2011) Fathers' involvement in child care and perceptions of parenting skill over the transition to parenthood. *Journal of Family Issues*, 32, 1500–1521.

Behnke, A., Taylor, B. and Parra-Cardona, J. (2008) I hardly understand English, but...": Mexican origin fathers describe their commitment as fathers despite the challenges of immigration. *Journal of Comparative Family Studies*, 39, 187–205.

Besemer, S. and Farrington, D. (2012) Intergenerational transmission of criminal behaviour: Conviction trajectories of fathers and their children. *European Journal of Criminology*, 9, 120–141.

Biggart, L. and O'Brien, M. (2010) UK fathers' long work hours: career stage or fatherhood? *Fathering*, 8, 341–361.

Bocchicchio, A. (2006) Fathers in the workplace: the use of EAP core technology functions in assisting fathers with work/family balance. *Journal of Workplace Behavioral Health*, 22, 89–102.

Booth, A., Scott, M. and King, V. (2010) Father residence and adolescent problem behavior: Are youth always better off in two-parent families? *Journal of Family Issues*, 31, 585–605.

Bronte-Tinkew, J. and Horowitz, A. (2010) Factors associated with unmarried, nonresident fathers' perceptions of their coparenting. *Journal of Family Issues*, 31, 31–65.

Bronte-Tinkew, J., Moore, K., Matthews, G. and Carrano, J. (2007) Symptoms of major depression in a sample of fathers of infants: Sociodemographic correlates and links to father involvement. *Journal of Family Issues*, 28, 61–99.

Bronte-Tinkew, J., Ryan, S., Carrano, J. and Moore, K. (2007) Resident fathers' pregnancy intentions, prenatal behaviors, and links to involvement with infants. *Journal of Marriage & Family*, 69, 977–990.

Bronte-Tinkew, J., Ryan, S., Franzetta, K. *et al.* (2009) Higher-order fertility among urban fathers. *Journal of Family Issues*, 30, 968–1000.

Buckley, C. and Schoppe Sullivan, S. (2010) Father involvement and coparenting behavior: Parents' nontraditional beliefs and family earner status as moderators. *Personal Relationships*, 17, 413–431.

Bzostek, S. (2008) Social fathers and child well-being. *Journal of Marriage & Family*, 70, 950–961.

Cabrera, N., Fagan, J. and Farrie, D. (2008) Explaining the long reach of fathers' prenatal involvement on later paternal engagement. *Journal of Marriage & Family*, 70, 1094–1107.

Cabrera, N., Shannon, J., Vogel, C. *et al.* (2004) Low-income fathers' involvement in their toddlers' lives: Biological fathers from the early head start research and evaluation study. *Fathering*, 2, 5–30.

Cabrera, N., Cook, G., McFadden, K. and Bradley, R. (2011) Father residence and father-child relationship quality: peer relationships and externalizing behavioral problems. *Family Science*, 2, 109–119.

Caldwell, C., Bell, L., Brooks, C., Ward, J. and Jennings, C. (2011) Engaging nonresident African American fathers in intervention research: What practitioners should know about parental monitoring in nonresident families. *Research on Social Work Practice*, 21, 298–307.

Cancian, M., Meyer, D. and Han, E. (2011) Child support: Responsible fatherhood ad the quid pro quo. *The Annals of the American Academy of Political and Social Science*, 635, 140–162.

Capps, R., Bronte-Tinkew, J. and Horowitz, A. (2010) Acculturation and father engagement with infants among Chinese and Mexican-origin immigrant fathers. *Fathering*, 8, 61–92.

Carlson, M. (2006) Family structure, father involvement, and adolescent behavioral outcomes. *Journal of Marriage & Family*, 68, 137–154.

Carlson, M., McLanahan, S. and Brooks-Gunn, J. (2008) Coparenting and nonresident fathers' involvement with young children after a nonmarital birth. *Demography*, 45, 461–488.

Cheadle, J., Amato, P. and King, V. (2010) Patterns of nonresident father contact. *Demography*, 47, 206–225.

Cherlin, A. (2010) *Marriage go round*. New York: Vintage.

Choi, J.-K. (2010) Nonresident fathers' parenting, family processes, and children's development in urban, poor, single-mother families. *Social Service Review*, 84, 655–677.

Chuang, S. and Moreno, R. (eds) (2008) *On New Shores: Understanding Immigrant Fathers in North America*. Lexington, Lanham.

Claxton-Oldfield, S., Garber, T. and Gillcrist, K. (2006) Young adults' perceptions of their relationships with their stepfathers and biological fathers. *Journal of Divorce & Remarriage*, 45, 51–61.

Coleman, J. and Franiuk, R. (2011) Perceptions of mothers and fathers who take temporary work leave. *Sex Roles*, 64, 311–323.

Coley, R.L., Votruba-Drzal, E. and Schindler, H. (2009) Fathers' and mothers' parenting predicting and responding to adolescent sexual risk behaviors. *Child Development*, 80, 808–827.

Craig, L. (2006) Does father care mean fathers share? A comparison of how mothers and fathers in intact families spend time with children. *Gender & Society*, 20, 259–281.

Craig, L. and Mullan, K. (2011) How mothers and fathers share childcare: A cross-national time-use comparison. *American Sociological Review*, 76, 834–861.

Crouter, A., Davis, K., Updegraff, K. *et al.* (2006) Mexican American fathers' occupational conditions: Links to family members' psychological adjustment. *Journal of Marriage & Family*, 68, 843–858.

Dariotis, J., Pleck, J., Astone, N. and Sonenstein, F. (2011) Pathways of early fatherhood, marriage, and employment: a latent class growth analysis. *Demography*, 48, 593–623.

Davis, S. and Wills, J. (2010) Adolescent gender ideology socialization: Direct and moderating effects of fathers' beliefs. *Sociological Spectrum*, 30, 580–604.

Day, R. and Padilla-Walker, L. (2009) Mother and father connectedness and involvement during early adolescence. *Journal of Family Psychology*, 23, 900–904.

DeBell, M. (2008) Children living without their fathers: Population estimates and indicators of educational well-being. *Social Indicators Research*, 87, 427–443.

Dommermuth, L. and Kitterød, R.H. (2009) Fathers' employment in a father-friendly welfare state: Does fatherhood affect men's working hours? *Community, Work & Family*, 12, 417–436.

Doucet, A. (2006) Estrogen-filled worlds: Fathers as primary caregivers and embodiment. *Sociological Review*, 54, 696–716.

Dyer, J., Pleck, J. and McBride, B. (2012) Imprisoned fathers and their family relationships: A 40-year review from a multi-theory view. *Journal of Family Theory & Review*, 4, 20–47.

Fagan, J. and Palkovitz, R. (2011) Coparenting and relationship quality effects on father engagement: variations by residence, romance. *Journal of Marriage & Family*, 73, 637–653.

Fitzgerald, M., Roy, K., Anderson, E. and Letiecq, B. (2012) The effect of depressive symptoms on low-income men in responsible fathering programs. *Fathering*, 10, 47.

Forste, R. and Jarvis, J. (2007) 'Just like his dad': Family background and residency with children among young adult father. *Fathering*, 5, 97–110.

Furstenberg, F. (2011) Comment: How do low-income men and fathers matter for children and family life? *Annals of the American Academy of Political and Social Science*, 635, 131–139.

Futris, T., Nielsen, R. and Olmstead, S. (2010) No degree, no job: adolescent mothers' perceptions of the impact that adolescent fathers' human capital has on paternal financial and social capital. *Child & Adolescent Social Work Journal*, 27, 1–20.

Geller, A., Cooper, C., Garfinkel, I. *et al.* (2012) Beyond absenteeism: Father incarceration and child development. *Demography*, 49, 49–76.

Glauber, R. and Gozjolko, K. (2011) Do traditional fathers always work more? Gender ideology, race, and parenthood. *Journal of Marriage & Family*, 73, 1133–1148.

Goldberg, A. (2012) *Gay Dads: Transitions to Adoptive Fatherhood*. NYU Press, New York.

Goodman, W.B., Crouter, A., Lanza, S. and Cox, M. (2008) Paternal work characteristics and father-infant interactions in low-income, rural families. *Journal of Marriage & Family*, 70, 640–653.

Goodman, W.B., Crouter, A., Lanza, S. *et al.* (2011) Paternal work stress and latent profiles of father-infant parenting quality. *Journal of Marriage & Family*, 73, 588–604.

Gregory, A. and Milner, S. (2008) Fatherhood regimes and father involvement in France and the UK. *Community, Work & Family*, 11, 61–84.

Guzzo, K. (2009) Maternal relationships and nonresidential father visitation of children born outside of marriage. *Journal of Marriage & Family*, 76, 632–649.

Guzzo, K. and Hayford, S. (2010) Single mothers, single fathers: Gender differences in fertility after a nonmarital birth. *Journal of Family Issues*, 31, 906–933.

Haas, L. and Hwang, P. (2008) The impact of taking parental leave on fathers' participation in childcare and relationships with children: Lessons from Sweden. *Community, Work & Family*, 11, 85–104.

Haldane, E., Mincy, R. and Miller, D. (2010) Racial disparities in men's health and the transition to marriage among unmarried fathers. *Journal of Family Issues*, 31, 1183–1210.

Hardesty, J., Khaw, L., Chung, G. and Martin, J. (2008) Coparenting relationships after divorce: Variations by type of marital violence and fathers' role differentiation. *Family Relations*, 57, 479–491.

Harmon, D. and Perry, A. (2011) Fathers' unaccounted contributions: Paternal involvement and maternal stress. *Families in Society*, 92, 176–182.

Hawkins, D., Amato, P. and King, V. (2007) Nonresident father involvement and adolescent well-being: father effects or child effects? *American Sociological Review*, 72, 990–1010.

Henwood, K., Shirani, F. and Coltart, C. (2010) Fathers and financial risk-taking during the economic downturn: Insights from a QLL study of men's identities-in-the-making 21st century society. *Journal of the Academy of Social Sciences*, 5, 137–147.

Herzog, M., Umaña-Taylor, A., Madden-Derdich, D. and Leonard, S. (2007) Adolescent mothers' perceptions of fathers' parental involvement: Satisfaction and desire for involvement. *Family Relations*, 56, 244–257.

Hofferth, S. (2007) Residential father family type and child well-being: Investment versus selection. *Demography*, 43, 53–77.

Hohmann-Marriott, B. (2009) Father involvement ideals and the union transitions of unmarried parents. *Journal of Family Issues*, 30, 898–920.

Hohmann-Marriott, B. (2011) Coparenting and father involvement in married and unmarried coresident couples. *Journal of Marriage & Family*, 73, 296–309.

Holmes, E. and Huston, A. (2010) Understanding positive father-child interaction: Children's, fathers', and mothers' contributions. *Fathering*, 8, 203–225.

Huang, C.-C. (2009) Mothers' reports of nonresident fathers' involvement with their children: Revisiting the relationship between child support payment and visitation. *Family Relations*, 58, 54–64.

Huang, C.-C., Mincy, R. and Garfinkel, I. (2005) Child support obligations and low-income fathers. *Journal of Marriage & Family*, 67, 1213–1225.

Kalmijn, M. (2007) Gender differences in the effects of divorce, widowhood and remarriage on intergenerational support: Does marriage protect fathers? *Social Forces*, 85, 1079–1104.

Kane, P. and Garber, J. (2009) Parental depression and child externalizing and internalizing symptoms: Unique effects of fathers' symptoms and perceived conflict as a mediator. *Journal of Child & Family Studies*, 18, 465–472.

Kaufman, G., Lyonette, C. and Crompton, R. (2010) Post-birth employment leave among fathers in Britain and the United States. *Fathering*, 8, 321–340.

Kenyon, D. and Koerner, S. (2008) Post-divorce maternal disclosure and the father–adolescent relationship: Adolescent emotional autonomy and inter-reactivity as moderators. *Journal of Child & Family Studies*, 17, 791–808.

King, V. (2006) The antecedents and consequences of adolescents' relationships with stepfathers and nonresident fathers. *Journal of Marriage & Family*, 68, 910–928.

Knoester, C., Petts, R. and Eggebeen, D. (2007) Commitments to fathering and the well-being and social participation of new, disadvantaged fathers. *Journal of Marriage & Family*, 69, 991–1004.

Kwon, Y.I. and Roy, K. (2007) Changing social expectations for work and family involvement among Korean fathers. *Journal of Comparative Family Studies*, 38, 285–305.

Lamb, M., Pleck, J., Charnov, E. and Levine, J. (1985) Paternal behavior in humans. *American Zoologist*, 25, 883–894.

Lee, C.-Y. (2007) Marital satisfaction and father involvement during the transition to parenthood. *Fathering*, 5, 75–96.

Lee, C., Sansone, F., Swanson, C., and Tatum, K. (2012) Incarcerated fathers and parenting: Importance of the relationship with their children. *Social Work in Public Health*, 27, 165–186.

Lewis, C., Jr, Garfinkel, I. and Gao, Q. (2007) Incarceration and unwed fathers in fragile families. *Journal of Sociology & Social Welfare*, 34, 77–94.

Loper, A., Carlson, W., Levitt, L. and Scheffel, K. (2009) Parenting stress, alliance, child contact and adjustment of imprisoned mothers and fathers. *Journal of Offender Rehabilitation*, 48, 483–503.

Lopez, V. and Corona, R. (2012) Troubled relationships: high-risk latina adolescents and non-resident fathers. *Journal of Family Issues*, 33, 715–744.

Lundberg, S., McLanahan, S. and Rose, E. (2007) Child gender and father involvement in fragile families. *Demography*, 44, 79–92.

Manlove, J., Logan, C., Ikramullah, E. and Holcombe, E. (2008) Factors associated with multiple-partner fertility among fathers. *Journal of Marriage & Family*, 70, 536–548.

Månsdotter, A. and Lundin, A. (2010) How do masculinity, paternity leave, and mortality associate? A study of fathers in the Swedish parental & child cohort of 1988/89. *Social Science & Medicine*, 71, 576–583.

Marsiglio, W. and Hinojosa, R. (2007) Managing the multifather family: Stepfathers as father allies. *Journal of Marriage & Family*, 69, 845–862.

Marsiglio, W. and Roy, K. (2012) *Nurturing Dads: Social Initiatives for Contemporary Fatherhood*. Russell Sage Foundation, New York.

Martin, A., Ryan, R. and Brooks-Gunn, J. (2010) When fathers' supportiveness matters most: Maternal and paternal parenting and children's school readiness. *Journal of Family Psychology*, 24, 145–155.

Matta, D. and Knudson-Martin, C. (2006) Father responsivity: Couple processes and the coconstruction of fatherhood. *Family Process*, 45, 19–37.

McKay, L. and Doucet, A. (2010) Without taking away her leave: A Canadian case study of couples' decisions on fathers' use of paid parental leave. *Fathering*, 8, 300–320.

Merla, L. (2008) Determinants, costs, and meanings of Belgian stay-at-home fathers: An international comparison. *Fathering*, 6, 113–132.

Meyer, D. and Cancian, M. (2012) 'I'm not supporting his kids': Nonresident fathers' contributions given mothers' new fertility. *Journal of Marriage & Family*, 74, 132–151.

Miller, A. (2010) Young adult daughters' accounts of relationships with nonresidential fathers: Relational damage, repair, and maintenance. *Journal of Divorce & Remarriage*, 51, 293–309.

Modecki, K. and Wilson, M. (2009) Associations between individual and family level characteristics and parenting practices in incarcerated African American fathers. *Journal of Child & Family Studies*, 18, 530–540.

Murray, C. (2012) *Coming Apart: The State of White America, 1960–2010*, Crown Forum, New York.

Nepomnyaschy, L. (2007) Child support and father-child contact: Testing reciprocal pathways. *Demography*, 44, 93–112.

Nepomnyaschy, L and Waldfogel, J. (2007) Paternity leave and fathers' involvement with their young children. *Community, Work & Family*, 10, 427–453.

Nepomnyaschy, L. and Garfinkel, I. (2010) Child support enforcement and fathers' contributions to their nonmarital children. *Social Service Review*, 84, 341–380.

Nesteruk, O. and Marks, L. (2011) Parenting in immigration: Experiences of mothers and fathers from Eastern Europe raising children in the United States. *Journal of Comparative Family Studies*, 42, 809–825.

Nielsen, L. (2011) Divorced fathers and their daughters: a review of recent research. *Journal of Divorce & Remarriage*, 52, 77–93.

Nobles, J. (2011) Parenting from abroad: Migration, nonresident father involvement, and children's education in Mexico. *Journal of Marriage & Family*, 73, 729–746.

Noonan, K., Reichman, N. and Corman, H. (2005) New fathers' labor supply: Does child health matter? *Social Science Quarterly (Blackwell Publishing Limited)*, 86, 1399–1417.

Offer, S. and Schneider, B. (2011) Revisiting the gender gap in time-use patterns: Multitasking and well-being among mothers and fathers in dual-earner families. *American Sociological Review*, 76, 809–833.

Palkovitz, R. and Palm, G. (2009) Transitions within fathering. *Fathering*, 7, 3–22.

Parker, K. 2007. "Being Dad May Be Tougher These Days, but Working Moms Are Among Their Biggest Fans." Pew Social and Demographic Trends Report. Washington, DC: Pew Research Center, June 13. http://pewsocialtrends.org/pubs/510/fathers-day.

Paulson, J., Dauber, S. and Leiferman, J. (2011) Parental depression, relationship quality, and nonresident father involvement with their infants. *Journal of Family Issues*, 32, 528–549.

Perlesz, A. (2006) Fathers cannot easily be de-gendered: Response to Silverstein and Auerbach. *Journal of Feminist Family Therapy*, 18, 93–97.

Perry, A. (2009) The influence of the extended family on the involvement of nonresident African American fathers. *Journal of Family Social Work*, 12, 211–226.

Perry, A. and Bright, M. (2012) African American fathers and incarceration: Paternal involvement and child outcomes. *Social Work in Public Health*, 27, 187–203.

Perry, A., Harmon, D. and Leeper, J. (2012) Resident black fathers' involvement: A comparative analysis of married and unwed, cohabitating fathers. *Journal of Family Issues*, 33, 695–714.

Peters, B. and Ehrenberg, M. (2008) The influence of parental separation and divorce on father-child relationships. *Journal of Divorce & Remarriage*, 49, 78–109.

Plantin, L. (2007) Different classes, different fathers? *Community, Work & Family*, 10, 93–110.

Pleck, J. (2010) Paternal involvement: Revised conceptualization and theoretical linkages with child outcomes, in *The Role of the Father in Child Development*, 5th edn (ed M. Lamb), Wiley, New York, pp. 59–93.

Pleck, J. and Masciadrelli, B. (2004) Paternal involvement by U.S. residential fathers: Levels, sources, and consequences, in *The Role of the Father in Child Development*, 4th edn (ed M. Lamb), Wiley, Hoboken, pp. 222–271.

Pougnet, E., Serbin, L., Stack, D. *et al.* (2012) The intergenerational continuity of fathers' absence in a socioeconomically disadvantaged sample. *Journal of Marriage & Family*, 74, 540–554.

Raley, S., Bianchi, S. and Wang, W. (2008) When do fathers care? Mothers' economic contribution and fathers' involvement in child care. *American Journal of Sociology*, 117, 1422–1459.

Ransford, C., Crouter, A. and McHale, S. (2008) Implications of work pressure and supervisor support for fathers', mothers' and adolescents' relationships and well-being in dual-earner families. *Community, Work & Family*, 11, 37–60.

Raphael, S. (2011) Incarceration and prisoner reentry in the United States. *The Annals of the American Academy of Political and Social Sciences*, 635, 192–215.

Ravanera, Z. (2007) Informal networks social capital of fathers: What does the social engagement survey tell us? *Social Indicators Research*, 83, 351–373.

Romano, A. and Dokoupil, T. (2010) Men's Lib. *Newsweek* (Sep 10), http://www.thedailybeast.com/newsweek/2010/09/20/why-we-need-to-reimagine-masculinity.html (accessed October 30, 2013).

Rosin, H. (2010) The End of Men? *The Atlantic* (Jul/Aug), http://www.theatlantic.com/magazine/archive/2010/07/the-end-of-men/308135/ (accessed October 30, 2013).

Roy, K. and Lucas, K. (2006) Generativity as second chance: Low-income fathers and transformation of the difficult past. *Research in Human Development*, 3, 139–159.

Roy, K. and Burton, L. (2007) Mothering through recruitment: Kinscription of nonresidential fathers and father figures in low-income families. *Family Relations*, 56, 24–39.

Roy, K. and Dyson, O. (2010) Making daddies into fathers: Community-based fatherhood programs and the construction of masculinities for low-income African American men. *American Journal of Community Psychology*, 45, 139–154.

Roy, K., Buckmiller, N. and McDowell, A. (2008) Together but not together: Trajectories of relationship suspension for low-income unmarried parents. *Family Relations*, 57, 197–209.

Roy, K., Vesely, C., Fitzgerald, M. and Buckmiller Jones, N. (2010) Young fathers at work: The influence of parental closeness and contact on employment. *Research in Human Development*, 7, 123–139.

Ryan, R., Kalil, A. and Ziol-Guest, K. (2008) Longitudinal patterns of nonresident fathers' involvement: the role of resources and relations. *Journal of Marriage & Family*, 70, 962–977.

Sayer, L., Bianchi, S. and Robinson, J. (2004) Trends in mothers' and fathers' time with children. *American Sociological Review*, 110, 1–43.

Schindler, H. (2010) The importance of parenting and financial contributions in promoting fathers' psychological health. *Journal of Marriage & Family*, 72, 318–332.

Schindler, H. and Coley, R. (2007) A qualitative study of homeless fathers: Exploring parenting and gender role transitions. *Family Relations*, 56, 40–56.

Schmeer, K. (2009) Father absence due to migration and child illness in rural Mexico. *Social Science & Medicine*, 69, 1281–1286.

Scott, M., Booth, A., King, V. and Johnson, D. (2007) Postdivorce father-adolescent closeness. *Journal of Marriage & Family*, 69, 1194–1209.

Scott, M., Bronte-Tinkew, J., Logan, C. *et al.* (2010) Subsequent fertility among urban fathers: The influence of relationship context. *Fathering*, 8, 244–267.

Sheftall, A., Schoppe-Sullivan, S. and Futris, T. (2010) Adolescent mothers' perceptions of the coparenting relationship with their child's father: A function of attachment security and trust. *Journal of Family Issues*, 31, 884–905.

Sinkewicz, M. and Garfinkel, I. (2009) Unwed fathers' ability to pay child support: New estimates accounting for multiple partner fertility. *Demography*, 46, 247–263.

Sinkewicz, M. and Lee, R. (2011) Prevalence, comorbidity, and course of depression among black fathers in the United States. *Research on Social Work Practice*, 21, 289–297.

Smeeding, T., Garfinkel, I. and Mincy, R. (2011) Young disadvantaged fathers: Fathers, families, poverty, and policy. *Annals of the American Academy of Political and Social Science*, 635, 6–21.

Strier, R. and Roer-Strier, D. (2010) Fatherhood in the context of immigration, in *The Role of the Father in Child Development*, 5th edn (ed M. Lamb), Wiley, New York, pp. 435–458.

Sum, A., Khatiwada, I., McLaughlin, J. and Palma, S. (2011) No country for young men: Deteriorating labor market prospects for low-skilled men in the United States. *Annals of the American Academy of Political and Social Science*, 635, 24–55.

Tamis-LeMonda, C. and McFadden, K. (2010) Fathers from low-income backgrounds: Myths and evidence, in *The Role of the Father in Child Development*, 5th edn (ed M. Lamb), Wiley, New York, pp. 296–318.

Thomas, B. (2010) In the absence of their fathers: The impact of male migration on children. *Journal of Social Welfare & Management*, 2, 119–124.

Townsend, N. (2002) *The Package Deal: Marriage, Work and Fatherhood in Men's Lives*. Philadelphia: Temple University Press.

Updegraff, K., Delgado, M. and Wheeler, L. (2009) Exploring mothers' and fathers' relationships with sons versus daughters: Links to adolescent adjustment in Mexican immigrant families. *Sex Roles*, 60, 559–574.

Utrata, J. (2008) Keeping the bar low: Why Russia's nonresident fathers accept narrow fatherhood ideals. *Journal of Marriage & Family*, 70, 1297–1310.

Vuori, J. (2009) Men's choices and masculine duties: Fathers in expert discussions. *Men & Masculinities*, 12, 45–72.

Walker, L. (2010) 'His mam, my dad, my girlfriend, loads of people used to bring him up': The value of social support for (ex) offender fathers. *Child & Family Social Work*, 15, 238–247.

Waller, M. and Swisher, R. (2006) Fathers' risk factors in fragile families: Implications for "healthy" relationships and father involvement. *Social Problems*, 53, 392–420.

Wallerstein, J. and Lewis, J. (2008) Divorced fathers and their adult offspring: Report from a twenty-five-year longitudinal study. *Family Law Quarterly*, 42, 695–711.

Weinman, M., Buzi, R., Smith, P. and Nevarez, L. (2007) A comparison of three groups of young fathers and program outcomes. *School Social Work Journal*, 13, 1–13.

Yamato, R. (2008) Impact of fathers' support and activities on mothers' marital satisfaction by income contribution during economic recession in Japan. *Fathering*, 6, 149–168.

Yocum, A. and Nath, S. (2011) Anticipating father reentry: A qualitative study of children's and mothers' experiences. *Journal of Offender Rehabilitation*, 50, 286–304.

22

Aging Families and the Gendered Life Course

PHYLLIS MOEN, JACK LAM AND MELANIE N.G. JACKSON

Introduction

The (Kenneth) Burke theorem states that "A way of seeing is also a way of not seeing – a focus upon object 'A' involves a neglect of object 'B'" (Burke, 1935, p. 70). Most family scholars focus on "young" families, as young adults move into marriage and parenthood and as working families negotiate paid work while simultaneously raising children. And yet, increased longevity, together with the aging of the Boomer cohort in North America and Europe, meant that growing numbers of contemporary families are "older" families, including older adults whose own aging parents are increasingly frail. While family scholars key in on the early stages of the adult life course (Burke's "A") and gerontologists concentrate on aging (and often infirm) individuals (another "A"), there is remarkably little emphasis on "B" – older families.

This chapter takes a *gendered life course* approach to understanding contemporary families in later adulthood. We draw on a gender perspective together with four interrelated life course themes (Elder, 1974; Moen, 2001; Mortimer and Shanahan, 2003; Moen and Spencer, 2006; Shanahan and Macmillan, 2007): (i) *historical timing, policy contexts, and social change*; (ii) *transitions and trajectories*, including the cumulation of advantage and/or disadvantage with age; (iii) *linked lives*, recognizing that families constitute patterned, interconnected relationships over time that shift with age, age-graded expectations, and exigencies; and (iv) *strategic (and often gendered) family adaptive strategies*, as older family members respond to changing resources and claims.

We use these interconnected themes to promote understanding of circumstances that (i) are being transformed at the macro-level of society in ways that make contemporary families in later adulthood historically unique, (ii) reflect an ongoing interaction between families and institutions (especially work and retirement), and (iii) are apt to characterize micro-level relationships in the later stages of the family course. Specifically, this

The Wiley Blackwell Companion to the Sociology of Families, First Edition.
Edited by Judith Treas, Jacqueline Scott, and Martin Richards.
© 2014 John Wiley & Sons Ltd. Published 2017 by John Wiley & Sons Ltd.

chapter employs these four life course themes to capture the nature and experiences of contemporary aging families around three main substantive areas: *family composition*, *families in transaction* with the institutions of work and retirement, and *intergenerational as well as intragenerational relations*, including caregiving, widowhood, and aid to younger generations. While we recognize considerable heterogeneity and inequities by race/ethnicity, nativity, and class in the experience of later family life, given space limitations, we focus here on gender distinctions and potential differences in the contemporary later family course compared to prior cohorts. The focus in this chapter centers largely on the United States, though we also draw on some empirical research on other countries. Clearly, the emerging later family course is an important issue for research throughout the developed as well as the developing world.

Changing Family Composition

Historical context and trends in family demography

Three demographic trends – longer and healthier lifespans, the aging of the large Boomer cohort (born 1946–1964), and delays as well as declines in marriage and fertility – have changed age structures of families, with rising numbers now constituting "older" families. A report by the Organization for Economic Cooperation and Development (OECD) underscores how life expectancy has increased remarkably over the past decades (OECD Family Database, 2011). In 2009, women at age 65 in OECD countries could expect to live another 20.5 years, while men could expect another 17.2 years. This reflects an increase since 1960 of an average of 5.6 years for women and 4.4 years for men. Living longer increases the risk of disability, and a greater proportion of women's than men's lives are lived with disability, even though disability at older ages is declining (Robine, Romeiu, and Cambois, 1997; Laditka and Laditka, 2002; Cutler and Wise, 2009).

Relationships take on added significance given increases in longevity, since both couple and intergenerational ties can extend over many years. For example, 18% of children born in 1900 were likely to be orphaned by the time they were 18 years old, whereas 68% of children born in the United States in 2000 were likely to still have four living *grand*parents by the time they reached 18 (Bengston, 2001). Three- or four-generation families are increasingly prevalent. Thus, the new longevity translates into long marriages and long intergenerational ties, the availability of extended kin such as grandparents and great-grandparents as resources for children, but also more older parents, grandparents, and others requiring care, often for longer periods of time (Bengston, 2001).

Ryder (1965) described social change as occurring through a process of cohort succession, as each cohort moves through the life course. Today's older families in the United States consist of the large Boomer cohort, born from 1946 through 1964, and the War cohort just preceding them, born from 1942 through 1945, as well as the Silent Generation, born from 1925 through 1941 (Soldo *et al.*, 2007). By 2030, all Boomers will be at least 65 years old, with 71 million adults in this age range (Centers for Disease Control and Prevention, 2010). The aging of the Boomer cohort is transforming what it means to be old, and to be an older family, in contemporary society.

Transitions, trajectories, and linked lives

Reuben Hill (1970) and his colleagues laid the groundwork for the study of family development by theorizing the orderly flow of families through *life cycles*, that is, the patterned sequence as families move through formation (marriage), childbearing, child-raising, child-leaving, and dissolution (widowhood). Hill's life cycle approach was foundational in that it emphasized the temporal nature of family life. Where families are located in biographical and family time (the ages of children and parents) and in social and institutional time is crucial to understanding their functioning. Hill investigated whether family members felt they were "ahead" of or "behind" normative clockworks as to when key transitions should take place. But identifying the stages of a "typical" family cycle was seen by some (O'Rand, 1996) as *pre*scriptive, that is, a prototype of how families *should* be. Moreover, today, the "typical" family cycle reflects the experience of an ever smaller portion of contemporary families.

As early as the 1970s, life course scholars began to build upon and extend the life cycle framing of families to capture *multiple paths* through lives, the dynamics, and diversities of arrangements within and across families. The *life course* itself can be thought of as a series of role entries, trajectories, and exits that, taken together, constitute both people's biographies and their family life course (Settersten and Owens, 2002; Elder, Johnson, and Crosnoe, 2003; Kohli, 2007; Elder and Giele, 2009).

Today, there is no "normal" family course. Marriage and children have come to be more of an option than an inevitability. Younger adults (Millennials born 1980–2000 and Gen Xers born 1965–1979) are marrying later or not at all, postponing parenthood, having fewer children or none at all, and moving in and out of jobs and in and out of schooling, while older adults (Boomers born 1946–1964 and members of the Silent Generation born 1925–1942) are also moving in and out of marriage and in and out of retirement. Older families represent the fallout from earlier choices as to whether and when to have children, whether and when to break up existing marriages or partnerships, whether or when to be in or out of the labor market, and whether and when to live close or far from extended family.

Thus, the later family course is characterized by considerable heterogeneity. There are older parents in their 50s, 60s, and 70s whose adult children have moved back home given economic downturns; older adults unexpectedly caring for infirm parents, siblings, and spouses; "old" new parents who have children later in life; couples negotiating two retirements; single mothers with adult children; grandparents caring for grandchildren; and fictive kinships with friends who are more "family" than not. In the context of the recession, the Pew Research Center (Parker, 2012) reports a steady upward trend in the percentage of young adults (ages 25–34, Millennials) living in multigenerational households, from 11% in 1980 to 21.6% in 2010. Most cite economic reasons for moving back. Other forms of shared households, including living with nonrelatives, have also increased (Mykyta and Macartney, 2012). Whereas in the past, the typical older family consisted of marital dyads, growing numbers of families are "stem" or "beanpole" families, consisting of relationships between older parents and adult children or between grandparents and grandchildren (Bengston, 2001; Fischer, 2011).

Adaptive strategies

As concrete repositories and constellations of roles, resources, risks, and relationships, families are where abstract national and global economic, technological, political, and demographic forces play out in real time. Studying family and individual adaptive strategies provides a useful point of entry for rendering visible what are often outdated shared cultural understandings and taken-for-granted rules, roles, and risks within and across the institutions of family, labor markets, business, and social policy development and regulation.

Given the variability in family lifestyles and the growing social acceptance of singlehood and divorce, contemporary older (as well as younger) couple relationships may be more by choice than by custom. Prior family decisions (or nondecisions) also shape family life in later adulthood. Having fewer children reduces the potential pool of caregivers for aging families (Hagestad and Uhlenberg, 2007). In young adulthood, the adaptive strategy of postponing parenthood to advance careers may result in childlessness in older age. Older divorced men estranged from their children may find their adult children feel no filial obligation to care for them (Solomou *et al.*, 1998; Jong Gierveld and Dykstra, 2002; Shapiro, 2003). Divorce and remarriage have long-term intergenerational consequences. College-age children in stepparent families receive less help with college costs than those living with both biological parents (Henretta *et al.*, 2012).

Older Families in Transaction with Institutions

Historical and policy contexts and institutional shifts

The experiences of older families are shaped by fundamental institutional structures around paid work based on the breadwinner/homemaker family form – the nature of career paths, pensions, social security provisions, unemployment, and disability insurance – along with the clockworks of workdays, workweeks, workyears, and the rewards accruing to those who follow them (Moen, 2012). Key to the family economy is paid work and retirement income, as well as social welfare supports in the form of social security and other protections. The historically constructed division of paid work from unpaid family work and community service has had enormous implications for family functioning and family well-being, as well as for gender inequality (Arber and Ginn, 1995; Moen and Roehling, 2005). In the United States, most contemporary older families consist of members of Boomer, War, and Silent Generation cohorts who in the prime of life took for granted the male "career mystique" that continuous full-time work throughout most of adulthood was the only path to success and life quality (Moen and Roehling, 2005). Accordingly, labor market and social security policies and practices were developed in the mid-twentieth century with seniority leading to job security and benefits tied to whether employees worked full time and full year in "permanent" jobs.

Given that family obligations typically fall on to women, few wives and mothers in the Boomer or prior cohorts have been able to pursue this ideal. Accommodating family life by moving in and out of jobs, in and out of full-time and part-time work, has been costly for women's wages, job security, pensions, and advancement;

these costs become especially apparent in the second half of the life course (Arber and Ginn, 1995; Harrington Meyer and Herd, 2007). Moreover, many older families of minorities, immigrants, and those with little education reap the disadvantages of having been in the secondary labor market. Moving to a global, highly competitive, information economy has meant that career prospects are now less predictable, secure, or stable for Americans, regardless of gender, race, or education, and this insecurity is intruding into the European experience as well. The old "contract" between employers and employees (awarding job and retirement security to workers in return for their commitment) is quickly disappearing (Sweet, Moen, and Meiksins, 2007).

Older families are now living in contexts that upended conventional retirement scripts, enduring gender schema that continue to prioritize women's family obligations, a growing older workforce that is more educated and healthy than in previous and perhaps future generations, and a volatile global economy eroding traditional job security and retirement protections. Unlike their parents or grandparents, contemporary older families in the United States are increasingly facing two retirements, the husband's and the wife's, in policy and economic contexts challenging taken-for-granted blueprints around the timing and nature of "retirement." Sweet *et al.* (2007) found that 9 in 10 middle-class couples report some risk in at least one spouse's job. In only 1 in 10 couples were both husbands and wives confident they would be able to keep their jobs.

Another key source of uncertainty and risk concerns the dismantling of the pension system and retirement protections. Systematic changes in retirement practices (O'Rand, 2003; Hacker, 2006) include employers switching from defined benefits to defined contribution plans. In the United States, defined benefit plans were historically designed so that workers were entitled to receive a given income once they retired. The amount retirees are entitled to in defined contribution plans varies depending on the performance of the fund investment, subject to the volatility of the stock market, as well as the amount employers and employees invest in them. Therefore, defined contribution plans are far more risky than defined benefit plans (Hacker, 2006), contributing to the economic uncertainty of older families. While nonstandard workers – part-timers and contractors – have been shut out of employer pension systems, even full-time employees in the United States are increasingly at risk; 44% of full-time workers in their 50s have neither a defined benefit nor a defined contribution pension plan from their employer (GAO, 2011).

Transitions, trajectories, and linked lives

A significant and growing number of Boomer women in the United States are not married; their work and retirement circumstances differ from those of wives, in that they cannot count on other sources of income or resources. Men's and women's lives today are more contingent than orderly, regardless of one's location in the social structure. Ambiguities and uncertainties about the future abound, coloring the sensibilities of older employees and their families as they face the realities of forced early retirements, layoffs, reduced benefits, and greater workloads. Growing numbers of Boomers find themselves unexpectedly "retired" from their primary career jobs in their 50s and early 60s, frequently as a result of corporate restructuring, mergers, and bankruptcies, or poor health. Looking at members of the pre-Boomer cohort in the United States found that most older workers left their career jobs earlier than they had expected as a result of early retirement packages or health difficulties (Han and Moen, 1999, 2001). And there is considerable heterogeneity in the age at which women and men even began planning for retirement.

Rather than being an individual status passage, retirement is a family transition, one that changes the roles, relationships, resources, and identities of all family members. Retirement based on the (male) family breadwinner had implications for homemaking wives and widows, showcasing the interdependencies of family relations. Today, the linking of lives around retirement is evident when two family breadwinners in the same household try to arrange joint retirements or else realign relationships and expectations when one retires and the other spouse does not (Moen, Kim, and Hofmeister, 2001; Kim and Moen, 2002; Moen, Sweet, and Swisher, 2005; Moen et al., 2006). Given many uncertainties, the retirement transition is a time of life without blueprints for couples moving to and through the retirement transition years, as well as for older singles (mostly women) with or without children.

Research on decision making and planning around retirement has focused on individuals' expectations and preferences. Midlife work experiences, in particular, have been linked with retirement intentions and the ability to realize later-life employment arrangements. In midlife, precarious employment (e.g., with low earnings and without private pension plans or health insurance coverage) predict preferences for later retirement (Raymo et al., 2012), likely because workers do not anticipate having adequate retirement income. Realizing one's preferences is contingent on a number of prior employment circumstances and is similar for both men and women; those with private pension coverage were less likely to realize preferences for working full time but more likely to realize preferences for not working (Raymo et al., 2010). Men with shorter job tenure and lower incomes expected to work longer but also reported lower life satisfaction when expectations were not met (Clarke, Marshall, and Weir, 2012). For 11 European countries where public retirement benefits have been more adequate, workers in lower social positions were more likely to report early retirement intentions (Wahrendorf, Dragano, and Siegrist, 2012). Expectations for later retirement are reflected in behavior. Using HRS data, Banerjee (2011) reports that fewer Americans are now expecting to retire "early" at ages 62 and 65. In 2006, 7.4% of people over 50 (leading-edge Boomers and Silent Generation cohorts) expected to stop working by 62, but by 2010, this number had dropped to 4.9%. Analyzing social security claims, Johnson (2012) reports that only 26.9% of adults aged 62 and older and eligible to claim early retirement benefits in 2011 did so, the lowest since 1976.

While about a quarter of middle-aged and older respondents believe their standard of living in retirement will be better than the previous generation, nearly half believed that it would be worse (Rix, 2011). In this sample, 67% were working for pay, 16% were not working but looking for work, while 18% were neither working nor looking for work. One concern tied to retirement timing in the United States has to do with the availability of healthcare. Fully 15% of men and women between ages 50 and 64 in 2010 were uninsured (Smolka, Multack, and Figueriredo, 2012). Early retirement (before eligibility for Medicare) is more likely for those having retirement health insurance (Nyce et al., 2011).

Many members of older families continue to work for the income it provides. Job earnings in fact provided 30% of income for adults over 65 in 2008 (Federal Interagency Forum on Aging-Related Statistics, 2010). Other major sources are social security (37%), pensions (19%), and asset income (13%). Others (often the college educated) choose to remain in the labor force because they enjoy working. For retirees who continued to work, 92% report they want to stay active, and 86% report enjoying the work (Helman, Copeland, and VanDerhei, 2011). Of course, fully 90% also provided a financial reason, such as a decrease in savings and investment (72%), needing to make ends meet (59%), or in order to keep health insurance or other benefits (40%). Many older family members (as individuals and as couples) volunteer for community organizations or else take on low-wage jobs for nonprofits, seeking new meaning and social purpose through employment or volunteer work (Freedman, 2007, 2012; Bank, 2010; Moen and Flood, 2012).

Adaptive strategies
What a gendered life course perspective brings to the research and policy agenda is the recognition of the fact that families are in constant transaction with the labor market as "role budgeting centers" (Goode, 1960), allocating family members' hours, days, and years to both paid work and unpaid domestic care work. In both North America and Europe, one retirement strategy is to take part time, part year, contract, or bridge jobs, including self-employment, in the move from full-time employment to full-time leisure (Cahill, Giandrea, and Quinn, 2006; Ebbinghaus, 2006; Wang *et al.*, 2008; Giandrea, Cahill, and Quinn, 2009; Van Solinge, 2012).

But these are often gender strategies, reproducing gender distinctions and disparities (Moen and Roehling, 2005). Because there are few options regarding the kinds of labor market attachments that provide good incomes and health insurance, couples often prioritize one job per family, typically the husband's (Pixley, 2008), which leads to gender inequality throughout the later life course (Arber, 2004; Moen and Spencer, 2006; Harrington Meyer and Herd, 2007). The timing of retirement is also a strategic choice. Putney and Bengtson (2003) find work–family conflict associated with greater odds of men and women preferring not to work or to work only part time (vs. working full time) 10 years in the future. Men and women with high work–family conflict when employed report a marked decrease in depressive symptoms upon full or even partial retirement (Coursolle *et al.*, 2010).

Relationships and Caregiving

Historical and policy shifts shaping later-life families

If retirement is one challenge of later life, another is caregiving. In European countries, the concern is that state provision of goods and services might "crowd out" family assistance to their aging members; the evidence suggests this is not the case (Künemund, 2008). Given the absence of extensive public supports in the United States, informal/family caregivers (family members, friends, and neighbors) provide the bulk of care for older adults (Family Caregiver Alliance, 2008); approximately 42.1 million family members in the United States in 2009 assisted adults with daily activities (Feinberg *et al.*, 2011). "Primary" caregivers assume the majority of caregiving obligations, including completing everyday tasks and errands. "Secondary" caregivers provide assistance to primary caregivers in a range of domains including emotional, instrumental, and financial support. Tertiary caregivers periodically provide assistance when the primary caregiver requires it, as well as assisting high-functioning care recipients, but are not usually involved in the decision-making aspects of care (Bourgeois *et al.*, 1996; Dilworth-Anderson, Willliams, and Cooper, 1999; Gaugler, Kane, and Kane, 2002; Jackson and Gaugler, 2014). As these definitions suggest, the bulk of the caregiving falls on one individual within a family, the primary caregiver. This has significant implications for both the health and psychological well-being of the caregiver, as well as implications for the quality of care that family member is able to provide.

The closest and most accessible family members tend to become caregivers in what is called the hierarchical compensatory model (Cantor, 1979; Gaugler *et al.*, 2003). Spouses are typically first in line, followed by adult children; then other relatives, friends, and neighbors; and finally formal support services. Besides assistance in activities of daily living (ADLs) tasks, caregivers also help with more cognitively demanding instrumental activities of daily living (IADLs), which can include managing medication, shopping, and housework (Szinovacz and Davey, 2008; Liu and Gallagher-Thompson, 2009; Jackson and Gaugler, 2014; The National Long Term Care Survey). Caregivers are primarily women, typically in their 40s, providing care for relatives who are in their 70s. What is unique to the contemporary caregiving experience is that most family caregivers are also in the workforce.

Caregiving for family members impacts the caregivers' psychological, emotional, and physical well-being, but this may depend on whether the caregivers perceive their role positively or negatively. Additionally, members of different cohorts perceive caregiving differently in terms of how they view the role as well as their willingness to access services and resources to aid in the care of older relatives. Boomers in Canada insisted they sacrifice far less to be caregivers than had their mothers' generation, emphasizing other aspects of their lives besides caregiving (Guberman *et al.*, 2012). They were concerned with maintaining their own autonomy, providing less hands-on care and being less willing to sacrifice their work lives in the face of caregiving demands. Nonetheless, they believed that being a caregiver made them less egotistical and more selfless compared to their counterparts not providing care. In contradiction to Guberman *et al.* (2003), Gans and Silverstein (2006) found US Boomers reported having stronger filial norms than their parents or grandparents reported.

Demographic trends throughout the life course – marrying later or not at all, postponing parenthood, having fewer children or none at all, and divorce – will impact the availability of family members to care for aging Boomers. Boomers are less likely than prior generations to have spouses or children to care for them. The circumstances of Boomers (delayed marriage, reduced fertility) are more similar to an older generation – the parents of the Depression and WWII cohorts (born 1905–1921) – than to the Boomers' own parents' generation (born 1922–1940) (Ryan *et al.*, 2012). Depression and WWII cohorts were less likely than the parents of Boomers to be married and to live within 10 miles of one of their children. Boomers will be less likely to have spouses or children to care for them.

They have more siblings, but it is unclear whether they will be able to compensate for closer relations.

Transitions, trajectories, and linked lives

As the principle of linked lives states, individuals' lives are interrelated, and the actions of one family member influence the experiences of others. The illness of a parent or spouse can precipitate key turning points as family members move in and out of caregiving, take in an older family member, place an infirm relative in a nursing home, or experience the death of a loved one. These transitions often have significant impacts on the psychological and emotional well-being and social lives of the caregivers. Seltzer and Li (2000) found that participation in leisure activities declined for wives who became caregivers, but daughters who became caregivers increased their social participation. Thus, caregiving may be more disruptive to wives' family and marital relations, whereas daughters' primary family relationships with their own husbands and children remain relatively unchanged. Daughters were more likely to exit caregiving by placing their infirm parent in a group residence, whereas wives only exited the role through the death of their husbands. When daughters institutionalized a parent, they reported a significant decrease in burden (while wives tended to continue to care for their husbands at home). Every indication is that caregiving is more demanding and all-consuming for wives than daughters.

When relationship quality is perceived to be high between family members, the transition to caregiving is less emotionally and psychologically disruptive. High relationship quality likely reduces how burdensome the role is perceived. Because burden predicts institutionalizing, higher relationship quality may also reduce the likelihood of institutionalization. Marks *et al.* (2008) found caregiving sons, but not daughters, showed greater depressive symptoms compared to sons who were not providing care. Lower relationship quality prior to becoming a caregiver, however, resulted in lower psychological well-being for caregiving daughters and sons. In dual-earner couples, caregiving was also associated with psychological distress, but men's well-being was enhanced when they moved into parental caregiving, possibly taking over caregiving responsibilities from their wives (Chesley and Moen, 2006).

Widowhood is another major transition of later life. Although women are more likely to experience widowhood, widowed or divorced men are more likely to remarry than are widowed or divorced women (Carr and Bodnar-Deren, 2009), providing them with socioemotional support that buffers some of the negative experiences associated with widowhood. Although widows are less likely to regain social support from remarriage, they are more likely to receive support from several sources, such as children, friends, neighbors, and religious groups (Hahn *et al.*, 2011).

Widowed women's psychological distress was tied to their financial strain, whereas lack of close relationships was linked to widowed men's psychological distress (Carr, 2004). Men's self-esteem decreased in the short term if they had been highly dependent on their wives for homemaking tasks.

Not all consequences of widowhood are negative for women. Widowed women have higher self-esteem than married women, perhaps from the confidence of having coped with a significant event (Carr, 2004). Widows also report higher levels of "personal growth" than widowers, which is positively related to the availability of emotional support. If the spouse had been in poor health, widowed men and women reported experiencing significantly more "personal growth" after widowhood. As with caregiving relationships, relationship quality shapes whether widowhood is experienced positively or negatively. Widowed persons expressed greater anger 6 months post loss if they had rated their marriages more positively than their spouses had in contrast to couples with similar marital assessments (Carr and Boerner, 2009). Women who remarry show an increase in psychological and emotional well-being, as also seen in earlier results with men who remarried. Widowed women who have an interest in remarriage are younger and unhappier than widows not interested in remarriage (Moorman, Booth, and Fingerman, 2006). Additionally, remarried widows are less depressed and less worried about finances. This is consistent with research on widowhood conducted internationally, which also shows limited interest by widowed women in remarriage. Dutch data find that only 11% of widowed individuals desire a new partner relationship (Stevens 2002). As in the United States, Dutch widowers were more likely to want a new partner than widows; about 20% of the Dutch sample had some sort of partnership with another person.

Because women are less likely to remarry, they appear to be more likely to seek social support from other relatives. Adult children are most likely to be a source of support for widowed women. Kalmijn (2007) found that widowed mothers in the Netherlands were more apt to receive support and contact from their children than were married mothers, while widowed fathers received the same amount of support but had less contact with their children than married fathers. Widowed parents who remarried received less support from their children than did widowed parents who lived alone – with remarried fathers receiving the least support.

Strategies of adaption

Hill (1966) theorized family stress adaptation in the face of crises and ongoing strains and laid the groundwork for the contemporary life course "cycles of control" model (Elder, 1985; Elder, Johnson, and Crosnoe, 2003). Specifically, when needs or pressures outstrip the available resources with which to manage them, individuals and families seek to regain equilibrium using strategies of adaptation. These strategies include ways of providing care, dealing with the ambivalence of relationships, and helping out between generations.

Caregiver strategies

Family members strategize as to who will provide care to infirm relatives and the kind of care they provide. Ward-Griffin *et al.'s* (2007) qualitative study of 15 mother–adult daughter dyads in Canada found that mothers and daughters identified four types of relationships: custodial, combative, cooperative, and cohesive. Custodial relationships were defined by the idea of duty, with a high expectation of care but a low expectation of emotional support. Within combative relationships, mothers and daughters competed for control over the care process. Daughters were more controlling of their mother's behaviors and ADLs, which increased tensions in the relationship. This type of relationship was more likely to lead to neglect and abuse. Cooperative relationships had reciprocity as a key defining characteristic, with both mothers and daughters having a strong family network they could rely on for support. Cohesive relationships were also strength based and positive, with daughters attentive to their mother's need for independence, which both mothers and daughters found to be rewarding.

When caregiving becomes too burdensome, caregivers identify strategies to reduce the burden, such as retiring from the workforce or institutionalizing the care recipient. Another adaptive strategy is to shift caregivers. Daughters caring for mothers were more likely than those caring for fathers to exchange caregiver responsibilities with another relative (Szinovacz and Davey, 2007). This, along with a study by Ward-Griffin et al. (2007), suggests that there may be specific challenges for caregiving relationships between mothers and daughters. Having more siblings, particularly more sisters, increased the probability of switching caregivers. This provides further evidence for the concept of linked lives, since the decision of one sibling to leave the role of primary caregiver has a direct impact on the lives of the other siblings.

Another strategy for managing caregiving demands is to exit the workforce. This can create a nonnormative, off-time transition for caregivers. Caregiving responsibilities and health/stress factors led Canadian women to retire earlier than expected (Zimmerman et al. 2008). In a US study, husbands caring for their wives were less likely than noncaregiving men to retire, while wives caring for husbands were five times more apt to exit their jobs than other wives (Dentinger and Clarkberg, 2002). Gender expectations may account for this difference.

Other strategies for care include moving infirm relatives to assisted living facilities (ALFs). Kemp (2008) studied 20 couples relocating to ALFs, finding couples transitioned to ALFs together, even though the healthier spouse could have continued to live independently. The transition to ALFs began with an illness diagnosis for one or both spouses. The diagnosis required a transition for the couple, because the caregiving partner was unable to meet the increasing burden of caring for their partner on their own and the couple wanted to be together. Adult children, who were seen as the "lifeline" for the couple, were involved in the decision regarding relocation. In these cases, adult children were the ones who would investigate options, locate facilities, and arrange relocation.

Parents and *children intergenerational relations*
Adaptive strategies can involve providing support for one's adult children (or vice versa) but also (re)defining the situation, say, feeling more or less ambivalent regarding intergenerational relationships. Typically, there appears to be less ambivalence between older parents and adult children when the children are married and not experiencing significant challenges. In relationships with their adult children, mothers were more ambivalent if they still provided financial support for adult children but less ambivalent toward adult children who had completed college and were married (Pillemer and Suitor, 2002). Mothers voiced more ambivalence toward children who experienced major problems in adulthood (serious illnesses or injury, serious mental or emotional problems, problems with drinking or drugs, and problems with the law) and toward children they felt took more than they gave back (Pillemer et al., 2007).

What is less frequently discussed is the effect that adult children have on the well-being of older parents. Greenfield and Marks (2006) assessed whether parents' well-being was impacted by adult children having 10 types of problems: chronic disease or disability, frequent minor illnesses, emotional problems, alcohol or substance problems, financial problems, problems at school or work, difficulty finding or keeping a job, marital or partner relationship problems, legal problems, and difficulty getting along with people. Parents with children having more problems reported lower levels of well-being, less positive affect, more negative affect, less self-acceptance, and more family strain. Married parents experienced smaller declines in positive affect in relation to their children's problems than did single parents. In another study, African American parents were more likely than white parents to have high levels of depression in relation to negative treatment by their (adult) children and their children's unemployment, as well as higher anger following a child's illness (Milkie, Bierman, and Schieman, 2008). Children's divorce, however, decreased anger for African American parents. Pillemer and Suitor (1991) also report a significant relationship between children and parents' depression and conflict.

Grandparents and grandchildren intergenerational relations
In light of the new family demography, most children in North America and Europe have several living grandparents (Hagestad and Uhlenberg, 2007), but a study in Italy shows they have less contact when the grandparents are divorced, widowed, or repartnered, compared to those in stable marriages (Albertini and Saraceno, 2008). In the United States, there were approximately 6.7 million grandchildren under the age of 18 living with a grandparent in 2009, and 2.7 million of these grandparents served as the primary caregivers for their grandchildren, assuming responsibility for their basic needs (United States Census Bureau, 2009). Kohli and Albertini (2008) examined European families' support (financial transfers, social support) for their adult children's own family projects. They found differences in support strategies across countries (Sweden, Germany, France, and Spain), but that both social support (including caring for grandchildren) and the combined strategy of social support and financial transfers increased when adult children transitioned into parenthood (see also Silverstein, 2006).

Typically, when the literature refers to the prevalence of grandparenting, it most often refers to the care provided by grandmothers (Arber and Timonen, 2012). Being the primary care provider to a grandchild can be seen as a nonnormative transition, yet other cultural values and contexts may characterize this as an expectable, on-time transition. Landry-Meyer and Newman (2004) interviewed grandparents who had legal custody of their grandchild. This was usually an unanticipated role, but they felt greater clarity regarding the roles once they had legal custody. Participants reported not feeling like a grandparent, however, because they were parenting their grandchildren. The literature also gives less emphasis to grandparents with older grandchildren.

As with children, relationships seem to depend on the younger generation fulfilling expectations. Grandparents and grandchildren both report higher-quality relationships when grandchildren enroll in college than when grandchildren do not enroll in college (Crosnoe and Elder, 2002). This also suggests support for the generational stake hypothesis proposed by Bengston, Schaie, and Burton (1995).

Given the increased longevity and the rising likelihood of chronic illnesses with age, older adults are increasingly likely to become dependent on not only their children but also their grandchildren for care. Approximately 8% of family caregivers of older adults in the United States are grandchildren (Foundation for Accountability and Robert Wood Johnson Foundation, 2001). The increased likelihood of single motherhood, divorce, and widowhood means diminished marital ties that reinforce the beanpole family form of older adults and their descendants. Of course, these relationships differ by class, race/ethnicity, and gender. As Swartz (2009, p. 207) points out, "Intergenerational support, while offering real help, also becomes a largely hidden mechanism by which privilege or disadvantage is transferred through families from generation to generation."

Conclusions: Implications for Theory and Future Research

We began with the Burke theorem, that a focus on "A" excludes "B" and vice versa. Scholars from a range of disciplines have until recently based their theoretical arguments and empirical investigations of paid work, family work, work–family issues, mobility and inequality on conventional taken-for-granted mental maps, and framings of families raising children. These mental maps are useful heuristics, but they direct our attention to some things, and not others. By contrast, a gendered life course approach to aging families puts both work and family in motion and in context, moving the focus beyond families raising children to families of adults living lives in tandem with their aging parents. It also captures the dynamics of family experience in transaction with the labor market and retirement.

The four life course themes organizing this chapter – historical context, transitions and trajectories, linked lives, and adaptive strategies – are both overlapping and interdependent. On the historical context, more needs to be known about these processes in contemporary cohorts regarding families of different composition, race/ethnicity, and class, even as evidence from studies of previous cohorts may well be out of date. Demographic changes, technological advances in communications, immigration, and economic uncertainty, for instance, are challenging assumptions about aging and families based on past cohorts. These social forces necessitate a complex but rich theoretical and research agenda on the contemporary experiences of older families in transaction with larger institutions. For example, as the gendered nature of family, work, and retirement "careers" as they unfold and intersect in later adulthood, they invite examination of families and labor markets as institutionalized processes intersecting and shifting over the life course. These changes have enormous implications for gender – and other – inequalities in resources, status, and future prospects in later adulthood, within and across families and societies.

Transitions and trajectories capture the importance for future research linking life stages, examining the impacts of early experiences (including the biographical pacing of family formation, parenthood, and labor market attachments) on later-life families. The concept of adaptive strategies (Elder, 1974; Hareven, 1982; Moen and Wethington, 1992; Elder, Johnson, and Crosnoe, 2003; Moen et al., 2013) has enabled life course scholars to consider families as decision units, even as they are enabled or constrained by existing (and often outdated) institutional arrangements. This points to the value of investigating ways contemporary older family members are making strategic choices regarding employment, residential mobility, and caregiving, in response to constraints, challenges, and opportunities.

The gendered life course framing of families in the second half of life demonstrates that family members' adaptive strategies cannot be captured by simply examining individual experiences separately. Recognizing linked lives, they require couple-level and family-level conceptualization and analysis. Historical, cultural, and institutional forces provide a backdrop of constraint, uncertainty, and risk. Work, family, community, and personal ties, as well as demands and resources, shift over the life course, *as do their meanings*. Constraints and strategic adaptations earlier in the life course play out in and often produce gender, race/ethnic, nativity, and class inequalities in the later adult years. What life course scholars find in both men's and women's biographies are more discontinuities than continuities – in family relationships, in paid work and retirement, in personal experience and development, and across cohorts (Rindfuss, Swicegood, and Rosenfeld, 1987; Elder and O'Rand, 1995; Settersten and Mayer, 1997; Han and Moen, 1999, 2001; Pavalko and Smith, 1999).

Acknowledgments

The authors thank the McKnight Foundation for supporting the research and Jane Peterson for her help in preparing the manuscript for publication.

References

Albertini, M., and Saraceno, C. (2008) Intergenerational contact and support: the long-term effects of marital instability in Italy, in *Families, Ageing, and Social Policy* (ed C. Saraceno), Edward Elgar Publishing, Cheltenham, pp. 194–217.

Arber, S. (2004) Gender, marital status and ageing: linking material, health and social resources. *Journal of Aging Studies*, 18 (1), 91–108.

Arber, S. and Ginn, J. (1995) *Connecting Gender and Ageing: A Sociological Approach*, Open University Press, Buckingham.

Arber, S. and Timonen, V. (eds) (2012) *Contemporary Grandparenting: Changing Family Relationships in Global Contexts*, Policy Press, Bristol.

Banerjee, S. (2011) Retirement age expectations of older Americans between 2006 and 2010. *Employee Benefit Research Institute Notes*, 13 (12), 2–12.

Bank, D. (2010) Encore careers and the economic crisis. *Generations*, 33, 69–73.

Bengston, V.L. (2001) The burgess award lecture: beyond the nuclear family: the increasing importance of multigenerational bonds. *Journal of Marriage and Family*, 63 (1), 1–16.

Bengston, V.L., Schaie, K.W. and Burton, L.M. (1995) *Adult Intergenertational Relations: Effects of Societal Change*, Springer, New York.

Bourgeois, M.S., Beach, S., Schulz, R. and Burgio, L.D. (1996) When primary and secondary caregivers disagree: predictors and psychosocial consequences. *Psychology and Aging*, 11 (3), 527–537.

Burke, K. (1935) *Permanence and Change: An Anatomy of Purpose*, University of California Press, Berkley.

Cahill, K.E., Giandrea, M.D. and Quinn, J.F. (2006) Retirement patterns from career employment. *The Gerontologist*, 46 (4), 514–523.

Cantor, M.H. (1979) Neighbors and friends: an overlooked resource in the informal support system. *Research on Aging*, 1 (4), 434–463.

Carr, D. (2004) Gender, preloss marital dependence, and older adults' adjustment to widow-hood. *Journal of Marriage and Family*, 66 (1), 220–235.

Carr, D. and Bodnar-Deren, S. (2009) Gender, aging and widowhood, in *International Handbook of Population Aging*, vol. 1 (ed P. Uhlenberg), Springer, the Netherlands, pp. 705–728.

Carr, D. and Boerner, K. (2009) Do spousal discrepancies in marital quality assessments affect psychological adjustment to widowhood? *Journal of Marriage and Family*, 71 (3), 495–509.

Centers for Disease Control and Prevention (2010) Healthy People, http://www.cdc.gov/nchs/healthy_people.htm (accessed August 30, 2010).

Chesley, N. and Moen, P. (2006) When workers care: dual-earner couples' caregiving strategies, benefit use, and psychological well-being. *American Behavioral Scientist*, 49 (9), 1248–1269.

Clarke P., Marshall, V.W. and Weir, D. (2012) Unexpected retirement from full time work after age 62: consequences for life satisfaction in older Americans. *European Journal on Ageing*, 9 (3), 207–219.

Coursolle, K., Sweeney, M.M., Raymo, J.M. and Ho, J.H. (2010) The association between retirement and emotional well-being: does work-family conflict matter? *Journals of Gerontology*, 65B, 609–620.

Crosnoe, R. and Elder, G.H., Jr. (2002) Life course transitions, the generational stake, and grandparent-grandchild relationships. *Journal of Marriage and Family*, 64 (4), 1089–1096.

Cutler, D.M. and Wise, D.A. (eds) (2009) *Health at Older Ages: The Causes and Consequences of Declining Disability Among the Elderly*, University of Chicago Press, Chicago.

Dentinger, E. and Clarkberg, M. (2002) Informal caregiving and retirement timing among men and women: gender and caregiving relationships in late midlife. *Journal of Family Issues*, 23, 857–879.

Dilworth-Anderson, P., Williams, S.W. and Cooper, T. (1999) The contexts of experiencing emotional distress among family caregivers to elderly African Americans. *Family Relations*, 48, 391–396.

Ebbinghaus, B. (2006) *Reforming Early Retirement in Europe, Japan and the USA*, Oxford University Press, Oxford.

Elder, G.H., Jr. (1974) *Children of the Great Depression: Social Change in Life Experience*, University of Chicago Press, Chicago.

Elder, G.H., Jr. (1985) Perspectives on the life course, in *Life Course Dynamics: Trajectories and Transitions, 1968–1980* (ed G.H. Elder, Jr.), Cornell University Press, Ithaca, pp. 23–49.

Elder, G.H., Jr. and O'Rand, A.M. (1995) Adult lives in a changing society, in *Sociological Perspectives on Social Psychology* (ed K.S. Cook, G.A. Fine and J.S. House), Allyn and Bacon, Boston, pp. 452–475.

Elder, G.H., Jr. and Giele, J.Z. (2009) *The Craft of Life Course Research*, Guilford Press, New York.

Elder, G.H., Jr., Johnson, M.K. and Crosnoe, R. (2003) The emergence and development of the life course, in *Handbook of the Life Course* (eds J.T. Mortimer and M.J. Shanahan), Plenum, New York, pp. 3–19.

Family Caregiver Alliance (2008) Family Caregiver Alliance: National Center on Caregiving.www.caregiver.org (accessed June 18, 2008).

Federal Interagency Forum on Aging-Related Statistics (2010) Older Americans 2010: key indicators of well-being. U. S. Government Printing Office, Washington, DC. Retrieved from www.agingstats.gov (accessed October 30, 2013).

Feinberg, L., Reinhard, S.C., Houser, A. and Choula, R. (2011) *Valuing the Invaluable: 2011 Update. The Growing Contributions and Costs of Family Caregiving*, AARP Public Policy Institute, Washington, D.C., pp. 1–28.

Fischer, C.S. (2011) *Still Connected: Family and Friends in American Since 1970*, Russell Sage Foundation, New York.

Freedman, M. (2007) *Encore: Finding Work That Matters in the Second Half of Life*, Public Affairs, New York.

Freedman, M. (2012) *The Big Shift: Navigating the New Stage beyond Midlife*, Public Affairs, New York.

Gans, D. and Silverstein, M. (2006) Norms of filial responsibility for aging parents across time and generations. *Journal of Marriage and Family*, 68, 961–976.

GAO (2011) *Income Security: Older Adults and the 2007–2009 Recession*, U. S. Government Accountability Office, Washington, DC.

Gaugler, J.E., Kane, R.L. and Kane, R.A. (2002) Family care for older people with disabilities: towards more targeted and interpretable research. *International Journal of Aging and Human Development*, 54 (3), 205–231.

Gaugler, J.E., Wackerbarth, S.B., Mendiondo, M. *et al.* (2003) The characteristics of dementia caregiving onset. *American Journal of Alzheimer's Disease and Other Dementias*, 18 (2), 97–104.

Giandrea, M.D., Cahill, K.E. and Quinn, J.F. (2009) Bridge jobs: a comparison across cohorts. *Research on Aging*, 31 (5), 549–576.

Goode, W.J. (1960) A theory of role strain. *American Sociological Review*, 25 (4), 483–496.

Greenfield, E.A. and Marks, N.F. (2006) Linked lives: adult children's problems and their parents' psychological and relational well-being. *Journal of Marriage and Family*, 68 (2), 442–454.

Guberman, N., Nicholas, E., Nolan, M. *et al.* (2003) Impacts on practitioners of using research-based career assessment tools: experiences from the UK, Canada and Sweden, with insights from Australia. *Health and Social Care in the Community*, 11 (4), 345–355.

Guberman, N., Lavoie, J.-P., Blein, L. and Olazabal, I. (2012) Baby boom caregivers: care in the age of individualization. *The Gerontologist*, 52 (2), 210–218.

Hacker, J.S. (2006) *The Great Risk Shift*, Oxford University Press, New York.

Hagestad, G.O. and Uhlenberg, P. (2007) The impact of demographic changes on relations between age groups and generations: a comparative perspective, in *Social Structures, Demographic Changes and the Well-Being of Older Persons* (ed K.W. Schaie and P. Uhlenberg), Springer Publishing Co., New York, pp. 239–261.

Hahn, E.A., Cichy, K.E., Almeida, D.M. and Haley, W.E. (2011) Time use and well-being in older widows: adaptation and resilience. *Journal of Women & Aging*, 23 (2), 149–159.

Han, S.-K. and Moen, P. (1999) Clocking out: temporal patterning of retirement. *American Journal of Sociology*, 105, 191–236.

Han, S.-K. and Moen, P. (2001) Coupled careers: pathways through work and marriage in the United States, in *Careers of Couples in Contemporary Societies: From Male Breadwinner to Dual Earner Families* (ed H.-P. Blossfeld and S. Drobnic), Oxford University Press: Oxford, pp. 201–231.

Hareven, T.K. (1982) *Family Time and Industrial Time*, Cambridge University Press, Cambridge.

Harrington Meyer, M. and Herd, P. (2007) *Market Friendly or Family Friendly? The State and Gender Inequality in Old Age*, Russell Sage, New York.

Helman, R., Copeland, C. and VanDerhei, J. (2011) The 2011 retirement confidence survey: confidence drops to record lows, reflecting "the new normal." Issue brief no. 355, Employee Benefit Research Institute, Washington, DC.

Henretta, J.C., Wolf, D.A., Van Voorhis, M.F. and Soldo, B.J. (2012) Family structure and the reproduction of inequality: parents' contribution to children's college costs. *Social Science Research*, 41, 876–887.

Hill, R. (1966) Contemporary developments in family theory. *Journal of Marriage and the Family*, 28 (1), 10–28.

Hill, R. (1970) *Family Development in Three Generations*, Schenkman Publishing, Cambridge.

Jackson, M.N.G. and Gaugler, J.E. (2014) Family involvement in residential long-term care, in *Long-Term Care in an Aging Society* (ed P.B. Teaster and G.D. Rowles), Delmar, New York.

Johnson, R.W. (2012) Social security claims edged down in 2011. Retirement security data brief no. 5), Urban Institute, Washington, DC.

Jong Gierveld, J. and Dykstra, P.A. (2002) The long-term rewards of parenting: older adults' marital history and the likelihood of receiving support from adult children. *Ageing International*, 27 (3), 49–69.

Kalmijn, M. (2007) Gender differences in the effects of divorce, widowhood and remarriage on intergenerational support: does marriage protect fathers? *Social Forces*, 85 (3), 1079–1104.

Kemp, C.L. (2008) Negotiating transitions in later life: married couples in assisted living. *Journal of Applied Gerontology*, 27, 231–251.

Kim, J. and Moen, P. (2002) Retirement transitions, gender, and psychological well-being: a life-course, ecological model. *Journal of Gerontology*, 57B, P212–P222.

Kohli, M. (2007) The institutionalization of the life course: looking back to look ahead. *Research in Human Development*, 4 (3), 253–271.

Kohli, M. and Albertini, M. (2008) The family as a source of support for adult children's own family projects: European varieties, in *Families, Ageing, and Social Policy* (ed C. Saraceno), Edward Elgar Publishing, Cheltenham, pp. 38–58.

Künemund, H. (2008) Intergenerational relations within the family and the state, in *Families, Ageing, and Social Policy* (ed C. Saraceno), Edward Elgar Publishing, Cheltenham, pp. 105–122.

Laditka, S.B. and Laditka, J.N. (2002) Recent perspectives on active life expectancy for older women. *Journal of Women and Aging*, 14 (1/2), 163–184.

Landry-Meyer, L. and Newman, B.M. (2004) An exploration of the grandparent caregiver role. *Journal of Family Issues*, 25 (8), 1005–1025.

Liu, W. and Gallagher-Thompson, D. (2009) Impact of dementia caregiving: risks, strains, and growth, in *Aging families and Caregiving* (ed S.H. Qualls and S.H. Zarit), Wiley, Hoboken, pp. 85–111.

Marks, N.F., Lambert, J.D., Jun, H. and Song, J. (2008) Psychosocial moderators of the effects of transitioning into filial caregiving on mental and physical health. *Research on Aging*, 30 (3), 358–389.

Milkie, M.A., Bierman, A. and Schieman, S. (2008) How adult children influence older parents' mental health: integrating stress-process and life-course perspectives. *Social Psychology Quarterly*, 71, 86–105.

Moen, P. (2001) The gendered life course, in *Handbook of Aging and the Social Sciences* (ed L. George and R.H. Binstock), Academic, San Diego, pp. 179–196.

Moen, P. (2012) Constrained choices: the shifting institutional contexts of aging and the life course, in *Perspectives on the Future of the Sociology of Aging* (ed L. Waite), National Research Council, Washington, DC, pp. 81–119.

Moen, P. and Wethington, E. (1992) The concept of family adaptive strategies. *Annual Review of Sociology*, 18, 233–251.

Moen, P. and Roehling, P. (2005) *The Career Mystique: Cracks in the American Dream*, Rowman and Littlefield, Boulder.

Moen, P. and Spencer, D. (2006) Converging divergences in age, gender, health, and well-being: strategic selection in the third age, in *Handbook of Aging and the Social Sciences* (ed R. Binstock and L. George), Elsevier Academic Press, Burlington, pp. 127–144.

Moen, P. and Flood, S. (2012) Limited engagements? Time working/volunteering in the third age of the (gendered) life course. Revise and Resubmit. *Social Problems*, 60 (2), 1–28.

Moen, P., Kim, J.E. and Hofmeister, H. (2001) Couples' work/retirement transitions, gender, and marital quality. *Social Psychology Quarterly*, 64, 55–71.

Moen, P., Sweet, S. and Swisher, R. (2005) Embedded career clocks: the case of retirement planning. *Advances in Life Course Research*, 9, 237–265.

Moen, P., Huang, Q., Plassman, V. and Dentinger, E. (2006) Deciding the future: do dual-earner couples plan together for retirement? *American Behavioral Scientist*, 49 (10), 1422–1443.

Moen, P., Lam, J., Ammons, S. and Kelly, E.L. (2013) Time work by overworked professionals: strategies in response to the stress of higher status. *Work & Occupations*, 40 (2): 79–114.

Moorman, S.M., Booth, A. and Fingerman, K.L. (2006) Women's romantic relationships after widowhood. *Journal of Family Issues*, 27 (9), 1281–1304.

Mortimer, J.T. and Shanahan M.J. (eds) (2003) *Handbook of the Life Course*, Plenum, New York.

Mykyta, L. and Macartney, S. (2012) Sharing a household: household composition and economic well-being: 2007–2010. United States Census Bureau. Current Population Report, June 2012, 60-242. http://www.census.gov/hhes/www/poverty/publications/P60-242.pdf (accessed August 30, 2012).

Nyce, S., Schieber, S., Shoven, J.B. *et al.* (2011) Does retiree health insurance encourage early retirement?. NBER working paper no. 17703, National Bureau of Economic Research, Washington, DC.

OECD Indicators (2011) Life expectancy and healthy life expectancy at age 65, in *Health at a Glance, 2011*. http://www.oecd-ilibrary.org/social-issues-migration-health/health-at-a-glance-2011/life-expectancy-and-healthy-life-expectancy-at-age-65_health_glance-2011-66-en (accessed August 2, 2011).

O'Rand, A.M. (1996) The precious and the precocious: understanding cumulative dis/advantage over the life course. *The Gerontologist*, 36 (2), 230–238.

O'Rand, A.M. (2003) The future of the life course: late modernity and life course risks, in *Handbook of the Life Course* (ed J.T. Mortimer and M.J. Shanahan), Plenum, New York, pp. 693–701.

Parker, K. (2012) The boomerang generation: feeling ok about living with mom and dad. *Pew Social Demographic Trends*. http://www.pewsocialtrends.org/2012/03/15/the-boomerang-generation/ (accessed August 16, 2012).

Pavalko, E.K. and Smith, B. (1999) The rhythm of work: health effects of women's work dynamics. *Social Forces*, 77, 1141–1162.

Pillemer, K. and Suitor, J. (1991) 'Will I ever escape my child's problems?' effects of adult children's problems on elderly parents. *Journal of Marriage and Family*, 55 (3), 585–594.

Pillemer, K. and Suitor, J. (2002) Explaining mothers' ambivalence toward their adult children. *Journal of Marriage and Family*, 64 (3), 602–613.

Pillemer, K., Suitor, J., Mock, S.E. *et al.* (2007) Capturing the complexity of intergenerational relations: exploring ambivalence within later-life families. *Journal of Social Issues*, 63 (4), 775–791.

Pixley, J.E. (2008) Life course patterns of career-prioritizing decisions and occupational attainment in dual-earner couples. *Work and Occupations*, 35, 127–163.

Putney, N.M. and Bengtson, V.L. (2003) Intergenerational relations in changing times, in *Handbook of the Life Course* (eds J.T. Mortimer and M.J. Shanahan), Plenum Publishers, New York, pp. 149–164.

Raymo, J.M., Warren, J.R., Sweeney, M.M. *et al.* (2010) Later-life employment preferences and outcomes: the role of midlife work experiences. *Research on Aging*, 32, 419–466.

Raymo, J.M., Warren, J.R., Sweeney, M.M. *et al.* (2012) Precarious employment, bed jobs, labor unions, and early retirement. *Journals of Gerontology*, 66B (2), 249–259.

Rindfuss, R.R., Swicegood, C.G. and Rosenfeld, R.A. (1987) Disorder in the life course: how common and does it matter? *American Sociological Review*, 52, 785–801.

Rix, S.E. (2011) 50+ and worried about today and tomorrow: older Americans express concerns about the state of the economy and their current and future financial well-being. *AARP Public Policy Institute Fact Sheet*, November 2011.

Robine, J.-M., Romieu, I. and Cambois, E. (1997) Health expectancies and current research. *Reviews in Clinical Gerontology*, 7, 73–81.

Ryan, L.H., Smith, J., Antonucci, T.C. and Jackson, J.S. (2012) Cohort differences in the availability of informal caregivers: are the boomers at risk? *The Gerontologist*, 52, 177–188.

Ryder, N.B. (1965) The cohort as a concept in the study of social change. *American Sociological Review*, 30 (6), 843–861.

Seltzer, M.M. and Li, L.W. (2000) The dynamics of caregiving: transitions during a three-year prospective study. *The Gerontologist*, 40 (2), 165–178.

Settersten, R.A., Jr. and Mayer, K.U. (1997) The measurement of age, age structuring, and the life course. *Annual Review of Sociology*, 23, 233–261.

Settersten, R.A. and Owens, T.J. (eds) (2002) *Advances in Life Course Research: New Frontiers in Socialization*, vol. 7. Elsevier Science, London.

Shanahan, M.J. and Macmillan, R. (2007) *Biography and the Sociological Imagination: Contexts and Contingencies*, Norton, New York.

Shapiro, A. (2003) Later-life divorce and parent-adult child contact and proximity: a longitudinal analysis. *Journal of Family Issues*, 24 (2), 264–285.

Silverstein, M. (2006) Intergenerational family transfers in social context, in *Handbook of Aging and Social Sciences* (eds R. Binstock, L. George, S. Cutler, J. Hendricks and J. Schulz), Elsevier, Oxford, pp. 165–180.

Smolka, G., Multack, M. and Figueiredo, C. (2012) Health insurance coverage for 50- to 64-year-olds. Insight on the issues no. I59, AARP, Washington, DC.

Soldo, B., Mitchell, O.S., Tfaily, R. and McCabe, J.F. (2007) Cross-cohort differences in health on the verge of retirement, in *Redefining Retirement: How will the Boomer Fare?* (eds B. Madrian, O.S. Mitchell and B.J. Soldo), Oxford University Press, Cambridge, pp. 138–158.

Solomou, W., Richards, M., Huppert, F.A. *et al.* (1998) Divorce, current marital status and well-being in an elderly population. *International Journal of Law, Policy and the Family*, 12, 323–344.

Stevens, N. (2002) Re-engaging: new partnerships in late-life widowhood. *Ageing International*, 27 (4), 27–42.

Swartz, T.T. (2009) Intergenerational family relations in adulthood: patterns, variations, and implications in the contemporary United States. *Annual Review of Sociology*, 35, 191–212.

Sweet, S., Moen, P. and Meiksins, P. (2007) Dual earners in double jeopardy: preparing for job loss in the new risk economy. *Research in the Sociology of Work*, 17, 445–469.

Szinovacz, M.E. and Davey, A. (2007) Changes in adult child caregiver networks. *The Gerontologist*, 47 (3), 280–295.

Szinovacz, M.E. and Davey, A. (2008) The division of parent care between spouses. *Ageing and Society*, 28, 571–597.

The Foundation for Accountability and the Robert Woods Johnson Foundation (2001) A Portrait of Informal Caregivers in America, 2001. http://www.rwjf.org/files/publications/other/CaregiverChartbook2001.pdf (accessed October 30, 2013).

The National Long Term Care Survey. http://www.nltcs.aas.duke.edu/ (accessed November 17, 2013).

United States Census Bureau (2009) Facts for Features-Grandparents Day. http://www.census.gov/newsroom/releases/archives/facts_for_features_special_editions/cb11-ff17.html (accessed October 30, 2013).

Van Solinge, H. (2012) Explaining transitions into self-employment after (early) retirement. *NETSPAR discussion paper DP 09/2012-036*.

Wahrendorf, M., Dragano, N. and Siegrist, J. (2012) Social position, work stress, and retirement intentions: a study with older employees from 11 European countries. *European Sociological Review*. doi: 10.1093/esr/jcs058.

Wang, M., Zhan, Y., Liu, S. and Shultz, K.S. (2008) Antecedents of bridge employment: a longitudinal investigation. *Journal of Applied Psychology*, 93 (4), 818–830.

Ward-Griffin, C., Oudshoom, A., Clark, K. and Bol, N. (2007) Mother-adult daughter relationships with dementia care: a critical analysis. *Journal of Family Nursing*, 13 (1), 13–32.

Zimmerman, L., Mitchell, B., Wister, A., and Gutman, G. (2008) Unanticipated consequences: a comparison of expected and actual retirement timing among older women. *Journal of Women and Aging*, 12, 109–128.

Part VI

Families in Context

23

Public Policy and Families

PERNILLA TUNBERGER AND WENDY SIGLE-RUSHTON

Introduction

If we think of public policy as an effort to move from "how things are" to "how we would like them to be," it becomes clear that we cannot understand policy logics without reference to the context in which they were developed. Certain aspects of "how things are" will be taken for granted, and others will be deemed an essential part of the problem that policy is trying to solve, and this will vary substantially across time and place. When the object of study is family policies and their gendered consequences, the need to take context into account in this way is immediately apparent. Family policies incorporate assumptions about how families operate, they make assumptions about the right and proper organization of earning and caring, and they attempt to effect change. The wider context informs, modifies, and constrains each of these in nontrivial ways. Moreover, intended effects can be bolstered or weakened to the extent that they resonate with prevailing social norms and institutional structures.

The aim of this chapter is to describe and compare the trends and innovations of family policies in the European Union (EU) and the United States, from the latter part of the twentieth century to the present day, taking into account cross-national differences in the wider political objectives, the underlying policy logics, and the consequences for different population groups. For ease of presentation and to facilitate our analysis, we consider two broad periods: the period of rapid social and economic change that took hold from the early to the mid-1970s, when attempts to respond to and manage change led to significant cross-national variations in the way welfare states have understood, constructed, and interacted with the family, and the period from the mid-1990s, when developments in the EU, perhaps because of its limited remit in areas of social policy, resulted in European family policy becoming more closely linked to economic and fiscal concerns. In addition, developments of the

The Wiley Blackwell Companion to the Sociology of Families, First Edition.
Edited by Judith Treas, Jacqueline Scott, and Martin Richards.
© 2014 John Wiley & Sons Ltd. Published 2017 by John Wiley & Sons Ltd.

EU approach to social policy such as the Open Method of Coordination (OMC) provided space for cross-national policy sharing and peer evaluation (Heidenreich and Bischoff, 2008), the result of which was some level of convergence in policy frames and, to a lesser extent, policy approaches. Nonetheless, previously well-established patterns of gendered and social stratification persist.

Diverging Models of Earning and Caring

From their earliest stage of development, most advanced welfare states made efforts to support families by subsidizing the costs of raising children. Motivated by concerns about poverty and inequality and, in some countries, by the desire to increase birthrates, most advanced welfare states developed redistributive mechanisms that targeted fathers' earnings (Shaver and Bradshaw, 1995). For the most part, these family policies originated in a setting where the male breadwinner/female carer gendered division of labor was either taken as given or deemed optimal. Even in countries with relatively high rates of female labor market participation such as France, family policies were developed that often presumed that mothers of (young) children would withdraw from the labor market and care for them at home (Misra and Jude, 2008; Jenson and Kantrow, 1990). As a consequence, family policies aimed to make it easier for men to maintain an economically dependent wife and children (Shaver and Bradshaw, 1995).

During the economic boom that followed World War II, many countries suffered from labor shortages. While some relied mostly on guest workers to provide the labor needed, others actively chose to also promote female labor market participation, including that of mothers (Rosenbluth, Light, and Schrag, 2002). Most formal guest worker programs were closed by the early 1970s (Castles, 2006), but their legacy left an important mark on European societies. The differing strategies chosen effectively created, or reconfirmed, different notions of the family as an institution, the gendered division of labor within it, and the division of labor between family, state, and market.

In subsequent years, rapid social and economic change saw the logic and the desirability of the male breadwinner/female carer family substantially undermined. Economic stagnation and labor market changes, driven in part by increased global competition and social dumping, made male employment less well remunerated and far more unstable. In addition, increasingly high rates of family dissolution meant that many children lived apart from their fathers. As a consequence, family policies which presumed a steadily present and continuously employed male breadwinner increasingly failed to reflect the reality of people's lives. Although female employment increased markedly in all countries, albeit to very different extents, the need to accommodate caring responsibilities meant that the pay, hours, and continuity of women's employment, mothers' employment in particular, often fell far short of the (historic) male standard, contributing to the economic vulnerability of the growing number of single-mother families. While these trends touched all advanced welfare states to some extent, they were more pervasive in some than in others. The pace (and, to some extent, the nature) of family change in Italy, for example, lagged behind other wealthy countries (Perelli-Harris et al., 2010, 2012). Moreover, policymakers interpreted and sought to manage these changes in different ways. Nordic countries, Denmark and Sweden in particular, had started promoting female labor market participation much earlier, but during the 1970s, the institutional framework meant to facilitate women's work–family reconciliation and to deliver greater economic independence to women was strengthened. Antidiscrimination and sexual harassment legislation in the United States removed institutional barriers to female employment while leaving the negotiation of work and care to the family and the market, creating very different living conditions and possibilities for women in different family structures and socioeconomic positions (O'Connor, Orloff, and Shaver, 1999; Orloff, 2006). In contrast to the other two approaches, which attempted to accommodate change in one way or another, Continental European welfare states, by and large, continued to actively subsidize a male breadwinner/female carer family (Sigle-Rushton and Kenney, 2003; Misra and Jude, 2008).

Classifying divergent models

The increasingly divergent logics characterizing these increasingly divergent policy trajectories, and the notions of the family they represented, have been the object of extensive feminist scholarship. Reacting to the gender blindness of mainstream welfare regime scholarship (in particular, the work of Esping-Andersen, 1990), feminist scholars criticized the relatively limited attention accorded to the family and to institutional support for particular gendered divisions of labor within it (for an overview, see Orloff, 2009). Some researchers sought to integrate family and gender issues more explicitly (see, e.g., Lewis, 1992; Orloff, 1993; Lister, 1994). Others have used divergent policy trends to motivate the development of frameworks that summarize cross-national variations in outcomes that are likely to be linked to divergent family policy trends (Sigle-Rushton, 2009). For example, taking the social foundations of variations in the development of direct care services by the welfare state as her point of departure, Pfau-Effinger (2005) devised a framework to describe broad cross-national similarities and differences in the way paid work and care is organized or arranged at the societal level. *The dual-earner/state-carer* arrangement, which characterized the Nordic approach, outsources important parts of care work to the state through institutionalized child and elderly care, while all adults are encouraged and expected to participate in paid labor. In the *modernized male breadwinner* arrangement, found in the United Kingdom and parts of Continental Europe, state support for child and elderly care is relatively underdeveloped, and the presumption seems to be that women's labor market participation will accommodate and be organized around their housework and caring responsibilities. As a consequence, large gender gaps in hours worked or Full-Time Equivalent (FTE) employment rates, both between men and women and between mothers and childless women, are observed. The third arrangement, *the dual earner/family carer*, is also characterized by poorly developed state services and so appears to leave responsibility for care work to families. In contrast to the modernized male breadwinner arrangement, however, gender differences in employment participation and hours worked are narrower. This arrangement has tended to emerge in settings with low levels of social spending combined with high levels of wage inequality (making an economically dependent wife, even if the "ideal," out of reach for many families), such as the United States and

Southern European countries. Although the framework was devised to summarize cross-national variations in gendered time allocations, the two latter models might also coexist in the same country, particularly when economic pressures for welfare state retrenchment are strong and the generosity of state support is reduced. Those families who can afford to live on one income have a greater possibility to choose which model to follow, while families who need two incomes are more limited to the dual-earner/family-carer model.

Pfau-Effinger (2005) classifies countries according to the extent to which they provide institutionalized childcare and promote women's paid work, and it is noteworthy that the framework does not address men's employment patterns or their allocation of time between work and care. To some extent, this is not surprising. It reflects the most salient differences in family policy logics up until the early 1990s, which seemed to take men's full-time employment and their unavailability for care work as given. Looking cross-nationally, the most relevant fault lines concerned whether and how much the employment of women (or more precisely mothers) should be encouraged and how much the work of the housewife could and should be provided outside of the family and the private sphere. Although in recent years, European trends have been more in the direction of convergence toward a modified, modernized male breadwinner arrangement with strong emphasis on some level of labor market participation of all adults, and there has been some discussion of whether and to what extent policies should incentivize a redistribution of some portion of men's time from paid work to care, the level and generosity of state care services continues to shape, reinforce, and differentiate the (classed and) gendered allocations of paid work and care in advanced welfare states in important ways.

New policy logics and emerging challenges

The effectiveness of policies which presume and support the male breadwinner/ female carer model to provide income security is conditioned upon children being born within marriage (or some other formally recognized union), union stability, as well as male employment security. Similarly, the new policy logics that characterize the family policy regimes that began to emerge since the 1970s presume and rely on certain ambient conditions in order to achieve their intended effects. When those conditions change, the logic of the approach is contradicted, and there is likely to be pressure for policy approaches to adapt to and accommodate change.

Similarly to the male breadwinner/female carer model, the modernized male breadwinner model still presupposes that women will be financially dependent on men and thus relies on men's ability to specialize in paid employment and on the stability of marriage (or some other formally recognized union) – a risky strategy for women since neither can be taken for granted (Sigle-Rushton, 2010). The dual-earner/family-carer model relies on high rates of employment for both women and men, and also on the possibility to organize care work without the help of the state. Grandparent care was common as rates of female labor market participation increased, but its availability is likely to be reduced as grandmothers increasingly participate in the labor market themselves, and the age of retirement is increased in many countries (Sigle-Rushton and Kenney, 2003). Relying on the formal or informal market for care provision is another solution, where countries with greater wage dispersion on the formal labor market, and less strict employment regulation, such as the United States, offer greater possibilities for purchasing care on the formal market. In many European countries, families have, in recent years, turned to the informal market, and similarly to the United States, migrants have supplied a low-cost supply of care workers (Hochschild, 2000; Parreñas, 2001; Lutz, 2002; Ungerson, 2004; Bettio *et al.*, 2006; Simonazzi, 2009). The dual-earner/state-carer model, finally, depends heavily both on the employment security for women and men and on the state providing extensive childcare services available to all and of satisfactory quality; if the middle class starts choosing other ways of organizing their childcare, political support for public financing is likely to decline, effectively compromising the system (cf. Korpi and Palme, 1998).

The coherence and effectiveness of any particular arrangement will likely change as a consequence of changing surrounding institutions, just as in the case of the male breadwinner/female carer model, potentially leading to missed policy goals and/or unwanted side effects such as decreasing birthrates or the undermining of the public care sector. Changes in surrounding institutions, moreover, can work to reinforce or undermine policy efforts. Limited possibilities for productivity gains in the labor-intensive care sector (sometimes referred to as the "cost disease"; see Donath, 2000; Himmelweit, 2007) that all advanced welfare states have had to grapple with as economies globalized, fertility declined, and the relative size of the working-age population stabilized and began to fall pose particular problems for the dual-earner/state-carer arrangement. A failure to increase productivity in line with more capital-intensive sectors means that the cost of care services relative to other types of goods increases, an outcome which, at face value, can be interpreted as a failure on the part of the welfare state. However, attempts to increase productivity will likely result in reduced quality (Himmelweit, 2007), which also risks undermining support for the system. Family dissolution and long spells of single motherhood, on the other hand, pose particular problems for the modernized male breadwinner arrangement. In the absence of a male breadwinner's income, the costs will be especially high either fiscally (in terms of providing income support) and/or socially (in terms of unacceptably high child poverty risks). A different challenge is labor market flexibilization and the greater difficulties for especially young adults to acquire permanent employment and the economic security needed to set up independent households and form families (Blossfeld *et al.*, 2005). Especially in Southern Europe, the lack of employment security for young adults seems to prolong transitions to adulthood and to depress birthrates (Bernardi and Nazio, 2005; Mills *et al.*, 2005; Esping-Andersen, 2007).

Family policy and labor market structure

Although Pfau-Effinger's (2005) framework distinguishes different levels of state involvement in the provision of care, and this is clearly a key policy variable, the framework does not explicitly incorporate either differences in the distribution of care work that is not provided by the state or differences in the structure and organization of the labor market. As a consequence, countries which Pfau-Effinger classified as having the same arrangement are somewhat heterogeneous in how they organize care. For example, where care work is not taken on as a state responsibility, in some countries, families tend to purchase care on the market, while in others, there is a stronger reliance on informal care arrangements. So although each of the arrangements suggests particular behavioral and material consequences for families with children, and particular policy challenges in the face of change, the broader social and economic context is also important for understanding their relationship with patterns of gender inequality and social stratification in any particular setting.

Using the concept of *care regimes* (Bettio and Plantenga, 2004), which more explicitly address the division of care labor between the family, the state, and the market, Bettio *et al.* (2006) and Simonazzi (2009) illustrate important variations in terms of both the female labor market participation and the creation of formal and informal markets for care work. Their work demonstrates how the structure of the labor market makes certain ways of organizing care work more feasible than others (Donath, 2000; Morgan, 2005). This is an important observation because it suggests that responses to similar (or even the same) policies (or lack of policies) may well differ both within and across welfare states. For example, high levels of wage inequality allow more people to purchase care on the market, potentially facilitating women's labor market participation at both the higher (as purchasers) and lower ends (by providing job opportunities) of the pay scale. At the same time, such a structure requires greater intragender inequality and, as a consequence, greater socioeconomic inequality. Poor women are most likely to take the caring jobs with the lowest pay. Such care chains will furthermore inevitably leave some children or elderly at the end of the chain without adequate care (Hochschild, 2000; Parreñas, 2001). A more compressed wage composition, on the other hand, means the cost of purchasing care will be expensive relative to women's earnings. The state must step in to provide care, or women will be forced to stay out of paid work and specialize in unpaid care work – thereby entrenching gender inequality at all socioeconomic levels.

In order for women (and men) to be able to combine earning and parenthood (or other care responsibilities), it must therefore be affordable to outsource care in some way, meaning that it must be possible to combine work and care and it must "pay to work." The literature offering a gendered analysis of the theory of varieties of capitalism (Hall and Soskice, 2001) argues that generous family policy can make work pay less for women in general by turning mothers into less reliable workers and, as a consequence, encouraging structural discrimination of all women (Mandel and Shalev, 2009; Mandel, 2010; see also Estevez-Abe, 2009; Folbre, 2009 and Rubery, 2009). The argument is that generous maternity leave tends to be a feature of more generous welfare states, which in turn typically coincide with what is labeled Coordinated Market Economies (CMEs). CMEs, typically found in Continental Europe, are characterized by labor markets based on workers with specialized skills, strong employment protection, and each employee being an important investment for the employer. These economies offer stronger protection for workers than Liberal Market Economies (LMEs) – such as the United States and the United Kingdom – which are characterized by workers with general, transferrable skills, low employment protection, greater wage dispersion, and high labor market mobility. Companies in CMEs are assumed to search for highly committed workers and therefore to be reluctant to employ women if they are likely to take long maternity leaves or to lack commitment to the organization. This suggests that the kind of jobs women, and different groups of women, are able to take – and what conditions those jobs come with – depends to a great extent on how care work is organized, the labor market, and the welfare system.

By considering the labor market structure and family policy as part of a wider system, it becomes clear that the gendered and classed outcomes can vary substantially across countries that are classified, according to Pfau-Effinger's (2005) framework, as having the same earning and caring arrangement. The modernized male breadwinner model relies on the possibility for a family to live on one income, and therefore on high wage levels and/or social transfers subsidizing that type of arrangement. In an LME, such a model is likely to coexist with the dual-earner/family-carer model, given that greater wage dispersion will make it difficult for those at the lower end of the scale to live on one income. A typical CME is more likely to actively subsidize the modernized male breadwinner arrangement, as Germany did until fairly recently, making it affordable for a greater share of the population. The dual-earner/family-carer model combined with greater wage dispersion and low employment protection likely results in market-based care where quality is a function of purchasing power – creating socioeconomic inequality but reducing gender inequality in employment outcomes, at least for the groups able to pay for decent care. Where compressed or low wage levels and employment regulation make it difficult to purchase care on the market, as is more likely to be the case in a CME, low levels of state provision force most families to rely on grandparent care or to search for other informal care solutions.

The dual-earner/state-carer model, finally, would be hard to combine with an LME, given that it requires a strong, interventionist state and substantial tax revenues. This model facilitates women's labor market participation, as can be seen in the Nordic countries, and has been argued to compensate for any tendency toward greater structural discrimination of women in CMEs (Englund, Ferrarini, and Korpi, 2010). It reduces socioeconomic inequality in the Nordic countries by offering the same affordable high-quality childcare for all and freeing all adults for participation on a labor market with relatively compressed wages, and consequently, women are able to achieve some level of economic independence from men. Nonetheless, women still tend to work part time (long part time at around 30 hours per week, but still less than men), and consistent with some of the predictions of the (gendered) varieties of capitalism literature regarding CMEs, they choose public sector jobs (created with the expansion of state services) with slightly lower pay than in the private sector, and in very small numbers are able to reach the highest career positions. Public childcare provision is important, but most care work is still carried out in the family, and it has remained disproportionally the responsibility of women. In a differently structured labor market, however, where in order to carry out the remaining care work, women would have to take insecure, "flexible" jobs, it would be even clearer that this model does not in fact produce a truly equal or equitable gendered division of labor.

Different combinations of labor market regulations, family policy, and state intervention can allow women a *capacity to form and maintain autonomous households* (Orloff, 1993), or their *defamilialization* (Lister, 1994), but with different consequences for different groups of women. It is notable that all models (sometimes implicitly) rely on women to reconcile earning and caring in the end, albeit in different ways, while men's lives are assumed to remain largely focused on paid employment. When this is the case, gender equality is implicitly understood as the extent to which the lives of women can come to resemble those of men. The achievement of greater gender equality in paid employment may therefore come with a crisis of care (Hochschild, 1995).

Female Employment and Birthrates: Converging Goals, Diverging Outcomes?

In more recent years, a common objective in both the United States and European policies has been the labor market activation of (in the case of the United States, mostly poor) women and mothers – irrespective of caring responsibilities – by using carrots, sticks, or both. An important difference between the United States and Europe, however, is that European countries have been more preoccupied with below-replacement-level birthrates (with perhaps the exception of the United Kingdom; see Sigle-Rushton, 2008). In Southern, Central, and Eastern Europe, in particular, we find patterns of lowest-low fertility (defined as a total fertility rate of 1.5 or lower (Billari and Kohler, 2004)). Although all European countries have below-replacement-level birthrates, single-child families have become increasingly common, and in Southern Europe in particular, this coincides with low rates of female labor force participation – the worst of both worlds when viewed through the lens of demographic challenges to long-term welfare state sustainability. This is because low fertility and a shrinking tax base may exacerbate trends toward higher dependency ratios and the fiscal challenges to welfare state budgets that accompany them. In the next few decades, aging populations mean that most advanced welfare states will experience increasing demand for, and a reduced tax base available to fund, welfare state programs. This is one of the most important explanations for the recent trends in family policy logics at the EU level.

Since the early to mid-1990s, family policy logics in advanced welfare states, European nations in particular, have again become more similar. Rather than provide support for a dependent spouse and caregiver, family policies have developed, which attempt to encourage and facilitate mothers' paid employment without obstructing the realization of their fertility ambitions. Rather than simply providing financial compensation for the costs of raising families, policy documents began to emphasize the need to address issues of parents' (often mothers') work–family reconciliation by providing job-protected time to care and childcare services, both of which are aimed at maximizing labor market participation rates (but not, as a general rule, at achieving gender parity in FTE rates). There is some consensus that meeting the challenges that accompany Europe's changing demographic profile and its aging population requires policies that support both higher birthrates and female labor market participation – to the extent that the potential for men to fill care gaps has come onto the policy agenda. The EU has played an important role in these developments by setting out common social policy goals that countries are encouraged to promote. Of course, the outcome for gender as well as socioeconomic equality will depend on how any new policy approaches interact with the social and economic setting, previous policy logics, and deep-seated norms and values, as well as with the surrounding institutional setting such as the labor market structure and the family.

Although at the level of rhetoric, the previously rather distinct models of gender arrangements found in the policy documents and (to a slightly lesser extent) policy packages (Ferragina *et al.*, 2013) of European countries appear increasingly blurred, most academic scholarship has continued to emphasize cross-national variations, often with reference to the policy logics that were adopted in earlier decades. There has been relatively less interest in documenting and explaining trends toward policy convergence, even those which involve substantial deviations from what expectations of path dependency would lead us to predict. In the following sections, we consider some of the most prominent trends toward convergence of policy logics and policy instruments, taking into account cross-national variations in approaches and likely outcomes.

Convergence in approaches to work–family reconciliation

Recent innovations in work–family reconciliation policies in EU countries have often been in the direction of convergence. Continental European countries, Germany in particular, have developed policies that moved in a Nordic direction, albeit in different ways, while Sweden has moved toward a more continental model. France was a forerunner in the development of policies that provide families with financial support for the costs of childcare without discriminating between different solutions. In what may be seen as a move toward encouraging female labor market participation over full-time informal childcare, France is now moving toward Nordic-style public childcare offering guaranteed institutionalized childcare from a young age (Morel, 2007; Lewis *et al.*, 2008). In contrast, Germany, having relied heavily on the male breadwinner/female carer family for work–family reconciliation, has only just recently begun to reconsider the link between their historically strong institutional support for the male breadwinner/female carer division of labor and their low fertility rates (Streeck, 2009). Evidence suggests that the low German birthrate is driven by a clear divide between women who focus on paid work and have very low fertility and the (declining number of) women who forego paid work in order to specialize in childcare (Cooke, 2004). In response, a Nordic-style income-related parental leave insurance was recently implemented, with the hope of increasing fertility among middle-class women (Lewis *et al.*, 2008; Streeck, 2009).

Sweden has a long tradition of promoting a dual-earner/state-carer model based on publicly subsidized and organized childcare combined with income-related parental leave. Recent reforms have, however, offered more ambiguous incentives framed as increasing parental choice in the organization of childcare and include a benefit paid to parents of children under three who are not enrolled in publicly financed childcare (Tunberger and Sigle-Rushton, 2011). The "cash-for-care" policy, which has been adopted by other Nordic countries as well, has been criticized as a "women's trap," especially for groups of women already poorly integrated into the labor market (Nyberg, 2010). But it has also been framed as a way of providing parents, and especially mothers, with a wider set of options, particularly in combination with an also recently implemented tax deduction for domestic services that can also be used to pay for home-based childcare. Even though institutional support for the dual earner/state carer remains strong at all income levels, the result may be a greater diversification of childcare arrangements according to socio-economic status, the long-term consequences of which might mean a decline of political support for publicly financed childcare (if the wealthy increasingly opt out) and/or increasing social gradients in children's developmental outcomes (if poorer women decide to look after their children at home and their children are denied the pedagogic stimulation of high-quality care) (Tunberger and Sigle-Rushton, 2011). In any case, these developments represent rather dramatic deviations from path dependency and toward a middle ground, one which supports a wider range of choices about how families organize their lives.

While this policy convergence indicates a wish to facilitate both women's choice to enter the labor market, but still maintaining (or creating) a feasible choice to provide full-time care, whether there is a real choice will also depend on the structure of the labor market. Swedish wages do not normally allow families to live on one income, and the cash-for-care scheme is not generous enough to change that (Tunberger and Sigle-Rushton, 2011). The compressed wages furthermore make the possibility to purchase care on the private market difficult for all but high-income families. In countries such as Germany, where large groups of women have remained outside the labor market, the question is whether it pays for mothers to work once childcare costs and the remaining subsidies for single-earner families are considered – that is, whether mothers can find good enough jobs, especially when part-time work is desired, or whether these remain reserved for men and childless women (cf. Cooke, 2004, Sigle-Rushton and Waldfogel, 2007). Poor employment options may keep mothers who can afford to stay at home out of the labor market, and women who cannot afford to do so might instead choose to forego motherhood – which would further reduce birthrates. The ability to exercise choice is likely to be constrained by the socioeconomic context and labor market structure in important ways, and similar policies may well result in dissimilar outcomes. It is clear that different ways of balancing and distributing earning and caring, actively or passively, will have varying consequences for both socioeconomic and gender equality. But these cannot be understood without reference to the wider social and economic context. Examining policies, or even policy packages, in isolation could well be misleading.

Making men care: Converging goal, diverging outcomes?

The division of labor remains gendered all over Europe as well as the United States, but different arrangements of paid work and care shape women's economic independence by conditioning the quantity and quality of women's paid work relative to that of men. As policymakers have sought to address these issues, the behavior of men was rarely deemed problematic. Recognizing that this might be an important oversight, political philosopher Nancy Fraser (1994) proposed a model called the Universal Caregiver model, in which society would be organized around an individual resembling today's woman – that is, one with both earning and caring responsibilities. The rhetoric of the Nordic countries and the EU comes closest to embracing this vision and aspiration, and there have been some modest efforts to develop policies to support and effect this sort of change, at least among fathers of young children.

While the US welfare state provides limited care services, effectively leaving it to women and the market (where other women make up the care labor), male caregiving is, to some extent, being encouraged at the EU level, possibly due to increasing evidence that it could help raise both the low European fertility rates and female labor market participation (Sigle-Rushton, Goisis, and Keizer, 2013). Indeed, a growing body of evidence, across a wide range of European countries, demonstrates that fathers' share of care of the first child is positively associated with the likelihood of having a second child (Cooke, 2004, 2008; Duvander and Andersson, 2005; Esping-Andersen, 2007; and Duvander *et al*, 2010). The authors of these studies argue that an increase in fathers' involvement in childcare works to reduce women's opportunity costs of having children, facilitating their work–family reconciliation and thereby making them more inclined to have larger families. Increasing fathers' involvement in childcare has been identified as a means of helping to increase fertility rates and women's paid work; so European men are to an (albeit very limited) extent being asked to assume more responsibility, for childcare.

The most important EU intervention to encourage fathers' caregiving was the 1996 parental leave Directive (96/34/EC), obliging all EU member states to create an individual right to leave for each parent for a minimum period of time that has recently been extended from 3 to 4 months, and 1 month has been made nontransferrable between the parents. As with all EU Directives, the legislation sets out a minimum level of requirements, but many aspects of the policy design, including the conditions of the leave, are left to each member state to decide as they transpose the directive into new or amended national law. This has resulted in a diversity of arrangements when it comes to both the flexibility of the leave and whether, and to what extent, it is paid. Sweden exemplifies a more generous parental leave consisting of 480 days out of which 390 days are paid at 80% of previous income up to a ceiling and the rest is paid at a flat statutory rate. Two months are reserved for each parent, and an equality bonus that increases the more equally the parental leave is allocated is meant to make up for the oft-cited economic loss related to fathers taking leave and encourage parents to share the leave (Nyberg, 2010; Tunberger and Sigle-Rushton, 2011). As we might expect from an LME, the United Kingdom exemplifies a minimal application of the directive, but there are nonetheless some signs of convergence toward a more European approach. Despite vehement opposition to efforts to introduce parental leave legislation at the EU level in the 1980s, the United Kingdom has, since the early 1990s, increasingly extended the length of both paid and unpaid maternity leave entitlements, while the United States continues to offer no statutory maternity leave at all. In contrast to other EU countries which have extended parental leaves, the United Kingdom has taken a more gendered approach and has one of the longest maternity leaves in the EU, while the gender-neutral parental leave entitlements remain more limited (Lewis and Campbell, 2007; Sigle-Rushton, Goisis, and Keizer, 2013). Only since 2011 has the United Kingdom provided the option of "additional paternity leave" of up to 26 weeks during the child's first year. However, this conditioned upon the mother "returning" to work and so effectively relies on the mother's eligibility for and her willingness to transfer any "additional maternity leave" to which she was previously entitled to her male partner.

The policy goal of increasing fathers' caregiving is, at least in theory, shared by EU member states, but the policy commitment and the policy instruments used vary substantially. The extent to which policies have effected change in men's behavior also varies to some extent. Despite some progress, Swedish men still only use a small share of the total parental leave entitlement, and outside the Nordic countries, fathers make even less use of their possibilities for leave. A partial explanation may be that even with generous legal entitlement, economic considerations (men tend to be higher earners) and strongly gendered norms both in the workplace and in the family make it difficult for some men to take (a large portion of) leave (Lammi-Tuskola, 2006).

Women's time allocations vary to a much greater degree across countries, however, as depending on the demand for and availability of part-time employment, how much care work is assumed to be provided by the family in different contexts, and depending on how easy it is to outsource that care work to the market or other family members, the fact that men provide so little care work will have very different consequences for women and their ability to enter the paid labor market.

Poor single mothers: From caring to earning

As part of the policy goal of increasing female labor market participation, countries that have traditionally offered social transfers to poor single mothers in order to allow them to specialize in full-time caring, including the United Kingdom, the United States, and the Netherlands, are reforming policy to instead make them enter paid employment. In the United States, the 1996 TANF reform made the eligibility requirements for social benefits (or "welfare") stricter, pushing many poor single mothers into work (Martin and Caminada, 2011). Although more enabling and less coercive than US approaches (Korteweg, 2006; Gregg, Harkness and Smith 2009), both the Netherlands and the United Kingdom have implemented reforms with the similar aim of moving poor single mothers into paid employment and away from welfare state dependence; the UK Welfare Reform Act 2012 aims to further strengthen work incentives.

The effects of these reforms depend heavily on the kind of wages low-skilled single mothers can earn on the labor market and on the extent to which their wages or working hours constrain their ability to access affordable and good-quality childcare. While LMEs might offer more employment opportunities, the wages offered might be too low to lift families above the poverty line. The United Kingdom, even if usually classified as an LME when it comes to the labor market and welfare state organization, generously subsidizes low-wage earners in various ways, especially when they have dependent children and even when they work part time. This distinguishes the United Kingdom from the United States, where the low-wage labor market largely offers less-than-living wages, making single mothers risk having to take more than one job in order to make ends meet (Ehrenreich, 2001; Korteweg, 2003). At the same time, they have less access than their European counterparts to affordable and high-quality childcare, leading to some level of concern about the consequences the reform might have for the children. In a CME such as the Netherlands, on the other hand, the difficulty might not be so much the wages earned as finding work in the first place, but also challenging ambivalent, if not resistant, attitudes about working mothers (Knijn and van Wel, 2001). Again, therefore, we see that although policy logics and policy goals have been moving in the direction of convergence, the outcome is dependent on wider policy constellations and the socioeconomic context. In the future, some of the most perplexing and important questions about family policy will be less about cross-national variations in policy design (which often implicitly assumed a rather simplistic relationship between policy incentives and behavioral change) and more focused on explaining diverse outcomes in a context of convergence.

Conclusion

Having previously followed different models of organization of earning and caring, encouraging female labor market participation to very different extents, advanced welfare states have more recently started to pursue more similar policy goals of increasing women's, and especially mothers', labor market participation and, in Europe, simultaneously to increase, or at least sustain, birthrates. It is plausible that the convergence of policy goals is linked to the similar economic and demographic challenges facing advanced welfare states and to supranational institutions setting policy targets and providing institutional support for policy sharing. While there is still discernible variation in both goals and instruments across advanced welfare states, and countries across the EU still provide different family policy packages, there is also some evidence of increasing convergence.

In the past couple of decades, efforts to classify countries into different regimes or typologies have yielded important insights. The point of such efforts is simplification, allowing us to see patterns in the complexity of comparative public policy. We know, of course, that reality is more complex; countries belonging to the same regime are not identical and will not necessarily respond in the same manner to similar policy instruments. Surrounding institutional settings make up differing contexts within which policy is supposed to move us to "how we would like things to be." Differences between countries following different models will likely be greater still. When classifications of countries integrate or are combined with analyses of how different models interact with related institutions, the usefulness of this analytical tool becomes evident. What we have seen in this chapter is that even if policy goals are similar, and in fact even when policy instruments are similar, outcomes may very well differ. Previous policy logics will be "sticky" to some extent, having created a society where the family is assumed to operate in a certain way, where men and women are supposed to take on certain roles, where earning and caring are assumed to be organized in a certain manner. Surrounding institutions, such as the labor market and the family, will have evolved in ways that inform and are informed by previous gender settlements and so shape the impact of subsequent policy innovations in important and complex ways. This underscores the need to examine family policies or policy packages not in isolation but as part of a wider policy constellation, which is modified by the wider social and economic context.

The outcome of the policy efforts to increase female labor market participation across the United States and Europe, and of work–family reconciliation across the EU, is therefore likely to vary in terms of gender equality but also of socioeconomic equality. While some systems are good at offering relatively equal living conditions among women, this has come at the price of very few women reaching the highest positions. Other countries seem better able to create gender equality among high earners – but at the price of greater inequality among women. This raises questions about whether economic equality among women is incompatible with economic equality between men and women: whether gender equality is incompatible with socioeconomic equality. One way or another, some form of gendered inequality seems unavoidable (cf. Rubery, 2009).

So how best to promote both gender equality and socioeconomic equality? Hakim (1995) argues that Nordic women have no choice but to work for pay, which might seem to explain the prevalence of the "choice" to combine paid work with mothering. What Hakim does not explain, however, is why Nordic women do not seem willing to forego children for their careers; pronatalist policies or not, it is arguably a free choice to have children. The relatively low fertility rates of the highly educated women in countries like the United Kingdom (Sigle-Rushton, 2008) or Germany also raise questions about whether systems that allow women to compete on men's terms, and climb the career ladder to the same extent, are in fact characterized by gender equality among high earners or simply by some women choosing to live as men – that is, without caring responsibilities. Is a model in which men are able to combine top careers with family life while women often enough have to choose one that has really delivered gender equality? Where wage dispersion is greater, as in the United States, it is easier for high-income women to purchase full-time childcare and in that way live lives similar to men, but in other contexts, such a solution might not be economically feasible, and, in any case, the gender equality offered high-income women might not have much to offer other women. Moreover, the incompatibility of caring responsibilities with high-status labor market positions remains unresolved in such a model, with gender equality being equated to women being able to live like men simply underscoring the higher status awarded by society to a "male" lifestyle compared to a "female" one. The conclusion must be that there is no clear answer as to what model is best for women, or for promoting gender equality in families; women cannot be seen as a homogeneous group when discussing gendered consequences of public policy. Instead, different groups of women gain from different policy instruments, with consequences at both the individual and the societal levels.

References

Bernardi, F. and Nazio, T. (2005) Globalization and the transition to adulthood in Italy, in *Globalization, Uncertainty and Youth in Society* (eds H.P. Blossfeld, E. Klijzing, M. Mills, and K. Kurz), Routledge, London, pp. 359–383.

Bettio, F. and Plantenga, J. (2004) Comparing care regimes in europe. *Feminist Economics*, 10, 85–113.

Bettio, F., Simonazzi, A. and Villa, P. (2006) Change in care regimes and female migration: the 'care drain' in the Mediterranean. *Journal of European Social Policy*, 16, 271–285.

Billari, F.P. and Kohler, H.-P. (2004) Patterns of low and lowest-low fertility in Europe. *Population Studies*, 58, 161–176.

Blossfeld, H.-P., Klijzing, E., Mills, M. and Kurz, K. (eds) (2005) *Globalization, Uncertainty and Youth in Society*, Routledge, London.

Castles, S. (2006) Guestworkers in Europe: a resurrection? *International Migration Review*, 40, 741–766.

Cooke, L.P. (2004) The gendered division of labor and family outcomes in Germany. *Journal of Marriage and Family*, 66, 1246–1259.

Cooke, L.P. (2008) Gender equity and fertility in Italy and Spain. *Journal of Social Policy*, 38, 123–140.

Donath, S. (2000) The other economy: a suggestion for a distinctively feminist economics. *Feminist Economics*, 6, 115–123.

Duvander, A.-Z. and Andersson, G. (2005) Gender equality and fertility in Sweden: a study on the impact of the father's uptake of parental leave on continued childbearing. Working paper 2005-2013. Max Planck Institute for Demographic Research.

Duvander, A.-Z., Lappegård, T. and Andersson, G. (2010) Family policy and fertility: fathers' and mothers' use of parental leave and continued childbearing in Norway and Sweden. *Journal of European Social Policy*, 20, 45–57.

Ehrenreich, B. (2001) *Nickle and Dimed: On (Not) Getting by in America*, Metropolitan Books/Henry Holt and Company, New York.

Englund, S., Ferrarini, T. and Korpi, W. (2010) Women's opportunities under different constellations of family policies in western countries: inequality tradeoffs re-examined. LIS working paper series: 556. Swedish Institute for Social Research (Stockholm University).

Esping-Andersen, G. (1990) *The Three Worlds of Welfare Capitalism*, Princeton University Press, Princeton.

Esping-Andersen, G. (ed) (2007) *Family Formation and Family Dilemmas in Contemporary Europe*, Fundacion BBVA, Bilbao.

Estevez-Abe, M. (2009) Gender, inequality and capitalism: the 'varieties of capitalism' and women. *Social Politics*, 16, 182–191.

Ferragina, E., Seeleib-Kaiser, M. and Tomlinson, M. (2013) Unemployment protection and family policy at the turn of the 21st century: a dynamic approach to welfare regime theory. *EJPR*, 47 (7), 783–805.

Folbre, N. (2009) Varieties of patriarchal capitalism. *Social Politics*, 16, 204–209.

Fraser, N. (1994) After the family wage: gender equity and the welfare state. *Political Theory*, 22, 591–618.

Gregg, P., Harkness, S. and Smith, S. (2009) Welfare reform and lone parents in the UK. *The Economic Journal*, 119, F38–F65.

Hakim, C. (1995) Five feminist myths about women's employment. *British Journal of Sociology*, 46, 429–455.

Hall, P. and Soskice, D. (2001) *Varieties of Capitalism: The Institutional Foundations of Comparative Advantage*. Oxford University Press, Oxford.

Heidenreich, M. and Bischoff, G. (2008) The open method of co-ordination: a way to the europeanization of social and employment policies? *JCMS: Journal of Common Market Studies*, 46, 497–532.

Himmelweit, S. (2007) The prospects for caring: economic theory and policy analysis. *Cambridge Journal of Economics*, 31, 581–599.

Hochschild, A.R. (1995) The culture of politics: traditional, postmodern, cold-modern, and warm-modern ideals of care. *Social Politics*, 2, 331–345.

Hochschild, A.R. (2000) Global care chains and emotional surplus value, in *On the Edge: Living with Global Capitalisation* (eds W. Hutton and A. Giddens), Sage Publishers, London, pp. 130–146.

Jenson, J. and Kantrow, R. (1990) Labor market and family policy in france: an intersecting complex for dealing with poverty, in *The Feminization of Poverty: Only in America?* (eds G.S. Goldberg and E. Kremen), Greenwood Press, New York, pp. 107–155.

Jenson, J. (2009) Lost in translation: the social investment perspective and gender equality. *Social Politics*, 16, 446–483.

Knijn, T. and van Wel, F. (2001) Careful or lenient: welfare reform for lone mothers in the Netherlands. *Journal of European Social Policy*, 11, 235–252.

Korpi, W. and Palme, J. (1998) The paradox of redistribution and strategies of equality: welfare state institutions, inequality and poverty in the Western Countries. *American Sociological Review*, 63, 661–687.

Korteweg, A.C. (2003) Welfare reform and the subject of the working mother: 'get a job, a better job, then a career'. *Theory and Society*, 32, 445–480.

Korteweg, A.C. (2006) The construction of gendered citizenship at the welfare office: an ethnographic comparison of welfare-to-work workshops in the United States and the Netherlands. *Social Politics*, 13, 313–340.

Lammi-Tuskola, J. (2006) Nordic men on parental leave: can the welfare state change gender relations? in *Politicising Parenthood in Scandinavia: Gender Relations in Welfare States* (eds A.L. Ellingsaeter and A. Leira), The Policy Press, Bristol, pp. 79–100.

Lewis, J. (1992) Gender and the development of welfare regimes. *Journal of European Social Policy*, 2, 159–173.

Lewis, J. and Campbell, M. (2007) Work/family balance policies in the UK since 1997. *Journal of Social Policy*, 36, 365–381.

Lewis, J., Knijn, T, Martin, C. and Ostner, I. (2008) Patterns of development in work/family reconciliation policies for parents in France, German, the Netherlands, and the UK in the 2000's. *Social Politics*, 15, 261–286.

Lister, R. (1994) She has other duties' – women, citizenship and social security, in *Social Security and Social Change: New Challenges to the Beveridge Model* (eds S. Baldwin and J. Falkingham), Harvester/Wheatsheaf, New York, pp. 31–44.

Lutz, H. (2002) At your service madam!: The globalisation of domestic service. *Feminist Review*, 70, 89–104.

Mandel, H. (2010) Winners and losers: the consequences of welfare state policies for gender wage inequality. *European Sociological Review*, 28, 241–262.

Mandel, H. and Shalev, M. (2009) Gender, class and varieties of capitalism. *Social Politic*, 16, 161–181.

Martin, M.C. and Caminada, K. (2011) Welfare reform in the U.S.: a policy overview analysis. *Poverty & Public Policy*, 3, 1–38.

Mills, M., Blossfeld, H.-P. and Klijzing, E. (2005) Becoming an adult in uncertain times: a 14-country comparison of the losers of globalization, in *Globalization, Uncertainty and Youth in Society* (eds H.-P. Blossfeld, E. Klijzing, M. Mills and K. Kurz), Routledge, London.

Misra, J. and Jude, L. (2008) Do family policies shape women's employment? A comparative historical analysis of France and the Netherlands, in *Method and Substance in Macrocomparative Analysis* (eds L. Kenworthy and A. Hicks), Palgrave Macmillan, Houndmills, pp. 91–134.

Morel, N. (2007) From subsidiarity to 'free choice': child- and elder-care policy reforms in France, Belgium, Germany and the Netherlands. *Social Policy and Administration*, 41, 618–637.

Morgan, K.J. (2005) The 'production' of childcare: how labor markets shape social policy and vice versa. *Social Politics*, 12, 243–263.

Nyberg, A. (2010) Cash-for-childcare schemes in Sweden: history, political contradictions and recent developments, in *Cash-for-Childcare: The Consequences for Caring Mothers* (eds J. Sipilää, K. Repo and T. Rissanen), Edward Elgar, Cheltenham.

O'Connor, J.S., Orloff, A.S. and Shaver, S. (1999) *States, Markets, Families: Gender, Liberalism and Social Policy in Australia, Canada, Great Britain and the United States*, Cambridge University Press, Cambridge.

Orloff, A.S. (1993) Gender and the social rights of citizenship: the comparative analysis of gender relations and welfare states. *American Sociological Review*, 58, 303–328.

Orloff, A.S. (2006) From maternalism to employment for all: state policies to promote women's employment across the affluent democracies, in *The State after Statism* (ed J. Levy), Harvard University Press, Cambridge, MA, pp. 230–268.

Orloff, A.S. (2009) Gendering the comparative analysis of welfare states: an unfinished agenda. *Sociological Theory*, 27, 317–343.

Parreñas, R.S. (2001) *Servants of Globalization: Women, Migration and Domestic Work*, Stanford University Press, Stanford.

Perelli-Harris, B., Sigle-Rushton, W., Kreyenfeld M. *et al.* (2010) The educational gradient of childbearing within cohabitation in Europe. *Population and Development Review*, 36, 775–801.

Perelli-Harris, B., Kreyenfeld, M., Sigle-Rushton, W. *et al.* (2012) Changes in union status during the transition to parenthood in eleven European countries, 1970s to early 2000s. *Population Studies*, 66, 167–182.

Pfau-Effinger, B. (2005) Welfare state policies and the development of care arrangements. *European Societies*, 7, 321–347.

Rosenbluth, F., Light, M. and Schrag, C. (2002) *The Politics of Low Fertility: Global Markets, Women's Employment, and Birth Rates in Four Industrialized Democracies*, Department of Political Science, Yale University, Mimeo.

Rubery, J. (2009) How gendering the varieties of capitalism requires a wider lens. *Social Politics*, 16, 192–203.

Shaver, S. and Bradshaw, J. (1995) The recognition of wifely labour by welfare states. *Social Policy and Administration*, 29, 10–25.

Sigle-Rushton, W. (2008) England and Wales: stable fertility and pronounced social status differences. *Demographic Research*, 19, 459–502.

Sigle-Rushton, W. (2009) Comparative methods in research on gender and welfare states. *21st Century Society*, 4, 137–148.

Sigle-Rushton, W. (2010) Men's unpaid work and divorce: reassessing specialization and trade. *Feminist Economics*, 16, 1–26.

Sigle-Rushton, W. and Kenney, C. (2003) Public policy and families, in *Blackwell Companion to the Sociology of Families* (eds J. Scott, M. Richards and J. Treas), Blackwell, New York.

Sigle-Rushton, W. and Waldfogel, J. (2007) Motherhood and women's earnings in Anglo-American, Continental European, and Nordic countries. *Feminist Economics*, 13, 55–91.

Sigle-Rushton, W., Goisis, A. and Keizer, R. (2013) Fathers and fatherhood in the European Union, in *Handbook of Father Involvement: Multidisciplinary Perspectives* (eds C.S. Tamis-LeMonda and N. Cabrera), Lawrence Erlbaum Associates, Mahwah, pp. 81–96.

Simonazzi, A. (2009) Care regimes and national employment models. *Cambridge Journal of Economics*, 33, 211–232.

Streeck, W. (2009) Flexible employment, flexible families, and the socialization of reproduction. MPIfG working paper 09/13. Max Planck Institute for the Study of Societies.

Tunberger, P. and Sigle-Rushton, W. (2011) Continuity and change in Swedish family policy reforms. *Journal of European Social Policy*, 21, 225–237.

Ungerson, C. (2004) Whose empowerment and independence? A cross-national perspective on 'cash for care' schemes. *Ageing and Society*, 24, 189–212.

24

Family Policy and Wives' Economic Independence

Hadas Mandel

The topic of the welfare state and gender equality has attracted much scholarly attention in recent decades. During this period, researchers have developed typologies, conceptions, and theories linking welfare state activities to gendered outcomes, alongside cross-country comparative databases of policy measures. The literature on the welfare state and gender highlights the effectiveness of welfare state interventions in reconciling the tension between mothers' paid and unpaid work. Thus, the theoretical conceptions, and consequently their measures, tend to focus on work–family reconciliation policies – that is, those policies that help mothers participate in paid work. Most common among them are policies that reflect the state's responsibility to provide mothers with the necessary conditions to care for their infants after birth, in the form of maternity or parental leaves, and to combine work with family responsibilities afterwards, in the form of childcare facilities (Gornick and Meyers, 2003). Because these policies are targeted at benefitting families with children, they are defined in the literature as "family policies." In practice, however, these policies mostly affect the labor market behavior of mothers and rarely, or only indirectly, affect the behavior of fathers (Morgan and Zippel, 2003).

In order to better understand the implications of family policies for gender equality, two important issues, both of which have been insufficiently discussed to date, need to be addressed. The first is the extent to which family policy contributes to the economic gains of women, beyond its effect on their labor market participation rates. This examination is important because the effect of family policy on gender equality may vary substantially for different parameters of equality. In fact, comparative research has shown that family policy may promote certain aspects of gender equality and, at the same time, impede others (see Mandel, 2009; Stier and Mandel, 2009).

A second, and no less important, issue is whether family policy affects all women similarly. To probe this, we must take socioeconomic characteristics into account in

The Wiley Blackwell Companion to the Sociology of Families, First Edition.
Edited by Judith Treas, Jacqueline Scott, and Martin Richards.
© 2014 John Wiley & Sons Ltd. Published 2017 by John Wiley & Sons Ltd.

our discussion of equality between men and women. With the massive entry of women into the workforce over the past three decades, inequality among women has grown rapidly (McCall, 2007). While it is true that all women struggle to negotiate between market demands and domestic work, this conflict takes different forms for women of different classes (Williams and Boushey, 2010). Because of these disparities, generous family policy, which is beneficial for some women, can be very costly for others (Mandel, 2011, 2012).

In this chapter, I shed light on these two neglected issues by considering the cross-country variation in the economic contribution of married (or cohabiting) women to household income (hereinafter, wives' contribution). The first issue is examined by analyzing the effect of family policy on the economic gains of wives, beyond its effect on women's participation rates. I will show that the cross-country variation in wives' contribution is highly related to the cross-country variation in female labor market participation. This is not surprising because a working woman, even if she earns very little, contributes more to her family income than does a non-working woman. Given the effectiveness of family policy in raising women's particip-ation rates (e.g., Gornick, Meyers, and Ross, 1997; Korpi, 2000; Van der Lippe and Van Dijk, 2002), the cross-country variation in wives' contribution is expected to be positively related to the cross-country variation in family policy. However, the effect of family policy on the economic resources of women who already work is more complicated. Family policy will foster the economic contribution of women already in the labor market only to the extent that it increases their occupational and earning attainments – an empirical question that has yet to be clearly answered.

The second issue, which has received even less attention than the first, is whether family policy affects all women similarly. In this chapter, I will argue that the effect of family policy on the economic contribution of educated women is very different from its effect on less educated women. Family policy may enhance wives' contribution in two ways: (i) by raising women's odds of being economically active (labor market participation) and (ii) by increasing women's occupational and earning attainments in the labor market. Both mechanisms are strongly related to socioeconomic character-istics. In the case of the former, developed family policy – such as childcare facilities, and long and subsidized parental leave – is expected to increase the economic contri-bution of low-educated women, but not that of high-educated women. Family policy reduces the reservation wage of mothers, the minimum compensation that makes their participation in paid employment economically profitable. For women with low earning potential, this is critical. In contrast, the biggest incentive for participation in paid employment for high-skilled women is their relatively high earning potential. Thus, family policy is expected to increase the participation rates of low-educated women, and therefore their economic contribution, but not the participation rates of high-educated women, whose labor market attachment and participation are high regardless of state assistance.

As for the latter – increasing women's occupational and earning attainments – the answer, again, depends on education and skill levels. In the case of low-educated women, family policy increases their economic contribution not only by easing their access to paid employment, but also by promoting their work continuity, which increases their labor market rewards. In contrast, to the extent that state assistance fosters employers' reluctance to hire women for, and promote them to, lucrative positions (Albrecht *et al.*, 1999; Mandel and Semyonov, 2006; Mandel, 2009, 2012; Ruhm, 1998), developed family policy is expected to *decrease* the relative economic gains of high-educated women and, thus, to lower their economic contribution to the household income.

Using microdata from the Luxembourg Income Study (LIS) for 21 advanced countries, this study analyzes the relative economic contribution of both low- and high-educated women to household income. The findings for low-educated women met expectations fully: among dual-earner couples with low-educated wives, all indicators of family policy showed that family policy increases wives' contribution, above and beyond its effect on participation rates. In contrast, according to these indicators, family policy had no effect – neither positive nor negative – on the contribution of high-educated women.

The implications of these findings and the extent to which they correspond with previous findings are discussed in the context of welfare state and gender theories, and in the context of men and women's tendency to marry partners who resemble them both culturally and socioeconomically (homogamy). Distinguishing between groups of women, and disentangling the effect of family policy on participation rates from its effect on labor market attainments, elucidates the social mechanisms that underlie how welfare states affect gender equality, in general, and women's economic contribution, in particular.

Theoretical Considerations

Wives' economic contribution to family income

Scholars of the sociology of the family emphasize the importance of women's access to market resources for determining women's position of power within the family and allocation of household tasks (Shelton and John, 1996; Bittman *et al.*, 2003; Breen and Cooke, 2005; Treas and de Ruijter, 2008). Access to independent resources such as income from paid work increases women's power in two important dimensions, referred to as "voice" and "exit" (Hirschman, 1970; Hobson, 1990). First, economic resources allow women to affect family decisions – to have a "voice" within the family about the division of household labor (Brines, 1994; Bianchi *et al.*, 2000; Treas and Tai, 2012). Second, it allows women to exit a relationship that they are not satisfied with (Oppenheimer, 1997). Thus, the extent to which married women are economically independent is an important indication of equality within the family and has important implications for family functioning (see also Bolzendahl and Myers, 2004).

The sharp increase in women's economic activity in recent decades has been the prime promoter of women's rising economic independence (Sorensen and McLanahan, 1987; Van Berkel and De Graaf, 1998). However, whereas access to paid work, and thus to an independent income, is considered the main contributor to women's economic independence, women's occupational and earning achievements in the labor market play a crucial role in determining their *level* of economic independence. While the number of households with wives entirely dependent on their spouses' income has dramatically declined, most women in dual-earner households still earn much less than their spouses, and households in which wives earn more than their husbands are relatively few (Winkler, McBride, and Andrews, 2005).

The economic inferiority of working women relative to their spouses can be attributed to their work patterns and their limited access to high-paying jobs. In many European countries, a substantial portion of working women work part time (Blossfeld and Hakim, 1997). For example, in the Netherlands, a country with high rates of part-time work, the economic dependence of married women is four times higher among part-time workers than among full-time workers (Van Berkel and De Graaf, 1998). Yet women who work full time still earn less than men (Persson and Jonung, 1998). In the United States, Sorensen and McLanahan (1987) found that only half of married women's economic dependence on their husbands is the fault of low work hours. Rather, working women contribute less to household income mainly because they receive lower returns for their work hours (see also Winkler, McBride, and Andrews, 2005). Thus, while the increase in women's labor force participation rates has significantly contributed to lowering women's economic dependence over time, considerable inequality within families remains due to women's limited access to highly paid positions and limited work hours.

The effect of family policy on wives' economic contribution to family income

How can family policy affect the relative contribution of wives to their households? The comparative empirical research on family policy and gender inequality has tended to deal with the implications of family policy from a particular viewpoint: because generous family policy aims to reconcile the inherent tension between paid and unpaid work, its success is usually measured by the extent to which it supports the employment of mothers. Thus, the traditional criterion for assessing the effect of family policy on gender equality is women's participation in the labor market, because women's participation in paid employment is thought to promote their economic independence within the family, either by reducing the unequal division of labor between spouses in dual-earner households or by helping single women establish an independent household (Breen and Cooke, 2005; O'Connor, 1996; Orloff, 1993). Thus, countries with high participation rates of women, especially mothers, are usually considered the most egalitarian.

The correspondence between women's participation rates and economic independence leads to the conclusion that every policy that directly or indirectly increases women's labor force participation will reduce wives' economic dependence. However, while almost every employment-supportive policy, by definition, reduces economic dependence, such policies do not necessarily foster gender equality within the family (Stier and Mandel, 2009). In fact, some of these policies may enhance women's economic dependence by harming the economic achievements of working mothers.

The prevailing indicators of family policy in comparative analyses are parental leave and subsidized childcare (Gornick, Meyers, and Ross, 1997; Gornick and Meyers, 2003), but their expected effects on women's attainments are not identical. The effect of paid maternity leave on women's market achievements is complicated. On the one hand, maternity leave may enhance women's pay by increasing women's attachment to the labor market. That is, paid maternity leave can help mothers maintain employment with the same employer, and, as a result, promote their job continuity. Paid maternity leave also encourages mothers to return to the labor force earlier and protects them against the loss of labor market skills (Waldfogel, 1998; Sigle-Rushton and Waldfogel, 2007). On the other hand, extended maternity leave encourages women to withdraw from paid employment and, consequently, reduces their work experience, erodes their labor market skills (Edin and Gustavsson, 2008), and aggravates employers' discrimination against women (Ruhm, 1998; Albrecht *et al.*, 1999; Mandel and Semyonov, 2005, 2006).

In their discussion of parental leave policies, Gornick and Meyers (2003) claim that as long as parental leave continues to be used almost exclusively by women, it will weaken women's labor force attachment and thus exacerbate gender inequality. Similarly, Mandel and Semyonov argue that "adjusting the demands of employment to women's home duties or allowing working mothers reduced working hours and long leaves from work, are likely to preserve women's dominant roles as mothers and wives" (2006, p. 1911). Women's tendencies "to take parental leave are likely to restrict their opportunities for occupational mobility as they foster employers' reluctance to hire women and to promote them" (pp. 1914–1915).

Subsidized childcare, however, has the potential to advance economic gender equality. Childcare facilities can improve women's economic resources by enabling mothers of young children to participate in paid work and by allowing working women to allocate more of their time and effort to paid employment. In contrast to parental leave, there are no theoretical reasons to expect unfavorable consequences from subsidized childcare. Nevertheless, although the effect of childcare on women's economic independence via increased participation rates is obvious, it is not clear to what extent childcare facilities contribute to the earnings of mothers who already work. Rather than support gender equality, childcare facilities aim to socialize, educate, and nurture preschool children (Morgan, 2005). As a result, they are not designed to match women's work hours, especially not those of career-oriented women.

The effect of family policy on wives' contribution among different groups of women: Argument and expectations

The literature reviewed thus far leads to the expectation that the implications of family policy, in general, and maternity leave and public childcare, in particular, for the economic dependence of wives are twofold: as an employment-supportive policy, family policy reduces economic dependence by definition, because it promotes mothers' access to a paycheck. However, the implications of family policy above and beyond its effect on participation rates are not entirely clear. Theoretically, both parental leave and subsidized childcare have the potential to decrease working women's economic dependence by supporting women's work continuity, labor market attachment, and, consequently, occupational and earning attainments. However, as noted earlier, the positive implications of parental leave on women's labor market attainments are doubtful. In the case of childcare, the positive implications depend on the extent to which those facilities match the regular employment hours of women.

The key argument developed in this chapter is that the effects of both mechanisms are strongly related to women's education and skill levels. Both maternity leave and subsidized childcare are not expected to influence the economic contribution of women from different class positions uniformly. Women with low labor market attachment – usually women with low education and low labor market skills – are more likely to be influenced by family policy. In fact, family policy is often a critical factor in determining their labor market participation (Hakim, 2002). Paid maternity leave enables low-skilled women to return to the same employers, which, in turn, increases their labor market continuity. Furthermore, even after taking extended maternity leaves, low-educated women are less exposed to employers' discrimination in hiring (Mandel, 2012): being less skilled, they are candidates for positions that require relatively short (and less expensive) training periods.

The availability of subsidized childcare is also crucial in the decisions of low-educated women to participate in paid employment. Because low-skilled women have low earning potential, expensive childcare makes their paid work economically unprofitable. Therefore, although public childcare reduces the costs of maternal employment for all women, the marginal profit for low-skilled women is much higher. Moreover, subsidized childcare is expected to contribute to the labor market continuity of those who already work. Both types of family policy, therefore, appear to increase the economic independence of low-skilled women, and consequently to improve women's relative standing within the family.

Reconciliation policies also have important implications for overall family welfare. Family policy is expected to benefit low-educated women twice: first, by helping them join the labor market and, second, by providing them with better economic rewards within the labor market. By helping mothers to become economically active, and to increase their economic gains, family policy is expected to benefit the economic standing of the entire family, raising total family income and, as a result, family standard of living.

The expected effects of family policy on high-educated women are very different. High-educated women are equipped with higher labor market skills and thus with greater earning potential. Their labor market attachment is high even without state assistance, which makes employment-supportive policies much less relevant for their decisions to participate in the labor market. Family policy, then, can decrease the economic dependence of high-skilled women on their spouses only to the extent that it supports their occupational and earning attainments in the labor market.

However, as noted earlier, parental leave tends to restrict, rather than encourage, the access of high-skilled women to lucrative job positions. Because of the relatively long training periods that attractive jobs require, the cost of a new worker (as a *locum tenens*) in these cases is high in contrast to jobs that require little or no on-the-job training. As the theory of statistical discrimination teaches us, having limited information on new candidates' characteristics and future productivity, employers seeking to fill jobs with high training costs are likely to discriminate against applicants belonging to groups with statistically lower average levels of expected productivity (Aigner and Cain, 1977). Employers, thus, prefer male employees for well-paid jobs, because men are perceived as more stable workers (Estevez-Abe, 2005; Mandel and Semyonov, 2005, 2006). Consequently, although long absenteeism from paid employment may increase discrimination in hiring against all women, advantaged women, the potential candidates for elite positions, suffer most from statistical discrimination. Indeed, Mandel (2012) found that family policy increases the earning gap among advantaged men and women, but not among the disadvantaged. She concluded that the perverse effects of family policy on women's occupational and earning attainments exist only for advantaged workers.

This is not to say that high-educated women, being the primary caregivers in their families, do not benefit from state assistance (Williams and Boushey, 2010). They, however, are less reliant on state assistance and are in a better position to purchase private solutions for the work–family tension (Morgan, 2005; Shalev, 2008). While the marginal effect of subsidized public childcare, for example, is weaker for high-paid women relative to low-paid women, other solutions, such as tax credits for childcare or antidiscrimination legislation, are more advantageous for educated and economically well-off women (O'Connor, Orloff, and Shaver, 1999; Shalev, 2008).

To sum up, the effect of family policy on the economic independence of educated women is very different from its effect on noneducated women. Developed family policy, such as long and subsidized parental leave and childcare facilities, is expected to reduce the dependence of low-educated women, but not that of high-educated women. Family policy reduces mothers' reservation wage, the minimum compensation that makes it economically profitable to participate in paid employment. For low-skilled women with low earning potential, this is critical. In contrast, the biggest incentive for high-skilled women to participate in paid employment is their relatively high earning potential. Furthermore, to the extent that long maternity leave restricts the occupational and earning attainments of high-skilled women, developed family policy is expected to decrease, rather than increase, the relative household economic contribution of high-skilled women.

Data and Measurement

Data for this study were obtained from waves four and five of the LIS (1991–1999). The specific year for each country appears in Table 24.1 (see detailed information on the archive in http://www.lisdatacenter.org). The analyses are based on data for couple-headed households (married or cohabiting), aged 25–60 years, from 21 countries (see list of countries and years in Table 24.1). Data on family policies were collected from various sources and were added to the household-level file.

The dependent variable, a measure for women's economic independence, was based on the relative contribution of wives to household income, as proposed by Stier and Mandel (2009) and described in the following:

$$\text{Economic contribution} = \frac{\text{earn}w}{(\text{earn}h + \text{earn}w)}$$

where earn$w$ is wife's earnings and earn$h$ is husband's earnings. This fraction is multiplied by 100, and consequently the range is from 0 (where 0 indicates that the wife is totally dependent on her husband) to 100 (where 100 indicates that the husband is totally dependent on his wife).

Table 24.1 Women's earning contribution to household income, by education[a]

	All women	High education	Low education	Gap between high and low education
Finland (1991)	40.80	41.90	40.66	1.25
Denmark (1993)	38.98	39.42	38.78	0.64
Hungary (1994)	38.54	44.40	38.24	6.17
Sweden (1995)	38.28	41.15	37.83	3.32
Norway (1995)	36.99	42.67	36.06	6.61
Czech Republic (1996)	34.57	35.21	34.52	0.69
Slovakia (1992)	34.32	38.27	33.92	4.35
Canada (1997)	31.38	36.97	30.39	6.57
United States (1997)	30.45	33.99	29.12	4.87
France (1994)	30.03	35.93	29.61	6.33
United Kingdom (1999)	29.77	36.31	28.47	7.84
Israel (1997)	28.74	33.95	27.27	6.68
Australia (1994)	27.69	35.96	26.44	9.52
Germany (1994)	27.17	33.57	26.77	6.80
Belgium (1997)	26.52	38.37	25.81	12.56
Austria (1997)	23.42	36.28	22.82	13.46
Ireland (1996)	22.83	39.70	20.72	18.99
Italy (1995)	22.29	39.64	21.18	18.46
Spain (1995)	19.83	38.90	15.56	23.33
The Netherlands (1994)	18.08	28.06	16.22	11.84
Luxemburg (1994)	17.25	31.36	16.67	14.69
Average	29.43	37.24	28.43	8.81
SD	7.11	3.89	7.69	6.23
Correlation with the first row		0.63	0.99	−0.84

Source: Data from LIS and Danish Leisure Study (1993).
[a]All microdata files are from the LIS, except the data from Denmark.

Two types of explanatory variables were introduced to the models: household-level and country-level characteristics. The household-level variables are presence of pre-school-aged children in the household (=1); number of children aged 18 or younger in the household; wife's age; age difference between spouses (husband's age minus wife's age); wife's work hours[1]; and couples' relative education. To compute relative education levels within couples, husbands and wives were ranked first on an ordinal scale, according to their country-specific educational categories. The relative education of the couple was then measured using a dummy variable, where a value of 1 indicates that a wife is more educated than her husband, and 0 indicates that she is not.

At the country level, four different indicators of family policy were employed in the analysis. The first two, childcare arrangements and maternity/parental leave, are the most prevalent measurable indicators of family policy and are thus useful for large-scale comparative studies (Gauthier, 1999; Kamerman, 2000; Meyers and Gornick, 2000; Gornick and Meyers, 2003). Childcare arrangements are measured as the percentage of children aged 0 to 3 in day care. In contrast to the percentage of preschool-aged children in day care, day care for infants is more clearly aimed at facilitating women's employment (Korpi, 2000). Parental leave is measured by the number of paid weeks of either maternity or parental leave. Because maternity and parental leaves are both income-related benefits, which are both widely (and almost exclusively) used by mothers, this indicator ensures the best comparability across countries (Morgan and Zippel, 2003). Table 24A.1 displays the values of the two variables for each country.

The other two indicators of family policy are more general: type of welfare state regime and an integrated index of family policy. The incorporation of welfare regimes is based on the assumption that countries classified under the same ideal welfare regime type share similar policy packages, which differ from the policies of countries in other welfare regimes. If, indeed, welfare state policies affect the economic contribution of women, then the similarities and dissimilarities across countries in wives' contribution should relate to welfare regime type (Mandel, 2009). Welfare state regimes are classified on the basis of Esping-Andersen's typology (1990, 1999). The four Scandinavian countries, all of which fall under the heading of the social democratic regime, are characterized by dual-earner strategies that promote gender equality through universal benefits to working mothers, social services, and public employment. The four Anglo-Saxon countries, all classified as having market-oriented liberal regimes, have the least developed family policies, which is typical of welfare state models that rely on private market solutions. All other countries, including the Czech Republic and Slovakia, which are grouped together with the Continental and Mediterranean countries, are considered part of the third group, the conservative welfare states. The conservative welfare states, according to Esping-Andersen, are characterized by their heavy reliance on family for care services.[2]

The integrated index of family policy used here was designed by Mandel and Semyonov (2005, 2006). The index captures the role of the state in mitigating the work–family conflict by means of three components: the number of fully paid weeks of maternity/parental leave, the percentage of preschool-aged children in public childcare institutions, and the size of the public service sector. Each of these components captures a different aspect of family policy. The size of the public service sector indicates the role of the state as a "family-friendly" employer, offering convenient working conditions for mothers (Kolberg, 1991). Parental leave and childcare help women combine paid with unpaid work, as explained at the outset. The index ranges from 0 to 100, where 0 is assigned to the country with the most limited family policy (Switzerland) and 100 to the country with the most generous one (Sweden). Table 24A.1 displays the family policy indicators by country.

The distinction between more and less advantaged women is based on education, a valid proxy for workers' potential and actual earning power. Because education is an indicator of skill and, thus, a key factor in labor market advantage, this type of operationalization enables valid comparisons across countries. Nonetheless, categorizing education is somewhat problematic because education groupings in most LIS data files are not harmonized across countries. In an effort to identify categories that are comparable, this analysis limits itself to two: *low education* (up to and including some postsecondary education) and *high education* (college graduate or higher). The low-educated group is very large and heterogeneous, which may lead to an underestimation, rather than overestimation, of the true effect in this group.[3]

Analytical Strategy

To estimate the net effect of family policy on women's earning contribution to the household, I use multilevel modeling, where the dependent variable is wife's earning contribution and both household-level and country-level variables serve as independent variables (Bryk and Raudenbush, 1992). The household-level variables were introduced to control for cross-country variation in the composition of these covariates, so that the net effect of policies on the relative standing of women within their households could be estimated.

At the country level, the dependent variable is the net average level of a wife's earning contribution, and its variation across countries is modeled as a function of family policy (e.g., childcare facilities, maternity leave, integrated index of family policy, and welfare state regime). The regressions were run separately for the sample of households in which the wife has an academic degree and the sample in which the wife does not. According to the theoretical rationale of this study, the effect of family policy on wives' economic contribution is expected to be negative in the case of the former and positive in the latter (see Appendix 2 for a formal presentation of this model).

Findings

Descriptive statistics: Wives' economic contribution and labor force participation

Table 24.1 displays the average levels of wives' earning contribution to household income. The first column displays the earning contribution of all (working and non-working) wives. The second and third columns display the earning contribution of wives with and without an academic degree, respectively, and the last column displays the gap in earning contribution between the two groups (second column minus third column). The average wives' contribution across all countries is less than 30%. That is, across all countries, women contribute less than a third to household economies, while men contribute more than two thirds. However, the variation between countries is substantial. Whereas in countries such as Finland, Denmark, Sweden, and Hungary, wives' earning contribution is around 40%, women in Spain, the Netherlands, and Luxemburg, on average, contribute less than 20% to total family income.

As expected, education levels are key in determining women's economic contribution to the household. The average contribution is nearly 40% for women with an academic degree, and cross-country variation among educated women is much lower. In contrast, the economic contribution of wives without a degree is lower by nearly 10 percentage points. Because the majority of women do not have a college education, the average economic contribution of low-educated women is very similar to the aggregate contribution of all women, as demonstrated by the very high correlation between the two distributions, presented in the bottom row. The economic contribution of high-educated women only partly correlates with the aggregate levels.

The last column displays the gaps between the average economic contributions of more and less educated women. Cross-country variations in the gaps are indeed

Figure 24.1 The gap in women's earning contribution between women with and women without college degree, by labor force participation.

very high. While in some countries (Denmark, the Czech Republic, Finland, and Sweden), the gaps between the two groups are negligible, in others (Spain, Italy, and Ireland), the gaps are very high. For example, in Denmark, the country with the smallest gap, the difference in economic contribution between women with high and low education levels is less than 1%. In contrast, in Spain, the country with the biggest gap, it is as high as 23%.

Obviously, access to paid work, and thus to an independent income, is the main contributor to women's economic independence. Therefore, the gap in earning contribution between the two groups of women is expected to be closely related to their labor force participation rates. Figure 24.1 plots labor force participation rates of women (x-axis) together with the gaps in economic contribution between more and less educated women (y-axis). Indeed, the cross-country variations in women's participation rates relate strongly and negatively to these gaps (Pearson $r = -0.87$). That is, the gaps are highest in countries with relatively low participation rates of women, such as Spain, Italy, and Ireland. In contrast, in countries with relatively high participation rates, such as the social democratic countries and the Czech Republic, Canada, and the United States, the gap between the average earning contributions of high- and low-educated women is relatively low. In fact, cross-country correlations are so strong that it looks as if the differences in economic contribution across countries depend exclusively on the extent to which a country succeeds in encouraging women's participation in paid employment.

However, small gaps in the economic contributions of more and less educated women can result from either relatively high participation rates of low-educated women or relatively low participation rates of high-educated women. Figure 24.2 plots the cross-country variations in the average rates of women's labor force participation (x-axis) with the average earning contributions of more and less educated women (y-axis). Country names are italicized and colored light grey for low-educated women and colored black for high-educated women. Indeed, the figure shows the

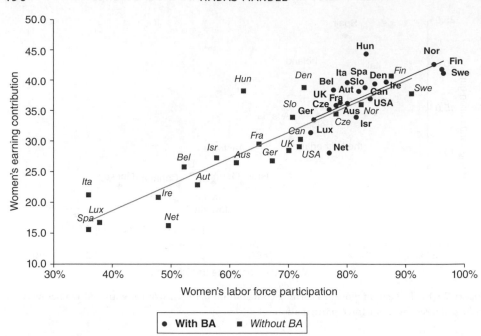

Figure 24.2 Women's earning contribution by labor force participation, for women with and women without college degree.

very strong cross-country correlations between participation rates and household economic contribution for the two groups of women. However, the variations on both axes are much lower among high-educated women, who tend to work in high proportions even in countries with relatively low participation rates. Consequently, their relative earning contribution is high regardless of their country. In contrast, the economic contribution of low-educated women correlates almost perfectly with their participation rates. Given the expansion of the education system in recent decades and the growing number of women with academic degrees, the findings imply that women's labor market participation rates, and consequently women's economic independence, will continue to increase even without state assistance.

Multilevel analysis: The impact of family policy on wives' economic contribution

As mentioned at the outset, an extensive array of literature has provided solid empirical evidence that developed family policy increases the labor market participation rates of women (Esping-Andersen, 1990; Korpi, 2000; Gornick and Meyers, 2003; Misra, Budig, and Moller, 2007). The strong cross-country correlations between participation rates and women's average economic contribution to the household lead to the expectation that policies that promote women's employment also reduce women's economic dependence (Bianchi, Casper, and Peltola, 1999). Thus, in the following analysis, the sample is restricted to dual-earner households. By limiting the sample to employed men and women, cross-country variations in women's participation rates are eliminated, and the effect of family policy on wives' contribution is examined net

Table 24.2 Predictions of the relative earning contribution of women in dual-earner households (standard errors in parentheses), results of multilevel regression

	Women without college degree			
Household-level variables	Model 1	Model 2	Model 3	Model 4
Intercept	13.987**	13.771**	13.403**	14.174**
	(0.867)	(1.135)	(1.028)	(0.836)
Presence of preschool children	0.137	0.137	0.136	0.137
	(0.194)	(0.194)	(0.194)	(0.194)
Number of children	−0.950**	−0.948**	−0.949**	−0.948**
	(0.075)	(0.075)	(0.075)	(0.075)
Woman more educated	3.057**	3.057**	3.056**	3.056**
	(0.154)	(0.154)	(0.154)	(0.154)
Age	−0.018*	−0.018*	−0.018*	−0.018**
	(0.01)	(0.010)	(0.010)	(0.010)
Spouses' age difference (male–female)	−0.061**	−0.061**	−0.06**	−0.061**
	(0.018)	(0.018)	(0.018)	(0.018)
Woman's weekly work hours	0.678**	0.678**	0.678**	0.678**
	(0.007)	(0.007)	(0.007)	(0.007)
Country-level variables				
% Children 0–3 in day care	0.104**			
	(0.036)			
Weeks of parental leave		0.079*		
		(0.042)		
Integrated index of family policy			0.051**	
			(0.019)	
Social democratic countries[a]				4.062**
				(1.314)
Conservative and Eastern Europe countries[a]				1.742*
				(1.035)
N (Countries)	35,937 (19)	35,937 (19)	35,937 (19)	35,937 (19)

[a]Relative to the liberal countries.
**$p < 0.01$, *$p < 0.05$, one tailed.

of its effect on labor force participation. According to the theoretical reasoning of this study, employment-supportive policies are expected to promote the economic contribution of low-educated women (net of the effect on participation rates), but not that of high-educated women.

To examine these hypotheses, I distinguish between households with wives that have an academic degree and those with wives that do not. Table 24.2 and Table 24.3 present the results of a series of multilevel regression models that predict women's earning contribution in dual-earner households. In each analysis, the sample is restricted to one of the two groups, and the coefficients reflect the effect of household- and country-level variables. Table 24.2 displays the results for households with low-educated wives. As for the household-level variables, although having a young child in the household does not significantly affect wives' contribution, each child decreases this contribution by about 1% ($b = -0.949$), when other indicators are held constant.

Table 24.3 Predictions of the relative earning contribution of women in dual-earner households (standard errors in parentheses), results of multilevel regression

Household-level variables	Women with college degree			
	Model 1	Model 2	Model 3	Model 4
Intercept	20.376**	19.928**	19.907**	19.652**
	(1.532)	(1.739)	(1.692)	(1.446)
Presence of preschool children	1.020**	1.019**	1.019**	1.025**
	(0.432)	(0.432)	(0.432)	(0.432)
Number of children	–1.182**	–1.183**	–1.184**	–1.183**
	(0.172)	(0.172)	(0.172)	(0.172)
Woman more educated	5.648**	5.649**	5.650**	5.648**
	(0.338)	(0.338)	(0.338)	(0.338)
Age	–0.025	–0.025	–0.025	–0.025
	(0.022)	(0.022)	(0.022)	(0.022)
Spouses' age difference (male–female)	–0.185**	–0.185**	–0.185**	–0.185**
	(0.045)	(0.045)	(0.045)	(0.045)
Woman's weekly work hours	0.614**	0.614**	0.614**	0.613**
	(0.016)	(0.016)	(0.016)	(0.016)
Country-level variables				
% Children 0–3 in day care	–0.008			
	(0.054)			
Weeks of parental leave		0.017		
		(0.055)		
Integrated index of family policy			0.009	
			(0.026)	
Social democratic countries[a]				–0.067
				(1.807)
Conservative and Eastern Europe countries[a]				2.298
				(1.551)
N (Countries)	7638 (19)	7638 (19)	7638 (19)	7638 (19)

[a]Relative to the liberal countries.
**$p < 0.01$, *$p < 0.05$, one tailed.

In households in which women are more educated than their spouses, wives' contribution is higher ($b = 3.056$). As expected, wives' contribution increases with work hours ($b = 0.678$), but decreases with age ($b = -0.018$), and also with age gaps between the spouses ($b = -0.061$). Because age may serve as a proxy for work experience, the age gap between spouses is indicative of the gap in their work experience (in favor of the male partner). Also, large age differences may reflect traditional gender ideologies and, thus, a conservative division of paid and unpaid labor within the family.

Household-level characteristics, however, affect the earning contribution of high-educated wives differently. As displayed in Table 24.3, unlike in the case of low-educated women, having preschool-aged children, surprisingly, increases the economic contribution of high-educated women. However, the negative effect of each additional child on wives' contribution is significant, so in this case, the two variables cancel each other out. In households with women who are more educated than their spouses, women's contribution is greater by nearly 6% ($b = 5.65$). Moreover, contrary to the effect among low-educated women, the economic contribution of high-educated women does not decrease with age, but it does decrease with an increasing age gap between the spouses $(b = -0.185)$. Similar to the explanation given earlier, because age is a proxy for work experience, a wider age gap is indicative of greater work experience for the male partner. Not surprisingly, here too, the average contribution of wives increases with increasing work hours $(b = 0.614)$.

Household-level variables were introduced into the equation as controls, to allow the estimation of the net effect of family policy on the economic contribution of women. Family policy was measured, at the country level, by four indicators. The results of the multilevel analyses, presented in Table 24.3, are in line with the main theoretical expectations. Among dual-earner families in which the wife has no academic education, all indicators of family policy have positive and significant effects on wives' contribution. Specifically, long periods of paid parental leave and public facilities for young children increase this contribution. Also, in countries located at the top of the family policy index (such as the social democratic countries), the economic contribution of low-educated women is higher relative to countries at the bottom (such as the liberal countries).

To get a sense of the magnitude of these effects, consider the following: after controlling for the variations in household characteristics across countries, the predicted contribution of wives in Sweden, the country at the top of the family policy index, is 5 percentage points higher than that in Australia, the country at the bottom of the index. Likewise, in the country with the largest percentage of children in day care (Denmark), the predicted contribution is higher by nearly 5 percentage points than that in countries with the smallest percentage of children in day care (Ireland and the United Kingdom). In the case of maternity leave, the gap between the country with the most (Sweden) and least (the United States and Australia) generous family policy is 4 percentage points, in favor of the former.[4]

The coefficients of the two dummy variables for welfare regimes, represented in Model 4, lead to similar conclusions. The reference category is the liberal welfare regime, the regime with the least developed family policy (see the location of liberal countries at the bottom of the family policy index, and their relatively low values for maternity leave and childcare in the Table 24A.1). Indeed, the predicted average economic contribution of low-educated wives in liberal regime countries is 4% lower than that in social democratic countries and nearly 2% lower than that in conservative regimes. Given that all the country-level effects are net of household-level characteristics – that is, they relate to households with the same characteristics – these effects are considerable.

In sharp contrast to the results for low-educated wives, none of the family policy indicators exert significant effects on the economic contribution of high-educated women. Table 24.3, which is limited to households in which the wife has an academic degree, reveals that neither childcare facilities nor maternity leave helps high-educated wives increase their relative earnings in the labor market. Also, in countries at the top of the family policy index, such as the social democratic ones, the relative economic standing of high-educated women is not different from their standing in other countries.

These findings are not surprising given the expected implications of family policy described at the outset. Educated women are equipped with more labor market skills, which is a significant determinant of their (relativity high) earning levels.

However, previous studies suggest that developed family policy, and, in particular, long absenteeism from paid work, may restrict their access to attractive and prestigious positions, and therefore reduce their potential earnings (Ruhm, 1998; Albrecht et al., 1999; Mandel and Semyonov, 2005; Mandel, 2006, 2012). Contrary to these findings, however, in the present study, maternity leave did not decrease the relative economic contribution of high-educated wives, nor was their contribution lower in countries with developed family policy.

In sum, the results of the multilevel analyses stress the importance of distinguishing between groups of women in the study of family policy and gender equality. Within the comparative context of the welfare state and gender, this distinction is crucial for understanding the impact of welfare state policies on women's economic dependence. From the perspective of family welfare, this approach emphasizes and reveals that family policies are particularly effective for low-income families. Because family policy helps low-educated women both join and gain better economic rewards in the labor market, it affects both their standing within the family and the economic standing of the family as a whole. Both these effects on low-income families are in line with the goals of state supportive policies and will be discussed further in the conclusion. As for high-educated women, the findings suggest that family policy has a negligible effect on their economic independence. These findings deviate from previous studies, which found family policies to have negative implications for women. In the following and concluding section, I refer to the trend of homogamy between married couples in order to help explain this discrepancy and discuss the broader implications of family policy.

Conclusions

Employment-supportive family policies have been implemented in most advanced societies in recent decades. Most of these policies aim to reduce the tension between paid and unpaid work, by providing accessible childcare arrangements and allowing women to take leave when their children are young. Indeed, the effectiveness of these policies in raising women's participation in the labor market has been proven in many comparative cross-country studies (e.g., Gornick, Meyers, and Ross, 1997; Korpi, 2000; Van der Lippe and Van Dijk, 2002). The integration of women into the paid labor force is a prime condition for advancing gender equality. Access to market resources increases women's power within the family and allows them to successfully negotiate task allocation (Shelton and John, 1996; Bittman et al., 2003; Breen and Cooke, 2005; Treas and de Ruijter, 2008). Moreover, in addition to reducing women's economic dependence in dual-earner households and contributing to a more equal division of labor between spouses, women's access to independent economic resources helps single women establish independent households and protects them from poverty (Misra, Budig, and Moller, 2007).

For all these reasons, the effect of employment-supportive policies on the economic dependence of women draws the attention of both sociologists of the family and scholars of the welfare state and gender equality (e.g., Bianchi, Casper, and Peltola, 1999; Stier and Mandel, 2009). Yet despite the considerable scholarly attention given to the effect of family policy on gender equality, two questions have been largely neglected. The first is the extent to which family policy contributes to the economic gains of women, beyond its effect on their participation rates (but see Stier and Mandel, 2009). The second, which has received even less attention, is whether family policy affects all women similarly.

This chapter sheds light on these two unheeded issues by disentangling the outcome of labor market attainment from labor market participation and by distinguishing between advantaged and disadvantaged women. According to the theoretical reasoning of this study, the effect of employment-supportive policies on the economic contribution of wives is conditioned by their education and skills. For low-educated women with low earning potential, family policy reduces economic dependence by assisting paid employment, which gives women access to a paycheck, and by promoting work continuity, which increases their labor market attainments. In contrast, state assistance is less likely to affect the participation rates, and thus the economic independence, of high-educated women. High-educated women have relatively high earning potential, which is the strongest incentive behind their labor market participation. Furthermore, to the extent that reconciliation policies foster employers' reluctance to hire and promote women to lucrative positions, these policies are expected to decrease the relative economic gains of high-educated women (the candidates for these positions) and, as a result, their economic contribution to the household.

The findings of this study fully met expectations regarding low-educated women. First, cross-country variations in wives' economic contribution correlate almost perfectly with cross-country variations in female labor market participation, especially among the low educated. Moreover, all four indicators of family policy were found to increase the economic contribution of low-educated wives, above and beyond the effect on labor market participation. That is, family policy helps low-educated women join the labor market, and also increases their economic rewards within it.

These results have significant implications not only for gender inequality, but also for class inequality. From the gender perspective, family policy increases women's relative economic gains and, consequently, their relative standing within the family (Shelton and John, 1996; Bittman *et al.*, 2003; Breen and Cooke, 2005; Treas and de Ruijter, 2008). From the class perspective, because low-educated women are mostly from low-income families, family policy – in increasing women's economic rewards – benefits total family income in low-income families. In doing so, family policy reduces the poverty risk for poor families and improves their standard of living and well-being. Yet while the implications of family policy for the gender aspects of inequality have been widely echoed, the important implications for class inequality have not. Mandel and Shalev (2009) relate this blind spot to the analytical distinction between gender and class inequality; each tends to be linked to different welfare state policies: the former to family policy, the latter to social policy.

In contrast to the results among low-educated wives, none of the family policy indicators were found to affect the economic contribution of high-educated wives. These results are not in line with previous studies, which found that generous family policy restricts women's access to powerful and desirable positions (Mandel and Semyonov, 2005, 2006; Mandel, 2011), promotes gender wage gaps among advantaged men and women (Mandel, 2012), increases sex segregation (Estevez-Abe, 2005), and increases the gender gaps in workplace authority (Wright, Baxter, and Birkelund, 1995).

The conflict between these findings may be rooted in the different ways that women's labor market attainments are measured. As opposed to previous studies, the dependent variable in this study is the relative contribution of wives' earnings. At first glance, cross-country variations in the gender pay ratio, and cross-country variations in women's economic independence, may seem to be strongly related, as both variables compare the labor market rewards of men and women. However, while the former analysis considers the average earnings of all working men and women, the latter considers the earnings of husbands and wives in dual-earner families. The gap in earnings between all economically active men and women may be very different from the gap in earnings between husbands and their wives. This is because one of the most distinctive characteristics of married couples is homogamy, the tendency of men and women to marry partners who resemble them both culturally and socioeconomically. In recent decades, with the expansion of the education system, educational homogamy has become a significant feature of married couples in all advanced societies (Blossfeld and Timm, 2003).

Homogamy is expected to reduce the gap in spouses' earnings because high-educated women, with relativity high earning potential, tend to marry high-educated men, and vice versa. Indeed, in the current data, the correlation between the education levels of spouses is very high, as is the correlation between their earnings. The Spearman correlation, computed for the pooled sample, for the education level of a wife and her husband is 0.71, while the Pearson correlation for their earnings is 0.86.

If work–family reconciliation policies restrict women's access to high-paid positions, as previous findings have argued, then in less developed welfare states, the average economic gains of educated women are expected to be higher than in more developed ones, and the gender wage gaps, therefore, should be lower (other things being equal), as indeed found in Mandel (2012). Women's increased access to lucrative positions, however, may raise the average earnings of all women, but it does not necessarily increase the relative household contribution of wives, if their husbands earn even more. For example, suppose that in the United States, 30% of high-educated women are in the top earning quintile, while in Sweden, only 20% are. The high representation of women in lucrative positions in the United States will decrease the gender wage gaps there, but will not necessarily increase women's earning contribution relative to their (also highly paid) spouses. Moreover, the higher wage ceilings in the United States and other liberal countries could encourage even greater gaps between spouses, because men dominate the top positions. Therefore, cross-country variations in gender earning gaps are likely to be much more affected by the wage of highly paid women than cross-country variations in wives' economic contribution. This is because in the case of the latter, the advantages of highly paid women may be masked by their spouse's earnings.

Several conclusions arise from this study. First, family policy impacts wives' relative household economic contribution, not only by facilitating women's labor market participation, but also by affecting women's earnings. In the case of low-educated families, family policy is doubly advantageous: for one, it significantly supports wives' participation in the labor market, and, for another, it increases the relative earnings of working women. In doing so, family policy contributes to reducing gender inequality within families, as well as to reducing class inequality between high- and low-educated families. In high-educated families, family policy has a lower effect on participation and neither a positive nor negative effect on the relative earnings of working women.

This is because mothers in high-educated families tend to work in high proportions, even in countries with relatively undeveloped family policy.

Second, the impressive rise in women's education in recent years in all countries is expected to reduce the cross-country variations in female labor force participation. Based on the different effects of family policies on low- versus high-educated women, the effect of family policy on women's participation rates, and, consequently, on wives' relative earnings, is also expected to decrease over time. Finally, the cross-country distributions of wives' relative economic contribution to the household are distinct from the distributions of gender earning gaps. Welfare state policies, therefore, do not affect these two aspects of gender inequality similarly. As suggested here, homogamy between spouses may explain these differences.

Acknowledgment

I would like to thank the Israel Science Foundation (ISF) for its generous financial support of this project (Grant no. 281/10).

Appendix 1

Table 24A.1 Family policy indicators, by country

	Index of family policy[a]	% Children 0–3 in day care[b]	Weeks of paid maternity/ parental leaves[c]
Sweden	100	33	52
Denmark	93	50	28
Finland	57	27	44
Israel	56	22	12
Belgium	50	30	15
France	50	23	16
Hungary	50	8	24
Spain	43	5	16
Italy	41	6	21
Luxemburg	30	2	16
Czech Republic	30	8	28
The Netherlands	27	8	16
United Kingdom	27	2	18
Austria	23	3	16
Germany	20	5	14
Ireland	18	2	18
Canada	10	5	25
United States	4	5	0
Australia	2	5	0

Country-level data are from the following sources:
[a]Mandel and Semyonov (2006).
[b]Gauthier (1999) and Meyers and Gornick (2000).
[c]Clearinghouse (2004) and Kamerman (2000).

Appendix 2: Method of analysis

The two-level model is represented by a set of equations. The first is a within-country equation, which models wives' earning contribution as a function of household characteristics, as illustrated in the following:

$$(\text{Wife's earning contribution})ij = \beta_{0j} + \beta X + \varepsilon ij \qquad (24\text{A}.1)$$

The dependent variable is wife's earning contribution in household i and country j; β_{0j} is the intercept, denoting the average contribution level; X is the vector of all household characteristics (i.e., relative education, work hours, age, children); and β is the vector of their coefficients. The error term εij is assumed to be normally distributed with a mean of zero. The household-level variables – which constrained to be the same across countries – were introduced to control for cross-country variation in the composition of these covariates. Thus, the effect of policies on the relative standing of women within their households is estimated net of the possible effect of household-level characteristics.

In Equation (24A.2), the intercept β_{0j}, which is derived from Equation (24A.1), constitutes the dependent variables:

$$\beta_{0j} = \gamma_{00} + \gamma_{01}(\text{maternity leave})_j + ... + v_{0j} \qquad (24\text{A}.2)$$

The intercept represents the net variation in the average level of wife's earning contribution across countries and is modeled as a function of family policy. In each regression, a distinctive measure of family policy is employed (e.g., childcare facilities, maternity leave, integrated index of family policy, and welfare state regime). The regressions were run separately for the sample of households in which the wife has an academic degree and the sample in which the wife does not. For example, a positive sign for γ_{01} in the low-educated sample group would support the claim that in countries with generous maternity leave policy, the economic contribution of wives is higher.

Notes

1   Norway and Slovakia were excluded from the regression analyses due to missing data for work hours.
2   As can be seen in Table 24A.1, the East-European countries are more similar to the conservative regime than to the other two regimes with regard to family policy (see their rank on the integrated index, as well as on the components of the index). Nevertheless, historically, the rates of female labor force participation in the East-European countries are high compared to those in the conservative countries.
3   This is because the great diversity in the category "low-educated women" – which groups women with little or no education together with women with some, or even relatively high, education – may mitigate, or conceal, the true impact of family policy.
4   The differences were estimated by multiplying the coefficient of each variable by the gap between the values for the most and least generous country for that variable (see values in Table 24A.1).

References

Aigner D.J. and Cain, G.G. (1977) Statistical theories of discrimination in labor markets. *Industrial and Labor Relations Review*, 30, 175–187.

Albrecht, J.W., Edin, P.A., Sundstrom, M. and Vroman, S.B. (1999) Career interruptions and subsequent earnings: a reexamination using Swedish data. *Journal of Human Resources*, 34, 294–311.

Bianchi, S.M., Casper, L.M. and Peltola, P.K. (1999) A cross-national look at married women's earnings dependency. *Gender Issues*, 17, 3–33.

Bianchi, S.M., Milkie, M.A., Sayer, L.C. and Robinson, J.P. (2000) Is anyone doing the housework? Trends in the gender division of household labor. *Social Forces*, 79, 191–228.

Bittman, M., England, P., Folbre, N. *et al.* (2003) When does gender trump money? Bargaining and time in household work. *American Journal of Sociology*, 109, 186–214.

Blossfeld, H.-P. and Hakim, C. (1997) *Between Equalization and Marginalization: Women Working Part-Time in Europe and the United States of America*, Oxford University Press, New York.

Blossfeld, H.-P. and Timm, A. (2003) *Who Marries Whom? Educational Systems as Marriage Markets in Modern Societies*, Kluwer Academic, Dordrecht/Boston.

Bolzendahl, C.I. and Myers, D.J. (2004) Feminist attitudes and support for gender equality: opinion change in women and men, 1974–1998. *Social Forces*, 83, 759–790.

Breen, R. and Cooke, L.P. (2005) The persistence of the gendered division of domestic labour. *European Sociological Review*, 21, 43–57.

Brines, J. (1994) Economic dependency, gender, and the division-of-labor at home. *American Journal of Sociology*, 100, 652–688.

Bryk, A.S. and Raudenbush, S.W. (1992) *Hierarchical Linear Models: Applications and Data Analysis Methods*, Sage, Newbury Park.

Clearinghouse (2004) Clearinghouse on International Development in Child, Youth, and Family Policies. 2004. Table 1.11 Maternity and Parental Leaves, 1999–2002. www.childpolicyintl.org (accessed October 30, 2013).

Edin, P.A. and Gustavsson, M. (2008) Time out of work and skill depreciation. *Industrial & Labor Relations Review*, 61, 163–180.

Esping-Andersen, G. (1990) *The Three Worlds of Welfare Capitalism*, Princeton University Press, Princeton.

Esping-Andersen, G. (1999) *Social Foundations of Postindustrial Economies*, Oxford University Press, New York.

Estevez-Abe, M. (2005) Gender bias in skills and social policies: the varieties of capitalism perspective on sex segregation. *Social Politics*, 12, 180–215.

Gauthier, A.H. (1999) Historical trends in state support for families in Europe (post-1945). *Children and Youth Services Review*, 21, 937–965.

Gornick, J.C. and Meyers, M. (2003) *Families That Work: Policies for Reconciling Parenthood and Employment*, Russell Sage Foundation, New York.

Gornick, J.C., Meyers, M.K. and Ross, K.E. (1997) Supporting the employment of mothers: policy variation across fourteen welfare states. *Journal of European Social Policy*, 7, 45–70.

Hakim, C. (2002) Lifestyle preferences as determinants of women's differentiated labor market careers. *Work and Occupations*, 29, 428–459.

Hirschman, A.O. (1970) *Exit, Voice, and Loyalty; Responses to Decline in Firms, Organizations, and States*, Harvard University Press, Cambridge.

Hobson, B. (1990) No exit, no voice: women's economic dependency and the welfare state. *Acta Sociologica*, 33, 235–250.

Kamerman, S.B. (2000) *Parental Leave Policies: An Essential Ingredient in Early Childhood Education and Care Policies*. A Publication of the Society for Research in Child Development, Ann Arbor.

Kolberg, J.E. (ed) (1991) *The Welfare State as Employer*, M.E. Sharpe, Inc, London.

Korpi, W. (2000) Faces of inequality: gender, class, and patterns of inequalities in different types of welfare states. *Social Politics*, 7, 127–191.

Luxembourg Income Study Database (LIS) (1991–1999), www.lisdatacenter.org (multiple countries – see Table 1 for surveys' year), LIS, Luxembourg.

Mandel, H. (2009) Configurations of gender inequality: the consequences of ideology and public policy. *British Journal of Sociology*, 60, 693–719.

Mandel, H. (2011) Rethinking the paradox: tradeoffs in work-family policy and patterns of gender inequality. *Community, Work & Family*, 14, 159–176.

Mandel, H. (2012) Winners and losers: the consequences of welfare state policies for gender wage inequality. *European Sociological Review*, 28, 241–262.

Mandel, H. and Semyonov, M. (2005) Family policies, wage structures, and gender gaps: sources of earnings inequality in 20 countries. *American Sociological Review*, 70, 949–967.

Mandel, H. and Semyonov, M. (2006) A welfare state paradox: state interventions and women's employment opportunities in 22 countries. *American Journal of Sociology*, 111, 1910–1949.

Mandel, H. and Shalev, M. (2009) How welfare states shape the gender pay gap: a theoretical and comparative analysis. *Social Forces*, 87, 1873–1912.

McCall, L. (2007) Increasing class disparities among women and the politics of gender equity, in *The Sex of Class: Women Transforming American Labor* (ed D.S. Cobble), ILR Press, Ithaca, pp. 15–34.

Meyers, M.K. and Gornick, J.C. (2000) Early childhood education and care (ECEC): cross national variation in service organization and financing. Paper presented at A Consultative Meeting on International Developments in Early Childhood Education and Care: An Activity of the Columbia Institute for Child and Family Policy, New York.

Misra, J., Budig, M.J. and Moller, S. (2007) Reconciliation policies and the effects of motherhood on employment, earnings and poverty. *Journal of Comparative Policy Analysis*, 9, 135.

Morgan, K.J. (2005) The 'production' of child care: how labor markets shape social policy and vice versa. *Social Politics*, 12, 243–263.

Morgan, K.J. and Zippel, K. (2003) Paid to care: the origins and effects of care leave policies in Western Europe. *Social Politics*, 10, 49–85.

O'Connor, J.S. (1996) From women in the welfare state to gendering welfare state regimes. *Current Sociology*, 44, 1–124.

O'Connor, J.S., Orloff, A.S. and Shaver, S. (1999) *States, Markets, Families: Gender, Liberalism, and Social Policy in Australia, Canada, Great Britain, and the United States*, Cambridge University Press, Cambridge/New York.

Oppenheimer, V.K. (1997) Women's employment and the gain to marriage: the specialization and trading model. *Annual Review of Sociology*, 23, 431–453.

Orloff, A.S. (1993) Gender and the social rights of citizenship – the comparative analysis of gender relations and welfare states. *American Sociological Review*, 58, 303–328.

Persson, I. and Jonung, C. (1998) *Women's Work and Wages*, Routledge, London.

Ruhm, C.J. (1998) The economic consequences of parental leave mandates: lessons from Europe. *The Quarterly Journal of Labor Economics*, 113, 285–317.

Shalev, M. (2008) Class divisions among women. *Politics & Society*, 36, 421–444.

Shelton, B.A. and John, D. (1996) The division of household labor. *Annual Review of Sociology*, 22, 299–322.

Sigle-Rushton, W. and Waldfogel, J. (2007) Motherhood and women's earnings in Anglo-American, Continental European, and Nordic countries. *Feminist Economics*, 13, 55–91.

Sorensen, A. and McLanahan, S. (1987) Married women's economic dependency, 1940–1980. *American Journal of Sociology*, 93, 659–687.

Stier, H. and Mandel, H. (2009) Inequality in the family: the institutional aspects of women's earning contribution. *Social Science Research*, 38, 594–608.

Treas, J. and de Ruijter, E. (2008) Earnings and expenditures on household services in married and cohabiting unions. *Journal of Marriage and Family*, 70, 796–805.

Treas, J. and Tai, T.O. (2012) How couples manage the household: work and power in cross-national perspective. *Journal of Family Issues*, 33, 1088–1116.

Van Berkel, M. and De Graaf, N.D. (1998) Married women's economic dependency in the Netherlands, 1979–1991. *British Journal of Sociology*, 49, 97–117.

Van der Lippe, T. and Van Dijk, L. (2002) Comparative research on women's employment. *Annual Review of Sociology*, 28, 221–241.

Waldfogel, J. (1998) The family gap for young women in the United States and Britain: can maternity leave make a difference? *Journal of Labor Economics*, 16, 505–545.

Williams, J.C. and Boushey, H. (2010) The three faces of work-family conflict: the poor, the professionals, and the missing middle. Retrieved from the Center for American Progress, website: http://www.americanprogress.org/issues/2010/01/pdf/threefaces.pdf (accessed October 30, 2013).

Winkler, A.E., McBride, T.D. and Andrews, C. (2005) Wives who outearn their husbands: a transitory or persistent phenomenon for couples? *Demography*, 42, 523–535.

Wright, E.-O., Baxter, J. and Birkelund, G.-E. (1995) The gender gap in workplace authority: a cross-national study. *American Sociological Review*, 60, 407–435.

25

Assisted Reproduction, Genetic and Genomic Technologies, and Family Life

Martin Richards

Introduction

While the claim that we are living in the biotech century may overplay an argument, it is undoubtedly true that the new genetic and reproductive technologies are increasingly playing a part in our daily lives. Those whose family medical histories suggest that a genetic disease may be running in their family can now take a DNA test which will tell them whether or not they carry the relevant gene mutation and so their personal risk. In other contexts, DNA tests are being used to determine the liability to pay child support, settle paternity disputes, or trace ancestral origins. And it is now a commonplace of police work that crime scenes are searched for traces of DNA which may then be linked to DNA profiles of suspects. A growing list of reproductive technologies may be used to provide children for the infertile or those without a reproductive partner. As I write, there is a public consultation underway (in the United Kingdom) about whether we should allow the development of new *in vitro* fertilization (IVF) technique which could be used by women to avoid passing on genetically inherited mitochondrial disease to their children. The technique involves modifying a mother's embryo or egg with material from eggs or an embryo from another woman. It is a form of genetic modification which could change children in subsequent generations and so is currently not permitted in most countries and will require a decision of Parliament if it is to be used in Britain (see Nuffield Council on Bioethics, 2012).

In this chapter, I will discuss some of the ways in which genetic and reproductive technologies are being used, how they may influence family life, and how our attitudes and assumptions about the family may, in turn, shape the development and use of these technologies. The chapter begins with a discussion of DNA relationship testing and then considers some of the assisted reproductive technologies (ARTs). Attention is then turned to some of the medical genetic technologies, and the chapter

The Wiley Blackwell Companion to the Sociology of Families, First Edition.
Edited by Judith Treas, Jacqueline Scott, and Martin Richards.
© 2014 John Wiley & Sons Ltd. Published 2017 by John Wiley & Sons Ltd.

concludes with a consideration of cultural assumptions and public attitudes to current and future technologies.

Relationship Testing

Until 1987, paternity and other genetic relationship testing was carried out using blood-group proteins. Such tests could exclude a child's potential father, but a match only indicated paternity with a degree of probability. DNA tests are much more accurate than this. Apart from cases involving monozygotic ("identical") twins, DNA tests can establish parent–child genetic relationships with a degree of accuracy that amounts to certainty for all practical purposes. These tests analyze parts of our chromosomal DNA which do not constitute genes and which are relatively variable in sequence from family to family. Samples from a child and a potential father(s) are compared to see whether various sections of the DNA sequence match. Initially, these tests, which have been developed and provided commercially, used DNA extracted from the white cells in a blood sample, but today they may be based on hair follicles, cells collected from the inside of the cheek, a smear on a drinking glass, or, indeed, almost any tissue in our body or from the material we excrete or leave around in the environment. Do-it-yourself postal kits are available, and the technology makes it easy for a sample to be collected without someone's knowledge or consent.

The most widely used of all DNA tests are paternity tests (Rothstein *et al.*, 2005). In the United Kingdom, about 10,000 tests were done in 2002, the majority on behalf of the state, but today, numbers are probably much higher than this. The largest user has been the Child Support Agency, for the purposes of settling contested paternity where there may be a liability to pay for child support. The second major government use is for the immigration control when eligibility depends on family membership. Other use arises from a wide variety of familial situations where testing involves consenting adults and court-sanctioned testing of children. A best-interests standard is used by the courts to decide whether children should be tested. Until recently, the judicial view was that testing was usually best avoided because it can potentially disturb established family relationships, but today, there is more emphasis on a child knowing his or her genetic parentage (Steiner, 2006; Bainham, 2008). This shift in attitude may have been encouraged by both the easy availability of DNA testing and cases where the results of web-based, unregulated testing have been used to bargain in the shadow of the law, as well as changing attitudes to an individual's need, or even right, to know the identity of their biological parents and the importance of this to their knowledge of their origins. In the child maintenance situation, there are cases where men have received repayment of child support payments after DNA testing has shown them not to be the genetic father of the relevant child. Such situations can lead to a child losing a social father without gaining access to or knowledge of their biological father (Lynch *et al.*, 2008). Similar disruptions of familial relationships have been reported as a result of using DNA testing for immigration control (Taitz, Weekers, and Mosca, 2002). In many countries, there are categories for immigrants that depend on family relationships, and DNA testing is widely used to provide proof of such blood relationships.

As social scientists have often observed, while maternity is seldom in doubt, paternity can be much less certain: a point that has been at the foundation of some theories of the family and the state (e.g., Engels, 1884). Indeed, functionalist explanations of marriage patterns, the seclusion of women, and much else have been based on this observation – as has a lot of speculation by sociobiologists and evolutionary psychologists. However, in the new moral order where a conscientious lawyer may suggest DNA tests as a sensible preliminary before a divorcing husband considers any child support issues, we may be witnessing a cultural shift. Under English common law, there is a presumption that a child born to a married couple is a "child of the family," and both mother and father have the rights and duties of parents regardless of the biological origins of a child, unless one of them is able to prove nonpaternity. There are comparable arrangements for most children of unmarried parents. However, it can be argued that in the era of DNA testing, there has been a shift to a situation in which parenthood becomes nearly coterminous with parentage and where the latter is defined by shared DNA sequences (Freeman and Richards, 2006).

The DNA techniques discussed thus far can establish whether or not there is a biological link between two people. Other techniques have been developed which can be used to trace family lineages. Male lines can be traced by investigating the degree of similarity of Y-chromosomes. Because the male's Y-chromosome is unpaired, unlike all their other chromosomes, it is passed down over generations almost unchanged. This means that men with a common ancestor will have almost identical Y-chromosomes. Y-chromosome tests are available from several companies and are proving popular with genealogists and those interested in family history, as well as providing a powerful research tool for studying human populations. The test may be used, for example, to see if families with the same surname are biologically related. A use of the test which received wide publicity was in the case of the American President Thomas Jefferson and the long-standing accusation that he had fathered a child with Sally Hemings, one of his slaves. Jefferson did not have a legitimate male descendant, so Y-chromosome analysis was carried out on five male (living) descendants of his paternal uncle, Field Jefferson. These were compared with an analysis of DNA from Sally Hemings' great-great-great-grandson. The Y-chromosomes did match, so that we know that Jefferson (or possibly a blood relative of Jefferson's) fathered Sally Hemings' child. DNA testing has the power to rewrite our family history – at least insofar as biological parentage is part of that history – and for some, revised family histories may cause discomfort and changed attitudes toward their forebears.

Similar analyses can be carried out on female lineages using mitochondrial DNA. Female X-sex chromosomes are paired, so would be unreliable for this kind of analysis. However, mitochondria, which are small cell organelles, are passed from a mother to her children in her eggs. Mitochondria have their own genome which can be analyzed and compared in the same manner as the Y-chromosome and can be used to track female lineages. A well-known use of this technique was the identification of the remains of the Romanovs, who had been executed in 1918 during the Russian Revolution. Because the mitochondrial DNA from one female body, recently exhumed, matched that of the Duke of Edinburgh, the body was identified as Nicholas II's Tsarina, Alexandra. Her maternal grandmother was Queen Victoria who was also a direct ancestor of the Duke of Edinburgh.

Nash (2004) has investigated how ideas of gender, reproduction, nation, "race," and relatedness are being shaped and deployed within new discourses of genetic kinship which are being established through the use of ancestor testing. Here, notions of family relations provide a "grammar" for translating the complexities of molecular genetics with the biosocialities in the form of Y-chromosome brotherhoods and mitochondrial DNA clan membership. The use of these techniques both by those interested in their family history and by researchers exploring connections of human populations, like DNA paternity and relationship testing, encourages ideas of genetic essentialism and enhances the iconic status of DNA (Nelkin and Lindee, 1995). Necessarily, they equate lineage and kin with a genetic connection, and in confirming notions of the power of DNA, they also underpin a cultural concept of kinship which is biological or, perhaps more accurately, natural at its roots (Schneider, 1980). Schneider in his studies of American kinship describes how natural ties define identity and are a relationship of identity, while love provides a more diffuse familial solidarity. It is, of course, common ground for many theorists (e.g., Giddens, 1991) to point to the declining role of kinship as notions of individualism and independence have grown. But in this context, it is worth drawing attention to the enormous growth in interests in family history in Western Europe and those parts of the world which have received immigrants from the region. Now, the use of official and family records for genealogical inquiry can be supplemented and extended using DNA techniques. Clearly, interest in the connections of descent and kin remain strong and seem likely to receive reinforcement through the possibilities of search and verification provided by DNA techniques.

Assisted Reproduction Techniques

The oldest of the practices of assisted reproduction are collaborative practices which involve third-party progenitors. The Old Testament (*Genesis*, 16: 2–3 and 30: 3–5) provides an example in the account of the family of the patriarch, Abraham. His wife, Sarah, had not produced the prophetic son who God had promised. She suggested to Abraham that he should lie with her handmaiden, Hagar, who in due course bore a son, Ismail. Collaborative reproduction raises difficult and controversial issues about the status of the children produced and their place in genealogies – as with the rival claims of Ismail and Isaac, the later born natural son of Abraham and Sarah, which reverberate through religious disputes to this day.

As well as full surrogacy, as we would now term Hagar's involvement, there is the possibility of artificial insemination and, following the development of IVF, egg and embryo donation and gestational surrogacy (where a woman carries an embryo created with sperm and egg from the commissioning couple). And as well as for the infertile, these techniques are used increasingly by those without an appropriate reproductive partner – single women (and possibly men) and same-sex couples.

Historically, we see resistance to the introduction of all these practices, essentially on the basis of the violation of the moral order of conjugal reproductive intercourse. In Britain, artificial insemination by donor (AID) became part of medical infertility treatment in the 1930s, though there has been earlier suggestion for its use for eugenic improvements (couples using sperm from superior men) or as a way that World War I widows could bear children without "the sin" of sexual intercourse (Richards, 2008). Its medical use in the United States began somewhat earlier, and its products were known as test-tube babies, the children of science rather than married love. In Britain, accounts of the practice in medical journals led to a growing, and largely hostile, public debate. A Commission set up by the Church found that AID

> "involves a breach of the marriage. It violates the exclusive union set up between husband and wife. It defrauds the child begotten and deceives both his putative kinsmen and society at large. For both donor and recipient the sexual act loses its personal character and becomes a mere transaction. For the child there must always be the risk of disclosure, deliberate or unintended, of the circumstances of his conception."
>
> (Wand, 1948, p. 58)

There was also much concern that masturbation was involved. And the Commission called for criminalization (Richards, 2014).

But despite all the disapproval, which was common beyond the Church, the practice grew, not least because there were declining numbers of babies for adoption, which was the only other alternative for couples where the husband was sterile. By the late 1950s, the practice was accepted in the National Health Service, and a decade later, it was given legal recognition so that the couple were the legal parents and all rights and duties of parenthood were removed from the sperm donor.

The United States pioneered the commercial cryobanking of sperm with the first sperm bank opening in 1977. By the 1990s, there were a few large operators dominating a $164 million-a-year industry (Mamo, 2005). Following the development of IVF, companies were set up to supply egg donors. But what is striking about this reproductive industry are the sharp differences between the sperm and egg trades. In an analysis of the US market for sex cells, Almeling (2011) found that while both women and men are drawn to "donation" for financial reasons, egg agencies and sperm banks do business in different ways. Sperm donors are encouraged to think of the money as remuneration for an easy "job," while women, who are better paid, are urged to regard egg donation in feminine terms, as the ultimate "gift" between women. And very significantly, the men and women saw their connection with the children produced in different ways. Most men stated that the offspring were their children, while only a tenth of the women said this. Sixty percent of the women were explicit – these were not their children; only 15% of men said this. Another way of describing the difference is in the use of kin language (parents, grandparents, siblings). Eighty-five percent of the sperm donors used kin language in contrast to 42% of the women.

Looking at egg and sperm donation more internationally, we see a great diversity of regulation and practice. In a few countries, like the United States, there are commercial markets, where sex cells are directly traded for money – commodification as some would term it. But elsewhere, trade in human tissue is banned, and instead, egg and sperm donation is rewarded through the payment of "expenses." In a few situations, donation is indeed a gift, and no money changes hands, as in most intrafamilial donation. In Britain, for example, intrafamilial egg donation is not uncommon, with sisters or sisters-in-law being the most usual donors (Vayena and Golombok, 2012).

But the practices of sex cell donation are themselves widely regulated, and there are countries that ban either egg or sperm donation or both (Gűrtin and Vayena, 2012). And this, coupled with variations in costs, has produced a growing phenomenon of transnational donation (Pennings and Gűrtin, 2012).

The birth of the first IVF baby in Britain (Steptoe and Edwards, 1978) was world-wide news, but reactions were mixed. As with sperm donor children earlier, these were also called test-tube babies – signaling the conception as disembodied and the product of science. For the cover of Time Magazine, Roger Hysser famously echoed Michelangelo's creation of Adam from the ceiling of St Peters in Rome, but he added the hand of a scientist to that of God, pointing to a test tube containing a fertilized egg. Some regarded this new technology as a further threat to the natural order of marital congress and conception and the institutions of marriage and family, while some feminists saw "a great technological fuck" (Raymond, 1994) and an attempt to stabilize patriarchal social relations (Spallone, 1987).

There is now a considerable body of research on the families and children born of IVF and collaborative assisted reproduction (e.g., Golombok *et al.*, 2002a, b; Blake, Richards and Golombok, 2013). Very broadly speaking, in terms of parent–child relationships and the development and well-being of children, few differences have been found between IVF families and those with traditional conception. Some studies have found that IVF mothers may see their children more positively and are seen to be more affectionate. This has been attributed to couples' prior infertility and strug-gles to conceive – these are special children. Where reproductive donation has been used "as if," families may be created by a systematic misrecognition (Bharadwaj, 2003), and in Britain, for instance, most children are not told of their donor origin and are brought up allowing children to assume that they are the natural children of their parents. It is often clinical practice to "match" donors and recipients, in the hope that there will not be any striking physical dissimilarity between children and parents which might cause doubt to be cast over parentage.

There has been ethnographic work on "kinning" where parents actively seek to realign biological and social accounts of reproduction (Grace and Daniels, 2007). Thompson (2001) has described "doing kinship" in US fertility clinics. So, for example, a mother who had used donor eggs from a friend stressed the small percentage of pregnancy involving the gamete and embryo stage, so minimizing the biological contribution of the egg, while emphasizing the biological significance of her gestational role. She also pointed out that she and her friend (the donor) shared a common genetic pool as they came from the same ethnic background. The bonds of friendship between the donor and the mother allowed the donor's relationship to the baby to be seen as an enhancement of that friendship. In another case where a husband's sister was the gestational surrogate, she was seen as having a custodial role only – providing a location and nurture for fetal development. "The children were fine with their auntie but could not wait to be reunited with their parents."

Perhaps the deepest divide in opinion regarding collaborative reproduction – and especially sperm donation – is whether or not children should be told of their donor origin or the identity of their donor. In the early days in the United Kingdom (and elsewhere), it was assumed by all parties that the whole practice would be based on secrecy. Parents would know nothing of the donor, who in turn would learn nothing of the outcome of the use of his sperm. Children would not be told of their donor origin to protect them from knowledge of their (then) illegitimate status and fathers from wider knowledge of their infertility. Later, when the legal situation was changed, and when attitudes toward male infertility had perhaps modified and it was less often seen as threatening manhood, it was increasingly believed that children should know the manner of their conception (but not the identity of their donor). The main arguments for this were that it would avoid family secrets and the children would learn their genealogy and full life story. It was also seen as a way of preventing unwitting incest – that a donor offspring might meet and marry another child of the same donor. Chances of that would, of course, be very remote, but it has been one of the persistent anxieties about AID and has led to restriction in the number of times sperm from a donor could be used. Anthropologist Janet Carson (2004) has noted that contemporary social worries about transgressive assisted reproductive practices are often phrased in terms of familiar anxieties about kin relationships such as those surrounding incest, adultery, divorce, and adoption. When AID was regulated in the United Kingdom under the Human Fertilization and Embryology Act of 1990, arrangements were put in place to record information about donors. When donors' children reach adulthood, they are able to access that donor information – but not names. But since that time, arguments have moved on. Increasingly, claims have been made that children have a "right" to knowledge of the identity of their donor. By this period, the nature of the link between donor and offspring was typically described as a "genetic" connection. And a new claim arose, that a child would not have a complete "genetic identity" if they did not know the identity of their donor. Such claims carried the day, and regulations changed and donor anonymity was ended – as had happened in a number of other countries. Space here does not permit a detailed analysis of the concept of genetic identity (but see Richards, 2014). But, suffice it to say, while it might sound rather significant and important, it is an empty concept, born of DNA and paternity tests and essentialist notions of DNA genetics – comparing DNA samples may provide a way of identifying people, but DNA genetics do not make us who we are; genes are not us.

However, not all arguments for openness in donation rest on the flawed concept of genetic identity. Wilson (1997), for example, put forward a plausible "narrative" notion of identity in which she sees identity as the different threads of narrative which people use to represent and to reflect on their lives. It is a notion of identity which is influenced by interactions and relationships with others and which helps to explain the significance of the past (including, of course, the manner of their conception) to many people's feeling of identity.

Of course, some children do grow up with knowledge of their donor origins and sometimes know who their donor is. The little evidence available on the matter suggests that when children are brought up with knowledge of their origins, this can have a beneficial effect on parent–child relationships (Golombok et al., 2002a; see also Haimes, 1998). It is also worth pointing out that though most children may not know about their biological origins, most parents tell other family members or friends about the manner of their conception (Golombok et al., 1996). This means, together with easy access to DNA relationship testing and the growth of clinical genetic testing, that children are increasingly likely to discover their "non-paternity." Those who discover their origins (or are told) as teenagers or adults may be angry and resentful of the way they have been misled by their parents and the professionals involved (Donor Conception Support Group of Australia, 1997; Turner and Coyle, 2000).

In the United Kingdom, as in many other countries, there are differences in the ways in which the children of donor conception and those of adoption are regarded. Almost all adopted children are told of their origins and given information about their birth parents. Increasingly, adoption is "open," with the possibility of continuing contact for children with their birth parents. Research suggests that adopted children benefit from openness (e.g., Grokevart and McRoy, 1998). In the United Kingdom, adopted children at 18, following counseling, have access to their birth certificates, and significant numbers use this information to try and trace their birth parents. The most common motive for doing this is for a sense of genealogical connectedness with forebears (Howe and Feast, 2000). There also may be issues for them about self-worth related to the reasons why their birth parents gave them up for adoption, and for some, there is the possibility of a continuing relationship with the birth parent(s). In Howe and Feast's (2000) study, a third of those who tried to make contact were either rejected by the birth parents or found the contact unsatisfactory, but even these young people said they were glad to have made the search and to have "completed the jigsaw." Eight years after having made a satisfactory contact with a birth mother, more than half the adopted children maintained a relationship with her. Strathern (1992) suggests that kinship talk is about the manner in which social arrangements are based on and provide the cultural context for the natural processes of reproduction and, we might add, also the less than natural arrangements that are made for the use of assisted or "artificial" reproductive technologies.

Testing for Genetic Disease

Since the mid-1990s, there have been intensive efforts, accelerated by the information from the Human Genome Project, to identify the genes with mutations that are associated with the Mendelian or single-gene diseases. Identification of the genes and their mutations opens up the possibility of genetic testing, which is now available for many of the 5000 or so of these genetic diseases. All are rare, and many are only recorded from a handful of families, but taken together, they may affect up to 5% of the population. In terms of causation, these diseases may be regarded as a genetic spanner in the works. A fault in the gene – a changed DNA sequence – which may be passed from parent to child, means that the protein which the gene is involved in producing is changed, so that it cannot perform its usual functions, and hence the disease. In the dominantly inherited Mendelian diseases, having a single faulty gene is usually sufficient to cause the disease.

One of the first genes associated with a dominantly inherited disease to be identified is that associated with Huntington's disease. This is a degenerative disease of the central nervous system which generally develops in middle age (most dominantly inherited diseases are adult onset). After about 15 years of increasing physical and mental disability, the disease is invariably fatal. Since predictive genetic testing has been available for Huntington's disease, families with the condition have been studied by social scientists (Marteau and Richards, 1996; Cox and McKellin 1999a, b). These families have been called the "moral pioneers" of the new genetic era (Cox and

Burgess, 2000; see also Rapp, 2000), facing novel decisions about genetic testing, communicating test results to relatives, and, more generally, living their lives in the shadow of a fatal genetic disorder which remains incurable. As with any dominantly inherited disorder, children of an affected parent have a 50% chance of inheriting the mutated form of the gene which leads to the disorder. Probably, about 10% of those in that situation have chosen to take the genetic test which tells them whether or not they have the gene mutation (Marteau and Richards, 1996; Harper, Lim, and Craufurt, 2000). "While there is uncertainty, there is hope" is the way one family member described their decision about testing (Wexler, 1979). In these families, as those with other gene diseases, communication about the disease is primarily undertaken by the women. They are the "kin keepers" or "genetic housekeepers" and are more likely to use genetic testing than the men (Richards, 1996, 1998). Perhaps more surprising is the very limited use made of fetal genetic testing by affected parents. Perhaps there is an issue of identity here. To abort a fetus that has the gene mutation is to destroy an individual that has the same gene mutation as the affected parent.

With the recessively inherited diseases, only those with mutations in both their copies of the relevant gene develop the disease; those with a single copy are normal carriers. These are diseases which typically develop at or soon after birth. Better-known examples here are thalassemia (particularly common in Mediterranean and Middle Eastern populations), cystic fibrosis (northwest Europe), and Tay–Sachs disease (Ashkenazi Jewish populations). Carriers of recessive disease may have an evolutionary selective advantage over noncarriers in these conditions. Thus, carriers of thalassemia and sickle-cell disease have resistance to malaria, while cystic fibrosis carriers are thought to be resistant to typhoid. This evolutionary advantage (despite the likelihood of producing children with the disease) may account for the relatively high frequency in carriers in certain populations.

In some of these cases, population-screening programs have been set up. In Cyprus, where about a fifth of the population are carriers of thalassemia, couples are screened before marriage. When both are carriers, they then use prenatal diagnosis and abortion. This has virtually eliminated the birth of affected children on the island. Previously, healthcare of the affected children during their short lives had accounted for a significant proportion of the island's total healthcare budget (Cowan, 2008). In parts of the United Kingdom, pregnant women are tested for cystic fibrosis carrier status; if they test positive, their partner is tested, and where both are positive, prenatal diagnosis with the possibility of an abortion of an affected fetus follows. But in most parts of the United Kingdom, such screening is not offered, and most carrier couples discover their status when a child with cystic fibrosis is born. This may then pose a profound dilemma for couples who want further children. Should they use prenatal diagnosis and abortion to avoid the birth of another child with the same condition as their existing child?

In some orthodox Jewish communities in North America and elsewhere, where prenatal diagnosis and abortion are not acceptable, young people are screened for Tay–Sachs carrier status. To avoid the possible damage to self-esteem that knowledge of carrier status can bring, or of blighting marriage prospects, results are not given to the young person but to the matchmakers that some communities use, who then avoid coupling two carriers. Where matchmakers are not used, there are schemes which offer young people a choice of receiving their own results or a personal identification number. This number then can be used together with that of a potential partner to determine whether or not both are carriers. In this way, young people avoid learning their carrier status except when both they and a potential partner are carriers.

Another way of avoiding the birth of affected children without the use of abortion is to employ preimplantation diagnosis. This involves IVF, and a genetic test is carried out on the embryos before implantation. Only those embryos not carrying the relevant gene mutation are then implanted. But, partly because of the low success of IVF programs (not much more than 20% of IVF treatments for couples lead to a pregnancy) and the high cost, this technology is not very widely used.

The recessively inherited conditions also provide one of the very rare examples of a genetic disease for which there is a cure (more or less) brought about through environmental manipulation. This is phenylketonuria (PKU). Those affected lack an enzyme which is necessary to digest a commonly occurring food component. This leads to accumulation of by-products in the body which may cause permanent brain damage, especially during childhood while the brain is still developing. But, by avoiding the relevant dietary constituent in childhood, brain development is largely normal. In many countries, babies are screened at birth (a Guthrie heel-prick blood test), and affected children (approximately 1 in 10,000) are then put on a special diet (Paul, 2002).

The final category of Mendelian single-gene disease which should be mentioned is the X-linked diseases such as Duchenne muscular dystrophy or fragile X syndrome. These diseases result from mutations from genes on the X-chromosome, one of the sex chromosomes. While women have paired X-chromosomes, men have an X and a Y. This means that if there is a gene with a potential disease producing on one of a woman's X-chromosomes, it is likely that she will have a normal copy of the gene on her other chromosome and hence no disease. But, if a man inherits an X-chromosome to "balance" this, disease results. Thus, X-linked conditions are generally confined to males but are inherited from their mothers. As has been reported in psychosocial studies of families which carry Duchenne muscular dystrophy, this gendering of the disease can produce difficult and complex dynamics in families (Parsons and Bradley, 1994).

As these new genetic technologies have been developed and deployed, there has been a systematic exploration of the lived impact of genetic understanding with families with genetic disorders, how they may communicate, or not, about their shared heritage, and such work has not only opened to scrutiny, a little explored aspect of family life and kinship, but has provided a knowledge base from which to develop genetic counseling and other aspects of clinical genetic services (Featherstone *et al.*, 2006).

Novas and Rose (2000) suggest that the key event in the development of genetic testing has been the creation of the person genetically at risk. This risk, it is argued, induces new and active relations to one's self and one's future as it generates new forms of "genetic responsibility" placing affected individuals and those at risk within new communities of obligation and identification. This may, it is claimed, transform the relations between patient and expert. "The birth of the person 'genetically at risk' is part of a wider reshaping of personhood along somatic lines and mutation in conceptions of life itself" (p. 486). Others have argued that a new kind of public health practice is being created based on a new concept of genetic risk (Petersen and

Lupton, 1996; Petersen and Bunton, 2002). Whether or not there is a wider issue of geneticization at play here is an issue we will return to later.

Our discussion thus far has focused on the relatively rare genetic diseases. However, there has also been a major research effort, largely through the genome-wide association studies, to identify genetic variants which might be associated with common "complex" diseases such as coronary heart disease, diabetes, and Alzheimer's disease. Many common genetic variants have been linked to such diseases. However, these tend to be weak associations, so predictive power of genetic tests using these variants is generally low. However, such tests have been developed for genome profiling which are now offered in direct-to-consumer personal genome testing by companies such as deCODEme and 23andMe. While these promise information which will empower prevention of common diseases, the useful information they may provide at present remains rather limited (Richards, 2010).

In the clinic, we begin to see the use of whole exome sequencing (ES) which is a targeted approach to sequence the coding regions of the human genome to identify genes associated with disorders (Biesecker, 2010). At present, ES is being used on a more or less research basis in situations where there are indications of an inherited disorder but the genetic basis is unknown. But critically, while the approach may identify the genetic basis of a condition, it will also reveal a great deal of information about other possibly significant genetic variations which may have clinical relevance to the patient and other family members. The first social science studies of this approach are just beginning, so we may be able to learn something of the impact of such developing genetic technologies. What is clear is that we are still only at the threshold of an era of medical genetic technology which may yield significant information regarding our health.

The development and implications of contemporary genetics have been a focus for both debate and research within sociology and other social sciences. Much of this research has proceeded under the influence of the geneticization thesis. Abby Lippman introduced this in the early 1990s (Lippman, 1991, 1992). Geneticization was defined as

> An ongoing process by which differences between individuals are reduced to their DNA, with most disorders, behaviours and psychological variations defined, at least in part, as genetic in origin. It refers as well to the process by which interventions employing genetic technologies are adopted to manage problems of health. Through this process, human biology is incorrectly equated with human genetics, implying that the latter acts along to make us each the organism he or she is.
>
> (Lippman, 1991, p. 19)

The claims inherent in this definition are clearly far reaching, and it is not surprising that this spawned considerable theoretical and empirical research. However, most of this concerns biomedicine and healthcare and is beyond the scope of this chapter on family life (but see, e.g., Weiner, Richards, and Martin, 2013). However, a popular but contested site for the claims of geneticization has been kinship and family relationship. Finkler (2001) has argued that kinship has been medicalized or geneticized (Gibbon, 2002) by the family pedigrees (or histories) which are created in genetic clinics. However, we should note that these pedigrees are not a recent creation of the DNA genetics but have been a central part of medical genetic practice since its inception in the 1940s and, indeed, were the stock in trade of the early twentieth-century eugenic movements in the United States, Britain, and elsewhere (Bashford and Levine, 2010). More generally, common themes in nineteenth-century fiction concern inheritance in families and secrets of descent and forebears, as well as madness and other "bad blood." Contemporary preoccupations with inheritance may have developed new narratives and themes with the DNA technologies (Nelkin and Lindee, 1995), but the metaphorical DNA, genes, and chromosomes of the twenty-first century (Richards, 2001) resonate strongly with the good and bad blood of Victorian culture and the ideology of eugenics in the twentieth century.

Biomedical Technology: Deployment and Cultural Assumptions

Of course, biomedical researchers do not simply set out to understand our biological world; they also wish to change it. As debates illustrate, public responses and attitudes to new developments are often complex (Gaskell and Bauer, 2001). In discussing attitudes to reproductive and genetic technologies, I want to argue that we are concerned with a particular set of values and a culture concerned with the maintenance of the boundary between the natural sphere of reproduction and the social sphere of family and kinship. Strathern (1992) and Edwards *et al.* (1999) have suggested that human reproduction is seen, at least in Europe and societies derived from these, as belonging to the domain of nature, not the domain of society, and the two are connected by concepts of kinship. It is important to note that the domain of nature referred to here is not the scientific world of biology but rather a cultural conception of nature (see Yanagisako and Delaney, 1995). Where technologies threaten to shift this boundary and extend the reach of society into the domain of nature, there is unease and resistance. In the modern period, the first major assault on this boundary was the increasing use of contraception, or the *artificial* methods of birth control, as they were termed, from the latter part of the nineteenth century onward. In 1877, there was the famous case in which Annie Besant and Charles Bradlaugh were convicted for distributing a book which described methods of birth control which was held to be obscene. After some initial hesitation that the availability of birth control might encourage the genetically well endowed to have smaller families, eugenicists did much to increase the knowledge and availability of contraception in many countries. In Britain, Marie Stopes set up her clinic for mothers in a poor part of London in 1921 as part of the activities of her Society for Constructive Birth Control and Racial Progress. Such efforts were swept along by the rising tide of eugenics, which, of course, also forcibly controlled the reproduction of those deemed unfit through the policies of institutional segregation and sterilization (Kevles, 1985; Paul, 1998; Bashford and Levine, 2010). However, there was continuing opposition from sections of the population that regarded (artificial) birth control as unnatural and against nature. In Britain, it was not until 1974 that contraception, as it was now known, and which by then included the pill, was generally available through doctors in the National Health Service. Today, the right to "found a family" is included in the Human Rights Act of 1998, and there was a general acceptance of a notion of reproductive autonomy allowing individuals the freedom to choose to have or not to have children (Jackson, 2001).

From the 1950s onward, the development of techniques for prenatal screening and diagnosis provided new methods for choosing what kinds of children to have or not have. There has been extensive research on attitudes toward the use of these techniques. In Britain, as elsewhere, there is strong endorsement for the availability of fetal tests and abortion for serious disease and disability (see Richards, 2002). But support falls off when conditions that develop later in life are involved, or those involving, for example, a restriction of growth. Data from the British Social Attitudes Survey indicate that, while almost 90% of respondents thought it was right for women to have an abortion if a fetus they carried had a serious mental or physical disability, this fell to 60% if a healthy fetus carried a condition likely to lead to death in their twenties or thirties and 48% if a healthy fetus would be restricted throughout life to the height of an 8-year-old child (Statford, Marteau, and Bobrow, 1999). Many opinion surveys on these issues have included questions about the use of techniques to select the sex of a baby. These show that an overwhelming majority of both the public and professionals reject the use of such techniques for sex selection, and this is banned in many regulated systems (McMillan, 2002). Given that in countries such as the United Kingdom, where the predominant preference of parents is to have children of both sexes and the use of sex selection is unlikely to distort the sex ratio or be damaging in other ways (Steinbock, 2002), at first sight, the strength of the opposition to this use of technology is perhaps surprising. However, here, we are concerned with what are widely termed "designer babies." Attitudes are very different toward the use of technology to avoid the birth of babies with serious conditions and cases where the aim is in some way to enhance or choose a baby's characteristics. Overall, there is a strong public approval of the use of biotechnology to prevent or treat disease (Gaskell and Bauer, 2001). However, to use techniques to determine any attributes of an unborn child is seen as something quite different. Once again, it is the boundary between the social and the natural domains which is violated. Here, using biotechnology is seen as "playing God," or being against "nature" or the natural order of things (Wagner et al., 2002). The other area of reproductive technologies where we find strong public and governmental opposition is with reproductive cloning. Here again, the natural order is disturbed. Cloning – assuming of course it becomes possible – would permit a predictability of the reproductive outcome as well as the foregoing of the natural union of egg and sperm. An inherent characteristic of the natural processes of reproduction is a capricious uncertainty of the outcome. Broadly speaking, children show a mixture of the characteristics of their parents. They demonstrate familial traits. However, the combinations and mixtures lead to unpredictable and unique characteristics. When at birth, a baby first enters the visible world, the same questions reoccur – "Is it a girl?," "Is it a boy?," and "Is it all right?" – and mothers as well as doctors and midwives count fingers and toes. Of course, other technologies, first X-rays and ultrasound, have made the unborn baby potentially visible (Oakley, 1984). But, interestingly, while these techniques are used to reveal physical abnormality as part of prenatal screening, in many situations, parents do not learn the sex of their unborn child. This is either kept hidden from them or they do not choose to know it before the birth. And, of course, the personality and physical appearance of babies remain unseen until after birth. The social child remains invisible. So, a boundary between the social world and nature remains intact.

We may also notice that birth provides a boundary after which the enhancement of bodily and mental functions becomes commonplace, in contrast to the general rejection of such possibilities before birth. Even young children may be subjected to cosmetic surgery or have their height enhanced with growth hormones. We pin back ears, fix teeth, or even provide adolescents with breast enhancement. But modification before birth – except to correct serious malformation – is not done, nor is any modification of the genes to be passed to future children permitted. Birth marks a boundary. We permit (in the United Kingdom, under license) genetic therapy of the already born – though, as yet, success in such experimental therapy has proved largely elusive – but modification of future children through germline therapy is not permitted. Yet, it is difficult to see why there should be objections were we able to safely restore the function of the gene in devastating disorders such as Huntington's disease.

We could argue that the commodification of gametes in IVF and donor insemination is part of this same boundary maintenance. Reducing the reproductive processes of the production and donation of eggs and sperm to the provision of "genetic material" denies and excludes the social actions of donors from a part of the "natural" reproduction by the couple receiving treatment. They are effectively written out of the story of the origins of the child, and so an apparently natural process of reproduction has taken place. Strategies for "naturalizing kinship" in IVF clinics may be seen in the same way (Thompson, 2001).

Of course, current boundaries may shift, and indeed, many have suggested that they will do so. In the end, pragmatism may rule for many. However, there may be a boundary which will prove robust. What is certain on the basis of current practice is that almost all parents, despite the possibilities of using gametes from all manner of desirable sources, prefer to have their "own" children conceived by their own egg and sperm brought together through sexual intercourse (Richards, 2002).

Conclusions

The new DNA technologies have not been with us for very long, and we have only begun to observe and analyze the ways in which they may play a part in family life. In the words of the old country song, "we are living in the future, where we have never been before," and it is not possible to see ways forward very clearly. DNA relationship testing allows a new explicitness in familial (genetic) connections, and I have suggested that their use may serve to further emphasize, and indeed define, relationship in terms of shared DNA sequences. Here, as with the use of reproductive technologies, international markets become important. A country may attempt to regulate access to certain technology, but its citizens are free to travel or to access global markets from their homes using the Internet. In the case of the United Kingdom, the use of ARTs has been controlled in line with past practice and, as far as possible, with the model of "natural" heterosexual reproduction. But medical tourism allows visits to the uncontrolled marketplaces; for example, gay men may seek egg donors (at a price) and birth mothers. Many travel from Europe to the unregulated clinics of the United States and the Far East, just as others surf the Net and travel to find babies for adoption, or sources where they can buy body parts for transplantation.

I have suggested that we see resistance where new technologies threaten to change the boundary between the social world of human actions and activity and the unseen domain of nature. "Artificial" birth control has shifted that boundary, and what was once discouraged by law has been renamed contraception and has become part of conventional medical practice, commerce, and family life. With the exception of some minority religious dissent, contraception has become an accepted part of daily life. Perhaps we shall see a similar shift in the boundary which currently determines the acceptability of gene and reproductive technologies. There is a wide acceptance of the genetic technologies which permit diagnosis and prediction of genetic disease and the possibility of avoiding the birth of affected children by using prenatal diagnosis and abortion or preimplantation diagnosis and embryo selection. Similarly, postnatal somatic gene therapy, while still largely a biotechnological aspiration, enjoys wide public support and encouragement. The current boundaries for resistance lie where prenatal selection (or treatment) moves from avoiding serious disease to the selection on the basis of social preference and prenatal enhancement. It is acceptable for parents to choose to select against a fetus with a serious genetic or congenital abnormality, but not for them to choose to use sex selection (or indeed, for deaf parents to choose to produce their desired deaf child). Having avoided predictable abnormality, reproduction is left to the vagaries of natural uncertainty, but wherever possible using parental sperm and eggs. "Designing" a baby to have desired characteristics or replicating an individual by reproductive cloning (were this to become technically feasible) is seen as steps too far. Indeed, approaching this boundary is usually seen as the beginning of the slide down a "slippery slope" which may lead to the boundary being shifted. However, if the history of contraception is any guide here, we may indeed be on a slippery slope, and one day, prenatal enhancement and the design of babies will become accepted social practice, assuming that there are widespread social pressures for these. When techniques become available which allow selection or modification of the unborn in ways that are seen to be socially desirable or useful, their use is likely to become acceptable. Then, a further part of the natural world will have been successfully colonized by the social.

Acknowledgments

My thanks are to Sophie Zadeh for her helpful comments on a draft of this chapter and to Gill Brown for her secretarial assistance and to Alison Krauss, The Be Good Tanyas, Blueflint, The Cox Family, Buddy Holly, The Low Anthem, The Flatlanders, Kitty Wells, The Everly Brothers, and Roy Acuff for their support.

References

Almeling, R. (2011) *Sex Cells. The Medical Market for Eggs and Sperm*, University of California Press, Berkeley.
Bainham, A. (2008) Arguments about parentage. *Cambridge Law Journal*, 67, 322–351.
Bashford, A. and Levine, P. (eds) (2010) *The Oxford Handbook of the History of Eugenics*, Oxford University Press, Oxford.

Bharadwaj, A. (2003) Why adoption is not an option in India: the visibility of infertility, the secrecy of donor insemination and other cultural complexities. *Social Science and Medicine*, 56, 1867–1880.

Biesecker, L. (2010) Exome sequencing makes medical genetics a reality. *Nature Genetics*, 42, 13–14.

Blake, L., Richards, M. and Golombok, S. (2013) The families of assisted reproduction and adoption, in *Family-Making: Contemporary Ethical Challenges* (eds. F. Baylis and C. McLoed), Oxford University Press, Oxford.

Carson, J. (2004) *After Kinship*, Cambridge University Press, Cambridge.

Cowan, R.S. (2008) *Heredity and Hope: The Case for Genetic Screening*, Harvard University Press, Cambridge.

Cox, S.M. and McKellin, W.H. (1999a) "There's this thing in our family": predictive testing and the social construction of risk for Huntington's disease, in *Sociological Perspectives on the New Genetics* (eds. P. Conrad and J. Gabe), Blackwell, Oxford.

Cox, S.M. and McKellin, W.H. (1999b) "There's this thing in our family": predictive testing and the construction of risk for Huntington's disease. *Sociology of Health and Illness*, 21, 622–646.

Cox, S.M. and Burgess, M.M. (2000) Victims, heroes or pioneers: moral experiences of hereditary risk and illness. Paper presented at the Canadian Bioethics Society Conference, Quebec.

Donor Conception Support Group of Australia (1997) *Let the Offspring Speak: Discussions on Donor Conception*, Donor Conception Support Group of Australia, Genges Hill.

Edwards, J.D., Franklin, S., Hirsch, E. *et al.* (1999) *Technologies of Procreation. Kinship in the Age of Assisted Conception*, 2nd edn, Routledge, London.

Engels, F. (1884) [1986] *The Origin of the Family, Private Property and the State*, Penguin Books, London.

Featherstone, K., Atkinson, P., Bharadwaj, A. and Clarke, A. (2006) *Risky Relations. Family Kinship and the New Genetics*, Berg, Oxford.

Finkler, K. (2001) The kin in the gene: the medicalization of family and kinship in American society. *Current Anthropology*, 42, 235–263.

Freeman, T. and Richards, M.P.M. (2006) DNA testing and kinship. Paternity, genealogy and the search for the 'truth' of genetic origins, in *Kinship Matters* (eds. F. Ebtehaj, B. Lindley and M. Richards), Hart Publishing, Oxford.

Gaskell, G. and Bauer, M.W. (eds) (2001) *Biotechnology 1996–2000*, Science Museum, London.

Gibbon, S. (2002) Re-examining genetization: family trees in breast cancer genetics. *Science as Culture*, 11, 429–457.

Giddens, A. (1991) *Modernity and Self-Identity: Self and Society in the Late Modern Age*, Polity, Cambridge.

Golombok, S., Brewaeys, A, Cook, R. *et al.* (1996) The European study of assisted reproduction families. *Human Reproduction*, 11, 2324–2331.

Golombok, S., Brewaeys, A., Cook, R. *et al.* (2002a) The European study of assisted reproduction families. The transition to adolescence. *Human Reproduction*, 17, 830–840.

Golombok, S., MacCallum, F.M., Goodman, E. and Rutter, M. (2002b) Parenting and contemporary reproductive technologies, in *Handbook of Parenting*, 2nd edn, vol. 3 (ed. M.H. Barnstein), Lawrence Erlbaum, Mahwah.

Grace, V.M. and Daniels, R.R. (2007) The (ir)relevance of genetics: engendering parallel worlds of procreation and reproduction. *Sociology of Health and Illness*, 5, 692–710.

Grokevart, M.D. and McRoy, R.G. (1998) *Openness in Adoption. Exploring Family Connections*, Sage, New York.

Gűrtin, Z.B. and Vayena, E. (2012) Reproduction donation: global perspectives and cultural diversity, in *Reproductive Donation. Practice, Policy and Bioethics* (eds. M. Richards, G. Pennings and J. Appleby), Cambridge University Press, Cambridge.

Haimes, E. (1998) The making of "the DI child": changing representations of people conceived through donor insemination, in *Donor Insemination: International Social Science Perspectives* (eds. K. Daniels and E. Haimes), Cambridge University Press, Cambridge.

Harper, P.S., Lim, S. and Craufurt, D. (2000) Ten years of pre-symptomatic testing for Huntington's disease: the experience of the UK Huntington's disease consortium. *Journal of Medical Genetics*, 37, 567–571.

Howe, D. and Feast, J. (2000) *Adoption, Search and Reunion*, Children's Society, London.

Jackson, E. (2001) *Regulating Reproduction. Law, Technology and Autonomy*, Hart, Oxford.

Kevles, D.J. (1985) *In the Name of Eugenics*, Knopf, New York.

Lippman, A. (1991) Prenatal genetic testing and screening: constructing needs and reinforcing inequalities. *American Journal of Law and Medicine*, 17, 15–20.

Lippman, A. (1992) Led (astray) by genetic maps: the cartography of the human genome and health care. *Social Science and Medicine*, 35, 1469–1471.

Lynch, M., Cole, S.A., McNally, R. and Jordan, K. (2008) *Truth Machine. The Contentious History of DNA Fingerprinting*, Chicago University Press, Chicago.

Mamo, L. (2005) Biomedicalizing kinship: sperm-banks and the creation of affinity ties. *Science as Culture*, 14, 237–262.

Marteau, T. and Richards, M.P.M. (eds) (1996) *The Troubled Helix*, Cambridge University Press, Cambridge.

McMillan, J. (2002) Sex selection in the United Kingdom. *Hastings Center Report*, 32, 28–31.

Nash, C. (2004) Genetic kinship. *Cultural Studies*, 18, 1–34.

Nelkin, D. and Lindee, S. (1995) *The DNA Mystique*, Freeman, New York.

Novas, C. and Rose, N. (2000) Genetic risk and the birth of the somatic individual. *Economy and Society*, 29, 485–513.

Nuffield Council on Bioethics (2012) *Novel Techniques for the Prevention of Mitochondrial DNA Disorders: An Ethical Review*, Nuffield Council on Bioethics, London.

Oakley, A. (1984) *The Captured Womb: A History of the Medical Care of Pregnant Women*, Blackwell, Oxford.

Parsons, E. and Bradley, D. (1994) Ethical issues in newborn screening for Duchenne muscular dystrophy, in *Genetic Counselling, Practice and Principles* (ed. A. Clarke), Routledge, London.

Paul, D. (1998) *Controlling Human Heredity: 1865 to the Present*, Humanity Books, Amherst.

Paul, D. (2002) PKU and procreative liberty. *Philosophy and Medicine*, 65, 171–190.

Pennings, G. and Gűrtin, Z.B. (2012) The legal and ethical regulation of transnational donation, in *Reproductive Donation. Practice, Policy and Bioethics* (eds. M. Richards, G. Pennings and J. Appleby), Cambridge University Press, Cambridge.

Petersen, A. and Lupton, D. (1996) *The New Public Health: Health and Self in the Age of Risk*, Sage, London.

Petersen, A. and Bunton, R. (2002) *The New Genetics and the Public's Health*, Routledge, London.

Rapp, R. (2000) *Testing Women. Testing the Fetus: The Social Impact of Amniocentesis in America*, Routledge, New York.

Raymond, J.G. (1994) *Women or Wombs: Reproductive Technologies and the Battle Over Women's Freedom*, Spinifex, Melbourne.

Richards, M.P.M. (1996) Families, kinship and genetics, in *The Troubled Helix: Social and Psychological Implications of the New Human Genetics* (eds. T. Marteau and M.P.M. Richards), Cambridge University Press, Cambridge.

Richards, M.P.M. (1998) Annotation: genetic research, family life and clinical practice. *Journal of Child Psychology and Psychiatry*, 39, 291–305.

Richards, M.P.M. (2001) How distinctive is genetic information? *Studies in the History of Biological and Biomedical Sciences*, 32, 663–687.

Richards, M. (2002) Future bodies: some history and future prospects for human genetic selection, in *Body Lore and Laws* (eds. A. Bainham, S. Day-Sclater and M. Richards), Hart, Oxford.

Richards, M.P.M. (2008) Artificial insemination and eugenics: celibate motherhood, entelegenesis and germinal choice. *Studies in the History, Philosophy of Biology and Biomedical Sciences*, 39, 211–221.

Richards, M.P.M. (2010) Reading the runes of my genome. A personal exploration of retail genetics. *New Genetics and Society*, 29, 291–310.

Richards, M.P.M.(2014) A history of collaborative reproduction and the rise of the genetic connection. In *Relatedness in Assisted Reproduction: Families, Origins and Identities* (eds. T. Freeman, F. Ebtehaj, S. Graham and M. Richards). Cambridge University Press, Cambridge.

Rothstein, M.A., Murray, T.H., Koebnick, G.E. and Majumder, M.A. (eds) (2005) *Genetic Ties and the Family*, John Hopkins Press, Baltimore.

Schneider, D. (1980) *Kinship: A Cultural Account*, University of Chicago Press, Chicago.

Spallone, P. (1987) Reproductive technology and the state: the Warnock report and its clones, in *Made to Order: The Myth of Reproductive and Genetic Progress* (eds. P. Spallone and D.L. Steinberg), Pergamon, Oxford.

Steinbock, B. (2002) Sex selection. Not obviously wrong. *Hastings Center Report*, 32, 23–28.

Steiner, E. (2006) The tensions between legal, biological and social conceptions of parenthood in English law. *Electronic Journal of Comparative Law*, 10, 3–14.

Steptoe, P. and Edwards, R.G. (1978) Birth after the replacement of a human embryo. *Lancet*, ii, 366.

Stratford, N., Marteau, T. and Bobrow, M. (1999) Tailoring genes, in *British Social Attitudes. The 16th Report* (eds. R. Jowell *et al.*), Ashgate, Aldershot.

Strathern, M. (1992) *Reproducing the Future: Essays on Anthropology, Kinship and the New Reproductive Technologies*, Manchester University Press, Manchester.

Taitz, J., Weekers, J.E.M. and Mosca, D.T. (2002) DNA and immigration: the ethical ramifications. *Lancet*, 359, 794.

Thompson, C. (2001) Strategic naturalizing kinship in the infertility clinic, in *Relative Values. Reconfiguring Kinship Studies* (eds. S. Franklin and S. McKinnon), Duke University Press, Duke.

Turner, J. and Coyle, A. (2000) What does it mean to be a donor offspring? *Human Reproduction*, 11, 2041–2051.

Vayena, E. and Golombok, S. (2012) Challenges in intra-family donation, in *Reproductive Donation. Practice, Policy and Bioethics* (eds. M. Richards, G. Pennings and J. Appleby), Cambridge University Press, Cambridge.

Wagner, W., Kronberger, N., Gaskell, G. *et al.* (2002) Nature in disorder. The troubled public of biotechnology, in *Biotechnology 1996–2000. The Years of Controversy* (eds. G. Gaskell and M.W. Bauer), Science Museum, London.

Wand, J.W.C. (1948) *Artificial Human Insemination*, Society for the Propagation of Human Knowledge, London.

Weiner, K., Richards, M. and Martin, P. (2013) Have we seen the geneticization of society? Expectations and evidence. *Sociology of Health and Illness*, submitted.

Wexler, N.S. (1979) Genetic "Russian roulette": the experience of being "at risk" for Huntington's disease, in *Genetic Counselling: Psychological Dimensions* (ed. S. Kessler), Academic, New York.

Wilson, S. (1997) Identity, genealogy and the social family: the case of donor insemination. *International Journal of Law, Policy and the Family*, 11, 270–297.

Yanagisako, S. and Delaney, C. (1995) Naturalizing power, in *Naturalizing Power* (eds. C. Delaney and S. Yanagisako), Routledge, New York.

26

Sex, Family, and Social Change

JUDITH TREAS AND THOMAS ALAN ELLIOTT

Any general account of contemporary families must come to terms with revolutionary changes in sexual attitudes and behavior. These family changes are seen in new customs for courtship and coupling, which are exemplified both by greater sexual self-determination among the young and by rising unmarried cohabitation at all ages. New ideas about sexual conduct are evident not only in the rise in births to unmarried parents but also in marital fertility so tightly controlled that even the timing and spacing of a woman's one or two babies is a matter of careful calculation. Changing ideas about sex are revealed in the more diversified portfolios of sexual practices which individuals report. Perhaps no recent change is as dramatic as the greater acceptance of sex between two men or two women, acceptance increasingly ratified in marriage law.

As these changes indicate, sex lives have been the place where the grand ideas of Western culture have played out for hundreds of years. Dating to The Enlightenment, cultural values of individualism offer the moral rationale for greater sexual autonomy (Lesthaeghe and Surkyn, 1988). Born of affluence, a postmaterial ethos has liberated individuals from the restrictions of kin, church, and community and sanctioned the pursuit of individual fulfillment (Inglehart, 1997). By offering women an alternative to patriarchy, feminism has framed sexuality as an area ripe for gender parity (Budig, 2004). The upshot of these sweeping ideational developments is that sex between consenting adults is subject to much less social regulation today than in the past.

To investigate the interplay of change in sex and family, this chapter begins with a focus on the young, whose behavior continues to be of significance to their families and whose formative experiences shape their subsequent lifestyles and life chances. Although tolerance of premarital sex has increased, sexual relationships are still seen as posing special risks for young people – risks that may justify parental guidance and invite broader social concerns. Sexual behavior in adolescence sets the stage for adult sexual relations, which are characterized today by greater sexual experience,

The Wiley Blackwell Companion to the Sociology of Families, First Edition.
Edited by Judith Treas, Jacqueline Scott, and Martin Richards.
© 2014 John Wiley & Sons Ltd. Published 2017 by John Wiley & Sons Ltd.

more varied sexual practices, and growing openness to sexual expression. An exception is the still strong expectation of sexual fidelity in committed relationships, especially heterosexual ones. The contraceptive revolution accounts for much of the shift from procreation to pleasure in sexual relationships, but scientific advances, combined with aggressive marketing, have extended the promise of sexual gratification over the life course. For gays and lesbians, the most revolutionary development is social – the growing public acceptance of same-sex relations. It remains to be seen whether the institutional forces of marriage will ultimately alter the nature of same-sex sexual relationships by imposing the same normative and practical constraints as they do on heterosexual couples.

Sex Early in the Life Course

Adolescence typically marks the beginning of sexual experience. Surveying 14 countries on five continents, one study finds that young people in most places become sexually active before they are out of their teens (Singh *et al.*, 2000). For adolescent women, high rates of sexual activity are seen not only in wealthy countries like the United States and Britain but also in impoverished sub-Saharan Africa. Lower rates are found in Asia with Latin American countries falling somewhere in between. Globally, sexual activity for young women – in contrast to young men – is still apt to take place within marriage (Singh *et al.*, 2000). When teenage women in the United States and United Kingdom have sex, however, it is apt to be before they are married. In North America and Western Europe, age at first sex has declined by about 3 years since the 1950s – even as age at first marriage has increased (Teitler, 2002). The end result of trends has been reductions in age-at-first-sex differences between countries, between social classes, between early and late initiators, and between men and women (Teitler, 2002). In Canada, the historical double standard, the earlier sexual initiation for males than females, virtually disappeared (Maticka-Tyndale, Barrett, and McKay, 2000).

Although premarital sex is widely accepted for adults (Gubernskaya, 2010), teen sex is often regarded as problematic. In 1994, fully 71% of Americans and 67% of the British said sex between young teens (ages 14–16) was "always wrong" (Widmer, Treas, and Newcomb, 1998). Elsewhere, disapproval ranged from high levels in Catholic populations to moderate levels in Scandinavian countries: 84% in Ireland, 81% in Northern Ireland, 71% in New Zealand, 61% in Australia, 58% in Italy, 55% in Canada, 45% in the Netherlands, and 32% in Sweden. If anything, the percent answering "always wrong" has increased over the last 20 years (Smith, 2008). Concerns about the long-run ramifications of early sexual activity arise not only from moral objections but also from cultural assumptions about minors' immaturity and vulnerability to exploitation.

Formative sexual experiences do resonate across the life course. American women who, as children, had sexual contact with an adult are at greater risk of sexually transmitted disease (STD), teenage childbearing, and multiple sex partners as an adult (Browning and Laumann, 1997). There is a growing appreciation that the low status of women and children makes them vulnerable to forced sex in much of the developing world (Farr, 2004). Around the globe, such concerns have led to stronger laws protecting children against sexual abuse, even as there has been a general trend to legal decriminalization of sex between consenting adults (Frank, Camp, and Boutcher, 2010). Of course, child protection may run at cross-purposes with efforts to support teenagers' sexual self-determination, as illustrated by American laws insuring that adolescents need not get their parent's permission to obtain contraceptives (Cook, Erdman, and Dickens, 2007). Cross-national variation in rates of sexually transmitted disease and pregnancy points out, however, the extent to which the broader social context buffers the risks associated with early sexual activity.

Sexually transmitted diseases

Adolescents are at higher risk than their seniors for STDs, but large cross-national differences in STDs suggest big gaps in the efficacy of education and prevention efforts. In the middle of the 1990s, the gonorrhea infections reported per 100,000 young people, ages 15–19, numbered 596 in Russia, 572 in the United States, 77 in England and Wales, 59 in Canada, and only 2 in Sweden (Panchaud et al., 2000). Providing protection against both STDs and pregnancy, condom use has been increasing, but only 54% of women, 15–19, in Australia and in the United States reported using a condom when they last had sex (Bearinger et al., 2007).

Higher STD rates map to higher numbers of sexual partners although, ironically, girls in the developing world are often placed at risk of STDs by unprotected sex with their husbands (Bearinger et al., 2007). At least in developed countries, unmarried adolescents are at risk because they are likely to have multiple partners (Bearinger et al., 2007), due to their relationships being of relatively short duration. In 2002, 23% of American men, ages 15–19 years old, and 21% of their female counterparts reported multiple partners in the last 12 months (Mosher et al., 2005). Even if they have ever had sex, of course, unmarried teens do not have particularly high levels of sexual activity, because they have relatively low frequencies of intercourse and long periods between partners (Sonenstein, Pleck, and Ku, 1991; Singh et al., 2000).

Teen pregnancy

Besides STDs, unprotected sex puts young women at risk of pregnancy. In the developing world, such as sub-Saharan Africa where maternal mortality remains high, early pregnancies pose threats to the life and health of teenage girls and their babies (Bearinger et al., 2007). In the developed world, children of teen mothers are disadvantaged in terms of birth weight and cognitive development (Alan Guttmacher Institute, 1994), but the concerns with early motherhood also focus on the implications of teen pregnancy for social and economic well-being.

In the West, nonmarital pregnancies historically resulted in marriage, but today, they result in nonmarital births. In Asia, such births remain rare (Jones, 2007). In Europe, children are often born into stable, cohabiting unions, and youngsters benefit from living in supportive welfare states (Teitler, 2002). In the United States, welfare provisions are more limited, and the relationships between young, unmarried parents are often unstable and short-lived (Edin and Kissane, 2010). Roughly 40% of American children are born to unmarried women (Hamilton, Martin, and Ventura, 2009), half of whom are cohabiting (McLanahan and Beck, 2010).

Only one-third of parents who were cohabiting at the birth of their child were still together 5 years later (McLanahan and Beck, 2010; Kamp Dush, 2011).

In the United States, early twentieth-century social reformers were alarmed that sexual activity would damage a young woman's reputation and marital prospects, thus consigning her to poverty (Nathanson, 1991). Today, having children outside of marriage reduces the chances a woman will marry (Upchurch, Lilliard, and Panis, 2001), but low marriage and high divorce rates mean that marriage no longer offers the security it once did. Contemporary concerns with teenage motherhood focus not on marriage market penalties, but rather on career costs from disrupted schooling and careers (Nathanson, 1991).

Since the mid-1970s, teen childbearing has declined in Europe as well as the United States, Canada, New Zealand, and Australia (Teitler, 2002). US rates remain markedly higher than those of other developed countries. The 42 babies born to every 1000 American women, ages 15–19, in 2006 represented a 32% drop in the teen birthrate since 1991 (Santelli and Melnikas, 2010). Still, this remains high compared to 35 in England and Wales, 14 in Canada, and 6 in Sweden (McKay and Barrett, 2010). While teen childbearing has been declining among African Americans, the rate is still three times higher than white teens (Singh, Darroch, and Frost, 2001; Kost and Henshaw, 2012). Teen childbearing is lower for immigrants, a pattern that also holds for Canada (Maticka-Tyndale, Barrett, and McKay, 2000) and Britain (Singh, Darroch, and Frost, 2001).

Americans' lack of candor about sexual matters has been faulted for sending mixed messages that contribute to teen pregnancy (Jones, 1986). Disadvantage, however, increases the likelihood of early childbearing in both the United States and Britain (Singh, Darroch, and Frost, 2001). The US teen pregnancy rates stand out, in part, because the United States has proportionately more poor people than Britain. Regardless of socioeconomic level, American teens are less likely to use contraceptives and more likely to have a baby than their British counterparts. This fact points to American policy differences – less access to contraception due to the historical lack of a national health system and less government effort to reduce the socioeconomic disadvantages that shape the childbearing choices of young people (Singh, Darroch, and Frost, 2001).

Sexual relationships of young people

Relationships early in the life course set the stage for later life. In France, those who were younger when they first had sex were less likely to marry, less likely to stay married, and more likely to have multiple sex partners (Bozon, 1996). Negative assessments, of course, discount the extent to which adolescent sexual relationships are a learning ground not only for sexuality but also for intimacy, communication, and other life skills (Bay-Cheng, 2003).

In the developed world, time spent in romantic relationships before first sex seems to have increased, leaving young people better equipped to communicate and manage their sexual debuts than in the past (Teitler, 2002). American teenagers who postponed sex are more likely to have used contraception than those who had sex for the first time at younger ages (Rapsey and Murachvery, 2006). Although first sexual experiences are often spontaneous, contraceptive planning for first sex has been on the rise (Abma *et al.*, 1997). Sexual scripts for young people are also changing. More adolescent males in the United States report heterosexual genital contact than report vaginal sex *per se* (Mosher *et al.*, 2005; Lindberg, Jones, and Santelli, 2008). Males, ages 15–19, were significantly more likely to have been masturbated by a female in 1995 than in 1988, even though they were less likely to have had vaginal intercourse (Gates and Sonenstein, 2000; Mosher *et al.*, 2005). American high school students who ever had sexual intercourse decreased from 54% in 1991 to 48% in 2007 (CDC, 2008).

Perhaps the most noteworthy change in sexual scripts in the United States has taken place on college campuses, where changing sexual lifestyles have given rise to the "hookup," a casual sexual encounter that could include anything from kissing to intercourse (Heldman and Wade, 2010). As many as three-quarters of US college students hookup at some point; about a quarter of those do so 10 or more times over their college career (Heldman and Wade, 2010). Although hooking up offers a normative framework for sex at a point in the life course when marriage is far in the future (Armstrong, Hamilton, and England, 2010; Heldman and Wade, 2010; Armstrong, England, and Fogarty, 2012), the practice generates something akin to moral panic in many quarters.

The hookup culture, for instance, is faulted for putting young women at risk of sexual coercion and assault (Wade and Heldman, 2012). At large campus parties where women can wind up stranded for the night, hookups are promoted by heavy drinking and the social expectation of friendliness toward the hosts (Armstrong, Hamilton, and Sweeney, 2006). The sex may leave something to be desired – at least for women who report an orgasm in only 11% of first-time hookups compared to 67% of relationship sex (Armstrong, England, and Fogarty, 2012). Few hookups prompt lasting connections, a disappointment for women hoping for a stable, ongoing relationship (Bogle, 2008). When hookups lead to dating, however, greater commitment may follow (England, Shafer, and Fogarty, 2008). In fact, most college seniors had a relationship that lasted longer than 6 months (England, Shafer, and Fogarty, 2008; Armstrong, England, and Fogarty, 2012). After they graduate, young people seem to adopt more formal dating practices as they move toward marriage age (Bogle, 2008).

Families and communities as contexts

As seen in the example of college campuses, young people's sexual attitudes and behaviors are shaped by their context. Families are an important influence. Schalet (2011) observes that Dutch parents tolerate teens having a romantic sleepover that would be forbidden by American parents. Framed as an issue of family cohesion, teen sex is normalized in the Netherlands. In the United States, it is dramatized in ways that can promote conflict between parents and children.

Research identifies numerous antecedents of teen sexual activity and teen pregnancy, including psychological dispositions, hormone levels, partner dynamics, poverty, school problems, risk-taking (e.g., substance abuse), religious beliefs, and community context (Udry, 1988; Brewster, Billy, and Grady, 1993; Mott *et al.*, 1996; Kirby, 2001; Singh, Darroch, and Frost, 2001; Chen, Thompson, and Morrison-Beedy, 2010). Negative consequences are mitigated when sexual activity happens within a romantic relationship (McCarthy and Grodsky, 2011). Although peers are important, families play critical roles. Parents determine the broad circumstances of upbringing, communicate and model their own values, and monitor their offsprings' behavior. Through various pathways, family disruption leads to sex at an earlier age (Kiernan and Hobcraft, 1997). Because low parental education and family disruption contribute to teen pregnancy, the ups and downs in teen birthrates in the United States have been driven, in part, by demographic trends in broader family structure (Manlove *et al.*, 2000).

Teens are less likely to pursue risky sexual behavior when they have a good relationship with a parent who disapproves of such conduct. Positively perceived mother–child relationships, maternal disapproval of teen sex, and maternal discussion about birth control deter sexual activity and promote consistent contraceptive use among African American teens (Dancy and DiIorio, 2012). Fully 70% of young black and Hispanic adolescents in the United States say that parents have discussed STDs with them, but fewer report parent–child conversations about contraception and other aspects of sexuality (Miller *et al.*, 1998). Teenagers talk about sex more readily with their mothers than with their fathers (Miller *et al.*, 1998), a finding that holds not only for heterosexuals but also for gay, lesbian, and bisexual youngsters (D'Augelli, Hershberger, and Pikington, 1998). Growing up in an unfavorable family environment (e.g., living apart from parents before age 14 or having parents who drank heavily or used illegal drugs) greatly increases the likelihood of sexual abuse (Moore, Nord, and Peterson, 1989). On the other hand, parental support and monitoring reduces the number of sex partners, especially for teens with troubling histories of sexual exploitation (Luster and Small, 1997).

Few people view families as sufficient to prevent teen pregnancy or STDs. Americans favor sex education in the schools nearly seven to one (National Opinion Research Center, 2002). Conservatives advocate "Just Say No" abstinence programs, but others support candid instruction about sexuality and safe sex methods. Evaluation studies show that abstinence-only programs do not delay the initiation of sex, decrease the number of sex partners, or increase the return to abstinence after having had sex. Comprehensive sex-education programs have been shown to delay initiation of sex, decrease number of sex partners, and increase the use of contraceptives (Kirby, 2007). Effective programs give the facts about the risks of unprotected sex and methods of protection (Kirby, 2007). They have specific goals, such as changing behavioral norms (rather than just giving students neutral information) (Kirby, 2001). They have committed and trained teachers who teach strategies for communicating, negotiating, and resisting peer and partner pressure. Since teens facing poor schooling and job prospects are at high risk of pregnancy, youth development programs offering counseling, tutoring, and job placement can also affect adolescent sexual choices. Whatever their content and efficacy, sex education is a staple of American adolescence. Although only 51% of women, 40–44, had had formal sex education by age 18, the figure stood at 96% for women and 97% for men, ages 15–19, in 2008 (Martinez, Abma, and Copen, 2010).

From Procreation to Pleasure

Each new generation knows more about physiology, reproduction, and sexual practices than did their own parents. This is, in part, a consequence of the spread of family planning, which includes at least a rudimentary dose of sex education.

There is also greater openness about sexual matters. In the 1930s, US decency codes dictated that movies show married couples in separate beds. After the 1950s, sexually explicit material, ranging from birth control pamphlets to pornographic films, became widely available in the United States after court cases confirmed Constitutional protections of free speech.

Compared to their grandparents' generation, today's couples come to marriage with more firsthand sexual experience. While the honeymoon was once a momentous sexual initiation, 70% of men and 58% of American women in 1963–1974 (post-baby boom) birth cohorts report having had vaginal intercourse with their mate before marriage (Laumann *et al.*, 1994). Only 6% of male and 16% of female respondents in Britain reported that they first had sexual intercourse at marriage (Wellings *et al.*, 1994). Sex is an integral part of courtship. By the late 1980s, half of recently married Americans had cohabited (Bumpass and Sweet, 1989). As more conservative cohorts were replaced by younger, more permissive generations in the United States (Treas, 2002) and Britain (Scott, 1998), public opinion came to accept sex before marriage. As the sexual practices of single and married people converged, sexual advice books stopped being called marriage manuals, and sex videos were marketed to couples as educational entertainment.

Couples have elaborated their sexual scripts to include more sexual practices. Although leveling off for recent cohorts, lifetime experience with oral sex increased sharply between the Great Depression cohorts (born 1933–1937) and the cutting edge of the baby boom (1948–1952). Among 25–29 year old American women in the 1992 National Health and Social Life Survey, 76% reported ever having given oral sex as compared to 39% of women, 55–59 (Laumann *et al.*, 1994). More recently, the gap between generations has closed, with 89% of American women, ages 25–29, having ever given oral sex, compared to 80% of women, ages 50–59 (Herbenick *et al.*, 2010). British data confirm similar trends in experience with oral sex (Wellings *et al.*, 1994; Johnson *et al.*, 2001).

Some groups remain relatively conventional in their sexual practices (Mahay, Laumann, and Michaels, 2001). Americans display greater variation in sexual behavior than do the British (Michael *et al.*, 2001). Even controlling for factors like age, marital status, and education, white Euro-Americans in the United States are significantly more likely to have oral sex than are Mexican Americans and African Americans (Leichliter *et al.*, 2007). Within racial groups, college-educated Americans follow less conventional sexual scripts than do persons with less schooling (Chandra *et al.*, 2011). Similarly, in Britain, social class is positively associated with oral, anal, and nonpenetrative sex for both men and women (Wellings *et al.*, 1994).

Marital sex

Although couples may be more adventurous than earlier generations, husbands and wives settle into fairly routine, if reportedly satisfying, sex lives. Married people have higher coital frequency than do singles. Having a regular sex partner, married people in Britain have sex more often than do the unmarried (although the coital frequency of married persons is slightly lower than that of cohabitors) (Wellings *et al.*, 1994). Among British informants who had vaginal sex in the past year, however, married people are less likely to report having oral, anal, and nonpenetrative sex than their cohabiting or unmarried counterparts (Wellings *et al.*, 1994). In the United States, married people are, if anything, *less* likely than unmarried people to have incorporated oral sex into their *last* sex act (Laumann *et al.*, 1994), perhaps because married people devote less time to their sexual encounters than singles do. Only 9% of married men said their last sexual event lasted an hour or more compared to 38% of noncohabiting, never-married men (Laumann *et al.*, 1994).

There is not much evidence that the married have more physically pleasurable sex than others, but married women do say that they derive more emotional satisfaction from their sexual relations than do cohabiting or single women (Waite and Joyner, 2001). There is popular agreement that sex contributes to a successful marriage. The percent of respondents citing a happy sexual relationship as "very important" ranges in the 70s for Mexico, Chile, France, the United States, Brazil, and Hungary to 28% in Japan (Yodanis, 2010). However, about 16% of coresident married people in the United States (excluding those who were sick, had recently given birth, or were pregnant) admitted that they had not had sex in the last month. Couples that never have sex tend to be unhappy and to have thought about separating (Donnelley, 1993; Sprecher and Cate, 2004), but coital frequency, however, is a poor gauge of marital quality. High levels of sexual activity also occur in violent marriages, where husbands use physical threats to extort sex from their wives (DeMaris, 1997).

Having preschool children can interfere with a couple's sex life (Donnelley, 1993). Coital frequency also declines with duration of marriage (Wellings *et al.*, 1994), no doubt reflecting both habituation (i.e., novelty wears off) and biological effects of aging. Men, 50–59, are three times more likely to say that they were disinterested in sex or had erection problems than were younger men, 18–29 (Laumann, Paik, and Rosen, 2001). For women, sexual dysfunction is correlated with physical health and relationship quality, not age (Laumann, Das, and Waite, 2008).

Certainly, couples no longer take it for granted that menopause or advancing years mark the end of sex. According to one US survey, over 40% of married people, 75–85, were still sexually active (Waite and Das, 2010). Until recently, erotic interests among older people were regarded as humorous and unseemly, and their physical attractiveness and capacity for sex were discounted. Just as Viagra and hormone replacement therapy reduced the physical impediments to sex in later life, a host of popular sex books by physicians and scientists offered up an enthusiastic prognosis for sex in middle and old age. Conveniently, *Love and Sex after 60* was published in a large-print edition (Butler and Lewis, 1996).

Technology in the bedroom

Couples' sex lives reflect not only their culture but also the technologies available to them. Separating sexual pleasure in marriage from its reproductive consequences stands as an important achievement in family life. Birth control, once unthinkable and tainted by its association with illicit sex, found a place within the realm of conscious choice and domestic respectability. At the end of the eighteenth century, even as the Reverend Thomas Robert Malthus fretted about improper arts employed to avoid the reproductive consequences of sexual relations, married couples in rural France were altering their sexual practices – using abstinence and withdrawal to prevent pregnancy. Today, couples are the beneficiaries of a long political struggle to legalize the distribution of birth control information as well as many scientific advances in contraceptive methods. Partners enjoy less obtrusive and more reliable contraception. Couples can and do have spontaneous, pleasure-oriented sex without giving much thought to the possibility of unwanted pregnancy. Indeed, coital frequency increased among married Americans in the 1970s when legal abortion and the pill reduced the fear of pregnancy (Ryder and Westoff, 1977).

There remain few, if any, differentials in contraceptive practice in the United States. Whites and blacks, Catholics and Protestants, married and cohabiting are equally and universally likely to use modern family planning (Sweeney, 2010). Nor is contraception just a stopping strategy that couples adopt after reaching their desired family size. Contraception is used to prevent premarital pregnancy, time the first birth, and space later ones – in short, to synchronize biology with the complex timetables of family, work, and leisure. While couples once structured their sex lives to avoid pregnancy, many couples must now self-consciously reorganize their sexual activities to make babies. (In this volume, Martin Richards (Chapter 25) explores the ways in which assisted reproductive technology has figured in.) Ironically, with fertility control so reliable, the United States, in particular, continues to have a high number of unplanned births (Morgan and Rackin, 2010) – a testimony to the cultural ambivalence toward sex and a healthcare system that has impeded access to contraception.

If contraceptive technology has permitted relationships to be more erotic, so have the development, marketing, and rebranding of technologies to remedy perceived sexual dysfunctions. While initial marketing of hormonal contraceptives stressed their efficacy in preventing pregnancy, 1990s' advertising extolled their benefits in controlling weight gain and acne, reducing menstrual bloating, and eliminating the inconvenience of menstruation altogether (Watkins, 1998, 2012). Oral contraceptives came to be viewed as a lifestyle drug, addressing quality of life issues that might discourage sex, rather than just averting pregnancy.

A similar shift occurred for drugs treating erectile dysfunction (ED). In 1998, when Viagra was introduced to America, it was marketed to older men whose sex lives were seriously compromised by ED. By the early 2000s, Viagra was being promoted as a performance-enhancing drug for otherwise healthy, middle-aged men (Irvine, 2006). Preying on fears of failed masculinity, the ads suggested that anything less than optimal sexual performance required treatment (Loe, 2001). By 2008, Cialis was introduced as a daily drug that preserved spontaneity by not requiring advance planning for sexual activity (Cialis, 2012). Young men without ED, especially those having sex with men, have increased their recreational use of ED medications (Kim, Kent, and Klausner, 2002; Korkes *et al.*, 2008; Harte and Meston, 2011).

Sexual exclusivity

Despite widespread acceptance of premarital sex, sexual exclusivity in heterosexual relationships is scarcely questioned. The percent saying faithfulness is very important for a successful marriage ranges from 72% in Russia to 94% in the United States and Northern Ireland (Yodanis, 2010). Fully 80% of Americans and 60% of the British say extramarital sex is "always wrong." Similar views are voiced in Australia (65%), Ireland (66%), Japan (48%), the Netherlands (54%), New Zealand (66%),

Sweden (61%), and other Western countries (ISSP Research Group, 2008, tabulated by authors). Although extenuating circumstances sometimes justify extramarital sex, virtually no respondents say that extramarital sex is "not at all wrong." Nor are moral judgments on extramarital sex softening. British condemnation remains high (Scott, 1998). If anything, disapproval has increased in the United States since the mid-1980s (Treas, 2002), and the gender gap narrowed as men adopted harsher views (Scott, 1998).

Sexual infidelity has a high cultural profile. On American television, extramarital sex is almost as common as marital sex (Lowry, 2000). A recent series, *Big Love*, features an obscure polygamous cult offering a mix of religious piety and unconventional sexual arrangements. Media preoccupation may explain why married Americans believe that other married people do not take fidelity as seriously as they do (Greeley, 1991). In fact, fully 99% of married Americans say they expect their partner to be sexually exclusive; the figure (94%) is nearly as high for cohabiting heterosexuals (Treas and Giesen, 2000). By and large, couples practice what they preach. In the United States, estimates for the percent of married persons with a secondary sex partner in the last year range from 1.5% to 3.6% (Smith, 1991; Leigh, Temple, and Trocki, 1993; Choi, Catania, and Dolcini, 1994;). According to Allen and Atkins (2012), 7% of women and 14% of men, currently married and not previously divorced, *ever* had sex with anyone except their spouse while married. In Britain, 4.5% of married men, 16–59, and 1.9% of comparable women reported two or more heterosexual partners in the last year (Wellings *et al.*, 1994). Cohabitors are at higher risk of sexual infidelity, even controlling for the shorter duration of their unions and their more permissive sexual values (Treas and Giesen, 2000). This is generally attributed to cohabitors being less invested in their unions – and having less to lose – than married people. While sexual infidelity is undoubtedly underreported, any lack of candor simply underscores the strength of sexual exclusivity norms.

Men are more likely to be unfaithful than are women (Treas and Giesen, 2000). Although social class is positively associated with sexual infidelity among the British (Wellings *et al.*, 1994), socioeconomic factors do not much matter for Americans' extramarital behavior (Treas and Giesen, 2000). At elevated risk for infidelity are those who have greater interest in sex, more sexual experience, and less conservative sexual values. Regardless of personal preferences, opportunities to meet potential sex partners increase the likelihood of infidelity. Americans whose jobs bring them into intimate contact with others are more likely to be unfaithful. British men and women who work away from home overnight are more likely to have had multiple sex partners (Wellings *et al.*, 1994). By contrast, intimate social networks can encourage fidelity. In-laws, for example, monitor behavior, stabilize the union with support, and generally constitute an asset that would be put at risk by marital indiscretions. Individuals who know and enjoy their partner's family and friends are more likely to be sexually exclusive than are individuals without such intimate ties (Treas and Giesen, 2000). Participating in a religious community also buffers against the risk of infidelity.

Sexual infidelity is regarded as a danger to ongoing unions (Lawson, 1988), because it taps deeply held feelings of sexual jealousy and partner possession, diverts time and energy from the marital relationship, poses risks to health and reputation, and compromises sex as a basis for pair bonding. Women, who tend to view affection as a requisite for sex, are more likely than men to describe extramarital sex as a threat to the relationship (Glass and Wright, 1992). By the same token, a married woman having an extramarital relationship is more likely to be perceived as being in love, committed, and ready to marry than is a man (Sprecher, Regan, and McKinney, 1998).

Infidelity has been linked to lower marital satisfaction (Treas and Giesen, 2000). A recent longitudinal study found that infidelity tends to follow decreases in marital satisfaction but also further lowers happiness within the marriage (Previti and Amato, 2004). As for infidelity as a cause of divorce, 40% of recently divorced Americans said their spouse was involved with someone else before the marriage ended, but only 15% of these respondents admitted that they themselves had an extramarital relationship (South and Lloyd, 1995). Divorced and separated persons who have had extramarital sex insist that their own infidelity was caused by marital problems, even as they maintain that their spouse's infidelity was a cause of their marital difficulties (Spanier and Margolis, 1983).

Sympathetic analyses frame infidelity as a mismatch between the biological quest for novelty, the psychological desire for emotional commitment, and the unrealistic cultural ideologies that equate love with sexual exclusivity (Anderson, 2012). Occasionally, organized challenges to sexual exclusivity have emerged. In the middle of the twentieth century, there was "swinging," a couple-oriented lifestyle of recreational sex. Swinging was succeeded by another social movement promoting "polyamorous" relationships, which reject expectations of sexual *and* emotional exclusivity (Wosick-Correa, 2010). Individual couples who agree to open relationships work out rules to maintain the emotional exclusivity of the primary relationship while allowing sexual inclusivity. Extradyadic, three-way sex, for instance, is a way of discouraging undesirable emotional bonds with outsiders. Certain acts, times, and/or places may be defined as off-limits for secondary relations in order to underscore the strength of the primary emotional commitment. Although some people fall short of the ideal, the notion that married people should limit their sex lives to marriage goes largely uncontested.

Same-Sex Relationships Going Mainstream

Gay men are less likely than straight couples or lesbians to practice monogamy (Gotta *et al.*, 2011). While some gay men see monogamy as a relationship ideal, if not always achievable, many regard sex with other partners as personally liberating and even as beneficial to the primary relationship. Though data are limited, monogamous and nonmonogamous gay couples report similar rates of relationship satisfaction (Bonello and Cross, 2009). Comparing life histories of straight and gay men, Green (2006) suggests that gay men are pushed into sexual experimentation and dyadic innovation, because legal marriage is not always available to them. Without the protections and presumed continuity of formal marriage, partners – homosexual or not – have less incentive to make long-run investments in a relationship (Brines and Joyner, 1999). Because they cannot rely on ready-made scripts based on gender differences to govern their relationships, gay and lesbian partnerships are organized along more egalitarian lines than heterosexual unions. Same-sex partners have more autonomy than heterosexual ones (Gotta *et al.*, 2011).

Marriage and family in the lives of nonheterosexuals have gained greater prominence and public recognition. This development raises an important question: Will
nonheterosexuals' growing incorporation in traditionally heterosexual family institutions alter the distinctive features of gay and lesbian relationships, sexual and familial?
Legal marriage might change the nature of gay relationships if gay married couples
conform to the social expectations of the institution, including perhaps its inhibiting
sexual norms. There is some evidence of convergence toward the heterosexual
domestic model of fidelity in the United States. Besides the decrease in reports of sex
outside their relationship (83% of gay men in 1975 and 59% in 2000), fewer couples
say they have explicit, nonmonogamy agreements (Gotta *et al.*, 2011). Alternatively,
if marriage does not change gay relationships, will gay marriage change the broader
institution of marriage, say, by introducing relationship models placing greater stress
on equality and less emphasis on sexual exclusivity?

This tension between sexual lifestyles and marital conventions is only the latest
chapter in the domestication of same-sex relations. So long as gays and lesbians
remained a marginalized minority, the heterosexual public saw them in largely
sexual terms – unfamiliar sexual practices, deviations from gender norms, and
even psychological pathology. Little thought was given to the possibility that gays
and lesbians even had families, much less confronted some of the same family
challenges as heterosexuals. Disapproval of same-sex relations, however, has
declined dramatically (Scott, 1998; Treas, 2002; Halder, 2012). Since World War
II, there has been a shift to the decriminalization of sodomy (Frank, Camp, and
Boutcher, 2010). As documented earlier, even the sexual repertoires of heterosexuals now routinely include practices once associated with homosexuals. Public
discourse on gays and lesbians no longer focuses on sex *per se*, and there is a
growing research literature on nonheterosexuals as partners and parents (Oswald,
2002; Lambert, 2005; Gotta *et al.*, 2011; Moore, 2011; Biblarz and associates
(Chapter 6) in this volume).

In contrast to the growing tolerance of premarital sex, which was due to the
generational replacement of earlier conservative generations by more recent liberal
ones, the greater open-mindedness on same-sex relations came about because cohorts
became more tolerant over time (Treas, 2002). In a striking illustration of the diffusion
of cultural innovations, less educated Americans moved closer to the permissive views
of college graduates. All but the most frequent American churchgoers softened their
views on same-sex relations. Men are still less tolerant than women, perhaps because
misogyny and homophobia are the cornerstones of hegemonic masculinity (Kimmel,
2003). Women's interest in the emotional content of relations may account for their
greater empathy for same-sex relationships (Scott, 1998). The importance of love is
often cited by those who would call couples "family" regardless of sexual orientation
(Powell *et al.*, 2010).

Barriers to same-sex unions have begun to fall (Chamie and Mirkin, 2011).
New legislation has extended marriage rights to nonheterosexual unions. In the
last 20 years, 15 Western European countries have legally recognized same-sex
unions (Kollman and Waites, 2009). In the United States, the federal government recognizes same-sex marriages issued by the states and, to date, 17 states
permit same-sex marriages. Others offer domestic partnerships or civil unions to

same-sex couples. Today, more Americans support same-sex marriage than those who do not (Saad, 2012).

Despite progress, nonheterosexuals have not achieved parity with heterosexuals when it comes to family life. Only 32% of Americans agree that two men can be called a family although the figure (59%) is higher when the two men are described as having a child (Powell *et al.*, 2010). In 2006, only 32% of the overall European Union population supported adoption rights of gay and lesbian couples (Hollekim, Slaatten, and Anderssen, 2012). Continuing resistance to incorporating gays and lesbians into American life is seen in a social movement that cites homosexuality as a threat to families (Stone, 2011). Backlashes from religious groups are seen in other nations as well, especially in formally colonized Africa and in the Middle East (Kollman and Waites, 2009).

The families formed by gays and lesbians highlight features which may challenge heterosexual family conventions but also draw nonheterosexuals into the regime of these institutionalized norms. First, children in lesbian families are usually the product of one partner's earlier heterosexual union (Black *et al.*, 2000), but younger gay and lesbian couples have children born within the context of their relationship (Patterson and Riskind, 2010). While often capitalizing on new reproductive technologies, both parents are experientially closer to heterosexual "birth parents" than earlier generations. Second, sometimes in response to rejection by kin, gays and lesbians often define family to include voluntary ties of affection incorporating lovers, former sex partners, friends, and others. Stressing broad networks of supportive friendships forged out of affection and reciprocity (Weston, 1991; Nardi, 1999; Weeks, Heaphy, and Donovan, 2001), this families-of-choice notion was a self-conscious effort by lesbians and gays not only to distinguish their family lives from those of their heterosexuals but also to argue for the superiority of their more voluntary and egalitarian relationships. As public debates about parenting qualifications illustrate, constructions of family difference based on sexual orientation run afoul of arguments for equality. Whether unique aspects of same-sex family and couple relations are sustained in the face of marriage equality and declining discrimination remains to be seen.

Conclusion

Family control of sexuality once meant avoiding out-of-wedlock births and social disapproval by restricting sexuality to suitable marriages. Norms about sexual behavior have changed, upending the life course of adolescents and young adults. Fewer and fewer young people expect that marriage will necessarily occur before having sex, living together, becoming pregnant, or siring children. Because age at first sex has declined and age at first marriage has risen, there is now a period of years that young people fill by exploring various sexual practices with different sexual partners. This behavior is not without risks, especially in the United States, where unprotected sex results in higher rates of teen pregnancy and STD. Rather than discrediting the family's control of sexuality, these changes serve to highlight the importance of family structure, parent–child communication, and parental values for young people, who navigate their early sexual experiences more successfully when they have a positive family context.

Early sexual experience echoes through the life course, affecting subsequent sexual behavior and even the likelihood of marriage and divorce. Premarital sex spills over into marriage. Given greater sexual sophistication, more reliable contraception, and a companionate ideal of marriage, twenty-first-century marriage has become more erotic. Couples come to marriage with a much broader repertoire of sexual experience and practices than in the past. Committed – at least ideologically – to sexual fidelity, married couples today can expect to have mutually satisfying physical relations that will continue well into old age. Thus, most of the life course – from early adolescence to advanced old age – is sexualized. Disapproval of same-sex relations has also declined. Paradoxically, as heterosexual unions became sexier, same-sex relationships – once defined almost exclusively by sexual practices – came to be seen through a domesticated lens of marriage equality. As gay marriage is legalized, it remains to be seen whether these unions will embrace such heterosexual ideals as monogamy or whether their more autonomous and egalitarian model will be taken up by more heterosexual couples.

References

Abma, J.C., Chandra, A., Mosher, W.D. *et al.* (1997) Fertility, family planning, and women's health: new data from the 1995 National Survey of Family Growth. *Vital and Health Statistics*, 23 (19), 1–114.

Alan Guttmacher Institute (1994) *Sex and America's Teenagers*, The Alan Guttmacher Institute, New York.

Allen, E.S. and Atkins, D.C. (2012) The association of divorce and extramarital sex in a representative U.S. sample. *Journal of Family Issues*, 33, 1477–1493.

Anderson, E. (2012) *The Monogamy Gap: Men, Love, and the Reality of Cheating*, Oxford University Press, Oxford.

Armstrong, E.A., England, P. and Fogarty, A.C.K. (2012) Accounting for women's orgasms and sexual enjoyment in college hookups and relationships. *American Sociological Review*, 77, 435–462.

Armstrong, E.A., Hamilton, L. and Sweeney, B. (2006) Sexual assault on campus: a multilevel, integrative approach to party rape. *Social Problems*, 53 (4), 483–499.

Armstrong, E.A., Hamilton, L. and England, P. (2010) Is hooking up bad for young women? *Contexts*, 9 (3), 22–27.

Bay-Cheng, L.Y. (2003) The trouble of teen sex: the construction of adolescent sexuality through school-based sexuality education. *Sex Education: Sexuality, Society and Learning*, 3 (1), 61–74.

Bearinger, L.H., Sieving, R.E., Ferguson, J. and Sharma, V. (2007) Global perspectives on the sexual and reproductive health of adolescents: patterns, prevention, and potential. *The Lancet*, 369, 1220–1231.

Black, D., Gates, G., Sanders, S. and Taylor, L. (2000) Demographics of the gay and lesbian population in the United States: evidence from available systematic data sources. *Demography*, 37 (2), 139–154.

Bogle, K.A. (2008) *Hooking Up: Sex, Dating, and Relationships on Campus*, New York University Press, New York.

Bonello, K. and Cross, M.C. (2009) Gay monogamy: i love you but i can't have sex with only you. *Journal of Homosexuality*, 57, 117–139.

Bozon, M. (1996) Reaching adult sexuality: first intercourse and its implications: from calendar to attitudes, in *Sexuality in the Social Sciences* (eds. M. Bozon and H. Leridon), Dartmouth, Aldershot, pp. 143–175.

Brewster, K.L., Billy, J.O.G. and Grady, W.R. (1993) Social context and adolescent behavior: the impact of community on the transition to sexual activity. *Social Forces*, 71, 713–740.

Brines, J. and Joyner, K. (1999) The ties that bind: principles of cohesion in cohabitation and marriage. *American Sociological Review*, 64, 333–355.

Browning, C.R. and Laumann, E.O. (1997) Sexual contact between children and adults: a life course perspective. *American Sociological Review*, 62, 540–560.

Budig, M. (2004) Feminism and the family, in *The Blackwell Companion to the Sociology of Families* (eds. J. Scott, J. Treas and M. Richards), Blackwell Publishers, Oxford, pp. 416–434.

Bumpass, L.L. and Sweet, J.A. (1989) National estimates of cohabitation. *Demography*, 26, 615–625.

Butler, R.N. and Lewis, M.I. (1996) *Love and Sex after 60* (Rev. ed.), G.K. Hall, Thorndike.

CDC (2008) Trends in HIV- and STD-related risk behaviors among high school students – United States, 1991–2007. *Morbidity and Mortality Weekly Report*, 57 (30), 817–819.

Chamie, J. and Mirkin, B. (2011) Same-sex marriage: a new social phenomenon. *Population and Development Review*, 37 (3), 529–551.

Chandra, A., Mosher, W.D. and Copen, C. (2011) Sexual behavior, sexual attraction, and sexual identity in the United States: data from the 2006–2008 National Survey of Family Growth. *National Health Statistics Report*, 36, 1–28.

Chen, A.C.-C., Thompson, E.A. and Morrison-Beedy, D. (2010) Multi-system influences on adolescent risky sexual behavior. *Research in Nursing & Health*, 33, 512–527.

Choi, K.-H., Catania, J.A. and Dolcini, M.M. (1994) Extramarital sex and HIV risk behavior among American adults: results from the national AIDS behavior survey. *American Journal of Public Health*, 84, 2003–2007.

Cialis (2012) Cialis for daily use, http://www.cialis.com/Pages/cialis-for-daily-use-for-ed.aspx (accessed August 8, 2012).

Cook, R.J., Erdman, J.N. and Dickens, B.M. (2007) Respecting adolescents' confidentiality and reproductive and sexual choices. *International Journal of Gynecology and Obstetrics*, 98, 182–187.

D'Augelli, A.R., Hershberger, S.L. and Pikington, N.W. (1998) Lesbian, gay, and bisexual youth and their families: disclosure of sexual orientation and its consequences. *American Journal of Orthopsychiatry*, 68, 361–371.

Dancy, B. and DiIorio, C. (2012) Mothers: the major force in preventing HIV/STD risk behaviors, in *Family and HIV/AIDS: Cultural and Contextual Issues in Prevention and Treatment* (eds. W. Pequegnat and C.C. Bell). Springer, New York.

DeMaris, A. (1997) Elevated sexual activity in violent marriages: hypersexuality or sexual extortion? *Journal of Sex Research*, 34, 361–373.

Donnelley, D.A. (1993) Sexually inactive marriages. *Journal of Sex Research*, 30 (2), 171–179.

Edin, K. and Kissane, R.J. (2010) Poverty and the American family: a decade in review. *Journal of Marriage and Family*, 72, 460–479.

England, P., Shafer, E.F. and Fogarty, A.C.K. (2008) Hooking up and forming relationships on today's college campuses, in *The Gendered Society Reader*, 3rd edn (ed. M. Kimmel), Oxford University Press, New York, pp. 531–593.

Farr, K. (2004) *Sex Trafficking: The Global Market in Women and Children*, Worth Publishers, New York.

Frank, D.J., Camp, B.J. and Boutcher, S.A. (2010) Worldwide trends in the criminal regulation of sex, 1945 to 2005. *American Sociological Review*, 75, 867–893.

Gates, G.J. and Sonenstein, F.L. (2000) Heterosexual genital sexual activity among adolescent males: 1988 and 1995. *Family Planning Perspectives*, 32, 295–297, 304.

Glass, S.P. and Wright, T.L. (1992) Justifications for extramarital relationships: the association between attitudes, behaviors, and gender. *Journal of Sex Research*, 29 (3), 361–387.

Gotta, G., Green, R.-J., Rothblum, E. *et al.* (2011) Heterosexual, lesbian, and gay male relationships: a comparison of couples in 1975 and 2000. *Family Process*, 50 (3), 353–376.

Greeley, A.M. (1991) *Faithful Attraction*, Tom Doherty Associates Book, New York.

Green, A.I. (2006) Until death do us part? The impact of differential access to marriage on a sample of urban men. *Sociological Perspectives*, 49 (2), 163–189.

Gubernskaya, Z. (2010) Changing attitudes toward marriage and children in six countries. *Sociological Perspectives*, 53, 179–200.

Halder, M. (2012) The influence of world societal forces on social tolerance. A time comparative study of prejudices in 32 countries. *The Sociological Quarterly*, 53, 211–237.

Hamilton, B.E., Martin, J.A. and Ventura, S.J. (2009) Births: preliminary data for 2007. *National Vital Statistics Report*, 57 (12), 1–23.

Harte, C.B. and Meston, C.M. (2011) Recreational use of erectile dysfunction medications in undergraduate men in the United States: characteristics and associated risk factors. *Archives of Sexual Behavior*, 40, 597–606.

Heldman, C. and Wade, L. (2010) Hook-up culture: setting a new research agenda. *Sexuality Research and Social Policy*, 7, 323–333.

Herbenick, D., Reece, M., Schick, V. *et al.* (2010) Sexual behavior in the United States: results from a national probability sample of men and women ages 14–94. *Journal of Sexual Medicine*, 7 (suppl 5), 255–265.

Hollekim, R., Slaatten, H. and Anderssen, N. (2012) A nationwide study of Norwegian beliefs about same-sex marriage and lesbian and gay parenthood. *Sex Research and Social Policy*, 9, 15–30.

Inglehart, R. (1997) *Modernization and Postmodernization: Cultural, Economic, and Political Change in 43 Societies*, Princeton University Press, Princeton.

Irvine, J.M. (2006) Selling viagra. *Contexts*, 5, 39–44.

ISSP Research Group (2008) Religion III. Distributor: GESIS Cologne Germany.

Johnson, A.M., Mercer, C.H., Erens, B. *et al.* (2001) Sexual behaviour in Britain: partnerships, practices, and HIV risk behaviors. *The Lancet*, 358, 1835–1842.

Jones, E.M. (1986) *Teenage Pregnancy in Industrialized Countries: A Study*, Yale University Press, New Haven.

Jones, G.W. (2007) Delayed marriage and very low fertility in Pacific Asia. *Population and Development Review*, 33 (3), 453–478.

Kamp Dush, C.M. (2011) Relationship-specific investments, family chaos, and cohabitation dissolution following a nonmarital birth. *Family Relations*, 60, 586–601.

Kiernan, K.E. and Hobcraft, J. (1997) Parental divorce during childhood: age at first intercourse, partnership and parenthood. *Population Studies*, 51, 41–55.

Kim, A.A., Kent, C.K. and Klausner, J.D. (2002) Increased risk of HIV and sexually transmitted disease transmission among gay or bisexual men who use viagra, San Francisco 200–2001. *AIDS*, 16 (10), 1425–1428.

Kimmel, M.S. (2003) Masculinity as homophobia fear, shame, and silence in the construction of gender identity, in *Race, Class, and Gender in the United States: An Integrated Study* (ed. P.S. Rothenberg), Worth Publishers, New York, pp. 81–92.

Kirby, D. (2001) Understanding what works and what doesn't in reducing adolescent sexual risk-taking. *Family Planning Perspectives*, 33, 276–281.

Kirby, D. (2007) *Emerging Answers: Research Findings on Programs to Reduce Teen Pregnancy and Sexually Transmitted Diseases*, The National Campaign to Prevent Teen Unplanned Pregnancy, Washington, DC. http://www.thenationalcampaign.org/ea2007/ (accessed October 31, 2013).

Kollman, K. and Waites, M. (2009) The global politics of lesbian, gay, bisexual, and transgender human rights: an introduction. *Contemporary Politics*, 15 (1), 1–17.

Korkes, F., Costa-Matos, A., Gasperini, R. *et al.* (2008) Recreational use of PDE5 inhibitors by young healthy men: recognizing this issue among medical students. *Journal of Sexual Medicine*, 5, 2414–2418.

Kost, K. and Henshaw, S. (2012) *U.S. Teenage Pregnancies, Births and Abortions, 2008: National Trends by Age, Race and Ethnicity*. Guttmacher Institute. http://www.guttmacher.org/pubs/USTPtrends08.pdf (accessed October 31, 2013).

Lambert, S. (2005) Gay and lesbian families: what we know and where to go from here. *The Family Journal*, 13, 43–41.

Laumann, E.O., Paik, A. and Rosen, R.D. (2001) Sexual dysfunction in the United States: prevalence and predictors, in *Sex, Love, and Health in America: Private Choices and Public Policies* (eds. E.O. Laumann and R.T. Michael), University of Chicago Press, Chicago, pp. 352–376.

Laumann, E.O., Das, A. and Waite, L.J. (2008) Sexual dysfunction among older adults: prevalence and risk factors from a nationally representative U.S. probability sample of men and women 57–85 years of age. *Journal of Sexual Medicine*, 5, 2300–2311.

Laumann, E.O., Gagnon, J.H., Michael, R.T. and Michaels, S. (1994) *The Social Organization of Sexuality: Sexual Practices in the United States*, University of Chicago Press, Chicago.

Lawson, A. (1988) *Adultery: An analysis of Love and Betrayal*. Basic Books, New York.

Leichliter, J.S., Chandra, A., Liddon, N. *et al.* (2007) Prevalence and correlates of heterosexual anal and oral sex in adolescents and adults in the United States. *The Journal of Infectious Diseases*, 196, 1852–1859.

Leigh, B.C., Temple, M.T. and Trocki, K.F. (1993) The sexual behavior of U.S. adults: results from a national survey. *American Journal of Public Health*, 83 (10), 1400–1408.

Lesthaeghe, R. and Surkyn, J. (1988) Cultural dynamics and economic theories of fertility change. *Population and Development Review*, 14, 1–45.

Lindberg, L.D., Jones, R. and Santelli, J.S. (2008) Noncoital sexual activities among adolescents. *Journal of Adolescent Health*, 43, 231–238.

Loe, M. (2001) Fixing broken masculinity: viagra as a technology for the production of gender and sexuality. *Sexuality & Culture*, 5 (3), 97–125.

Lowry, B. (2000) Study: Sex Has Few Consequences in TV, Film. *Los Angeles Times*, March 29, F3.

Luster, T. and Small, S.A. (1997) Sexual abuse history and number of sex partners among female adolescents. *Family Planning Perspectives*, 29, 204–211.

Mahay, J., Laumann, E.O. and Michaels, S. (2001) Race, gender, and class in sexual scripts, in *Sex, Love, and Health in America: Private Choices and Public Policies* (eds. E.O. Laumann and R.T. Michael), University of Chicago Press, Chicago, pp. 197–238.

Manlove, J., Terry, E., Gitelson, L. *et al.* (2000) Explaining demographic trends in teenage fertility, 1980–1995. *Family Planning Perspectives*, 32, 166–175.

Martinez, G., Abma, J. and Copen, C. (2010) Educating teenagers about sex in the United States. *NCHS data brief*, no 44, National Center for Health Statistics, Hyattsville, http://www.cdc.gov/nchs/data/databriefs/db44.htm (accessed October 31, 2013).

Maticka-Tyndale, E., Barrett, M. and McKay, A. (2000) Adolescent sexual and reproductive health in Canada: a review of national data sources and their limitations. *Canadian Journal of Human Sexuality*, 9 (1), 41–65.

McCarthy, B. and Grodsky, E. (2011) Sex and school: adolescent sexual intercourse and education. *Social Problems*, 58 (2), 213–234.

McKay, A. and Barrett, M. (2010) Trends in teen pregnancy rates from 1996–2006: a comparison of Canada, Sweden, U.S.A., and England/Wales. *The Canadian Journal of Human Sexuality*, 19 (1–2), 43–52.

McLanahan, S. and Beck, A.N. (2010) Parental relationships in fragile families. *The Future of Children*, 20 (2), 17–38.

Michael, R.T., Wadsworth, J., Feinleib, J.A. *et al.* (2001) Private sexual behavior, public opinion, and public health policy related to sexually transmitted diseases: a U.S.-British comparison, in *Sex, Love, and Health in America: Private Choices and Public Policies* (eds. E.O. Laumann and R.T. Michael), University of Chicago Press, Chicago, pp. 439–453.

Miller, K.S., Kotchick, B.A., Dorsey, S. *et al.* (1998) Family communication about sex: what are parents saying and are their adolescents listening? *Family Planning Perspectives*, 30, 218–222, 235.

Moore, M. (2011) *Invisible Families: Gay Identities, Relationships, and Motherhood Among Black Women*, University of California Press, Berkeley.

Moore, K.A., Nord, C.W. and Peterson, J.L. (1989) Nonvoluntary sexual activity among adolescents. *Family Planning Perspectives*, 21, 110–114.

Morgan, P.S. and Rackin, H. (2010) The correspondence between fertility intentions and behavior in the United States. *Population and Development Review*, 36 (1), 91–118.

Mosher, W.D., Chandra, A. and Jones, J. (2005) *Sexual Behavior and Selected Health Measures: Men and Women 15–44 Years of Age, United States, 2002*. Advanced Data From Vital and Health Statistics, No. 362, National Center for Health Statistics, Hyattsville.

Mott, F.L., Fondell, M.M., Hu, P.N. *et al.* (1996) The determinants of first sex by age 14 in a high-risk adolescent population. *Family Planning Perspectives*, 28, 13–18.

Nardi, P.M. (1999) *Gay Men's Friendships: Invincible Communities*, Chicago University Press, Chicago.

Nathanson, C.A. (1991) *Dangerous Passage: The Social Control of Sexuality in Women's Adolescence*, Temple University Press, Philadelphia.

National Opinion Research Center (2002) *General Social Survey 1972–2000 Cumulative Codebook*. NORC, Chicago.

Oswald, R.F. (2002) Resilience within the family networks of lesbians and gay men: intentionality and redefinition. *Journal of Marriage & the Family*, 64, 374–383.

Panchaud, C., Singh, S., Feivelson, D. and Darroch, J.E. (2000) Sexually transmitted diseases among adolescents in developed countries. *Family Planning Perspectives*, 32, 24–32, 45.

Patterson, C.J. and Riskind, R.G. (2010) To be a parent: issues in family formation among gay and lesbian adults. *Journal of GLBT Family Studies*, 6 (3), 326–340.

Powell, B., Bolzendahl, C., Geist, C. and Steelman, L.C. (2010) *Counted Out: Same-Sex Relations and Americans' Definitions of Family*, Russell Sage Foundation, New York.

Previti, D. and Amato, P.R. (2004) Is infidelity a cause or consequence of poor marital quality? *Journal of Social and Personal Relationships*, 21 (2), 217–230.

Rapsey, C. and Murachvery, R. (2006) Adolescent sexuality, in *Sex and Sexuality, Volume 1: Sexuality Today: Trends and Controversies* (eds. R.D. McAnulty and M.M. Burnette), Praeger Publishers, Westport, pp. 61–100.

Ryder, N.B. and Westoff, C.F. (1977) *The Contraceptive Revolution*, Princeton University Press, Princeton.

Saad, L. (2012) U.S. acceptance of gay/lesbian relations is the new normal. *Gallup*. http://www.gallup.com/poll/154634/Acceptance-Gay-Lesbian-Relations-New-Normal.aspx (accessed September 19, 2012).

Santelli, J.S. and Melnikas, A.J. (2010) Teen fertility in transition: recent and historic trends in the United States. *Annual Review of Public Health*, 31, 371–383.

Schalet, A. (2011) *Not Under My Roof: Parents, Teens, and the Culture of Sex*, University of Chicago Press, Chicago.

Scott, J. (1998). Changing attitudes to sexual morality: a cross-national comparison. *Sociology*, 32, 815–845.

Singh, S., Darroch, J.E. and Frost, J.J. (2001) Socioeconomic disadvantage and adolescent women's sexual and reproductive behavior: the case of five developed countries. *Family Planning Perspectives*, 33, 251–259.

Singh, S., Wulf, D., Samara, R. and Cuca, Y.E. (2000) Gender differences in the timing of first intercourse: data from 14 countries. *International Family Planning Perspectives*, 26, 21–28, 43.

Smith, T.W. (1991) Adult sexual behavior in 1989: number of partners, frequency of sexual intercourse and risk of AIDS. *Family Planning Perspectives*, 23 (3), 102–107.

Smith, T.W. (2008) *Changes in Family Structure, Family Values, and Politics: 1972–2006*, NORC, Chicago.

Sonenstein, F.L., Pleck, J.H. and Ku, L.C. (1991) Levels of sexual activity among adolescent males in the United States. *Family Planning Perspectives*, 23, 162–167.

South, S.J. and Lloyd, K.M. (1995) Spousal alternatives and marital dissolution. *American Sociological Review*, 60 (1), 21–35.

Spanier, G.B. and Margolis, R.L. (1983) Marital separation and extramarital sexual behavior. *Journal of Sex Research*, 19, 23–48.

Sprecher, S. and Cate, R.M. (2004) Sexual satisfaction and sexual expression as predictors of relationship satisfaction and stability, in *The Handbook of Sexuality in Close Relationships* (eds. J.H. Harvey, A. Wenzel and S. Sprecher), Lawrence Erlbaum Associates, Mahwah, pp. 235–256.

Sprecher, S., Regan, P.C. and McKinney, K. (1998) Beliefs about the outcomes of extramarital sexual relationships as a function of gender of the 'cheating spouse'. *Sex Roles*, 38 (3–4), 301–311.

Stone, A.L. (2011) *Gay Rights at the Ballot Box*, University of Minnesota Press, Minneapolis.

Sweeney, M.M. (2010) The reproductive context of cohabitation in the united states: recent change and variation in contraceptive use. *Journal of Marriage and Family*, 72, 1155–1170.

Teitler, J.O. (2002) Trends in youth sexual initiation and fertility in developed countries: 1960–1995. *Annals of the American Academy of Political and Social Science*, 580, 134–152.

Treas, J. (2002) How cohorts, education, and ideology shaped a new sexual revolution on American attitudes toward non-marital sex, 1972–1998. *Sociological Perspectives*, 45, 267–283.

Treas, J. and Giesen, D. (2000) Sexual infidelity among married and cohabiting Americans. *Journal of Marriage and the Family*, 62, 48–60.

Udry, J.R. (1988) Biological predispositions and social control in adolescent sexual behavior. *American Sociological Review*, 53, 709–722.

Upchurch, D.M., Lilliard, L.A. and Panis, C.W.A. (2001) The impact of nonmarital childbearing on subsequent marital formation and dissolution, in *Out of Wedlock: Causes and Consequences of Nonmarital Fertility* (eds. L. Wu and B.L. Wolfe), Russell Sage Foundation, New York, pp. 344–380.

Wade, L. and Heldman, C. (2012) Hooking up and opting out: negotiating sex in the first year of college, in *Sex for Life: From Virginity to Viagra, How Sexual Changes Throughout Our Lives* (eds. L.M. Carpenter and J. DeLamater), New York University Press, New York, pp. 128–145.

Waite, L.J. and Joyner, K. (2001) Emotional and physical satisfaction with sex in married, cohabiting, and dating unions: do men and women differ?, in *Sex, Love, and Health in America: Private Choices and Public Policies* (eds. E.O. Laumann and R.T. Michael), University of Chicago Press, Chicago, pp. 239–269.

Waite, L.J. and Das, A. (2010) Families, social life, and well-being at older ages. *Demography*, 47, S87–S109.

Watkins, E.S. (1998) *On the Pill: A Social History of Oral Contraceptives 1950–1970*, The Johns Hopkins University Press, Baltimore.

Watkins, E.S. (2012) How the pill became a lifestyle drug: the pharmaceutical industry and birth control in the United States since 1960. *American Journal of Public Health*, 102 (8), 1462–1472.

Weeks, J., Heaphy, B. and Donovan, C. (2001) *Same Sex Intimacies: Families of Choice and Other Life Experiments*, Routledge, New York.

Wellings, K., Field, J., Johnson, A.M. *et al.* (1994) *Sexual Behavior in Britain: The National Survey of Sexual Attitudes and Lifestyles*, Penguin Books, London.

Weston, K. (1991) *The Families We Choose: Lesbians, Gays, Kinship*, Columbia University Press, New York.

Widmer, E.D., Treas, J. and Newcomb, R. (1998) Attitudes toward nonmarital sex in 24 countries. *Journal of Sex Research*, 35 (4), 349–358.

Wosick-Correa, K. (2010) Agreements, rules and agentic fidelity in polyamorous relationships. *Psychology and Sexuality*, 1 (1), 44–61.

Yodanis, C. (2010) The institution of marriage, in *Dividing the Domestic: Men, Women and Household Work in Cross-National Perspective* (eds. J. Treas and S. Drobinc), Stanford University Press, Stanford, pp. 175–191.

27

The Global Chaos of Love: Toward a Cosmopolitan Turn in the Sociology of Love and Families

Ulrich Beck and Elisabeth Beck-Gernsheim

It is common knowledge that globalization has brought about major changes in economics, politics, and the labor market. But what about love, intimacy, and families in the global age, what transformations are we witnessing here? What was our book the *Normal Chaos of Love* (Beck and Beck-Gernsheim, 1995) all about? What is the *global chaos of love* all about?

With the rise of cohabitation, single parenthood, divorce, and serial monogamy; with the growing number of patchwork families, same-sex couples, ex-husbands, and ex-wives; with living together, living apart, living apart together, and transnational families; with surrogate mothers and collaborative assisted reproduction with donor egg and sperm; etc., in short, with the rapidly increasing variety of lifestyles, seemingly simple questions may change their color and old answers will no longer do. For example, what is a *couple* if we can no longer define it by a marriage license, or by having sex, or by living together? French sociologist Jean-Claude Kaufmann (1992) came up with a truly modern answer: a couple exists when *two* people buy *one* washing machine; for at that moment, they move beyond romance. The business of everyday joint life begins and with it a series of entanglements, negotiations, and confrontations. What counts as "dirty" clothes? Who does the washing for whom? Is ironing a waste of time? And so on.

Yet obviously, in a constellation of *distant* love, the criteria "two people, one washing machine" does not work. Kaufmann's approach, though indeed innovative, does not engage with the transformations of love and family that come with globalization and produce the *global* chaos of love.

In the following, we want to explore a topic that is of growing importance but as yet only rarely dealt with by family sociology: *Distant Love* (Beck and Beck-Gernsheim, 2014). To introduce this subject, we will present some characteristic constellations and suggest some first ideas toward building a theoretical framework. We start from the idea that in the field of love and family, a major transformation

The Wiley Blackwell Companion to the Sociology of Families, First Edition.
Edited by Judith Treas, Jacqueline Scott, and Martin Richards.
© 2014 John Wiley & Sons Ltd. Published 2017 by John Wiley & Sons Ltd.

is taking place. Increasingly, lovers do not share the same territory or roots. Love has become cosmopolitan. While the national chaos of love was based in a polarized vision of the world – either us or them, either here or there – today, this polarized notion seems to be on the wane and is gradually vanishing from the horizons of love. Be it skin color, nationality, religious affiliation, or geographical distance – these characteristics that were used to draw definite lines of demarcation have begun to lose some of their power. And for an increasing number of people, they have even gained a specific appeal. Men and women feel drawn by the vision of new horizons, by the romantic appeal of the global other. The great divides of former times, seemingly set in stone, now seem to be differences that can be dealt with, and indeed are being dealt with, in the everyday lives of many families in many places.

Cosmopolitan Families: Characteristics and Constellations

To analyze these ongoing transformations, we suggest a differentiation between two models – On the one hand, the social model of *national* love and families and, on the other, the social model of *cosmopolitan* love and *world* families. This is a contrast on the conceptual level; in real life, many families are somewhere in-between, some closer to the national model and some closer to the cosmopolitan model. It is the latter model, the new landscapes of love, family, and household, that we will explore here. We start from the following idea: at the beginning of the twenty-first century, the national or territorial face-to-face model of "the" family – defined by the trinity of territory, passport, and language – is breaking down. In its place, we witness the rise of many varieties of cosmopolitan love and globally mediated love (Internet, netscape etc.), from marriage migration to migrant domestic workers and from transnational romance to transnational households and to transnational parenting.

Basically, this new model of "world families" (Beck and Beck-Gernsheim, 2014) encompasses a broad range of family constellations which transcend national, cultural, ethnic, and religious boundaries. Two major types stand out. In the first type, family members live together in the same place yet come from different national backgrounds (for instance, a binational couple, he French and she English, both living with their children in Paris). In the second type, all family members belong to the same national or other group but have come to live in different countries or even continents (for instance, a Mexican couple who work and live in the United States while their children stay behind in rural Mexico).

To characterize the many diverse forms of world families, we suggest the concept "cosmopolitization" (Beck, 2006, 2011; Beck and Sznaider, 2006). By this, we mean more than globalization or transnationalism. Cosmopolitization in this sense refers to a much deeper, more personal, and intimate relationship. It means a basic interconnectedness between "us" and "them," an "enmeshment" with the global other. It means that we have come closer to those labeled "others," and "they" have come closer to us. Cosmopolitization takes place in many areas of our day-to-day lives, from job to education, to leisure, to love, and it takes place whether we like it or not. It brings with it a "fusion of horizons," a "dance of understanding" (Charles Taylor), sometimes resulting in more misunderstanding and a clash of horizons. Yet whether strengthening mutual understanding or mutual misunderstanding, the global age is the age of interconnectedness (Held *et al.*, 1999; Delanty, 2009), with interaction taking many forms: from face-to-face, direct, and personal relations to indirect and mediated ways such as TV, movies, and Internet. The outcome reaches deep into our personal lives, our mental and emotional landscapes. Be it the majority population or a minority group, be it natives or migrants, peoples' identities are being touched. Inner transformations are set into motion, in sometimes subtle and sometimes more open and direct ways. Religious beliefs, political ideologies, personal hopes, and ambitions begin to change.

Furthermore, with the rapid spreading of global capitalism, "long-distance love" and "world families" are no longer marginal phenomena. They have long since taken root at the heart of the "majority society." Cosmopolitan love and world families embody the antagonisms of the world, and these antagonisms are worked out in them. Not all families embody all antagonisms, but most families embody some of them. For example, with binational couples, political tensions between their respective countries may translate into personal conflicts, while in immigrant families, the tensions between the center and the periphery, between the West and "the rest," may come to the fore and cause irritation, resentment, or open hostility. World families may become the battleground where contrasting national narratives and national myths, with all their respective blind spots and spins, come to confront each other. Be it colonial rule and exploitation, violence against minorities, or wars of conquest against neighboring nations: in cosmopolitan love and families, the personal is political, and the political is personal. History is present, is alive, and sometimes is explosive.

Seen like this, when speaking of cosmopolitan couples and world families, we do not refer to a small elite of people who are educated, sophisticated, culturally ambitious, and economically well positioned. Quite to the contrary, more often, these families are the victims of global violence and global economic misery, some wealthy and most of them not, some with academic credentials and some barely literate, and many on the run from persecution and poverty and hoping to build a better future elsewhere.

To explore the inner dynamics of such families, in the next section, we will give a short introduction to what we call "cosmopolitan theory."

Cosmopolitan Theory

So far, family sociology has paid little attention to globalization and cosmopolitization. By ignoring some of the most powerful trends of recent years, it remains trapped in the unholy trinity of territory, state, and nation, in "methodological nationalism": a frame of reference that equates society as such with nationally organized societies (Wimmer and Glick Schiller, 2002; Beck, 2006; Beck and Sznaider, 2006).

Yet today, this frame of reference is rapidly becoming anachronistic. It cannot deal with the rise of ever more forms of personal life and relationships that extend across (national) borders. First, it is blind to the relationships and lifestyles of a growing number of people within the population at large. Second, its concepts, while reflecting the vantage point of the majority society in the center, implicitly claim universal validity. The results are characteristic blind spots, biased interpretations, and flawed conclusions.

For these very reasons, sociological research on love and families needs a "cosmopolitan turn." But what does "cosmopolitan" mean in terms of social theory?

Cosmopolitanism is a classic set of ethical and political ideas, dating back to Greek and Roman antiquity. At its center is the duality of human existence, the duality of "cosmo-polis": on the one hand, every human being is a member of the "cosmos," the unity of nature and humanity; at the same time, she/he is a member of the "polis" – that is, different states, ethnicities, gender, religions.

This idea was revived by the philosophies of the European enlightenment, most notably by Immanuel Kant who foretold a future era of polite civilization, commerce, and global peace. By the twentieth century, however, cosmopolitanism virtually disappeared as a major intellectual, let alone political, position. In its place, power-centered "realism" gained priority in politics and social science, resonating the raging nationalisms of the era, the trauma of two world wars and a Cold War of superpowers competing for global dominance.

With the emergence of "globalization" as a master concept in the social sciences, cosmopolitanism regained currency within the academy. But in the process, cosmopolitanism also refashioned itself, moving beyond political theory, its conventional home, and spreading widely across anthropology, cultural studies, literary criticism, legal studies, and social history. New, more or less reflexive cosmopolitanisms have since proliferated. First, these are preoccupied with squaring the circle of abstract universalism by paying respect to human diversity and, second, with expanding the boundaries of the circle to include (if not to favor) those for whom cosmopolitanism is not a lifestyle choice, but a tragic state endured by the refugee or the otherwise dispossessed.

To make these concepts useful for the study of global intimacy and world families, we have to bring social science in. For a start, the crucial point is to see the difference between, on the one hand, "*cosmopolitanism*" in the normative sense, top-down, from above, from God's eye, and a concept of philosophy and, on the other hand, "*cosmopolitization*" from below, impure, ordinary, part of everyday life, the enmeshment with "the other" in our midst, a concept of social science, and a program for empirical research (Beck, 2006, 2011). Put differently: cosmopolitanism is about *ethics*, and cosmopolitization is about *facts*, about social life in the global age. Be it for the study of love and family relations or for the study of the labor market, religion, class, nation-state, global risk, climate change, etc., the cosmopolitan approach points to the erosion of distinct boundaries dividing markets, states, civilizations, and cultures and focuses on the interconnectedness of people, groups, and nations around the globe.

Cosmopolitan love in this sense does *not* mean that the individuals in love are becoming cosmopolitans. Cosmopolitan love is not a personal attribute or attitude but love that comes with a specific epoch in social history. In this context, the difference between the perspective of the *actor* and the perspective of the social science *observer* is of major importance. "Cosmopolitan" is a category of social theory, essential for analyzing the moral and political dynamics of today – be it in world families or in respect to global risks. With cosmopolitization, with the other in our midst, and with people from diverse backgrounds coming geographically close, established beliefs, norms, and ideas become contested areas. The "end of geographical distance" may mark not the beginning of eternal peace, but rather the proliferation of cultural clashes and cultural wars. Ever more controversies arise, and sometimes explode, in many areas, not the least in respect to love and family life: What is right or wrong, decent or obscene? How do we define moral duty? Should tradition be honored and obeyed, or does it conflict with basic human rights? Is homosexuality a perverse disposition and a criminal act, to be despised, punished, and banned, or a lifestyle to be accepted and respected? What about arranged marriages: parents' right and responsibility or an act of cruel oppression coming from the dark days of patriarchy? And what about circumcision: an act of physical violence, inflicting pain and emotional trauma, or a symbol of belonging, a medically safe measure with special health benefits?

With these basic elements of cosmopolitan theory, we have built a first framework for analyzing world families. Out of the many diverse forms of such families, in what follows, we shall present two. First, we shall take a closer look at the transnational shadow economy of care and, second, at transnational motherhood and the emergence of global care chains. In recent years, these constellations have increasingly come into the focus of social science, even if not into the focus of family sociology. Yet in other fields, and especially so in anthropology and migration research, we find numerous studies exploring the inner dynamics in such families. From the material presented there, we build the analysis of the following paragraphs.

The Rise of a Transnational Shadow Economy

When speaking of the family, we mostly think of emotions, of love and belonging and desire, and of anger and hatred. Sometimes, we romanticize the family as a "haven in a heartless world" (Lasch, 1977). Sometimes, we see it as a place filled with secrets and lies. Yet quite some time ago, feminists brought into focus that the family is not only a site of emotions but also a site of work. This work includes a broad range of activities, often summarized by the label the "Three Cs": caring, cooking, and cleaning. And, of course, far into the twentieth century, these tasks were considered to be women's work, assigned to them by the will of God or by nature.

Then, in the 1960s, in many Western countries, a new role model for women began to make its way, slowly and accompanied by many heated debates. No longer should women be confined to the home. Instead, they should take part in higher education, hold jobs, and earn their own salaries. Feminists, fiercely criticizing the polarized sexual division of labor, proclaimed a new gender order. Both men and women, so they claimed, should be active in the labor market *and* in the family household. In particular, men should do their share of family work, for instance, cleaning floors, sorting rubbish, changing nappies.

The stalled revolution

We know what has become of such claims. In recent years, the sexual division of labor has been the subject of numerous studies, in different countries and for couples of varying backgrounds. From among the results, two trends stand out. First, yes, men have been changing. Men of the younger generation, when compared to their fathers or grandfathers, take much more part in the upbringing of their offspring, from taking them to kindergarten to sports or playground activities. Second, so far, the changes are modest in scope (except, maybe, in the Scandinavian countries). Women still bear most responsibilities in regard to childrearing tasks. And in the field of household activities, men's participation is even lower. Except for some rare heroic souls, routine activities such as changing sheets or doing the laundry are not on the male menu (Risman, 2010).

In past decades, women have been changing faster than men. American sociologist Arlie Hochschild argues that while women have ventured beyond the confines of "woman's place," men's moves into family work lag behind, in short, a gender gap or, as Hochschild and Machung (1989) puts it, a "stalled revolution" in gender matters.

With little support from their male partners, women who try to combine both, motherhood and holding a job, have to bear high personal costs – for instance, sleep privation, constant stress, and no time for free time. For a survival strategy, many of these women resort to delegating some of the family work to female helpers of all kinds, from grandmothers to neighbors to cousins, and, in recent years, more and more often to another group, migrant women.

From this constellation, so we suggest, results the cosmopolitization of many middle-class households, the outsourcing (or insourcing) of family work to women from countries of the so-called Second or Third World, or, to put it differently, the rise of a transnational shadow economy (Hochschild, 2000; Hondagneu-Sotelo, 2001; Ehrenreich and Hochschild, 2003; Rerrich, 2006).

From mother's task to migrants' job

When speaking of migrant domestic workers, we speak of women from all over the globe: women from Mexico who work in California as nannies, women from the Philippines who care for the elderly in Italy, and women from Poland who clean houses and do the laundry for German families.

Faced with high rates of unemployment in their home countries, and no prospects to earn a decent living there, these women have decided to look for work in the wealthier regions of the world, hereby following the millions of "guest workers" of earlier decades. Yet meanwhile, most Western countries have severely restricted migration; in particular, options for legal labor migration have been cut down drastically.

But women in the poorer countries, desperately looking for ways to earn some money, are not put off easily. Rather, many multiply their efforts, trying just the harder to find some backdoor or sideway to the West. Here, they make use of the communication networks that have come with globalization. Via such channels, news spread that in spite of official restrictions, in the domestic sector, there are plenty of jobs to be found. Furthermore, because this sector is shut off from outside view, there is little risk of control. Here, workers need no papers, no certificates, and only little knowledge of the local language.

In this way, the needs of two different groups of women meet. Lacking help from their male partners, women of the First World resort to outsourcing: turning over some of the care for their children, elderly parents, and homes to women from the Third World. And for the same reason, women of the Third World can find a way to earn money. While men's activity in household is modest at best, the workload has to be coped with, no matter what, hence the market solution: job offers to fill the gap.

Seen like this, a perfect fit. Supply and demand correspond closely. But a closer look reveals a massive flaw to this solution. Its main characteristic is a massive imbalance of risks and profits for the parties involved. Obviously, the migrant workers have to bear most of the risks. They are trapped in a semilegal shadow economy. Because they often have no visa, no work permit, and no residence rights, their position is fragile and vulnerable. In most countries, these women have no access to public health services, unemployment benefits, and pension rights. They are vulnerable to exploitation; they can be fired without notice. Last but not least, their political rights are severely restricted.

By silent agreement

Of course, this is why migrants are hired: because they are efficient and because they are cheap. At first sight, it is the middle-class women of the First World who profit; but when looking closer, we find that their male partners profit just as much and probably even more. More than the women, the men are set free to follow their ambitions and pursue careers without being disturbed by tedious tasks. We suggest the following constellation:

In many middle-class families today, both men and women are well aware that the gender issue is a sensitive area and that the "stalled revolution," if not handled carefully, might escalate into explosive conflicts. And many of these couples have come to a similar strategy of conflict management: they have reached a kind of silent treaty, an implicit agreement. If women see to it that the family household is functioning at a reasonable level, then men consent to their venturing out of the home and into the labor market, even to pursue some career of their own. And vice versa: if their men "allow" them a career of their own, then the women consent to provide, as best they can, for the functioning of household and family affairs and to do so by outsourcing the family work, not by constantly claiming male participation.

To illustrate this point, imagine just for a moment the following situation. What if all of a sudden, all migrant domestic workers would disappear; what if they did what politicians in Western countries officially expect them to do, namely, return to their respective home countries – to Poland or Romania, to Mexico or Honduras? By all probabilities, it would then no more suffice that German men, or US men, talked high of gender equality. In this emergency, women would no longer keep to their implicit agreement, and instead, they would demand loudly that men do their share of family work. If this analysis holds true, here is a major area of hidden benefits – not for the migrants, but for their employers. By relieving Western families of some of their workload, migrant domestic workers stabilize – and contribute to – the precarious peace in the arena of gender.

At this point, we might come to ask, what about *their* families?

Transnational Motherhood and Global Care Chains

With methodological nationalism, our analysis could stop here. Yet, methodological cosmopolitanism demands that we go further and ask: What about families at the periphery, in the Philippines, in the Ukraine, and in Poland? What are the transformations going on there? What happens to the children, partners, and parents of migrant domestic workers?

This is a question that we – natives of the West – mostly ignore. Yet it is no minor matter concerning but a few. Quite to the contrary, many of the women working abroad have families of their own, back in their home countries. These women have left partners, children, and whoever else there is to go abroad and earn a living. In fact, it is often the children, or rather their responsibility toward them, that motivates women migrants to go abroad; the mothers want a better future for their sons and daughters, free from hunger and constant poverty. For this hope, they are willing to accept long separations and the lonely life in a far-away country.

Yet this behavior means no more, no less than a revolution of basic rules. In the old times, it was proof of your love that you would stick together, no matter what. Yet now, in a globalized world, for many, the opposite holds true. The new rule says: if you truly love your family, you must leave them. You must go to some distant part of the world, wherever there is money to be made, because this is the only way to lift your family out of the misery and desperation at home. Or to quote from a novel by Michelle Spring: "For migrant domestic workers all over the globe, love means, first of all: having to go away" (Spring, 1998, p. 63).

But how does this work? How are the children of migrant mothers cared for? According to recent studies (Hondagneu-Sotelo and Avila, 1997; Gamburd, 2000; Parreñas, 2005; Madianou and Miller, 2012; Rerrich, 2012), the answer is that another division of labor is being established, starting in the respective home-lands of female migrants and again involving women only. For instance, often migrant women rely on the help of other women in their hometown (for instance, grandmother, sister in-law, neighbor). By sending them money and other gifts from abroad, migrant mothers hope to grow a sense of responsibility among the recipients of such favors and make them willing to look after their children's well-being and care.

In this way, new patterns of motherhood are being created, named "transnational motherhood" in recent studies. They result in the so-called global care chains, based on elaborate networks and spanning over countries and continents. To give a typical example: in some family of the Second or Third World, the eldest daughter is responsible for looking after her younger siblings; this sets her mother free to take care of some third woman's children, and thus earn a little money; while the third woman has migrated to some Western country and is nanny to the baby boy of a family resident there. Transnational care chains are to be found, for instance, when we look at the migration flows between Eastern Europe and Western Europe. Women from Poland go to Germany, cleaning the houses of middle-class families there; at the same time, women from the Ukraine go to Poland, managing the household and family tasks of the Polish migrant women at work in Germany.

A global hierarchy of care

While these care chains spread into many directions, crossing borders, mountains, and oceans, connecting the most diverse places, they do so in no accidental way. On the contrary, they follow a distinct pattern, rooted in social inequality. As American sociologist Arlie Hochschild (2000) puts it: "Motherhood is passed down the hierarchy of nation, ethnicity, race." This statement brings into focus that the age of globalization creates a new hierarchy, a global hierarchy of delegation. The work implied by the Three Cs – caring, cleaning, and cooking – is cast off along the lines of nationality, color, and ethnicity.

Above all, children, old people, and disabled or ill people have to bear the consequences. With each step downward, the chances for receiving adequate help and good care are being diminished. If Polish women leave their homes to work for German families and women from Ukraine leave their homes to work in Polish households, who then will do the caring–cleaning–cooking in Ukraine?

Empirical studies have found that, indeed, those at the bottom of the hierarchy often have to bear the costs of delegating. Take, for instance, the children of migrant mothers. Often, their grandmothers, aunts, and elder sisters are burdened by numerous responsibilities – or too old, too tired, too sick – to master yet another task. Even if they try hard, the children left in their charge are more or less on their own, lacking proper care and proper meals. At the same time, there is little help to expect from the fathers. Some men disappeared years ago, taking leave from family bonds and family duties. And of those who stayed, many find it hard now to come to terms with the role reversal. The women working abroad and being the breadwinners: this turn of events is threatening their male identity. Because many men are preoccupied with their own sense of crisis, they are hardly able to offer emotional support and protection. The effect is that many children lack a stable base, feel lonely, and desperately long for their mother.

Loss and Gain: Cosmopolitan Comparisons

Exploitation, misery, and loneliness, these ingredients come up in studies on transnational motherhood and transnational families time and again. Yet when looking closer, a few studies also point out moments of a different shade. While by no means ignoring the loss and pain that comes with geographical separation, these studies question the "dismal view of transnational households" (Parreñas, 2005a) and caution against the "dramatizing features" (Rerrich, 2012) and the "horror story genre" (Gamburd, 2000) made of abused women, incapable fathers, and neglected children. The stories they present speak of "ambivalence" (Madianou and Miller, 2012), not total loss, but, along with the loss, also some gains.

So what might these gains be? How do we explain that, as said by a Filipina migrant, having come to London was "the greatest blessing" of her life (Madianou and Miller, 2012)? For a preliminary answer, in the material given in empirical studies, we find two major groups of positive effects:

First is a way out from an unhappy relationship (Gamburd, 2000; Hochschild, 2003; Madianou and Miller, 2012). Quite often, women migrants, when describing their life back home, speak of relationships gone sour (drunken husband, domestic violence, etc.). Yet in the Philippines, one of the major countries of female migration, there is no legal divorce. In other countries, divorce, though legal, comes with a heavy social stigma for women, and having a child outside marriage brings a similar loss of reputation. So in their native countries, these women have been trapped. In a context dominated by a traditional family model and a gender-based division of labor, their prospects for finding a husband, or finding a better husband, are severely reduced. At the same time, they are also deprived of the economic benefits that come with marriage and a male provider. For these women to start a new life, a new relationship, and maybe even a new family, there is only one option: the way out. Looking for a better future means leaving behind their native country and trying their luck elsewhere.

Second, migrant women, whether running away from a dysfunctional relationship or not, may enjoy further benefits. Often for the first time, they gain some independence. In the new country, they may have to follow the whims and wishes of their employers yet are no more subject to the direct control of husband, father, or wider kin. For some women at least, their identity begins to transform, in subtle yet deep ways (Madianou and Miller, 2012).

They begin to enjoy their new independence and personal freedom (Sassen, 2003). Over the years, they find ways to adapt to their new surroundings, making new friends, learning to appreciate the geographical distance to everyday life in the close-knit family, and sometimes maybe even appreciating the anonymity of urban life. For working long hours and working hard, the women migrants receive little money. Yet it is money nonetheless and, what is more, their own money and, even better, money at their own disposal. They decide how much to send home and how much to keep and how much to spend now and how much to save for the future. In the new country, they are labeled "illegal" and stuck at the low end of the social hierarchy. Yet in their home country, migrant women gain social status and authority. Because most prove loyal to their families, sending money home regularly and often also sending generous gifts, the reputation of transnational migrants rises, changing from "morally dubious" to "successful and hardworking." In their family, neighborhood, and native village now, they are met with respect (Madianou and Miller, 2012).

Seeing with the eyes of the respective "other"

Even though we have touched the subject of benefits only briefly, it has become obvious that transnational migration is not a story made of monochrome and total suffering. On the contrary, along with the personal suffering come also some personal gains or at least the potential for them. Arriving at the center, women confront global capitalism and its many diverse ways of exploitation, oppression, etc. Yet they may also find more autonomy in the new place, and at the same time, more status and respect in their native country. Cleaning floors in London may not be a dream job and yet may be better than being beaten up by a drunken husband or being raped by his brother-in-law. Living in a tiny apartment in a shabby neighborhood may bring loneliness and longing and yet may give women some kind of personal freedom and an opportunity to go beyond the narrow confines of traditional gender roles and the gender-based division of labor.

In short, the cosmopolitan approach calls for a methodology of cosmopolitan comparisons, involving what might be called a cosmopolitan theory of social relations. One of its crucial prerequisites is learning to see with the eyes of the respective "other," in our context: looking at migration through migrants' eyes (Beck-Gernsheim, 2009). Instead of taking the Western way of life, Western values and aspirations as the universal standard of measuring, we need to start from the *migrants'* situation, comparing their prospects in the country of origin with those in the country of arrival. The difference between these two is what counts for the migrant. This difference is his or her frame of reference, his or her answer to the question of loss or gain.

Conclusions

The forces that globalization sets into motion are not confined to economy or politics, but reach deep into the family. On both sides of the global divide, among rich and among poor nations, families are being transformed. While in some ways, they are drawn together, becoming mutually dependent, at the same time, they grow further apart, moving into opposite directions. New hierarchies are building up, both within families (middle-class families of the West hiring servants from the global "rest") and also among families (a care drain from poor to rich nations).

Coming back to the beginning, we can now see why we need a cosmopolitan turn in family sociology. When keeping within the national, Western perspective, we see only one part of the ongoing transformations: it is only by switching from a national to a global perspective that these two diverse yet closely interconnected trends of family change come into view.

From this, a methodological imperative follows. In the twenty-first century, in an age of ever-increasing transnational connections and interdependencies, sociology becomes anachronistic if it sticks to a framework of nation-states as separate entities. Instead, sociology has to overcome such restrictions and move beyond methodological nationalism. To put it in a nutshell, a cosmopolitan turn is needed. For conclusions, we come back to the question we started out with and add another one. Taken together, they read: What happens when globalization hits home? And when will family sociology tell us about it?

References

Beck, U. (2006) *The Cosmopolitan Vision*, Polity Press, Cambridge.

Beck, U. (2011) We do not live in an age of cosmopolitanism but in an age of cosmopolitisation: the 'global other' is in our midst. *Irish Journal of Sociology*, 19(1), 16–34.

Beck, U. and Beck-Gernsheim, E. (1995) *The Normal Chaos of Love*, Polity Press, Cambridge.

Beck, U. and Sznaider, N. (2006) Unpacking cosmopolitanism for the social sciences: a research agenda. *British Journal of Sociology*, 57(1), 1–23.

Beck, U. and Beck-Gernsheim, E. (2014) *Distant Love*, Polity Press, Cambridge.

Beck-Gernsheim, E. (2009) Preface: looking at immigration through immigrant eyes, in *From Guest Workers into Muslims. The Transformation of Turkish Immigrant Associations in Germany* (ed. G. Yurdakul), Cambridge Scholars Publishing, Cambridge.

Delanty, G. (2009) *The Cosmopolitan Imagination: The Renewal of Critical Social Theory*, Cambridge University Press, Cambridge.

Ehrenreich, B. and Hochschild, A.R. (eds) (2003) *Global Woman: Nannies, Maids, and Sex Workers in the New Economy*, Granta Books, London.

Gamburd, M.R. (2000) *The Kitchen Spoon's Handle: Transnationalism and Sri Lanka's Migrant Housemaids*, Cornell University Press, Ithaca.

Held, D., McGrew, A., Goldblatt, D. and Perraton, J. (1999) *Global Transformations: Politics, Economics and Culture*, Polity Press, Cambridge.

Hochschild, A.R. (2000) Global care chains and emotional surplus value, in *On the Edge: Living with Global Capitalism* (eds. W. Hutton and A. Giddens), Jonathan Cape, London.

Hochschild, A.R. (2003) Love and gold, in *Global Woman: Nannies, Maids, and Sex Workers in the New Economy* (eds. B. Ehrenreich and A.R. Hochschild), Granta Books, London.

Hochschild, A.R. and Machung, A. (1989) *The Second Shift: Working Parents and the Revolution at Home*, Viking, New York.

Hondagneu-Sotelo, P. (2001) *Domestica. Immigrant Workers Cleaning and Caring in the Shadows of Affluence*, University of California Press, Berkeley/Los Angeles/London.

Hondagneu-Sotelo, P. and Avila. E. (1997) "I'm here, but I'm there": the meanings of Latina transnational motherhood. *Gender and Society*, 11(5), 548–571.

Kaufmann, J.–C. (1992) *La Trame Conjugale. Analyse du Couple par Son Linge*, Nathan, Paris.

Lasch, C. (1977) *Haven in a Heartless World: The Family Besieged*, Basic Books, New York.

Madianou, M. and Miller, D. (2012) *Migration and New Media: Transnational Families and Polymedia*, Routledge, London.

Parreñas, R.S. (2005a) *Children of Global Migration: Transnational Families and Gendered Woes*, Stanford University Press, Stanford.

Parreñas, R.S. (2005b) Long distance intimacy: class, gender and intergenerational relations between mothers and children in Filipino transnational families. *Global Networks*, 5(4), 317–336.

Rerrich, M.S. (2006) *Die ganze Welt zuhause. Cosmobile Putzfrauen in privaten Haushalten*, Hamburger Edition, Hamburg.

Rerrich, M.S. (2012) Migration macht Schule. Herausforderungen für Care in einer rumänischen Gemeinde. *Mittelweg*, 36, 73–92.

Risman, B.J. (ed) (2010) *Families as They Really Are*, W.W. Norton, New York.

Sassen, S. (2003) Global cities and survival circuits, in *Global Woman: Nannies, Maids, and Sex Workers in the New Economy* (eds. B. Ehrenreich and A.R. Hochschild), Granta Books, London.

Spring, M. (1998) *Running for Shelter*, Orion, London.

Wimmer, A. and Glick Schiller, N. (2002) Methodological nationalism and beyond: nation-state building, migration and the social sciences. *Global Networks*, 2(4), 301–334.

Index

The Wiley Blackwell Companion to the Sociology of Families, First Edition.
Edited by Judith Treas, Jacqueline Scott, and Martin Richards.
© 2014 John Wiley & Sons Ltd. Published 2017 by John Wiley & Sons Ltd.